Improving Student Learning

Improving Students as Learners

Edited by Chris Rust

Published by
THE OXFORD CENTRE FOR STAFF & LEARNING DEVELOPMENT
Helena Kennedy Building
Oxford Brookes University
Headington Hill Hall Campus
Headington
Oxford
OX3 OBP

Improving Student Learning –
Improving Students as Learners

ISBN 1 873576 59 5

British Library Cataloguing-in-Publication Data.
A catalogue record for this book is available from the British Library.

Printed 1998

Designed and Typeset in Palatino by Ann Trew

Printed in Great Britain by
Oxonian Rewley Press Ltd
Oxford

Printed on paper produced from sustainable forests.

Preface

The appeal of the Improving Student Learning Symposium continues to grow both in terms of numbers and international appeal, and this 5th Symposium in 1997 at the University of Strathclyde, Glasgow was the biggest yet attracting 230 participants from over 15 countries.

The major aim of the Symposium is to provide a forum which brings together those who are primarily researchers into learning in higher education and those who are primarily practitioners concerned more pragmatically with improving their practice, but from whichever starting point, papers are only accepted if they take a sufficiently scholarly, research-based approach.

This year, with its theme of Improving Students as Learners, the Symposium was organised around eight sub-themes which ran in parallel over the two days, and they can be found as the various sections from Part III to Part X of these proceedings. In most themes there were seven or eight contributions, but a few were less popular. This left space for this to be the first Symposium where a separate IT theme was identified, reflecting the increase in submissions in this area. Obviously these sessions tended to be more practical and "hands on" but nevertheless most have been written up and are included here in Part XI.

At the end of the first day of papers and works-in-progress, there was also an optional workshop offering a more participative process. Despite its more light-hearted approach however it dealt with a serious theme - the overcrowded curriculum - and has been included as an Appendix.

After its successful introduction the previous year, this Symposium again also included an optional extra day prior to the main events devoted to research methods. A choice of four parallel half-day sessions covered aspects of both quantitative and qualitative methodologies and were aimed primarily at those just starting to be interested in pedagogic research but also possibly for those with some experience but wanting to develop or extend their repertoire. These sessions were largely practical but one has been written up and can be found in Part II.

The Symposium was opened and closed by two excellent but contrasting keynote addresses. The opening keynote by Phil Candy, Deputy Vice-Cahncellor (Scholarship) at University of Ballarat in Australia, took a global look into the crystal ball to consider the way the world is rapidly changing in the development of an "information society", the subsequent creation and need for what he called "knowledge workers", and the implications for the role of universities in developing such people. Stephen Brookfield, Distinguished Professor, University of St Thomas (St Paul, Minnesota) in the USA, closed the Symposium with a keynote which focussed very much on the individual student, and in particular on the needs of those students "who just don't get it". In a presentation peppered with entertaining anecdotes, often of a personal nature and made amusing at Stephen's expense, he nevertheless made some very serious and telling observations about what makes good teaching. Both these keynotes can be found in Part I.

I inherited responsibility for chairing this Symposium part way through the year when Graham Gibbs left our Centre to return to the Open University, and was honoured to do so. I believe the continued and growing success of ISL is a testimony to his vision in seeing the need for such a forum. I would also like to publicly acknowledge the invaluable contribution to both the organisation of the symposia and the production of these proceedings played by Felix Lam.

Chris Rust
Oxford Centre for Staff and Learning Development, Oxford Brookes University, July 1998.

Contents

PART III   IMPROVING STUDENTS AS INDEPENDENT, LIFELONG LEARNERS

PART IV   IMPROVING STUDENTS' GENERIC
TRANSFERABLE SKILLS

PART V IMPROVING STUDENTS' STUDY SKILLS

PART VI   IMPROVING PEER TUTORING, PEER
SUPERVISION AND PEER ASSESSMENT SKILLS

PART VII   IMPROVING STUDENTS' ABILITY TO LEARN FROM EXPERIENCE

PART VIII   IMPROVING STUDENTS AS RESEARCHERS

PART IX   BUILDING SKILL DEVELOPMENT INTO THE CURRICULUM, AND ASSESSING SKILLS

PART XI   INNOVATIVE APPLICATIONS OF IT

APPENDIX: WORKSHOP

1 Knowledge navigators and lifelong learners: producing graduates for the information society

Philip C. Candy
University of Ballarat

1.1 Overview

In recent years, considerable attention has been paid, at least at the policy level, to the need for graduates to be 'lifelong learners'. Although this concept means different things in different cultural contexts, there is more or less general agreement that graduation really only marks the beginning of the graduate's need for continuing personal and professional learning and, moreover, that it is the responsibility of universities and other institutions of higher education to equip their graduates with the skills and attitudes to help them to continue learning throughout their lives.

The emergence of an information-rich 'knowledge society' has made this even more of an imperative. The rapid and pervasive spread of information and communication technologies, coupled with increasing globalization, the democratization of knowledge production – once assumed to be largely the preserve of universities – and what has been dubbed the 'information explosion' collectively mean that most citizens of advanced industrialized countries are, or will soon become, 'knowledge workers'. Accordingly, many graduates, whether they work in educational or other contexts, are likely to be involved in 'knowledge-intensive' activities, for which they need to be prepared. But what does this mean in practice, and what are we to do about it?

In 1990, the late Dr Ernest Boyer, in his book *Scholarship Reconsidered: Priorities of the Professoriate*, proposed a fourfold division of academic work into what he labelled the *scholarship of discovery*; the *scholarship of application*; the *scholarship of integration*; and, finally, the *scholarship of teaching*. This opening chapter suggests that each of these four aspects of scholarship has a direct counterpart outside the university, and that accordingly they might be taken as a way of considering the attributes of graduates as well as of academics. The chapter suggests a necessary symmetry between the teaching and other scholarly work carried out within the university and the development of such abilities and predispositions in graduates from a variety of fields who might not otherwise consider themselves to be destined for 'scholarly' work.

1.2 Introduction

In 1776, the American Colonies wrested their independence away from Britain, to become the bastion of free market economics and individualism which the United States remains to this day. In the same year, a book appeared which, like the American War of Independence, was to have repercussions down the centuries. That book was the *Inquiry into the Nature and Causes of the Wealth of Nations* (or, as it is more commonly known today, *The Wealth of Nations*) by Adam Smith, one of the world's earliest and best-known economic theorists.

Smith's notion of political economy included two precepts which have since become central in conventional economics: first, that if people are allowed to follow their individual self-interests this will provide an 'invisible hand' which will automatically solve the problem of bringing supply and demand into alignment; and, second, that people (and nations) are more productive if they concentrate on a small subset of a total task. To illustrate this latter principle, he uses the manufacture of pins as an example:

> A workman not educated to this business . . . nor acquainted with the use of the machinery employed in it . . . could scarce, perhaps, with his utmost industry, make one pin in a day, and certainly could not make twenty. But in the way in which this business is now carried on, not only the whole work is a peculiar trade, but it is divided into a number of branches of which the greater part are likewise peculiar trades. One man draws out the wire, another straights it, a third cuts it, a fourth points it, a fifth grinds it at the top for receiving the head; to make the head requires two or three distinct operations; to put it on is a peculiar business, to whiten the pins is another; it is even a trade by itself to put them into the paper; and the important business of making a pin is, in this manner, divided into about eighteen distinct operations. . .
>
> (Smith 1776 p5)

Having outlined how such an apparently simple process could be subdivided into a dizzying range of smaller steps, each the responsibility of an individual worker, Smith then went on to show the advantages of such a system in terms of efficient production:

> I have seen a small manufactory of this kind where ten men only were employed, and . . . [although] . . . indifferently accommodated with the necessary machinery, they could, when they exerted themselves, . . . make among them upwards of forty-eight thousand pins in a day. Each person, therefore, making a tenth part of forty-eight thousand pins might be considered as making four thousand eight hundred pins in a day. But if they had all wrought separately and independently, and without any of them having been educated to this peculiar business, they certainly could not each of them have made twenty, perhaps not one pin in a day; that is, certainly not the two hundred and fortieth, perhaps not the four thousand eight hundredth part of what they are at present capable of performing in consequence of a proper division and combination of their different operations.
>
> (Smith, 1776 p5)

Extending this principle to companies, and ultimately to entire countries, economists have argued that 'specialization' is the most efficient way of organizing production and, in the two hundred years since Smith first wrote about this principle, it has come to dominate western society. There has been a proliferation of increasingly specialized institutions, each with its own esoteric knowledge, its particular equipment and its distinctive ways of operating.

Educational institutions, including universities, have been part of this general process of progressively differentiating themselves from other social institutions, so that today they are distinguished from one another, and from other social structures in terms both of what they attempt to do and how they do it. However, in the past few years, this has tended to change: public universities are being challenged not only by private universities, but also by further education colleges and community colleges. There is, as it were, an epochal shift away from universities as specialized providers of learning opportunities, even for so-called 'higher learning'. In such a fluid and challenging context, universities are having to adapt, and very quickly, to a world in which they have lost, or are losing, their special status as producers and disseminators of knowledge (Gibbons, Nowotny, Limoges *et al.*, 1994).

1.3 The information society

Universities are far from the only social institutions to experience this sort of dislocation and change. Indeed, due to the development and rapid spread of 'convergent technologies', the whole higher-education sector is itself being challenged for people's time, money and attention by other sectors, notably the entertainment industry on the one hand and the media on the other. In 1985, the Social Science Council of Canada published a report with the evocative title *The Uneasy Eighties: The Transition to an Information Society*. It opens with these words:

> Printing, the water wheel, electricity, the automobile – all were at one time new technologies, all had profound social and economic consequences. Today, the new technologies of microelectronics and computing are transforming societies, particularly those of the industrialised West.

> (Cordell, 1986, p. 3)

In the decade since then – which might be termed the 'nervous Nineties'! – the concept of an information society has become increasingly familiar. In 1991, Hague suggested that the UK was fast becoming an information society (or what he termed a 'knowledge society') along with other advanced industrial economies such as the United States (Drucker, 1993), and in the same year, the Australian House of Representatives Standing Committee for Long Term Strategies produced a report entitled *Australia as an Information Society: Grasping New Paradigms*, which traced the movement back even further:

> Most technologically advanced societies and economies have experienced, since the 1960s, an unprecedentedly rapid increase in the use of and dependence on information, information technologies and communications systems generally, marked by the growth of electronics, especially computing. Australia is no exception.

> (Jones, 1991, p. 5)

In fact, it is not only what we conventionally think of as 'technologically advanced' industrial economies which are being transformed. Perhaps in sympathy with Australia's alliterative aspiration to become a 'clever country', Singapore has adopted the slogan, the 'intelligent island'. Under the leadership of Prime Minister Dr Mahatir, Malaysia too has developed an ambitious 'Multimedia Super Corridor' which, in the words of the Australian Minister of Communications, Senator Richard Alston,

> involves an industrial development zone, designed to boost industrial growth, as well as a new international airport, a new administrative capital (Putrajaya) and the Kuala Lumpur City Centre, a high-tech IT enabled centre in the heart of the city. Companies locating in the Super Corridor will receive tax concessions and grants, and will have access to a high speed telecommunications network.

> (Alston, 1997, p. 4)

Other Asian economies are likewise being affected by the information revolution: Thailand, Indonesia, Hong Kong, Korea, the Philippines, China and India are all undergoing massive restructuring based on what has come to be called 'Information Technology and Advanced

Telecommunications' or ITAT. Indeed, while I was preparing this paper, the following article appeared in Melbourne's major daily newspaper, *The Age*:

> Used to make transistors and semiconductors, silicon has altered our lives and turned a relatively poor, overcrowded Asian island into Silicon Island, the world's third biggest information technology producer with annual exports worth billions of dollars. Taiwan has risen Phoenix-like from the ashes over about 40 years, moving from a primarily agricultural society to become an industrial *tour de force* and the world's 14th biggest trading nation.
>
> On the doorstep of South-East Asia, mainland China, Korea and Japan, the country has risen to the top rung of Asian development . . . Fast becoming a manufacturer on a global scale, the country exports more computer mother boards than any other nation, and has plans for the next millennium as an Asia-Pacific regional operations centre for manufacturing, research and development and marketing.
>
> (Spinks, 1997, p. B8)

In the light of accomplishments such as these, it seems more than mere rhetoric when the highly influential Bangemann Report – *Europe and the Global Information Society* – begins with the words:

> Throughout the world, information and communications technologies are generating a new industrial revolution already as significant and far-reaching as those of the past.
>
> (Bangemann, 1994)

In fact, Bangemann discusses the effects of this 'new industrial revolution' on: citizens and consumers; content creators; regions; governments and administrations; large, medium and small business enterprises; telecommunications operators, including satellite, microwave and cable companies (keywords: interconnectivity and interoperability); and computer companies – both hardware and software industries. In short, whether in the mind-numbing statistics of the growth of the Internet; the rollout of cable TV; the penetration of computers into schools, homes and offices; or the profound re-calibration of established social and economic relationships, it is clear that modern technologies are reaching – some would say insidiously – into every corner of our lives. Affecting the home and the workplace, banking, government services, shopping, communications, entertainment and education, there are few aspects of our lives which lie beyond the reach of the information explosion. The Bangemann Report, for instance, highlights the following ten applications which are required 'to launch the information society' in Europe, each of which is explained in detail in the Report:

1. teleworking;
2. distance learning;
3. a network for universities and research centres;
4. telematic services for Small and Medium Enterprises (SMEs);
5. road traffic management;
6. air traffic control;
7. healthcare networks;

8. electronic tendering;

9. trans-European public administration network;

10. city information highways.

One of the consequences of this revolutionary turmoil has been that it has brought 'new capacities to human intelligence, and . . . changes [to] the way we work together and the way we live together' (Bangemann, 1995, p. 3). Not all of these changes have been beneficial, however; one unanticipated and unwanted side-effect of the information revolution has been the creation of groups of 'information rich' and 'information poor'. Clearly it is a social responsibility of governments to ameliorate, as far as possible, the emergence of differences between the 'haves' and 'have nots' in this, as in other aspects of cultural capital.

Another consequence of the rapid and pervasive development of convergent technologies has been the blurring of what were once defined and dependable boundaries between various sectors of economic activity. To take but one example:

> In the United States, the telephone and cable television companies compete to monitor air conditioning, lights and home security, and soon they will be competing with the mail service. The telegraph, printing, travelling, computer, mail, package delivery, airline, movie and broadcasting industries are overflowing into each other's territories.

> (Cordell, 1985, p. 7)

This blurring of boundaries, or 'overflowing into each other's territories', has, if anything, intensified in the years since the appearance of that report; a phenomenon of enormous significance to universities and other providers of learning opportunities. This is a theme to which I alluded previously, and to which I will return later in this chapter.

1.4 Knowledge-based workplaces

If one changes the lens, and increases the magnification, it is apparent that the availability of new technologies and consequently of new business opportunities, has also impacted at the level of individual organizations, and even of occupations. Both in their external relationships and their internal structures, few, if any, domains of economic activity have escaped the combined effects of the information explosion and modern technologies.

The first and most obvious examples are to be found in the professions – including accountants, doctors, lawyers, architects and engineers – who, partly because of increased client expectations but principally because of the dramatically increased complexity of their professional knowledge base, have had to change the way in which their practices are managed. One aspect of the knowledge revolution for professionals has been the tendency to form linkages with other professionals, often in related areas, in recognition of the need for a range of expertise which transcends their narrow specialism. For instance, in the case of doctors, there has been a move towards the establishment of health-care clinics embracing a range of experts including dietitians, nurse practitioners, physiotherapists, pharmacists and even lifestyle counsellors. Because of the growing complexity and interdependence of these fields, similar aggregations of related professionals are also be found in other domains.

For many, the professions represent the quintessential knowledge-based occupations, and it is hardly surprising that they would be affected by the information society. However, at the other end of the spectrum, many conventional organizations – even those engaged in extractive, construction or 'value-adding' production industries – have also become more knowledge-dependent than ever before. As a consequence, they have had to forge distinctive, knowledge-based relationships with their customers, their suppliers, and occasionally, through joint ventures, even with their competitors (for which a new word has been coined: 'cooperatition'!).

This practice perhaps reaches its most extreme form when organizations locate staff permanently within an enterprise with which they frequently deal in order to ensure that tailor-made products and services are delivered on time and to their specifications. As Hirschhorn and Gilmore put it in their paper on 'boundary-less organizations':

> The problem is that [the] traditional organisational map describes a world that no longer exists. New technologies, fast-changing markets, and global competition are revolutionising business relationships. As companies blur their traditional boundaries to respond to this more fluid business environment, the roles that people play at work and the tasks they perform become correspondingly blurred and ambiguous.
>
> (Hirschhorn and Gilmore, 1992, p. 105)

The move to an information society has not only transformed existing, but has also given rise to entirely new, enterprises and workplaces. There has been a striking proliferation of entities which concentrate on the production, collection, analysis, transformation, storage or dissemination of information in some form or other, and which derive their competitive advantage from a combination of the technologies on which they are based and the special expertise they bring to bear. Setting aside the dramatic changes which have occurred in familiar fields such as publishing, journalism, banking, insurance, meteorology, scientific research, education and librarianship, it is evident that the information society has brought into existence completely new occupations – such as management consulting, software production, information systems design, various forms of technical writing and media production, and telecommunications engineering – and employment niches which did not formerly exist.

Without wishing to get bogged down in complex and pedantic linguistic analyses, it is worth noting that the trend towards the emergence of knowledge-rich workplaces has given rise to a new vocabulary within the organizational literature. Some commentators refer to 'knowledge-intensive firms' (or KIFs), a usage which

> imitates the economists' labelling of firms as capital intensive or labour intensive. These labels describe the relative importance of capital and labour as production inputs . . . labelling a firm as knowledge intensive implies that knowledge has more importance than other inputs . . .
>
> (Starbuck, 1992, p. 715)

Starbuck goes on to point out that 'knowledge intensive' is not the same as 'information intensive' and that, since all organizations are based to some extent on knowledge, 'one should not label a firm as knowledge intensive unless exceptional and valuable expertise dominates' (Starbuck, 1992, p. 716).

Others refer instead to 'knowledge-based organizations' which they distinguish from

> organisations of knowledge workers such as publishing houses where a tangible, reproducible commodity is produced on the one hand, and from groupings of artists, academics and scientists on the other, where there is very little standardisation
>
> (Winch and Schneider, 1993, p. 924)

In recent years, yet another term has come into use. Swedish author, consultant and theorist, Karl-Erik Sveiby, has referred to 'knowhow companies', partly to make the point that 'knowing' is an active process of constructing meaning, whereas 'knowledge' has come to be thought of as an artefact or commodity that can, like other more tangible entities, be acquired, preserved and even traded. In discussing the characteristics of such a company, Sveiby writes:

> It is an organisation where the majority of the employees are highly educated, where the 'production' does not consist of goods or services but complex non-standardised problem-solving. The problem-solving process involves a lot of information processing (not necessarily computerised) and the end result is normally a report or process delivered orally or as hard copy. The customers are treated individually . . .
>
> (Sveiby, 1992, p. 170)

Taken together, these terms not only signal a newfound sophistication and thoughtfulness within the organizational literature, they also capture a more complex view of the nature of knowledge itself. Spender comments: 'These days, knowledge is less about truth and reason, and more about intervening knowledgeably and purposefully in the world' (Spender, 1996, p. 64), and Blackler, Reed and Whitaker go so far as to observe:

> the notion of a 'knowledge society' must be redefined . . . It is no longer enough to analyse the 'knowledge society' in terms of objective reflection, or merely in terms of the economic importance of commodifiable, theoretical knowledge. Rather, the 'knowledge society' should be analysed in terms of established and emerging areas of crucial uncertainty. Attention should be focused on the nature of such uncertainties, how they are recognised and negotiated, and above all, on the demands they are making on individual, organisational and institutional knowledge.
>
> (Blackler, Reed and Whitaker, 1993, p. 857)

In another paper, Blackler makes a similar point when he contrasts two distinct epistemological positions. On the one hand, he writes:

> it has been commonly assumed [that people] possess objective knowledge and can be expected to act in accordance with their considered judgements. This is a personal matter which takes place within individuals' heads; decisions on complicated issues will be well thought through and logical; plans are central to purposive action.

On the other hand, however,

> Compare this to an approach which blurs the distinctions between the psychological and social, between thought and action and between theory and practice, and which emphasises the limits of articulation, the cultural basis of knowledge, its indeterminacy, and the active nature of the processes through which knowledge is managed.
>
> (Blackler, 1993, p. 864)

It is evident that the knowledge revolution has affected virtually every sphere of economic activity, transforming existing organizations and professional occupations, bringing into existence new enterprises and occupations, and forcing much more careful attention to what we mean by 'knowledge' in the workplace. It has also led to the emergence of a new class of workers called 'knowledge workers', who are increasingly dominant in both new and continuing industries.

1.5   Knowledge workers

In 1991, the previously mentioned study on Australia as an Information Society showed a dramatic increase in the proportion of the workforce in the information sector.

> A generation ago [it argued] people might have identified a shearer or wheat farmer as a typical Australian worker. It would not have been accurate even then, but the view would have been widely shared. More recently, a blue collar worker in a factory might have been identified – but they now comprise [only] between one-sixth and one-seventh (15 per cent) of the labour force.

According to that report, by 1981,

> 41.5 percent of 'economically active' Australians were in the information labour force, [a fact which] suggests there has been a paradigm shift away from traditional areas of employment based on muscle power and the use of energy and raw materials towards employment based on information/knowledge.
>
> (Jones, 1991, p. 7)

More recently, a report by the Provincial Government of Nova Scotia in Canada – a place conventionally associated with traditional occupations such as agriculture and fishing – argues that in 1992 29.2 per cent of the workforce in the Province were working as knowledge workers, and that 'industries with the largest concentrations of knowledge workers were Education (64%), Business (57%), Health (49%), and Government (50%)' (Nova Scotia Department of Finance, 1993). No doubt, statistics such as these would be found in virtually all OECD countries, and many others besides, which raises the question: 'What, precisely, do knowledge workers do?'

Because the term 'knowledge work' is being used to describe a novel and rapidly changing phenomenon, the most logical way to assess its contemporary usage is to look for references to it on the World Wide Web. This demonstrates that it has already begun to take on a variety of meanings. At least some use the term to refer to 'web work' or other forms of high-technology or multimedia communication. For others, it is evidently a synonym for any kind of work involving intangible services such as consulting or even real-estate sales(!), while for the US military it refers to a particular category of clerical and logistical work which facilitates the 'mission accomplishment' of the armed services.

Setting aside such idiosyncratic meanings, it is evident that many professionals, whether working alone, in firms of practitioners, or in other organizational settings, would qualify as knowledge workers on the basis that they are immersed in large, complex and growing bodies of knowledge with which they need to keep up-to-date (and to which they often contribute) through the pursuit of their calling (Eraut, 1985; Svensson, 1990). People such as software engineers and management consultants have an esoteric body of knowledge which, like that of other 'traditional' professionals, is constantly changing and growing and which likewise provides the basis of their particular competitive advantage. For instance, in a study of three different contexts in the US – a policy-oriented think-tank, a firm of business consultants, and a highly specialized firm of research lawyers – Starbuck found that people working in these settings 'gather information through interviews or reading; they analyse and interpret this information; and they make written and oral reports to clients and colleagues'. Yet, despite what Starbuck describes as 'the strong overt similarities across people, sites and projects':

experts themselves describe their activities diversely. Some say that they are applying old knowledge to new problems, others that they are creating new knowledge, and still others that they are preserving knowledge that already exists. Experts who see themselves as producing new knowledge emphasise the recency or originality of their data and the differences between their findings and those of predecessors. They may classify such work either as basic scientific research or as applied research on markets, products or processes. Other experts see their work mainly as applying existing knowledge to current problems. For instance, when most lawyers do research, they analyse and interpret previous cases and they emphasise the continuity over time of knowledge and its meaning. To gain acceptance of their rulings, most judges de-emphasise the innovative quality of their reasoning.

The distinction between *creating* knowledge and *applying* it is often hard to make. Lawyers may be more successful if they reinterpret precedent cases imaginatively, or if they conceive original strategies. In a particular case study the Garden Company's engineers were applying known techniques, but they were applying them to products no one else had imagined. Basic research may have direct application, and applied research may contribute fundamental knowledge. When it comes to systems as complex as a human body or an economy, people may only be able to create valid knowledge by trying to apply it.

(Starbuck, 1992, pp. 721–2, emphasis added)

Even in conventional industries, process workers are now becoming 'knowledge workers'. In many, perhaps most, factories or assembly plants, it is increasingly common to find production processes and workflows controlled by computers. This is much more than simply the modern-day analogue of the automated workplace; instead the computer converts it into the 'informated' workplace, where the technology provides a rich source of data for workers to manipulate and utilize in order not simply to 'push buttons', but instead to 'push the business':

The proper interpretation of information as it appears on a video screen is rarely self-evident. Whenever the viewer perceives something unusual or potentially problematic, there are soon four or five people crowded around the screen, each offering hypotheses and suggesting methods for testing them. In addition, it frequently requires individuals from several disciplines – systems engineers, process operators, instrumentation specialists – to generate the best solutions.

Traditional training methods are appropriate for teaching people *what to think* ... If they are to get the most out of informating technologies, people also need to learn *how to think*. Learning how to think means developing the intellective skill required for original, independent problem-solving.

(Schuck, 1996, p. 205, emphasis added)

Thus, the informated workplace also provides a vehicle for workers to exchange knowledge and insights and, as Schuck (1996, p. 203) puts it, 'to ask "why" and "what if" questions'. This theme of independent problem-solving is also more vital in other even more information-intensive work settings. It would seem, then, that there are certain underlying similarities in the nature of knowledge work, irrespective of where it occurs. In fact, in his study of knowledge-intensive organizations, Sveiby claims that the four main features of production are:

- non-standardization;

- creativity;

- high dependence on individuals; and

- complex problem solving (Sveiby, 1992, p. 170).

Although using different language, this perspective is strongly reminiscent of Schön's conception of 'reflective practice', elaborated in his two books *The Reflective Practitioner* (1983) and *Educating the Reflective Practitioner* (1987) in which he advances a compelling critique of positivist approaches to professional practice, or what he terms the 'technical rational paradigm'.

Clearly, preparing graduates to work in such complex, fluid and unpredictable settings is a challenge for universities and other educational providers; indeed many employers are now taking responsibility for 'training' their own employees, often because, in their view, universities have been slow to acknowledge the dramatic transformations in the economic, social and technological environments in which their graduates will work. However, one possible way out of this dilemma might be to examine the work of universities as if they themselves are knowledge-intensive organizations, because in this way it might be possible to apply to their graduates some of the insights and developmental practices which are relevant to academic staff.

1.6 Academics as knowledge workers

As the concept of knowledge work has evolved and gained greater currency and clarity, it would appear that universities fit precisely within the ambit of knowledge-based organizations, and, moreover, that academics are quintessentially knowledge workers. While there is a great deal of both speculative and empirical information about the nature of the academic role, arguably the clearest and most cogent contemporary analysis is to be found in the work of the late Ernest Boyer, President of the Carnegie Foundation for the Advancement of Teaching, in particular in his widely acclaimed monograph *Scholarship Reconsidered: Priorities of the Professoriate*.

Instead of the arid and simplistic typification of academic work as comprising a tug-of-war between teaching and research, or even the slightly richer but nevertheless still incomplete three-way split of teaching, research and community service, Boyer proposes that academics actually have four major, complementary aspects of their scholarly work. These four he labelled the *scholarship of discovery*; the *scholarship of application*; the *scholarship of integration*; and, finally, the *scholarship of teaching*.

This typology helps to conceptualize the work of universities and, it is argued, other knowledge-based entities, in a potentially fruitful way. It allows us to consider universities as networks of overlapping and interlinked activities which, while they draw strength and vitality from one another, can nevertheless be 'unbundled' or 'disaggregated' from one another. In the sections which follow, each of the four domains is examined in greater detail, with a view to demonstrating their relevance to other knowledge-based organizations.

1.6.1 The scholarship of discovery

For many, research is the heart and soul of the university, and the purity of disinterested enquiry is the essence of what it means to be an academic. While there is an element of truth to this, and it certainly captures one aspect of research, in practice the discovery of new insights which have commercial applicability is every bit as intellectually demanding, as resource-intensive and as scholarly as its 'pure' or 'basic' counterpart. Indeed, the dividing line between pure and applied research is far from clear. Often basic and applied research will be conducted within the same laboratory or even within the same project. A study which starts out with an applied focus might well throw up novel insights of wider scientific interest and importance. Likewise, a research project conceived and paid for under a research grant may suddenly and unexpectedly yield knowledge which can be commercially exploited. Research assistants who are employed on 'applied' projects may produce scholarly papers which enhance their reputation and that of the institution, thereby increasing the chances of obtaining further competitive grant money. Even the infrastructure which is used to undertake research will be paid for using funds derived from a mixture of both public and private sources.

Thus research within universities demonstrates much the same blurring of boundaries which seems to exemplify the conduct of enquiry in other parts of the knowledge economy and, as universities have become more entrepreneurial, more commercially oriented and more financially sophisticated, not only are various forms of collaboration possible (Turpin, 1996), but indeed academics are seen to exhibit and to exemplify the qualities needed by other knowledge workers as well.

1.6.2   The scholarship of application

The scholarship of application may usefully be thought of as having two components. The first is the familiar territory of 'community service' whereby institutions provide access to their buildings, libraries and sporting facilities, and academics bring to bear their specialist knowledge through activities such as public lectures, social commentary and critique and the elucidation and solution of 'problems' in the community – all without charge. Since public universities are paid for out of the public purse, society at large expects universities and academics to perform such services as part of their civic obligation. This feature is sometimes thought of as unique to universities; however, many companies and firms also undertake various types of community service as part of their role as corporate citizens.

The second aspect of application relates to the university's bringing to bear its specialist knowledge, including research and other infrastructure, in the service and solution of 'real-world' problems for which others are prepared to pay. Ever since the emergence of the modern university in the middle of the nineteenth century there has been debate about the extent to which universities should be 'applied' in their focus. Whatever the merits of these historical arguments in terms of academic autonomy, social critique and institutional independence, the fact is that today universities are seen very much as part of the mechanisms which enhance a country's innovation and international competitiveness. This does not mean that they should forsake their socially critical role, that they should be uncritical servants of any cause which offers money, or that they should become entirely dependent on short-cycle, commercially driven expediencies of the commercial world. However, it does mean that they should see themselves as a vital part of the economic and industrial infrastructure of the region and, more broadly, of the nation.

It is within this domain of application that universities should be prepared to enter fully into partnerships, to charge for their services (businesses are for the most part willing to pay for outside expertise) and to undertake consultancies. It is through application that universities can enhance their practical reputation, develop income flows to subsidise other aspects of their work, and, perhaps most significantly, obtain new insights which may be expected to enrich their teaching and research work. Since there is a clear analogy here with other enterprises in the knowledge economy, there is a direct comparison between academics and other knowledge workers in this regard.

1.6.3   The scholarship of integration

The scholarship of integration has at least three main aspects. First, there is integration, *within* a discipline or field of study, of knowledge claims derived by different research approaches, or at different times or in different parts of the world. This sort of 'integrative scholarship' is vital, and involves an intimate familiarity with the traditions and major lines of development in the field, as well as a high degree of intellectual sophistication. In a post-modern world characterized by fragmentation and an over-abundance of information, such integration provides much-needed synthesis and offers a platform both for the conduct of further inquiry and for practical application of consolidated outcomes and insights.

The second aspect of integration involves the incorporation of new knowledge acquired in real-world settings into the intellectual apparatus of the disciplines. This in turn can be particularly useful in training people for the professions. In his paper on entrepreneurial universities, Formica writes:

> The holistic model moves away from the notion of technology transfer as a one-time handout from the university and research institutions to the firm, replacing it by a broader vision, which encompasses an ongoing multiway exchange between the partners.
>
> (Formica 1996 p.255)

In the case of university partners, the incorporation of such insights and new knowledge developed by industry is part of the scholarship of integration.

Third and finally, integrative scholarship may involve drawing together insights from different disciplines or fields of study. Most real-world problems do not present themselves neatly labelled according to a discipline, which after all is little more than a conventional way of dividing up the complexity of the world into administrative or cognate areas of study. Instead, real-world problems span several different disciplines and solutions are often found through the juxtaposition of those fields. Moreover, it is also true that fruitful lines of enquiry and speculation often arise in multidisciplinary or cross-disciplinary teams; thus integrative scholarship can throw up productive new insights which can be of use to more than one field of practice at a time.

Clearly, integration is a hallmark of much knowledge work both inside and outside universities, and the intellectual capabilities and organizational infrastructure required are virtually the same in both cases.

1.6.4   The scholarship of teaching

Unfortunately, many regard teaching as a relatively routine and undemanding practice, in which information is transmitted from the teacher to the learner in a unidirectional flow which leaves both parties largely unchanged. This, however, is a narrow and restricted view of what teaching actually entails. Not only is it a demanding form of scholarly endeavour, but one which starts with what the teacher knows, and reaches out to the learners to 'create a common ground of intellectual commitment'. Teaching aims to 'stimulate active, not passive, learning and encourage students to be critical, creative thinkers, with the capacity to go on learning after their college days are over'. It requires the teachers to be 'well informed, and steeped in the knowledge of their fields', and that their work be 'not only transmitting knowledge, but *transforming* and *extending* it as well'. Through such inspired and inspirational practice, teachers and learners 'keep the flame of scholarship alive' (Boyer, 1990, pp. 23–4).

On the surface, this may seem to have little to do with organizations not having an explicitly educational mandate, and might provide no direct analogy with other forms of knowledge work. However, it turns out that many knowledge workers have a significant element of what might be called 'teaching' in their roles. Health professionals, for instance, must instruct their patients, and engineers and lawyers their clients; management and other consultants are actually engaged in teaching their principals new ways of behaving or viewing the world; and accountants and auditors do much more than simply process information – they also have a significant role in raising standards of practice and probity in the enterprises with which they deal.

Managers, too, have a responsibility to facilitate learning:

> Inquiry – asking questions – is the first step on the road to creating new meanings and thus new business insights. In an environment of inquiry, people talk to one another and play with ideas. They pose problems, generate hypotheses, test, experiment, and reflect on the outcome . . .

> (Schuck, 1996, p. 206)

Thus, increasingly, managers and practitioners in all manner of knowledge-based workplaces have an almost analogous responsibility to create a climate of enquiry whereby people expand their repertoire of skills and manage to solve problems as they arise.

1.7   Role of universities in developing knowledge workers

A comparison of the activities of knowledge workers and academics, therefore, yields the intriguing insight that academic work – including research, application, integration and teaching – is remarkably like that performed in a variety of other knowledge-intensive settings. Not only does this provide a language with which to describe knowledge work generally, it also suggests that the activities of universities might usefully provide a framework for the development of those attributes – both generic and discipline-specific – which employers and the professions increasingly claim they expect of graduates. With the blossoming of knowledge-based and knowledge-intensive organizations, and the transformation of professional practice, it is argued that the universities have a leadership role in producing graduates who are not only attuned to the need for, and equipped with the skills of, continuing lifelong personal and professional development (Candy, Crebert and O'Leary, 1994), but who also:

1.   are capable of finding things out for themselves through disciplined enquiry;

2.   can apply what they know to the solution of non-recurrent problems and the betterment of society;

3.   are able to bring to bear insights and methods derived from various field of study and practice; and

4.   can explain what they know to patients, clients, colleagues and members of the public.

In other words, there is a unique and distinctive role for universities in developing in their graduates the ability and predisposition to take the values of scholarship to the communities which they serve.

1.8   Conclusion

I began this chapter with a discussion of specialization, and argued that universities have evolved as specialized providers of specialized learning. In recent years, however, their distinctive role has been under attack from at least two different directions. On the one hand, their position as 'specialized providers' of both vocational and general education has been challenged by a plethora of competitors including many non-traditional entrants to the higher education scene. On the other hand, the provision of specializedlearning has also been eroded to some extent, not only by the practice of employers and others providing in-house training, but more generally by the widespread criticism that many of their programmes were excessively narrow and specific (this notwithstanding the fact that the highly vocational focus was commonly in the name of increasing the employability of graduates at the behest of those very professional associations and employers which actually accredit university courses in the first place (Higher Education Council, 1996)).

Faced with this 'pincer movement', universities are having to reinvent themselves and redefine their role in the production, preservation and dissemination of knowledge. They are having to rethink their missions with respect both to other agencies, and to their own internal ways of operating. Universities have had to become more entrepreneurial, more managerial and more flexible. In common with other organizations and entities, they have entered into joint ventures and collaborative arrangements with other institutions of higher learning, with business and industry, with research organizations and with other cultural organizations such as libraries and theatres.

Ironically, this very adaptability has proven to be a double-edged sword. Some have argued that universities are manifestly irrelevant, because each part of their role is performed at least to some extent by other social agencies. Others have taken the view that their irrelevance derives instead from the fact that that much of what universities teach is available more cheaply from other educational providers – such as community colleges or colleges of further education – or, even more ominously, from the World Wide Web. Others again have lamented what they see as a loss of autonomy through surrendering a distinctive mandate to what might be seen as the demands of 'the market'.

Perhaps counter-intuitively, however, there has been at least one positive consequence of the blurring of universities' boundaries. Although it might be true both that some of their direct instructional functions have been superseded by the media, and in particular by the World Wide Web, and that aspects of their role as producers of knowledge have been usurped by other agencies (Gibbons, Nowotny and Limoges *et al.*, 1994), collaborating with other education and training providers has actually thrown into sharp relief those features of their work which are distinctive; indeed those which actually make higher education higher in the first place.

While other aspects of society might indeed provide access to learning opportunities, and might even help to lay the foundation of learning competence, it is apparent that universities also perform other valued social functions. In the preservation of much of our cultural heritage, in the informed critique of social trends and issues, and through the profoundly important socialization function of education, universities have the responsibility to model the highest standards of probity and rigour with respect to the development and wise use of knowledge.

Universities have a distinctive and enduring educative role in the production of lifelong learners and of graduates capable of informed action. Far from being rendered redundant or superfluous by the move to an information society, universities are in fact needed more now than ever, because, in a world dominated by knowledge, they represent knowledge work at its highest.

1.9   References

Alston, Senator R. (1997) Speech at the launch of IBM's Asia Pacific Geoplex, Ballarat, 8 August 1997.

Bangemann, M. (Chair) (1994) Europe and the global information society: Report to the European Council by the High-Level Group on the Information Society. Brussels: European Council. (http://www2.echo.lu/eudocs/en/report.html, accessed 31 July 1997).

Blackler, F. (1993) Knowledge and the theory of organisation: organisation as activity systems and the reframing of management, *Journal of Management Studies*, 30(6), 864–84.

Blackler, F. (1995) Knowledge, knowledge work and organisation: an overview and interpretation, *Organisation Studies*, 16(6), 1021–46.

Blackler, F., Reed, M. and Whitaker, A. (1993) Editorial introduction: knowledge workers and contemporary organisations, *Journal of Management Studies*, 30, 851–62.

Boyer, E.L. (1990) *Scholarship Reconsidered: Priorities of the Professoriate*, Princeton, NJ: Carnegie Foundation for the Advancement of Teaching.

Candy, P.C., Crebert, R.G. and O'Leary, J. (1994) *Developing Lifelong Learners through Undergraduate Education*, National Board of Employment, Education and Training Commissioned Report No. 28, Canberra: AGPS.

Cordell, A.J. (1985) *The Uneasy Eighties: The Transition to an Information Society* (Summary of Background Study 53), Ottawa: Science Council of Canada.

Darrah, C.N. (1995) Workplace training, workplace learning: a case study, *Human Organisation*, 54(1), 31–41.

Drucker, P.F. (1993) *Post-Capitalist Society*, Oxford: Butterworth Heinemann.

Eraut, M. (1985) Knowledge creation and knowledge use in professional contexts, *Studies in Higher Education*, 10(2), 117–33.

Formica, P. (1996) Innovative players of economic development: 'Learning' companies and 'entrepreneurial' universities in action. In M. Guedes and P. Formica (eds.) *The Economics of Science Parks*. Brazili, Brazil: ANPROTEC, Universidade de Brazila. pp. 233-268

Gibbons, M., Limoges, C., Novotny, H. *et al*. (1994) *The New Production of Knowledge*, London: Sage.

Hague, D. (1991) Knowledge society university challenge, *Marxism Today* (September 1991).

Higher Education Council (1996) *Professional Education and Credentialism*, Canberra: AGPS.

Hirschhorn, L. and Gilmore, T. (1992) The new boundaries of the 'boundary-less' company, *Harvard Business Review*, 70(3), 104–15.

Jones, Hon., B.O. (Chair) (1991) *Australia as an Information Society: Grasping New Paradigms*, Report of the House of Representatives Standing Committee for Long term Strategies, Canberra: AGPS.

Nova Scotia Department of Finance (1993) A working paper on knowledge workers and industries in Nova Scotia (http://www.gov.ns.ca/fina/stats.div/papers/know/ accessed 29 July 1997).

Pogson, P. (1997) The university and intellectual capital: rethinking our strategies for the arrival of the knowledge era. Paper presented at the *6th Australasian Higher Education Development Conference*, Adelaide, South Australia, July 1997.

Schön, D.A. (1983) *The Reflective Practitioner*, New York: Basic Books.

Schön, D.A. (1987) *Educating the Reflective Practitioner*, San Francisco: Jossey-Bass.

Schriesheim, J., von Glinow, M-A. and Kerr, S. (1977) Professionals in bureaucracies: a structural alternative, *Studies in the Management Sciences*, 5, 55–69.

Schuck, G. (1996) Intelligent technology, intelligent workers: a new pedagogy for the high-tech workplace. In K. Starkey (ed.), *How Organisations Learn*, London: International Thomson Business Press.

Slaughter, R.A. (ed.) (1996) *New Thinking for a New Millennium*, London: Routledge.

Smith, A. (1776/1910) *An inquiry into the nature and causes of the wealth of nations* (2 vols) London: J. M. Dent & Sons

Spender, J-C. (1996) Organisational knowledge, learning and memory: three concepts in search of a theory, *Journal of Organisational Change Management*, 9(1), 63–78.

Spinks, P. (1997) Island with mother of all economies, *The Age*, 25 July 1997, p. B8.

Starbuck, W.H. (1976) Organisations and their environments. In M. D. Dunnette (ed.), *Handbook of Industrial and Organisational Psychology*, Chicago: Rand McNally.

Starbuck, W.H. (1993) Learning by knowledge-intensive firms, *Journal of Management Studies*, 29(6), 713–40.

Stoffle, C.J. (1996) The emergence of education and knowledge management as major functions of the digital library, *1996 Follett Lecture*, 13 November 1996, University of Cardiff (http://www.ukoln.ac.uk/follett/stoffle/paper.html accessed 21 January 1997).

Sveiby, K-E. (1992) The knowhow company: strategy formulation in knowledge-intensive industries, *International Review of Strategic Management*, Chichester, West Sussex/Chichester, New York: John Wiley, 167–86.

Svensson, L.G. (1990) Knowledge as a professional resource: case studies of architects and psychologists. In R. Torstendahl and M. Burrage (eds), *The Formation of Professions: Knowledge, State and Strategy*, London: Sage.

Turpin, T. et al. (1996) Knowledge-based Cooperation: University-Industry Linkages in Australia, *EIP Report 96/17*, Canberra: AGPS.

Winch, G. and Schneider, E. (1993) Managing the knowledge-based organisation: the case of architectural practice, *Journal of Management Studies*, 30(6), 923–37.

2 On the certainty of public shaming: working with students 'who just don't get it'

Stephen Brookfield
Distinguished Professor, University of St Thomas (St Paul, Minnesota)

2.1 Introduction

I'd like to begin by stating three foundational assumptions about helping students learn that I imagine many readers of these proceedings believe to be self-evident. These are that:

- good teaching is teaching that is critically reflective;
- good teaching focuses on helping students learn;
- the most important knowledge we need to teach well is an awareness of how our students are experiencing their own learning.

Let me take each of these in turn . . .

2.2 Assumption 1: Good teaching is teaching that is critically reflective

This assumption holds that good teachers regard their practice as open-ended and developmental, always changing in response to new circumstances. Instead of regarding teaching as the standard application of set behaviours across contexts, critically reflective teachers know that each new group of students represents a new milieu. The particular mix of abilities, personalities, histories, experiences, cultural backgrounds and genders that a class represents never repeats itself. This means that we have constantly to review, research and critique how we think and act as teachers to ensure that what we're doing has the effects we intend.

Critically reflective teachers constantly research the assumptions that inform their practice by seeing this practice through four complementary lenses: the lens of their own autobiographies as teachers and learners, the lens of students' eyes, the lens of colleagues' perceptions and the lens of theoretical, philosophical and research literature. Reviewing practice through these lenses makes us more aware of those submerged and unacknowledged power dynamics that exist in classrooms and staffrooms. It also helps us detect the hegemonic assumptions that frame how we teach.

Hegemonic assumptions are assumptions that we think are in our own best interests but that actually work against us in the long term. As developed by the Italian political economist Antonio Gramsci (1978), the term hegemony describes the process whereby ideas, structures and actions come to be seen by the majority of people as wholly natural, preordained and working for their own good, when in fact they are constructed and transmitted by powerful minority interests to protect the status quo that serves these interests so well. The subtle cruelty of hegemony is that over time it becomes deeply embedded, part of the cultural air we breathe. One cannot peel back the layers of oppression and point the finger at an identifiable group or groups of people who we accuse as the instigators of a conscious conspiracy to keep people silent and disenfranchised. Instead, the ideas and practices of hegemony become part and parcel of everyday life – the stock opinions, conventional wisdoms or commonsense ways of seeing and ordering the world that people take for granted. If there's a conspiracy here, it is the conspiracy of the normal.

Hegemonic assumptions about teaching are eagerly embraced by teachers. They seem to represent what's good and true and therefore to be in their own best interests. Yet these assumptions actually end up serving the interests of groups that have little concern for teachers' mental or physical health. The dark irony of hegemony is that teachers take pride in acting on the very assumptions that work to enslave them. In working diligently to implement these assumptions, teachers become willing prisoners who lock their own cell doors behind them. If we could but stand outside our practice and see these assumptions from another perspective we would realize that they are actually destroying us and working to serve the interests of others. Critically reflective teachers are alert to hegemonic assumptions. They can uncover ideas about good teaching that seem obvious, even desirable, yet that end up harming and constraining them. They are able to see the insanity of aspiring to ways of teaching that end up seriously threatening their own well-being.

Let me give an example of a hegemonic assumption – the assumption that teaching is a vocation. Many teachers speak of their work as answering a vocational calling. Thought of this way, teaching becomes work that implies that its practitioners are selfless servants of their students and institutions. That teachers sometimes eagerly accept concepts of vocation and conscientiousness to justify their taking on backbreaking loads is evident from Campbell and Neill's (1994a,b) studies of teachers' work. A sense of calling becomes distorted to mean that they should deal with larger and larger numbers of students, regularly teach overload courses, serve on search, alumni and library committees, generate external funding by winning grant monies and make occasional forays into scholarly publishing. And they should do all of this without complaining, which is the same as whining.

Teachers who take the idea of vocation as the organizing concept for their professional lives may start to think of any day on which they don't come home exhausted as a day wasted. Or, if not a day wasted, then at least a day when they have not been all that they can be (it's interesting that so many teachers have adopted a slogan to describe their work that first appeared in commercials for U.S. army recruitment). Diligent devotion to the college's many ends (some of which are bound to be contradictory) may come to be seen as the mark of a good teacher.

So what seems on the surface to be a politically neutral idea on which all could agree – that teaching is a vocation calling for dedication and hard work – may be interpreted by teachers as meaning that they should squeeze the work of two or three jobs into the space where one can sit comfortably. 'Vocation' thus becomes a hegemonic concept – an idea that seems neutral, consensual and obvious, and that teachers gladly embrace, but one that ends up working against their own best interests. The concept of vocation ends up serving the interests of those who want to run colleges efficiently and profitably while spending the least amount of money and employing the smallest number of staff that they can get away with.

A critically reflective teacher can stand outside her practice and see what she does from a wider perspective. She knows that curriculum content and evaluative procedures are social products that are located in time and space, and that they probably reproduce the inequities of the wider culture. She is able to distinguish between a justifiable and necessary dedication to students' wellbeing, and a selfdestructive workaholism. She has a well-grounded rationale for her practice that she can call on to help her make difficult decisions in unpredictable situations.

This rationale – a set of critically examined core assumptions about why she does what she does in the way that she does it – is a survival necessity. It anchors teachers in a moral, intellectual and political project and gives them an organizing vision of what they are trying to accomplish. By prioritizing what is really important in their work a critical rationale helps teachers keep in perspective their own tendency to translate a sense of vocation into meaning that they have to do everything asked of them.

Finally, teaching with a critically reflective stance makes us mistrustful of grand theories and grand narratives of what 'good' teaching looks like. We realize the contextuality of all practice and the limitations of universal templates such as behavioural objectives, conscientization, outcomes or competency-based education, and so on. For more on the ideas discussed in this section see *Becoming a Critically Reflective Teacher* (Brookfield, 1995a).

2.3 Assumption 2: Good practice is whatever helps students learn

If we believe that the focus of our efforts is student learning, and if we judge whether or not something qualifies as good teaching by the extent to which it helps students learn, then this shifts our attention far away from exemplary models of teacher performance. The range of behaviours that is subsumed under notions of good teaching becomes broadened to include such things as the teacher not talking, the teacher leaving the room, the teacher refusing to give detailed directions, and so on. Under certain conditions these things might be exactly what some students need in order to learn something. Letting students wrestle with complexity, ambiguity and uncertainty and not jumping in to help them out is painful, both for them and us. But in the long run this may be the only way they'll learn to engage with complex concepts or consider perspectives and information that challenge their familiar ways of thinking and acting. Yet most institutions would look askance at teachers who left the room and refused to give directions to students. These actions would be judged to be a dereliction of professional duty rather than a spur to students' learning.

Thinking of good practice as whatever helps students learn also calls on us to reconsider our knee-jerk, instinctive dismissal of lecturing. Sometimes students need to attend carefully to a lecture in order to make informed choices and decisions regarding their own selfdirected learning. As Freire and Shor (1987) recognize, there is nothing inherently oppressive or demagogic about lecturing, and nothing inherently liberating about discussion. A lecture can be critically reflective and stimulating, offering challenging perspectives to students. Conversely, a discussion can be an insidious manipulation of the group by the leader to make students agree with the leader's predetermined views. Just putting students in a circle will not change the flow of power in the room.

Gore (1993) and Usher and Edwards (1994) all make the point that the experience of being in a circle is ambiguous. For students who are confident, loquacious and used to academic culture, the circle holds relatively few terrors. It is an experience that is congenial, authentic and liberating. But for students who are shy, aware of their different skin colour, physical appearance or form of dress, unused to intellectual discourse, intimidated by disciplinary jargon and the culture of academe, or conscious of their lack of education, the circle can be a painful and humiliating experience. These students have been stripped of their right to privacy. They have also been denied the chance to check teachers out by watching them closely before deciding whether or not they can be trusted. Trusting teachers is often a necessary precondition to students speaking out. This trust only comes with time as teachers are seen to be acting consistently, honestly and fairly. Yet the circle, with its implicit pressure to participate and perform, may preclude the time and opportunity for this trust to develop.

So beneath the circle's democratic veneer there may exist a much more troubling and ambivalent reality. Students in a circle may feel an implicit or explicit pressure from peers and teachers to say something, anything, just to be noticed. Whether or not they feel ready to speak, or whether or not they have anything particular they want to say, becomes irrelevant. The circle can be experienced as mandated disclosure, just as much as it can be a chance for people to speak in an authentic voice. This is not to suggest that we throw the circle out and go back to the dark days of teachers talking uninterruptedly at rows of desks. I continue to use the circle in my own practice. But critical reflection makes me aware of the circle's oppressive potential and reminds me that I must continually research how it is experienced by students.

One last point about this assumption. Of all the mistakes staff developers make, perhaps the most common is to castigate as neanderthals any of their colleagues who choose to use lecture methods. The impression is given that anyone who gives a lecture combines the moral sensitivity of Adolf Hitler with the democratic impulses of Josef Stalin. Since most college and university teachers lecture at some time or another, this implies that of all the people working in academe today it is only those in charge of staff development centres who really understand the dynamics of teaching and learning. If any hint of this kind of attitude is picked up by those whom we are hoping will critically examine their own teaching, then we (as staff developers) are dead in the water. We need to demonstrate that our own commitments to experiential methods, small-group activities and multiple learning modalities are themselves viewed as problematic and subjected by us to constant critical analysis.

2.4 Assumption 3: The most important knowledge teachers need to do good work is a knowledge of how students are experiencing learning and perceiving their teachers' actions

To me an awareness of what's happening to students in my classrooms is the first order, framing knowledge I need to teach well. Without this knowledge all the pedagogic skill in the world is irrelevant. I may have a terrific command of computer-assisted instruction (I don't), be a charismatic lecturer (I'm not), design tests that assess exactly what students have learned (not bad at this), or be able to create lively, democratic discussions (occasionally) but without knowing what's going on inside my students' heads I have no way of knowing when, in what way, and with whom these different methods (and others) should be used.

This assumption has several problems embedded at its core. One is the fact that it is impossible to enter another's consciousness and experience this in exactly the same way as it's being experienced by the other. We can listen to students' words, but we can never know exactly the complex flow of thoughts, feelings, and impulses that comprise their experience. Not only is it existentially inconceivable to experience another's particular configurations of experience, it is also highly labour-intensive to try! How on earth can any college teacher be expected to develop an awareness of the multiple ways in which her many students experience her classrooms? The kinds of phenomenographic explorations advocated by Marton (1988) are probably beyond the capacities of most harried university lecturers carrying course and advisement loads that are already way out of proportion to the time they have available.

Another difficulty is that when we get inside students' heads we find things there that complicate our life immeasurably. We find that there are more students operating at low levels of comprehension or competence than we had imagined. We find that students have a far greater variety of learning preferences and forms of cognitive processing than we were aware of. We discover that the aspects of our teaching that we're proudest of, and that we put great store by, are hardly noticed by many students. Conversely, we learn that exercises we did almost as an afterthought are found to be extremely helpful by students. It is demoralizing to find that teaching actions we have invested with great significance pass students by, while other actions that to us are incidental are viewed by students as rife with profound meaning. So finding out what's inside our students' heads does not lead immediately to clarity or common understanding. In the short term it probably adds to any frustration or confusion we already feel.

Added to this is the difficulty raised by the fact that we teach what we like to learn. Most people end up as teachers of subjects and skills that they were good at as students and that they took pleasure in learning. It would be a masochistic (or very unlucky) teacher who ended up teaching something she hated and had a history of failing to learn. Lee Andresen, an Australian educator, claims that the reason many people go into teaching is vicariously to re-experience the primary joy they experienced the first time they learned something they loved (Andresen, 1993). By introducing others to the pleasure involved in such learning they relive the primary joy they themselves experienced as students.

If this is true (and I'm sure that for many of us it is) then this means that most teachers have never been in the same unfortunate position faced by many of their own students the position of 'just not getting it'. 'I just don't get it' describes the experience that settles on many students who can't seem to grasp the essential manoeuvres, the defining operations, of something your autobiography as a learner tells you is simple to grasp. R.S. Peters's (1967) concept of the grammar of the activity is useful here. The grammar of any activity comprises the foundational building blocks, the crucial cognitive or psychomotor procedures that comprise a skill set or area of knowledge. If we have learned this grammar then we grasp the central criteria which allow us to determine that something has been understood properly or practised well. Students who just don't get it lack the grammar of the activity they are studying. They are strangers in a strange land.

If you teach a subject or skill you like and are good at, the chances are that you learned the grammar of your activity fairly quickly and easily. Consequently you will never have had the sustained experience of struggle, demoralization and total mystification that settles on students who just don't get it. You have never known what it feels like not to be able to understand the simplest organizing principles of a subject or to be unable to meet the standards for the demonstration of a minimum level of skill competence. This means that when you meet students who tell you that they 'just don't get' your subject you are perceptually challenged. At a rational level of analysis you know what these words mean: for example, that students are having difficulties decoding your words and actions, that they are struggling to understand conceptual ideas and apply these to context, or that the ability to write and think critically is lacking. But it is one thing to know these things rationally, quite another to know them viscerally.

When teachers are faced with students who just don't get it they often follow a predictable series of responses. First, they slow down their explanation of a concept or their demonstration of a skill, in the hope that this will give students the necessary time to develop the required level of understanding. But the student responds by saying 'I'm sorry, I don't know what you mean/what you want me to do – I just don't get it.' The teacher then takes a deep breath, and with an increasingly surreal sense of frustration, demonstrates the manoeuvre again and again, or repeats the principle using a variety of examples and analogies. These pedagogically diverse strategies are only met with the same blank look. The basic problem the teacher faces here is that because she has never had this extended experience of 'just not getting' the subject or skill she teaches, she has no autobiographical experiences of struggle on which to draw. She is powerless to help her own students who are in this position because she has never lived through their experience of being 'blocked' and unable to grasp the fundamentals of her discipline. Rapidly she reverts to what we might call the Nike school of pedagogy. When a student says for the third or fourth time 'Sorry, I just don't get it', the teacher cries out in frustration, 'for God's sake, *just do it!'*

How can we get ourselves out of this box? One way is to use different classroom research techniques to survey students so that on a weekly basis we get some information about what's happening to them. We can then use this information to make more informed pedagogic decisions and to take actions that are grounded in an accurate reading of the emotional and cognitive tenor of our classrooms. In my own teaching I use a weekly, anonymous critical incident questionnaire (the CIQ) to solicit written information from students about the moments during the week's classes in which they were most engaged or distanced, the actions they found most helpful or puzzling, and the ways in which they were taken by surprise. I report this information back to students at the start of each new week and use it to guide much of my practice. A fuller description of this instrument together with some examples of its use is contained in Brookfield (1995a). American variants of classroom research are available in Angelo (1991), Angelo and Cross (1993), and Cross and Steadman (1996). In Britain important work has been done by Hammersley (1986, 1993) and Hopkins (1993).

The other way to resolve this problem and the one I want to explore in this chapter is to decide that on an annual basis we will deliberately put ourselves in the position of being a student who 'just doesn't get it'. This means that we will volunteer to learn something that we find intimidating or threatening because we know we lack the grammar of that activity. We do this in the sure knowledge that what awaits us in this learning is a sustained experience of private shaming and public humiliation. As we go through this experiential analog of what many of our own students suffer, we keep a journal of the engaging and distancing moments in our learning. We notice what it is that our teachers do that puts us at our ease or emboldens us, and what it is they do that insults, embarrasses or demeans us. We reflect on these matters in the company of colleagues and then interpret our own practice as teachers from this new vantage point. Seeing our actions through the eyes of a terrified student who has no idea of the basic grammar of the learning activity shocks us into a realization of what we should, and should not, do when we meet such learners as a teacher.

Let me give an autobiographical example of what I mean.

2.5   Memoirs of a digitally challenged adult learner

It's the mid-1980s and I'm wishing, deeply and fervently, that I had been born into the predigital age. All around me people are babbling on about the Information Superhighway. As far as I understand this idea, the conversion of information into digital impulses combined with the use of telephone lines is about to turn the world into one giant communication party with everyone able to locate (sorry, 'access') any person or piece of information they want at a moment's notice. As far as this Information Superhighway metaphor is concerned, I think of myself as roadkill festering on the hard shoulder of the off ramp to the Information Superhighway – a squashed skunk, stinking to high heaven before I ever got going.

My colleagues compound my feelings of insecurity by telling me that typewriters are old technology. Wordprocessors (remember them?) are the new thing. If I just switch from a typewriter keyboard to a wordprocessor keyboard (so I'm assured) my publishing output will triple overnight. I will be able to list three times as many books, articles and monographs on my curriculum vitae as would otherwise be possible. Since I am coming up to face a tenure decision in a year or so, this seems a prospect worth investigating. I wrote my first books and articles in longhand which, when I admit it, makes me sound like Dickens or Keats. So the process of writing everything out in script and then typing it, with all the cutting and pasting and whiteout fluid this entails, certainly seems unnecessarily time-consuming.

One day a senior colleague gives me an Apple IIE wordprocessor with a soupedup hard disk drive that does all kinds of things I couldn't begin to explain. He hands me the manual explaining the workings of this mystery machine and assures me that all I need to do is read it and all will be revealed. 'Apple makes processors for idiots It's a simple menu-driven program, all you need to do is choose what you want from a list of menu options that will appear on the screen,' he confidently declares. The machine doesn't look much like a sympathetic waiter, but I decide to give it a try.

I try doing what the manual says but keep running into problems. Basically I follow every instruction carefully only to discover that the machine doesn't respond to my instructions the way it should. Then, I get on the phone to my friend Warren (a technological avatar) and ask him what I'm doing wrong. Patiently he takes me through the procedures I've just attempted assuring me I must have missed something along the way. 'Impossible' I reply, with an indignation that masks my feelings of failure. But, sure enough, he's right. Although I could have sworn that the instruction wasn't there the first time I read the page, and that between reading it and speaking to him it has mysteriously materialized, I have to admit I *did* miss out an intermediate stage. When I do what he tells me the machine snaps to attention and brings me my order.

These phone calls continue for about a week until Warren tells me we can't go on like this. I'm phoning him every hour or so with an elementary query about the AppleWorks word-processing program I'm using and he needs to get back to his own life. 'What you need' he assures me 'is to take an introductory wordprocessing class. They'll explain all these basic things there and you'll be able to work the program on your own.' As it happens my college is offering an 'Introduction to AppleWorks' class the next week at lunchtime. I sign up.

A week passes and the fateful day arrives. As I close the door to my office and start the 100 yard walk across campus to the computer lab where the class is to be held I am a confident academic who has spent his adult life in institutions of higher education. Not only that, I've already published two books on adult learning and teaching. By the time I enter the computer lab and sit at the terminal waiting for the class to start I am terrified. It is as if during the 100 yard walk I have experienced a process of infantilization and regressed to the state of terror of a new pupil in his first day at primary school.

As I sit at the computer terminal I'm having a frenetic inner dialogue around the question 'Should I go or should I stay?' I feel like I've made a terrible mistake ever showing up for this class because I know, with every fibre of my being, that at the end of the class I'll still be trying to work out the first instruction the teacher gave 60 minutes earlier. In my mind's eye everyone else in the group will be forging ahead, their fingers flying confidently over the keyboard in a way that shows their command of processing. I, on the other hand, know that I'm the one person in the whole class who just won't get it. The one thing I know with any degree of certainty is that by volunteering to attend this class I've let myself in for a degree of public shaming, humiliation and embarrassment that I'd never before thought possible.

So I'm having this internal conversation on 'shall I go or shall I stay?' I think to myself that I could leave before the class starts and that the other students who are now wandering in will conclude that I'm some sort of computer trekkie – a whizz kid who saw that he'd wandered in by mistake to a beginner's class and who'd decided to leave until he could have the lab back to perform all sorts of unimaginable technological feats. (It occurs to me later that many students in my own classes are probably having this same sort of interior dialogue on the first day of a new course.) But I know I have to stay. The alternative is to go back to my office, try to follow the manual, and end up calling avatar Warren again bringing me full circle and right back to the point at which he told me I needed to take this class.

While I'm pondering my dilemma I notice a switch on the side of the computer marked 'On/Off'. I lean over and move the switch from 'Off' to 'On'. In response the computer goes 'blip' and words appear on the screen. 'That's nice' I think to myself, 'at least I've got it humming'. At the same moment as I'm thinking this a human thunderbolt hurtles across the room with the unexpected power of summer lightning. It turns out that this is the instructor for the course. He's a nondescript-looking person, a grey blur at the edge of the room who could be a janitor, a student, or the teacher. When he reaches me he starts slapping me on the back and complimenting me lavishly on my willingness to interact with the machine without any direction from him. 'It's so wonderful', he tells me, 'to have at least one student in the group yourself who's obviously used to being around these machines. You won't believe this but quite a few students are really threatened by the idea of computers so it's great for me when I get someone like you who's a natural. You're obviously a selfdirected technological learner who feels confident around all this hardware and I'm sure that your sense of confidence is going to rub off on your less confident peers.'

As I hear these remarks I'm flooded with a sense of wellbeing. The teacher likes me! Not only that, he says I'm a natural! I never knew I had all this latent potential as a technological learner! As soon as he says all these things my interior dialogue of 'shall I go or shall I stay?' is resolved. Of course, I'm staying. Why am I staying? Because the source of all objective power and authority where computer learning is concerned – the teacher – has laid his hands on me and declared me to be in a state of technological grace. If he says I'm fine, then I'm fine. The fact that I wrote my PhD thesis on independent learning, and that I've just published an edited collection on self-directed learning (Brookfield, 1985) that is highly sceptical of teacher authority, never enters my head. If teacher says I'm good, then I'm good.

It's a while after the class ends before I start to think about this interaction. Two things strike me.

2.5.1 Insights so far

1. If I, who am used to academic settings and have mostly been successful in them, feel completely intimidated when I'm enrolled in a continuing education class in my own institution, then many of my own adult students (many of whom have been away from education for a considerable time) are probably terrified on the first day of class. Although they don't show this terror, I must assume it exists.

2. It's astonishing to me how much the teacher's approval meant to me. His noticing what I'd done and complimenting me on it made all the difference to my confidence level and convinced me to stay in the course.

2.5.2 Meanings for my practice

1. I need to find a way of acknowledging and addressing the fear that many adult students feel the first day of a new course of being found to be the one idiot in the group who doesn't get it while everybody else does. This is the sense of impostorship I subsequently wrote about in *The Skillful Teacher* (1990). I decide that the way to do this is to start off any new course by inviting a panel of adults who were formerly students in any course to attend the first class of a new course. I will ask the visiting students to talk about the way they felt when they attended the first day of class a year or two before. Chances are they will each talk about their sense of being sure that they were the only one's who wouldn't understand the simplest command while all the rest of the class forged ahead.

2. I need to do what my computer teacher did for me that first day. I must try to notice something that each of my students does the first day of class and proceed to compliment them on their accomplishment. This will probably help them resolve the 'should I go or should I stay?' question in favour of staying. So I start to think about creating a 'failure proof' exercise for the first day of every new course. This would be a task that every member of a new course could complete successfully. On successful completion of this task I would then compliment the students on a job well done.

Of course I know these things rationally. I know it's important to build confidence early on in a learning episode. I know that confidence is a self-fulfilling spiral – the more confident you feel the more confidence you gain. But though I know these things rationally I don't know them viscerally. It took my being on the other side of the mirror, looking at teaching through the eyes of a terrified student, to learn them viscerally.

2.6 Taking the plunge

It's the mid 1980s. I'm pushing 40, living in Manhattan and getting flabby. What exercise I get – walking along Broadway after dark – is conducted amidst car exhausts, requests for money made two or three times per block, and the ever-present danger of ending up under the wheels of a cab driven by an over zealous (let's be kind and not say maniacal) New York cabbie. This is all extremely stimulating and I never face the problem of boredom that accompanies taking most forms of exercise. However, I've decided that I need to do something safer and healthier, so I decide I'll do some regular swimming, maybe three times a week. The only problem is, I can't swim. So, I've decided to enrol in a swimming class for adult nonswimmers.

Why am I doing this? Well, the woman I am spending a lot of time with suggested I take the class. I protest, saying I don't need it and that I can learn to swim selfdirectedly, thank you very much. She points out that selfdirected learning where swimming is concerned isn't getting me very far. I describe to her how I've been working on selfdirected swimming since I was in my teens. On each vacation, when the chance arises, I watch people swim in hotel pools, lakes and oceans during the day and observe and remember exactly what it is that they do. Then, under cover of darkness, when everyone else is asleep or eating, I slip out of my room like some aquatic vampire and make my way to the water, a Bela Lugosi figure with a towel draped around my shoulders rather than a black cape. I slide into the pool, lake or ocean and do my best in near darkness to mimic what I've observed other people do during the bright light of day. Needless to say, I've spent several years floundering (literally as well as figuratively) in this self-directed learning project.

When my woman friend hears me describe my autobiography of learning to swim she gently points out that my 'natural' learning style – selfdirection – is, in this case, severely dysfunctional for me. (In spite of this humiliatingly penetrating insight we get married a little later.) She says that what I'm really afraid of is looking stupid in front of other people. All this self-direction is a cover for my innate shyness and my arrogant conviction that I can learn anything I want without others assisting me. What I need, she tells me, is to switch from my preferred learning style into a situation where I'm getting some expert instruction. I should study swimming with someone who can break down this extremely complex skill into manageable, but increasingly complex, operations. If this happens, I'm assured, the confidence I will derive from mastering some basic skills will lead me to increase my efforts until, before I know it, I am swimming. I protest that what she's saying is ridiculous, all the while knowing that she's right (a marital dynamic that continues to this day).

2.6.1   Insights so far

1   Sometimes the last thing learners need is for their preferred learning style to be affirmed. Agreeing to let people learn only in a way that feels comfortable and familiar can restrict seriously their chance for development. If I had stayed within my own habitual pattern of self-directed swimming I never would have moved beyond the point of staying afloat for a couple of seconds.

2.   Self-directed learning – something I have championed unquestioningly for several years – can spring from much darker psychic wellsprings than I had imagined. Instead of representing an admirable resilience and a desire to exercise independent control, it can also betoken a certain arrogance and a fear of public failure.

2.6.2   Meaning for my practice:

I must think again about my unquestioned belief that good teachers find out the preferred learning styles of their students early on in a course and then spend the rest of the course designing methods and forms of evaluation that connect to these. I realize that this is important to do for some of the time so that students feel affirmed by ways of learning that are comfortable and familiar. But it is equally important for me to spend other parts of the course deliberately exposing students to ways of learning that are unfamiliar for them and that will make them uncomfortable, at least initially.

Part of a good educational experience involves broadening the range of learning styles with which students are familiar. No one is likely to be able to spend most of their time learning only in the way they like, so giving students some experience in a range of styles is really in their own best long-term interests. From now on I will try to mix methods and evaluative options that strike an equitable balance between affirming students' preferred learning styles and introducing them to alternative ways of learning. My unalloyed reliance on what are thought of as self-directed learning formats (learning contracts, independent studies, individual projects) will have to be balanced with more directive and more collective forms of teaching, learning and evaluation.

2.7   The story continues . . .

A few weeks later I am in a tiny changing cubicle at a swimming pool. It's the first evening of a class for adult non-swimmers and, while I'm stripping down to my swimming trunks, a number of thoughts are darting through my mind. One is that I hate to show my pale, pimply, naked Englishman's body in public. Its torso and legs are so skinny and underdeveloped and its stomach is so flabby. Another is that I'm probably the only man in America who doesn't know how to swim. I already know I'm the only man in America who doesn't know how to drive (I eventually pass my test when I am 44 after being taught expertly by my wife a tale that requires a book in itself). Somehow, my lack of aquatic ability embodies my problems dealing with the world of artefacts and the psychomotor domain in general (I have to ask my wife to tell me which is the Phillips screwdriver in the tool box).

A third thought is that it's taking some nerve for me to show up at this class and make a public admission that I don't know how to swim. I think, 'If it's difficult for me to show up at an adult non-swimming class, what must it be like for a nonreader to show up at an adult literacy class? What an act of courage that really is.' As I step out from my cubicle to the poolside I look around at the other students in my class. They are all women. Right then and there I know that my suspicion that I was the only man in the whole country who didn't know how to do this was well founded.

Over the next few weeks I splash around in a fairly unconvincing fashion. Matters aren't helped much by our having two instructors. One I find much more intimidating than the other. The one I dread meeting is a young man. His athleticism, his muscles, his youth and the aquatic abilities he exhibits have already prejudiced me against him before he has opened his mouth. He seems to bounce rather than walk into the pool area, a pedagogic version of A.A. Milne's Tigger, the kind of muscular jock I hated in school. Moreover, he looks 16 years old, a fact that causes me to refect ruefully that when teachers and cops start to look to you like adolescents, you're really hitting mid-life.

Matters are made very difficult by his teaching method, one I would describe as 'charismatic demonstration'. Charismatic demonstration means that he believes that if he shows us how terrifically well he is able to swim, this will inspire in us an uncontrollable desire to match his exemplary performance. On the first night, for example, his first action is to jump in the pool at one end, cut through the water with stunning power, aquatic grace and fluidity and emerge from the water at the other end. As he levitates out of the water he tells us that we should try to do what he does. He shouts things like 'You see how easy it is, that's all there is to it, in ten weeks you'll be doing this too!'

This creates a crashing dissonance since for me to do anything vaguely resembling what I've just seen is an action so far beyond my comprehension that I feel like throwing in the towel (literally and figuratively). I pull him aside one night and explain that the problem for me – the thing that's really stopping me learn how to swim – is that I hate to put my face in the water. Each time I do this I feel like I'm drowning. The universe becomes a white chlorinated haze, with all my usual reference points totally obscured. I'm reminded of how it used to be when I was having dental treatment in England as a young boy and the dentist would give me gas to knock me out entirely. There was the same sense of being out of control and the inability to stop oneself from being submerged by an onrushing, smothering force. Putting my face into the swimming pool is as close to a near-death experience as I can have while still remaining reasonably sentient.

I ask him if I can do the backstroke (which will at least ensure that my face is out of the water) but he tells me that the crawl stroke is the stroke of choice and that's what *real* swimmers learn to do. He then says something to me that I forget but his whole body language conveys to me one unequivocally expressed message: 'For God's sake, grow up. For once in your life act like a man.'

2.7.1 Insight so far

The best learners people for whom learning a skill comes entirely naturally often make the worst teachers. This is because they are, in a very real sense, perceptually challenged. They cannot imagine what it must be like to struggle to learn something that comes so naturally to them. Because they have always been so successful in their learning it is impossible for them to empathize with learners' anxieties and blockages. I visualize my swimming instructor as learning to swim through some kind of aquatic Suzuki method whereby he was thrown in the deep end of the pool at three years of age to find out to his surprise that he actually already knew how to swim. Because he didn't experience the terror I feel at putting my head in water, he can't offer any good insights from his own experiences of learning how to swim that might help me keep my fears under control.

Following this line of reasoning I realize that the best teachers are probably those that have achieved their skill mastery, knowledge and intellectual fluidity only after periods of struggle and anxiety. Because they know what it's like to feel intimidated, and because they have often been convinced that they'll never learn something, they are well placed to help students through their learning difficulties. From now on, when I'm on search committees to appoint teachers, I'll make sure that as I review candidates' CVs I'll look for academic records that start off relatively undistinguishedly but that improve over time. That will probably indicate that the candidate has a history of struggle as a learner on which she can draw when thinking how to help her own students with their difficulties.

2.7.2 Meaning for my practice

As a teacher I need to find a way of revisiting the terror most people associate with learning something new and difficult. Only if I do this will I be able to help my students with their own problems in learning something that I enjoy teaching. This seems, on the face of it, to be impossible.

I think about ways I could do this. One would be to bring in students from my earlier classes to talk to new students about the emotional difficulties they faced in their own learning. Another would be to find ways of entering my students' emotional worlds, so that I can get some sense of the ways they're reacting to learning (this is the purpose of my classroom critical incident questions described in Brookfield (1995)). Maybe the best way would be for me just to keep finding ways of putting myself in the situation of my students; that is, of being a learner in an area of skill or knowledge that is new and intimidating to me.

It occurs to me also that in my work with other teachers I should find ways of helping them to do this (this idea eventually becomes the ELICIT faculty project development described in Brookfield (1995a).

2.8 Final scene . . .

One night about half way through the semester a colleague in the swimming class to whom I am complaining about my fears and lack of progress hands me her goggles and says, 'Try these on, they might help.' I slip them on, put my head in water, and the effect is amazing! At a stroke the universe has been returned to me! True, the chlorine sting is still in my nose, but the awful white haze has disappeared. I can see the tiling at the bottom of the pool, the lines marking the lanes, even bubbles from my own breathing. I begin my usual attempt at the crawl stroke, trying to coordinate arms, legs and breathing, and after a while I feel my hand hit tiling. 'Damn', I think to myself, 'I thought I could see where I was going with these goggles but I must have swum across the pool again, swum a width rather than a length, and all the lap swimmers will be glaring at me for messing up their laps again.'

I raise my head out of the water and I'm astounded at what I see. I'm at the other end of the pool from where I started a couple of minutes before. I've swum a length, not a width! With this realization I feel a startling jolt of pride, an unalloyed rush of pure happiness. I can't believe it ! I thought I'd never see this moment. I've actually swum a length of a swimming pool without stopping at least once to touch the bottom of the pool and make sure I'm still in my depth, all the while pretending that I'm casually treading water. At some level I knew, or thought I knew, that this day would never come. Now that it's arrived I start to think that maybe I'm not the psychomotor dolt I always thought I was, and that maybe all aspects of the physical world are not totally closed off to me.

Getting tenure, winning awards for books, having a nice round of applause from an audience after a speech, notes of appreciation from students, learning to play the academic game by getting published in prestigious scholarly journals – all these things are nice and affirming, but they pale into visceral insignificance when compared to this moment. By any index, this is a 'critical incident' in my autobiography as a learner; a transformative marker event when I look at myself as a learner in a completely different way and realize a host of new and alternative possibilities for myself.

2.8.1 Final insights

1. If it hadn't been for the suggestion of another student that I try on her goggles I'd still be splashing around in frustration. Her insight and practical suggestion about how to deal with my fears made all the difference in the world to my learning.

2. On almost any scale imaginable by which one could measure aquatic excellence, my performance is pathetic. People forty years my senior are zooming past and my own actions are an uncoordinated mess of huffing, puffing and unsightly struggling. Yet, in terms of my own estimation of the significance this event has in my history as a learner, this means more than anything that has happened to me for quite a time. So, my subjective assessment of how well I've done probably bears no relation to the instructor's external assessment of my efforts. To him I'm still a dismally uncoordinated wimp who expends many more times the amount of energy than is actually needed to get down to the end of the pool. But external evaluations mean nothing next to my own sense that I've done something really significant. Swimming that length is a learning achievement of intergalactic

proportions in terms of my own autobiography.

2.8.2 Meaning for my practice

1   I must remember that a student's suggestion that I wear goggles was crucial for my own progress as a learner. I need to remember that the experts on learning are often learners themselves. Within any learning group students should learn to see each other as resources who can help with learning difficulties. After all, the formally recognized 'expert' in the class – the teacher – was of no help whatsoever in getting me past the major blockage to my learning. The person who did most to help me through my anxieties was another learner. I decide I have to find a way of fostering the formation of peer learning groups in my own classes. It's something I believe in, but I need to pay more explicit attention to how I might help these groups form more quickly. It's just been demonstrated to me how crucial a peer's contribution was to my own learning.

2.   As an evaluator of my students' learning I must be careful to remember that what I might judge to be a miniscule, insignificant amount of progress by a student, or even a total lack of movement, may be perceived by that person as a major learning event. Subjective assessments of the meaning of learning to learners may be very different from the objective assessments made by external evaluators. I need to find a way of introducing self-evaluation methods so that students can document in their own terms how and what they have learned.

I decide that whenever I can I will use two evaluative approaches, each of equal importance. I will use my own judgment about the significance of a learner's accomplishments, and also a learner's judgment of how much she has learned. This leads me to experiment with participant learning portfolios as an evaluative tool in which students demonstrate and document how far they've travelled in terms of their own histories as learners. I also start experimenting with peer evaluations; that is, with students giving narrative evaluative commentary to each other. This is partly to increase the number of evaluative measures and perspectives possible for an act of learning. Partly, too, it's a way of giving students some experience in evaluating learning that will help them when they come to compile their own participant learning portfolios.

2.9   Afterword . . .

Joining an adult swimming class is, in the grand scheme of things, a pretty prosaic event. My learning to swim didn't decrease the amount of injustice in the world and it didn't result in any social change. It counted for very little compared to the significant personal learning that people point to as being the most important in their lives. Yet, as a result of this one engagement in an act of learning, I was provoked into challenging and changing some assumptions about my teaching that up to that point I had viewed as axiomatic. Instead of believing that it was my duty to cater consistently to students' preferred learning styles I now knew that I had to try and strike a balance between affirming these styles and making sure that students were exposed to other ways of learning. No longer would I insist on only self-directed modes of teaching and learning.

Instead of believing that the people who could learn something the best were also the best people to teach it, I now knew that naturally talented learners could be perceptually disabled when it came to understanding the source of students' anxieties about learning. This meant that the best learners sometimes made the worst teachers for students in struggle. Finally, I was granted a new insight into the contradictory, yet internally consistent, interpretations that students and teachers could make of the same learning effort. I knew that what to my eyes were apparently minor actions taken by students could, to them, be events of transformative significance. Knowing this made me a more even-handed, empathic evaluator of students and led to my experimenting with forms of self and peer evaluation.

2.10 References

Andresen, L. (1993) On becoming a maker of teachers: journey down a long hall of mirrors. In D. Boud, R. Cohen and D. Walker (eds), *Using Experience for Learning*, Milton Keynes: The Open University Press.

Angelo, T.A. (ed.) (1991) *Classroom Research: Early Lessons from Success*, New Directions for Teaching and Learning, no. 46, San Francisco: JosseyBass.

Angelo, T.A. and Cross, K.P. (1993) *Classroom Assessment Techniques: A Handbook for College Teachers*, San Francisco: JosseyBass.

Brookfield, S.D. (ed.) (1985) *Self-Directed Learning: From Theory to Practice*, San Francisco: JosseyBass.

Brookfield, S.D. (1990) *The Skillful Teacher*, San Francisco: JosseyBass.

Brookfield, S.D. (1995a) *Becoming a Critically Reflective Teacher*, San Francisco: JosseyBass.

Brookfield, S.D. (1995b) Changing the Culture of Scholarship to the Culture of Teaching: an Amercian Perspective. In T. Schuller (ed.), *The Changing Univesity?* Milton Keynes: Open University Press

Campbell, J. and Neill, S.R. (1994a) *Primary Teachers at Work*, London: Routledge.

Campbell, J. and Neill, S.R. (1994b) *Secondary Teachers at Work*, London: Routledge.

Cross, K.P. and Steadman, M.H. (1996) *Classroom Research: Implementing the Scholarship of Teaching*, San Francisco: JosseyBass.

Freire, P. and Shor, I. (1987) *A Pedagogy for Liberation*, Westport, CT: Bergin & Garvey.

Gore, J.M. (1993) *The Struggle for Pedagogies: Critical and Feminist Discourses as Regimes of Truth*, London: Routledge.

Gramsci, A. (1978) *Selections from the Prison Notebooks*, London: Lawrence & Wishart.

Hammersley, M. (1986) *Case Studies in Classroom Research*, Milton Keynes: Open University Press.

Hammersley, M. (ed.) (1993) *Controversies in Classroom Research*, Milton Keynes: Open University Press.

Hopkins, D. (1993) *A Teacher's Guide to Classroom Research*, Milton Keynes: Open University Press.

Marton, F. (1988) Phenomenography: a research approach to investigating different understandings of reality. In R.R. Sherman and R.B. Webb (eds), *Qualitative Research in Education: Focus and Methods*, London: Falmer Press.

Peters, R.S. (1967) *The Concept of Education*, London: Routledge & Kegan Paul.

Usher, R. and Edwards, R. (1994) *Postmodernism and Education: Different Voices, Different Worlds*, London: Routledge & Kegan Paul.

3 Analysing student performance

Roger Lindsay[1]
Department of Psychology, Oxford Brookes University

3.1 Chapter objectives

- To justify the analysis of student performance as a distinctive methodology
- To describe how to investigate student learning using performance measures
- To identify important techniques and pitfalls associated with student performance studies
- To illustrate the use of student performance data using a wide range of case studies
- To provide an opportunity for readers to explore the appropriateness of performance analysis to issues of interest to them

3.2 Background models

It is helpful to have available a theoretical framework within which empirical research can be contextualized and understood. The general framework within which the analysis of student performance data can be interpreted is probably that of scientific realism, i.e. the view that there exists an objective, physical world to which access is publicly shared, and which can be investigated by a variety of discovery procedures. But the study of student performance data also has a more specific methodological identity as an investigative procedure. For example, while sharing some features with *secondary data analysis* (the re-analysis of data originally collected for some other purpose), student performance data are not initially accumulated for any scientific purpose. Additionally, many kinds of data which are susceptible to secondary analysis, including much interview and questionnaire data, cannot be classified as performance data because they consist exclusively of phenomenological reports. Again, while performance data are in some respects like data produced by *experimental procedures*, particularly in their objective character, they differ dramatically from experimental data in that they are not generated under artificial laboratory conditions and are not therfore exposed to many of the biases and artefacts associated with experimentation (Lindsay, 1997).

Because the analysis of student performance data appears to constitute a methodology which is in a variety of respects unique, it is useful to have in mind some local models which draw attention to these specific virtues of performance data. I have found it useful to operate with three such local models which do not closely integrate with one another, but do severally draw attention to important features of performance data and seem jointly capable of coexisting within the scientific realist framework.

3.2.1 Performance as behaviour

For much of the twentieth century Behaviourism was the dominant theoretical paradigm in psychology and education and during the time of its hegemony only the study of behaviour was regarded as legitimate. From the mid-1950s onwards the cognitive approach began to replace the rigid and intolerant, animal-oriented behaviourist theories, and in studies of student learning in the 1980s the pendulum swung completely to the opposite extreme as a result of the work of Ference Marton (Marton, 1981; Marton and Saljo, 1984). Marton's work emphasized the importance of accessing the private, phenomenal world of the learner in seeking to understand the student experience, and course-evaluation work in the world of higher education has subsequently come to be almost exclusively dominated by phenomenologically oriented methods such as interviews, focus groups and course-impression questionnaires.

The defects of theoretical behaviourism remain as real as ever, and the value of direct accounts of first-hand experience is unlikely to diminish But it is sometimes forgotten that phenomenological methods too have their difficulties, and that objective data did not become worthless along with behaviourist theory.

An example which makes this point is the use of phenomenological measures to evaluate psychoanalytic treatments. It is widely reported that patients exposed to psychoanalytic treatment regimes almost invariably develop the impression that they have benefited as a result. Evaluation procedures which tap into patient phenomenology are very likely to produce positive outcomes for psychoanalysis as a result. However, where objective measures of a condition under treatment exist, for example with eating disorders, alcoholism, drug addiction, and phobic/obsessive behaviour, evaluation procedures based upon them tend consistently to show that psychoanalysis produces little improvement.

It is no part of my case to insist that psychoanalysis works, or that it doesn't. The value of the example lies in its power to illustrate the fact that phenomenological methods do not say all that there is to be said. Certainly, the phenomenological experience of the student is of central importance, and was for far too long neglected. In course marketing, the student experience may be all that matters, in the sense that if customers are content that they are getting good value for money, there is little more to be said. As educators, however, there are questions to be asked which go beyond phenomenology: a course may be producing an acceptable experience for the student but failing to achieve worthwhile objectives. 'Is it liked?' is one question. 'Does it work?' is another one entirely.

The first of my three informal models, then, is the idea of performance data as coming not from the world of subjective impressions, but from the world of objective behaviour. It enables us to address questions about the causal efficacy of professional practices and principles of course design which cannot be answered using phenomenological methods.

This is in no sense a plea to make the clock run backwards. The central role of phenomenological analyses of the client experience cannot sensibly be challenged. Rather my plea is that we acknowledge the fact that performance data has become neglected, perhaps because it is wrongly seen as an alternative to impression measures, when in truth it is an essential complement.

3.2.2 Performance data as 'trace' measures

The second background model which is useful in understanding the value of performance data is the idea of 'trace' measures developed and expounded by Webb, Campbell, Schwartz and Sechrest (1966). In their classic of methodology *Unobtrusive Measures*, Webb *et al.* argue that in addition to phenomenological techniques and behaviour in real-time, there is a third source of data available to psychologists consisting of the physical traces which behaviour leaves behind – an illustration might be fossilized dinosaur footprints left in ancient rock.

Webb *et al.* provide a multitude of examples of the use of trace measures in the social sciences. Investigators interested in the quantity of alcohol consumed in households might think about counting empty cans and bottles discarded in dustbins (an 'accretion' measure), to counter the tendency that people have to under-report consumption when directly asked. Authorities responsible for monitoring the relative popularity of exhibits on public display can do so by using floor tiles which wear away readily and uniformly (an 'erosion' measure). Though the associated error component must be quite large, Webb *et al.* even suggest that TV audience size can be estimated from the surge in demand for power experienced by generating facilities, when a programme ends and viewers simultaneously switch on kettles across the nation.

The central core of the arguments put forward by Webb *et al.* is that all research in the social sciences (and education) is plagued by the twin evils of bias and reactivity. Bias is the contamination of variables we want to measure by irrelevant variables. Reactivity is the effect of a measurement process itself upon the variable measured. Bias afflicts all measurement operations, and the surest palliative (for there is no cure) is *triangulation*. This is the use of multiple measurement procedures each prone to different biases to confirm a result. Trace measures can often make useful contributions to triangulation procedures just because they are often very different from more conventional measures.

More important, however, is the use of trace measures as an antidote for reactivity. Consider how reactivity arises in studying learning processes. An investigator asks a group of students whether they use rote leaning to prepare for an examination, or whether instead they make an 'effort after meaning'. Many students will try to give the response which they think will elicit most approval. Which would you expect this to be? Probably, like me, you think of rote learning as superficial, mindless, and mechanical. 'Deep' learning organized around meaning on the other hand, is intelligent, creative, and altogether superior. Bright students who want to give a good impression of themselves may well claim to use deep learning even if they don't, because of the social characteristics of the measurement situation.

How do trace measures help? Suppose the investigator collected together the revision notes used by a sample of students. One batch might be characterized by the use of organizing diagrams, paraphrases, summaries, revision questions and cross references. Another might consist of a multiplicity of attempts at verbatim recall. Now the situation is quite different because the revision notes are traces left by the procedures actually used. Because the students had no idea that the traces that would form the substance of an investigation when they were actually created, the traces cannot have been designed to influence that investigation.

Anyone who has carried out, or even been subject to, evaluation studies in the area of student learning will know from experience that reactivity is a major problem. Students don't want to get lecturers into trouble; they don't want to cause offence; they don't want to rubbish courses on which they have gained good marks; they want to perceive their experience as positive; they want to make a good impression. And each of these positive forms of reactive response has a negative counterpart.

The trace measure model reminds investigators that there are solutions to the reactivity problem, and one of them lies in the use of the physical traces left by performance.

3.2.3 Academic courses as ecosystems

Zoologists and anthropologists, as well as psychologists, are used to the idea that many aspects of behaviour are conditioned by the environment in which they occur. Ducks don't try to swim on land, conspicuously placed surveillance cameras deter crime; sexual intimacy has a raised probability of occurrence in warm, dark, comfortable environments such as bedrooms and cinemas.

What we often forget, however, is that in designing a university course, complete with rewards and incentives, punishments and penalties, we are designing an ecosystem which conditions the behaviour of people operating within it. The rules and processes associated with a course are likely to have considerable influence over the extent of learner effort and when and where it is applied, the probability of cheating, the pattern of course choices, and even the marks and grades which students achieve. Conversely, the observable manifestations of choice and cheating and achievement can potentially be used to examine whether the course as implemented is achieving its design objectives.

Crudely put, unless the formal characteristics of a course are entirely without effect upon student behaviour, then either they assist in producing an intended effect or they help to produce an unintended effect. Course features thought to assist in producing an intended effect may in fact not do so, and features causing unintended effects may cause effects which are positively undesirable (e.g. an excessively heavy workload accompanied by severe penalties for failure might predispose towards cheating). The analysis of student performance data often allows inferences to be made about the way in which student behaviour is shaped by the course structures within which their behaviour occurs, just as a zoologist can isolate effective features of the local ecology upon the behaviour of an organism, and determine the behavioural effects which are produced.

3.3 What is student performance?

On the basis of discussion so far it seems useful to think about student performance data as physical traces left by objective behaviour which enable inferences to be made about features of the course environment which have helped to shape that behaviour.

Necessary conditions for studies of this kind include the following.

3.3.1 Student performance analysis requires records of behaviour

This condition is not sufficient in itself, because it also embraces course evaluation questionnaires and tape-recorded feedback interviews which are both prone to reactivity and phenomenologically oriented.

3.3.2 Student performance analysis requires data to be subjected to second-order analysis

'Second-order' is intended to mean something unusual here, namely that it is interpreted in terms of objectives which differ from those which the behaviour was originally intended to achieve. To give an example: if class attendance records are kept, it might be reasonable to use these records to infer which of two versions of a course is best preferred by students. Of course, controls against bias must be incorporated by ensuring that discipline content, teacher identity, time of term, external factors operating on students etc. are kept constant as far as possible. The point is, however, that attendance is a behavioural measure not a phenomenological report, and can therefore be used to check that phenomenological reports have objective validity. And as the analysis is second-order, reactivity effects are unlikely because participants could not have known that attendance data would later be used as a satisfaction measure. In any event they would probably be unlikely to use relative attendance frequency (in comparison with another group) as a method of eliciting social approval or of pleasing the instructor.

3.3.3 Studies of performance data are (usually) retrospective

While this is not a logically essential condition, prospective performance studies re-introduce many of the dangers of response bias and reactivity, particularly if the investigator is aware of expected outcomes and is likely to interact with participants. Prospective studies which involve intervention cease to be analyses of performance data and simply become experimental studies of student performance, which are in term subject to their own hazards of bias.

3.3.4 Examples of performance data

These include:

- course marks and grades;
- examination scripts;
- coursework (essays, practical reports, projects);
- video-recorded seminar performance; and
- attendance and withdrawal records.

3.4 Why study student performance?

3.4.1 Performance data has high intrinsic validity

Performance data is characterized by high validity in part because of the relative absence of reactivity effects, and in part because it is a common-sense assumption that preferences expressed when consumers 'vote with their feet' are a better guide to their underlying values than opinions elicited by deliberate canvassing. Just as important, however, is the fact that performance data includes the institutionalized proxies for whatever educators are trying to optimize. For example: imagine that Notown University (NU) uses unseen end-of-course examinations, marked on a percentage scale, as its proxy for student attainment. An investigation carried out in NU shows that students who are given a three-month period without teaching in their final year get higher percentage marks in their final examinations than students who receive uninterrupted teaching.

No separate argument is now required to show that the dependent variable used in the investigation is a valid predictor of performance because the validity is intrinsic: the dependent variable *is identical with* the performance measure the value of which NU seeks to maximize via its educational provision. If a course evaluation questionnaire or interviews had been used, this certainly would not have been true, and the normal tedious round of arguments about validity and sampling would distract from the impact of the findings.

3.4.2 High communicative credibility

For reasons implicit in the discussion above, it is far easier to persuade members of an institution that the variables implicated as effective by an investigation really do matter, if they can be shown to make a difference to performance indicators which are already embedded in institutional practice. It is reasonable to respond: 'OK, so your questionnaire study shows that students say such-and-such. Why should I change?' It is much less reasonable to respond: 'OK, so your study shows that students get worse degree results if I do such-and-such. Why should I change?' The lamentation is often heard that evaluation work in education usually gets ignored. Too frequently, this is explained by the fact that investigators use measures which have high credibility among investigators who are in touch with the latest trend in educational theory, but much less so to busy academics who are not.

3.4.3 Avoidance of bias

Well-known response-bias effects in educational evaluation include halo effects, faking good, evaluator ingratiation, uninformed responses and yea- and nay-saying. Most of these are unlikely to affect performance data. Of course there are plenty of other bias effects to worry about, but at least it is valuable to have one technique in the triangulation repertoire which is largely unaffected by biases of social origin.

3.4.4 Good data availability

Most studies of performance data are retrospective, and indeed much of the attraction of performance data analysis comes from the fact that considerable quantities of data already exist in the form of administrative and academic records. Particularly where such records are available in computer databases, it is often possible to gain relatively easy access to datasets which vastly exceed the size and scope of anything which could be financed as a study involving the collection of original data. Incidentally, course authorities who have a gatekeeping role over access to records, are much more likely to cooperate in studies involving the analysis of objective data than in other kinds of evaluation. Certainly, this has never been a problem at Oxford Brookes University.

3.4.5 Data is readily quantifiable

The purposes and conventions of administrative and academic record-keeping usually require clearly defined and accurate data in a standard format. This is generally numerical or categorical in form. Data of either type is readily susceptible to statistical analysis.

3.4.6 Powerful analytic techniques are available

During the 1990s, PC-based statistical packages have become increasingly powerful, flexible and user-friendly. There is now a range of well-known and readily accessible packages which can cope with very large datasets and which allow a wide variety of transformations to be applied to input data to extend the statistical operations which can be applied.

3.5 Approaching student performance

In detail, there are no doubt as many ways of approaching performance data analysis as there are investigators or problems, but in outline there are some easily stated principles which should assist in getting a study established. To begin with, there are two quite different starting points:

1. data-driven research: locate a body of accessible data and consider what issues it can be used to illuminate;

2. problem driven research: identify a significant problem and consider what data is required to address it.

While with data-driven research there will necessarily be a body of available data, there is no guarantee that the data will support generalizations of any great importance. The investigator must therefore develop a thorough knowledge of the course structure and procedures, in order to understand how they might shape the form of the data, and a thorough knowledge of the data in order to establish what features they have which might require explanation.

With problem-driven research the challenge is rather different. The investigator begins with a problem chosen because of its interest or importance, so there is no difficulty here. The challenge, rather, is to imagination and ingenuity in locating and gaining access to some kind of record or trace of behaviour which might illuminate the problem.

3.5.1 Try to establish hypotheses

There are a number of reasons for establishing hypotheses at the outset of an investigation. The first is to make the expectations of the investigators explicit. It is always best to begin by knowing what you think will be discovered. This knowledge can then be used to guard against modifications and interpretations of the data which favour expectations. It is much harder to take precautions against expectations which go unacknowledged.

Another virtue of hypotheses is that they create a locus of engagement with existing knowledge. Expectations about what might be discovered often arise not from the convictions of the investigators but from the results of earlier studies. Learning about a particular course is undoubtedly an important motivation for analysing performance data. In some contexts, however, it may be as or more important to use performance data from a particular course to examine theories or beliefs or policies which are of greater generality. In case study 3.3 (below) the interest of the finding that students undertaking paid work during termtime gain worse average marks than those who do not work derives from its probable relevance to the population of all full-time students involved in paid work.

Finally, the existence of prior hypothesis enables the full power of statistical hypothesis testing techniques to be used, including associated probability levels. Without prior hypotheses, statistical techniques can still be used as powerful tools for exploring data, but great care (and often expert advice) must be taken in evaluating the strength of the evidence which results.

3.5.2 Establish a useable database

Data must be offered to statistical packages in a form which those packages are able to handle. This means that the data must have a reasonably *uniform structure* (e.g. values on the same variables for all cases). For most purposes investigators should aim for a 'flat rectangular' database, that is, where there are a fixed number of cases each with a value on a fixed number of variables yielding data in an $n \times n$ matrix. Many institutional records are now maintained in spreadsheet formats, and spreadsheet files can often be directly read by statistical packages (for example Microsoft EXCEL is widely used for assessment records and EXCEL files can be read by SPSS for Windows).

Data must also be reasonably *complete*, having relatively few missing values. Statistical packages commonly exclude cases or variables with missing values from many kinds of analysis, and it is annoying to find that a very large sample with few missing values in absolute terms becomes a very small sample once whole cases with missing values are excluded. To give an example, a database with 200 cases and 200 variables per case will collapse to a single case if all cases but one have a missing value for just one of the 200 variables and the missing value happens to be on a different variable each time. This dramatic reduction in usable data is caused by only 199 empty cells out of 40,000 – less than 0.5 per cent. The moral is that not only the number of missing values but their distribution is important: better to have many missing values on a few cases than few missing values on many cases. Finally, data must be reasonably 'clean' (as few cases as possible where values have been modified or 'doctored' in some way). This should not be taken as an implication that anything improper has occurred but a reminder that, for example, when using student assessment data, all manner of discretionary, extenuation and penalty procedures can play a part in determining the final mark. These processes may not be affected by variables under scrutiny in the same way as conventional learning and investigators must therefore be aware of the size of the contribution they make.

3.5.3   Locate a set of appropriate analytic techniques

Examples of appropriate analytic techniques are:

* correlation for exploring co-variation between pairs of variables;

* cross-tabulation for nominal scale data, and chi-squared and log-linear modelling for examining associations between variables;

* tables of means, *t*-tests and analysis of variance for interval scale data.

Though statistical packages frequently offer menus of daunting size and richness, most of the routines contained there have highly technical niche applications. A relatively small number of statistical methods is used with great frequency and a very large number of methods is used relatively rarely. There is also a definite and quite low upper bound on the complexity of techniques which it is profitable to use when seeking to communicate with a general audience (Lindsay, 1989). In general, unfamiliar techniques tend to create a barrier to understanding and distract from the data. All sorts of complicated statistical techniques may be employed for data exploration, but simplicity should be sought in communicating results.

3.5.4   Interpreting probability levels with caution

Be prepared to use statistical methods for exploring data, but to ignore or adjust conventional significance levels.

Significance or 'alpha' levels generally assume that a particular number of hypothesis tests, (usually one), is being carried out. If this number is exceeded, the significance level is no longer valid. With a *t*-test for example, the 5 per cent significance level can legitimately be quoted in connection with a result only if no other *t*-test is performed at the same time. This is not an argument for rejecting the use of multiple *t*-tests in exploring data, where the practice can be very useful. It is an argument for interpreting the associated probability levels with caution. While their relative size is as informative as ever, their absolute interpretation becomes problematic, and at the very least some adjustment must be made to significance levels to allow for the number of comparisons. Obviously, associated probability levels generated when multiple comparisons are made in tandem should never be quoted as if only one comparison has been made.

3.6 Analysing performance data

3.6.1 'Clean' data set

Remember that the most time-consuming research task is establishing a 'clean' data set.

Once a clean and regular data set with tolerable quantities of missing data has been established, the actual analysis can usually be accomplished very rapidly. Often an appreciable body of output can be produced in minutes or hours, though the process of understanding what is generated and returning to the data to carry out cross-checks, test further hypotheses etc. arising from initial analyses can take much longer. However, the establishment of a satisfactory data can be immensely time-consuming. It may, for example, involve an initial audit in conjunction with someone who is very familiar with the original format of the data. In a worst case, data may then need to be input *ab initio* or modified using a special purpose language. Once the data is available in spreadsheet form, quality checks can begin but the result may well be that further modifications of the data are necessary. The fact that performance data analysis projects are front-end loaded in this way should be taken into account at the planning stage.

3.6.2 Develop data quality control procedures

There are invariably a host of problems with performance data of which first-order users are unaware. Sometimes this is because they use the data for different purposes than the investigators and the problems are not significant from this perspective. Sometimes it is because users brief investigators on general principles underlying data characteristics and forget about exceptions. It is essential that problems affecting the integrity (missing and clean values) of the data are located early on because statistical hypothesis testing is typically cumulative. This usually means that data corruption discovered late on will force a recalculation of all values generated up until that point. Typical quality control procedures are missing value counts, data tests (e.g. are there any non-numerical values entered for the variable 'age'), range tests (e.g. are all age values for students within the band 17–65 years?), and frequency counts (e.g. are the expected 70 per cent, or whatever, within the age-band 18–22).

3.6.3 Use descriptive statistics to understand and double-check the data

Quality-control checks are general and almost content-independent. More subtle errors may depend on a through understanding of the data. For example, all of the numbers for age may look OK, but there appear to be 10 per cent more 18-year-old males in the sample than females when it is known that more males choose to defer university study. This may suggest that there is an error in the coding schedule which has resulted in the values for males and females (often coded quite arbitrarily as '1' and '0') becoming reversed. There is nothing internal to the data set which could reveal this kind of error, although when carried through to the report stage, the error would appear gross to an informed audience. There is no alternative to gaining a thorough understanding of the dataset, seeking inconsistencies and checking major data features with well-informed course administrators or academics. Descriptive statistics are immensely invaluable at this stage.

3.6.4 Watch out for confounded variables and try to locate 'natural controls' when they are discovered

Confounded variables exist when two variables covary with a third. If the two variables covary exactly then they are completely confounded. An example which arises in a number of the case studies presented below is that in Oxford Brookes' University's Modular Course there tends to be a relatively small number of 'Basic' ('introductory') modules in a discipline, which are compulsory. There is a much greater number of Advanced modules which are usually optional. Basic modules do not usually count towards a student's degree classification. If an investigation focuses on class-size, for example as a correlate of module marks, there is an immediate confounding with module level (because Basics tend to have larger classes than Advanced) and with incentive/motivation (because Basics don't usually contribute to class of award). This can be handled, for example, by dropping Basic modules from the sample. Where confoundings are not complete, it is sometimes more satisfactory, however, to use partially confounded variables as *natural controls*, for example, by comparing the effect of class-size on Basic and Advanced modules separately. Basic modules are a natural control for the hypothesis that incentive (operationalized as counting towards award-class) is a critical determinant of the relationship between class-size and performance. Similarly, Basic modules which do count towards degree class can be used to separate the effect of incentive from the effect of level. The general form of a natural control is: *If the value of dependent variable DV covaries with independent variables IV^1 and IV^2 try to locate a subset of cases with variation in IV^1 and not in IV^2 or with variation in IV^2 and not in IV^1.*

3.7 Case studies

In the rest of this chapter, data is presented from a number of case studies which illustrate various features of student performance analysis as described above. Data presented is selected only to illustrate the methodology and some of the purposes and benefits of analysing student performance data. In all cases one or two data tables are chosen from a much greater number in the original reports. Only a small proportion of printed results were tabulated and by no means all of the analyses carried out were printed. Inevitably the reader will not be able to recover all of the essential features of the studies described from the fragments presented here.

Case study 3.1 Student performance in the first year of a modular course

Case study 3.1 is from a study carried out by Paton-Saltzberg and Lindsay (1986) on the first full-time year of Oxford Polytechnic's Modular Course. It employed data from standard summaries of Results for Modules published by the Modular Course Administration between 1981–2 and 1983–4. Data were entered manually onto the institution's mainframe computer and analysed using the Bio-Medical Data Processing statistical package (BMDP).

Over the period sampled, first-year students were required to pass 10 of 12 modules taken, in order to proceed into the second year. Much internal debate centred on the issue of the value of the 'take 12' rule. Organizational functionalists tended to argue that 'pass 10' was sufficient, while liberal educationalists, who were probably in the majority, contended that 'take 12, pass 10' gave permission to fail and encouraged students to explore new subjects without fear of 'sudden death'. Table 3.1 presents the percentage of each of five grades achieved each term averaged over three years.

GRADE	A (=/>70)	B+ (60-69)	B (50-59)	C (40-49)	F (<40)
TERM 1	37.0	34.0	31.0	30.0	18.0
TERM 2	29.0	30.0	33.0	36.0	25.0
TERM 3	34.0	36.0	36.0	34.0	57.0

Table 3.1   Percent of students obtaining each of five grades, in their first year in, HE according to the academic term in which they were examined. Analysis of variance (+ post-hocs) showed Term 1 means to be higher than other terms. (23,826 assessments; 384 modules)

The main feature of interest is the percentage of F (Fail) grades in term 3. The course rules seemed to be creating a situation in which by term 3 most students had passed 8 or 9 modules and needed only one or two more to make up the required 10. They were therefore, quite rationally, investing little or no effort in the two 'surplus' modules and accepting fail grades. The results of this study illustrate at least two points made earlier in the chapter. First, the way in which course regulations create a cognitive ecosystem which constrains student decision-masking and determines some aspects of their observed performance. Secondly, the way in which data with high intrinsic validity can assist the process of course evolution by virtue of its credibility among people involved in delivering the course. In the present case, a debate which was initially quite charged and ideologically loaded was substantially defused by the realization that the 'take 12' rule was not broadening the education of students, but instead was creating phantom registrations and pointless administration.

	YEAR A	YEAR B	YEAR C	YEAR D
TERM 1	54.9	55.8	55.5	55.2
TERM 2	52.7	53.2	53.9	52.8
TERM 3	51.8	52.9	53.1	52.7

Table 3.2   Mean marks awarded to first year students in four successive years, according to the academic term in which they were examined (23,826 assessments; 384 modules)

Data in Table 3.2 excludes marks for modules awarded fail grades. The reason is that if students have decided not to invest effort in some modules because of the 'take 12' rule, mark averages which include these results will be very misleading. The *a-priori* expectation here was that average module marks would show a term 3 dip resulting from the same constellation of factors which produce the high term 3 failure rate. In fact, term 3 results do not differ significantly from those for term 2. *But term 1 results differ from both.* Analysis of variance showed that the difference between terms was significant and independent of years, i.e. the same effect of term was found in every year (F = 4.89; df = 5; p < 0.001). Separate variance post-hoc *t*-tests with Bonferroni adjustments to significance levels for the number of comparisons showed that, indeed, the difference came from higher means in term 1 than in the other two terms.

This finding was completely unexpected and its explanation remains uncertain. Paton-Saltberg and Lindsay (1986) discussed three possibilities: that teaching was better after the summer vacation, that students do better when they have less examinations (Table 3.3 shows that less modules are examined in term 1) and that student uncertainty about standards in their first term results in their setting them high initially and subsequently lowering them in the light of feedback. The third explanation, with its implication that higher expectations from assessors would produce higher levels of student achievement, is perhaps the most alarming.

TERM	TERM 1	TERM 2	TERM 3
PERCENT OF STUDENTS EXAMINED	30%	32%	38%

Table 3.3   Percentage of total number of first year assessments falling in each academic term (23,826 assessments; 384 modules)

Table 3.3 drew the attention of course organizers to an additional feature of the course structure which had gone largely unnoticed. In addition to one-term single credit modules, the Oxford Brookes Modular Course also recognizes two-term double modules and three-term triples. If single modules are randomly distributed across terms, there will be heavier assessment burdens in successive terms just because two-term modules can only be examined in terms 2 and 3, and three-term modules can only be examined in term 3. Institutionally this was undesirable because it meant that most first-year assessments were occurring in the term in which graduating students were also being dealt with. The clear administrative moral was that single Basic modules should be most frequent in term 1 and least frequent in term 3. It is unlikely that this point would have become quite so obvious without the analysis of performance data.

Case study 3.2   Effects of class-size on student performance in advanced modules

It is extremely surprising how little is known about basic features of student performance in HE even though many of the strategic debates about student funding depend critically upon assumptions about the relationship between teaching input (TI) and student performance (SP). The reason for this lack of basic facts seems to be the attention paid by researchers to theory rather than performance. Figure 3.1 below illustrates a number of possible forms the function relating teaching input with student performance might take, though it should be emphasized that there are an infinite number of theoretical possibilities.

Curve 1   Illustrates the 'elitist' model on which the greater the amount of teaching input, the greater are the returns from each further unit invested. This model might naturally lead to lots of contact time with very low staff-student ratios.

Curve 2   Illustrates the commonsense model (and the author's expectations) with high initial returns on teaching input diminishing with successive increases. This model might lead to high concentrations of teaching contact early in courses, attenuating as the course progressed.

Curve 3   Illustrates the optimistic professional teacher's model with constant performance gains for each unit of teaching input invested.

Curve 4   Illustrates the cynical educational consultant's model with each increment in teaching input causing student performance to deteriorate (because teaching 'induces dependence' or 'impairs autonomy').[2]

All of the curves below are completely hypothetical. They are presented here to illustrate ignorance rather than knowledge, and it is highly likely that in practice there is not one, but a family of TI/SP curves for different categories of student, teaching method and so on. Too often, however, political and educational debate assumes not that the situation is more complicated than the hypothetical curve suggests, but much simpler, with one faction arguing that increasing teaching input is bound to be disastrous and another that it is bound to be beneficial. There is probably general agreement that the intercept of the TI/SP function is positive and greater than zero, that is, without any teaching at all students would get some marks. Beyond this there is only opinion. Even if the form of the TI/SP were known, it would still be an open question where on the curve universities are currently located. Thus for example, if Curve 2 does describe the underlying function, are we presently located on the early section of the curve, which shows high returns on further investment, or on the later part where further investment is relatively unprofitable?

The relation between TI and SP can be approached through the use of performance data to examine the effect of various contingencies which cause reductions in teaching input. Together with various colleagues at Oxford Brookes I have made a number of attempts to evaluate such contingencies. Case studies 3.2 and 3.3 illustrate what has been found.

One factor which probably causes reduced levels of teaching input per student is the number of students who enrol upon a course. There is wide variation in module enrolment on Oxford Brookes Modular Course and a huge quantity of data accumulated within the University's computerized course and student record system. Table 3.4 presents an analysis of some of this data carried out by Lindsay and Paton-Saltzberg (1989).

The main features of the data are that the percentages of A and B+, the highest grades, show a progressive decline as enrolment size gets larger. The percentage of C grades by contrast increases steadily as enrolment size increases. Though there is an apparent reversal in the effects of enrolment size on A grade frequency for classes over 60, subsequent investigation revealed that the source of this reversal was a small number of modules in catering and languages which enrolled students on large modules but taught them entirely in smaller groups.

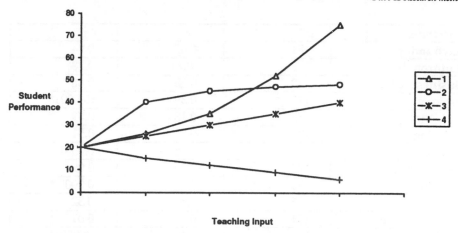

Figure 3.1   Hypothetical relationships between quantity of teaching input and student performance

Class Size	A =/>70	B+ 60-69	B 50-59	C 40-49	F <40
<11	10.1	31.1	34.0	15.7	9.2
11-20	9.7	29.5	35.9	16.6	8.4
21-30	8.5	27.4	37.0	18.3	9.0
31-40	6.9	25.6	38.8	19.6	9.1
41-50	6.2	26.9	38.1	20.0	8.9
51-60	4.8	24.9	40.1	21.5	8.7
61-70	6.5	24.3	38.1	21.6	9.5
71-80	6.9	21.3	38.1	21.6	9.3

Table 3.4   Percentage of students achieving each of 5 grades in advanced modules according to the number taking the module. Multi-way chi-squared showed differences to be significant. Main discrepencies between observed and expected frequencies come from A and C grades. 36,984 assessments; 1516 modules)

Table 3.3 shows that the negative relationship between module enrolment and average module mark was observed in 27 out of 32 disciplines, with 16 negative correlations reaching an unadjusted 5 per cent significance level, compared with only two positive correlations. It is hard to resist the conclusion that large enrolments are associated with poorer student performance.

Discipline	df	r	p
Accounting	81	-0.07	0.94
Anthropology	53	+0.21	0.13
Business Admin	39	-0.28	0.08
Biology	143	-0.39	<0.0001*
Env. Biology	85	-0.13	0.89
Catering	128	-0.06	0.51
Computing	119	-0.35	0.0001 *
Cartography	73	-0.20	0.09
Economics	90	-0.39	0.0001 *
Education	85	-0.11	0.32
Appl. Education	101	-0.01	0.01 *
English	116	-0.40	<0.0001*
French	139	-0.10	0.27
German	177	+0.23	0.01 *
Geography	84	-0.04	0.72
Geology	122	-0.32	0.001 *
Hist. of Art	71	-0.24	0.04 *
History	103	-0.12	0.23
Law	88	-0.36	0.001 *
Mathematics	83	-0.18	0.09
Micro-electronics	31	+0.03	0.89
Music	50	-0.19	0.17
Nutrition	65	+0.03	0.82
Physics	85	-0.63	0.001 *
Planning	80	-0.30	0.01 *
Politics	77	+0.26	0.02 *
Psychology	109	-0.43	<0.0001 *
Publishing	94	-0.35	0.001 *
Sociology	73	-0.33	0.01 *
Tourism	25	-0.41	0.03 *
Visual Studies	119	-0.20	0.03 *

Table 3.5   Correlations between average module mark and number of enrolled students for 31 disciplines. (Data from Fearnley, 1995)

Case study 3.3 Effects of paid employment on student performance in advanced modules

A second angle on performance effects of reducing teaching input comes from looking at cases in which the university maintains a constant level of provision but students reduce their own exposure to it. This occurs to an appreciable extent when students undertake paid work during termtime. Many previous studies have carried out questionnaire-based surveys of the effects of working on students, with most reporting adverse consequences but such data is easily dismissed as subjective, based on small samples and capturing only self-serving complaints. Negative effects based on recorded assessment data are more difficult to brush aside, particularly as information on the employment status of students was not available to assessors awarding the marks. Paton-Saltzberg and Lindsay (1993) again took advantage of Oxford Brookes' computerized record system to look at the effects of working during termtime on objective performance data having these characteristics.

The chosen methodology was to distribute postal questionnaires to students asking such questions as whether they undertook paid work, when they did it, how many hours they worked, what the nature of the work and the rate of pay was, what was their level of debt and how working affected their studies. Respondents were also asked to give their student number so that their academic progress could be examined.

Using questionnaire information from 193 respondents (5.5 per cent of second- and third-year enrolment), student numbers were used to access administrative records and obtain the average marks achieved by working and non-working students. Table 3.6 shows that the mean difference between the two groups is almost 3 per cent, with working students gaining lower marks. Paton-Saltzberg and Lindsay (1993) were able to estimate that, as a result of this difference, about 250 students would be expected to gain an award which was one class lower than they would otherwise have achieved.

	Stage I Average	Stage II Average
Termtime working	57.01 n = 110	57.56 n = 110
No termtimeworking	57.63 n = 83	60.25 n = 83

Table 3.6 Difference in average marks across all courses taken for students who work in termtime during Stage II, and those who do not. The difference in average mark between Stage II students who were working and those who were not is significant (t = 2.41; df = 184; p<0.02). There was no difference in Stage 1 average between those students who were working and those who were not. (Total n = 193). Data from Paton-Saltzberg and Lindsay (1993).

Failure-rate data was also considerably elevated, being three times higher among working than non-working students. There was also a calculable consequence to the university of the higher failure rate, in terms of compensatory re-enrolments. The 1993 estimate of this cost was around £250,000. One design feature of this study worth drawing attention to is the use of Stage I (first-year) performance as a control for motivation and ability. On the assumption that students are less likely to work in their first year because of lower indebtedness and lack of familiarity with work opportunities in the town, Stage I performance was used to compare performance between the working and non-working students when work effects were not present. Table 3.5 shows that at this stage in their university career there was no difference between the two groups. While case studies 3.2 and 3.3 do not definitively prove that reductions in exposure to teaching at university cause poorer student performance, they do tend to shift the onus of proof to those who would deny that the relationship is such. In both cases objective evidence indicates that a reduced quantity of teaching input is associated with lower marks.

Case study 3.4   Effects of supplemental instruction

Supplemental Instruction (SI) consists of the use of students who have already completed a course or course component to assist in supporting the learning of students who are taking it presently. There are a multitude of models for implementing SI, varying in terms of whether formal teaching is allowed, how much contact occurs, whether student instructors are rewarded, and how, to name but a few. SI is of considerable interest in the context of the present chapter for several reasons. The first is the possibility of using performance data as a measure of whether SI is effective. Secondly, performance data can also be used to seek learning transfer beyond the particular course on which SI was administered. Thirdly, provision of SI constitutes a *prima facie* increase in teaching input and so is relevant to the issue of the relationship between TI and SP. If SI produces learning benefits, then either this is evidence that increasing teaching input produces learning benefit, or it becomes necessary to argue that SI is not teaching input.

Case study 3.4 uses data from an SI scheme[3] offered as an optional element of Stage I (first FT year) provision by Oxford Brookes University's School of Business. Students enrolled for the three modules on which SI was offered were invited to attend from one to four sessions on any or all of the three modules. Students providing SI were given no financial reward, but could use the experience as part of an exercise attracting academic credit. SI providers were given training and were clearly informed that they were not there to provide orthodox teaching. Their role was to try to communicate to current candidates what they had learned about approaching study and assessment on the modules. Table 3.7 presents background data on the population of students involved in the study. Data was taken from the University's administrative records, anonymizing it as it was extracted. The data shows that there are no apparent differences between candidates who elected to take SI ('SUPPINST') and those who did not ('NOSUPPINST') with respect to pre-university indicators of achievement such as GCSEs and A-levels. Candidates who elected to take SI were slightly older. Associated probability levels are uncorrected and should be interpreted conservatively because of the number of comparisons made. Table 3.7 illustrates both the risks and the benefits of using conventional hypothesis-testing techniques for the purposes of data exploration.

Effects of supplemental instruction on student performance

	SUPPINST	NOSUPPINST
NO. OF GCSEs	7.4	7.5
A LEVEL POINTS	15.8	14.9
AGE	23.5***	22.1 t=2.95;df=563;p<0.005
STAGE I AVERAGE	57.9***	55.8 t=3.31;df=164;p<0.005
STAGE II AVERAGE	58.6	57.6
MODULE 7001	58.9*	55.9 t=2.12;df=429;p<0.05
MODULE 7002	59.0***	54.1 t=3.31;df=398;p<0.001
MODULE 7003	56.5****	45.2 t=4.04;df=189;p<0.0001

Table 3.7   Comparisons between attenders and non-attenders at supplemental instruction sessions on a Business Administration course. SUPPINST means that cases have attended at least 1 SI session. (Data from Price and Rust 1995).

For the purposes of the present study, data reported in Table 3.7 suggest that SI is associated with better performance in the three first-year modules, 7001, 7002 and 7003. This superior performance does not appear to arise from pre-existing differences in ability between candidates. The data in Table 3.7 also suggest a more general tendency for students who elect to take SI to get better average marks across Stage I modules as a whole. This suggestion is very difficult to evaluate, however, because the averages used were taken without modification from Oxford Brookes University's administrative records. As a consequence, the overall Stage I averages already include marks from modules 7001, 7002 and 7003. For transfer of effect to be demonstrated, it is necessary to find a measure of performance which excludes these three modules. Stage II average is independent of the three stage I modules on which SI was available, but many of the Stage II modules included in the average were remote from the academic content of 7001, 7002 and 7003, and indeed in many cases were in different academic discipline altogether. The finding that there is no difference between SUPPINST and NOSUPPINST groups with respect to Stage II average was therefore a weak test of the transfer hypothesis, and unsurprising.

Effects of supplemental instruction on Stage II performance

GROUP	NO SI	SI
MEAN STAGE II MARK	48.8	54.9
SAMPLE SIZE	57	31

Table 3.8   Mean marks achieved by students on a sample of 4 modules selected for comparability and relevance, according to whether they had attended at least one session of SI. (Data from Price and Rust 1995).

Table 3.8 reports data from a subset of Stage II modules to which material in modules 7001, 7002 and 7003 was relevant. This time the difference between means was significant ($t = 2.09$; df = 86; $p < 0.05$), and correspondingly there does seem to be some evidence for transfer of effect. The disappointingly small numbers result from the need to track students onto a shared set of largely optional Stage II modules. The fragility of this evidence obviously does not detract from its value as an illustration of the methodology of performance data analysis.

While the evidence that SI is associated with improved student performance is of interest in its own right, it does also raise further questions concerned with the mechanism by which the improvement in performance is produced. Some progress was made in answering this further question by analysing the data presented in Table 3.9.

Effects of supplemental instruction on examinations and coursework

	SI		NO SI	
	EXAM	CWORK	EXAM	CWORK
SAMPLE SIZE	45	45	333	333
MEAN MARK	30.7 (61.4%)	29.7 (59.4%)	31.0 (62.0%)	28.0 (56.0%)

Table 3.9   Mean marks achieved by students on the coursework and examination components of an introductory module, according to whether they had attended at least one SI session. (Data from Price and Rust 1995).

In interpreting data summarized in Table 3.9, the following points should be noted:

- Analysis was confined to comparison of coursework and examination marks for module 7001. Data was not available for other modules.

- 'SI' here was operationalized as 'attended at least one session of SI in association with module 7001'.

- SI had a significant effect on coursework marks ($t = 2.22$; df = 376; $p < 0.05$).

- SI had no effect on examination marks.

- When SI was operationalized to mean 'attended at least two sessions of SI in association with 7001' the significant effect of coursework was lost.

- The difference between examination and coursework marks with SI (mean difference = 2.8) and without SI (mean difference = 0.9) was also significant (t = 1.99 ; df = 372; $p < 0.05$). SI attendance associated with a reduced difference between examination and coursework marks, and improved marks for coursework.

In summary, performance data analysis was of considerable assistance in evaluating effects of SI, and suggests that student performance benefits from SI; that the benefits are produced by SI itself, not because more able students elect to take it; that the effects of SI generalizes to other courses taken later in a student's career; and that the source of the benefit is the transfer of experience which assists in preparing assessed coursework exercises. While it remains an open question whether student performance would have benefited more or less by investing equivalent resources in providing instruction sessions led by members of the teaching staff, the SI data also suggests that at least in the School of Business, Oxford Brookes students are still located on the TI/SP curve at a point at which increased TI produces detectable improvement in SP.

Case study 3.5   Effects of academic research on student experience of teaching

Case study 3.5 deals with another issue of concern in the area of university resourcing and student performance in HE. For many years there was a broad consensus that university academics learned from research and transmitted the results of their learning to students via teaching. As the participation rate in HE has increased, so the cost of resourcing research has come under increasing scrutiny, and the view has been urged that at best research contributes nothing to teaching and may even affect the quality of teaching negatively (Ramsden and Moses, 1992).
    While this is a message that universities, particularly new universities, might well wish to hear, the evidence upon which it is based is deeply suspect. The basic methodology is to develop an 'extent' measure of academic research by, for example, counting publications or asking academics to rate their own or peers' productivity. The extent measure of academic research is then correlated with student satisfaction-ratings of the same individuals as teachers. Though there are some null findings and the occasional weak positive relationship, the bulk of studies of this kind report low negative correlations. This data has been taken to demonstrate that at best academic research doesn't benefit teaching, and that it may either impair it or be associated with cognitive characteristics which are not conducive to producing high levels of student satisfaction. The difficulty with this methodology lies in its employment of an extent or productivity measure as a proxy for research. The problem is whether the apparent negative impact of research on teaching has anything to do with research *per se*, but might rather be produced by the amount of time that research takes up. If academics' time is fixed, then anything will impair teaching if it takes up enough time. Naturally enough, high-productivity researchers will have less time for teaching, but this does not support the conclusion that there is any intrinsic lack of compatibility between the two. It seems that the correlational evidence may involve a confounding between variables. The straightforward way to untangle the confounding is to ask students whether and why they think academic

research is bad for university teaching.

Lindsay, Paton-Saltzberg, Blackman and Jenkins (1997) used an interview-based methodology, but, because the focus of interest was in consensually held views rather than idiosyncratic opinions, a semi-structured group interview of the form often referred to as a focus group was employed. In planning the study, it became clear that discipline-related differences might be expected, differences associated with how long students had been at university, and differences related to how much research was carried out in the students' department. To investigate these possibilities fairly elaborate sample structure was used consisting of eight focus groups each made up of 4–6 students from a different discipline. Each group was composed entirely of first years or entirely of third years. Some groups came from disciplines ranked low in the 1992 RAE, some from disciplines ranked high, and some from disciplines with intermediate rankings. All of the groups were asked the same set of 'trigger' questions in the same order, and given the same prompts if discussion dried up. The questions were contributed by the investigators but modified in the light of a pilot study, data from which was not used in the final analysis.

The focus group data was examined in two quite different ways. The first approach was to focus on the content of participant contributions using qualitative analysis techniques. Using this approach, there was no doubt that students sometimes held negative views about research. What they were, and the extent to which they were shared, are summarized in Table 3.10. These negative views could be subdivided into three classes: *Minority and infrequent complaints*, of the kind in the three leftmost data columns in Table 3.10, are of little importance just because they were infrequent and atypical. *Theoretical problems* are presented in the three rightmost columns. These were not problems that students claimed to have experienced but ones they thought might arise. *Shared grievances* are presented in the two middle columns of Table 3.10. What this data suggested was that students were not disaffected by lecturer-research because it impaired their teaching but because students knew that lecturers were involved in research but weren't being told what it was about. And, as we suspected, students were also unhappy because when lecturers were doing research they weren't available to students.

A difficulty with qualitative research is its subjectivity. All of the investigators involved in the present study became concerned that perhaps they were picking out comments which fitted with their prior beliefs or which contradicted other beliefs with which they disagreed. To circumvent this unease, the data was also in a quite

	Boring	Resource Gambling	Undergrad Neglect	Not Disclosed	Reduces Availability	Threatens Relevance	Increases Intolerance	Distorts Priorities
Biology	YES			YES	YES	YES		
Adult Nursing				YES	YES	YES		YES
Planning	YES		YES	YES	YES	YES	YES	YES
Hosp. Man.				YES	YES	YES		
English				YES	YES	YES	YES	
Anthrop.				YES	YES	YES	YES	YES
Bus. Admin.		YES		YES	YES	YES		
Education				YES	YES	YES	YES	

Table 3.10 Reasons why research activity might have negative consequences for teaching given by students from eight different academic disciplines.

different way. A research assistant was hired and asked to go through transcripts of the focus groups, sentence by sentence, classifying each sentence as positive negative or neutral about teaching, and positive negative or neutral about research. The results are presented in Table 3.11.

RAE RATING	Research +	Research -	Research 0	Teaching +	Teaching -	Teaching 0
HIGH	34	21	45	20	14	66
MEDIUM	26	9	65	17	10	73
LOW	18	8	74	16	7	77

Table 3.11   Percentage of sentences categorised as Positive, Negative, and Neutral towards teaching and research, used by students in focus group discussions categorised according to the 1992 RAE rating of their discipline.

Data in the two columns with minus signs at the top show that the percentage of negative comments about research, and about teaching, increase as RAE rating gets higher. Just as the correlational studies apparently suggest, the more research active a department is, the less satisfied students are with teaching quality. But Table 3.11 also provides some new information suggesting a very different interpretation of the data. The new information is contained in the columns headed by plus signs. They too increase with RAE rating, including positive comments about teaching. Furthermore, the positive percentages are consistently considerably larger than the negative percentages. This is quite incompatible with the conclusions drawn from the correlational studies that students are less satisfied with the teaching of academics who engage in research.

With the qualitative data available as well, reasonable sense can be made of these results. Students are positive about teachers who do research because involvement makes them enthusiastic, it 'brings ideas alive' and it creates confidence that they 'know what's going on' in the discipline. Students are negative about research because they find that teachers are inexplicably absent or frequently unavailable and most ironically because they feel excluded from it and poorly informed about it. These conclusions are almost opposite to the ones drawn from the correlational literature alone. Tables 3.12 and 3.13 show that this pattern is found right across a broad range of disciplines. It was also noted in first- and third-year groups alike.

From the perspective of the present chapter, the interest of the data presented in Tables 3.11, 3.12, and 3.13 lies not so much in its capacity to illuminate a particular debate in the domain from which the data is drawn, but in its value as an illustration of the use of performance data analysis. In both case studies 3.1 and 3.2 the performance data which was analysed existed entire and complete before the study commenced, but case study 3.1 provides an example of how performance data can be used to modify course environments rationally, while case study 3.2 is offered as an example of how performance data can illuminate issues of general or at least national significance. In case study 3.3, the existing average mark data was organized in terms of a grouping variable (termtime working versus no-termtime working) which only became available as a result of (the questionnaire) part of the study itself, but which gave the data rather more meaning than it originally possessed. Case study 3.4 illustrates how student performance data can be used to monitor and evaluate experiments in education without distorting the processes involved or making guinea pigs of students. Case study 3.5 pushes the idea of performance data to its very limit, by suggesting that even qualitative methodologies can, incidentally, produce physical traces such as recorded speech, which can be objectively studied as performance data. Case study 3.5 also suggests that this methodology can in some circumstances produce an illuminating outcome. There is here perhaps some slight promise that the apparently unbridgeable gulf between the subjective world of qualitative phenomenological data and the public world of physical objective data may, if only in a small way, occasionally be traversed.

Discipline	Positive Sentences	Negative Sentences	Neutral Sentences
Biology	207	61	465
(%)	(28)	(8)	(64)
Adult Nursing	95	58	116
(%)	(35)	(22)	(43)
Planning	85	43	236
(%)	(22)	(15)	(63)
Hospitality Mngmnt.	101	101	470
(%)	(16)	(7)	(77)
English	143	51	707
(%)	(16)	(6)	(78)
Anthropology	161	64	937
(%)	(14)	(6)	(80)
Business Admin.	26	13	692
(%)	(4)	(2)	(94)
Education	175	106	541
(%)	(21)	(13)	(66)

Table 3.12   Number of sentences categorised as Positive, Negative, and Neutral towards research, used by students from a variety of disciplines in focus group discussions.

Discipline	Positive Sentences	Negative Sentences	Neutral Sentences
Biology	130	77	526
(%)	(18)	(11)	(72)
Adult Nursing	67	28	174
(%)	(25)	(10)	(65)
Planning	38	35	306
(%)	(10)	(9)	(81)
Hospitality Mngmnt.	53	17	544
(%)	(9)	(3)	(88)
English	78	68	755
(%)	(9)	(8)	(84)
Anthropology	120	68	974
(%)	(10)	(6)	(84)
Business Admin.	131	30	570
(%)	(18)	(4)	(78)
Education	141	91	590
(%)	(17)	(11)	(72)

Table 3.13   Number of sentences categorised as Positive, Negative, and Neutral towards teaching, used by students from a variety of disciplines in focus group discussions (percentages in brackets).

3.8   References

Lindsay, R.O. (1989) Review and evaluation. In D. Watson (ed.) *Managing the Modular Course*, Milton Keynes: SRHE and Open University Press.

Lindsay, R.O. (1997) Designing experiments on student learning. In C. Rust and G. Gibbs (eds), *Improving Student Learning: Improving Student Learning through Course Design*, Oxford: Oxford Centre for Staff and Learning Development.

Lindsay, R.O., Paton-Satltzberg, R., Blackman, T. and Jenkins A. (1997) Academic research and student learning – towards an explanatory model. In preparation.

Lindsay R.O. and Paton-Saltzberg R. (1987) Resource changes and academic performance at an English polytechnic, *Studies in Higher Education*, 12(2), 213–17.

Marton, F. (1981) Phenomenography – describing conceptions of the world around us. *Instructional Science*, 10, 177–200.

Marton, F. and Saljo, R. (1984) Approaches to learning. In F. Marton, D. Hounsell, and N. Entwistle (eds), *The Experience of Learning*, Edinburgh: Scottish Academic Press.

Paton-Saltzberg, R. and Lindsay, R.O. (1986) An Analysis of Academic Performance in Stage I. *Report to Modular Managment and Review Committee MARCO 86/14, Oxford Polytechnic.*

Paton-Saltzberg, R. and Lindsay, R.O. (1993). The Effects of Paid Employment on the Academic Performance of full-time students in Higher Education. *Report to Academic Standards Committee, Oxford Brookes University.*

Price, M. and Rust, C. (1995) Laying firm foundations: the long-term benefits of supplemental instruction for students on large introductory courses. *Inovations in Education and Training International*, 32 No. 2, May.

Ramsden, P. and Moses, I., (1992) Associations between research and teaching in Australian Higher Education. *Higher Education*, 23, 273-295.

Webb, E. J., Campbell, D.T., Schwartz, R. D. and Sechrest, L. (1996) *Unobtusive Measures: Nonreactive research in the social sciences.* Chicago: RandMcNally.

Notes

1 Most of the data discussed in this chapter results from studies carried out in collaboration with Renée Paton-Saltzberg. It is a pleasure to acknowledge that if the ideas in the chapter are of any interest or value, then a great deal of the credit is hers.

2 It is doubtfull whether anyone would explicity endorse this model. However, some educational consultants appear prepared to advise universities that cutting teaching input will improve student learning, a message that financially stretched university managers will sometimes pay to hear. Such advice may be justified if both the teaching input/student performance function and the location of the university upon it are known. As this is not the case, advice that cutting TI will have positive effects upon TP must presumably rest upon the assumption that cutting TI is good for SP whatever the position of the university upon the TI/SP function. This is the relationship expressed by Curve 4.

3 Data reported here were collected as part of a study by Margaret Price and Chris Rust (Price and Rust 1995). The author of the present chapter advised on design and carried out much of the data analysis on a consultancy basis. The author is grateful to the original authors for permission to use their data. The purposes for which the data are used here, are not necessarily the same as those of the original report.

4

The value of self and peer assessment to the developing lifelong learner

Kay Sambell and Liz McDowell
University of Northumbria at Newcastle

The past 25 years have seen considerable discussion and promotion of the importance of lifelong learning. The term means different things to different people, and throughout the literature it has at times been used as a synonym for adult education, recurrent education and open learning (Knapper, 1991, p. 21). For the purposes of this chapter, however, we are concerned with the ways in which lifelong learning has become linked with a particular set of educational principles or guidelines which seek to create the notion of an ideal learner who is sufficiently autonomous, independent and motivated to continue self-regulated learning throughout life. Paragraph 23 of the summary of the UK National Committee of Inquiry into Higher Education (1997), for instance, outlines the need to create a 'learning society', which will 'benefit the economy and society' and to shape 'a democratic, civilised, inclusive society' by inspiring and enabling individuals 'to develop their capabilities to the highest potential levels throughout life, so that they grow intellectually, are well equipped for work, can contribute effectively to society and achieve personal fulfilment'.[1]

We will draw upon Knapper's model of lifelong learning to highlight more precisely the meanings we attach to the term.

Knapper (1991) proposes the following definition of an idealized lifelong learner, who will:

1. be strongly aware of the relationship between learning and real life;

2. be aware of the need for lifelong learning;

3. be highly motivated to continue lifelong learning;

4. possess a self-concept which favours lifelong learning;

5. possess the necessary skills for lifelong learning (p. 45).

There are two aspects of this model which are of particular interest to us. First, the model is underpinned by the learner's *attitudes* towards learning and study. According to Knapper these are 'vital prerequisites' that influence adults' willingness to engage fully in a process of lifelong learning. In other words, items 1—4 of the model concern learners' disposition or preparedness not only to accept but genuinely to value the business of learning. For instance, if learners regard learning as a worthless activity, lack confidence in their ability to learn effectively or cannot see the relevance of a particular learning activity then they would scarcely be expected to show great enthusiasm or aptitude for lifelong learning. On the other hand, those people who see learning as interesting and worth while (in terms which they can relate to their own lives), and who feel confident in their own competence to learn, possess what Knapper describes as 'personal prerequisites for learning' which will heighten their potential to engage in lifelong learning. In short, successful lifelong learning depends upon a particular mental set, which includes positive values and attitudes towards the principles of lifelong learning and a particular self-image as an active, autonomous learner.

Secondly, according to Knapper, the capacity for lifelong learning depends greatly on what might be called *competencies* or *study skills* (p. 44). These include, for example, the capacity to work without the direct supervision of a tutor; skill at locating information; effectiveness in applying knowledge already possessed; skill in using learning resources such as libraries. For our present purposes it is important to recognize that some of the skills to which Knapper draws specific attention are directly concerned with learners' capacity to monitor and evaluate their own learning. Knapper's definition of the idealized lifelong learner possesses the following important abilities:

- capacity to set personal objectives in a realistic way;

- efficiency in evaluating one's own learning (p. 45).

This is important because there is a clear link here between the skills and qualities needed by the effective lifelong learner, and the skills and qualities which many would argue are fostered and developed by involvement in self- and peer-assessment activities. The link between the idea of the 'ideal' self-determining learner and the need for that learner to be effective in self-assessment is clearly apparent in Heron's (1988) definition of an 'idealized' educated individual, for example. For him, an educated individual is

> a person who is self-determining – who can set his own learning objectives, devise a rational programme to attain them, set criteria of excellence by which to assess the work he produces and assess his own work in the light of these criteria

(p. 79)

4.1 The role of assessment in developing lifelong learners

The skill of self-monitoring and evaluation is, then, crucial to the development of lifelong learning and autonomous individuals. Self and peer assessment is viewed by some to encourage the development of these particular abilities.[2] For example, Boud and Falchikov (1989) claim

> there has been a principled desire on the part of teachers for learners to take greater responsibility for their own learning through involvement in a crucial act of learning: assessing one's own competence.

In other words, self and peer assessment are being proposed as major tools by which to develop lifelong learners. It is hoped that by promoting one particular study skill – the ability to assess one's own achievement – learners will be encouraged to assume greater levels of responsibility and see themselves differently, as independent learners, rather than relying on traditional dependency on a teacher figure. This therefore involves an attempt to alter learners' attitudes and values towards themselves as learners, and corresponds to the 'prerequisites' of Knapper's model.

If lifelong learners are wanted, then formal education must play a part in preparing them and supporting their development (Boud, 1995a, p. 14). The question is, how far can self and peer assessment play a valuable role in this development and in educating students as lifelong learners? In this paper we will explore the issue from the student perspective, presenting the results from a number of case studies investigating student perceptions of innovative assessment in theory and in practice.

4.2 The Impact of Assessment project

The Impact of Assessment research project was set up to investigate the ways in which a variety of assessment techniques influence students' perceptions, behaviour and learning. Thirteen case studies of instances of assessment practice have been conducted across the University of Northumbria, over half of which have included at least an element of self and/or peer assessment. In-depth interviews and observation studies have been conducted with a sample of students involved in these activities.

4.2.1 The role of assessment in student learning

The project sought to build upon the ample research evidence that has revealed the importance of assessment with regard to student learning in higher education contexts (for example, Gibbs, 1992; Ramsden, 1992; Miller and Parlett, 1974; Entwistle and Entwistle, 1992). The project's novelty lies in its specific aim of exploring the issues surrounding innovative assessment from the student perspective.

4.2.2 'Alternative' or 'innovative' assessment

Empirical investigations into innovative assessment have become increasingly pertinent because of what Birenbaum (1996) has described as a shift from a 'testing culture' towards an 'assessment culture'. Unlike the 'testing culture', the new 'assessment culture' places strong emphasis on the integration of assessment and teaching, on assessing processes rather than just products of learning (see, for example, Fazey, 1993), and on measuring individual progression. Importantly the notional position of the student has also shifted from that of powerless, mystified subject to whom assessment is being done by somebody else, to the role of an active participant who shares responsibility not only in the learning process, but also the assessment process (Brown and Knight, 1994, p. 52). Assessment practices that are meaningful and varied are being sought, so that they more nearly coincide with the goals of the 'alternative approach' to active learning (McDowell, 1996). As Birenbaum summarizes

> all these changes are . . . meant to develop self-motivated and self-regulated learners and intended to make learning a more mindful and meaningful experience which is responsive to individual differences among the learners.

> (p. xiii)

The increasing introduction of alternative or innovative assessment raises interesting questions of student empowerment and a shift from assessment (as marking) being done to learners (for the purposes of certification and grading) through a spectrum of additional goals in which assessment is being done *on behalf of* learners (to provide them with feedback to improve their learning, for example) and eventually done *by* learners. In the final stage of this model it is obvious why self and peer assessment are regarded as having a vital role to play.

The fact remains, however, that some teaching colleagues have been disappointed with the application of self and peer assessment and they fear that it does not always work (McDowell and Mowl, 1995). As staff developers we are sometimes told by lecturing staff that they have experimented with it and that it has apparently, from their perspective, met with student rejection and even sometimes hostility. This is undoubtedly because, as Boud (1995b, p. 40) points out, it can be conducted in ways that ironically undermine the principled educational goals it aims to achieve, and that what matters is how students *interpret* the context of assessment. The Impact of Assessment project was designed to illuminate and probe the student perspective to explore the explicit and implicit 'messages' students receive from their involvement in various assessment tasks.

4.3 Self and peer assessment and lifelong learning: student perspectives

Six of the 13 cases we studied included peer and/or self assessment in the grading of work, while three others encouraged students to make judgements about their own work and that of their peers on an informal, formative basis. In all of these cases it was striking that the students were, with one noticeable exception which we will report later in the paper, generally in favour of the idea of their becoming more involved in the assessment process, and could perceive potential benefits of becoming assessors themselves. It was not uncommon to find students expressing the view that

> we ought to get the opportunity to do more of this sort of thing.

That is not to say that students were unreservedly satisfied with the practicalities of the situations in which they found themselves and complaints about the procedures were commonplace (see McDowell and Mowl, 1995). But it is fair to say that, as a general principle, the wide range of students we interviewed were in favour of staff attempting to continue with the innovation, or could see ways in which it might in future become a fruitful exercise, given suitable development. In other words, most made clear distinctions between seeing the point of self and peer assessment as an aid to learning, and its practical implementation in their particular case.

4.4 Student perspectives on self and peer assessment: developing the skills necessary for lifelong learning

Despite their reservations, from their perspective students were very aware that self and peer assessment had the capacity to develop and foster useful abilities and skills, which we would argue relate directly to the skills necessary for lifelong learning outlined above. We identified four main ways in which students' evaluative skills were enhanced.

4.4.1 Reflecting upon how judgements are made

When invited to talk about their perception of the point of the exercises in which they found themselves situated, students frequently suggested that they were learning how to evaluate their own learning achievements more effectively. They often recognized that this was because they were being placed in a situation in which they were being required (paradoxically forced!) to reflect upon their own learning and that of their peers. For example, here is a student describing the way in which involvement in peer assessment made her consider the business of essay writing more deeply:

> It [peer assessment] improved my understanding of how judgements are made about work because before . . . I thought I knew what constituted a good essay and a bad essay, and then I went into it in more detail.

This student is describing how she believes peer assessment has improved her evaluative skills because she has moved from an impressionistic and unreflective view of a 'good essay' to a more thorough, reasoned approach. She went on to describe how this had impacted on her future approach to academic work, because she had consciously attempted to address some of the aspects ('detail') of which she had now become aware. She described her attempt to think of each assessment criterion when writing her next essay, and how she tried to bear in mind the good and bad points of other essays she had seen while being involved in peer assessment exercises:

> I think it was generally quite good . . . to go away and think to yourself 'Well, I should do that in my essay, I shouldn't do that.' So I think it was a good exercise.

We see her belief that her own skills, especially her ability to set herself personal objectives in a realistic way, have been improved by the more sophisticated evaluative model with which her involvement in peer assessment has now equipped her.

4.4.2 Developing skills by talking to fellow students

The following extract is drawn from an observation of a tutorless student-group discussion. Before the session students had read two model essays and had been asked to consider the strengths and weaknesses of each. In the workshop, they were placed in tutorless groups to discuss their views with each other, and to decide collectively upon grades and, most importantly, the reasons for those grades, in order to generate criteria to be used in follow-up exercises. It shows its participants entering actively and energetically into an illuminating dialogue about the various ways in which it is possible to evaluate learning achievement:

> A: It's got a much better structure, they've really thought about it
>
> B: But it's got no facts in it. You can't just say something and then not back it up . . .
>
> C: It'd be better if it had some of the figures from the first essay.
>
> A: But it is good, because it has a good introduction and a conclusion . . .
>
> B: Yes, but it makes sweeping statements.

In a follow-up interview these students highly valued what they saw as an 'opportunity' to reflect collaboratively upon the ways of evaluating learning, first because they felt it increased their understanding of the assessment mechanism by giving them an 'insider's view', but also because they discovered that they were not alone in their individual uncertainty as to what differentiated a good and a poorer essay. They valued the chance to discuss this more fully and to reflect upon it in the relatively 'safe' environment of their peers. Several students expressed surprise that, as a result of their discussions, they had been able to mark accurately the two pieces of work under scrutiny, and their confidence as successful evaluators had been significantly boosted. This is an important point to which we will return later in the paper.

4.4.3 Using evaluative skills to enhance the communication of learning

There was evidence to suggest that students were being more careful and thorough in the preparation and evaluation of their own work when they knew that their fellow students would be involved in its assessment. Here, for example, is a student describing how the knowledge that her peers would be observing and questioning her during an oral seminar presentation prompted her to take what seems to be a deeper approach to learning in order to prepare for this form of innovative assessment:

> You always find that you really know the stuff that you've done seminars [oral presentations] on . . . You try to cover all the angles, make sure you're ready for any question, whereas with an essay there's no comeback.

Some described how the effect of having to communicate their learning to their peers, rather than an 'expert' tutor, had a significant effect on the way they approached learning for peer assessment:

> Well, you have to take it seriously because, at the end of the day, you know that someone is going to see it, and you don't want to look a total idiot in front of your friends . . . Whereas with an essay you give it in and it just goes into a black hole, no one actually sees it, and you can forget about it because you don't get it back for weeks on end . . .

This not only suggests that having 'real' people as an audience for your learning achievements (note that lecturers are not deemed to be real people!) prompts some students to reflect more conscientiously upon their work and attempt to evaluate their own achievement more seriously, but also demonstrates the point that, paradoxically, learners often have to be forced to assume more responsibility for their own work. This feeling of compulsion is expressed by the following student quote:

> If I do an essay I just, you know, I just tend to do it. I think that because I knew that someone from my peer group was going to mark it . . . it *made me think* about what I was actually writing . . . I thought 'What would someone else think?', which you should do really, because, I mean, someone else is marking it. But I used to just go ahead . . . just do it [when an essay is staff marked] (author's emphasis).

It is important to stress that the student claimed that 'being made to think' was a positive aspect of her involvement in self and peer assessment and was seen as developing a useful skill.

4.4.4   Developing skills in self evaluation by broadening your repertoire

Other students described how useful it was to have access to a range of ways of performing tasks which then acted as a benchmark against which to evaluate one's own learning achievements. In the following example, the student shows how this not only broadens her potential repertoire in future, but allows her to perceive the strengths of her own work in a realistic light:

> You were able to jot down things [while peer marking] which you thought would be good in your essay . . . At first [when I read someone else's essay] I thought 'Oh no! I didn't do it like that . . . I had more graphs and illustrations in mine, and she'd just written it all [in prose]. But I won't say it was loads better than the one I did, it was just completely different.

Although self and peer assessment did help students to develop evaluative skills, many told us that they found self and peer assessment 'difficult', not just because of embarrassment at having to judge their friends, but because they were unaccustomed to putting themselves in the shoes of the assessor and reflecting in such detail on learning. Acquiring a feel for appropriate standards was especially difficult.

> Grading is hard anyway, getting away from the fact that you know them and that's hard. But just to sit down and know whether you give them a 2 or a 4, I've no idea how to draw the line. I just know if something is good or bad.

Again, this point relates strongly to the levels of student confidence and their self-concept as capable assessors, to which we will now turn. It is important to recognize and bear in mind, however, that most students find the assessment process complex and taxing. The following section considers two case studies to illustrate the point, and to draw attention to the implications in terms of the developing lifelong learner. In this section we place less emphasis on the *skills* required and instead draw attention to the related capacity of self and peer assessment to encourage what Knapper calls the *prerequisites*, the attitudes and values, need by the lifelong learner. We believe that students' reactions to what, at the outset, appeared to be very similar self- and peer-assessment exercises reveal important insights into self and peer assessment's potential to foster (or hinder) the development of the prerequisites necessary for effective lifelong learning.

4.5 Developing the prerequisites for lifelong learning: the importance of students' perceptions of the assessment criteria

In this section of the chapter we intend to concentrate our attention on two specific cases of self and peer assessment because, although they initially appeared to involve students in strikingly similar activities and the staff, when interviewed, expressed very similar aims, students reacted to the activities in markedly different ways. In each case students were offered the opportunity of attending workshops, designed to prepare the students to become effective assessors. The sessions were introduced as opportunities to help students to improve their future work by giving them insights into the process of assessment and by encouraging them to reflect upon their work in greater detail. Staff aimed to share the assessment criteria and to build student confidence, promoting independence as an educational goal. Group A, who were social-science students, were being prepared to contribute to the marking of essays to be produced at the end of the unit, via self and peer assessment. They were involved in generating assessment criteria and had practice in applying criteria to model answers. Group B, who were studying a modern language as part of their course, were given staff-produced assessment criteria during their workshop, which they used to provide feedback to their peers during a 'trial run' of an oral presentation, which was ultimately to be staff-marked.

While Group A responded very positively to their introduction to self and peer assessment and expressed similar comments to those reported above, Group B responded extremely negatively. We identified three significant features of students' perceptions of the criteria used in self and peer assessment which could foster or hinder their development as independent learners:

1. control and ownership of assessment criteria;

2. understanding of criteria;

3. application of criteria.

We believe these inter-related aspects are important because they contribute significantly to these learners' self-concept, that is, their own perceptions of their ability to evaluate effectively their own, and others', learning. This in turn may well affect their own self-confidence as effective and autonomous learners themselves. In this way we would postulate that in these case studies we are gaining some insight into the complexities of the ways in which Knapper's 'prerequisites' for lifelong learning may be fostered or obstructed by the practical realities of self and peer assessment in these specific contexts.

4.5.1 Students' perceptions of their control of the assessment criteria

Group A was asked to generate its own criteria which, in negotiation with the lecturers, were then written down for future use in peer- and self-assessment activities. It was important that the criteria were then in the students' own language (Orsmond *et al.*, 1996). Students were involved in substantial dialogue about these criteria, and were encouraged to interrogate the meanings of each one. Below we will draw upon the ample evidence that they subsequently tried to use the criteria to evaluate work. Group B was simply given the tutor's criteria to use. The lack of ownership of the criteria felt by Group B is clear in the following quote:

> We all got these lists of things to consider – numbers to circle – well, what I did was to get a general idea of whether someone's presentation was good or not, and then I went down giving them a 4 or a 3 for everything – no matter what the little bit I was supposed to be thinking about was.

Note how this student expresses her receipt of the criteria in passive terms ('we all got these lists') and how she feels that the 'list' is fairly meaningless ('numbers to circle'). This then appears to have an impact in the way the student describes tackling the assessment: she does not really use the criteria at all.

4.5.2 Understanding of the assessment criteria

During their workshop Group A were encouraged to develop their own criteria by being asked to evaluate two specimen essays, and to consider and discuss what they felt to be good and bad points about each. One described how it was important to reflect upon the criteria by comparing the merits of 'real' essays rather discussing them in an abstract way, which in turn improved her confidence as an assessor:

> you could just have one essay in front of you and think 'Yeah, that's quite good', but you need something to compare it against . . . through that you can see the good points in that essay and the good points in that essay.

The positive nature of these comments contrast markedly with a member of Group B, who confesses that she did not understand the criteria

> I didn't understand what half of the things we had to circle meant anyway . . . So basically what I put down for one I put down for them all. So I didn't mark it properly at all.

We would draw attention to the way in which the student re-emphasizes the feeling of compulsion and being out of control ('we *had* to circle') and the subsequent feelings of inadequacy and incompetence within the situation she finds herself ('I didn't mark it properly').

4.5.3　Application of the assessment criteria

When we interviewed members of Group A about how they had tackled the peer assessment, each had clearly attempted to apply each criterion individually, using them as a more sophisticated model of evaluating learning than had hitherto been the case. Here, for example, a student describes her approach to marking a peer's essay by using each criterion as a 'heading', whereas previously she had simply formed a general impression:

> I actually put those headings down . . . and went through to see if she had included all of those.

By contrast, as we have already seen, no one in Group B talked of seeking to apply an individual criterion:

> Well, perhaps [the tutor] finds it easy to break it [assessment] all down into sections – that's up to her. But I just get a general feeling, myself.

Here the student is clearly aware of a significant gap between the tutor's procedures and her own: and the tutor's principled attempt to allow students to become 'insiders' in the assessment process has actually resulted in students who are even more aware of the inequalities between staff and student.

4.5.4　Self confidence: perceptions of dependence or independence as learners

It was very striking that Group B ended up feeling dejected or resentful, convinced that they were unable to effectively evaluate the learning, either of their peers or themselves, whereas Group A felt confident and highly motivated to carry forward and apply their improved skills to new contexts. During interviews and observation studies Group A often talked of using the insights from the workshops to improve their future essays in ways which showed they were confident in their ability to continue assessing independently and with self-direction, without the direct supervision of staff. Group B, however, was far from inclined to experiment independently with self-evaluation and to apply it to subsequent academic work:

> I can't say that it helped me [with future preparation]. I ended up doing exactly what I did for the last one.

From this student's point of view, undertaking self and peer assessment has had little impact on learning. Their lack of confidence led Group B to rely on staff to assess their learning achievements, exemplified by the following quote, in which a student explains why she 'took no notice' of feedback from her peers and depended purely on the tutor's comments:

> She actually knew what she was doing and the rest of us didn't.

4.6　Conclusions

What we hope above all to emphasize is the point that self- and peer-assessment activities relate to students' effectiveness in evaluating and monitoring their own learning in important and extremely complex ways. If we aim to develop lifelong learners who are better able to evaluate their own learning and have an increased capacity to set their own personal objectives in realistic ways, then we must heed the implicit messages that students receive from the activities in which we involve them. We hope to stress the crucial role of the assessment criteria being used, which play a major part in equipping students with vital information and guidance to allow them to develop their skills. How students relate to the criteria; the measure of control they feel able to exercise over them; the ways in which they understand them; the purposes for which they feel able to use them are, we believe, important keys to enabling students to exercise a sufficient degree of confidence and control to become more autonomous, developing the important prerequisites of the lifelong learner.

4.7   References

Birenbaum, M. (1996) Introduction. In M. Birenbaum and F.J.R.C. Dochy (eds), *Alternatives in Assessment of Achievements, Learning Processes and Prior Knowledge*, Dordrecht: Kluwer Academic Publishers.

Boud, D. (1995a) What is learner self assessment? In *Enhancing Learning through Self Assessment*, London, Kogan Page, ch.2, 11–23.

Boud, D. (1995b) *Enhancing Learning through Self Assessment*, London, Routledge

Boud, D. and Falchikov, N. (<??? date ???>) Quantitative studies of student self-assessment in higher education: a critical analysis of findings, *Higher Education*, **18**, 529–49.

Brew, A. (1995) What is the scope of self assessment? In D. Boud, *Enhancing Learning through Self Assessment*, London: Kogan Page, 48–62.

Brown, S. and Knight, P. (1994) *Assessing Learners in Higher Education*, London, Kogan Page.

Candy, P., Crebert, G. and O'Leary, J. (1994) *Developing Lifelong Learners through Undergraduate Education*, NBEET Commissioned report No. 28, Canberra; Australian Government Publishing Service.

Entwistle, N.J. and Entwistle, A. (1992) Experiences of understanding in revising for degree examination results, *Learning and Instruction*, **2**, 1–22.

Fazey, D. (1993) Self assessment as a generic skill for enterprising students: the learning process, *Assessment and Evaluation in Higher Education*, **18**(3), 235–50.

Gibbs, G. (1992) Improving the quality of student learning through course design. In R. Barnett (ed.), *Learning to Effect*, Milton Keynes: SRHE and Open University Press, 149–65.

Heron, C. (1988) Assessment revisited. In D. Boud (ed.), *Developing Student Autonomy in Learning*, 2nd edn, London: Kogan Page.

Knapper, C.K. and Cropley, A.J. (1991) *Lifelong Learning and Higher Education*, 2nd edn, London: Kogan Page.

McDowell, L. and Mowl, G. (1995) Student perceptions of innovative assessment; a pilot study. In Gibbs, G. (ed.), *Improving Student Learning*, Oxford: Oxford Centre for Staff Development.

McDowell, L. (1996) Enabling student learning through innovative assessment. In G. Wisker, G. and Brown, S. (eds), *Enabling Student Learning: Systems and Strategies*, London: Kogan Page, 158–65.

McDowell, L. *et al* (1997) *Improving the Quality of Education: The Impacts of Subject Specialist Assessor Experience*, HEFCE.

Miller, C.M.L. and Parlett, M. (1974) *Up to the Mark: A Study of the Examination Game*, Guildford: SRHE.

The National Committee of Inquiry into Higher Education (1997) *Higher Education in the Learning Society*, Summary Report.

Orsmond, P., Merry, S. and Reiling, K. (1996) The importance of marking criteria in the use of peer assessment, *Assessment and Evaluation in Higher Education*, **21**(3), 239–50.

Ramsden, P. (1992) *Learning to Teach in Higher Education*, London: Routledge.

Notes

1. Birenbaum (1996) argues that we now see the prevalence of an 'alternative approach' to education as we approach the twenty-first century. Massive cultural, economic and social changes now demand flexible, adaptable, autonomous individuals. (see also Brew, 1995). Learners, accordingly, are increasingly seen as active agents rather than passive subjects. In a recent survey of HEFCE Assessors (1997) the authors discovered that this ideal of the active learner was indeed prevalent among this group of academics.

2. See, for example, Boud (1995a) p. 13; Boud (1995b); Candy *et al.* (1994).

5 Independent learning confronts globalization: facilitating students' development as learners

Terry Evans[i] and Alistair Morgan[ii]
(i) Faculty of Education, Deakin University, Australia;
(ii) Institute of Educational Technology, Open University, UK

5.1   Introduction

As both researchers and teachers we are concerned with issues of student learning. We are especially concerned with research and teaching in the adult open and distance education sector, where the majority of students are 'mature-age' and part-time (see, for example, Evans, 1994; Morgan, 1994). The university contexts in which we work, as is the case for many other colleagues in other educational institutions, have been influenced by the rhetoric and realities of new technologies. In the case of our work in universities, there is a concern for constructing what might be called the 'new educational technologies' in ways which encourage and sustain educational dialogues between teacher and students (Evans and Nation, 1993; Morgan, 1997). Most of the new educational technologies are based on computer and communications equipment, and the technologies which surround them, in the world at large. The surge of computer and communications technologies is said to be 'globalizing' economic, social, and political relations, and drawing educational institutions and systems into the fray.

Our aim in this chapter is to consider critically issues of globalization and relate these to issues about independent learning and lifelong learning, and to raise matters and questions concerning educational practice in a 'globalized' and/or 'globalizing' field. The tensions which flow from the above matters will be related to the need for a critical appraisal of the ways in which teachers, administrators and student support staff facilitate learners' development. We argue that these ways will need to be consistent with the 'new times' – the emerging cultural and technological contexts. Facilitating student development as learners requires a consideration, not only of the diverse contexts and needs of students, but also of the potential resources and strategies which are emerging: these include forms of collaborative and peer group learning mediated through new information technologies.

5.2   Globalization

The term 'globalization' abounds in the popular press and, particularly, in the rhetoric of government and business leaders. Despite, or perhaps because of, all this popular rhetoric, settling the term conceptually is not an easy task. Often, it seems, in education and elsewhere, the terms 'globalization' and its derivations are used interchangeably with the term 'internationalization' and its derivations. However, the terms cannot be synonymous, logically, although they have some important shared elements. We can clarify the position by drawing on some of the collected work of Bartlett, Evans and Rowan (Evans, 1995, 1997; Evans and Rowan, 1997a, 1997b, 1997c; Rowan and Bartlett, 1997; Rowan, Bartlett and Evans, 1997). They have recognized the problematic nature of the concepts of globalization and, for them, its corollary 'localization'. It can be seen that the process of globalization is derived historically from the development of transport and communications – especially those involving electronic, digital, satellite and/or computer-based systems. This has contributed to what Giddens (1991) and others have called a 'time-space compression' to the extent that people may now 'feel' connected to remote and distant events by virtue of the immediacy of the mediated representations they can experience of those events. For example, satellite or Web-based news and information services connect people in Glasgow with events which occur in other 'connected' parts of the globe irrespective of the distances involved. Although the rhetoric of globalization is usually expressed in economic and financial terms – there is no doubt that these are very significant elements – we contend that, for educators at least, it is the social and cultural aspects which turn 'globalization' into a meaningful entity for people in general. It is in this sense that they become citizens of the 'globe' and interact, usually virtually and often vicariously, with their fellow citizens.

5.3 Globalization and forms of open and distance education

It can be understood that forms of open and distance education are both potentially, and evermore actually, players in globalizing education. Traditionally, these forms of education have often seen that their 'distances' included ones of an international kind which renders them amenable to global practices. Likewise, their 'liberation' from having to see their practices as being bounded by the walls of an institution, or the boundaries of a campus, means that they often have educational and administrative practices and values which are adaptable and amenable to global operations. However, it is important for us to state that we are not only addressing institutions which call themselves 'open universities' or say that they are distance teaching organizations. We contend that, partly due to the technologies and consequences of globalization, all universities are shifting some of their practices into forms of open and distance education. They are all doing so partly to use computer and communications means to create their institutions into, at least partially, 'global' educational entities (see, Edwards, 1994; Evans, 1989, 1995, 1997).

Evans and Rowan have argued that:

> The non-dependence on contiguity of the educational practices of open and distance education institutions – coupled with the increasing pressure to find 'new markets' and sources of income, and the 'competitive threats' of other institutions in 'their marketplace' – has led these institutions to contemplate policies and actions which can be seen to operate simultaneously on two levels. At the first level they respond to the processes and procedures of a concept widely defined as globalisation. At the second level they negotiate contextual issues associated with both their own location and the site(s) and context(s) of their educational activities – 'localisation'. They therefore respond to a need to be 'globally competitive', as well as racially, culturally and 'locally' sensitive.
>
> (Evans and Rowan, 1997c, p. 1).

We wish to take this position a step further by considering the needs and contexts of learners within globalizing forms of education and relating this to ideas from independent and lifelong learning. Our reason for so doing is that, if we recognize that there is a need to be 'racially, culturally and "locally" sensitive', then this implies that understanding the needs and contexts of learners is crucial, and yet it appears to be an extremely problematic matter for those who wish to teach globally. It is not merely a matter of the global expanse itself, although this in itself is daunting, but rather the fluidity and diversity which the new educational technologies permit or encourage, are intensely problematic for those who advocate forms of, for example, student-centred learning. It seems that, on the one hand the new educational technologies permit greater capacities for interaction and communication (at a distance), but at the same time they sweep into the virtual classroom a potentially bewildering array of learners with whom most educators would find it perplexing to deal. At this point we should say that the conclusion we have just made about educators is based on our views about teaching and learning (see, Evans, 1994; Evans and Nation, 1989, 1993b; Morgan, 1983, 1993). These views eschew notions of behaviourist forms of programmed learning or instruction as being appropriate for the ways we like to teach (and learn) in the sorts of educational contexts we are discussing here. One of our motives for writing this chapter is that it seems probable to us that, given the difficulties of coping with a globally distributed and diverse student body, institutions will encourage or require their staff to look to forms of instruction which use only the conceptual and knowledge elements of their courses as the basis of their pedagogies, and ignore the students' needs, contexts and meaning-making capacities. In this sense, we fear that there is a danger that global forms of education will become 'programmed instruction' based entirely on the instructing institution's cultural, economic and political location and interests. Not only will this be an inferior education, in our view, but it will also contribute powerfully to a cultural hegemony which will crush local languages and cultures (see, George, 1997; Guy, 1997; Thaman, 1997; Wah, 1997).

Given these concerns it seems appropriate to consider how the theories and practices of independent and lifelong learning can be marshalled to construct forms of global education which value and incorporate the diversities of students, needs and contexts.

5.4   What is independent learning?

What is independent learning? Is it a coherent educational philosophy or is it such a broad term with so many meanings, a slogan even, that it offers little for theorizing our practice and improving our practice? Independent learning means all sorts of things, people use it with very different meanings and assumptions about the nature of learning and the aims and purposes of post-compulsory education.

For some people, independent learning means the separation of the teacher and learner, with the learner studying at home, in libraries, using new technology sources of information etc. Independence in this sense is a basic characteristic of open and distance education (ODE). Course teams in ODE put considerable effort into the design of self-instructional materials which are supported by various forms of tuition and counselling provided at the local level. With this meaning, any debate about a move towards independent learning is usually as a disguise for financial constraint and the worsening of provision for tutorial support. Financial cutbacks in conventional institutions are also likely to drive this notion of independent learning.

For other academic staff, independent learning means something very different. Students are taking greater responsibility for *what* they learn and *how* they learn it and are developing autonomy and self-direction in their learning, (Boud, 1981). A move to greater student autonomy in learning raises questions curriculum and assessment and particularly issues of power within educational institutions.

With these contrasting meaning of independent learning, ranging from a teacher-centred curriculum followed by a student in isolation, to a student-centred curriculum and lifelong learning, the term needs to be used with care if it is to be of any value for critical reflection on our practice. The discussion of variations in project-based learning (Morgan, 1983) around the dimensions 'curriculum construction' and 'control of learning' would seem relevant for examining the widely differing practices adopting a label of 'independent learning'. Curriculum construction, derived from the work of Bernstein (1971) on the classification and framing of educational knowledge, refers to whether the curriculum and learning activities are structured within academic disciplines and subject areas or around 'real-world' problems and issues. And the dimension of control of learning relates to whether students or teachers (or in negotiation) decide the content of the independent study, how it is to be tackled and how it is to be assessed.

A recent example of an independent study module (from the study of changing assessment practices in Scottish higher education) gives some idea of how some degree of learner autonomy can be designed into a university curriculum.

> The Independent Study Module – provides students with an opportunity to design, with support from and in negotiation with a specialist tutor, their own module. The module proposal, which includes learning outcomes, rationale for undertaking the module, pattern of study, resource requirement, has to meet formal requirements in terms of level of study, coherence and relevance to the rest of the student's approved degree programme. It does mean however, that the student has the opportunity to negotiate a set of learning outcomes which they can show evidence of achieving, through agreement of the kinds and forms of evidence that will be produced and the ways in which these will be assessed by the specialist tutor. After approval of the proposal the student works to produce the evidence required by the jointly designed assessment specification.
>
> (Hounsell *et al.*, 1996, p. 23)

In this case the student is taking some responsibility for the learning, within a broad framework of the institution. In practice most learning within institutional contexts will be some form of interdependent learning, certainly where assessment and accreditation are involved.

If we look further towards Candy's (1991) notion of self-direction and lifelong learning, he suggests the term includes personal autonomy, the capacity to manage one's own learning, a context to allow control by the learner and the independent pursuit of learning outside formal institutional settings; so only outside formal settings can we establish independent learning in the complete sense.

The concern or 'drive' for independent learning comes from a diversity of sources; these range from a long tradition of autonomy in learning in philosophy of education, to curricular reforms in the 1970s and demands for student-centred relevant curricula. In the late 1990s this concern comes from discussions about transferable skills, graduateness, vocational considerations and in the UK the Enterprise in Higher Education Initiative.

5.5 Students' development as learners

How do students change and develop as a result of their studies? How do they develop autonomy in learning and how can this be facilitated?

The research of Säljö (1982) on conceptions of learning and the longitudinal studies of Perry (1970) and Morgan and Beaty (1997) provide insights into the complex area of student development. The changes identified are that students move from holding absolutist conceptions of knowledge towards developing more relativistic conceptions of knowledge. There are changes in confidence, competence and control in learning. Students are changing from relying on the institution (or teacher) for control of their learning to exercising more of their own control over their learning. As students feel more confident and competent to make decisions for themselves, so they develop more independence from the teacher; they feel able 'to go it alone'.

The crucial question, is how can we as teachers facilitate these changes? The writings of Carl Rogers in *Freedom to Learn* still provide important insights for critical reflection on our teaching learning practices. Rogers stresses people's natural potential for learning and how this is realized when there is a personal intrinsic motivation and when externals threat are at a minimum. And to quote Rogers, (1969, p. 163):

> Independence, creativity, and self-reliance are all facilitated when self-criticism and self-evaluation are basic and evaluation by others is of secondary importance.

Research using approaches to studying and course perceptions questionnaires (Entwistle and Ramsden, 1983; Ramsden, 1992) show strong relationships between good teaching, freedom in learning, openness to students, realistic workloads and students adopting a deep approach to learning. So teaching learning activities which embody these characteristics within a supportive learning milieu or departmental style (Parlett, 1977) are likely to encourage reflection in learning and development of students' independence in learning.

5.6   Independent learning and new technology

There are many claims that learning with various forms of new technology will transform the quality of teaching learning and encourage student interaction in learning and help develop independence in learning. These forms of technology may be with multi-media instructional materials on CD-ROM or with computer mediated conferencing (CMC) between students and tutors or students selecting their own programmes on the WWW from the 'virtual universities'. There are predictions of a new paradigm for education, as Collis (1996) suggests:

> Tele-learning, connecting to resources and people via telecommunications, will be an important instrument of a new paradigm of educational organization and of new social conception of learning, in ways similar to the paradigm shifts accompanying the printing press and the popularization of books some centuries before.
>
> (Collis, 1996, p. 577)

New technology certainly provides challenges for students to engage in independent learning from the range of meaning associated with this term. However what are the realities of student's experience of learning with these new technologies, when viewed from the learner's perspective? It seems far from clear that aspirations of teachers and course designers will be met if we look at students' learning experiences in more depth.

A recent study of resource-based learning on CD-ROM with Open University students (MacDonald and Mason, 1996) highlights the problems some students encounter of being overwhelmed with vast amounts of information and unclear about their task as learners. Similar problems are likely to exist for students in conventional institutions as they are required to make greater use of global databases and electronic libraries available on the WWW. At one level these students could be seen as lacking certain 'information handling skills'. However, the underlying issue seems to be about how they perceive learning and their development as learners. These students seem to be constrained by a conception of learning which is concerned with a reproducing orientation to study, rather than seeing learning as a process of constructing meaning and going beyond the information provided.

If we look to virtual communities and collaborative learning online, what sorts of issues confront the independent learner, what are learners experiences? Is there the potential for local CMC groups to resist the globalizing pressures we suggest may occur? And how do online learning communities develop? These are of course complex questions which will be difficult to answer. The research of Wegerif (1995) into collaborative online learning identified that the 'construction of a community with a shared communication style' was the crucial factor the success on collaboration online. This may suggest how local communities could develop online and thus challenge globalizing tendencies from a global educational institution.

5.7   Conclusion

In this brief chapter we have raised some of the current concerns about gloabalization and localization and to what extent learners can both participate in a 'global university' as independent learners, as well as using the potential of computer mediated conferencing to counter tendencies of cultural hegemony. As educators, in designing our practice under the label of 'independent learning', we need to be aware of the assumptions we are making about the curriculum and who controls it. Learners will need 'just enough support' to enable them to move on and develop a degree of autonomy in learning, and the competence and confidence as lifelong learners.

5.8   References

Bernstein, B. (1971) 'On the classification and framing of educational knowledge' in M.F.D. Young (ed.), *Knowledge and Control*, Macmillan, London.

Boud, D. (ed.) (1981) *Developing Student Autonomy in Learning*, London, Kogan Page.

Candy, P.C. (1991) *Self-Direction for Lifelong Learning*, San Francisco, Jossey-Bass.

Collis, B. (1996) *Tele-learning in a Digital World*, London, International Thomson Computer Press.

Edwards, R. (1994) From a distance? Globalisation, space-time compression and distance education, *Open Learning*, 9(3), 9–17.

Entwistle, N. and Ramsden, P. (1983) *Understanding Student Learning*, London, Croom Helm.

Evans, T.D. (1989) Taking place: The social construction of place, time and space, and the (re)reading of distances in distance education, *Distance Education*, 10(2), 170–83.

Evans, T.D. (1994) *Understanding Learners in Open and Distance Education*, London, Kogan Page,

Evans, T.D. (1995) Globalisation, post-Fordism and open and distance education, *Distance Education*, 16(2), 241–55.

Evans, T.D. (1997) (En)countering globalisation: issues for open and distance education. In L.O. Rowan, V.L. Bartlett and T.D. Evans (eds), *Shifting Borders: Globalisation, Localisation and Open and Distance Education*, Geelong, Deakin University Press, 11–22.

Evans, T.D. and Nation, D.E. (1989) *Dialogue in practice, research and theory in distance education*, Open Learning, 4(2), 37–43.

Evans, T.D. and Nation, D.E. (1993a) Educational technologies: reforming open and distance education. In T.D. Evans and D.E. Nation (eds), *Reforming Open and Distance Education*, London, Kogan Page, 196–214.

Evans, T.D. and Nation, D.E. (1993b) Theorising open and distance education. In A.W. Tait (ed.), Key Issues in *Open Learning*, London, Longman, 45–62.

Evans, T.D. and Nation, D.E. (1996) Educational futures: globalisation, educational technology and lifelong learning. In T.D. Evans and D.E. Nation (eds), *Opening Education: Policies and Practices from Open and Distance Education*, London, Routledge, 1–6.

Evans, T.D. and Rowan, L.O. (1997a) Place matters: exploring issues of globalisation and localisation through sites of open and distance education. In T.D. Evans, D. Thompson and V. Jakupec (eds), *Research in Distance Education*, 4, Geelong, Deakin University Press (in press).

Evans, T.D. and Rowan, L.O. (1997b) Globalisation, localisation and distance education: issues for research. Paper presented at the Australian Association for Research in Education Globalisation and Education symposium, Brisbane, June 1997

Evans, T D & Rowan, L O (1997c) 'Globalisation, localisation and distance education: issues of policy and practice. Paper presented at the *Open and Distance Learning Association of Australia conference*, Launceston, September 1997.

George, R. (1997) Language and learning in open and distance education. In L.O. Rowan, V.L. Bartlett and T.D. Evans (eds), *Shifting Borders: Globalisation, Localisation and Open and Distance Education*, Geelong, Deakin University Press, 39–51.

Giddens, A. (1991) *The Consequences of Modernity*, Cambridge, Polity Press.

Guy, R.K. (1997) Contesting borders: knowledge, power and pedagogy in distance education in Papua New Guinea. In L.O. Rowan, V.L. Bartlett and T.D. Evans (eds), *Shifting Borders: Globalisation, Localisation and Open and Distance Education*, Geelong, Deakin University Press, 53–64.

Hounsell, D., McCulloch, M. and Scott, M. (eds) (1996) *The ASSHE Inventory, Centre for Teaching Learning and Assessment*, University of Edinburgh.

MacDonald, J. and Mason, R. (1997) *Information Handling Skills and Resource Based Learning, OTD Project No. 10*, Open University, Milton Keynes.

Morgan, A.R. (1983) Theoretical aspects of project-based learning in higher education, *British Journal of Educational Technology*, **14**(1), 66–78.

Morgan, A.R. (1993) *Improving Your Students' Learning: Reflections on the Experience of Study*, London, Kogan Page.

Morgan, A.R. (1997) Still seeking the silent revolution? Research, theory and practice in open and distance education. In T.D. Evans, V. Jakupec and D.C. Thompson (eds), *Research in Distance Education 4* Geelong, Deakin University Press (in press).

Morgan, A. and Beaty, E. (1997) The world of the learner. In F. Marton, D. Hounsell and N. Entwistle (eds), *The Experience of Learning, Edinburgh*, Scottish Academic Press.

Parlett, M. (1977) *The learning milieu, Studies in Higher Education*, **2**(2), 173–81.

Perry, W.G. (1970) *Forms of Intellectual and Ethical Development in the College Years: A Scheme*, New York, Holt, Rinehart & Winston.

Ramsden, P. (1992) *Learning to Teach in Higher Education*, London. Routledge.

Rogers, C. (1969) *Freedom to Learn*, Columbus Ohio, Merrill.

Rowan, L.O. and Bartlett, V.L. (1997) Feminist theorising on open and distance education: local and global perspectives. In L.O. Rowan, V.L. Bartlett and T.D. Evans (eds), *Shifting Borders: Globalisation, Localisation and Open and Distance Education*, Geelong, Deakin University Press, 117–34.

Rowan, L.O., Bartlett, V.L. and Evans, T.D. (eds) (1997) *Shifting Borders: Globalisation, Localisation and Open and Distance Education,* Deakin University Press, Geelong.

Säljö, R. (1982) *Learning and Understanding,* Goteborg Studies in Educational Sciences 41, Goteborg, Acta Universitatis Gothoburgensis.

Thaman, K. (1997) Considerations of culture in distance education in the Pacific Islands. In L.O. Rowan, V.L. Bartlett and T.D. Evans (eds), *Shifting Borders: Globalisation, Localisation and Open and Distance Education,* Geelong, Deakin University Press, 23–34.

Wah, R. Distance education in the South Pacific: issues and contradictions. In L.O. Rowan, V.L. Bartlett and T.D. Evans (eds), *Shifting Borders: Globalisation, Localisation and Open and Distance Education,* Geelong, Deakin University Press, 69–82.

Wegerif, R. (1995) *Collaborative Learning: Creating and On-Line Community,* CITE Report 212, Institute of Educational Technology, Open University, Milton Keynes.

6 Student-led not spoon fed: the co-curriculum and student learning and personal development

Gillian Winfield
Centre for Educational Development, Appraisal and Research (CEDAR), University of Warwick

Recent years have seen the idea of 'lifelong learning' become the main focus for current education policy developments and a popular subject for discussion in higher education literature (Knapper and Cropley, 1985; Duke, 1992). Those addressing its meaning have often focused on the role of higher education, both in terms of equipping graduates to continue learning in various settings throughout life and the ways the sector has had to develop as a provider of continuing education for adult learners. The effects of rapid expansion on teaching and learning issues has received much attention, and considerable effort has been exerted in creating a curriculum that enables lifelong learning (Entwistle, 1992). Yet, while in adult and vocational education much attention has been paid to the role of non-formal learning environments (Butler, 1993), these have not been applied to the study of higher education student learning.

Students' Unions in UK Higher Education Institutions are complex organizations with a wide range of activities and roles. Set up by students as representative organizations, they remain student-owned and student run through democratic structures. Union's generate income from their commercial activities and this profit is reinvested at the direction of the membership in order to fund welfare and representation services, as well as a range of organized student activities, from campaigning activity to clubs and societies formed by groups of students. Many unions have renewed their focus on these 'student activities' and their developmental nature for the students involved and now employ staff to provide a range of support facilities such as training, advice and guidance and accreditation. Student activities can be seen as a non-formal learning environment and has a role to play in lifelong learning. However, very little acknowledgement has been made of this co-curricular learning in the literature, which largely ignores any non-academic aspect of student life.

This chapter links theory, policy and practice through an analysis of the literature about student learning and development. It looks at work originating from the United States, that has interacted with student activities practice there, the literature on student learning, which focuses on the improvement of learning through curriculum development and literature on the graduate labour market, particularly from the viewpoint of the employers of graduates. This analysis reveals much marginalization of student activities which, if mentioned, is usually misrepresented. It is not even clear from published research in the UK that such learning exists. The most favourable portrayal of student activities available sees it as of value, yet inherently different from the curriculum. Whereas academic study leads to cognitive development, co-curricular development is seen as purely affective and behavioural. This chapter suggests that such divides are artificial and argues that these supposedly 'equal but different' developmental domains and the learning which results are more usefully seen holistically to make a contribution to the development of students as independent, lifelong learners.

6.2 Theories of student development

The theoretical defining of student development in the United States has resulted in the development of a vast literature on the area. The literature has developed alongside the professional field of student affairs: a term used to group together non-academic staff on US campuses working with students in the provision of services such as housing, counselling or campus activities with a distinct professional identity. The US literature can be characterized as a complex tapestry of interrelating theories and models of the processes that students move through in their development. These theories and models come together to make a significant statement about the purpose of higher education being to allow students access to these processes.

6.2.1 The problem of applying a diversity of theories

Over the years one writer's ideas have been progressed by another as incremental steps are taken, new models postulated and theories formed. However, the steps seem to have been taken web-like in a variety of different directions as the increasing volume of work and influences on the field led student development theories to fragment. There now exists a range of literature that is not so much incompatible as unrelated, with the once common core discredited. Early works read as though the writer is engaging in a perpetual quest for the definitive model to inform practice. Gradually, however, the view that such models did not adequately reflect the diversity of student populations has gained ground, and as variables such as gender, race and sexual orientation have been researched, the notion that one human development model can be found has been discredited. Yet rather than accepting the limitations of theory that this implies, the response to this seems to have been the creation of a different developmental theory for each variable, still failing to recognize the personal constructs of individual students.

6.2.2 Development across the whole student experience

One of the main features of the student development theory in comparison to that on student learning is the broad view it takes of the whole student experience while in higher education, whether that be the curriculum, organized student activities or the social peer interaction that occurs through campus life. However, throughout the US literature there seems to be a tendency in research design to view all out-of-class activities as one entity, rather than to focus explicitly on participation in student activities. George Kuh undertook a study looking at the impact of 'out-of-class' experience on outcomes of college attendance considered important by students, with experience categorized together as both social interaction with faculty and students and organized student activities. His starting point is other studies measuring importance of 'out-of-class' activities, e.g. Wilson estimates they lead to 70 per cent of what students learn during college, yet argues that previous research had been quantitative and has not looked at college outcomes from a student perspective. Kuh uses a qualitative methodology so the data depends on students' ability to divide their experience into class and out of class. He finds this problematic, as some interviewees were not able to identify the boundary:

most students found it difficult to bifurcate their college experience into two separate categories of learning: that is, one linked to experience outside the classroom and the other a function of the formal curriculum.

(Kuh, 1992, p. 279)

While the US literature focuses on the whole student experience rather than the curriculum, it largely persists in maintaining the firm boundary around the curriculum as the site of cognitive development, with behavioural or affective development a result of anything extra-curricular. However, 'The Student Learning Imperative' discussion paper published by the practitioner organization, the American College Personnel Association, in 1993 goes still further in justifying the extra-curricular. They are arguing for a paradigm shift, with a re-emphasizing of 'student learning and personal development as the primary goals of undergraduate education' (ACPA, 1993, p. 1) and a seamlessness between the two areas. They see student development as a term that encompasses both 'learning' and 'personal development' on the basis that many skills can't be categorized as cognitive or affective, that the student experience is holistic and that such divisions as to where learning took place are irrelevant after college.

students benefit from many and varied experiences during college and . . . learning and personal development are cumulative, mutually shaping processes that occur over an extended period of time in many different settings.

(ACPA, 1993, p. 3)

6.3   Student learning literature

While the literature on student development has originated from and largely stayed within the United States, there is an overlapping international field of 'student learning' theory more familiar to a UK audience. Here, discussion of how to improve the quality of student learning is isolated to the curriculum with an artificial and limiting focus on the cognitive.

6.3.1   Cognitive and affective development

The distinction between the cognitive and the affective is not an easy one to define. In his work *First Degree: The Undergraduate Curriculum*, (1990) Squires focuses on the 'general powers of the mind' as areas of cognitive development in response to their inclusion in the Robbins report's statement of the objectives of higher education. Squires argues that student development can only justifiably be examined in terms of the curriculum and defines it as 'first and foremost cognitive development, the development of the mind, or . . . "learning to think"' (Squires, 1992, p. 124). One of the few British writers who engages with the US 'student development' literature, he refers to its suggestion that student development is not simply cognitive but encompasses of 'ethical, personal, social and cultural development' (Squires, 1992, p. 135) portraying such broad parameters as a slippery concept.

6.3.2   Improving the quality of student learning through developing learner autonomy

A thread running through the literature on student learning is the view that it will be improved if students are empowered to become independent, lifelong learners, a state referred to here as learner autonomy. Many writers use different concepts and language in comparable typologies of student learning, such as active learners, deep and surface learning (Marton and Säljö, 1976, 1984) orientations to study (Entwistle and Ramsden, 1983). Boud (1981) uses learner autonomy as an educational goal and approach to encapsulate these typologies and innovations with the defining characteristics of 'the goals of developing independence and interdependence, self-directedness and responsibility for learning' (Boud, 1981, p. 8). He goes on to demonstrate that reorienting higher education to focus it towards that goal leads to an increasing emphasis on learning process over content, a process that takes students from dependence through counterdependence and independence to interdependence.

6.3.3 Autonomy as a goal and an approach

In the same way that typologies are seen as a difference in student intention rather than ability, Boud and others demonstrate the importance of recognizing that autonomy is a goal rather than something that can be assumed; that not all students are ready for self-directed learning and that these skills must be taught first. Boud writes that 'Student reticence and resistance to taking responsibility for learning are likely to be among the first problems a teacher will meet' (Boud, 1981, p. 11) and that a structure must be provided to assist the learner towards the goal.

In an analysis of his own innovative practice, Peter Carrotte reaches the same conclusion. In the light of his own commitment to developing autonomy, he introduced a problem-based learning element to his dentistry course. He concludes that students approached the innovation differently, largely due to their previous educational experience, and he should have preceded the innovation with some individual analysis on the basis that learners with a surface approach need guidance and support if they are going to change. He writes that 'I now realise that I 'hijacked' that [student] control and imposed my own will in promoting independent learning without any true student negotiation!' (Carrotte and Hammond, 1995, p. 71).

6.3.5 Student learning and student activities

Entwistle (1992) looks at the learning outcomes of a variety of different traditional and innovative teaching methods: lectures, Resource Based Learning, Computer Assisted Learning, discussion classes, peer teaching, supervised work experience and learning contracts. The latter two are consistent with co-curricular learning, involving identifying problems, generating solutions and working in a group. Work Based Learning requires academic knowledge to be applied in real situations:

> The type of learning which takes place in the work place also has a different character to course based learning. Students are forced to confront realistically complex professional situations where textbook answers will not suffice.
>
> (Entwistle, 1992, pp. 30–1)

The students not only see theoretical ideas being applied, but they have an exposure to all the interpersonal dimensions of everyday work and see at first hand the pressures and rewards of working life. However, the quote implies a difference in what is learnt in formal and nonformal settings. 'Knowledge', primarily gained through the formal curriculum, seems to be consistently prioritized as an outcome, yet as Boud has shown, autonomy in learning should see us focus on the process and the ability of students to continue in self-directed learning activity throughout life rather than the content of what they have been taught. Entwistle finishes by recommending a systems approach to learning as it results from 'complex interactions between the characteristics of the students, the nature of the teaching, and the whole learning environment provided by the department and institution.' (Entwistle, 1992, p. 42). But once again, he falls short of acknowledging that organized student activities are an element of the 'whole learning environment' worthy of specific attention.

6.4 Graduate labour market literature

Finally we turn to the literature focusing on the requirements of the economy from higher education, a subsection of the broader field of educational policy.

6.4.1 The employers agenda

The Employment Department funded 'Enterprise in Higher Education Initiative' (EHE) has been the major policy initiative in this area. Launched in 1987, its stated aim was to assist higher education, in close partnership with employers, to develop enterprising graduates. The term 'enterprise' was used to refer generally to the world of work, and hence the emphasis was on the development of those transferable or core skills commonly sought by employers.

With EHE underway throughout higher education, many employer organizations saw an opportunity to use their consequent increase in influence, and published reports such as the Confederation of British Industry's, *Thinking Ahead: Ensuring the Expansion of Higher Education into the 21st Century*, published in June 1994. The report explores ideal qualities in graduates, and they have clear cognitive and affective desired outcomes in mind as they seek 'creativity, analytical skills and problem-solving abilities' (CBI, 1994, p. 8). 'The intellectual skills of analysis and synthesis should be typical of the competent graduate, as should the ability and desire to continue learning' (CBI, 1994, p. 14) as well as 'core transferable skills' (CBI, 1994, p. 20).

The Quality in Higher Education report *Employer Satisfaction* (Harvey and Green, 1994) reports on research carried out at the University of Central England into the importance that various graduate attributes and qualities may have to employers, the levels of employer satisfaction with graduates and implications for policy. They have carried out a survey of the outcomes desired by employers, which are compressed into the following four broad areas of attributes; knowledge, willingness to learn, flexibility and adaptability and intellectual and innovative ability. Discovering that some attributes of graduates are worth more to the organization they work for than others, they then relate these criteria to the concept of adding value to an organization by defining an 'enhancement continuum' (Figure 6.1) which shows that while knowledge adds value to the organization, willingness to learn can transform it.

One of the most recent publications in this area is the Association of Graduate Recruiters *Skills for Graduates in the Twenty-First Century* (AGR, 1995). They are critical of previous approaches which have listed skills required in graduates for focusing too heavily on affective development as 'career management and effective learning skills are, at best, only included by implication' (AGR, 1995, p. 20). The model they promote is broader and more comprehensive than those included in previous publications and combines cognitive and behavioural change with much more intangible factors included such as 'political awareness' and 'development focus'. As well as skills they refer to qualities, knowledge, understanding and attitudes and define graduates' need to be 'self-reliant' in 'career and personal development' (AGR, 1995, p. 5). Their model of the 'complete graduate' is someone who is self-reliant, with specialist and generalist skills and knowledge as well as 'connected' through interpersonal skills (AGR, 1995, p. 21) arguing that this combination will 'put them in charge, instead of being at the mercy of their working lives' (AGR, 1995, p. 45).

6.4.2   The graduate labour market and student activities

The notes of guidance for second round institutions bidding for Enterprise in Higher Education funding contain the following remark, ostensibly recognizing the value of student activities:

> The importance and value of the Students' Union in both providing opportunities for enterprise related activities and in helping to ensure effective communication should not be overlooked.

> (Employment Department Group, 1988, p. 11)

However, the bids contained no proposals to enhance the development of skills through extra-curricular activity or in conjunction with Students' Unions. In practice, Students' Union involvement has been effected through union officers becoming members of Enterprise Units' Steering Groups. In its later years, the part of EHE that looked exclusively at the role of students in such changes did point to co-curricular activity as an area for development and Students' Unions as a place to embed many of their activities through provision of seedcorn funding, and in January 1994 a conference was held called 'Developing Potentials' where:

> the burning issue was how to ensure the continuation of student development . . . through student centred learning and extra-curricular activity after EHE funding had run out.

> (R. Watson in Assister, 1995, p. 48)

One of the outcomes of this conference was the creation of STADIA, a DfEE INOS, funded project designed to promote and support student development through student activities.

Harvey and Green also consider the influence of higher education beyond the curriculum when they raise the idea that outcomes such as the skills being identified by the research 'are implicit in, indeed the essence of, the undergraduate experience . . . based on a full time collegial experience with a stable peer group' (Harvey and Green, 1994, p. 55). Their recommendations acknowledge that 'extra-mural activity' has a developmental outcome but the language used reveals that they still see it as very much secondary. Interestingly, however, like much of the student learning literature, the same research centre has given overwhelming support to work-placements, which are related to but outside the curriculum and are likely to have broadly similar outcomes to student activities (Harvey *et al.*, 1997).

The AGR report goes some way towards acknowledging the need to view the student experience in broader terms than the curriculum in saying 'the challenge is to identify which skills should be integral to the teaching process and which should be facilitated outside the academic curriculum' (AGR, 1995, p. 26), and they advise students to make the most of student activities. However, it is clear again that the view is that there are separate things to be learnt inside and outside the curriculum.

These publications are helpful in putting Students' Unions growing interest in student development into a policy context. The opportunities for learning that exist through student activities have a role to play in generating the outcomes employers wish to see, as well as achieving the goals of higher education that the student development and student learning literatures wish to see.

6.5　The tension between theory and policy focused writing

The constant interrelation of theory, policy and practice can also be seen in tensions between stakeholders in higher education. The writers of the student learning literature seem very clear about their identity as members of the higher education community, writing from a theory-based position rather than responding to policy. As 'insiders', there seems to be resentment of the interference of other stakeholders such as government and employers in shaping higher education. Jon Nixon (Carrotte and Hammond, 1994) describes a marketplace model of higher education where 'judgements about what is to be taught, as well as about how effectively it is being taught, seem to lie with those who are to recruit university graduates, or with government authorities acting on their behalf' (p. 47) and quality is defined in terms of relationships with the various 'customers' of higher education. He juxtaposes the 'crude reductionism' (p. 48) of this model with the liberal notion of the ivory tower, where academics are purveyors of truth. He is right to be critical of a customer focused approach, for as a customer a student is still a passive recipient of the goods of higher education rather than a partner in a 'community of self-disciplined enquirers' (p. 50) and put forward a third model of the university as 'meeting place'.

Harvey and Green are also critical of a 'customers' approach: 'Education is not a service being sold to customers or supplied to clients; it is a process in which students are participants!' (1994, p. 67). They argue that academics should be more responsive to students and teach in ways that 'enhance and empower' them for lifelong learning. Their enhancement continuum demonstrates that hostility towards the policy-based literature is unhelpful and unnecessary as all sides are actually seeking the same outcome. The first of the four broad areas sought in graduates, knowledge and skills, can meet quality standards at the 'adding' end of the continuum, but only with the other three; willingness to learn, flexibility and adaptability and intellectual and innovative ability; can a graduate have a 'transforming' effect on an organization. It is precisely these latter attributes that autonomous learners will be able to demonstrate: 'deep' or 'transforming' learning approaches, self-direction as a lifelong learner and skills of critical analysis and synthesis. If students are empowered as partners in learning throughout the institution, they will be able to see their own development holistically and the outcomes all the literature's seek will be realized.

6.6　Conclusion: 'whole student: whole institution' holistic approach

The three areas of literature explored all have a different perspective on student activities. The first, student development, comes closest to recognizing its importance as a source of learning for students through its holistic view of the whole student experience and the development of the whole person: cognitively and behaviourally. The second, student learning, focuses on the curriculum and cognitive development and, despite acknowledging the importance of the whole learning environment on the development of learner autonomy, follows the student development literature in falling short of recognizing the role of organized student activities within that. The third, policy-based documentation, makes occasional acknowledgement of their developmental nature but clearly sees them as marginal to the curriculum, often misrepresents them, and subscribes to the traditional view that while some personal development occurs outside the curriculum, 'learning' only occurs within it.

Returning to the ACPA position paper's point about the seamlessness of the 'cumulative, mutually shaping processes' (ACPA, 1993, p. 3) of cognitive and affective development it can be argued that, to achieve true learner autonomy as Boud supports, the curricular and the co-curricular should not be treated as totally separate and distinct. Kuh's research conclusions about students' inability to 'bifurcate their college experience' (Kuh, 1992, p. 279) show that this divide is artificial. In stressing an emphasis on the process of developing skills in autonomous learning over content, Boud writes of empowering students and developing their confidence, which is also a direct outcome of participation in student-led student activities. Higgs also points out that the process of autonomous learning can bring about cognitive and behavioural change in that it sees not only completion of the learning task, but also 'development of learning and interpersonal abilities' and 'development of the learner as a person (e.g. in terms of increasing self-reliance and confidence in one's own abilities)'. She concludes 'As this development takes place, the learner gains abilities and confidence which will in turn enhance his or her performance in future learning activities' (Boud, 1980, p. 41).

Squires and Harvey and Green do make valid points about the need to ensure that the development that can be gained through student activities should be open to all students. While the curriculum is central to student life, not all students are involved in student activities. But the role of student activities needs to be recognized and steps taken to open these opportunities to more students. The need to redress the balance between the curricular and the co-curricular can be characterized as a 'parity of esteem' argument similar to that about education and training, based on the assumption that education is long-term attitudinal change and training leads to short-term behavioural change. Traditionally we have aligned the curricular with education and the co-curricular with training on this basis and also on the bases of the assumed cognitive/affective divide and that they are learnt in different environments, formal and informal. Yet co-curricular activity contributes to the educational process in that it empowers students as partners in learning. Furthermore, student activities run through student-led organizations give students input into their overall learning environment and the campus community, facilitating a 'whole institution approach' to learner autonomy. Boud supports such shifts in power in that autonomy in learning can only be fostered by adopting an approach which involves students in decision-making about their learning

> if students are denied opportunities to participate in decision-making about their learning, they are less likely to develop the skills they need in order to plan and organise for lifelong learning which depend on their decisions about their learning needs and activities.

(p. 22).

Kolb takes a controversial approach that is useful here by defining learning as 'the process whereby development occurs' (Kolb, 1984, p. 132) rather than seeing learning and development as two different concepts. His work on experiential learning integrates cognitive and behavioural models and defines it as 'the process that links education, work and personal development' (Kolb, 1984, p. 7). He writes 'It is more difficult to conceptualise the effect of the larger institutional context on student learning, although the effect is considerable' (Kolb, 1984, p. 205). His suggestion that integrative structures and programmes could provide a counter-balance to limiting academic specialization could be used to argue for the benefits of looking at the whole student's development (cognitive and affective) across their whole student experience (curricular and co-curricular): a 'whole student: whole institution' approach.

The outcomes sought by employers also support this view. The four attributes identified by Harvey and Green of knowledge, willingness to learn, flexibility and adaptability and intellectual and innovative ability cannot be neatly defined as either cognitive or affective. It is also not possible to pin point the exact source of any of them in terms of where it was learnt. The survey showed that the simple most important factor for employers was a graduate's willingness to learn which is a prerequisite for someone taking up a new student leadership post. Employers also reported a dissatisfaction with graduates' problem-solving ability and some graduates of having a lack of practical awareness and being unable to apply knowledge in a practical work situation. It is exactly this sort of experience that student activities has to offer. The skills of analysis, critical ability and synthesis encompassed by 'innovative and intellectual ability' are also used. Regarding innovation specifically, many employers cited dissatisfaction not with the ideas generated by graduates, but with their inability to implement change within an organization. Student leaders are already working in an organizational context and are getting additional experience of coping with pressure, stress and deadlines. Student activities are organized with students working in teams towards shared goals as opposed to competing as individuals in the classroom. Significant gaps exist both within the literature and the ways it has been used in practice. Empowerment of students as learners, and co-curricular activity as a means towards this, is not discussed fully or treated adequately by research and has not been fostered by practice. While student activities' strength is in its experiential nature, giving students the chance to learn and practise new skills and transfer them into a variety of settings, practitioners are only just beginning to make systematic attempts to enhance that learning. Maintaining artificial assumptions about what is learnt where, and not encouraging students to view their development as a whole, is inconsistent with the philosophical perspective I have taken that promotes lifelong learning, integrative development and empowering students as autonomous learners.

This chapter advocates shifting of the locus of power in higher education, so that students are enabled to act as autonomous learners with responsibility for their whole development. Policy-makers (national and institutional) should take note of the value of student activities and the 'whole institution' approach which treats students as partners in the learning environment. Those working with students should take note of the need to view the whole student's development. Finally, student development practitioners should enhance the potential political impact of their work (in that it embraces the 'whole student, whole institution' approach) by carrying out research and developing theories in conjunction with and for students. If students are supported and empowered as autonomous learners solely in their academic studies, but their development through co-curricular routes is not acknowledged a mixed message is being sent at institutional level that will undermine the most enlightened academic's attempt to treat them as partners in learning.

6.7   References and bibliography

Assister, A. (ed.) (1995) *Transferable Skills in Higher Education*, London: Kogan Page.

Association of Graduate Recruiters (1995) *Skills for Graduates in the Twenty-First Century*, Cambridge, AGR.

Boud, D. (ed.) (1981) *Developing Student Autonomy in Learning*, 2nd edn, London: Kogan Page.

Brown, R.D. and Barr, M.J. (1990) Student development: yesterday, today and tomorrow. In *New Directions for Student Services: Evolving Theoretical Perspectives on Students*, Jossey-Bass, Fall 1990.

Butler (1992) Unpaid work: taking the credit, *Adults Learning*, 4(4), Dec.

Carrotte and Hammond (eds) (1995) *Learning in Difficult Times: Teaching in Higher Education*, Sheffield: UCoSDA.

Confederation of British Industry (1994) *Thinking Ahead: Ensuring the Expansion of Higher Education into the 21st Century*, London: CBI.

Duke, C. (1992) *The Learning University*, Buckingham: SRHE/Open University Press.

Employment Department Group (1988) *Enterprise in Higher Education: Supplementary Notes of Guidance.*

Entwistle, N. (1992) *The Impact of Teaching on Learning Outcomes in Higher Education: A Literature Review* Sheffield: CVCP/USDU.

Entwistle, N. (1983) *Understanding Student Learning*, London: Croom Helm

Harvey, L. and Green, D. (1994) *Employer Satisfaction*, Quality in Higher Education Project, University of Central England in Birmingham.

Harvey, L., Moon, S. and Geall, V. (1997) *Graduates' Work: Organisational Change and Students' Attributes*, Birmingham, University of Central England/Association of Graduate Recruiters.

Kolb, D.A. (1984) *Experiential Learning: Experience as the Source of Learning and Development*, New Jersey, Prentice-Hall.

Knapper and Cropley (1985) *Lifelong Learning and Higher Education*, London: Croom Helm.

Kuh, G.D. (1992) In their own words: what students learn outside the classroom, *American Educational Research Journal*, 30(2), 277–304.

Marton, F., and Säljö, R. (1984) 'Approaches to learning' in Marton, F. Hounsell, D and Entwistle N. (eds) *The experience of learning*, Edinburgh: Scottish Academic Press

Moore, L.V. and Upcraft, M.L. (1990) Theory in student affairs. In *New Directions for Student Services: Evolving Theoretical Perspectives on Students*, Jossey-Bass, Fall 1990, 3–23.

Pascarella and Terenzini (1991) *How College Affects Students: Findings and Insights from Twenty Years of Research*, San Francisco, Jossey-Bass.

Squires, G. (1990) *First Degree: The Undergraduate Curriculum*, Buckingham, SRHE/Open University Press.

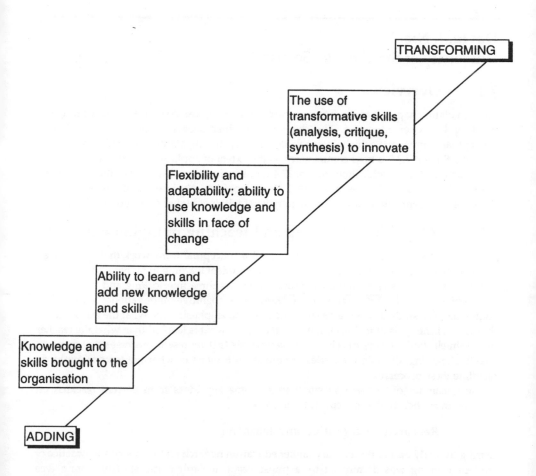

Fig 6.1:   'The Enhancement continuum', Harvey, L, & Green, D, 1994

7 Using research on learning to improve teaching practices in higher education

David. J. Nicol
University of Strathclyde, Scotland

7.1 Overview

The aim of this chapter is to show how research on learning can be used to improve teaching practices in higher education. The chapter is in three sections. Section 7.2 provides a conceptual framework which inter-relates the key findings from research on student learning. Section 7.3 is a brief commentary on the extent of application of the different areas of research in higher education. Section 7.4 gives some examples of how the framework described in section 7.2 has been used to increase the application of research at the classroom, academic department and faculty level within a higher education institution.

7.2 Research on learning and teaching in higher education

In a recent briefing paper Nicol (1977) provided a conceptual framework that synthesized the main findings from contemporary research on student learning in higher education. The framework, which is reproduced as Figure 7.1, shows three interlocking and overlapping perspectives or influences on student learning – cognitive, motivational and social-contextual. The student is at the centre of the figure to emphasize that what the learner does, thinks and believes is more important in determining what is learned than what the teacher does (Shuell, 1992). Inside the circles are key words that represent processes that result in effective learning. Outside the circles are broad indications of what the teacher might do facilitate these processes.

The remainder of this section summarizes some key ideas from current research on learning in relation to the conceptual framework.

7.2.1 Research on cognition and learning

During the early part of this century higher education research on the theory and practice of student learning was dominated by a transmission metaphor: the student's brain was assumed to be like an empty container into which the teacher poured, mainly through lectures, the facts and concepts of the discipline. Students memorized these facts and reproduced them in examinations. In this view the lecturer, as knowledge expert, is the key actor in higher education and students are passive recipients of transmitted input.

Contemporary research on learning has highlighted the weakness in this transmission conception (Ramsden, 1992). For students to be able to use knowledge to reason and to solve problems in new contexts they must learn, not by absorbing facts, but by interacting with and transforming received information so as to own it and make it personally meaningful.

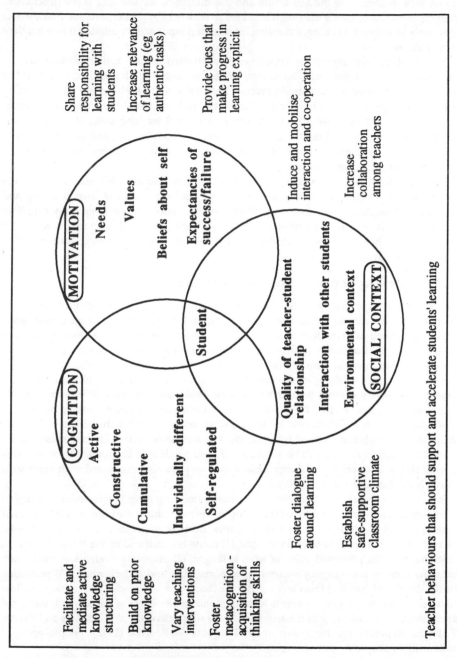

Figure 7.1: Research on learning: cognitive, motivation and social-contextural influences on learning (inside the circles) and their respective implications for teaching practices (outside the circles).

In this view students are the key actors and the metaphor for learning is constructivism. Students *construct* or create their own knowledge networks and interpretative frameworks by actively modifying, revising, extending information input and by relating it to what they already know.

The constructivist metaphor conceives the student as an active partner in the teaching–learning relationship. The lecturer or teacher might still transmit information but this is only a first step in the learning process. For students to develop deep understanding and useable knowledge, the teacher must think beyond this initial transmission and focus on ways of *facilitating active dialogue* by students around learning tasks (e.g. discussion, debate, questioning, explaining) and with learning materials both in and out of class. The teacher must provide students with opportunities to construct knowledge through personal exploration and discovery learning

Associated with the constructivist conception is recent research on metacognition – the importance of encouraging students to reflect on and explore their own thinking and knowledge construction so that they learn how to self-regulate their own cognitive processes. Raising students' awareness of *how* they learn (process) as opposed to *what* they learn (content) has been shown to develop critical thinking and lifelong learning skills (Biggs, 1985).

7.2.2   Research on motivation and learning

The constructivist theme, and the active role of students in mediating learning is also evident when we turn to the research on learning and motivation. In the past, motivation was either viewed as characteristic or trait inherent in students (with some having high and others low motivation) or as determined by factors in the environment (like getting good marks in assessments). In contrast, the current view of motivation is that it is neither a fixed trait nor determined solely by environmental events. Instead, motivation, like knowledge, is constructed by the student 'in a dynamic way based on a process of self-appraisal of situations' (Paris and Turner, 1994). Motivation is influenced by what students perceive as important – which is determined by *needs and values* – and what they believe they can accomplish – which is influenced by *expectations* of success or failure. From the research we know that students are likely to be motivated 'if their needs are being met, if they see value in what they are learning, and if they believe that they are able to succeed with reasonable effort' (McMillan and Forsyth, 1991).

This research shows that students' can be motivated to greater involvement and higher achievement by instructional behaviours and course structures that are sensitive to their needs. Practical suggestions to increase students' intrinsic motivation drawn from theory, research and experiences of teachers include: (1) using relevant and authentic learning tasks which increase the perceived value of what is taught; (2) involving students in curriculum decisions thereby encouraging ownership, responsibility and self-direction; (3) providing clearly structured learning tasks and regular feedback (not just grades and marks) to allow students to monitor progress towards learning goals (experiences of success); (4) using the interpersonal dynamics of group learning to create supportive learning climates and a sense of shared responsibility for group goals. To quote McKeachie (1992) 'people are . . . motivating to people'.

7.2.3   Research on the social context of learning

Research on the social context of learning takes a broader view than the cognitive or motivational research although it shares many principles with them, especially the importance attached to the active participation of students in their own education. This research stresses that learning takes place essentially through interaction with others and with the wider social culture in departments and higher education institutions. What and how students learn depends on how they interpret the social context of learning and in particular how they perceive and act out their relationships with teachers and other students.

Chickering and Gamson (1989) after examining 50 years of higher education research in the US extracted seven principles of good teaching, four of which were concerned with these relationships. They found that the effective teacher encourages contacts between students and faculty, develops reciprocity and co-operation among students, communicates high expectations and respects diverse talents and ways of learning. The teacher–student relationship is invariably found to be a significant variable in students' ratings of teacher effectiveness (see Marsh, 1987).

Research on the social context of learning has clearly demonstrated the benefits of collaborative and co-operative learning arrangements for the development of students' critical thinking (e.g. Qin, Johnson and Johnson, 1995), for the development of self-concepts, social skills, personal responsibility, values and attitudes (Johnson and Johnson, 1990). Group learning gives students practice in thinking and explaining; it exposes students to multiple viewpoints which helps them to make connections among concepts and ideas; it provides opportunities for 'scaffolding' (students supporting each other's learning); it often results in students teaching each other; it results in shared goals which can lead to increases in students' sense of responsibility and self-efficacy; it provides a supportive atmosphere for learning.

Learning is now understood to be 'situated' in academic and disciplinary contexts that influence not only how students construct their subject knowledge but also how they construct interpretations of how they are supposed to learn, what is worth learning and what it means to be a student (e.g. Marton, Hounsell and Entwistle, 1984; Stefani and Nicol, 1997).

This research on the social context of learning is a challenge to higher education institutions that wish to improve students' learning – especially given the current pressures to reduce teacher–student contact time. It raises questions about the higher-education tradition of individualistic and competitive learning. It suggests a need to re-conceptualize the basic learning unit in our institutions – away from individuals and towards learning cells comprising groups of students. The research on teacher–student relationships points to the need to redefine the conventional contracts (formal and informal) upon which teaching and learning are based – contracts that centre on a paternalistic teaching approach rather than on a shared exploration of learning. Overall this focus on the interpersonal relations in learning highlights the demand for new social arrangements in higher-education based on models which emphasize learning 'alliances', learning 'communities' and dialogue.

7.2.4   Interactions across the research domains

The conceptual framework introduced at the beginning of this section highlights the importance of not taking a single perspective on the research but of looking at interactions across the three research domains. How students feel about their studies (motivation) and how they interact while learning (social) has effects on how they process information (cognitive) and on their level of understanding (e.g. Boekaerts, 1993). Conceptualizing learning from a 'cold' cognitive perspective is too narrow. A broader, and more holistic, conception is necessary if the intention is to develop students' confidence and interest in learning and if we wish to encourage students to learn through their lifespan.

7.3 The application of learning research in higher education

Of the three areas of research on learning described above it is ideas mainly from the cognitive domain that have influenced teaching and learning in higher education. The idea that the teacher's role is to facilitate 'active' learning is prevalent in almost all current discussions in HE. Terms like active, participative and deep learning are now common in university mission statements. There are staff development workshops on active learning methods and teaching practices have altered as a result of this changed conception. For example, more teachers are using interactive lectures where there are breaks for student activity centred on problem-solving tasks or student-generated questions.

The situation with regard to the application of research from the social and motivational areas is less clear-cut. On the one hand, there are indications that group learning methods are on the increase as are teaching strategies (e.g. self/peer assessment) geared towards the sharing of responsibility for learning with students (Hounsell, McCulloch and Scott, 1996). More attention is also now being paid to how students perceive (and evaluate) teaching and their courses. On the other hand, learning in HE is still driven by examination grades rather than by activating students' interest and motivation. Classroom climates are still organized primarily around individual and competitive learning rather than around shared goals and learning partnerships. Management policies are not, on the whole, conducive to democratic participation by students in decision-making.

7.4 The conceptual framework as a tool to apply the learning research

This section provides three examples of how the conceptual framework (Figure 7.1) has been used as a tool to increase the application of the research on learning in a large higher education institution. The first example is a description of a chemical engineering design class that was planned using the framework. The second is an example of the use of the framework by the author while acting as a consultant on educational matters with staff from an academic department. The third example describes how graduate teaching assistants were trained to run tutorials using the learning research framework.

7.4.1 Example 1: Using the framework to develop student responsibility for learning in a chemical engineering design class

The conceptual framework described in this chapter was recently used by an individual lecturer to devise a new course to teach chemical engineering design to 60 students taking a third-year undergraduate class. The project arose because the lecturer, who had been asked to teach this new class, was concerned that learning to design in chemical engineering often 'involved marching students through design problems and solution paths that had been

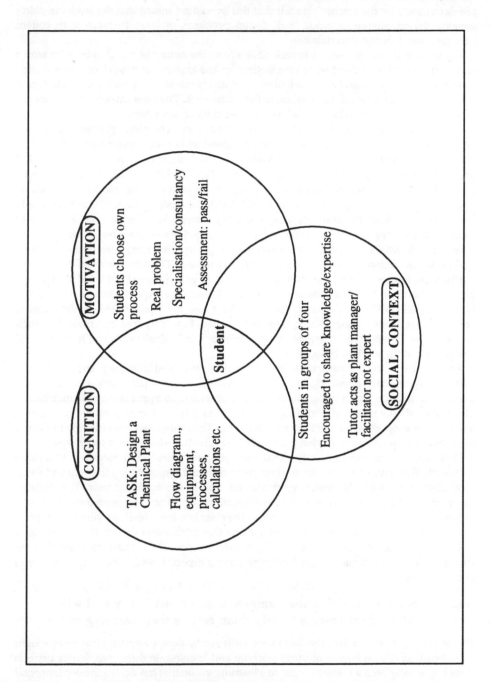

Figure 7.2   Developing Students' Responsibility for Learning in a Chemical Engineering
Design Class

pre-determined by the teacher'. He felt that this procedure meant that the students didn't develop the confidence to tackle 'real' design problems or learn to make independent decisions about design uncertainties.

The lecturer therefore decided to seek advice from the author of this chapter who works as an educational consultant within the institution and together they devised a new design class using the conceptual framework from the learning research. Figure 7.2 shows the main components of the new class in relation to the framework. The class involves 1–2 hours per week contact time every Thursday afternoon over the two semesters.

The students in groups of four chose their own chemical process to design (MOTIVATION). Subject to agreement being obtained within their own group each student was allowed to specialize in specific areas related to the design (e.g. chemistry, mathematics) and to offer their expertise to other groups (MOTIVATION/SOCIAL). The small groups planned their own work (MOTIVATION) using critical path analysis and they decided on and allocated tasks to individual members (SOCIAL). The design task itself was exceedingly complex: it involved the students in synthesizing subject knowledge from a variety of sources, discovering new information and using knowledge to solve a real design problem (COGNITIVE/MOTIVATION): they selected equipment (reactors), determined process flows and calculations all with minimal help from the tutor. The tutor assumed the role of a facilitator and resource provider (SOCIAL): since each group carried out a different design problem the tutor could not assume the role of knowledge expert. The assessment was PASS/FAIL (MOTIVATION). Students had to make a case for a pass based on three sets of criteria: what chemical engineering they had learned, how they had contributed to their group output (a report including design specifications and calculations) and how they had contributed to the work of other groups.

As indicated in the last paragraph, the design class embodied learning principles derived from the conceptual framework. The pass–fail system, choice, specialization, the authentic design task and the group responsibility were all intended to increase intrinsic motivation. The group collaboration and tutor facilitation were intended to increase individual learning and foster a supportive social climate for learning. The design task was intended to foster the active construction of knowledge by both the individual student and by groups.

This class was comprehensively evaluated using semi-structured recorded interviews with individual students and with the lecturer at different stages during the year and using focal discussions with the design groups at the end of the academic year. The students reported that this design class was the most significant learning experience they had had at university. Typical group comments were that the class involved 'teaching yourself' through 'synthesizing and applying prior knowledge' and that it 'prepared you for the real world of design . . . where no-one is going to tell you what to do'. The lecturer reported that the students' design submissions were far superior to his expectations for students at that stage in their study.

7.4.2 Example 2: Using the framework as a consultancy tool with whole departments to help them realize their learning vision

The learning framework has also been used with academic departments that have sought educational advice on how to improve teaching and learning. In these consultancy projects there has usually been a thematic focus or a learning vision that has driven the departmental improvement programme. Typical themes in recent times include increasing student independence or responsibility in learning, encouraging more reflective practice by students around learning and enhancing group work in learning. In each case the consultancy involves working with all the teaching staff in the department. Usually the research on learning and the conceptual framework are presented first within a context that emphasizes the departmental theme or learning vision.

After the learning framework and its relationship to the thematic concern are presented, follow-up meetings are organized at which teaching staff identify strategies in each of the three learning research areas that would support the improvement programme. The initial focus is often the first year of the course because this is seen as a foundation for the developments in later years. For instance, if the consultancy is about developing reflective practice, staff are encouraged to think through how they might lay a foundation for reflective practice in the first year. In this situation, the teachers would identify strategies they currently use to foster reflection and discuss them and relate them to the framework of learning research. Then they would identify new strategies that would strengthen the building blocks of their learning vision. In this way each strategy is analysed in terms of the learning research and the year-by-year curriculum is developed through a process that ensures staff ownership and consensus.

A key principle in this kind of departmental consultancy is the establishment among staff of a common understanding of what effective learning is and of how learning can be facilitated. (The latter also implies the establishment of a common language to talk about learning.) It is difficult to get all staff in a department to agree on what changes are necessary to improve learning if learning is never defined. The conceptual framework is useful in this respect because it is based on research and is therefore credible and it is systematic and reasonably comprehensive (it provides the big picture).

7.4.3 Example 3: Using the framework to train graduate teaching assistants

For the last eight years at the University of Strathclyde the Centre for Academic Practice has provided a course for graduate teaching assistants (GTAs) in the Faculty of Arts and Social Sciences. The primary task undertaken by these teaching assistants or tutors is to manage tutorial discussions in their subject discipline with groups of around 12 students.

The course for GTAs comprises five training workshops of two and a half hours. The first three of these are used to prepare the GTAs for their tutorial duties. Two of these sessions are provided before the beginning of the academic year and before GTAs begin tutoring. The third session occurs about five weeks later and is a review session designed to help the tutors reflect on their experiences of tutoring practice and to make improvements. Each workshop has both a practical teaching focus as well as the research-based theoretical focus. The conceptual framework described in this chapter is used in all three sessions.

GTAs are introduced to the research on learning and the conceptual framework in the first session. The course leader delivers a mini-lecture on the learning research using the framework and then asks the GTAs to form groups to discuss the implications of this research for tutorial teaching.

Tutors then plan how they would establish rapport and a safe psychological climate with a group of students attending a first tutorial and how they would clarify the tutor's role and what was expected of the students. The primary focus in this session is on the influence of motivation and social relations on group learning in tutorials.

In the second session the course leader models the design of a tutorial using the conceptual framework. Tutors are then asked to form disciplinary groups to create a written

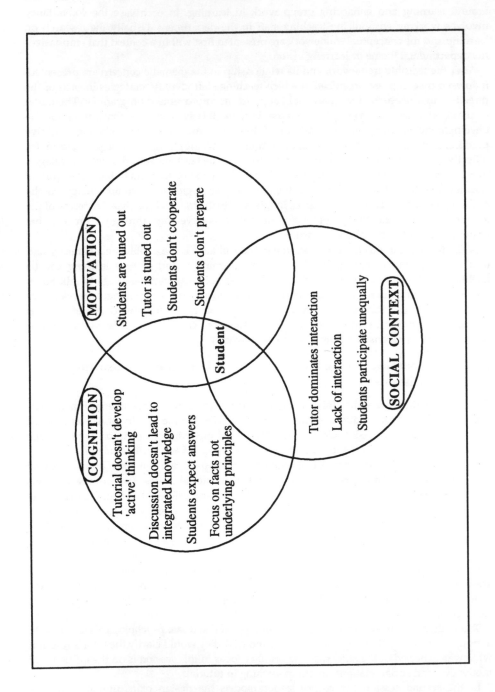

Figure 7.3:   Tutorial Problems and their Relation to the Learning Research

plan for a one hour tutorial using an actual tutorial topic. They specify the aims of the tutorial, the student preparation, the learning tasks, the subgroupings, what the tutor will do, the timings and how the session will open and close. The tutorial plans are presented in a plenary and justified in terms of the conceptual framework.

Tutors who take this course are encouraged to use task-based tutorials in their departments rather than spend all of the tutorial time leading an open discussion. This is intended to take the pressure off new tutors and to ensure that they don't do all the talking in tutorials. The conceptual framework is highly relevant to this kind of tutorial because the success of these tutorials depends on the tutor being able both to design learning tasks (that ensure active cognitive processing) and being able to design and manage groupwork (so as to harness intrinsic motivation and gain the benefits of collaborative learning).

In the third workshop session the tutors first work in groups to identify problems or challenges that they have experienced in tutorials. The conceptual framework drawn from the research and its relationship to small group tutoring is then reviewed by the course leader. Tutors are then invited to select an issue to work on drawn from the problems or challenges they have identified earlier. They form subgroups and use the learning framework to help devise their own strategies for tackling the issue. Each subgroup presents their strategies in a plenary and these are discussed by the workshop participants. This procedure keeps tutors focused on the relation between the research on learning and their own tutoring practices.

Figure 7.3 is an example of some of the issues identified by the tutors in relation to the different perspectives in the learning research. Although each issue has a specific locus in the figure the tutors are well aware that tutorial problems and strategies interact across the three perspectives. For example, when the learning climate (SOCIAL) is perceived as threatening to students (e.g. because tutor is perceived as dominating or because the students don't know one another) then students don't participate in discussion (MOTIVATION) and this invariably leads to less active involvement in disciplinary thinking (COGNITIVE).

7.5   Conclusion

Applying the research on learning to improve higher education teaching is not an easy task. The research is vast, exceedingly complex and no single research perspective is appropriate to all teaching and learning situations. Every educational issue could be analysed and interpreted using any one of a number of different lenses or perspectives. What is needed is a conceptual framework that incorporates more than one perspective on learning and teaching and that provides an up-to-date summary of contemporary research. The framework provided in this chapter tries to present the 'big picture' of the learning research using three key perspectives and their interactions. The chapter also describes how this framework has been used to help academic staff in higher education apply the research on learning to their own teaching practices.

7.6   References

References cited are just a sample of the extensive research in this area.

Biggs, J. (1995) The role of metalearning in study processes, *British Journal of Educational Psychology*, **55**, 185–212.

Boekaerts, M. (1993) Being concerned with well-being and with learning, *Educational Psychologist*, **28**(2), 149–67.

Chickering, A. W. and Gamson, Z.F. (1989) *Seven Principles for Good Practice in Undergraduate Education*, Racine, Wisc: Johnson Foundation.

Hounsell, D., McCulloch, M. and Scott (1996) *The ASSHE Inventory: Changing Assessment Practices in Higher Education*, University of Edinburgh, Napier University & UCoSDA.

Johnson, D.W. and Johnson, R.T. (1990) *Learning Together and Alone: Cooperation, Competition and Individualisation*, Prentice Hall.

McKeachie, W.J., Pintrich, P.R., Lin, Y.G. and Smith (1990) *Teaching and Learning in the College Classroom: A Review of the Research Literature*, National Center for Research to Improve Postsecondary Education.

McKeachie, W.J. (1992) Recent research on university teaching and learning: implications for practice and future research, *Academic Medicine*, **67**(10) 584–7.

McMillan, J.H. and Forsyth, D.R. (1991) What theories of motivation say about why learners learn. In R.J. Menges and M.D. Svinicki (eds), *College Teaching: From Theory to Practice*, Jossey-Bass

Marsh, H.W. (1987) Students' evaluations of university teaching: research findings, methodological issues and directions for future research, *International Journal of Educational Research*, **11**, 253–388.

Marton, F., Hounsel, D. and Entwistle, N. (1984) *The Experience of Learning*, Scottish Academic Press.

Nicol, D.J. (1997) *Research on Learning and Higher Education Teaching*, UCoSDA Briefing Paper 45, Universities' and Colleges' Staff Development Association (UCoSDA), Sheffield, UK.

Nicol, D.J., Kane, K. and Wainright C. (1994) Improving laboratory learning through group work and structured reflection and discussion, *Education and Training Technology International*, **31**(4), 152–68.

Paris, S.G. and Turner, J.C. (1994). Situated motivation. In P.R. Pintrich, D.R. Brown and C.E. Weinstein (eds), *Student Motivation, Cognition and Learning*.

Qin, Z., Johnson, D.W. and Johnson, R.T. (1995) Cooperative versus competitive efforts and problem solving, *Review of Educational Research*, **65**(2), 129–43.

Ramsden, P. (1992) *Learning to Teach in Higher Education*, Routledge.

Shuell, T.J. (1992) Designing instructional computing systems for meaningful learning. In M. Jones and P.H. Winne (eds), *Adaptive Learning Environments: Foundations and Frontiers*, Berlin: Springer-Verlag

Stefani, L. and Nicol, D.J. (1997) From teacher to facilitator of collaborative enquiry. In S. Armstrong, G. Thompson and S. Brown (eds), *Facing up to Radical Changes in Universities and Colleges*, Kogan Page, London.

8 Improving student learning through a focus on the teaching context

Keith Trigwell,[i] **Michael Prosser,**[ii] **Paul Ramsden**[iii] **and Elaine Martin**[iv]
(i) University of Technology, Sydney, (ii) La Trobe University, (iii) Griffith University, (iv) Royal Melbourne Institute of Technology

8.1   Introduction

In this chapter we describe the results of a study of the relations between students' approach to learning and their teachers' approaches to teaching in first-year university subjects. We also report the relations between the way teachers approach their teaching and their perceptions of their teaching context. We use the results to comment on the implications for improving student learning of a focus on the teaching context.

Extensive research studies have been conducted into the relations between students' perceptions of their learning environment and their approaches to learning (and learning outcome) (Entwistle and Ramsden, 1983; Ramsden, 1991, 1992). The results suggest that students' awareness of their learning environment is related to the approach to learning they adopt. That is, approaches to learning are relational. They show that students who perceive the nature of the assessment as encouraging memorization and recall, and who perceive the workload demands of a subject as high, are more likely to adopt a surface approach. A deep approach is found to be related to perceptions of high-quality teaching, some independence in choosing what is to be learned, and a clear awareness of the goals and standards required in the subject (Trigwell and Prosser, 1991).

These relations suggested a way of improving the quality of student learning. If it were possible to change the context, such that students perceived it to be affording a deep approach, they might adopt a deep approach. That context would need to be perceived to be offering some choice in what was to be learned, as involving good teaching, and as having clear goals and clear descriptions of the standard of work expected. And if it were possible to establish a context perceived by students to have an appropriate workload and assessment that encouraged understanding, then it is less likely that students would adopt a surface approach.

In this chapter we focus on the teaching factor in student learning and the context in which good teaching is afforded. We report the results of part of a study into relations between perceptions of academic leadership, approaches to teaching and student learning. We describe relations between teachers' perceptions of their teaching context and their approaches to teaching, and relations between their approaches to teaching and students' approaches to learning in 55 classes in 11 universities. This study of these two elements of the teaching–learning system links teachers' perceptions of their teaching context with their students' approaches to learning, which has not previously been reported.

Two of us recently described the results of an empirical study which shows that qualitatively different approaches to teaching are associated with qualitatively different approaches to learning (Trigwell, Prosser and Lyons, 1997). The study made use of a teaching approach inventory derived from interviews with academic staff, and a modified approach to learning questionnaire. In classes where teachers describe their approach to teaching as having a focus on what they do and on transmitting knowledge, students reported being more likely to adopt a surface approach to the learning of that subject. Conversely, students who report adopting significantly deeper approaches to learning than their colleagues are found to be taught by staff who report adopting approaches to teaching that are significantly more oriented towards students and to changing their conceptions. We concluded:

> Given the numerous studies that show correlations between students' deeper
> approaches to learning and higher quality learning outcomes, these results demonstrate
> the importance in attempts to improve the quality of student learning of encouraging
> higher quality . . . [s]tudent-focused approaches to teaching.

In an earlier exploratory study (Prosser and Trigwell, 1997) we reported that there are systematic relations between teachers' perceptions of their context and their approaches to teaching. Those relations suggest that the adoption of a conceptual change and student-focused approach to teaching is related to perceptions that the teacher has control over what is taught and how it is taught, as well as perceptions that the department values teaching and that class size is not too large.

In this study we sought confirmation of the relations found in both the earlier studies, and whether both sets of relations would be observable within the same sample.

8.2   Method

Our sample was 55 first-year courses in 55 departments in four fields of study (Arts and Social Sciences, Science and Engineering, Commerce and Law, and Health Sciences) in 11 Australian universities. The unit of analysis is the first-year course. On average eight teachers in each course completed the Approaches to Teaching Inventory (Trigwell and Prosser, 1996) and a Perceptions of the Teaching Environment (PTE) questionnaire (Prosser and Trigwell, 1997). The mean of the scores for the teachers in each course was used as the score for that course. On average, 150 students in each course completed a version of the Study Process Questionnaire (Biggs, 1987) which had been modified to suit the specific context of the study. The mean of the scores on the approaches to learning scales for the students in each course was used as the score for that course. Both teachers and students were asked to complete the questionnaires in relation to the particular lecture topic being taught to the students.

8.2.1   The Approaches to Teaching Inventory

The Approaches to Teaching Inventory contains two scales. Example items from each scale are given below:

Information Transmission/Teacher Focused scale items

32. I feel it is important to present a lot of facts in classes so that students know what they have to learn for this subject.

27. I design my teaching in this subject with the assumption that most of the students have very little useful knowledge of the topics to be covered.

Conceptual Change/Student Focused scale items

45. I feel a lot of teaching time in this subject should be used to question students' ideas.

36. We take time out in classes so that the students can discuss, among themselves, the difficulties that they encounter studying this subject.

8.2.2   The Perceptions of the Teaching Environment questionnaire

The Perceptions of the Teaching Environment questionnaire completed by the teachers contains five scales. Example items from each scale are given below:

Appropriate teacher workload

10. Academic staff here just don't have enough time to help students properly.

26. It is difficult to really assist students in this subject in the time we have available for teaching.

Class size

35. In large classes I give students less encouragement to see me.

40. In large classes I try to avoid questions from students.

Control of teaching

39. I feel a lack of control over what I teach in this subject.

29. I have very little say in the way this subject is run.

Student characteristics

30. Having a range of student talent in a lecture makes it difficult for me to appropriately direct my teaching.

48. Students have such variable skills that I find it hard to predict what they know and what they don't know.

Commitment to student learning

6   You get the feeling in this department that the staff really care for students.

14 The staff here make a real effort to understand the difficulties students may be having with their work.

8.2.3   The Study Process Questionnaire (SPQ)

The Study Process Questionnaire (SPQ) completed by the students contains two scales: a Deep Approach to Learning scale, and a Surface Approach to Learning scale. These scales, with items modified to reflect the relational focus of this research, were used in this study. So, for example, in item 28, 'in this subject' has been added to focus students' awareness on the topic of the study.

Surface Approach scale items

32. Although I generally remember facts and details, I find it difficult to fit them together into an overall picture.

35. The best way for me to understand what technical terms mean is to remember the textbook definitions.

8   *Deep Approach* scale items

28. I try to relate ideas in this subject to those in other subjects, wherever possible.

34. In trying to understand new ideas, I often try to relate them to real life situations to which they might apply.

Correlation and factor (principal components, followed by varimax rotation) analyses were conducted on the data for the 55 cases. Both forms of analysis look at the relations between variables and groups of variables. The factor analysis aims at combining variables into groups of variables. The groups account for the individual differences that exists between the variables. Each separate group of variables is replaced by a factor.

8.3   Results

The results of the correlation analyses between teachers' approach to teaching and students' approach to learning is shown in Table 8.1.

Variable	Variable			
	Deep	Surf	CCSF	ITTF
Deep	-	-.22	.38**	-.15
Surf		-	-.48***	.38**
CCSF			-	-.30
ITTF				-

*p<.05, **p<.01, ***p<.001, n=55
Deep: Deep Approach
Surf: Surface Approach
CCSF: Conceptual Change/Student-focused
ITTF: Information Transmission/Teacher-focused

Table 8.1   Correlation between teachers' approach to teaching and students' approach to learning

The table shows that the Deep approach to learning variable correlates positively and significantly with a Conceptual Change/Student-focused approach to teaching. A similar correlation is shown between a Surface Approach to learning and an Information Transmission/Teacher-focused approach to teaching.

The factor analysis of the same variables confirms these relations (Table 8.2). The two factors indicate the positive relationship that exists between the Conceptual Change/Student-focused approach variable and the Deep approach variable (Factor 1) and between the Information Transmission/Teacher-focused variable and the Surface approach variable (Factor 2).

Variable	Factors	
	1	2
Students' approaches		
Surface approach	-35	73
Deep approach	87	
Teachers' approaches		
Information Transmission/Teacher focused		85
Conceptual Change/Student focused	73	-39
n=55		

Table 8.2   Factor analysis of student approach to learning and teacher approach to teaching variables

Table 8.3 shows the factor analysis of the perceptions of the teaching context variables and the teachers' approach to teaching variables.

Variable	Factors	
	1 (CCSF/Deep)	2 (ITTF/Surf)
Perceptions of the teaching context		
Control of teaching	46	-66
Class size	83	
Student characteristics	80	
Commitment to student learning		-72
Appropriate teacher workload	70	
Approaches to teaching		
Information transmission/teacher focused		80
Conceptual change/student focused	43	-37

n=55
Deep: Deep Approach, Surf: Surface Approach, CCSF: Conceptual Change/Student-focused approach, ITTF: Information Transmission/Teacher-focused approach

Table 8.3   Factor analysis of teachers' approaches to teaching and perceptions of the teaching context

Table 8.3 shows the two-factor solution for the two sets of teacher variables. It shows that the Conceptual Change/Student-focused approach to teaching variable loads with an appropriate teaching load, enabling student characteristics, an acceptable class size and some control over what is taught and how it is taught. The Information

Transmission/Teacher-focused approach to teaching variable loads with perceptions that the department is not committed to supporting student learning and that there is insufficient control over what is taught and how it is taught.

8.4 Discussion

Studies in the 1970s on approaches to student learning (Marton and Säljö, 1976; Biggs, 1978; Entwistle and Ramsden, 1983) reported the differences between Deep approaches and Surface approaches to learning. Studies then and since have consistently shown that deeper approaches to learning are related to higher quality learning outcomes (Marton and Säljö, 1997; van Rossum and Schenk, 1984; Trigwell and Prosser, 1991; Ramsden, 1992; Prosser and Millar, 1989). The results reported above show that perceptions that the teacher has some control over what is taught, that there are enabling student characteristics, that the class size is not too large, and the teaching load is not too heavy are related to an approach to teaching (Conceptual Change/Student-focused) which is related to a deep approach to learning. As was the case with the results which showed relations between students' perceptions of their learning environment and their learning outcome, these results give those aiming to improve student learning, some guidance as to where to direct their attention. The relations found suggest that the teaching context as perceived by teachers may also be an important element on which to focus.

We have previously described Conceptual Change/Student-focused approaches to teaching as being more desirable than Information Transmission/Teacher-focused approaches because the former are more inclusive (Trigwell and Prosser, 1996). More options are available to teachers who adopt this approach, and more opportunities are available for student learning when teachers adopt this approach. The outcomes of this and the previous study on relations between teachers' approach to teaching and the quality of student learning suggest that teaching with a Conceptual Change/Student-focused approach may also be more desirable because it is associated with classes of students who report adopting more desirable approaches to learning.

Recently we concluded that research results which are similar to those reported here also contribute significantly to the debate on what constitutes good university teaching (Trigwell, Prosser and Lyons, submitted for publication).

> [A] Conceptual Change/Student-focused approach is one which has the student as the focus of activities. It matters more to the teacher what the student is doing and learning than what the teacher is doing or covering. The teacher is one who encourages self directed learning, who makes time (in formal 'teaching' time) for students to interact and to discuss the problems they encounter, who assesses to reveal conceptual change (not only to judge and rank students), who provokes debate (and raises and addresses the taken-for-granted issues), who uses a lot of time to question students' ideas, and to develop a 'conversation' with students in lectures. These are the specific areas covered by items in the Approach to Teaching Inventory. The qualitative studies from which the inventory evolved also indicate that teachers adopting a Conceptual Change/Student-focused approach are aware of the nature of the learning of their students.

These characteristics of good teaching complement those reported by Ramsden *et al.* (1995) in their investigation of the recognition of good university teaching.

Acknowledgments

The authors wish to acknowledge the support of the staff and students who participated in the study, the work of Kitty te Riele, and funding from the Australian Research Council.

8.85   References

Biggs, J.B. (1978) Individual and group differences in study processes, *British Journal of Educational Psychology*, **48**, 266–79.

Biggs, J. (1987) *Study Process Questionnaire Manual*, Australian Council for Educational Research, Melbourne.

Entwistle, N. and Ramsden, P. (1983) *Understanding Student Learning*, London: Croom Helm.

Marton, F. and Säljö, R. (1976) On qualitative differences in learning. I. Outcome and Process, *British Journal of Educational Psychology*, **46**, 4–11.

Marton, F. and Säljö, R. (1997) Approaches to learning. In F. Marton, D. Hounsell and N.J. Entwistle (eds), *The Experience of Learning*, 2nd edn, Edinburgh: Scottish Academic Press, 39–58.

Prosser, M. and Millar, R. (1989) The how and what of learning physics, *The European Journal of Psychology of Education*, **4**, 513–28.

Prosser, M. and Trigwell, K. (1997) Perceptions of the teaching environment and its relationship to approaches to teaching, *British Journal of Educational Psychology*, **67**, 25–35.

Ramsden, P. (1991) A performance indicator of teaching quality in higher education: The Course Experience Questionnaire, *Studies in Higher Education*, **16**, 129–50.

Ramsden, P. (1992) *Learning to Teach in Higher Education*, London: Routledge.

Ramsden, P., Margetson, D., Martin, E. and Clarke, S. (1995) *Recognising and Rewarding Good Teaching in Australian Higher Education*, Committee for the Advancement of University Teaching, Australian Government Publishing Service.

Trigwell, K., Prosser, M. and Lyons, F. (1997) Defining good teaching: relations between teachers' approaches to teaching and student learning. Paper presented at the *7th Conference of the European Association for Research in Learning and Instruction*, Athens.

Trigwell, K., Prosser, M., Lyons, F. and Waterhouse, F. (in press) Defining good teaching: relating student learning to teachers' approaches to teaching, *Higher Education*.

Trigwell, K. and Prosser, M. (1991) Relating learning approaches, perceptions of context and learning outcomes, *Higher Education* (special edition on Student Learning) **22**, 251–66.

Trigwell, K. and Prosser, M. (1996) Congruence between intention and strategy in science teachers' approach to teaching, *Higher Education*, **32**, 77–87.

van Rossum, E.J. and Schenk, S.M. (1984) The relationship between learning conception, study strategy and learning outcome, *British Journal of Educational Psychology*, **54**, 73–83.

9 Student attitudes to resource based learning

Janet Macdonald,[i] Robin Mason[ii] and Nick Heap[iii]
(i) Associate Lecturer, THD204, OU Scottish Region; (ii) Head, Centre for Information Technology in Education, IET, OU; (iii) Senior Lecturer, Dept Telematics, OU

9.1 Introduction

The move towards resource-based learning reflects a trend away from the transmission model of education towards a more student-centred approach where the individual has the responsibility for extracting relevant information from a variety of sources. The approach offers students greater freedom and the opportunities to develop new skills. But given the demands of a traditional assessment system for testing knowledge, as well as skill or conceptual depth, the need to lend credibility to a degree course, and the particular requirements on distance learning courses to establish the identity of students, the question arises as to how such courses should be assessed.

In the context of open and distance learning, recent advances in IT have increased opportunities for all students to make use of resource-based learning. Multimedia workstations allow students access to information in the form of text, graphics, audio or video clips. They can search for relevant information, using a variety of techniques; they can select from a wide range of material and concentrate their study on only those sections which are most appropriate; finally, they can cut and paste relevant sections into assignments or other work. In addition, modem access to the Internet means that students working from home can make use of a store of documents, news and other sources, in addition to communicating using electronic mail and conferencing with their tutor and other students.

9.2 'Information Technology and Society'

The Open University course THD204 'Information Technology and Society' is innovatory in these spheres. An interview survey and observations of 21 students (Macdonald and Mason,1997), on completion of the course in 1996, indicated that many aspects of resource-based learning appeal to OU students: choice, breadth of materials and the use of new technology for course delivery and support. The variety of readings and the media on which they were found engendered high interest levels, and students were enthusiastic about their increased independence and the ability to construct alternative arguments with ease, afforded by the searching facilities on the CD-ROM library . However, many students continued to find difficulty in selective reading and reported confusion as to what they should be studying. They described a sense of information overload and it seems likely that the information handling skills required to study in this way may need more time to develop than that available during a single course. Until there is more general practice of resource-based learning throughout the education sector, students will benefit from assistance with the development of these skills.

In addition, the findings suggest that students may experience conflict between the open ended process-oriented approach associated with resource-based learning and the demands of more traditional content-oriented assessments. Given that the source material provided for this course was extensive and that each student may have made a unique selection of reading material from their personal CD-ROM library, how were they to prepare appropriately for their assignments or indeed for a closed book exam? This study raises many interesting questions for course developers. How does one assess content in a resource-based course? Is it acceptable to assess such courses with a closed book exam? What role does revision play in the student's acquisition of an understanding of course content? What revision strategies are successful for a resource-based course? What skills do the students carry away with them and how best might these skills be assessed?

The project team has concentrated its evaluation on a range of approaches to assessment for resource-based learning, by tracking student reactions to the assessment of this resource-based course in 1997. They decided to concentrate on three objectives:

1. an evaluation of ways of enhancing and improving feedback on existing assessments;

2. an evaluation of an assessment which the pilot study indicated might be reflective of the aims and objectives of resource based learning;

3. an evaluation of the current traditional assessment strategy which tests other parts of the course.

The present assessment structure includes a series of six continuous assignments, which are both summatively and formatively assessed. The last of these is a collaborative project, in which the students research a topic, working together in small groups and using computer conferencing as a medium of collaboration. The course concludes with a closed book exam.

As a way of providing the project team with concurrent feedback from students on their attitudes to the assignments as they were encountered, data was gathered from three computer conferences, one run in parallel with the continuous assessments, one in the revision period and one after the exam. In line with objective 1, the first of these conferences also attempted to improve the formative aspects of existing assignments, in addition to its feedback function. Participants were supplied with model answers and marking notes after assignment submission dates and offered the opportunity to participate in a peer assessment trial, using electronic submission of scripts, as a formative adjunct to tutor marking.

It became apparent that the computer conferences provided a rich source of *ad hoc* and unprompted feedback on issues which students felt were of importance to them at the time. However, it was also a difficult and unpredictable way to extract information on specific questions, because students did not feel that they had to answer the questions, as they might in an interview, or indeed to respond at all. Preliminary evaluation indicates that the first conference (which ran in parallel with the coninuous assessment) was particularly well received by students, and could be a useful way of supplementing formative feedback on assignments in future. In addition, the fact that the students were given extra help with the interpretation of assignments meant that they were willing participants, and were eager to provide feedback.

The data from the conferences was supplemented by a total of 60 flexibly structured telephone interviews, some conducted with conference participants and others with students who had not joined in the conferences. The interviews were conducted at three stages in the course: after the first five continuous assessments, after the collaborative project and after the exam. They were important as a way of contextualizing the conference data and setting it in perspective, and of providing new insights into student behaviour and attitudes.

Preliminary analysis indicates that students experienced difficulties in the initial stages of the course, particularly in their interpretation of the requirements of assignments, and this was compounded by variations in their academic backgrounds. At this stage in the course, formative feedback was critical: the feedback from tutors was the subject of keen interest and reactions to additional feedback in the shape of model answers or marking schemes were enthusiastically received. The peer-assessment exercise was also found to be helpful as a learning experience, although since the process was time-consuming it was difficult to encourage many students to participate. Evaluation of the collaborative project indicated that it was successful in reinforcing the information-handling skills encouraged throughout the course and left the majority of students feeling at home with the prospect of researching a topic. The computer-supported collaboration, where successful, provided a supportive environment for individual study and encouraged a critical approach to reading. As for the final exam, it appeared that the revision period represented an important part of the course, in which many students came to an understanding of course aims and objectives. However, many also experienced severe problems in the selection of appropriate sources to revise, from the volume of information presented to them and expressed a need for more guidance at this stage. Finally, the demands of the closed-book exam left many students feeling bewildered and uncertain of its role in testing a course of this kind.

It is clear that the resource-based approach can be a successful and stimulating way to work for distance-learning students, but also requires particular care in the support and guidance of students. It is anticipated that the results of this study should provide a better understanding of the problems faced by students in studying in this way and should lead to the development of an assessment strategy appropriate for resource-based learning using technologies for open and distance learning.

9.3   Reference

Macdonald, J. and Mason, R (1998) Information handling skills and resource based learning in an Open University course, *Open Learning*, 13(1) 38–42.

10 Linking physics students' development as independent and reflective learners with changes in their conceptions of science

Cedric Linder and Delia Marshall
University of the Western Cape, South Africa

> I never used to read any of my textbooks, and I never applied anything at home, or on my way home. I can certainly say that I learned more from physics than any other thing in my life.
>
> (Physics student at UWC)

10.1   Introduction

In 1909 John Dewey wrote:

> Science teaching has suffered because science has been so frequently presented just as so much ready-made knowledge, so much subject-matter of fact and law, rather than as the effective method of inquiry into any subject-matter.

In the case of higher education physics, very little has changed since 1909 in terms of how physics is taught (for example, see Wilson, 1997). It appears that people who teach undergraduate physics often make unsubstantiated assumptions about how their students learn physics (for example, see McMillen, 1986) and are thus seldom in a position to promote independent lifelong learning.

One of the primary aims in a newly designed introductory undergraduate physics course we have been teaching is the promotion of independent, lifelong learning – widely held to be the central purpose of a higher education (for example, see Candy, 1991; Barnett, 1990). For students to become independent lifelong learners we argue that the ability *to be aware of, and to reflect on, one's own learning* (metacognition) is an important prerequisite. Consequently, when designing the course we developed specific strategies which focussed on fostering these reflective abilities. In a previous paper (Linder and Marshall, 1996) we described how we infused a set of metacognitive strategies into our course and how these strategies affected the students' experiences of learning. At this stage we noticed that our students had a tendency to link their conceptions of learning with their conceptions of science, and we decided to look at this outcome in a more systematic way. We framed our study by looking at two main interrelated dynamics which we felt most affected physics teaching and learning.

First, there were the teachers' perspectives of how students learn and conceptualize their physics. These perspectives would form an integral framing of an educators' teaching approach in relation to their 'personal' philosophy of how best to teach physics (cf. Prosser *et al.*, 1994). Science education commentary such as that of Bruner (1986, p. 128) argues that one cannot teach physics 'without transmitting a sense of stance toward nature and the use of mind', and research such as that done by Linder (1992) and Hammer (1995) supports the.

notion that such teaching approaches can give subtle epistemological messages which may have far-reaching consequences for physics learning.

Secondly there are the kinds of well-established perceptions, with which students arrive at university, of how physics teaching and learning *should* be experienced. We felt that significant influential factors in the construction of this perspective would be *how* they were taught physics in the past and what epistemological messages were carried in the physics-related material that they had read and studied. In this regard, probably the most pervasive philosophical view of the nature of science portrayed in science textbooks and professional scientific literature is one in which scientific activity is the 'discovery of truth' (Gauld, 1982; Hodson, 1985; Marquit, 1978; Otero, 1985). The problem with portraying such a perspective when teaching science is that it tends to undervalue the 'contributions of conscious mental or theoretical activity to the process of acquiring an understanding of the physical world' (Marquit, 1978, p. 785) and at the same time it supports 'the assumption that knowledge of facts provides an adequate psychological foundation for concept learning' (Otero, 1985, p. 364). This 'metaphysical realism' (Putnam, 1981) reflected by traditional science teaching thus adds an obstacle to the development of independent and reflective learners. For example, teachers holding such a metaphysical realism perspective would conceivably view content as *the* main criteria of the standard of a course. In such a scenario the amount of course content covered then takes on overriding importance and the rate of science instruction becomes typically so rapid that in-class reflection or discussion becomes impossible (see for example, McMillen, 1986; Tobias, 1986). Arons (1979) has delightfully characterized this fast content coverage with a 'length contraction' metaphor taken from Einstein's Special Theory of Relativity:

> It is the premise of the vast majority of introductory physics courses . . . that if one takes a huge breadth of subject matter and passes it before the student at sufficiently high velocity, the Lorentz contraction will shorten it to a point at which it drops into the hole which is the student's mind . . . The students have been 'told' but they have not made the concept part of their own . . . they have no understanding of the physics.
>
> (p. 650)

Consequently we felt that we needed to examine the kinds of epistemological influences which our students were experiencing in terms of how it influenced their *conceptions of learning* development and how this was interrelated to their *conceptions of science* development. To do this, we phenomenographically characterized the impact of our teaching strategies in terms of our students' experiences of learning and their experiences of the nature of science. We then used this analysis to explore the implications that the epistemological framing of a course may have for the orientation of science students towards independent and reflective learning.

10.2   Course design and background to present study

In a previous paper (Linder and Marshall, 1996) we described the design of a new introductory physics course taught at the University of the Western Cape and, in particular, a set of metacognitive strategies which were infused into the course design. These metacognitive strategies were aimed at getting students to reflect on their own learning, on the relevance of what they were learning and on the nature of their subject. We felt that such strategies were central to developing students' intellectual autonomy and their reflective and critical thinking abilities. In brief, the metacognitive strategies were as follows:

- *Strategies to foster a conceptual focus*
  - concept-mapping;
  - linking different parts of the course;
  - emphasis on qualitative reasoning;
  - note-taking discouraged.
- *Strategies to foster reflection on the nature of the discipline*
  - what physics is about, how it works and why we believe it, for example modelling.
- *Strategies to promote reflection on the value and relevance of what is taught*
  - links with societal/environmental/historical contexts;
  - using everyday examples.
- *Strategies to foster learner activity*
  - 'check-your-neighbour' in-class discussion;
  - using students in class-illustrations.
- *Strategies to get students to reflect on their own educational orientations*
  - generating discussions about issues such as what students expected to get in return for their fees, how their physics understanding impacted on their self-image as scientifically informed citizens exercising their rights in a modern democracy, and so on.
- *Strategies to make metacognition explicit*
  - making the metacognitive dynamic of the course explicit on a continual basis;
  - cartoons; and
  - songs.

Our previous research (Linder and Marshall, 1996) examined students' experiences of learning in this course. Using the 18-item Approaches to Studying Inventory as well as in-depth interviews, we found that our students' approaches to learning had shifted towards 'deeper' approaches. Furthermore, we were able to characterize phenomenographically the nature of these shifts in terms of students' epistemological perspectives. While looking at students' descriptions of their learning experiences, we noticed that many of the students interspersed their descriptions of learning with descriptions of science. This interrelationship between students' conceptions of learning and conceptions of science then became our subsequent research focus. Previous studies have indicated that students' approaches to learning are linked to their conceptions of the nature of science. For example, Edmondson and Novak (1993) showed that students who perceive scientific knowledge as a body of facts generally follow a passive, rote-learning approach, while those who perceive science as 'an ongoing process of concept development' tend to adopt a 'deep' approach.

In the next section we describe how we examined the impact that the metacognitive strategies outlined earlier had on students' conceptions of learning and conceptions of science, and we examine the links between the development of students' conceptions of learning and their conceptions of science.

10.3   Method

At the start of the course, all the students completed a short questionnaire requiring written responses to questions about their conceptions of learning and of the nature of science. Towards the end of the course students were asked to complete a similar questionnaire and a group of students were also chosen for in-depth interviews. The interviews were based upon a semi-structured interview protocol which was designed using the students' descriptions given on the questionnaires. All the interviews were transcribed verbatim.

All the students' *descriptions* of how they experienced science were used to construct phenomenographically (cf. Marton, 1981; 1988) qualitatively different *categories of description*. The phenomenographic process of constructing these categories involves hermeneutic iterations to generate the integration of important descriptive content and structure similarities – the characterization of the resultant *categories of description* are then characterized as *conceptions*. The *conceptions of science* were thus constructed. These are described later. It is necessary to point out that the resultant *conceptions of science* do not represent a sampling of *students* per se, but of qualitatively different *ways of experiencing science*.

Once all the conceptions of science categories were constructed, the students' interviews, and pre- and post-course questionnaires were then individually categorized using the Marton *et al.* (1993) *learning conceptions taxonomy*, and our newly constructed *conceptions of science taxonomy*.

10.4   Results

10.4.1   The conceptions of learning taxonomy

The conceptions of learning were characterized using the Marton *et al.* (1993) taxonomy, which has the following categories:

A   increasing one's knowledge;

B   memorizing and reproducing;

C   applying;

D   understanding;

E   seeing something in a different way;

F   changing as a person.

Since this framework is well described in the literature (see Saljo, 1979; Marton *et al.*, 1993) we will not discuss it further here, but do provide some illlustrative excerpts to give the reader a sense of how these conceptions of learning manifested themselves for our students.

10.4.2   Conceptions of science taxonomy

In this section, we describe students' conceptions of science that emerged from the iterative phenomenographic analysis. The conceptions we obtained were:

A   science as discovery or 'knowing about the world';

CONCEPTION OF LEARNING	ILLUSTRATIVE STUDENT DESCRIPTION
A Increasing one's knowledge	It is increasing the knowledge that I have.
	Learning's like getting to know more, really.
B Memorizing and reproducing	Before this year I sincerely believed that understanding work means learning it by heart, ... learning it the night before and getting good results.
	Learning means spending a lot of time in memorising the particular thing, just to obey its rules for the sake of knowing how to do it. Sometimes I have to learn the rule whereas it means nothing to me, but just for the sake of doing it.
	To store what I learnt
C. Applying	It means that you are capable of practising it.
D Understanding	It means to learn for deeper understanding which needs a lot of reflection.
	When you say 'you learn something', then that means that the meaning of the thing is new to me. It opens the way I think, and so I think differently from the things I knew before, or it makes it more clear.
	Learning' is discovering something new or something that I always took for granted, I actually *make sense* of it and *understand*.
E Seeing something in a different way	... it's having a broader outlook on how everything about the Earth falls into place.
	How to relate what I've learnt to life as a whole – to be aware of things around me so that they don't come as a surprise.
F Changing as a person	For me when I came here I had one thing in mind that was to become a better person in life, to have something to strive for in life.

Conceptions of science taxonomy

In this section, we describe students' conceptions of science that emerged from the iterative phenomenographic analysis. The conceptions we obtained were:

A) Science as discovery or 'knowing about the world'.

B) Science as an accumulation of facts, and explanations which explain how things are or how they work

C) Science as a process of inquiry undertaken by 'scientists'.

D) Science as an accessible way of looking at the world and, as such part of everyday life.

E) Science has a social dimension.

F) Science as empowering.

Figure 10.1   Ilustrative descriptions of students' conceptions of learning

B   science as an accumulation of facts and explanations of how things are or how they work;

C   science as a process of enquiry undertaken by 'scientists';

D   science as an accessible way of looking at the world and, as such part, of everyday life;

E   science has a social dimension;

F   science as empowering.

The primary characterizations of these conceptions are described below together with some illustrative student descriptions of their experiences. We do need to point out, however, that these descriptions are only examples and are not meant to represent fully any of the conceptions.

A   *Science as discovery or 'knowing about the world'*

This conception of science is characterized by vague descriptions of science in terms of 'a study of the world, of everything in the world', and in terms of science as 'being all around us'. For example:

- 'There is no limit to science because it deals with so many things.'
- 'Science is the study of life and what is going on around us.'
- 'Science is everything around us.'

The conception includes science as discovery of facts and theories 'out there', for example:

- 'Scientists are discoverers: they are always on the lookout for new information.'

However, the delimitation of this conception is that science is not seen as *part* of the students' life, but rather as 'mysterious and unfathomable'. In other words, although science is described as 'all around us', it is seen as being inaccessible to 'ordinary people' and belonging to laboratories where 'clever' scientists do their work, for example:

- 'Science is one of those far-fetched subjects . . . so far out of my league.'
- 'Science is a study of things that many people cannot understand.'
- 'Science is something we can't do anything about.'
- 'Scientists study most of the things which are peculiar to an average person.'

B   *Science as an accumulation of facts, explanations which explain how things are, or how they work*

This conception, like conception A, characterizes an experience of science as a body of accepted facts and theories. However, its delimitation now includes *explanation* of how things are and how they work in nature, but it is in a *detached* impersonal way. Science is experienced as a body of knowledge *separate* from the students in that science provides explanations which are essentially outside the realms of the students' life. As in conception A, it is the *scientist* who explains how things work, not the student. For example:

- 'Science to me is the study of material things. How everything works – how it doesn't work and the repairs and maintenance done to.'

- '. . . finding out how scientists have figured out how things work'.

The delimitation of the conception also includes the *usefulness* of scientific knowledge, not at an everyday *personal* level, but in a broad technological, utilitarian way. When students provided descriptions which included details of science's capacity to 'improve one's life', the framing was in terms of a depersonalized technology. For example:

- 'Science improves our standards of living to create new devices to help our country to become more powerful, technically advanced and economically strong.'

- 'Methods of making human life easier, i.e. ways to become more modernized.'

- 'Scientists are always busy formulating new theories that could bring about a change in certain areas of our daily lives.'

In other words, science's capacity to 'improve one's life' is described in a passive sense. It is science, as practised by scientists, that can improve life, in contrast to a later conception **D** in which 'ordinary people' can use science *themselves* to improve their own lives.

C   *Science as a process of enquiry undertaken by scientists*

This conception represents an experience of science which has moved from seeing science as a set of facts and theories to seeing science as a *process or method* of enquiry for scientists. The descriptions here are typically in terms of observation, hypothesis etc. – elements of a 'scientific method' that they most probably heard about at school. This is described in a depersonalized way, for example:

- 'Scientists test something, come up with results whether they correspond or not, discuss their results and conclude their results before they can be shown to the public.'

- 'Scientists do experiments and make hypotheses in a fixed way to prove things.'

D   *Science as an accessible way of looking at the world and, as such, part of everyday life*

This conception portrays science as a 'way of looking at the world' *that anyone can adopt.* There are descriptions of thinking logically and critically, of basing arguments on evidence, and of asking oneself questions. Students describe previously 'taking things for granted', but that they are now more critical, and don't just accept things. For example:

- 'I now just don't accept theories and hypotheses – I question them myself . . . and I now ask for proof or evidence to support one's statement.'

- 'Science is a way of thinking . . . to support yourself in your opinion.'

- 'How to estimate and ask myself questions about why this happens.'

- 'When one talks about science I thought I have to be in the lab, but now I can see that science is our everyday life; we are surrounded by it, but one cannot see that unless one can ask oneself questions – how this is done and what made it.'

This conception also represents an experience of science which the students describe as being part of their everyday life which is in contrast with the vague, depersonalized experience of science being 'all around us' as characterized in conceptions **A** and **B**. Examples of descriptions falling into the conception **D** category are:

- 'I never expected science to be part of our everyday lives.'

- 'And I've learnt about things that occur in my everyday life which I once didn't even give a thought about.'

The delimitation of this conception in the students' descriptions extends beyond that of the delimitation of conception **B**. In both cases students are describing science in terms of 'improving quality of life'; however, for conception **D** the experience of science is in terms of *personal decisions they may take in their lives*, instead of *improvement directed by scientists in terms of technological advancement*. In other words the experience is no longer a passive one, the students can improve their *own* lives through science. For example:

- 'I now have a better understanding of science. It is not something I leave in the classroom – I can take it all over and explain things to myself.'

- 'I *live science* – whatever I do I have a scientific explanation – whether I am walking in a circle, or baking bread, or taking a shower.'

E   *Science has a social dimension*

In conception **B** science is portrayed only in terms of positive benefits to 'quality of life', particularly in terms of technological advances. In this conception, the delimitation is extended to having an awareness of both the positive and negative aspects of science. Here, students' conceptions of science include social and ethical dimensions, and an awareness of the limitations of science, for example:

- 'Science is not just about calculations and formulas but about how it affects our lives – socially as well as politically. How the inventions in science can help us in good ways, as well as how those people who would exploit it as a means to have total power.'

- 'I see science now as a subject that informs me of our environment and how certain things affect our environment, without us knowing it.'

F   *Science as empowering*

In this conception, science is experienced in terms of the *positive personal impact* it has on students, and in terms of its *capacity to empower people*. For example,

- 'I can take [science] all over and explain things to myself. It actually is a calming thing which can help you find the reason for everything.'

- 'I always just thought of science as a lot of formulas that I'll never really use. But I've come to understand how science can empower me in my day to day life.'

- 'I see things differently now – science has helped me to be a better person. I've gained respect to the environment I'm living in. I'd not thought about science before in the way I see science now.'

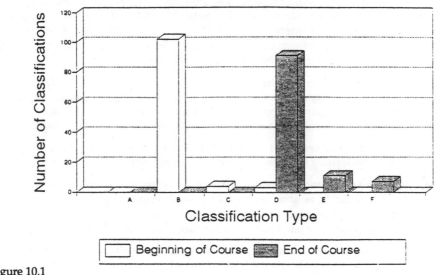

Figure 10.1

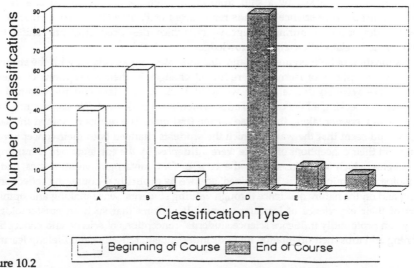

Figure 10.2

10.5 Discussion

This study was aimed at phenomenographically characterizing and categorizing our students' conceptions of science, and then looking at how changes in these conceptions were related to changes in their conceptions of learning.

Figure 10.1 shows the distribution of the students' conceptions of learning at the beginning and end of the introductory physics course. Most students began our course with conceptions of learning in categories **B** and **C**. Five months later, all of the students described experiencing learning in a more sophisticated way. Here are two typical examples of how students described their shifts in their conceptions of learning:

> Before this year I sincerely believed that understanding work means learning it by heart . . . learning it the night before and getting good results . . . [Now] understanding it and knowing it thoroughly and applying it to reality makes greater sense, and the knowledge that you gain remains with you until death – because you *understand* it.

> I used to just put numbers in formulas to pass and not understand what I am doing. Now, I think learning is reasoning solutions with understanding.

Figure 10.2 shows the distribution of the students' conceptions of science at the beginning and end of the course. In essence, we were able to characterize the predominant change being one from an 'authoritarian' conception of science (conceptions **A**, **B** and **C**) to a more humanized conception (**D**, **E** and **F**) which 'demystified' science, for example:

> I used to think that science is only for those who have intellectual ability higher than others. Now I have realised that it is for everyone in their everyday lives in order to make better decisions to make their life simpler.

> Science in general was for me what great scientists discovered in those days, and made it a fact that we would take for granted and accept as it is. Now, I try to understand many concepts and not just swat it for exam purposes or because Newton or Galileo said so, but to understand about daily life and how science plays a major role in it.

This change is also marked by a shift from an 'immutable' conception of science to a 'tentative' conception of science which is reminiscent of Perry's (1970) work on students' intellectual development during college years, which described students' shifts from absolute to more relativistic views of knowledge.

An examination of both Figures 10.1 and 10.2 indicates that associated with the students' changes in conceptions of learning were linked changes in their conceptions of science. These changes were so dramatic that we went back to our data and re-examined our analysis, cross-checking all the categorization which was not distinct. We also excluded any students who were not taking the course for the first time. The results remained the same. Thus it would seem that the way in which the students changed both their conceptions of learning and their conceptions of science were influenced by the epistemological framing of the strategies which we infused into the course. Our metacognitive strategies had an epistemological framing which 'humanized' science by explicitly encouraging reflection on learning and on the nature of science through valuing students' sense-making and opinions as part of their experience of learning science. It appears that such an epistemological framing can profoundly influence science students' conceptions of science and conceptions of learning and thus their orientation towards independent, reflective and lifelong learning.

10.6 References

Arons, A.B. (1979) Cognitive level of college physics students, *American Journal of Physics*, **47**(7), 650–4.

Barnett, R. (1990) *The Idea of Higher Education*, Buckingham: SRHE and OUP.

Bruner, J. (1986) *Actual Minds, Possible Worlds*, Cambridge, Mass: Harvard University Press.

Candy, P. (1991) *Self-direction for Life-long Learning*, San Francisco: Jossey Bass.

Dewey, J. (1909, repr. 1995) Science as subject-matter and as method, *Science and Education*, **4**, 391–8.

Edmondson, K. and Novak, J. (1993) The interplay of scientific epistemological views, learning strategies and attitudes of college students, *Journal of Research in Science Teaching*, **30**(6), 547–59.

Gauld, C. (1982) The scientific attitude and science education: a critical reappraisal, *Science Education*, **66**(1), 109–21.

Hammer, D. (1995) Epistemological considerations in teaching introductory physics, *Science Education*, **79**(4), 393–413.

Hodson, D. (1985) Philosophy of science, science and science education, *Studies in Science Education*, **12**, 25–46.

Linder, C.J. (1992) Is teacher-reflected epistemology a source of conceptual difficulty in physics? *International Journal of Science Education*, **11**, 491–501.

Linder, C.J. and Marshall, D.(1996) Introducing and evaluating metacognitive strategies in large-class physics teaching. Paper presented at the *4th International Improving Student Learning Symposium*, University of Bath, UK.

McMillen, L. (1986) The frustrations of a college physics class: some professors get to experience it, again, *Chronicle of Higher Education*, Oct., 18-19.

Marton, F. (1981) Phenomenography – describing conceptions of the world around us, *Instructional Science*, **10**, 177–200.

Marton, F., Dall'Alba, G. and Beaty, E. (1993) Conceptions of learning. *International Journal of Educational Research*, **19**(3), 277–9.

Marton, F. (1988) Phenomenography and 'The Art of Teaching All Things to All Men', *Fenomenografiska notiser 8. Publikationen fran institutionen for pedagogik*. A revised version of an invited address entitled 'Revealing Educationally Critical Differences in our Understanding of the World Around Us' presented to the American Educational Research Association,New Orleans, LA, April 1988.

Marquit, E. (1978) Philosophy of physics in general courses, *American Journal of Physics*, **46**(8), 784–9.

Otero, J.C. (1985) Assimilation problems in traditional representations of scientific knowledge, *European Journal of Science Education*, **7**(4), 361–9.

Perry, W.G. (1970) *Forms of Intellectual and Ethical Development in the College Years: A Scheme*, New York: Holt, Rinehart & Winston.

Prosser, M.,Trigwell, K. and Taylor, P. (1994) A phenomenographic study of academics' conceptions of science teaching and learning, *Learning and Instruction*, **4**, 217–31.

Putman, H. (1981) *Reason, Truth and History*, Cambridge: Cambridge University Press

Tobias, S. (1986) Peer perspectives on the teaching of science, *Change*, March/April, 36–41.

Wilson, J. (1997) *Conference on the Introductory Physics Course*, New York: John Wiley.

11 Curriculum innovation: assessing the effectiveness of the explicit teaching of communication skills in a large first-year accounting course

Linda English[(i)] and Tig Ihnatko[(ii)]
(i) Department of Accounting, University of Sydney, Australia;
(ii) Department of Econometrics, University of Sydney, Australia

11.1 Overview

Communication, intellectual and interpersonal skills have been identified as essential attributes of accounting graduates. This chapter reports on the evaluation of a project at the University of Sydney to integrate the explicit teaching of these skills and to promote lifelong learning skills in a large first-year accounting course. The chapter discusses the evolution of the course and its evaluation since 1994, when the curriculum redesign project was first introduced into the two-semester course. During 1994 the course was evaluated extensively. Evaluation from the students' perspective took several forms: quantitative and qualitative surveys, focus groups and interviews conducted by experienced outside facilitators. The chapter presents feedback from qualitative assessment and details revisions to the course in response to that feedback. Quantitative results in 1994, 1995, 1996 and 1997 suggest that revisions to the program in 1995 were favourably received by students and that students continue to perceive that they have benefited from the redesign project. In addition to presenting an account of student and staff evaluation procedures as a result of curriculum innovation of a component of one course at one institution, the chapter discusses the role of assessment, from both a theoretical and practical perspective.

Acknowledgements

Special thanks to Helen Bonanno for constructive criticism and to Cathie Paul for encouragement.

11.2 Introduction

Accounting educators in Australia are under pressure from professional bodies (Capelletto, 1993, Appendix A) and the market place (Higher Education Council, 1992, p. 23) to develop in their graduates intellectual and interpersonal skills and the ability to communicate orally and in writing. Similar concerns have been raised in New Zealand (McLaren, 1990), Canada (Whitely, 1993), the UK (Morgan, 1997) and the USA (American Education Change Commission, 1992; Andersen *et al.*, 1989; Lau and Rans, 1993; AICPA, 1988). The ultimate objective of teaching these skills has been identified as the development of the capacity and desire to learn throughout life (Candy *et al.*, 1994). Similar conclusions have been drawn in the US (Francis *et al.*, 1995; American Education Change Commission, 1990, Appendix A). A number of academics have responded to these calls with enthusiasm (Hirsch and Collins, 1988; Stocks *et al.*, 1992, Webb *et al.*, 1995). The challenge to educators is to determine where and how in an undergraduate degree these skills should be taught, and how to appraise their effectiveness in teaching desired learning outcomes.

This chapter is primarily concerned with the evaluation of a major curriculum redesign project to introduce the explicit teaching of the American Education Change Commission's skills inventory in a large first-year accounting course at the University of Sydney. The chapter is organized as follows. First, an outline of the theoretical underpinning of the pedagogical interventions which took place is presented. Discussion of approaches to evaluation is followed by consideration of methodologies appropriate to assess curriculum innovation. Qualitative methods utilized in 1994 to evaluate the project, from both a student and faculty perspective, in its first year are presented together with outcomes and an indication of our response to feedback in terms of revisions to the programme made in 1995. A section on demographics and discussion of the methodology adopted precedes the presentation of quantitative results from student surveys conducted at the end of the first developmental semester in the years 1994–97. The chapter concludes with a discussion of results and, more generally, of problems associated with the evaluation of teaching initiatives. Both qualitative and quantitative evidence suggests that the redesign of the curriculum has been successful in achieving its pedagogical objectives.

11.3   Rationale for interventions

Three areas of educational research underlie the project. Redesigning a programme around the learner's acquisition of skills and the acquisition of knowledge is strongly supported in the educational research literature. Educational research into approaches to learning suggests that the learner's motive/strategy can be categorized as: surface (meet requirements/rote learning), deep (intrinsic/search for meaning) and achieving (grade-oriented/sufficient to obtain high grades) (Biggs, 1987, p. 11). It is also known that learning is a function of both student and context (Trigwell and Prosser, 1991; Gow *et al.*, 1994). The nature of the course and the teaching within the course form part of that context. Thus, students' perceptions of both the teaching and the course requirements can affect their approaches to learning.

Secondly, research into metacognition or metalearning, that is the learner's awareness of his/her learning processes and control of those processes, suggests that even relatively young students can perceive the motive and strategy options associated with the three approaches to learning (Biggs, 1987: 97). There is evidence that accounting education has tended to encourage a surface approach to learning (Gray *et al.*, 1994).

These two research strands suggest that it *may* be possible to influence some students' approaches to learning in a particular course by designing teaching materials, assignments and assessment tasks, including examination questions, that promote quality learning, that is learning which involves students either in an intrinsic search for personal understanding or learning motivated by grades. However, students' approaches to learning are also influenced by their orientation to studying which, in turn, is related to their previous educational experiences (Ramsden, 1992, p. 82). Thus, it may not be possible to influence approaches to learning universally through the redesign of curricula and teaching materials. For students motivated by grades or those who may be more naturally inclined to be surface learners, perceptions of the requirements of the task is the paramount motivator (Ramsden, 1992, pp. 62–5). For such students it is imperative to discourage rote learning by ensuring that assessment tasks require the demonstration of understanding, analysis and critical evaluation. There is evidence that individuals adopt learning strategies which match their perceptions of the task at hand (Laurillard, 1984; Biggs, 1985; Ramsden, 1992).

A third strand of educational research influencing the development and design of teaching materials is Systemic Functional Linguistics which explains the role of language in representing a discipline (Halliday, 1985). It is through language that the learner accesses subject matter and, in becoming familiar with the subject, masters the language of the discipline. In using language to know, understand and, in turn, explain a subject, the learner develops the skills of consciously reflecting on learning that subject. Using language to know and understand a subject are usually products of the private domain of learning, and include reading, summarizing, drafting and self-testing. These processes also involve a measure of conscious reflection on the learning of the subject. When a student comes to explain a subject in the public domain, either in writing or orally, his/her level of understanding is demonstrated through the written or spoken presentation. The quality of the presentation will be a result not only of the student's approach to the task, but the nature of the task itself and the student's perception of the standard expected by teaching staff. The role of conscious reflection in learning is also stressed in the research into metacognition and metalearning. According to Biggs (1987, p. 98), an individual's control of his/her learning processes is related to maturity and experience, is not necessarily uniform, but *is* positively associated with high quality learning.

In helping the learner to develop the desired skills, a pedagogy which regards the learner as an active and reflective participant in the learning process is vital. Without the ability to reflect on one's own learning and to transfer skills to novel tasks, it is unlikely that the learner will develop skills for what Candy *et al.* (1994) refer to as 'lifelong learning' and Francis *et al.* (1995) 'intentional learning'. The capacity for lifelong learning is also related to students' learning strategies and motivation (Gianen and Locatelli, 1995, p. 60).

Figure 11.1 indicates diagrammatically the theoretical rationale for curriculum redesign and its evaluation. Given that the key to students' approaches to learning is determined by both previous experiences *and* orientation to studying, in addition to the context of learning, it is the context of learning that presents educators with a window of opportunity to promote change in the learning of their students. Figure 11.1 also indicates what we have attempted to assess: namely whether the first semester course affected approaches to studying, and students' perceptions of whether or not they had benefited from the explicit teaching of generic skills.

The pedagogy which evolved out of these theoretical perspectives draws together a number of principles: the staged progression of learning activities and tasks from lower order cognitive processes such as memory and recall to higher cognitive processes such as analysis and evaluation (Bloom, 1956); an attempt to lead the learner towards deep learning through the design of appropriate learning activities and assessment tasks (Ramsden, 1992, pp. 150–70); the elaboration of metacognitive learning strategies through modelling of thinking processes (Collins and Gentner, 1980); and the use of individual and peer review to foster reflection on learning activities and tasks.

11.3.1   Development of teaching materials

The first priority was to determine how to operationalize the AECC skills inventory into appropriately staged learning activities and tasks (English *et al.*, 1997). As Table 11.1 indicates, our approach was dictated by the primary need to understand the subject matter.

Figure. 11.1

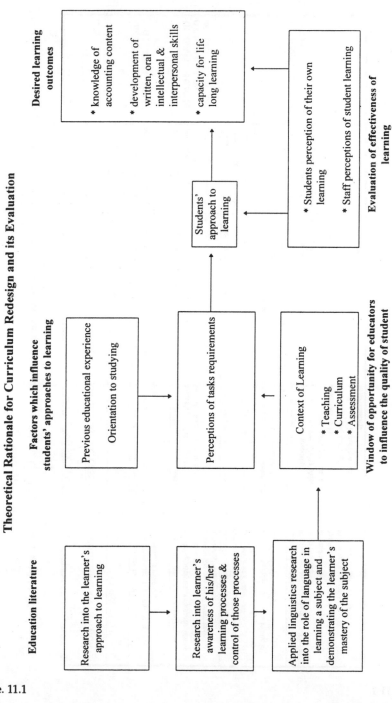

Theoretical Rationale for Curriculum Redesign and its Evaluation

Desired learning outcomes

* knowledge of accounting content
* development of written, oral intellectual & interpersonal skills
* capacity for life long learning

Factors which influence students' approaches to learning

Previous educational experience

Orientation to studying

Students' approach to learning

Evaluation of effectiveness of learning

* Students perception of their own learning
* Staff perceptions of student learning

Perceptions of tasks requirements

Context of Learning

* Teaching
* Curriculum
* Assessment

Window of opportunity for educators to influence the quality of student learning

Education literature

Research into the learner's approach to learning

Research into learner's awareness of his/her learning processes & control of those processes

Applied linguistics research into the role of language in learning a subject and demonstrating the learner's mastery of the subject

* This figure has been adapted from Ramsden 1992: 83

Operationalizing the AECC's skills inventory: the relationship between tasks facilitating the building of knowledge-based skills and the development of generic skills

GENERIC SKILLS	LEARNING OBJECTIVES	ENABLING SKILLS		
		KNOWLEDGE ACQUISITION & CONSERVATION — TASKS	KNOWLEDGE PROCESSING — TASKS	KNOWLEDGE APPLICATION — TASKS
THE DEVELOPMENT OF INTELLECTUAL SKILLS	To locate, interpret & apply relevant data in the discipline of accounting	• to read and understand tutorial readings, lecture notes and other course materials	• to complete reflective reading guides, • to analyse case study problems and recommend solutions	• to complete tutorial exercises • to analyse case study problems and recommend solutions
THE DEVELOPMENT OF COMMUNICATION SKILL	To develop factual and analytical writing in the context of conveying accounting information	• to summarise readings • to provide written descriptions of numerical data • to deconstruct model written answers	• to analyse the purpose of questions • to develop written argument and rationale in tutorial exercises	• to produce written case study reports involving analysis, recommendations and rationale • to assess the quality of team and individual writing
	To develop oral presentation skills in the context of conveying accounting information	• to take notes of group discussions • to practice technical aspects of oral presentations - visual aides, clear speech etc. • To present factual information informally on behalf of a group • to present group poster displays	• to devise evaluation criteria for oral presentations • to orally present the rationale for group recommendations • to prepare a group oral presentation • to prepare an individual oral presentation	• to apply evaluation criteria for oral presentations to group and individuals (self and peer evaluation) • to orally present case study problems with recommendations and rationale in teams and individually
THE DEVELOPMENT OF INTERPERSONAL SKILLS	To develop team and leader ship skills in the context of the discipline of accounting	• to discuss information about group roles, processes and dynamics • to understand the purpose of teamwork	• to form project teams • to organise team meetings • to select and control team objectives • to break down team projects into sequenced tasks • to allocate team tasks • to reflect and improve on team performances	• to document team processes • to assess the individual contribution of team members • to produce a practical survey • to produce a written case study report • to manage a tutorial with oral presentation and discussion

* This table is taken from Table 1 in English *et al* (1997): 123

Table 11.1

We concentrated on the cognitive progression required of the learner to acquire, conserve, process and apply knowledge in a novel discipline with (for the learner) initially uncertain expectations regarding standards. While we recognize that there *is* a place for rote learning when a student is introduced to a new topic, it was our intention to design teaching materials which progressively lead students beyond that necessary first stage towards the higher levels of cognition as identified by Bloom (1956): analysis and critical evaluation; and to make clear the standards, in terms of both content knowledge and skills development, required in written and spoken tasks. The framework adopted is represented in Table 11.1.

Learning activities and tasks were developed to help students acquire not only knowledge of the subject, but to give them strategies, through explicit examples, of how to tackle unfamiliar material and to indicate, through the provision of models, the standard of work required. Major innovations to the curriculum can be summarized as follows:

- Provision of interactive reading guides designed to develop understanding of, and a reflective and critical approach to, subject matter and to introduce students to the language of the discipline.

- Explicit development of writing to encourage not only an ability to write acceptably at university in a novel discipline, but also to foster the development of critical thinking and content analysis by focusing attention on an 'appropriate answer' to different types of questions in terms of subject matter, level of argument and structure. To enhance understanding, students are given models of, and prompted to analyse, 'unsuccessful' as well as 'successful' answers.

- Redesign of tutorial activities to allow more time for impromptu group discussions and informal presentations. Formal oral presentation skills are discussed in tutorials with students determining the hallmarks of successful oral presentations. These agreed criteria are used by students as benchmarks for their own presentations and to evaluate presentations by their peers.

- Formation of teams as a learning strategy to foster informal discussion and interpersonal skills in tutorials and outside class through the production of written and oral team assignments. To enhance understanding of group dynamics and differences in individual contributions, role-plays were developed.

- Establishment of formal peer and self-assessment processes to give formative feedback for students and the summative (graded) assessment system revised to give weighting to the explicit teaching of the AECC skills inventory which became the focus of the course. For instance, predetermined marking criteria emphasize the importance of writing and presentation as well of content, argument and analysis and English grammar.

- Expectations are made explicit. For example, students are provided with models of successful responses to tutorial questions, faculty model an oral presentation, predetermined assessment sheets are provided as guides for assignment preparation and self-assessment of assignments as well as detailed assignment feedback from faculty.

The teaching strategy is to develop skills in the first semester course, and to permit students to demonstrate their mastery of those skills in the second semester. For instance, written and oral communication skills are taught explicitly in first semester and formative feedback always precedes summative (graded) feedback. In the second semester summative assignments are more complex; demanding a demonstration of mastery of subject matter and more complex cognitive tasks.

11.4   Assessing innovation in teaching

A major point of agreement in the accounting education literature appears to be that there is no one 'correct' methodology to evaluate innovation in teaching. There is also no agreed terminology. 'Assessment' is used in the US; in Australia and the UK the term 'evaluation' is preferred. In this chapter the terms will be used interchangeably with 'assessment' or 'evaluation' taken to mean the 'systematic collection, interpretation, and use of information on student characteristics, the educational environment and learning outcomes to improve student learning and satisfaction' (Gainen and Locatelli, 1995, p. 3). Assessment of teaching performance has two dimensions: its focus and its purpose (Ramsden, 1992, p. 222). In the case reported here, the focus is the tutorial programme of a first-year accounting course; the purpose to provide the project coordinators[1] with feedback about student and faculty perceptions of the redesign of the curriculum and, especially in 1994, with indications of how the innovations could be refined to better achieve the desired learning outcomes and higher levels of student satisfaction.

At one end of the spectrum Street (1995) advocates the use of experimental research to test the effect of innovative educational practices on student learning.[2] At the other end of the scale are Gainen and Locatelli (1995, p. 1) who argue that the recent emphasis on teaching communication skills and the enhancement of lifelong learning skills requires educators to create new methods to assess effectiveness of student learning. Underlying the Gainen and Locatelli definition of assessment is the notion of continuous improvement in teaching based on credible evidence systematically obtained.

The assessment procedures described and analysed in this chapter fall into the category of what Gainen and Locatelli (1996, p. 61) call 'naturalistic modes of inquiry', which they categorize as class-room centred and which include qualitative data and faculty-designed course-embedded instruments rather than standardized achievement tests. Such inquiry precludes the use of experimental designs which include pre- and post-testing and comparison groups. Gainen and Locatelli quoted with approval the Brigham Young University study into the AECC-funded junior year core programme which concluded that because 'the technical competencies in the new program are somewhat different from those in the traditional program, there is no way to obtain a comparable control group' (BYU, Vol. 1, 1992, p. 61, cited in Gainen and Locatelli, 1995, p. 61). We concur with this conclusion.

According to Gainen and Locatelli (1995, p. 5), the value of assessment procedures is 'not to provide numerical indicators of success or failure, nor to design the definitive curricular experiment'. Gainen and Locatelli (1995, p. 5), quoting Wolff, advocate the creation of 'a culture of evidence' to enhance interpretation of results. Their approach assumes rapid response by educators in terms of instruction and curriculum revision to information gathered from evaluation procedures. This is the approach adopted. In the discussion of the assessment of the tutorial programme of the first-year accounting course presented here, the framework has been adapted from Gainen and Locatelli. The Gainen and Locatelli (1995, p. 4) model links as inputs intended learning outcomes interacting with student characteristics and the educational environment to produce actual learning outcomes and client satisfaction. Table 11.2 associates this model with the evaluation methods adopted.

Table 11.2 Relationship between assessment framework, items assessed and methodology adopted for assessment purposes

ASSESSMENT FRAMEWORK (taken from Gainen & Locatelli, 1995:4)	ITEMS ASSESSED	EVALUATION METHODOLOGY USED
INPUTS		
intended learning outcome	development of written, oral, intellectual and interpersonal skills, approach to learning, attitude to program: student satisfaction & perception of faculty	a combination of quantitative and qualitative feedback
student characteristics	ability on entry	• TER
educational environment	explicit development of written, oral, intellectual and interpersonal skills and a capacity for lifelong learning in a small-group teaching environment	• quantitative student surveys, • qualitative student survey (1994 only) • student focus groups (1994 only) • student interviews (1994 only) • feedback from faculty
OUTCOMES		
actual learning outcomes	assignments and examinations	• anecdotal evidence from portfolio of assignments and examinations
client satisfaction	student perceptions of course faculty perceptions of effectiveness	• student surveys • feedback from faculty

As indicated in Table 11.2, the intended learning outcomes relate to the pedagogical objectives discussed earlier. No single instrument was used to measure their achievement; rather their achievement was inferred from analysis of the evaluation procedures described below.

11.5   Assessment of curriculum redesign

11.5.1   Qualitative data, 1994: student response

In 1994, the first full-year of implementation of the project, various qualitative methodologies were used to gain a deeper understanding of student responses to the programme and to elicit detailed suggestions as to how it could be improved. These included focus groups, individual interviews conducted by an independent interviewer and a qualitative survey at the end of second semester.

Focus groups in first and second semesters and individual interviews during second semester yielded detailed information on the functioning of teams, the reaction of students to teaching innovations, the methods of learning employed, opinions on workload and teaching. Despite inducements, both monetary and culinary, it proved difficult to persuade a representative sample of students to participate in focus groups and individual interviews. Nevertheless, the data from these sources was valuable. Ten students attended a focus group in the middle of 1994, eleven at the end of 1994. Fifteen students attended interviews in the second semester 1994. The poor response explains the rationale behind conducting a qualitative survey at the end of second semester 1994.

Feedback from focus groups and interviews on the development of writing skills indicated that, although summary work and team writing tasks had been helpful, improvements could be made in the composition of the requirements of the case studies in order to make it easier to distribute tasks within the team, that more assistance was needed in the area of writing for examinations and in structuring texts, and that plagiarism was a very real issue for first-year students of a new subject. Case studies were considered of high interest and an extremely good tool for understanding accounting concepts and issues, but were criticized as being, in some cases, too complex and time-consuming. (Faculty also gave feedback indicating that more careful staging of the level of complexity of case studies was required.) Comments were made about the perceived lack of balance between the development of oral and written skills, constructive suggestions made on how group conferencing of writing tasks could be facilitated, with more time to be spent on fewer tasks and more support for the development of a positive group dynamic. Qualitative feedback from the final questionnaire echoed these concerns.

Six questions designed to yield both quantitative and qualitative data about the tutorial programme were attached to a more general student survey at the end of second semester 1994.[3] Students were required to respond on a 5-point Likert scale to questions about the effectiveness of each of the programme's six specified objectives. Specifically, these were the development of: (1) the understanding of content, (2) reading, (3) writing, (4) oral communication, (5) teamwork and (6) peer- and self-assessment skills. Students were then asked to give *reasons* for their rating and suggestions for any changes, yielding the qualitative feedback. In order to focus students' responses, and as a basis for qualitative comments, the respondents were prompted about the strategies employed to facilitate their acquisition of the desired skills. For example, under a heading 'Development of writing skills' the question 'How effective has the tutorial program been for you in achieving this objective?', was accompanied by the reminders as to how the programme had attempted to develop writing skills. Overall, the results indicated that most students found the programme was effective in achieving its objectives, with responses clustering above the middle range (3) on the scale. Fifty per cent or more of students valued the programme's development of their content understanding, interpersonal skills, and written and oral communication skills as very or quite effective.

Despite its methodological flaw[4] (potentially leading the respondent), this survey yielded valuable qualitative data. Students were asked to explain the reasons behind their ratings on the achievement of objectives, and for suggestions of how to better achieve programme objectives. These responses provided a rich source of input to course revisions which took place prior to 1995. Reasons given for high ratings included: the effectiveness of the support offered in the development of reading and writing skills: for example, the helpfulness of reading guides, model summaries and model answers, and the usefulness of analysing those model answers. Other common themes were the value of individual oral presentations, and the effective learning situation provided by a team which worked well. Some examples of reasons for low ratings were, in the case of the development of reading skills, the difficulty of some tutorial readings; in the case of the development of oral communication skills, the need for more practice in both discussion and formal oral presentations; and in the case of the development of interpersonal skills through teams, the uneven distribution of tasks within groups.

Valuable suggestions were made by students to improve the course and their performance in many areas. The study groups/teams were a particular focus, as they were seen as a vital component in the assessment process and, where they worked effectively, as a source of support and collaborative learning. Members of ineffective teams made numerous suggestions about how to improve team effectiveness. These covered size and formation, ways of evaluating the contribution of individuals to group efforts, and the nature of group assignments. Peer assessment was unpopular with students, mainly because they found critical evaluation of their peers problematic and destructive of a positive group/tutorial environment. Students requested that more time be allocated to faculty to respond to both content and presentation of student material in tutorials, because they felt ill-equipped to evaluate their peers in terms of their grasp of subject matter. In the areas of tutorial readings and the understanding of content, students tended to suggest that short-cuts be provided in the form of summaries, prioritizing of content and solutions to exercises.

The qualitative feedback suggested that students are particularly sensitive to (1) the commitment of faculty, (2) the time devoted in class to clarification of content, (3) peer assessment requiring negative comment about peers and judgment about the efficacy of content, (4) the time devoted to the development of writing, (5) the amount of team work, including problems of arranging meetings outside class time and how to cope with freeriders, (6) the difficulty and complexity of case studies and (7) heavy workload.

11.5.2 Qualitative data, 1994: faculty response

The innovations made a number of demands on faculty which required them to reflect on their role and level of teaching skill. Not only did they need to develop the traditional teaching role of information delivery and clarification of content, but also to become discussion facilitators. The programme also made demands in areas which even experienced faculty found challenging.[5] The complex skills and roles required of faculty by the programme and the relative inexperience of the majority of faculty involved resulted in the establishment of a system of faculty support.[6]

Faculty also submitted written feedback on each tutorial. Essentially, faculty feedback reinforced comments made by students reported above. These informal reports were collated and used as a basis for recommendations for modification of individual tutorials in 1995. From written faculty feedback, comments at staff meetings and reports from students it became obvious that one member of faculty had consistently negatively questioned, in class, the objectives of the programme and its teaching methods.

11.5.3   Responding to qualitative assessment feedback: revisions in 1995

Many of the suggestions made by students and faculty guided the revision of the 1994 tutorial programme. Some of the suggestions for improvement put forward by students were unable to be incorporated into the programme in 1995 due to constraints of time and large student numbers; for example, the suggestion of two individual oral presentations per student per semester, and the suggestion that teams meet in course time. Suggestions relating to 'short-cuts' were rejected because they conflicted with desired learning outcomes.

11.6   Demographics and methodology: quantitative assessment, 1994–7

11.6.1   Student characteristics on entry

The majority of students completing the first-year accounting course are enrolled in a Bachelor of Commerce (B.Com) degree and come to the course straight from high school. The majority have not studied any aspect of accounting prior to entry. For all B. Com students the course is compulsory. Generally, 70 per cent of all those students who pass the first-year course elect to major in accounting. The majority of entering students are admitted on the basis of their performance in the NSW Higher School Certificate (HSC) examination which is marked and scaled to produce a Tertiary Entrance Rank (TER) for each student. The TER is a number between 0 and 100 which indicates each student's place in the State relative to all HSC candidates.[7]

11.6.2   Educational environment

Each week there are two lectures to introduce new material delivered to over 250 students at a time, one workshop containing about 70 students and a self-taught computer component to reinforce technical competence. To help students grasp content, interactive lecture notes are prepared to reduce the amount of student note-taking and increase the time spent by the lecturer explaining the material and answering questions. The purpose of the weekly tutorial is to enable consideration and discussion of underlying principles and the application of theory to practice. It is the site in which the development of communication, intellectual and interpersonal skills; and the capacity for lifelong learning takes place. Tutorials contain a maximum of 20 students. It is in the tutorial programme that the curriculum redesign took place. First-year accounting is a two-semester course; this chapter concentrates on reporting the evaluation of the changes introduced into the developmental first semester. In reality though, both semesters are devoted to the development of the generic skills. Numbers of students sitting for examinations at the end of first semester,[8] were: 1994 – 459; 1995 – 486; 1996 – 769; and 1997 – 820.

Faculty teaching the course comprised the course co-ordinator and part-time and casual staff with varying amounts of teaching experience. In 1994 and 1995 faculty were relatively stable and, for the most part, had taught the course both before and after the introduction of the innovations. In 1996, however, there was a large turnover of faculty, the majority of whom were newly graduated and concurrently completing a second undergraduate degree. Declining resources combined with the end of active involvement in the course by the educational experts on the project team (see note 1) meant that from 1996 faculty did not receive the level of training they had been given previously. From both student and staff feedback it was evident that one faculty member in 1994 and two in 1996 felt uncomfortable teaching the course and, in at least one case, actively promoted, in their own classes, their opposition to the teaching strategies adopted.

11.6.3   Quantitative surveys, 1994–97: methodology

A quantitative survey was completed by students at the end of the developmental first semester in 1994, 1995, 1996 and 1997. Direct comparison between the 1994 survey and those conducted thereafter was impossible as 1994 responses were measured on a 4-point scale (Always true for me (4); True for me (3); Sometimes true for me (2); and Not true for me (1)), but those for subsequent years offered respondents five possible choices (All of the time (5); Most of the time (4); Half the time (3); Little of the time (2) and None of the time (1)). Comparison between years could thus only be achieved via the adoption of several assumptions:

1. that identically phrased questions common to all three years were measuring the same underlying variable;

2. that these variables are continuous in nature, and that a discrete response (1, 2, 3 or 4) is an approximation of where the student's attitude falls on this continuum;

3. that a response of (1), (2), (3) or (4) (on a four point scale) places a student in either the first, second, third or fourth quartile on the variable's continuum. Similarly, the five-point alternative places the respondent in the appropriate quintile.

4. that responses are uniformly distributed within a given quartile.

Under these assumptions, the four-point responses of 1994 were rescaled to allow comparisons with subsequent years. The rescaling algorithm took 80 per cent of those responding (1) on the four-point scale and assigned them (1) on the five-point regime; while the remaining 20 per cent were assigned (2). Sixty percent of those responding (2) on the four-point scale were assigned (2) on the five-point regime and combined with the 20 per cent of the initial (1)s who were scaled to (2). As our interest lies only in the total prportion of (4) and (5) responses, the remainder of the rescaling algorithm is moot.

Having rescaled the 1994 data to allow comparisons to be made, the question arises as to how student attitude is best described or measured across the four years. Three alternative approaches were considered: a comparison of variances on any given question, a comparison of the mean response for each question, and a comparison of the proportion of students responding (4) or (5) to each question. Comparing the variation in responses may be a reasonable measure of outcomes, in that one would expect that as outcomes improved so would student satisfaction, and convergence in opinion should be observed. Changes in the mean response would also indicate any shift in student satisfaction in a given dimension. These two approaches, however, were rejected in favour of the third, as it was felt that comparing variances was perhaps an insufficiently concise measure of student attitudes, and the mean response was more sensitive to the choice of rescaling regime.'

Additionally, the assignment of a numerical indicator to a qualitative variable is ultimately arbitrary, that is, the five possible responses could have been identified as (A) through (E), or (11) through (15), leaving the interpretation of the mean response open to question. Hence, we focus on the proportion of 'reasonably satisfied customers' as measured by a 4 or 5 (rescaled where appropriate) response on the Likert scale on each question from 1994 to 1997.

11.7 Results

11.7.1 First semester student survey results: 1994–7

The purpose of the student surveys conducted at the end of first semester in 1994, 1995, 1996 and 1997 was to determine students' perceptions of the development of their written, oral, intellectual and interpersonal skills, their attitudes towards learning, and towards the course in general. Differences in questions between 1994 and 1995/96/97 in the first semester survey reflect the development of our interest in feedback as the project continued. As noted earlier, our commitment was to make explicit our expectations in all areas of concern prior to requiring summative assessment. Thus, the first semester course was designed as the vehicle to demonstrate what we wanted and to allow students to practice the development of their skills for purposes of (largely) formative assessment prior to facing summative (graded) assessment largely unprompted in the second semester. In the second semester we gave students much less help in tackling tasks, instead relying on them to take more responsibility for their own learning. This explains our interest in student perceptions at the end of the developmental first semester each year.

The rationale for including questions about students' approaches to learning is to try to determine our success in fostering the AECC's skills inventory and lifelong learning skills, and to gain some insight into our success in developing teaching materials which might stimulate deeper learning. Surface approaches to learning tend to be associated with assessment methods emphasizing recall or the application of trivial procedural knowledge, assessment methods that create anxiety, cynical or conflicting messages about rewards, an excessive amount of material in the curriculum, poor or absent feedback on progress, lack of independence in studying, lack of interest in and background knowledge of the subject matter and previous experiences of educational settings that encourage these approaches (Ramsden, 1992, 81).

Student attitudes towards the first semester course were measured by a survey designed in conjunction with the University's Centre for Teaching and Learning. A casual impression is that students were, by and large, more satisfied with the first semester course in 1995 than in 1994, and slightly more dissatisfied in 1996 than they had been in the previous year, but 1997 saw a rebound to the 1995 levels. A more rigorous statistical analyses of the survey results was attempted to allow comparisons of common questions across the four years. The questions could be grouped broadly into six categories, each associated with a key learning objective, student approaches to learning, or to ascertain general attitudes towards the programme.

Initially, for each common question, we tested the hypothesis:

$$H_0: \pi_{95} = \pi_{94} \qquad \text{vs.} \qquad H_1: \pi_{95} > \pi_{94}$$

where π is the proportion of responses that are either (4) or (5) in the indicated year. Rejection of H_0 suggests that students have positively shifted their attitudes towards the

Students' perceptions of the development of written, oral, intellectual skills; and their general attitudes towards the program: first Semester, 1994, 1995, 1996, 1997.

Question	% of Responses[1]					
	1994	1995	1996	1997	Chi-Sq[2]	Sens[3]
	4-5	4-5	4-5	4-5	95-97	Avg
Written communication skills						
The standard of written communication expected in the tutorial program is clear	35.3	54.7	55.7	52.8	0.46	0.91
Z - STATS		6.39	7.12	6.24		
My summarising skills have been developed through the tutorial program	n/a	21.4	20.4	21.0	0.11	-
Z - STATS		n/a	n/a	n/a		
The tutorial program has helped me improve my written communication skills	15.6	27.5	25.3	29.8	2.10	1.08
Z - STATS		4.63	4.02	6.58		
The reading guides helped me understand unfamiliar material	n/a	41.4	39.8	44.7	1.68	-
Z - STATS		n/a	n/a	n/a		
The model answers helped me develop my writing skills	n/a	45.8	46.9	46.3	0.06	-
Z - STATS		n/a	n/a	n/a		
Oral communication skills						
The standard of oral communication expected in the tutorial program is clear	40.9	66.2	66.1	62.5	0.74	1.02
Z - STATS		8.36	8.87	7.47		
I was encouraged to participate in tutorial discussions	47.5	65.5	58.3	55.4	3.78	0.77
Z - STATS		5.97	3.76	2.67		
The tutorial program has helped me improve my oral presentation skills	26.8	43.5	43.0	43.8	0.04	0.95
Z - STATS		5.67	5.78	6.52		
My level of confidence in participating in tutorial discussions has increased	38.1	52.5	47.2	49.1	1.21	0.75
Z - STATS		4.68	3.15	3.83		
The tutorial program has developed my discussion skills	26.6	47.4	42.6	49.9	3.34	1.13
Z - STATS		6.99	5.71	8.87		
Intellectual Skills						
The case studies helped me learn to apply knowledge in real world settings	n/a	60.7	58.3	60.3	0.28	-
Z - STATS		n/a	n/a	n/a		
The tutorial program has enabled me to apply the knowledge I have learned in the rest of the course	n/a	46.8	35.4	49.3	13.99	-
Z - STATS		n/a	n/a	n/a		
The tutorial program has developed my thinking skills	28.9	49.0	42.3	52.8	0.46	1.15
Z - STATS		8.39	9.20	8.83		
The case studies helped me to relate the course material to the real world	40.1	53.4	53.4	57.7	1.17	0.82
Z - STATS		4.29	4.57	6.01		
The tutorial program has improved my understanding of concepts and principles in this subject	28.7	53.7	52.0	53.7	0.19	1.07
Z - STATS		8.20	8.09	9.36		

Table 11.3

Question	% of Responses[1]					
	1994	1995	1996	1997	Chi-Sq[2]	Sens[3]
	4-5	4-5	4-5	4-5	95-97	Avg
Interpersonal skills						
Team projects helped me to develop team skills	n/a	59.6	55.3	68.4	8.32	-
Z - STATS		n/a	n/a	n/a		
Working in a team helped my learning	n/a	55.3	51.3	54.5	0.83	-
Z - STATS		n/a	n/a	n/a		
My team worked effectively	n/a	72.6	65.3	71.4	2.20	-
Z - STATS		n/a	n/a	n/a		
Student approaches to learning						
The tutorial program covers too much material4	34.2	32.5	27.7	24.6	4.90	0.22
Z - STATS		-0.58	-2.48	-3.43		
I generally put a lot of effort into trying to understand things with initially seem difficult	43.0	53.2	45.6	57.2	7.70	0.69
Z - STATS		3.36	0.91	4.90		
The tutorial readings were too difficult4	26.4	16.2	13.9	16.0	1.11	0.02
Z - STATS		-4.22	-5.80	-4.05		
The volume of work means that you can't comprehend it all4	32.1	22.7	26.9	25.3	1.49	-0.02
Z - STATS		-8.67	-7.64	-7.54		
The best way for me to understand technical terms is to memorise textbook definitions4	26.4	28.6	28.7	31.8	1.18	0.57
Z - STATS		0.81	0.90	2.10		
I usually set out to understand thoroughly the meaning of what I am asked to read	36.2	45.3	49.4	44.0	1.92	0.73
Z - STATS		3.03	4.63	2.77		
I find I have to concentrate on memorising a good deal of what we have to learn4	30.3	33.2	35.4	34.4	0.30	0.58
Z - STATS		1.00	1.83	1.48		

Table 11.3

Question	% of Responses[1]					
	1994	1995	1996	1997	Chi-Sq[2]	Sens[3]
	4-5	4-5	4-5	4-5	95-97	Avg
General attitudes towards the tutorial program						
The objectives of the tutorial program are clear	35.4	71.4	71.1	71.4	0.00	1.30
Z - STATS		12.03	12.84	12.88		
In this program I got a lot of help and advice on studying the tutorial material	15.4	28.7	25.8	29.4	1.45	1.02
Z - STATS		5.12	4.30	6.58		
As a result of the tutorial program, I feel confident about tackling new material	15.9	35.6	28.5	35.9	5.61	1.28
Z - STATS		7.05	4.97	9.00		
The teaching staff gave helpful feedback on how I was going	17.5	40.6	39.0	42.0	0.64	1.63
Z - STATS		8.08	7.90	10.92		
My tutor is well prepared for each tutorial	68.9	83.0	83.6	81.6	0.14	0.85
Z - STATS		5.51	6.31	4.63		
The tutorial program is not related to the rest of the course 4	n/a	19.1	22.0	16.0	5.38	-
Z - STATS		n/a	n/a	n/a		
I have learned a lot in this subject	n/a	42.3	44.2	50.2	3.57	-
Z - STATS		n/a	n/a	n/a		
The assessment criteria for the case study assignments were clear	n/a	57.1	58.3	52.6	1.78	-
Z - STATS		n/a	n/a	n/a		
Summary performance						
All things considered, how would you rate this tutorial program5	49.2	67.6	65.6	62.6	0.89	-
		5.84	5.51	4.35		
Sample size	200	346	581	601		
Course enrolment	459	486	769	820		
% responding	43.6	71.2	75.6	70.7		

1. **Based on a 5 point Likert scale where 5 indicated "true all of the time", 3 "true half of the time" and 1 "not true for me".**
2. **The Chi-Square statistic measures the homogeneity, or stability, of the distribution across the 1995 to 1997 period. A value greater than 5.99 shows a significant difference at the 5% level.**
3. **The average threshold for which the proportion of 1994 "3's" rescaled to "4's" leads to the loss of statistical significance. A value of 1.0 (or greater) shows the results is absolutely robust to the rescaling assumption.**
4. **Due to the nature of these questions, a high negative response was expected**
5. **Measured on a 7 point Likert scale; percentage responding 5, 6 or 7 reported.**
6. **Z statistic calculated to test H_0: Mean difference = 0 vs H, - Mean Difference > 0. A Z value > 2.33 indicates a statistically significant improvement at the 1% level.**

Table 11.3

course. (Several questions are phrased such that a (4) or (5) response is an undesirable outcome, hence for those questions we test the lower-tail alternative, that is, the proportion of 'dissatisfied customers' has decreased from 1994 to 1995.) The statistical results overwhelmingly indicate a substantial improvement in student satisfaction in the first semester between 1994 and 1995, as H_0 was rejected in 20 out of 23 tests, with the remaining three showing no change. That is, for 87 per cent of those questions common to the 1994 and 1995 surveys, a statistically significant (at the 5 per cent level) favourable change was observed.

To determine if such shifts were transient phenomena, we then compared 1994 to 1996 and to 1997 by testing

$$H_0: \pi_{96} = \pi_{94} \qquad \text{vs.} \qquad H_1: \pi_{96} > \pi_{94}$$

and

$$H_0: \pi_{97} = \pi_{94} \qquad \text{vs.} \qquad H_1: \pi_{97} > \pi_{94}$$

We found significant evidence of a favourable change in 21 of 23 (91%) tests comparing 1994 to 1996, and 22 of 23 (96%) in the 1994 to 1997 comparison.

The 95/96/97 period was then examined for stability via a chi square test where the null hypothesis is

$$H_0: \pi_{95} = \pi_{96} = \pi_{97} \qquad \text{vs.} \qquad H_1: \text{At least one proportion is different}$$

If the course interventions of 1995 increased the proportion(s) of satisfied customers when compared to 1994, we would expect those proportions to remain relatively stable over subsequent years, hence acceptance of H_0 augers for the success of the interventions. In the 23 questions common across the four years, H_0 was accepted in 22 instances (96%), and in 9 of the 11 remaining questions (82%).

The results are summarized on Table 11.4 which reports for each question the observed values of the Z test statistics comparing 1994 to 1995, 1994 to 1996, 1994 to 1997 and the chi square statistic for stability. An observed Z greater than 2.33 indicates the difference in proportions is statistically significant at the 1 per cent level (H_0 is rejected), i.e. a larger proportion of (4) and (5) responses were observed in the latter years than in 1994. (For those questions where (4) or (5) is an undesirable outcome, an observed Z less than -2.33 indicates a favourable change, that is, the proportion responding (4) or (5) has decreased.) A chi square value greater than 5.99 would lead to the rejection of the null hypothesis of stability across 1995/96/97 at the 5 per cent level.

Table 11.4 indicates that in response to the 23 questions common to the 1994 and 1995 surveys, a favourable change (statistically significant at the 5 per cent level) was observed in 20, and no significant change was observed in the remaining three. That is, students reported more favourably, and without reservation, about the development of their written and oral communication skills, intellectual skills and their general attitudes towards the tutorial programme. Students' perceptions of the development of their interpersonal skills through teamwork were not surveyed in 1994. It should be noted that all six hypothesis tests in which no significant change occurred (comparing the subsequent years to 1994) relate to student attitudes towards learning, survey opinion on pre-existing attitudes among students towards academic endeavour (e.g., 'I usually set out to understand thoroughly the meaning of what I am asked to read') and as such may be beyond the scope of the course

Comparison of responses to common questions: first semester 1994, 1995, 1996, 1997*

	94 - 95	94 - 96	94-97
Written communication skills			
Common questions	2	2	2
Numbers of favourable change	2	2	2
Numbers of unfavourable change	0	0	0
Number of no change	0	0	0
Oral communication skills			
Common questions	5	5	5
Numbers of favourable change	5	5	5
Numbers of unfavourable change	0	0	0
Number of no change	0	0	0
Intellectual Skills			
Common questions	3	3	3
Numbers of favourable change	3	3	3
Numbers of unfavourable change	0	0	0
Number of no change			
Student approaches to learning			
Common questions	7	7	7
Numbers of favourable change	4	5	6
Numbers of unfavourable change	0	0	0
Number of no change	3	2	1
General attitudes towards the tutorial program			
Common questions	5	5	5
Numbers of favourable change	5	5	5
Numbers of unfavourable change	0	0	0
Number of no change	0	0	0
Summary performance			
Common questions	1	1	1
Numbers of favourable change	1	1	1
Numbers of unfavourable change	0	0	0
Number of no change	0	0	0
Totals			
Common questions	23	23	23
Numbers of favourable change	20	21	22
Numbers of unfavourable change	0	0	0
Number of no change	0	0	0

Note "favourable", "unfavourable" and "no change" reflect positive, negative or neutral changes in respones at the 5% level of significance.

* There were no questions relating to the development of interpersonal skills in 1994, hence, these skills are not featured on this table

Table 11.4

interventions (Ramsden, 1992), i.e. no changes in response for these questions could be anticipated *a priori*. However, for 15 tests relating to student approaches to learning we do note a favourable change. This suggests positive movement towards a deeper approach to learning for some students which may have been stimulated by teaching materials and assessment tasks which required critical thinking and analysis.

We note that of the six tests for which favourable change is not found, five are associated with 'negative' questions for which a (1) or (2) response is desired. A common problem encountered in surveys is bias introduced by having the majority of questions written such that one type of response is favourable, interspersed with questions where the opposite is favourable. Some respondents give answers reflexively, without giving due consideration to the phrasing of the question. Given the otherwise overwhelming evidence suggesting that the changes in course design were highly successful, it is possible that we fail to obtain a significant improvement on these few questions because of this bias.

As perhaps the single best measure of satisfaction, students were asked 'All things considered how would you rate this tutorial program?' In 1995 and subsequent years there was a significant positive change, as measured by responses 5, 6, and 7 on a seven-point Likert scale. We conclude that the statistical results support the claim that the revisions to curriculum design introduced in 1995 were successful in improving student satisfaction with the first semester course, and that students perceived that they had developed the skills fostered in the programme.

11.7.2 Robustness of results

The results obtained from the first semester surveys are obviously reliant on the assumptions made as to the underlying distribution of 1994 results required for rescaling to a five-point response. Defining success as an increase in the proportion of (4) or (5) responses has a decided advantage over measuring success by the mean response where rescaling is required, in that two fewer assumptions are required. It is quite sensible to regard those who responded (4) on a four-point scale as responding either (4) or (5) given a five-point option. Similarly, it is only reasonable to assume those who answered (1) or (2) on a four-point basis would not have given a (4) or (5) reply under the five-point alternative. Thus, our results are sensitive only to the choice of the proportion of (3) responses who would have opted for (4), given the five-point opportunity. As outlined above, our results are based on an assumption of uniformly distributed responses in each class, which rescales 60 per cent of the 1994 (3)s to (4), leaving 40 per cent remaining as (3)s.

The initial results were then checked for their robustness to changes in this assumption. The proportion of 60 per cent was altered until the statistically significant difference disappeared. (That is, we would increase the proportion of 1994 (3)s rescaled to (4)s until the difference between 1994 and the comparison year (1995, 1996 or 1997) became statistically negligible.) The average threshold for each question is reported in Table 11.5, and range from 69 per cent to 163 per cent, with a mean threshold of 101 per cent. Note that a threshold of 100 per cent or more requires the allocation of (2)s on the four-point scale to (4)s on the five-point in order to eliminate statistical significance, clearly an implausible proposition. Hence, we conclude that our results are robust to any reasonable change to the underlying rescaling mechanism.

Students' perceptions of the change in the development of selected skills as a result of the first semester tutorial program: 1997

Question	Mean[1] Difference	Z - Stat[2]
Rate your written communication skills at the beginning of this year Indicate your level of written communication skills now	0.66	20.244
Rate your critical thinking skills at the beginning of this year Indicate your level of critical thinking now	0.80	21.059
Rate your capacity to work independently at the beginning of this year Rate your capacity to work independently now	0.57	14.43
Rate your interest in the subject at the beginning of this year Rate your interest now	0.62	10.244
Rate your oral communication skills at the beginning of this year Indicate the level if your oral communication skills now	0.74	21.945
Rate your team skills at the beginning of this year Indicate your level of team skills now	0.90	21.838
Rate your level of confidence at participating in tutorial discussions at the beginning of this year Indicate your level of confidence now	1.00	21.776

1   Based on a 5 point Likert scale where 5 indicated "very good", 3 "satisfactory" and 1 "very poor"

2   Z statistic calculated to test H_o: Mean difference = 0 vs H, - Mean Difference > 0.
      A Z value > 2.33 indicates a statistically significant improvement at the 1% level.

Table 11.5

11.8   Interpretation of results

In 1997 we attempted to gather additional evidence from students regarding their perceptions of the effect the programme actually had on the development of their skills. The 1997 survey was expanded to include the following general introduction:

One of the aims of the Tutorial Program in Accounting 1A is to assist students to develop a range of professional skills related to Accounting.

>We are interested in how you feel your skills have developed over the semester.
>   Please complete this questionnaire by first indicating with a cross (X) your level of skills at the beginning of the year, and then marking with a circle (O) your level of skills now:

Table 11.5 summarizes the results to seven general questions about the development of broad skills and their interest in the subject.

Table 11.5 indicates that, in general, students perceived their skills to have improved as a result of the tutorial programme. We can conclude that the shift in perceived improvement in the measured dimensions has been statistically significant at the 1 per cent level.

Using Gianen and Locatelli's assessment framework (see Table 11.1) we considered factors which may have impinged on results:

11.8.1   Student characteristics on entry

The results obtained overwhelmingly suggest improved student satisfaction in 1995, 1996 and 1997 in the revised course. However, as these tests do not identify precisely the cause of such improvement, further analysis was undertaken to control for differences across the four years in academic qualification as measured by the student's TER. Two objectives motivated such analyses:

1. Could the apparent improvement in student satisfaction observed between 1994 and 1995 be attributable to factors other than course changes; specifically, were students entering in 1995 significantly different in some measurable ways than those who entered in 1994?

2. To the extent that students were somewhat less satisfied in 1996 than they were in 1995 (although not nearly on the level of 1994 respondents), could this difference be reasonably attributed to the lowered admissions standard of the current year?

The summary statistics reported in Table 11.6 show the distribution TERs to be broadly comparable between 1994 and 1995 entrants, although the mean TER is significantly lower (at 5%) in 1995 than 1994. However, the distribution of TERs shifts significantly lower in 1996 and 1997 and becomes more variable compared to previous years. Our results suggest that the TER is not necessarily a good predictor of perceived learning or overall satisfaction with courses.

11.8.2   Educational environment

In 1996 there were several differences in the educational environment. Student numbers increased dramatically without a corresponding increase in resources to support quality teaching and learning. In 1997 resource levels improved slightly. The increase in student numbers in 1996 which caused pressures on both faculty and students probably contributed

Descriptive Statistics: TER Rankings, BEc/BCom 1994 - 1997

	1994	1995	1996	1997
Minimum	91	90	82	84
Maximum	99	99	99	98
Mean	93.74	92.76	87.45	88.74
Median	93.5	92	86.5	88
First Quartile	92	91	84	86
Third Quartile	96	95	90	91
Interquartile range	4	4	6	5
Range	8	9	17	14
Standard Deviation	2.24	2.47	4.24	3.88

Table 11.6

to the modest decline in satisfaction in some dimensions in 1996. The 1997 results confirm this observation. By 1997 faculty had developed strategies to deal with increased numbers.

While numbers in tutorial classes remained at approximately 1995 levels, the need to employ more faculty meant appointing a larger proportion than usual of people who had just completed their undergraduate commerce degree and who had no teaching experience. The appointment of relatively inexperienced faculty was compounded by a large turnover of faculty, with many of our experienced teachers moving on. Increased numbers of casual staff also made communication between staff more difficult than it had been previously. Resourcing issues negatively affected teaching through diminished time spent on training faculty, an inability in 1996 to pay faculty employed on a casual basis to attend the weekly meeting with a corresponding reluctance of some to attend regularly. The sensitivity of students to the commitment and experience of faculty has been alluded to earlier. Analysis of weekly feedback sheets from faculty and observation at the weekly faculty meetings combined with anecdotal evidence from students apparently affirmed by survey results suggests a growing disenchantment on the part of at least two members of faculty in 1996. A similar problem had occurred in 1994. This problem did not reoccur in 1997.

Dwindling resources also made it impossible to keep up the relationship developed over the previous two years with educational experts from the University's Learning Assistance Centre (LAC) (see note 1 below). Their ongoing commitment to the project had resulted in the development of remedial programmes exclusively targeting the first-year accounting students in need of supplementary oral and written communication development, in input relating to the development of teaching materials and production of the students' and faculty manuals. The LAC had also been primarily responsible for staff training in 1994 and 1995 and had attended weekly faculty meetings. Withdrawal of active involvement of the three-member LAC team meant that the responsibility for the project fell solely onto the shoulders of the subject expert. Although it was always intended that LAC withdraw its involvement, their support was missed. While the overall philosophy behind the curriculum revision remained unchanged, some teaching materials have to be revised each year to ensure that students (and faculty) do not get complacent. As the course has progressed it has became obvious that there were problems with the staging and complexity of case studies; this too had been a problem in 1994.

11.8.3   Actual learning outcomes

Each year a sample of assignments are photocopied prior to return to students. This portfolio suggests that the standard achieved by the majority of students is very high. In 1995 faculty was very pleased by the general standard of achievement exhibited in the examinations at the end of each semester. We feel that there was some backsliding in 1996. Students in 1997 seem to have produced a high standard in written and oral presentations. Overall, faculty have informally reported discerning positive change in written and oral communication skills, have praised the levels of discussion in class and the effort put into assessed assignments. They have also noted in students an increased interest in the business world and in the relationship between course content and what is reported in financial statements. In both 1995 and 1996 at the end of second semester students reported having gained a good understanding of how to interpret financial statements, and having developed skills needed by professional accountants.

11.8.4   Client satisfaction

As indicated, we believe that our survey results indicate a relatively high level of student satisfaction with the tutorial programme and indications that it has achieved its learning objectives. If we consider faculty teaching our students in later years as 'clients' of the course, we can also report that we have received favourable comments about the development of the desired skills observed as our students pass though other courses.

11.9   General conclusion

It appears from the evidence presented that it is possible, even in settings with large student numbers, to develop teaching strategies and materials to help students learn communication, intellectual and interpersonal skills. Encouraging the development of the capacity for lifelong learning through positively altering students' approaches to learning appears, not unexpectedly, more problematic. Our experience suggests that the gathering of a 'culture of evidence' (Gainen and Locatelli, quoting Wolff, 1995, p. 5) from both qualitative and quantitative sources is important, but in terms of revisions to curricula, qualitative evidence may be more valuable in assisting faculty to assess and fine tune innovation relating to skills development. It is also clear in retrospect, that planning *how* to assess innovation in teaching is as important as developing and implementing the innovation itself and the two should be planned in conjunction (Gainen and Locatelli, 1995).

In terms of further research, it would be interesting to correlate individual students' responses to survey questions to their own assessment of their skills on entry and actual outcomes in terms of assessment. This has not been possible, as for ethical reasons, all surveys have been anonymous.

Notes

1. The project team consisted of a subject expert (the course coordinator) and three educational experts from the University's Learning Assistance Centre (LAC), whose brief is to help students learn.

2. There are several practical and ethical problems in following Street's dictum to conduct laboratory research. While laboratory experiments offer the possibility of a controlled environment and sophisticated statistical analysis of results, the random assignment of experimental and control groups is often unrealistic in a live teaching context. Street acknowledges the potential ethical and design problems (Street, 1995, p.183). What she fails to consider is the methodological problems involved in the design of an experiment to test a range of major innovations introduced simultaneously as happened in the case reported here. Ethical issues resulting from teaching students differently could also raise potential problems for researchers.

3. The survey conducted at the end of second semester 1994 asked questions about other areas of the course, such as the workshops, lectures and computer components. There were some additional questions relating to the tutorial programme, but these have been omitted as they were not repeated subsequent years; may be difficult to interpret and do not add to comparative data.

4. We have not presented details of these results nor analysed them statistically because of the potential methodological weakness of the survey design.

5. Beginning in the first semester, the focus on discussion skills requires skills of classroom management and of the facilitation of group-work in order to foster a positive classroom dynamic as a preliminary to the formation of project teams. Later, in their role as team monitors, faculty need some detailed knowledge of how group dynamics work in order to act as arbiters and negotiators if required to do so. Faculty also need to develop skills enabling them to make judgments on communicative competence when assessing group and individual oral and written work. Finally, faculty need to familiarize themselves with the links between the different components of the first-year course in order to put the tutorial activities into perspective and ensure that students are fully informed about objectives and rationale. A Tutor's Manual is prepared each semester to help faculty in their role. It contains not only solutions to problems, but suggestions about how to facilitate students learning through group role, timing of activities etc.

6. In addition to the Tutor's Manual, there are two main forms of tutor support. First, specific training sessions are held at the beginning of each semester of the course. Faculty are also given practice in putting together a model presentation and in assignment grading. Experienced faculty are teamed with new faculty to discuss strategies for managing ongoing issues such as keeping students informed and motivated, managing peer assessment etc. Feedback on these training sessions indicate that faculty find them practical and helpful in identifying the objectives of the course and in managing the practical issues that can arise, and in providing a forum where expertise and experience is shared. The second form of faculty support is a weekly staff meeting where the tutorial programme is monitored and the faculty's roles discussed.

7. The calculation of the TER has changed over the period, largely due to the addition of new subjects and changes to scaling. In 1995 a major reform meant that, for the first time, the

TER, based on the aggregate of scaled marks in 10 units had to include at least one unit each of English, and one unit from each of two Key Learning Areas (Universities Admission Centre, 1996). Students sitting the HSC in 1995 entered the university in 1996. No research has been undertaken to determine the effect, if any, these reforms have had on the profile of entering students.

8. It is impossible to give exact enrolment numbers at the beginning of the first semester in any year. The figures given in the paper represent the number of students sitting for the final examination at the end of the semester. There is a drop-out rate each semester, but we are unable to determine its magnitude accurately.

9. Further analysis was pursued in these areas, the results of which support our findings. It must be acknowledged that any attempt at rescaling involves some arbitrary assumptions; however, such is the weight of the statistical evidence that any reasonable alternative rescaling scheme would not have led to substantially different conclusions.

11.10 References

Accounting Education Change Commission (1990) *Objectives of Education for Accountants*, Position Statement No. 1, AECC.

American Education Change Commission (AECC) (1992) *The First Course in Accounting*, Position Statement Number Two.

American Institute of Certified Public Accountants (AICPA) (1988) *Education Requirements for Entry into the Accounting Profession*.

Arthur Andersen & Co., Arthur Young, Cooper & Lybrand, Deloitte Haskins & Sells, Ernst & Whinney, Peat Marwick Main & Co., Price Waterhouse and Touche Ross (1989) <??? Perspectives ???> *Perceptives on Education: Capabilities for Success in the Accounting Profession*.

Biggs, J.B. (1987) Process and outcome in essay writing, *Research and Development in Higher Education*, **9**, 114–25.10

Biggs, J.B. (1985) The role of metalearning in study processes, *British Journal of Education Psychology*, **12**, 1, 73–85.

Biggs, J.B. (1987) *Student Approaches to Learning and Studying*, 1987 Australian Council for Educational Research.

Bloom, B. (ed.) (1956) *Taxonomy of Educational Objectives, the Classification of Education Goals – Handbook 1: Cognitive Domain*, David McKay, New York.

Candy, P.C., Crebert, G. and O'Leary, J. (1994) *Developing Lifelong Learners through Undergraduate Education*, National Board of Employment, Education and Training, Australian Government Publishing Service, Canberra.

Cappelletto, G. (1993) *Education Chartered Accountants in Australia*, Institute of Chartered Accountants in Australia.

Collins, A. and Gentner, D. (1980) A framework for a cognitive theory of writing. In L. W. Greg and E. R. Steinberg (eds), *Cognitive Processes in Writing*, Lawrence Erlbaum Associates, Hillsdale, New Jersey, USA: 51–72.

English, L., Webb, C., Bonanno, H. and Jones, J. (1996) *Learning to Write and Writing to Learn: The Development of Writing Skills as a Means and Outcome of Learning in a First-year Accounting Course*, University of Sydney, Department of Accounting 1996 Working Paper Series.

English, L., Bonanno, H., Jones, J. and Webb, C. (1997) Framing the curriculum: teaching communication, intellectual and interpersonal skills in a first-year accounting course. In Chris Rust and Graham Gibbs (eds), *ISL: Improving Student Learning through Course Design*, 120–43.

Francis, M.C., Mulder, T.C. and Stark, J.S. (1995) *Intentional Learning: A Process for Learning to Learn in the Accounting Curriculum*, Accounting Education Change Commission and American Accounting Association, Education Series, No. 12.

Gainen, J. and Locatelli, P. (1995) *Assessment for the New Curriculum: A Guide for Professional Accounting Programs*, Accounting Education Change Commission and American Accounting Association, Accounting Education Series, 11.

Gow, L., Kember, D. and Cooper, B. (1994) The teaching context and approaches to study of accounting students, *Issues in Accounting Education*, 9(1), 118–30.

Gray, R., Bebbington, J. and McPhail, K. (1994) Teaching ethics in accounting and the ethics of accounting teaching: educating for immorality and a possible case for social and environmental accounting education, *Accounting Education*, 3(1), 51–75.

Halliday, M.A.K. (1985) *An Introduction to Functional Grammar*, Edward Arnold, London.

Higher Education Council (1992) *Achieving Quality*, National Board of Employment, Education and Training, Australian Government Publishing Service, Canberra.

Hirsch, M.L. and Collins, J.D. (1988) An integrated approach to communication skills in an accounting curriculum, *Journal of Accounting Education*, 6, 15–31.

Lau, R. and Rans, D.L. (1993) They can add but can they communicate?, *Business Forum*, Summer: 24–6.

Laurillard, D.M. (1984) Learning from problem-solving. In F. Marton *et al.* (eds), *The Experience of Learning*, Edinburgh, Scottish Academic Press.

Ramsden, P. (1992) *Learning to Teach in Higher Education*, Routledge, UK.

McLaren, M.C. (1990) The place of communication skills in the training of accountants in New Zealand, *Accounting and Finance*, May, 83–94.

Morgan, G. J. (1997) Communication skills required by accounting graduates: practitioner and academic perceptions, *Accounting Education*, 6(2), 93–101.

Stocks, K.D., Stoddard, T.D. and Waters, M.L. (1992) Writing in the accounting curriculum: guidelines for professors, *Issues in Accounting Education*, 7(2), 193–204.

Street, D. (1995) Controlling extraneous variables in experimental research: a research note, *Accounting Education*, 4(2), 169–88.

Trigwell, K. and Prosser, M. (1991) Improving the quality of student learning: the influence of learning context and student approaches to learning on learning outcomes, *Higher Education*, 22, 251–66.

Universities Admission Centre (1996) *Guide*, NSW Government Printer.

Webb, C., English, L. and Bonanno, H. (1995) Collaboration in subject design: integration of the teaching and assessment of literacy skills into a first-year accounting course, *Accounting Education*, 4(4), 335–50.

Whitely, S. (1993) The society responds to employer expectations, *CMA Magazine*, July–August:2.

12 An action research evaluation of a first-year 'learning to learn' unit: the role of reflection and metacognition

Katherine Cuthbert
Dept of Humanities and Applied Social Studies, Manchester Metropolitan University

12.1 Overview

This chapter examines the implementation of a first-year, compulsory 'learning to learn' unit within the BA in Applied Social Studies by Independent Study at the Crewe+Alsager Faculty of Manchester Metropolitan University. An action research approach is used to investigate a three-year developmental cycle of implementation, review, modification and further implementation from 1994/95 to 1996/97.

12.2 'Learning to learn' in the higher-education context: important issues

A number of recent features of the higher-education context have led to increased concern about students' capacities to cope effectively with the demands of degree-level work and to manage studying and learning at this level. These include the much increased participation rate and the entry into higher education of students with a wider range of abilities and prior experience. There has also been pressure for graduates to have a stronger base of skills that will more effectively prepare them for successful employment and for continuing life-long learning.

These various influences have led to increased impetus for finding ways of better supporting students in the development of more effective studying and learning skills as well as more general transferable skills which will be of relevance in the world of work. The earlier focus on study skills has given way to a broader concern to encourage students to become more effective, autonomous and reflective learners both within and beyond the higher-education context. This brief review of current research and practice will be organized in terms of a number of issues which appear to be emerging in the literature, but which will also provide a basis for reviewing the experience of implementing the 'learning to learn' unit which is the focus of this article.

An essential consideration relates to the nature and content of any such intervention. Initial approaches to attempting to improve students' study skills were frequently didactic in character, focusing on procedures to improve particular aspects of the studying process. The work of Gibbs in the 1980s (Gibbs, 1981) involved a greater emphasis on a more student-centred, open-ended approach. The aim was to encourage students to discuss their own study strategies and work together to share and review these. These ideas, in conjunction with recent research into student learning, have led to an increased concern with metacognitive awareness as part of the 'learning to learn' process (e.g. Biggs, 1988). Thus, an important current issue is whether and how study skills and 'learning to learn' metacognitive approaches should be combined in any interventions in this area.

It is appropriate at this point to make some comment on the nature of metacognition. There seems to be a consensus that two sets of processes are involved. First, there is the awareness of our own cognitive processes, and secondly their control or regulation (Biggs, 1988; Norton and Crowley, 1995). Atkins, Beattie and Dockrell (1993) suggest that students with good metacognitive skills are likely to reflect productively on their ongoing learning experiences and be able to identify and adopt strategies which appear to be working successfully. Thus in this context 'learning to learn' represents the acquisition of these more complex, higher-level, adaptive skills rather than more simplistic, prescriptive, static study procedures. Earlier study-skills programmes were frequently free-standing and often available for students from a variety of discipline areas. Recent research and current thinking about metacognition suggest that study skills and 'learning to learn' have a stronger impact on students if there is integration with other components of their academic work (Martin and Ramsden, 1987; Zuber-Skerritt, 1987; Norton and Crowley, 1995).

However, this integration can be difficult to manage in a way that maintains coherence and avoids repetition, particularly in modular programmes of study. There are perhaps two main strategies whereby the links between study skills and 'learning to learn' and the remainder of students' academic work can be organized. The first of these might be called a 'distributed model'. In such an approach core skills would be distributed through the rest of the student's course units (e.g. Atlay, Harris and Assitter, this volume). This strategy has the advantage that the links with ongoing academic work are likely to be clear and strong. However, in a modular context there is likely to be some difficulty in ensuring that every student is exposed to all the skill areas and that, conversely, there isn't too much repetition or overlap. There is also the further question of whether the distribution of study skills and 'learning to learn' content through a programme will provide an appropriate context for the adequate development of reflective and metacognitive skills.

The second approach might be called a 'concentrated model' in which study and learning skills are made available in a more focused way within a single unit (e.g. Bloxham, 1997). This strategy is likely to have the advantage that study and learning skills can be made available in a more carefully planned way to avoid overlap and could be used to provide greater time and a more conducive context for the nurturing of reflective and metacognitive skills. The disadvantage of such an approach, especially when it is compulsory, is that students may be disenchanted by an overemphasis (as they might see it) on such material and lose interest and motivation. It also could be more difficult to ensure integration with the remainder of students' academic programmes since this will be contained within separate, substantive units.

12.3 Research aims and context

The aim of the research reported in this chapter has been to provide an action research evaluation of the implementation of a compulsory first-year 'learning to learn' unit, following a 'concentrated model' as identified above and to review the experience of implementing the unit in relation to the issues identified.

The unit, named the Independent Learning Module (ILM), is run as part of the BA in Applied Social Studies by Independent Study at the Crewe+Alsager Faculty of Manchester Metropolitan University. This degree is a multi-disciplinary programme in the social sciences. Teaching and learning during the first two years of the programme are relatively conventional in character, but in their third year students must complete a major independent project which may take up from two to five units out of the six units required for the final year of the degree.

Because of the nature and demands of this final-year project, there has always been a major concern that students should be properly prepared for this independent work, and this preparatory work has taken a number of forms through the years. During 1993/1994 there arose an opportunity to plan, for the first time, a whole compulsory first-year unit (one out of the six which would make up the student's first-year programme) which would have a role in providing a preparatory base for students to be able to work independently in their third year. The intention was to provide a broadly based foundation for autonomous learning within the degree and beyond.

12.4 The Independent Learning Module: nature, theoretical base and practice

The intention in this section of the chapter is to provide an overview of our aims and rationale for the unit, largely focusing on these as they existed at the initial planning and implementation stage.

12.4.1 Study skills

Although a primary aim of the unit has been to be concerned with reflective, metacognitive skills, it is difficult to work with these more abstract capabilities without drawing on more substantive study and transferable skills. In any case, these skills are of importance in themselves and provide a useful means of making links with substantive units. However, it was seen as important that the unit did not become just a study-skills programme, leaving no space for other material. The study-skills content of the unit has therefore been selective. It has focused particularly on writing and the supporting skill of word-processing, but also the library skills of literature search and the use of bibliographies and indices, the skills of group work and oral presentation. The intention has been to embed the work on study skills within a framework which is supportive of the development of metacognitive abilities.

12.4.2 Supporting reflection and metacognition

It is easy to emphasize the importance of metacognition but less easy to know how to provide a context which is conducive to its development. Our efforts in this direction involved the use of three strategies. Briefly, these relate to the choice of methods of teaching and learning and class management, making available to students relevant theoretical models of metacognitive processes and the use of assessment which will help to promote metacognitive thinking and practice.

In terms of teaching practice the sessions were discussion and exercise-oriented, rather than being didactic in character. There was very little formal, traditional teaching within the unit. The objective was to encourage students to reflect on, and discuss, learning experiences and exercise responses. Frequently students worked in small groups from pairs, up to around five or six, often after individual reflection on an issue, and then shared reactions in a plenary class session. This kind of relatively informal class teaching was possible because the 60–70 students following the unit were divided into classes of 20–25, with each class being led by one tutor and meeting weekly for around two hours.

Three theoretical models were used to support students' metacognitive understanding. These involved the work of Kolb and especially Boud and others on reflective learning (Kolb, 1975; Boud, Keogh and Walker, 1985), and secondly, models of self- regulation derived from Bandura's account of social cognitive learning theory and used in the educational context by Schunk and Zimmerman in particular (Bandura, 1986; Schunk, 1990; Zimmerman, 1988). Finally, of course, the inclusion of the seminal work of Entwistle and Ramsden and its development by many others was essential (Entwistle and Ramsden, 1983).

It is not appropriate or possible to provide a summary of these theories here. It is assumed that the first and last mentioned above are likely to be familiar to most readers of this chapter. The work of Bandura and colleagues is possibly less so and a brief overview would perhaps help to demonstrate its metacognitive relevance.

Bandura's account of self-regulation is concerned with our management of motivational processes through a sequence of constituent responses. These involve self-observation or self-monitoring (being aware of one's own ongoing behaviour and responses), goal-setting (effective goal-setting requiring an emphasis on shorter term, specific goals), progress checking (reviewing performance through social comparison, comparison with standard norms and self comparison) and reacting to performance through tangible and self reward. It is argued that all of us use these processes to manage various aspects of our lives, not just in the learning context, but we do so with varying degrees of effectiveness. In the educational context, Zimmerman suggests that self-regulated learners plan, seek advice, set goals, self-instruct during acquisition, self-monitor, self-evaluate at various points in the learning process and provide appropriate self-reinforcement at achievement (Zimmerman, 1990, p. 5).

As a full academic unit, formal assessment of the Independent Learning Module was necessary. This was also essential to convince students of its worth. However, as so many commentators have pointed out, it was also essential that this assessment was consonant with the aims of the unit. As is evident, one of our aims was to increase students' reflective awareness of their own learning experiences as a base for more informed metacognitive understanding.

Three assessment procedures were used in this attempt to promote reflective skills. Students were required to keep an ongoing learning log as a diary record of their experience (cf. Walker, 1985). The second piece of work involved the construction of a portfolio of achievements both from within and outside the curriculum. These two assignments were assessed only on a pass/fail basis. The third assignment took the form of a 'reflective learning review' in which students were expected to review discursively and in an organized and argued way their learning experience over the year. They were encouraged to identify strengths and weaknesses and produce an action plan for the future. Detailed assessment criteria were developed and this assignment was assessed formally on a percentage basis.

12.4.3   Integration with substantive academic content

As already indicated, a further important concern was to try to ensure that students would be able to make links between the experience and content of the ILM and their other more substantive units (cf. Martin and Ramsden, 1987; Sherman, 1991). There were two main approaches to achieving this end. First, the study skills components of the unit were linked to specific features of other first-year units within the degree. For example, group work skills were reviewed in relation to group work which would be completed within the ILM unit, but also in other units being taken by the students.

The second way of making links to more substantive content was to include, as part of the ILM unit, a problem-oriented project in which students worked in small groups to investigate the literature related to a student chosen topic area. It was hoped that this would encourage intrinsic interest and motivation. In the first implementation of the unit this group project was positioned in the second half of the unit after the completion of the study skills and 'learning to learn' content. The intention was that students would be able to use their developing learning skills during their work on this project. The overall topic area for each project was analysed and divided into subsidiary issues. Individual students then took primary responsibility for one of these topics and part of the unit assessment derived from the resulting project essay.

12.5   Research approach and issues

An action research approach was used to review, evaluate and modify the unit over successive implementations. As is usual in the action research context a variety of data gathering procedures have been used. These involved noting the ongoing informal reactions of students, administering a more structured, but still open-ended investigation of student reactions around mid-way into the academic year, and a more formal evaluation questionnaire to obtain more specific and quantifiable reactions at the end of the academic year. Research use has also been made of student performance and responses on two of the pieces of assessed work, that is the reflective learning review and the project essay. In addition, again as an accepted part of the action-research approach, discussion and reflection on the part of the researchers were seen as making an important contribution to our understanding of the successes and difficulties of implementing the unit (Winter, 1989). Regular tutor meetings (especially during the first run of the unit) provided an important context for this reflection.

As already indicated, the overall purpose of this research was to provide a general evaluatory review of successive implementations of the Independent Learning Module. Our experience of the first implementation of the unit led to our identifying more specific aspects for investigation. The main focus of this chapter is on the implementation of teaching strategies and assessment which are intended to promote student reflection and metacognition. A further aim has been to review the maintenance of student interest and motivation for this process-oriented unit. This issue provides the main focus of a separate research paper. It will be reported here only in so far as resulting adjustments made to the unit impact upon changes which relate to the promotion of reflection and metacognition.

12.6   Action research review of successive implementations

12.6.1   Maintaining motivation and making substantive links using a group-based project (a brief summary)

On the first implementation of the Independent Learning Module in 1994/95, mid-year open-ended feedback (i.e. feedback obtained after the initial 'learning to learn' component of the unit) was disappointingly negative. Fortunately, the structured feedback received at the end of the year showed some more positive appreciation of the unit, but it was still clear to the tutors teaching the unit that the project work, in its initial form and position had failed to provide a successful substantive focus for the unit.

Tutor reflection and discussion led to a proposal for revision, which, in retrospect, seemed very obvious. This was a plan to implement the group project alongside and in parallel with the study skills and 'learning to learn' content. Thus in the second implementation of the unit, in 1995/96, work on the group project began early in the first term. There were two important consequences of this change: first, there was from the beginning some substantive content to the unit besides the more process-oriented concern with studying and learning; secondly it became possible to make ongoing links between these two components of the unit.

The difference in student reactions in the second implementation of the unit was clear from very early on. At an informal, subjective level, tutors were agreed that the general class atmosphere was much more positive than in the previous year and the open-ended mid-year feedback was much more supportive of the unit. The clearest contrast with the previous year's feedback was demonstrated in the responses to the closed questions in the end of unit evaluation questionnaire. The percentage of students making positive responses over a number of questionnaire items increased quite markedly and the differences between responses in 1994/95 and 1995/96 were clearly statistically significant, frequently at the .005 level.

12.6.2 Encouraging reflection and metacognition

12.6.2.1 Use of journals, portfolios and reflective reviews

In the first implementation of the unit in 1994/95 students demonstrated a fair degree of impatience with the requirements of keeping the journal record and constructing the portfolio. Ongoing effort was required, particularly for the journal and the only outcome was a pass or fail grading. This dissatisfaction was clearly demonstrated in the questionnaire response that 69 per cent of students found it difficult to think of things to write about in their learning journals.

Responses to the completion of the reflective review were more positive in character but still with a relatively high proportion of neutral (37%) or negative responses (also 37%) made in response to the statement 'Writing a reflective review helped me to become more strongly aware of my strengths and weaknesses in relation to the learning process.'

Modifications were clearly needed to try to improve the overall commitment to the reflective process. It was decided to omit the journal and portfolio as required parts of the assessment for the unit but to continue to encourage them on a voluntary basis. It was judged that the compulsion was probably irksome and counter-productive for many students, and the pass/fail assessment was problematic but it didn't seem possible or appropriate to introduce clearer criteria for an essentially open-ended and unstructured assignment. We were usefully able to delay submission of the reflective learning review to right at the end of the unit because of the changed project arrangements. Feedback in relation to the completion of the reviews during the second implementation was more positive in character. This was demonstrated clearly by considerably increased support for the benefits of the review (57 per cent of students supporting its value in increasing awareness of strengths and weaknesses), the difference from 94/95 results being significant at the .005 level.

Open-ended feedback comment was varied and complex. At one end of the distribution, reaction was clearly negative or dismissive because of the other more important calls on time:

I thought it was a waste of time.

I considered it not to be relevant as I had three other assignments of greater importance to concentrate on.

I didn't enjoy doing it at all. I thought it was quite a tedious task.

At the other extreme there was enthusiastic support for the learning and understanding which had resulted from the exercise:

Enjoyable and helpful to see how you are coping.

Most enlightening! I actually learned something about myself.

Very useful and interesting to do.

More commonly, there was some frustration at the difficulty and challenge of the task, but then an almost grudging admittance of something useful learned:

I wouldn't want to do it again but it has provided some useful information.

I found it interesting but hard to look at myself.

Very hard to be reasonably objective. Self evaluation is much harder than I imagined.

There was also a recognition by some students that their reflection on their performance had been beneficial, but it was not something they would have addressed without the requirement of the assignment:

Made me aware of strengths and weaknesses and forced me to address those factors which needed attention and alteration.

It gave me the chance to examine my progress which otherwise I would not have had the time or inclination to do.

It was beneficial as it made me think and reflect over the work carried out.

Another way of demonstrating the value of the reflective review is in terms of their actual content. Although a full content analysis has not been completed, brief excerpts from these reviews can indicate the kind of thinking about their own learning experience that students were able to develop:

My problem in relation to reading stems from one of my successes . . . The problem was, I had read too much, made too many unconnected notes and consequently I found that I couldn't structure my essay to answer the question . . . My plan in this area is to sort out my time management of reading. I should plan it that I read widely perhaps for a week, then focus my reading, making notes in relation to the essay for a week and thinking how I am going to organise my ideas and finally leaving time to write my essay.

I find it quite hard to identify where I have used other peoples words or ideas . . . In this way I find it difficult to reference correctly . . . My problem of referencing stems from the rush in my essay towards the final drafting. So if from the early stages of drafting I keep a separate page of all the quotes I am going to use and properly reference them I think this problem would be overcome.

Prior to doing the Independent Learning Module I like many others didn't think about how we learn. The biggest change I have made now is an attempt to adopt a 'deep approach' to learning rather than a surface approach. I used to memorise a lot of work in order to learn but now when I read I set out to get a full understanding of the reading material . . . I find myself discussing more about subjects, questioning aspects and trying to relate to everyday life.

Although these comments do draw, as we would have expected and hoped, on the experience of the ILM, they are also clearly personal in character and relate to individual experience of studying and learning. In this sense they show support for the achievement of some of our aims for the unit.

12.6.2.2   Use of reworked essays

The introduction of the group project to run alongside the study skills and learning to learn content of the ILM unit in the 1995/96 implementation provided us with a new opportunity. Because the project work now took place over a longer period of time, it became possible to require each student to prepare two drafts of their project essay with each contributing to overall unit assessment.

The pragmatic rationale for the introduction of reworked essays was to provide a context for the provision of very detailed and thorough feedback on the first draft of the essay. At a more theoretical level, it can be argued that structured feedback, review and redrafting could have a metacognitive influence. Students will be supported in thinking about the writing process in ways which they might otherwise not have done. In the usual essay-writing situation there is no guarantee that students will use or even carefully read tutor feedback. In the redrafting situation they are forced to do so since the criteria for marking second drafts means that they will be penalized if the essay is resubmitted unchanged. The intention of the feedback was to provide clearer substantiation of earlier discussions about expectations and criteria for writing in the higher education context, but with a particular focus on the requirement for clear argument and taking up a position or 'point of view'. It is suggested that such focused feedback provides a form of 'expert scaffolding' (Kember and Gow, 1989; Wade and Reynolds, 1989) which can support the improvement of skill in this area.

Student reactions in relation to this aspect of the 95/96 implementation were very encouraging. Almost 90 per cent of students thought that feedback comment on the first draft of their contribution to the group project had been helpful in enabling improvement to the second draft (57% strongly agreed and 30% agreed). The remaining 13 per cent were undecided so no students disagreed. This level of support was continued in 96/97.

Inspection of student marks for the two drafts, produced by the 96/97 cohort, showed that improvement was reasonably substantial. Although the range of differences is considerable – from - to +29 and around a third of students only achieve a marginal improvement between drafts of 3 marks or less, just over 50 per cent demonstrate an improvement of 9 marks or more. Given the fairly demanding criteria for improvement this indicates a fair degree of successful learning.

12.7   Concluding discussion

This chapter has reviewed the experience of implementing a first year, compulsory, 'learning to learn' unit over a three-year period. Over this time considerable change was made to the structure and functioning of the unit. On the basis of the evidence reported above, I think it is reasonable to conclude that these changes have largely been positive ones which have had a real impact on the way in which the unit has been received by the student group to whom it was addressed. The considerable resistance to the unit which was encountered in the first year has been overcome so that it is now generally positively received and is enjoyable to teach. The use of project work in its parallel arrangement seems to have worked well to support student motivation and provide a substantive focus for the unit.

It is also important to compare the kind of unit represented by the ILM with other ways of promoting student learning. In the introductory section to this chapter a distinction was made between two forms of integrated 'learning to learn' provision, in terms of 'concentrated' (as in ILM) and 'distributed' models. Ultimately the evaluation of these two possible approaches must derive from a thorough, comparative examination of their advantages and disadvantages (although the two are not necessarily mutually exclusive). A particular aim for this present unit has been the promotion of reflective and metacognitive skills as part of the 'learning to learn' process. Although it is difficult to prove conclusively that there have been improvements in metacognitive awareness and control, the evidence that has been gathered in this review is suggestive that some such changes have taken place among at least a proportion of the students following this unit. It is perhaps questionable as to whether the kind of teaching strategies, or the assessment procedures that we have used to support the development of this awareness, could be managed within a 'distributed' provision.

The criticism might be offered that the ILM unit takes place within a somewhat unusual degree programme, the BA in Applied Social Studies by Independent Study. This is true to an extent and perhaps the ILM sits more easily within this programme than it might within a more conventional degree. However, it is likely that some of the ideas, teaching strategies and assessment procedures could be adapted for a more conventional setting. If we have a serious commitment to the promotion of effective student learning skills, then time within student programmes and energy on the part of tutors and course developers will be necessary. I hope that the experience and evaluation of the ILM unit can make a small contribution to this enterprise.

12.8   References

Atkins, M.J., Beattie, J. and Dockrell, W.B. (1993) *Assessment Issues in Higher Education*. Report commissioned by the Department of Employment, published by the School of Education, University of Newcastle-under-Tyne.

Biggs, J.B. (1988) The role of metacognition in enhancing learning. *Australian Journal of Education*, 32(2), 127–38.

Bloxham, S. (1997) Integrated learning skills training: an evaluation. In C. Rust and G. Gibbs (eds), *Improving Student Learning through Course Design*, The Oxford Centre for Staff and Learning Development, Oxford.

Boud, D., Keogh, R. and Walker, D. (1985) Promoting reflection in learning: a model. In D. Boud, R. Keogh and D. Walker (eds), *Reflection: Turning Experience into Learning*, London, Kogan Page.

Gibbs, G. (1981) *Teaching Students to Learn – A Student Centred Approach*, The Open University Press, Milton Keynes.

Kember, D. and Gow, L. (1989) A model of student approaches to learning encompassing ways to influence and change approaches. *Instructional Science*, 18, 263–88.

Kolb, D.A. (1975) Towards an applied theory of experiential learning. In C. L. Cooper (ed.), *Theories of Group Processes*, London: John Wiley.

Norton, L.S. and Crowley, C.M. (1995) Can students be helped to learn how to learn? An evaluation of an Approaches to Learning programme for first year degree students, *Higher Education*, **29**, 307–28.

Sherman, T.M. (1991) Creating a disposition to learn: promoting enduring effects from learning improvement programmes, *Research and Teaching in Developmental Education*, **8**(1), 37–47.

Schunk, D.H. (1990) Goal setting and self-efficacy during self-regulated learning, *Educational Psychologist*, **25**(1), 71–86.

Wade, S.E. and Reynolds, R.E. (1989) Developing metacognitive awareness, *Journal of Reading*, **33**(1), 6–14.

Walker, D. (1985) Writing and reflection. In D. Boud, R. Keogh and D. Walker (eds), *Reflection: Turning Experience into Learning*, Kogan Page, London.

Winter, R. (1989) *Learning from Experience: Principles and Practice of Action Research*, Falmer Press, Lewes.

Zimmerman, B. (1990) Self-regulated learning and academic achievement: an overview, *Educational Psychologist*, **25**(1), 3–17.

Zuber-Skerritt, O. (1987) The integration of university learning skills in undergraduate programmes, *Programmed Learning and Educational Technology*, **24**(1), 62–70.

13 Improvement of students' skills in a problem-based curriculum

Marie-Louise Schreurs and Jedidja van Vliet
Department of Educational Development and Research,
University of Maastricht, The Netherlands

13.1 Introduction

The educational approach in Maastricht University is problem-based learning (PBL). This non-traditional approach to education is characterized by the use of problems as a stimulus for learning, small group tutorials and much emphasis on the acquisition of practical skills necessary for future professional practice. Instead of teacher-controlled instructional methods, students are in charge of their own learning process. In a problem-based curriculum students learn from the beginning to cooperate in small groups, to solve problems and to work regularly and be goal-directed. These are important skills for students to finish their studies successfully but also for their future professional career.

Dolmans (1994) and Schmidt (1983) saw cooperating in groups, self-directed learning and problem-solving as the main characteristics of PBL. Barrows (1986) stated that four key objectives would be achieved in problem-based learning in a medical curriculum: motivating learning, developing effective clinical reasoning, structuring knowledge in clinical contexts; and developing self-learning skills.

Patel *et al.* (1993) conducted a study to compare the effects of conventional and problem-based medical curricula. The results indicated that students in the PBL curricula learned a systematic process of thinking that is explicitly taught by which they mean the specific strategy students learn to solve problems.

In the work of Belenky *et al.* (1986) different perspectives in the intellectual development of young adults are distinguished. Some students seem to benefit more from a certain learning environment than others. Subjective knowledge and constructed knowledge are important aspects in the learning strategies of females. As problem-based learning facilitates subjective knowledge and constructed knowledge may be that male and female students benefit in a different way from PBL.

Although it is presumed that students acquire social skills and problem-solving skills in a PBL curriculum, research mainly has focused on the cognitive aspects of learning in PBL compared to traditional curricula. The process of skills' acquisition within a problem-based curriculum has not been the subject of study. However, it seems important to know what students gain from this educational strategy.

13.2 Research topics

In order to gain insight into the process of skills acquisition of students in problem-based learning a study was conducted. The main research questions were:

1. To what extent do students develop problem-solving skills, leadership skills, cooperating skills and planning skills during their studies?

2. What is their opinion about the contribution of their education in the development of these skills?

3. Are there differences between male and female students in the development of skills in PBL and in the appreciation of this educational approach?

13.3 Methods

13.3.1 Subjects

Participants of this study were 141 first-year students and 212 students in the final stage of their studies at the faculty of Health Sciences of Maastricht University. The group of first-year students consisted of 34 men and 107 women. This ratio of 1 to 3 is the same as in the population of students in the faculty. The mean age was 19.

The first-year students had just finished the first three block periods and knew what skills were needed to work in problem-based learning. They had a training in study skills for PBL, with such themes as cooperating in groups, leading a group discussion, giving feedback etc.

In the group of fourth-year students there were 54 men and 158 women. The mean age was 25 years. These students were in the final stage of their studies and preparing to leave university and enter the labour market. Some of the students of this group were in the fifth or sixth year.

13.3.2 Instrument

A questionnaire Personal Qualities and PBL was designed as a self-assessment instrument for students. The questionnaire consisted of 49 assertions which described qualities or skills. Students filled in this questionnaire twice: the first time to mention to what extent the assertion applied to him or her. They could answer on a five-point scale; 1 meant that they strongly disagreed with the assertion and 5 meant they strongly agreed with it. The filled it in a second time to indicate the contribution of education to the development of these skills or qualities. Again they answered on a five-point scale: 1 meant that education didn't contribute to develop the skill; 5 meant that education contributed very much to it.

13.3.2.1 *Examples of items of this questionnaire*

- I am able to analyse problems
- I am able to work in a goal-directed way
- I can handle conflicts in a group
- Leading a group discussion is easy for me

By means of factor analysis and reliability analysis the questionnaire is divided into four subscales which refer to main abilities: problem-solving, planning, collaborating in groups and leadership skills.

In an open-ended question students were asked to mention other aspects they learned in PBL.

13.3.3 Procedure

The first-year students were informed about this study after a lecture about methodology, and asked to fill in the questionnaire. Unfortunately only half of the 300 first-year students attended this lecture, but most of the attendants participated in the study.

Another procedure was followed for the fourth-year students. The questionnaire was sent to all the students of the faculty who were in the final stage of their studies. Non-respondents received a reminder which led to a response percentage of 70.

The data was analyzed using SPSS.

13.4   Results

13.4.1   Students' self-assessment of skills

First- and fourth-year students were asked to rate themselves to what extent they possessed the qualities stated in the questionnaire. The results were clustered into four main skills or qualities: problem-solving, planning, cooperating in groups and leadership skills. In Table 13.1 the qualities of the first- and fourth-year students are compared; mean scores and standard deviations are presented. Differences were tested with a *t*-test.

	first year mean	SD	fourth year mean	SD
problem solving	3.6	.4 (n=120)	3.7	.4 (n=181)**
planning	3.8	.5 (n=127)	4.0	.5 (n=192)***
collaborating in groups	3.5	.4 (n=124)	3.6	.4 (n=196)**
leadership skills	3.6	.5 (n=128)	3.8	.4 (n=207)***

(* $p \leq .05$, ** $p \leq .01$, *** $p \leq .001$)

Table 13.1   Qualities of first year students versus fourth year students

Fourth-year students show overall higher scores on the four skills, although the differences between scores are small. A significant difference was found at all four qualities. Level of significance was highest for planning and leadership skills.

This suggests that, in their own opinion, students grow significantly through problem-solving, planning, collaborating in groups and in leadership skills during a problem-based curriculum.

Are there differences between male and female students? To answer this question the group was split up. In Table 13.2 qualities of male students are described and in Table 13.3 first- and fourth-year female students are compared.

	first year mean	SD	fourth year mean	SD
problem solving	3.6	.4 (n=27)	3.9	.4 (n=45)*
planning	3.6	.6 (n=30)	3.8	.5 (n=50)Ns
collaborating in groups	3.6	.5 (n=28)	3.7	.4 (n=50)Ns
leadership skills	3.7	.4 (n=29)	3.8	.3 (n=52)Ns

(* $p \leq .05$, ** $p \leq .01$, *** $p \leq .001$)

Table 13.2   Qualities of first year versus fourth year male students

In Table 13.2 we found only small differences on three of the qualities, which were not significant. Only problem-solving differs substantially. Male students reported a higher score on problem-solving in the fourth year compared to first-year students.

In Table 13.3 we found a different pattern. Female students differed significantly on all the four qualities. The differences were highest on planning and leadership skills. A high score was reported especially on planning. Fourth-year female students scored higher than first-year students on all four aspects.

	first year		fourth year	
	mean	SD	mean	SD
problem solving	3.6	.4 (n=92)	3.7	.4 (n=136)*
planning	3.8	.5 (n=96)	4.0	.5 (n=142)***
collaborating in groups	3.5	.4 (n=95)	3.6	.4 (n=146)*
leadership skills	3.6	.5 (n=98)	3.8	.4 (n=155)***

(* p≤ .05, ** p≤ .01, *** p≤ .001)

Table 13.3   Qualities of first year versus fourth year female students

13.5   Contribution of problem-based learning to the acquisition of skills

Another aspect of this study was to investigate the perceived role of education in the acquisition of qualities. To what extent did problem-based learning contribute to this process of skills acquisition? Students rated this in the questionnaire.

The results are presented in Table 13.4.

	first year		fourth year	
	mean	SD	mean	SD
problem solving	3.1	.6 (n=122)	3.3	.5 (n=179)**
planning	3.0	.8 (n=127)	2.8	.6 (n=186)Ns
collaborating in groups	3.0	.6 (n=127)	2.9	.5 (n=193)Ns
leadership skills	3.2	.5 (n=130)	3.2	.6 (n=208)Ns

(* p≤ .05, ** p≤ .01, *** p≤ .001)

Table 13.4   Contribution of problem based learning, according to first year versus fourth year students

In Table 13.4 the mean score is centred around 3.0, which is the average of the scale. On problem-solving only fourth-year students reported a higher contribution of PBL compared to first-year students. This difference was significant. On planning and collaborating in groups the first-year students rated the contribution of PBL higher than the fourth-year students, although the differences were not significant.

An open-ended question was asked for other positive and negative aspects of PBL.

Table 13.5 shows the positive aspects mentioned by first-year students and fourth-year students.

Some of the aspects are mentioned by first-year students as well as by fourth-year students. These are social skills, self-reliance, motivating and the development of a critical attitude.

First-year students also mention cooperating in groups and computer skills. Fourth-year students stress an open-minded attitude, self-confidence and problem-solving skills. Negative aspects are presented in Table 13.6.

Reported by first year students (n=46)	Reported by fourth year students (n=58)
• social skills	social skills
• cooperating	open minded attitude
• self-reliance	self-reliance
• motivating	motivating
• critical attitude	critical attitude
• computer skills	self-confident
	problem solving

Table 13.5   Positive effects of PBL

Reported by first year students (n=51)	Fourth year students (n=95)
• unclear what should be known	little basic knowledge
• blocktest is not representative	superficial knowledge
• dependence of group members and tutor	dependence groupmembers and tutor
• blocktest is not representative	missing overview of problem area
• dysfunctioning tutorial groups	dysfunctioning tutorial groups
	missing overview of problem area

Table 13.6   Negative effects of PBL

Weak points of PBL according to students concern the dependence on group members and the tutor in the tutorial. When a tutorial group does not function well, it is difficult to learn enough in that group. Students are also concerned about their knowledge: Do I know enough?

13.6   Discussion

13.6.1   Qualities of students

In the process of skills acquisition in PBL students develop problem-solving, planning, cooperating in a group and leadership skills from the first year of their studies. Self-assessment of students show significantly higher scores by fourth-year students compared with first-year students on the four categories, although the differences are small. However, the results from the open-ended questions support the positive effect of PBL on the development of social skills, a self-reliant attitude, the development of a critical attitude and problem-solving skills. Also the motivating aspect of learning in PBL is stressed in the open questions. Referring to the four key objectives in PBL distinguished by Barrows (1986), three of these aspects are supported by the subjects in this study. The fourth aspect, structuring knowledge in context , was not explicitly covered in this study.

13.6.2   Contribution of education

It seems that there are different topics for first- and fourth-year students. First-year students are concerned with cooperation in the tutorial group and planning skills. It seems that they are directed to the learning method in the tutorial. First-year students have to get used to this learning strategy. In secondary school most of the students have experienced a more teacher-centred learning system.

Fourth-year students are concerned with problem-solving and leadership. So it seems that they are more involved in their own learning process.

13.6.3   Differences between men and women

Differences between first-year students compared to fourth-year students in the self-assessment of skills were greater for female than for male students. It could be that female students appreciate this learning method more than males; that they like to work on concrete problems from professional practice together with peers in the tutorial, and to steer their own learning process. PBL seems to be an appropriate learning environment for female students.

These findings fit the work of Belenky *et al.* (1986) who describe the learning strategies of women. They distinguish different perspectives in the intellectual development of young adults. Subjective knowledge and constructed knowledge can be developed and applied in cooperation with peers in PBL. Students have to relate a problem to their own prior knowledge and have to build and construct new knowledge.

13.6.4   Future research

According to Thomas (1997) explicit and formal training in group and team skills is a neglected area in medical schools. Training in group processes would enhance students awareness of these mechanisms and their ability to handle dysfunctioning groups. In PBL students experience group work from the start of their studies and they benefit from this experience, as described in this chapter. Perhaps the effect could be enhanced by an explicit training in group dynamics, spread over the curriculum. Further research could be directed to this topic.

13.7   References

Barrows, H.S. (1986) A taxonomy of problem-based learning methods, *Medical Education*, **20**, 481–6.

Belenky, M.F., Clinchy, B.M., Goldberger, N.R. and Tarule, J.M. (1986) *Women's Ways of Knowing*, New York: Basic Books.

Dolmans, D.H.J.M. (1994) *How Students Learn in a Problem-based Curriculum*, Maastricht: Datawyse.

Foley, R.P., Polson, A.L. and Vance, J.M. (1997) Review of the literature on PBL in the clinical setting, *Teaching and Learning in Medicine*, 9(1), 4–9.

Patel, V.L., Groen, G.J. and Norman, G.R. (1993) Two modes of thought: a comparison of effects of conventional and problem-based medical curricula. In P.A.J. Bouhuijs, H.G. Schmidt and H.J.M. van Berkel, *Problem Based Learning as an Educational Strategy*, Maastricht: Network Publications.

Schmidt, H.G. (1983) Problem-based learning: problem and definition, *Medical Education*, **17**, 11–16.

Sharan, S. (1990) *Cooperative Learning: Theory and Research*, New York: Praeger.

Thomas, R.E. (1997) Problem-based learning: measurable outcomes, *Medical Education*, **31**, 320–9.

14 Learning teams: improving students' generic skills

Penelope Watson
University of Wollongong, Australia

14.1 Introduction

My aim in this chapter is to present some of my experiences in using teamwork in the Faculty of Law at the University of Wollongong, Australia, demonstrating how teamwork can be used to improve students' generic skills. The topic is approached from both a theoretical and a practical perspective.

Teams and teamwork have been a major theme in industry, especially in the USA, for the last two to three decades. Surveys report figures as high as 80 per cent for US businesses using some form of teamwork (McNerney, 1994, pp. 12–13). Interest is now strong in Australia and the UK as well. Higher education, in particular Law, has been slower to adopt the teamwork concept, tending instead to rely on an individualist or 'person-solo' model, that is, a model which 'views learning as primarily an individual activity that takes place in the head, [and overlooks] social aspects of learning and extra-cognitive factors' (Pacanowsky, 1995, pp. 36–51).

14.2 The learning teams model (LTM)

The teamwork model presented here proposes a methodology whereby generic skills can be incorporated into the curriculum, serving the needs of both Pericles and the plumber (Twining, 1967) and at the same time bringing a critical, rigorous, analytical and conceptual perspective to skill development, avoiding the dangers of 'soaring through theory unto the empty abstractions of a fancied law of nature' as well as those of 'sinking through practice into a soulless, unsatisfying handicraft' (Savigny). The model is founded upon an experiential, interactive and constructivist view of learning. Central features are the combination of explicitly taught theory[1] with practice, emphasis upon reflection and self-knowledge, integration of substantive and skills-based material, assessment which is a combination of authentic tasks (high correlation to workplace experience), process tasks and tasks designed to promote creative problem-solving and use of multiple thinking strategies (higher order cognitive skills), explicit team skills training and a sustained, managed exposure to working in teams.

LTM must be understood as a teaching/learning *methodology*, which aims to develop flexible learning skills in students, and promote flexible delivery by academic staff, through the use of teamwork. Sequenced application of the model in varying contexts, combined with reflective practice, assists learners to progress from novice to expert level more readily, and enhances transferability of newly acquired skills.

Teamwork has been chosen as the vehicle because team skills are inherently useful, being highly correlated with employability in a diverse range of occupations (thus vocational in the broadest sense), and also because the skills identified as necessary for effective teamwork are equally necessary for effective individuals.

14.2.1 The pilot studies

The Learning Teams model was trialled in 1996 and 1997 at the University of Wollongong in the Faculty of Law core compulsory subject of Torts. Both pilots consisted of 70–80 students, the majority in their third year of Law, organized for the 14-week semester into teams ranging in number from three to six individuals. Teamwork was compulsory and each team member received the same mark for assignments prepared jointly. Assessment related both to substantive (legal) and process (teamwork) tasks, and was a combination of team and individual work. Normal seminar classes were held for two of the five timetabled hours per week, one hour of lectures, and not less than two hours per week of team meetings, as required. All meetings were minuted, the minutes forming part of an assessable reflective journal. Many of these team meetings were conducted under formal and informal observation, either by teaching staff and/or other student teams, the observation reports also contributing towards final assessment. Readings were set each week for both law and teamwork, and the legal material was organized into a series of weekly modules consisting of 10–15 questions, problems, hypotheticals etc. Various specific team tasks, not all directly assessable, were set. In the first year an introductory, one-day workshop was held which included outdoor and indoor exercises and activities related to teamwork. The pilots were evaluated by means of student journals and surveys, and direct observation of team meetings and presentations.

14.3 What are learning teams?

There is considerable confusion in the literature, and in everyday speech, over terminology. Groups, teams, work groups, project groups, task forces, committees and self-directed work teams are just some of the overlapping terms commonly encountered.

The most useful approach to definition is to consider the presence or absence of various qualities. For present purposes, an effective learning team may be defined as:

- an intact and cohesive social system, formed for the purpose of 'deliberate' learning (Tough, 1979; Boud, Keogh, Walker, 1985) within an institutional context, and possessing the following attributes:

- clearly defined membership;

- small number of members;

- shared/rotating leadership;

- common commitment, individual and mutual accountability, interdependence;

- specific and common team purpose or mission, clearly articulated and developed by the team itself;

- definite task(s) to perform, collective work products;

- delineated criteria for success;

- clear and open communication, open-ended discussion, active problem-solving;

- agreed strategies, rules and procedures;

- direct and appropriate performance goals, and clear deadlines;

- suitable team based reward or assessment scheme;

- constructive conflict;

- differentiated member roles;

- appropriate expertise, training and complementary skills;

- adequate resources and support;

- balanced planned composition

(Katzenbach and Smith, 1993, p. 214; Taguiri, 1995; Hackman, 1990, pp. 4–5; Jacques, 1991, p. 130).

Thus it is clear that seminar groups, the basis of the 'small group' teaching method, are not teams, even when working as sub-groups in the form of dyads, triads, buzz groups, syndicates, role-play groups and so on. Nor is it likely that groups formed for the purpose of completing one assignment together over a fairly short period will go through enough of the developmental stages to become a real team. The essence of the distinction lies in the longer term, more committed, focused and cohesive nature of the team and, above all, in the concepts of interdependence, responsibility and accountability inherent in teamwork. Substantial time needs to be spent working together, in an environment in which high performance demands are placed upon the group, thus providing the necessary range and depth of experience needed to trigger transition to a true team. In a sequenced programme, groupwork of the types described above is a useful introduction to more intensive teamwork at later stages, and offers some of the benefits in terms of experience and skill development, but is conspicuously lacking in others.

14.4　Benefits of learning teams

14.4.1　Generic skills

The benefits associated with teamwork are greater educational autonomy and skill development for learners, enhanced employability[2] and, possibly, management savings in terms of staff resources in the medium term. The andragogical benefits provide the overriding justification, and these will be the main focus of the discussion.

There is much support for the view that the old-style exclusive emphasis on domain-specific knowledge, individually and competitively acquired, is an approach universities can no longer afford. In many fields of study, factual technical knowledge will be obsolete by the time the student graduates.

The ability to undertake continuous independent learning throughout one's life and career, to maintain employability, will be a key survival skill for the future, necessitating conscious awareness of the processes involved, together with attitudes supportive of ongoing learning and high levels of proficiency in the requisite skills. Capacity for rapid adaptation, flexibility and constructive change management will be vital.[3]

There have been numerous attempts to identify the range of skills required by Law graduates (Keyzer, 1994, pp. 3–4; de Groot, 1994; MacCrate,1992; Ayling and Costanzo,1984; Masters and McCurry, 1990). Necessary skills for all types of graduate can be grouped as:

job skills/ functional expertise; team and interaction skills (personal/ interpersonal); problem-solving and decision-making.

Many skills which would be regarded as generic in other contexts are usually classified as discipline specific for Law, for example, capacity for analytical and critical thought, problem solving, evaluating evidence, advocacy and negotiation etc. Skills which are generic may be taught in discipline specific ways, for example, the discipline specific skill of mooting (mock legal trial) is also an aspect of broader skills such as oral communication, construction of argument, and so on. The Learning Teams model focuses on generic skills specific to or essential for successful teamwork, which are either not taught using other delivery modes, or insufficiently taught. As will be evident, skills identified as necessary for effective teamwork are just as necessary for effective individuals. Communication skills, conflict management, leadership skills, meeting skills, personal and time management, record-keeping, goal-setting and prioritizing, decision-making, problem-solving, and above all, enhanced learning skills, are all benefits which result from successful teamwork, and can all be classified as generic skills.

14.4.2 Interactive deep learning

The team format offers the student increased opportunities for participation and interaction as compared with the usual small group teaching methods, thus promoting 'deep' learning, improved engagement with the subject matter, and construction of new knowledge. The significance of this will be discussed further under the heading of transfer. Retention rates for student learning have been determined as: 10 per cent of what they read, 26 per cent of what they hear, 30 per cent of what they see, 50 per cent of what they see and hear, 70 per cent of what they say, and 90 per cent of what they say as they do something (Lagowski, 1990). Studies conducted by Webb (1983) and Powell (1974) showed that even in so-called interactive seminar groups, tutors spoke approximately 60 per cent of the time, whereas in the absence of the tutor, student participation increased threefold, and participation time was more evenly shared. Findings quoted by Brown and Atkins (1988) (McNally, 1994) are even more damning. Two studies of small group teaching revealed that tutor talk reached 86 per cent of time spent; student interaction could be as low as 8 per cent; tutor used student ideas less than 2 per cent of the time; lecturing in small groups varied from 7 to 70 per cent of the time; asking questions varied from 1 to 28 per cent of the time; and mean time spent talking by tutors was 64 per cent.

The conclusion to be drawn from these figures is that active/interactive learning is demonstrably superior to lecture and other passive methods of direct instruction, at least as regards retention, yet it does not necessarily occur even in seminar and small group settings. Teamwork, where students are working in groups of around four peers (that is, there is no authority figure, presumed to have superior knowledge), cannot help but be more interactive and lend itself more readily to discovery and construction of knowledge.

14.4.3 Peer assisted learning

Research has consistently demonstrated that students learn more from the process of teaching others than from being taught (Clement, 1971; Annis, 1983; Bargh and Schul, 1980; McKeachie, 1986, pp. 196–7; see also Le Brun and Johnstone, 1994, 288–95) and this is true for learning by seminar, discussion, independent study through the use of essays, straightforward reading, or being taught by a peer (Goldschmid, 1970; Goldschmid and Shore, 1974; Schermerhorn, Goldschmid and Shore, 1975; McKeachie, 1986, p. 199; and

McKeachie, 1990, p. 193; see also Le Brun). Personal experience of teaching confirms this. It is an important point to reinforce, since it directly addresses a range of issues concerning fairness, appropriate roles for staff and students, and time pressures. Teaching others well requires students to transform information into knowledge, and develops analytical and communication skills.

The benefits of being tutored by peers are also well documented, both in the affective and cognitive domains (Goodlad, 1989, pp. 81–3). In a sufficiently supportive climate the opportunity exists to be honest about difficulties, with less fear of either losing face or losing marks, and places both tutors and tutees in a position to seek further assistance where needed. It must be stressed, however, that students who perceive significant disparities between themselves and other team members in terms of ability,[4] are likely to experience difficulty in being open, and require additional support. Careful monitoring by staff is important, through observation or classroom follow-up, to avoid such problems, including 'groupthink' (Janis, 1972), that phenomenon of concurrence-seeking behaviour and pressure towards social conformity which stifles critical analysis.

Sharing of knowledge and skills informally as well as in more structured ways is encouraged by the teamwork format. Peer-assisted learning promotes reflection upon the learning process, and develops an appreciation of different learning styles (Kolb, 1984; Honey and Mumford, 1986; Smith, 1982), an aspect which should be emphasized in prescribed readings.

14.4.4   Reflective practice

Training in reflective practice (Schon, 1987; Boud, Keogh, Walker, 1985; Peters, 1991; Mezirow, 1991; Holly, 1989; Martinez, 1990; Sparkes-Langer, 1990) enables learners to convert their individual experiences into more generalized theory. Reflection is the process which enables the learner to transform experience into knowledge, that is, to construct meaning and understanding from an experience, and maximize the benefits obtained. Reflection makes explicit the connection between theory and practice, and subjects to conscious scrutiny many things which to the learner may feel 'intuitive', thus enabling ideas and practices to be evaluated, and informed choices to be made. It is a conscious process of purposeful examination, of one's thoughts, feelings, actions and reactions, with a view to gaining greater self awareness leading to a continual upward spiral of improvement.

Initially this process will be fairly domain-specific and laborious, but as sophistication develops, transferability increases, that is, learning can be applied to new contexts, and further knowledge generated. The process of experiential learning (Kolb,1984) which forms the basis of the teamwork model, 'occurs in a cycle of experience (gathering information about events), reflective observation (bringing events to a conscious level), abstract conceptualization (making sense of events), and active experimentation (putting learning into practice)' (Ballantyne and Packer 1995, p. 11). Put another way, the four stages in the process link together to form the DATA model of Describe/Analyse /Theorize/Act (Peters, 1991).

14.5   Assessment

Assessment should be summative and formative, and related to both substantive and process objectives. Assessing learning summatively conveys the message that this is important, while formative assessment is necessary for diagnostic and feedback purposes. Thus what is assessed, as well as the methods chosen, has a significant impact on the type, content and extent of learning which occurs, and the assessment itself contributes to learning, rather than merely measuring it. Decisions about assessment also impact upon transferability of skills learned (see below).

14.5.1 Reflective journal

All students in our studies were required to submit a reflective assignment (team or individual), either in journal (Holly and McLoughlin,1989; Smith and Pape, 1990; Wedman and Martin, 1986) or other form. This demanded a theoretical understanding of reflection, and demonstrated ability to apply teamwork theory to individual experience. Choice of format was left to the students, some electing to make videos, others including allegorical stories, poems, even drawings, of team experiences. Unusual and creative projects were encouraged. Staff reviewed reflective journals at several stages, prior to the final assessment, making comments and suggestions. The journals were extremely useful for feedback and evaluation of the course, as well as for providing insight into process, and checking for disparities in contribution.

14.5.2 Peer and self assessment

Short written reports on team observations, both as observer (peer) and observed (self) were assessed as a follow-up to verbal feedback given contemporaneously. Preparation for both sides prior to conducting the observations included discussion of appropriate criteria for evaluating team processes, readings on giving and receiving constructive feedback, as well as the usual preparation of substantive material under discussion. Both teams received verbal feedback from the staff observer at the end of the process. The great majority of students reported very favourably on the peer observations as learning experiences, once the initial self-consciousness and 'staged' feeling had abated.

In the second year peer assessment of class participation was introduced. Despite careful preparation, this exercise would have to be acknowledged as a failure, generating strong student opposition and complaint. (See discussion of student attitudes to learning, below.)

Peer and self-evaluation play a valuable part in enhancing learning, with students being assisted to consider and articulate criteria for determining high-quality performance. The ultimate objective is, of course, to extend the individual's self knowledge and capacity for independent lifelong or continuous learning. Self assessment by means of a standard form was used, as well as via reflective journals.

14.5.3 Authentic (workplace related) assessment

The major legal component of the assessment was in the form of an authentic brief to counsel (that is, documents as supplied by a solicitor to a barrister for purposes of preparing for litigation, in a split legal profession). This required students to identify relevant facts from some 40 pages of primary source material, draft a statement of claim, and prepare written legal advice on various aspects. To construct such an assignment undoubtedly requires far more effort and time on the part of staff than drafting the usual hypothetical, but is well worth the investment. The unfamiliar and demanding nature of the task underlined more emphatically than anything else that it could have the benefits of working in teams, of having an extended pool of resources to draw on and colleagues with whom to discuss problems and share the workload. Working from primary sources in determining relevant facts was an important aspect, one usually overlooked in the appellate case method of teaching law. Feedback from students was overwhelmingly positive and enthusiastic, especially as regards the realistic, practical nature of the assignment, and some transfer of skills to the workplace (see below) could be expected.

14.5.4   Creative thinking task

Innovative applications of established principle to new contexts was the focus of another major assignment. Students were asked to develop an oral team presentation, critically examining ways in which tort law might be accessed in situations in which it traditionally would not be used, or would apply at the margins, and to assess modifications and extensions of the law needed to suit their purpose. A class debate on a controversial and topical legal subject was held, students being required to construct arguements from one of six different perspectives, based on De Bono's 'Six Hat Thinking' method (De Bono, 1993). The 'blue hat' (thinking about thinking) process which is engaged in jointly at the end of the exercise is a variation on reflection, promoting meta-cognitive learning. The debate was used to demonstrate structured and holistic thinking processes, to practise existing skills of argument construction in a novel way, as well as to contextualize and add currency to the law being studied.

14.5.5   Team and individual

All assessment tasks were initially envisaged as compulsory team products, in line with principles of mutual accountability, but this was reassessed to include a balance of team and individual components. Many students in the first trial reported that they felt the need for some acknowledgement of their individual input, even in successful teams. Inclusion of some individual tasks also serves a useful monitoring function, helping to allay concerns about unfair advantage and freeloading.

14.6   Transfer of skills

14.6.1   Lateral and vertical transfer

Transferability of knowledge, skills and attitudes refers to the extent to which things learned in one context can be transposed to a different context. Near or vertical transfer, that is, application of skills in a different but very similar context – for example, essay writing on different topics or advising on a legal hypothetical problem in different law subjects – is readily achieved with instruction, practice and feedback. Far or lateral transfer refers to the ability to apply previous learning in a markedly different context, and this is notoriously difficult to achieve (Thorndike and Woodsworth, 1901a, 1901b; Gibbs *et al*., 1993). The new context may well be an employment one, but need not be confined to this. Larkin (1989) argues that transfer means applying previous knowledge in a context different enough to require learning new knowledge. My view is that construction of new knowledge is an inevitable outcome of any transfer process, but that near transfer can be achieved with little new knowledge, and very limited depth of understanding, whereas far transfer cannot. Positive transfer refers to a situation in which prior learning assists rather than impedes performance of the new task.

14.6.2   Transfer across disciplines

Lateral transfer is at the heart of attempts to promote development of generic skills, so much so that a skill which is not transferable cannot be said to be generic. This is not to say, however, that successful transfer necessarily requires transfer outside the discipline, except at a very general level. Certainly, 'generic' skills will differ across different disciplines, taking different forms and assuming differing degrees of importance (Gibbs *et al.*, 1993). Ability to solve legal problems does not indicate ability to solve mathematical problems, for example, since both of these depend heavily on context-specific knowledge. Skills such as oral communication, although employed in many different forms in various disciplines, may be analysed in terms of the presence of common factors which are not context-dependent, such as self-confidence, clarity of thought, ability to reduce complex material to essential principles, awareness of audience and so on. Possessing these attributes (skills) makes it easier to gain proficiency in a dissimilar context, which is the essence of transfer, but does not guarantee it.

14.6.3   Experts vs novices

It is clear in the literature that experts, that is, individuals possessing large bodies of knowledge and experience in a given field, are better at problem-solving in that domain than novices. Experts have better organized and integrated knowledge structures, enabling them to grasp underlying principles and perceive relationships. They are also better monitors of their own thinking strategies. The development of expertise has been shown to depend upon repeated practice and the accumulation of strategies and prototypical responses (Misko, 1995). The implications of this for transfer are that novices are able to achieve less transfer than experts within a discipline and that improvements in transfer can be expected as expertise develops. Confining any skills-training methodology to one subject, therefore, is of limited utility, whereas integration in a sequenced programme promotes transfer.

14.6.4   Means to promote transfer

Transfer cannot be assumed to occur unaided. Examples of non-transfer are frequent in the literature. Training in computer programming does not improve 'rigour' in mathematics (Pea and Kurland, 1984); professional abacus users do not do well in pen and paper maths tests (Stigler, Barclay and Aiello, 1982); Brazilian street-vendor children able to calculate correct change for their customers are unable to do well on similar maths problems given in a school setting (Carraher, Carraher and Schlieman, 1977), and so on (all cited in Misko, 1995). Various writers advocate the teaching of general or abstract rules for activities such as reasoning, thinking, problem solving, and reading comprehension, arguing that these are common across domains (Ennis, 1990; Fong and Nisbett, 1990; Nickerson, Perkins and Smith, 1985; cited in Misko, 1995; De Bono, 1993). Positive transfer is frequently claimed to occur. Standard problem-solving methodologies such as the Dewey Reflective Problem Solving Process, or similar (see Keyzer, 1994) can be taught. Wilson (Wilson, 1993) offers a broad range specifically related to teams. Pacanowsky (1995) convincingly argues that such methods work well for the type of problem soluable through known algorithms, but are unsuitable for what he terms 'wicked problems', for example, the problem of illicit drug trafficking, urban town planning and so on. Approaches based on heuristics (general rules of thumb) training, such as De Bono's Cognitive Research Team (CoRT) thinking programme for problem-solving, or his Six Hat Thinking method, employ systematic structured approaches, seeking to make explicit each step in the thinking process. De Bono in particular is a strong advocate of brainstorming and similar techniques designed to promote creative and lateral thought, thus opening up a much broader range of possibile solutions, including redefinition or reconceptualization of the problem. Whilst his claims have been criticized on the grounds of lack of empirical evidence (McPeck, 1981), there are many examples of success in the corporate world using De Bono's methods, and feedback from students in our pilots on use of his techniques was extremely positive.

In summary, transfer can be promoted most effectively by a combination of experience, repetition (practice), variation of context, explicit analysis of experience through reflection or other forms of debriefing, including making connections to new applications visible, theory, sequenced integration with substantive material to contextualize knowledge and provide a purpose for the learning, and by persisting long enough for expertise to develop.

14.7   Conclusion

- ideal vehicle for generic skill development;
- make connections explicit to maximize transfer;
- promotes learner independence/autonomy;
- be trusting in allowing students an increasing measure of control;
- appropriate skills training and practice essential;
- balance of theory and practice – reflection;
- relate all activities to learning objectives;
- pay attention to process as well as product and seek an appropriate balance;
- ensure assessment rewards team behaviours;
- include a balance of individual components;
- monitor teams and individuals carefully, taking prompt remedial action where indicated;
- offer strong leadership and support;
- be prepared for some resistance – look to your own support networks;
- proceed gradually and consolidate;
- hang in there!

Notes

1. This includes theory relating to teamwork, reflective practice and learning (emphasis on gaining awareness of individual learning styles and needs).

2. Employers consider professional knowledge 'less important than the development of skills in communication, decision-making, problem-solving, the application of knowledge to the workplace, working under minimum supervision, and the ability to learn new skills and procedures' (Business/Higher Education Round Table, 1991, 1993). Both the B/HERT studies in Australia, a similar Coopers and Lybrand study in Queensland (1991) and another conducted by Sheffield University in the United Kingdom (McNally, in Thorley, 1994, pp. 113–20) ranked teamwork skills as one of the top six criteria of employability.

3. Most recently Dearing Report, UK, 1997.

4. This is frequently a matter of confidence and can be especially problematic for students from cultural minorities. Such students often feel very exposed working in teams.

14.8   References and bibliography

Abassi, S.M. and Hollman, K.W. (1994) Self management teams: the productivity breakthrough of the 1990s, *Journal of Management Psychology*, 9(7), 25–30.

Ballantyne, R. and Packer, J. (1995) *Making Connections: Using Student Journals as a Teaching/Learning Aid*, HERDSA Gold Guide No. 2, Higher Education Research and Development Society of Australasia.

Bond, C. and Le Brun, M. (1996) Promoting learning in law, *Legal Education Review*, 7(1, 1).

Boud, D. (ed.) (1981) *Developing Student Autonomy in Learning*, London: Kogan Page.

Boud, D., Keogh, R. and Walker, D. (1985) *Reflection: Turning Experience into Learning*, London: Kogan Page.

Boyatzis, R.E. and Kolb, D.A. (1995) From learning styles to learning skills: the executive skills profile, *Journal of Management Psychology*, 10(5), 3–17.

Buzan, T. (1993) *The Mind Map Book*, London: BBC Books.

Candy, P.C., Crebert, G. and O'Leary, J. (1994) *Developing Lifelong Learners through Undergraduate Education*, Commissioned Report of the National Board of Employment Education and Training No. 28, Canberra, AGPS.

Davis, J., Millburn, P., Murphy, T. and Woodhouse, M. (1992) *Successful Team Building*, London: Kogan Page.

De Bono, E. (1993) *Teach Your Child How to Think*, London: Penguin.

Downs, R.M. and Stea, D. (1977) *Maps in Minds: Reflections on Cognitive Mapping*, USA: Harper & Row.

Eales-White, R. (1995) *Building Your Team*, London: Kogan Page.

Gibbs, G. (ed.) *Improving Student Learning: Theory and Practice*, Oxford Centre for Staff Development.

Gibbs, G. , Rust, C., Jenkins, A. and Jacques, J. (1993) *Developing Students' Transferable Skills*, Oxford Centre for Staff Development.

Goodlad, S. and Hirst, B. (1989) *Peer Tutoring: A Guide to Learning by Teaching*, London: Kogan Page.

Hackman, J.R. (ed.) (1990) *Groups that Work (and Those That Don't)*, San Francisco: Jossey-Bass.

Holly, M.L.H. (1989) Reflective writing and the spirit of inquiry, *Cambridge Journal of Education*, 19(1), 71–80.

Holly, M.L.H. and McLoughlin, C.S. (1989) Professional development and journal writing. In M.L.H. Holly and C.S. McLoughlin (eds), *Perspectives on Teacher Professional Development*, The Falmer Press.

Honey, P. and Mumford, A. (1986) *Using Your Learning Styles*, 2nd edn, Maidenhead, Berkshire.

Honey, P. and Mumford, A. (1989) *The Manual of Learning Opportunities*, Maidenhead, Berkshire.

Jacques, D. (1991) *Learning in Groups*, 2nd edn, London: Kogan Page.

Janis, I.L. (1972) *Victims of Groupthink*, Boston: Houghton-Mifflin Company.

Katzenbach, J.R. and Smith, D. (1993) *The Wisdom of Teams – Creating the High Performance Organisation*, Boston: Harvard Business School Press.

Keyzer, P. (1994) *Legal Problem Solving*, Australia: Butterworths.

Kolb, D.A. (1984) *Experiential Learning: Experience as the Source of Learning and Development*, Englewood Cliffs, NJ: Prentice Hall.

Le Brun, M. and Johnstone, R. (1994) *The Quiet Revolution: Improving Student Learning in Law*, Sydney: Law Book Co.

McNally, J. (1994) Working in groups and teams. In L. Thorley and R. Gregory (eds), *Using Group Based Learning in Higher Education*, London: Kogan Page.

McNerney, D.J. (1994) The 'facts of life' for teambuilding, *HR Focus*, Dec.

Margerison, C.J. and McCann, D. (1991) *Team Management: Understanding How People Work Together*, Melbourne: Business Library.

Martinez, K. (1990) Critical reflections on critical reflection in teacher education, *Journal of Teaching Practice*, **10**, 20–8.

Maughan, C. and Webb. J. (1983) Taking reflection seriously: how was it for us?' in J. Webb and C. Maughan (eds) *Teaching Lawyers' Skills*, Australia: Butterworths.

Mezirow, J. *et al.* (1991) *Fostering Critical Reflection in Adulthood*, Jossey-Bass.

Misko, J. (1995) *Transfer: Using Learning in New Contexts*, NCVER, Australia.

Pacanowsky, M. (1995) Team tools for wicked problems, *Organisational Dynamics*, Winter, 36–51.

Pearce, E., Campbell, E. and Harding, D. (1987) *Australian Law Schools: A Discipline Assessment for the Commonwealth Tertiary Education Committee*, Canberra AGPS, Vol. 4 (Pearce Report).

Peters, J.M. (1991) Strategies for reflective practice. In R.G. Brockett, *Professional Development for Educators of Adults*, San Francisco: Jossey Bass.

Schon, D.A. (1983) *The Reflective Practitioner: How Professionals Think in Action*, New York: Basic Books Inc.

Schon, D.A. (1987) *Educating the Reflective Practitioner*, San Francisco: Jossey-Bass.

Senge, P. (1990) *The Fifth Discipline*, New York: Random House.

Sleigh, J. (1993) *Making Team Learning Fun*, Australia, CCH.

Smith, L.C. and Pape, S.L. (1990) Reflectivity through journal writing: student teachers write about reading events. Paper presented at the Annual Meeting of the National Reading Conference, Miami. ED 327 498.

Sparkes-Langer, G.M., Simmons, J., Pasch, M., Colton, A. and Stark, A. (1990) Reflective pedagogical thinking: how can we promote and measure it?, *Journal of Teacher Education*, **41**(4), 23–32.

Tagiuri, R. (1995) Using teams effectively, *Research Technology Management*, **38**(1), Jan.–Feb., 12–13.

Tough, A. (1979) *The Adult's Learning Projects*, Toronto: Ontario Institute for Studies in Education, 2nd edn.

Twining, W. (1967) Pericles and the plumber, *LQR*, **83**, 396.

Twining, W. (1989) Taking skills seriously, *Journal of Professional Legal Education*, **4**(1, 1). Also published in N. Gold, K. Mackie and W. Twining (1989) *Learning Lawyers' Skills*, Butterworths, UK.

Wedman, J.M. and Martin, M.W. (1986) Exploring the development of reflective thinking through journal writing, *Reading Improvement*, **23**(1), 68–71.

Wilson, G. (1993) *Problem Solving and Decision Making*, London: Kogan Page.

15 The acquisition and development of core skills: practices and perceptions

Elisabeth Dunne and Moira Fraser
University of Exeter, UK
ESRC Learning Society programme: The Acquisition and Development of Core Skills in Higher Education and Employment
Project Directors: Neville Bennett and Elisabeth Dunne

15.1 Project overview

The Acquisition of Core Skills project is one of 13 within a programme entitled 'The Learning Society'. This is a major national programme with the over-arching aim of examining the nature of a learning society and exploring ways in which it can contribute to economic development and progress. A central premise is the belief that it is only through equipping citizens with appropriate knowledge and skills that national prosperity can be assured. Crucial to this exploration is a critical understanding of the complex relationships of education, training and employment, and of the teaching and learning processes through which knowledge and skills are acquired. This study considers issues at the heart of such concerns by focusing on the acquisition, development and use of core and generic skills in higher education as well as in the workplace.

15.2 Introduction

Whereas higher education in the past has focused almost entirely on the development of disciplinary knowledge and skills, core skills are at present attracting considerable attention in Britain, particularly in post-compulsory education, since they are assumed by many to be central to the provision of effective, flexible learners and workers of the future. Those in higher education, rather than maintaining an assumption that a traditional education is appropriate, are expected to respond to a societal shift in concern about its nature and purpose. There is a perception that some part of its role is specifically and explicitly to prepare individuals for their future and for the world of work.

Slee (1989), of the Confederation of British Industry, set out the employer perspective:

> the common denominator of highly qualified manpower will . . . be the ability to think, learn and adapt. Personal transferable skills – problem-solving, communication, teamwork – rather than technical skills defined with narrow occupational ranges, will come to form the stabilizing characteristic of work. If higher education is to meet the needs of the economy and the individual it must seek actively to develop these generic core competences . . .

This is a view with which the government sympathizes, as well as lead bodies, university vice chancellors and many others. The change in conception of the role of higher education is not unique to Britain; similar perspectives are apparent across North America, Australia and much of Europe.

Major initiatives to innovate in this area seem not to have had the positive impact anticipated. Earlier research in one university (Dunne, 1995) highlighted a belief held by academics that 'the whole concept of a university education is based upon transferable skills' although there was little evidence of such skills being made explicit to students. Students seemed unable to articulate or to recognize their own development in this area. There also appeared to be problems in the utilization of core skills in workplace settings, and in the provision of appropriate training. It seemed that there was a need to explore further the whole area of core skills, in higher education and in the workplace.

15.3   Research design

To this end, data on teachers and students was collected in four universities (two 'old' or 'traditional' and two 'new' or historically more vocationally oriented) where 32 staff in 16 departments were targeted. The research programme focused on courses in which core or generic skills were deliberately and explicitly planned, in order to provide exemplars of appropriate models for the improvement of practice. A range of research methods has been used including detailed interviews of individuals and focus groups, observation and questionnaires. Courses have been studied in depth, focusing on teachers' conceptualizations, planning and intentions; how these were enacted; and the extent to which planned outcomes were achieved. Students' responses have also been gathered through questionnaires and group interviews, and the main study has been further developed to provide a phenomenographic analysis and account of the individual experiences of 40 students following core skill courses. In addition, data in employment settings is being acquired from 24 major national companies as well as from smaller enterprises in the South West region. The focus is on graduates in their first year of employment, in particular on their expectations and experiences, the skill demand in their different work or task contexts, and the opportunities for, and quality of, training in core skills.

All data is in the process of being analysed and the findings reported below represent only a small part of the whole study. Outcomes from higher education and the workplace are touched on, with the major focus being on student perceptions of core skill provision.

15.4   Outcomes

The conceptualization of core skills within higher education is complex and not easily articulated. There is no discrete and easily identifiable set of skills known as core skills. A priority for this project was to find a succinct means for describing core skill development while maintaining the variety in interpretation, as well as the differences in practice and the nature and explicit focus of any course. The first part of this chapter describes the development of frameworks or models which became, at an early stage of the project, an essential prerequisite to the clarification of conceptual and terminological difficulties. They have also underpinned data collection and interpretation, and analysis of the whole project.

15.4.1   A framework and a model

The framework for mapping transferable or generic skills (see Appendix 15.1) was developed during a prior study (Dunne, 1995). It suggests an essential core for student development: management of self, of others, of information and of the task. There is an implication in the use of the word 'management' that the onus is on the student to manage his or her own learning. These skills are generic in that they could potentially be applied to any discipline, to any course in higher education, to the workplace or to any other context. They might also be considered lifelong skills in that they could, at appropriate levels, underpin education and learning at any age or stage of development. Sets of subskills in each of the four management areas provide some idea of what university teachers state they consider appropriate to address in their programmes of study. When used as a tool for planning, it is intended that teachers should change or adapt these lists for their own purposes and in relation to their own courses and disciplines.

The centre of this framework outlines aspects of the learning environment which may be important factors in the fostering of such skills, enabling the student to manage learning effectively through the gaining of learning strategies, through assessment of skills, which has the potential for promoting appropriate self-evaluation, and through an understanding and awareness of the applicability and the transferability of skills.

This framework became a useful tool in promoting a shared vocabulary and understanding in the research programme and for illustrating different emphases in the range of courses observed. In courses which were specifically based on generic skills, there was often an associated focus on the processes of learning which tended to represent a move away from the teacher as always being a direct transmitter of knowledge to one promoting involvement in interactive contexts, with students expected to take greater responsibility for managing and evaluating their own learning. This was evidenced in the organization and monitoring of activities such as teamwork, project work or student-led presentations and discussions, often with a demand for students to evaluate their own involvement and progress. A focus on independent learning also promoted similar requirements for self-review. There was often a deliberate shift from teacher-centred to student-centred learning, with teacher assessment used as a device to ensure the valuing of skills by students. However, planning for transfer of these skills, or the requirement to use, practice and develop them on a regular basis throughout a degree, was rarely built into programmes of study. There is evidence of continued planning for disciplinary content rather than generic skills.

One of the difficulties of this project lay in the use of terminology. In higher education, the words 'core skills' are sometimes associated with the kinds of generic skill outlined above. However, the term is also used to describe those skills which are viewed as central to a specific discipline and which provide each discipline with its own characteristics; they are intricately bound with specific disciplinary content; they are the skills which make a lawyer different from a scientist, or an historian different from a mathematician. The dichotomy in usage rests in part in the conception of 'core skills', especially in further and vocational education as broad-based, cross-disciplinary skills, and this approach has recently been enshrined in a system of National Vocational Qualifications. However, the tradition of higher education, set firmly in the context of disciplinary study, tends to value as 'core' those skills which are central to the discipline.

The model we have developed in order to clarify the contexts of provision for skills (Dunne, Carré; and Bennett, 1997) is designed to suggest the centrality of conceptions of core skills to learning, no matter their interpretation or the extent to which they are integrated into disciplinary study. It also outlines a possibility for the drawing together of different strands of the higher education experience and for identifying overlap or connections between them. It allows recognition of core skills in courses which perpetuate a traditional awareness of disciplinary content and skills, as well as in those which create opportunities for developing generic skills in the absence of subject discipline. It enables exploration of vocational and non-vocational patterns of provision, and the complex amalgam, for example in vocational degree subjects, of workplace awareness and experience provided within a context of disciplinary content and skills. It is this kind of exploration which may allow a better conceptualization of producing learners equipped for the workplace.

The model identifies five major areas of student provision: disciplinary content, disciplinary skills, workplace awareness, workplace skills and generic skills. All courses observed for this project can be described within the five areas, but each will 'fit' the model in a different way according to objectives and to the processes and contexts used for learning. Practices which are believed by teachers to encompass core skills set centrally within the acquisition of disciplinary content can be accommodated as well as those set almost entirely outside a subject context.

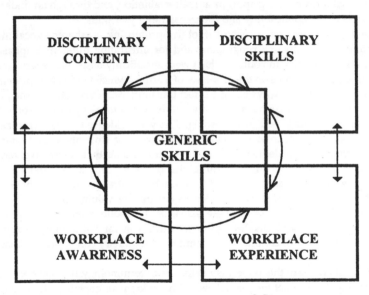

Figure 15.1   A model for the description, analysis and development of core skills

It is intended that this model can in future be used as a tool for more explicit planning for core skills, in its potential for the mapping of individual courses as well as departmental provision as a whole, in the assumption that if all students gain some planned experience in each of the five areas, they will be better prepared for employment. However, in educational terms, or in terms of learning, it may be the connections made between the areas and the experiences that are equally important, and which may promote understanding and even potential for transfer.

15.4.2   University teacher perspectives

The shift of emphasis advocated by government and employer groups, with a significant movement towards employment skills or employability, is not always shared by academics. Not uncommon are comments such as 'I fundamentally and categorically do not believe that these skills have anything to do with a university degree'; 'We shouldn't be a training shop for all kinds of skills – which we could be. If you want to set up a training shop you wouldn't fill it up with academics because they are not actually very good at that on the whole.'

A disappointment of the study is that university teachers do not seem able to talk either easily or explicitly about 'how students learn'; it is not, in general, an issue which they seem used to addressing. As one academic states: 'higher education institutions are simply not set up for this kind of discourse'. Academics (obviously) are used to discussing disciplinary knowledge – but, on the whole, not how to teach it; they are not trained as teachers and do not have the vocabulary of teachers. Yet a deep interest in such issues is apparent at the level of university teachers; there is a genuine and stated desire to work at the issues and questions raised by the core skills project, or to review their practice in the light of new ways of understanding, or to make use of feedback. As an example, one academic asked if he could complete a questionnaire for a second time:

> I thought I would do it very quickly and then I realized there were some fairly deep issues here . . . what your question did was make me think about it, so I want to go back over it again having thought about it more deeply.

Not being able to talk about teaching does not mean that there are no good teachers; but it may be important that the discourse of teaching is enabled to develop if a culture of 'reflective practitioners' is to be achieved, and the student learning experience to be enhanced as a consequence of this.

The notion of a 'learning society' (as in the title of this research programme) is not one that is familiar:

> Maybe it's to do with not being an elite any more, that the whole of society, or a broader section of society, is enabled to learn by having access to higher education, I'm just guessing here. It can't just be limited to the university as a learning society, it must refer to society as a whole taking part.

The title of the Dearing review, 'Higher Education in the Learning Society', may mean, however, that the concept of a learning society fostered both within, and by, higher education is one that will become increasingly important.

15.4.3 Student perspectives

Despite difficulties of conceptualization and vocabulary, many courses in higher education do now include elements designed to enhance generic skills, through, for example, group work, oral presentations or work placements. Despite the large amount of research relating to traditional higher education activities, there is less research which seeks to describe students' experiences of learning from more innovative and skills-based courses, and addressing such issues as:

- Why and how do students vary in the way they learn in skills-based courses?
- What affects the way a student approaches learning in these courses?
- What aspects of the learning environment seem to promote effective learning?

Scenarios (such as that painted by Wagner, 1996) of opportunities for lifelong learning best served by flexible systems (with preferably a breaking down of barriers between HE/FE) do not seem of central importance to students. In the departments surveyed so far, there is little evidence of students moving outside a chosen faculty or widely supporting options designed to offer breadth and interest. Discussion with mature students suggests that they opt for what they perceive looks most like a 'traditional' degree; having got into university they gain satisfaction from achievement in traditional academic terms. They report also being highly committed to their chosen discipline. Younger students give some evidence of not having the confidence to move beyond a selected discipline or the maturity to know what else might be of value to them. As an example, students selecting from a wide range of short options provided specifically to allow them to 'pick and mix' a broad-based curriculum, premised their choices on whatever 'looks easiest'; 'won't take up extra time'; 'has the shortest/easiest assessment'; or looked as if it would directly benefit their present studies – not on enabling them to become more employable or a better learner or having a wider knowledge base.

Students may also be unlikely to espouse the 'new rhetoric' of the purposes of higher education. A first run through of questionnaire data from half the sample observed (some 350 students) suggests that there is a strong tendency for responses to be conceived in terms of subject knowledge rather than skills. One academic comments: 'we are still failing to open our students' eyes to what they need to be fundamentally developing and practising and nurturing – what they need basically to get out of higher education.'

15.4.4   The study of individual students

The following descriptions have been gained from individual students who were participating in compulsory modules on transferable and generic skills. The aim of selecting such students was to investigate how they perceive the relevance of courses which may not have an obvious or direct relationship with the subject matter of their degree. Three courses, and student responses to them, are outlined.

15.4.4.1   *Core skills module: 'Personal and Professional Skills' (BSc. Computing and Informatics, Year 1)*

This module is compulsory and takes place in the first semester of year 1. Teaching methods used are lectures to the whole year group, followed up by small group work where students put skills into practice. Students are required to write a CV, give a group presentation and write a report on a non-computing subject.

15.4.4.2   *Core skills module: 'Transferable skills' (BSc. Geography, Year 2)*

This module is compulsory and takes place in the first semester of year two. It follows on from two previous transferable skills modules which covered study and laboratory skills, IT and writing skills. Teaching methods used are large group lectures, student handbooks on groupwork, verbal skills and career skills, and some small group classes. Students are required to give an individual oral presentation, conduct a group research project (with a report) and compose a CV and job application form.

15.4.4.3   *Core skills module: 'Professional Studies' (BA Fine Art, Year 2)*

This compulsory module consists of a series of lectures from professionals in art-related careers, followed by a project outside of the college environment. Projects were mostly carried out by individuals, although some did work in pairs or small groups. An initial list of possible projects was circulated, but they were free to propose their own project. Students were also required to propose their own learning outcomes and method of assessment, and submit a report.

15.4.5 Findings

Although this work is still in progress and much analysis is still to be done before firm conclusions can be drawn, there are a number of issues emerging from the three case studies. All three groups of students perceived core skills generally to be a valuable part of their academic programme. However, there was a variation in enthusiasm. For example, the geography and fine art students with highly academic orientations tended to see core skills more as something they 'had to do', whereas the computing students, who were more vocationally oriented, were inclined to show a greater personal interest in this area.

> As much as I'd like to do just art, at the same time all of those criteria [core skills] are very important and it would be silly not to have those skills included in a degree
>
> (fine art student)

> To start off with I thought, well, this has got nothing to do with computing, why? . . . and I sat here learning about how to take notes and talk to someone in an interview, but the point of getting a degree is so you can go and get a job in the first place . . . so if you haven't got any interpersonal skills . . . then there's no point in getting a degree, because no-one's going to want to employ you
>
> (computing and informatics student)

In general terms, it seems that student experiences and interpretation of core skill courses are likely to be affected by their degree subject and the extent to which such skills are perceived to be directly relevant to their needs. This, in turn, is likely to affect motivation for learning and the nature of feedback to tutors. The less core skills are perceived to be relevant, the less students are likely to be motivated or enthusiastic. However, teachers often work hard to create a relevance, to persuade students of the necessity of generic skills, and to reinforce this through assessment. This may be more difficult, but all the more important, in non-vocational degrees.

In all three modules, the skills which students felt they had learnt closely matched the intentions of the provider. However, students also recognized further skills which they employed in order to complete coursework. For example, the geography students added time management, research skills, information handling, report writing and project organization to those skills which were the specific focus, in the teachers' terms, of the module. Also, when asked what they believed the aims of the module to be, the computing students believed it was not only to help them vocationally and academically, but also personally (organizing themselves and their money) and socially (allowing them to meet other students). These were first-year students, and such perceptions may reflect their needs at that time.

Although students know that core skills will be useful in employment, they are not always sure in which ways this would be so. Fine art students, having experienced a taste of a working environment, were more clear about how their skills would be directly of use than the computing or geography students. Although they also had some idea that such skills would be useful in getting, or in doing, a job, they seemed less able to elaborate on this. There was a tendency to repeat lists of skills without providing personal insight into how they would use them.

> At the moment my work is interacting with the general public as opposed to an art audience, and working with pupils in a school as opposed to the general public is different. It's very important to have people observing what I'm doing and interacting, so it'll be valuable
>
> (fine art student with intended career in teaching)

research skills and problem solving and interpersonal skills, organization, groupwork – I think that's what you use in a working environment

(geography student)

apart from the application form . . . perhaps giving a talk, I don't know

(geography student)

Students saw staff as the key to providing an optimal learning environment. Aspects of this which were mentioned are: providing an informal or fun atmosphere; helping the students to feel personally involved; giving a clear indication of aims and objectives; providing a good example by demonstrating competence in core skills; showing commitment to the importance of core skills; giving adequate support while encouraging students to learn independently; and understanding the structure of the module, including assessment.

even when you saw him in the corridor, he'd say hello and use your name. The lectures were more laid back with all the little jokes and bits, and quotes that he'd put on the slides just to make them that little bit more interesting. One day he brought teddy bears in to illustrate some point, and yeah, I remember it

(computing and informatics student)

I think it's quite good that it's somebody who does geography [who runs this course] because then you get the impression that it's important, it's important to the geography department that we do it.

(geography student)

Any uncertainty on the part of staff was also picked up by students. Demonstrating a commitment to generic skills through teaching style and attitude seems to be a major factor affecting both the quality of students' experiences and their interest in skill development.

15.4.6   Employer perspectives

One finding of concern, if the notion of workplace experience is to be taken seriously, is an apparent lack of commitment from employers to partnership with higher education in developing student learning, especially among the smaller, local companies. This may be understandable in the present economic climate, and in Britain there is no history of this kind of community involvement except in some kinds of professional training. Finding students a placement for any kind of sandwich course, long or short, or even a vacation placement, can be difficult and is likely to get more difficult with increasing demands. In a meeting of local employers it was made clear that there was a desire to 'vet' students for placements in order to check for their acceptability and to ensure that only the 'best' students were taken. This perhaps runs counter to any requirement for more students to be given an opportunity in gaining workplace experience, especially those from disciplines where a vocational or professional training does not form some part of the degree. Further, it has been made clear that many employers are, in the main, not willing to give any length of time to students once in the workplace, that students' 'getting a job done' is more important than enabling them to reflect on their learning, and that assessing student competence is too difficult or time-consuming. There are, of course, some notable exceptions to this, and some students who have experienced a deep commitment to their development within the workplace.

Employers, despite the rhetoric of skills as being essential, also show a tendency to recruit graduates with at least 'upper second' degrees, preferably from the traditional universities, rather than those from 'new' universities – even when these graduates (as evidenced within our sample) have been provided with a firm grounding in generic skills.

15.5 Discussion

To date, the findings seem to raise more questions than they answer. For example, to what extent does a focus on generic skills mean that we risk losing the demand on students for conceptualization of deep learning and understanding of a discipline, which is the central purpose of a degree to many academics – including those who are open to change and who do not discount the value of skills for employment? How much is known about the relationship of changes in learning provision to the ability of graduates to be effective in employment in later years? Universities may have been guilty of ill-preparing students for the workplace and for an uncertain future, but many academics continue strongly to defend disciplinary study and the core skills deemed integral to this as being the most important preparation for any future.

Is it enough to consider that those who gain access to higher education are automatically set on the road of lifelong learning? To what extent should quality of learning and experience be addressed? How can informed decisions be made about structures, nature of provision, the role of generic skills? Whose voice is the most important – that of the student, the academic, the administrator, the employer? In recent years, higher education has been subjected to many changes; access has been widened, accountability and efficiency have become key concepts and structural changes have been achieved. However, none of these changes has been premised on a framework for learning, let alone on what it could mean to develop lifelong learners, with an ability to transfer useful knowledge and skills effectively between contexts. Much of the difficulty in the area of core skills is that approaches are set in a context of dogmatic views rather than healthy debate. This cannot be the most positive contribution to a learning society. The latest report from Dearing (1997), with its support for a functional approach to higher education to complement the more traditional knowledge-based curriculum, and with its emphasis on learning and professionalism in teaching, may be just the catalyst that is needed.

15.6 References

Slee, P. (1989) A consensus framework for higher education. In C. Ball and H. Eggins (eds), *Higher Education in the 1990s: New Dimensions*, SRHE/OUP.

Dearing Report (1997) *Higher Education in the Learning Society*, London: HMSO.

Dunne, E. (1995) *Personal Transferable Skills*, Report to Teaching Development Committee, University of Exeter.

Dunne, E., Carré, C. and Bennett, N. (1997) Working Paper, Core Skills Project, University of Exeter.

Wagner, L. (1996) *Lifelong Learning and the Relationship between Higher and Further Education*, Higher Education and Lifelong Learning, University of Newcastle upon Tyne, Department of Education.

Appendix 15.1 A framework for the development of generic skills

The core of this framework presents areas considered central to the promotion of effective learning experiences. The quadrants of the framework outline skills in key areas of personal development: management of self, of others, of the task and of information. The skills lists provided here do not preclude attention to more conventional lists including, for example, 'communication', 'problem-solving', 'independent learning', 'team/ group work', 'self-reliance' etc. but may be used in conjunction with them. It is intended that skills should be selected and combined from across the management quadrants according to context, purposes and required emphases. These lists serve as a starting point which may be supplemented and adjusted.

MANAGEMENT OF INFORMATION
- use appropriate sources of information (library, retrieval systems, people, etc)
- use appropriate technology, including IT
- use appropriate media
- handle large amounts of information / data effectively
- gather information from appropriate sources
- use appropriate language and form in a range of activities
- interpret a variety of information forms
- present information / ideas competently (orally, in written form, visually)
- respond to different purposes / contexts / audiences
- use information critically
- use information in innovative and creative ways
- persuade rationally

MANAGEMENT OF TASK
- identify key features
- conceptualise issues
- set and maintain priorities
- identify strategic options
- plan and implement a course of action
- organise sub-tasks
- use and develop appropriate strategies
- assess outcomes

MANAGEMENT OF SELF
- manage time effectively
- set objectives, priorities and standards
- take responsibility for own learning
- listen actively and with purpose
- use a range of academic skills (analysis, synthesis, argument, etc)
- develop and adapt learning strategies
- show intellectual flexibility
- use learning in new or different situations / contexts
- plan / work towards long-term aims and goals
- purposefully reflect on own learning and progress
- clarify personal values
- deal with constructive criticism
- cope with stress

MANAGEMENT OF OTHERS
- carry out agreed tasks
- respect the views and values of others
- work productively in a cooperative context
- adapt to the needs of the group
- defend / justify views or actions
- take initiative and lead others
- delegate and stand back
- negotiate
- offer constructive criticism
- take the role of chairperson
- learn in a collaborative context
- assist / support others in learning

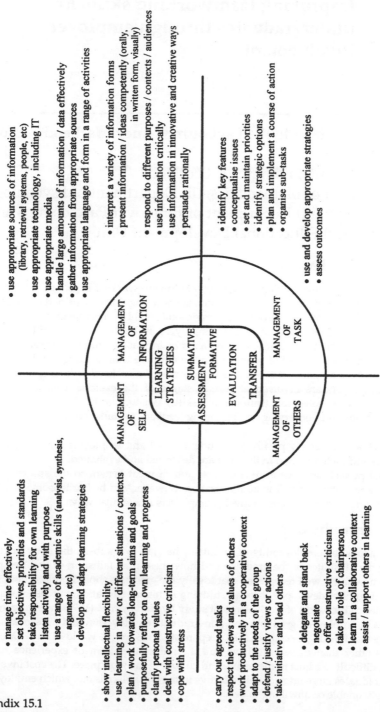

LEARNING STRATEGIES
SUMMATIVE
FORMATIVE
ASSESSMENT
EVALUATION
TRANSFER

Appendix 15.1

16 Improving teamworking skills in undergraduates through employer involvement

Judy Goldfinch[i], **Phyllis Laybourn**[ii], **Lucy MacLeod**[iii] **and Sheila Stewart**[iv]
Napier University, Edinburgh, Scotland
(i) Department of Mathematics; (ii) Department of Psychology and Sociology; (iii) Department of Employer Partnerships and Enterprise; (iv) Educational Development Unit

16.1 Overview

Frequently undergraduate project work involves students working in groups or teams. Such teamworking is often problematic due to poor teamworking skills on the part of the students involved, yet 'teamwork' is one of those generic skills highly prized by employers.

This study describes a pilot to involve employers in the development of teamworking skills in undergraduate students, with the aims of increasing student awareness of team dynamics and processes and of promoting more effective teamworking. Students work in small teams over a period of 6–8 weeks on a problem associated with the module being studied. Employers are involved at several stages of the exercise: contributing to the identification of key assessible teamworking skills; assisting in the design of the problem and, most importantly, observing and providing feedback to students on their teamworking skills.

The reactions (extremely positive) of students, staff and employers are presented. The procedures and methods used in the pilot are described and evaluated.

The pilot project has been a great success and of great benefit to the students. It will certainly be repeated again. The administration, however, can be burdensome and advice will be given for others wishing to involve employers in a similar way.

16.2 Introduction

Concerns about the employability of graduates has led to a substantial body of research exploring the attributes of the graduate and how these may fall short of what employers seek. It is now fairly well recognized that ideally the graduate should possess not only the intellectual abilities developed through studying in higher education, but also transferable skills related to the world of work. A recent study by Harvey *et al.* (1997) involving in-depth interviews of employers, graduate and non-graduate employees found agreement among employers that few degree courses fully prepare students for the world of work. Moreover, graduates other than those who have had a significant placement experience reported finding it difficult to adjust to the nature and culture of the workplace. The cost involved in making graduates more immediately effective in the workplace is one which employers are increasingly unable or unwilling to bear.

The present study concerns the development of teamworking – defined here as: working collaboratively with others and contributing to task management in order to achieve team goals – in undergraduate students, an interactive attribute highly valued by employers. There is a growing emphasis on teamwork in university courses and there is also an increase in research and other publications relating to development, management and assessment of student team project work. This demonstrates the increasing recognition of teamworking not only as a useful transferable skill assisting successful transition from graduate to employee but also as a co-operative vehicle for effective learning. However, recent research suggests this has yet to make a significant impact on the graduate profile as perceived by employers (Harvey *et al.*, 1997). Have these methods not been adopted widely enough or long enough to have made an impact, or is there an element of lack of sophistication in terms of how teamworking is developed, assessed and integrated within the curriculum? How can we effectively inculcate team working skills in higher education students? It is questions such as these which led us to embark on the current research initiative.

A key concern in educational research and practice is the identification of methods which actively and meaningfully engage the student in the learning process. Principles of active, student centred learning (Entwistle, Thompson and Tait, 1992) and deep learning (Marton and Säljö, 1976; Entwistle, 1988) were fundamental in informing the design and undertaking of the present study. A mathematics project was the vehicle for enabling students to gain experience in teamwork. In addition to demonstrating understanding and skills related to the mathematics topic, students were also expected to enhance awareness of team experience and processes and to promote more effective teamworking skills. These two separate but interrelated educational aims may be referred to as 'product' (mathematics project) and 'process' (teamworking skills).

In the present study the key innovative step is to involve employers at several stages in the project: contributing to the identification of key assessable teamworking skills; assisting in the design of the problem; observing and providing feedback to students on teamworking skills. To date there is little or no documented research in the UK in this area. In the USA, however, at Alverno College, Milwaukee the co-operation of local employers in the development and assessment of a range of skills has now become established practice (Alverno, 1994). The methods used to involve employers in the present study are influenced by the Alverno model but are less resource intensive. This study is part of a wider initiative: LANDSKAPE (Learning and Skills Achievement through Partnership with Employers) which is a major Scottish Higher Education Funding Council funded project at Napier University. Among other things, employer involvement makes the learning experience more meaningful for the student. It also establishes credibility and provides a motivational impetus raising the level of performance and reinforces the aims and objectives set by staff.

The active learning methods adopted to enhance teamworking skills are designed to provide the students with opportunities to engage in a 'natural' learning cycle (Kolb, 1983). The cycle depends on active participation ('doing'), to set in motion the learning process. The second stage, 'reflecting', is fundamental, linking practical experience with the interpretation of that experience ('thinking') and devising ways of profiting from that experience in future ('planning'). The importance of reflection is well recognized (Schön, 1983; Boud *et al.*, 1985). In this study the reflection process is engaged by creating opportunities for feedback and appraisal of activities. The general term 'reflection' relates to a more specifically defined cognitive process, that of metacognition (Flavell, 1970). Metacognition is associated with 'learning to learn' and the development of learning strategies (Nisbet and Shucksmith, 1986). Metacognitive processes are regarded as occupying a central, pivotal position. They are described as executive processes for example, monitoring, checking, revising and self-testing.

The current study utilizes three concurrent methods designed to enhance conscious awareness of skills and strategies involved in teamwork. First, students participate in tasks which require the selection, utilization and analysis of previously learned teamworking skills. Secondly, instructional materials are made available which will provide explanation of key team work skills and give suggestions about how to develop these. Thirdly, and most importantly, a number of experiences involving feedback and reflection are provided. One aspect of metacognition is the monitoring of current level of understanding. This requires developing and utilizing criteria for evaluating the adequacy of current performance. The value of feedback for self evaluation and aiding the establishment of internal criteria is well documented (Bransford, 1979). Thus in the present study, feedback from employers is used to enable the learner to confront and raise conscious awareness of their current level of understanding and skill in teamworking. Several other opportunities for reflection further enhance this process of raising conscious awareness and promote active and meaningful interpretation of experiences gained.

16.3   Method

The aims of the present study are: to increase awareness of team dynamics and processes; to promote more effective teamworking; to test procedures and methods for co-ordinating employer involvement; and to examine the effectiveness of video and face-to-face observation and feedback.

16.3.1   Design

The Department of Mathematics runs a module in quantitative methods for 35 second-year BA Accounting students which, for the first time, was to include an extensive assignment on project management, worth 50 per cent of the module marks and lasting for six weeks. The mathematical aim of this coursework was to develop the students' understanding of the topic and their skills in using Microsoft Project Manager by exposing them to a real project management problem. This problem was supplied by the finance company Standard Life and the set of associated tasks was jointly developed by them and the module team. The students worked in eight teams of four or five. They were assessed through a team report with individual marks assigned by peer assessment (Goldfinch, 1994). To help in the development of their teamskills, each student, individually, was asked to write a reflective essay on the experience worth 10 per cent of their coursework mark.

Key stages in the project were: a short student training session on teamworking in week one; employer's training session in observation and feedback – week one; observation and feedback session in week four; completion of evaluation questionnaires; and project submission.

16.3.2   Procedure

16.3.2.1   *Employer's forum*

One of the first steps in the LANDSKAPE project was to bring together a number of staff, students and employers to discuss the implications of involving employers in teamwork assessment. Approximately 60 people in total attended a three-hour discussion forum held in the university. Following discussion, the employers were canvassed regarding their possible future contributions to LANDSKAPE. A number of employers offered to take part in observation sessions and four volunteered to join an Employer's Working Group (EWG) and assist in the preparation of materials/feedback forms.

16.3.2.2 Development of observation forms

Two observation forms were developed for use in the Maths pilot: a team assessment form and an individual assessment form. First drafts were prepared by the CWG following:

- visits to/interviews with recruitment personnel from three large companies in Lothians and Fife;

- research into methods used at Alverno College, USA;

- review of current literature on developing transferable skills particularly in relation to team/team work.

These drafts were revised in the light of comments from the EWG. Further revisions were made following the use of the forms during the employers' training session (see below).

16.3.2.3 Arranging the employers

The number of employers required for the Maths pilot was determined by the following decisions on the part of the sub-group of the CWG and the module team:

(a) to use 1:2 observation (i.e. one employer for every two students);

(b) to have an additional observer to record and feedback on the performance of the team as a whole.

The aim was to recruit and train a minimum pool of 25. The employers were drawn from existing departmental databases; contacts provided by departmental placement tutors and personal contacts of the project team.

16.3.2.4 Employers' training session

Employer volunteers and members of the CWG were required to attend a training session two weeks before the date scheduled for the observation session. The programme consisted of small team discussions on personal experience of working teams; plenary session to raise concerns about teamworking; an introduction to the feedback forms; a simulated student teamwork exercise, during which two-thirds of the employers/CWG completed individual assessment forms and the remainder completed team assessment forms; team discussion and comparison of assessments; mini-lecture on giving feedback; and questions and discussion. Only people who attended this training session were permitted to act as observers.

16.3.2.5 Student training session

The two-hour training session took place in week one of the semester during normal class time. A short introduction summarized the aims of the project, supplied clear guidelines on how the project was to be run, identified its key stages and explained how it was to be assessed. The terms 'product' and 'process' were explained and related to the educational aims of the project. Some time was spent alerting students to the importance of teamwork as a generic skill strongly valued by employers. The role of employers as team observers supplying feedback was described. Students were then asked to split into teams of four or five to include one or more of the students who were absent from the class (24 of the 35 students taking the module attended).

Stage two of the training session was designed to enable students to draw on previous experience of team work, begin to relate this to teamskills and to evaluate previous team behaviour. It also gave students the opportunity to begin the process of team cohesion and to experience team communication and interaction. Choosing a team name served as an ice-breaker to this session. Students were then given a brief introduction to Belbin's team roles and were given forms (adapted from Gibbs, 1994) to focus their reflection on previous team experience. Individually, they were required to identify those roles which they felt applied or did not apply to them. Students then discussed their individual responses and identified team members who could fulfil each of the roles either as a primary or a secondary strength.

Students were then introduced to key jobs facilitating successful teamwork (leader, progress chaser, timekeeper, secretary) and asked to consider how their team would ensure these jobs were done. The penultimate task involved a brainstorming session which required reflection on previous team experience to describe ways of 'wrecking a team' (Gibbs, 1994). This ended with students giving feedback of examples of wrecking behaviours.

In the final task students began the process of drawing up a team management plan. They were asked to devise and agree on a set of ground rules (a code of conduct) to help the smooth operation of their team. Students displayed their rules on flip chart paper around the room for other teams to appraise and comment on. Students were then set the task, to be submitted at the next tutorial, of completing a team management plan arranged under the headings: ground rules; team communication; action plan and procedures; and monitoring and evaluation. They were issued with booklets on teamworking (Gibbs, 1994) and a one-page index to assist them to locate information on potentially important team issues. The session ended with students filling in a team evaluation form which encouraged reflection on how the team operated on key aspects of team process over the course of the training session.

16.3.2.6 *The observation session*

This session took place in week four. The students' normal mathematics tutorial was providentially followed by a free hour on their timetable so this two-hour slot was fixed for the observation session. The employers were invited in for a briefing half an hour beforehand, allocated to student teams and to type of observation (team or individual).

Students were required to prepare material before the observation session and, at the start of the observation, were provided with a sheet of questions to answer based on the prepared material, plus various tasks to perform such as preparing a difficult memo, deciding how to resolve various problems, and planning how to complete the rest of the project. They were given a time limit of 50 minutes. The observers sat round the team who were themselves sitting round a table. Each team was observed by one team observer who watched the team as a whole, and two individual observers who each observed two students as individuals. (A third observer was used for the fifth student in teams of five.) In addition, two of the student teams were videoed by means of a fixed camera. (Initially it had been intended to have no live observers for the videoed teams to see if this was less intimidating, but it was decided that (a) these students should not be deprived of instant feedback and (b) parallel live observation would allow checks on how well it was possible to observe using a video.)

After the observation, the employers recongregated to reflect and prepare feedback. Employers chose to discuss their observations in their groupings of three. Students completed identical forms to the employers on their own individual behaviour in their team to provide a starting point for the feedback discussion.

Thereafter, each student received 10 to 15 minutes' feedback from the employer who observed them as an individual, followed by feedback as a team from the observer who watched the team as a whole.

16.3.2.7 *Evaluation questionnaires*

Evaluation of the project was principally by a questionnaire posted out to all the observers immediately after the observation session, and a questionnaire completed by the students during the first mathematics lecture after the session. These questionnaires were designed to ascertain the employers' and students' feelings about the experience as a whole and contained the following headings:

Employers: Observation and feedback training session, general resources provided for observation event, observation and feedback forms, giving feedback, general comments.

A large proportion of the questions on the employers' form were open, asking for comments or suggestions for improvement.

Students: Observation session (how behaviour changed while being observed, feelings during observation), feedback session (positive aspects about receiving feedback, negative aspects about receiving feedback, the self-assessment form, whether there were improvements in how the team operated), general (views about involving employers, how the team behaved before the observation, general comments), being videoed (where applicable).

Questions on the student form were mainly closed with responses requested on a four-point scale from 'Not at all' to 'A great deal'. Some open questions were included to allow for unanticipated reactions, for comment, for detail and for explanations.

16.4   Results of the pilot

The project successfully recruited the required numbers of employers who came from organizations in the private, public and voluntary sectors. They held a range of positions within their organizations and different types of experience of recruitment practices and procedures. For those who attended both the training session and the observation session, the total time involved amounted to some six to eight hours. The project team were very encouraged by the response, enthusiasm and commitment displayed by all the employers. Several employers commented on how much they had enjoyed participating in the exercise and all said that were happy to be contacted again.

All forms of feedback were very positive, summarized by the comments 'the whole experience was most informative and well managed' from an employer and 'the whole experience was very worthwhile' from a student.

16.4.1   The employers' training session

The training session for the employer and staff observers was highly successful, giving employers familiarity and practice with the materials and increasing their confidence. The two-week gap between the training and the actual observation session was found acceptable but on the long side.

16.4.2   The student training session

This session was less successful. Since the activities of the session were designed to promote proper team development, it was unfortunate that most teams had several missing members. This was principally a problem of timing. Allowing students to form teams of their choosing but to include some of the absent students led to considerable discontent. Some of the absentees were apparently well known for their lack of participation in such projects and others resented having to include them. A later timing for the training would have allowed some preparatory work and allowed the alternative strategy (Standing, 1995) of staff allocating students into balanced teams.

The period of two hours was found to be rather short for the student training: a slightly longer session would have allowed time for more active participation and discussion. The time between the student training and the observation session, at three weeks, was determined by the work schedule of the module but would ideally have been slightly longer to allow teams to meet more often.

16.4.3   The observation session

16.4.3.1   Arrangements

In practice it proved impossible to obtain a separate observation room for each team and there were two cases of two teams at opposite ends of a large room. The observers reported that, though definitely not ideal, the situation had been just about manageable. Four of the six observers involved in room sharing reported problems of hearing the students speak. All but two of the observers felt that the 50-minute observation time was 'about right'; the other two felt it would have been better if it had been 10 minutes shorter.

All except three students attended the observation session and on time. The missing three formed three-quarters of a team that confessed afterwards to never having met. Only one observer was absent.

16.4.3.2   Student reactions

Students' feelings about being observed varied considerably. Several felt that they were quieter than usual, but a similar number said that they tried to say more than usual. One team, from now on called Team X, resented being observed, but none of the students from the other teams did. Team X was dominated by one student who 'disliked teamwork and had no wish to change'. His attitude that 'it was all a waste of time' spoilt the experience for the rest of his team. Students reported being more aware of judging their own actions and being very aware of the observers. However, several added that, after about ten minutes, they relaxed and 'blotted out' the observers or the camera.

16.4.3.3   Observation and feedback forms

The observation forms seemed to work well. One or two people found the scales difficult to use when the end criteria did not appear to be mutually exclusive or when an individual was rather passive and quiet. Several observers requested space for more comments. Many found the time they had to reflect and to complete the forms too short.

16.4.3.4   Student self-assessment forms

These were shown only to the individual observers who all found them useful, principally as a helpful starting point for feedback discussion but also as a reassurance for observers with less experience. Observers commented that student patterns often agreed with theirs but that the students tended to undermark themselves. This is not really surprising as people generally prefer to be told that they are better than they have stated. Team observers would have liked to see self-assessment forms, too. Students were rather more conservative on how useful they found completing the forms.

16.4.3.5   Feedback session

All except two students (both from Team X) found the employers' feedback very informative and almost all said it would be very useful to them in the future. Every student, even from Team X, felt that they had been shown ways that they could improve and practically all found that it increased their confidence considerably. Most said that it revealed aspects of their own behaviour that they had been unaware of and half found that it revealed aspects of other's behaviour that they had not been aware of. All but two students commented how valuable it was to have employers involved in such exercises, seeing them as impartial observers with 'real' experience.

A few of the employers would have liked longer for giving feedback, particularly for the weaker teams, and most would have welcomed a short general discussion session at the end of the morning to share experiences.

16.4.3.6.   Student use of the feedback

When asked if there had been any improvement to how their team operated after receiving feedback, all members of Team X felt that there had not. However, most other students felt that there had been definite improvements. Several commented that their team began to plan and work more efficiently, and even more commented on individual behaviour having improved such as being more assertive, listening more and being more aware of team needs.

Most students felt that the employers' assessment should be formative only and should not contribute to their module mark.

16.4.4   Videoed sessions

The videoed sessions were rather unsatisfactory with the students finding them stressful and the resultant videos being of poor quality. The observers who watched the videos found their sound so poor that they had serious doubts about their assessments. They also found that the fixed camera angle prevented the observer from seeing those whose backs were to the camera and also from seeing what the students were pointing to on the paperwork. They did, however, see great advantages to this form of observation in that there was no travelling involved, the video could be replayed where necessary, the observer did not feel 'himself' to be under observation, and several observers could assess the same performance. However, future videos would require every student to be seen and heard separately throughout.

16.4.5   Student comments from their reflective essays

In these essays students were asked to reflect on their team's development, their own role within the team, whether the feedback had helped, and how they would handle teamwork in the future. The essays were full of very encouraging and positive comments about the employers' feedback, going into considerable detail in some cases, and showing that the student had understood, appreciated and learnt from the experience.

Typical comments include:

> None of us thought that this was important until it was pointed out to us at the feedback session.

The feedback from the observers has helped me enormously. It is a key area which employers look at.

The feedback from the employer was very useful in that it gave a different point of view on how I was working in a team.

The feedback from the employers was very interesting and very good. For example, I did not realize that during the observation session that I was not allowing Craig to join in the discussion just through the position of my body.

16.4.6   The team project submissions

The marks awarded for the product of the teams did not correlate with how well the teams seemed to work together. However, all the teams managed to solve the problem and marks were lost for errors in the data entry or for poor presentation rather than for lack of success.

Students completed peer assessment forms to indicate how much of the success of the team was due to each member. Most teams reported little variation in the contribution between members. The only team showing a lot of variation between contribution levels was Team X, the team with the dominant, disaffected member.

16.5   Discussion

The present study has effectively tested a method of involving employers in student teamwork. It has also provided some evidence that these methods produce improvements in teamskills and increased awareness of team dynamics and processes.

It has clearly shown that the procedures and methods used were, on the whole, successful. The very nature of action research makes the likelihood of unforeseen difficulties arising greater and increases the value of pilot work to aid future planning. This study gave many insights into operational aspects of running this type of project and provided valuable indicators for future work. Good preparation and training of the observers played a key part in the success of the project. Observers were particularly positive about the training session and this seemed to provide good preparation for the demanding task of observing the students. The student training session was somewhat marred by absent team members. Delaying training by one week or imposing some attendance incentive/penalty system may alleviate this problem. Ideally more time should be allocated to this session. This would allow fuller debriefing of each exercise, thus encouraging students to reflect and review the process, aiding the structuring and reinforcement of learning experiences. Consideration will also be given to the option of using some screening questionnaire, e.g. learning styles, team roles to aid the formation of more balanced teams.

The observation and feedback session was reported to be a valuable and informative experience, providing clear direction on possible ways of improving, revealing aspects of individual and team behaviour that they had been unaware of and, with few exceptions, served to raise confidence. These comments reinforce the view that feedback aids reflection and provides a process for improvements in teamskills. Moreover, most teams reported improvements in their behaviour after feedback, indicating, perhaps, completion of the learning cycle. Analysis of the reflective essays further reinforced this view. There was evidence of students using and applying concepts relating to team process to analyse and evaluate personal and team behaviour in an appropriate way.

The project team's concerns about student performance being seriously disrupted as a result of observation seemed to have been unfounded. It was generally felt that while observation produced changes in behaviour, few resented observation taking place. The majority reported being more aware of their behaviour. This may have proved beneficial to the reflection process providing greater conscious appraisal of the interaction.

The video methods utilized tested facilities and equipment readily available to staff under normal teaching circumstances. Unfortunately the quality of recordings produced was poor. Clearly greater attention needs to be paid to layout, microphones and camera position. Future work will explore this while attempting to maintain costs at a feasible level.

Future work will explore the use of this technique in a larger sample of students incorporating cohorts who have differing levels of prior teamskill training. Control teams receiving all aspects of teamskill training except observation and feedback will be used for comparison. Measures will include questionnaire and focus team feedback, product mark and content of reflective essays. Additional comparisons between video and face-to-face observation, written and face-to-face feedback and, finally, staff and employer observers will be made.

16.6   References and bibliography

Alverno College Faculty (1994) *Student Assessment-as-Learning at Alverno College,* Milwaukee: Alverno College, 3.

Boud, D., Keogh, R. and Walker, D. (1985) *Reflection: Turning Experience into Learning,* London: Kogan Page.

Bransford, J. D. (1979) *Human Cognition: Learning, Understanding and Remembering,* Belmont, California: Wadsworth Publishing Company.

Entwistle, N. J. (1988) *Styles of Learning and Teaching,* London: David Foulton.

Entwistle, N. J., Thompson, S. and Tait, H. (1992) *Guidelines for Promoting Effective Learning in Higher Education,* Centre for Research on Learning and Instruction, University of Edinburgh.

Flavell, J. H.(1970) Developmental studies of mediated memory. In H. W. Reese and L. P. Lipitt (eds), *Advances in Child Development and Behaviour,* New York: Academic Press.

Gibbs, G. (1994) *Learning in Teams – A Student Guide; Learning in Teams – A Student Manual,* Oxford: The Oxford Centre for Staff Development.

Goldfinch, J. (1994) Further developments in peer assessment of team projects, *Assessment and Evaluation in Higher Education,* 19(1), 29–35.

Harvey, L., Moon, S. and Geall, V. with Bower, R. (1997) *Graduates' Work: Organisational Change and Students' Attributes,* Birmingham, Centre for Research into Quality.

Kolb, D. A. (1983) *Experiential Learning: The Experience as the Source of Learning and Development,* New York, Prentice Hall.

Marton, F. and Säljö, R. (1976) On qualitative differences in learning: I-outcome and process, *British Journal of Educational Psychology,* 46, 4–11.

Nisbet, J. and Shucksmith, J. (1986) *Learning Strategies,* Routledge & Kegan Paul.

Schön, D.A. (1983) *The Reflective Practitioner: How Professionals Think in Action,* London, Temple Smith.

Standing, T. (1995) Managing learning teams effectively, *Training Officer,* 31(3), 80–2.

17 Supporting first-year students: generic skills development strategies

Nancy Falchikov
Napier University, Edinburgh

17.1 Overview

There is a growing concern for the welfare of first-year students, in terms of the stress levels experienced by many students and in relation to under achievement and drop out rates. Some of these areas of concern are reviewed briefly, and a number of strategies designed to ameliorate the situation, recently implemented in higher education institutions world wide, are discussed. Many strategies for supporting first-year students emphasize the development of generic skills. Controversies concerning generic skills generally, and the 'best way' in which to provide opportunities for their development are addressed. Issues concerning the question of whether it is more beneficial to embed such training within specialist modules or to provide purpose-built modules are explored. The need for evaluation of the effectiveness of different approaches, in terms of both transferability of the skills developed and increased well-being of students, is stressed, and an evaluative research programme currently underway at Napier University, Edinburgh, is described.

17.2 The growing concern for the welfare of first-year students

There is a growing concern for the welfare of first-year undergraduates, in terms of the stress levels experienced by many students, and in relation to under-achievement and dropout rates. John Earwaker, a chaplain working within the student support services in a UK college of education, comparing his current experiences with those previous to his arrival in higher education, writes of his surprise on encountering an alarming number and variety of student problems.

> Like many teaching staff, I imagined that many students must find . . . a large institution daunting and perhaps alienating; that they might be lonely, anxious and afraid; and that they would appreciate it if someone was willing to befriend them, offer practical help and possibly some advice as well. That, of course, is all true, but it is not the whole truth' (Earwaker, 1992, p. viii).

Earwaker goes on to describe the numerous and complex problems he encountered on entering higher education, 'almost every problem imaginable' (p. viii) – drug addiction, alcoholism, suicide, imprisonment.

We are all familiar with some student problems, which can range from the serious to the apparently slight, though the latter category may also be a manifestation of something more important. For example, there is a growing amount of anecdotal evidence pointing to absenteeism in large first-year classes. However, Fisher (1994) found that missing lectures was a manifestation of homesickness. She described students who habitually missed lectures because they were unable to leave their rooms or to function properly. Moreover, 'they were also unlikely to report the experience . . . because they believed it to be "wimpish"' (Fisher, 1994, p. 45).

Another, more obviously serious problem for students, and one that is certain to become more acute in the future, is that of finance. Whatever our views on student contributions to tuition fees, student loans or graduate taxes, a direct consequence of these measures is that many of our students are now engaged in some kind of employment in addition to their full-time studies in order to pay their way. A recent survey of student employment in four years of six courses at Heriot-Watt University, Edinburgh (Taylor, 1997) found that only 8 per cent of students surveyed *did not work* at all. Students undertook vacation work and weekend work, they worked in the evenings during the week, and were engaged in paid employment during the weekdays. It is very likely that these secondary occupations will interfere with the quantity and quality of studying. Financial considerations may also influence dropout decisions. Certainly, attrition rates have given cause for concern at Napier University and in the higher education sector more widely (e.g. Johnson, 1996a and b; Raab, 1995).

17.3   The experience of transition to student life

Transitions involve a movement from one state or situation to another. Students now come into higher education not only from school, but also from work, from unemployment and, increasingly, from retirement. Thus, there is likely to be a wide variety of ways in which this particular transition will be experienced. Whatever the situation, the transition will involve complex pathways and interactions between factors of particular salience to any individual. Common to all experiences of transition is change and development. Earwaker (1992) proposed three dimensions of change involved in the transition to higher education: development as a person, development as a student and 'occupational socialization' (p. 17) or development in relation to some specific career. Successful adaptation to many aspects of the new situation presented by the new institution will require flexibility on the part of the student and the ability to cope with change.

All change is stressful, even change for the better. 'Change is, in fact, one of the monumental stress factors of our time', wrote Cooper *et al.* (1988, p. 123). Welcomed life events, such as buying a house, marriage or the birth of a child, carry with them increased levels of stress. Moreover, problems caused by the 'constantly changing world' (Cooper *et al.*, 1988, p. 124) multiply when one enters higher education. Taking up a place at university involves the new student in a series of changes and this has, for some, been found to 'have powerful negative effects on well being and health' (Fisher, 1994). Fisher's surveys of Scottish students found very high levels of homesickness (between 60 and 70 per cent). She has argued that the stress experienced during students' early weeks at university might be accounted for by transient loss of control over the new environment which is an inevitable consequence of moving into unknown surroundings. Similarly, our own work at Napier University has found not only disturbingly high levels of stress in first-year students but also that student approaches to studying tend to change for the worse during the first semester, particularly in terms of strategic approaches (Thomson and Falchikov, 1997). These changes, too, could be a consequence of the reduction in control experienced by the students on entry to the new strange environment of university.

17.4   Strategies for supporting students in higher education

A number of strategies for reducing failure and dropout have been attempted. For example, Tinto's (1975) model of student dropout, which incorporates demographic factors, measures of motivation and commitment to the institution and academic and social integration, has been found to provide a useful structure to aid in the development of strategies to support students during their very important first year.

It is possible to offer students support in a variety of areas of their experience at university: academic, financial, emotional and social. In general, Earwaker (1992) argues that institutions may rely on one of three sources of help: specialist professionals trained to provide for student welfare; academic staff who respond, formally or informally, to students in trouble; or voluntary and other informal arrangements. Specialist professionals are usually located in formal organizations such as student support services, student counselling services, housing associations, chaplaincies and student associations. Generally, professional counselling services operate 'on the margins' and support provided by these services is often seen as an extra-curricular activity. Informal support for students may also come from friends, family, peers or subject tutors. However, Earwaker (1992) questions whether amateur guidance, however well-meaning, is an appropriate course of action. He believes that some informal attempts at support may be 'positively dangerous' (p. 107) in that they may result in an unhealthy dependency or abuse of the teacher's power. Moreover, students readily recognize and resent paternalism which may characterize some tutor–student interactions. In any case, argues Earwaker, many teaching staff may have at least as many problems themselves as many of their students.

The question of whether support for students should be integral to the educational task or ancillary to it is one that continues to concern us. How may institutions provide help and support which is seen as a normal part of the student's experience rather than an extra-curricular activity? Many universities, particularly in the USA, now offer programmes designed to support first-year students, many of which emphasize the usefulness of the development of generic (or personal transferable) skills. For example, the American 'Freshman Seminar' includes reading and writing skills, library skills, study skills, time management and group working as essential elements in the first-year programme.

17.5   Models of provision: focus on problems and orientation issues

Institutions may provide support at various points in an undergraduate's career. We shall look briefly at some examples of pre-entry programmes and induction programmes. An example of a pre-entry strategy employed in the USA is a *summer orientation programme for freshmen*. During the course of this programme, early identification of potential problems and intervention to alleviate them takes place (Pickering *et al.*, 1992). Subsequently, this information is offered to catchment schools to enable them to improve the preparation of potential university students.

Many institutions of higher education organize *induction programmes for new students* which contain activities to provide practical advice and increase social support for students and their commitment to the institution. For example, Oxford Brookes University's induction programme contains a group orientation exercise, in which students are supplied with an orientation map of the university and a checklist of all key destinations (e.g. library, student union). Students then work out a route and travel to each. This seems a particularly useful exercise where destinations are geographically separated from each other (Bocher *et al.*, 1995).

We shall now look at some examples of alternative models of support programmes which focus on the development of generic skills.

17.6 Focus on generic skills development

17.6.1 What are generic skills and why are they thought to be important?

The terms 'generic skills' and 'personal transferable skills', or, more recently, 'core skills' or 'key skills', seem to be used interchangeably in the literature and, in a sense, are so familiar as not to require definition. However, some (e.g. Hyland, 1997) would argue that no common definition exists, questioning whether the term, 'generic skills' actually refers to outcomes of behaviour, ways of thinking, attitudes, values or personality traits in students. Others have argued that lack of definition of generic skills is a feature shared with cognitive elements. We do not have a definition of 'the precise nature of the cognitive elements each degree should develop', claims Atlay (1997, p. 15), yet this does not reduce the importance attached to the development of cognitive abilities. Thus, he argues, any lack of precise definition of 'generic skills' should, similarly, not act to devalue these skills.

We would do well to remember that many of the skills now labelled 'generic' or 'transferable' were found in higher education prior to their labelling as such by recent initiatives such as the Enterprise in Higher Education (EHE). Skills listed in Bloom's taxonomy (Bloom, 1956), such as analysis and synthesis or critical evaluation, are now frequently awarded a place on a list of generic skills. While not all educators would agree about the desirability of including some skills such as economics or accounting in a list of essential generic skills, oral communication has been identified as the skill most highly rated by employers in a variety of situations (e.g. Devon *et al.*, 1994). In addition, listening skills and team working are also rated highly by employers, academics and undergraduates alike (Heskin *et al.*, 1994).

17.6.2 Are generic or transferable skills truly transferable?

There is some agreement that generic skills can be applied in a variety of contexts and are, thus, subject-independent. Moreover, it is sometimes assumed (though less often demonstrated) that, once learned, these skills will transfer from the context in which they were acquired to another situation. While there is a well-established research literature in psychology concerned with the transfer of training (often focusing on laboratory experiments), there appears to be very little empirical evidence concerning the transferability of so-called transferable skills. Carter (1993) described the split between those who view critical thinking skills as generic or transferable and those who believe them to be domain specific, or contextualized, and posed a pertinent question which might apply to any transferable skill.

> Are there certain generic, one-size-fits-all critical thinking skills we can teach that our students will be able to transfer to new writing tasks? Or is the ability to think critically so tied to context as to be discipline dependent?
>
> (Carter, 1993, p. 86)

Courses in any skill deemed essential to the educated, Carter argued, tend to rest on assumptions that they can be 'decontextualized', and that students will be able to apply them to other domains, 'including their lives' (p. 86), and Weitzman (1997) has argued that, 'if academics cannot impart skills that can travel, they may, like Samson, bring their ivory towers crashing down over their heads' (p. 15). However, this may not happen in practice.

Such debates, while important as aids to reflection on our part and, no doubt, stimulating to the protagonists, should not divert us from the main concern of much generic skills training and development: helping and supporting students as they enter higher education.

17.6.3   Generic skills development – the embedding vs. stand-alone or purpose built module controversy

While there is surprising consensus within higher education about the desirability of helping students develop generic, transferable skills, there is less agreement about how this may be best achieved. For some, the solution lies in the provision of a stand-alone module or course designed to develop a skill or skills which learners are subsequently expected to apply to other contexts. For others, individual skills are developed within specialist modules or courses. In other words, the development is contextualized. There is debate about which of these two alternatives is most likely to succeed. We shall return to this issue later.

17.7   Strategies for generic skills development

In order to provide more support for first-year students, and as a response to unacceptable levels of attrition during first year at university (e.g. Raab, 1995; Johnson, 1996a, 1996b), Napier University, Edinburgh, took the decision to develop a 'Toolkit' of personal development skills programmes for use during this period. These programmes are designed to help students not only with specific skills, but also to 'prepare them for their survival and success within the University' (Toolkit skills guidelines). University policy now requires that, starting in semester I session 1997–98, by the end of the academic year, all first-year students be required to present a portfolio in which they have demonstrated their ability in the following key areas: study skills; quantitative skills; information skills; writing skills; and IT skills. It is the responsibility of each department to 'customize' the provision to make it suitable for their students and to plan and implement modules which are designed to achieve these ends.

17.7.1   Embedded approaches

Many strategies for generic skills development at Napier University and elsewhere employ an embedded approach, and generic skills are developed within specialist courses or modules. Research reports describe the embedding within specialist subject teaching of a variety of generic skills: application of theory to practice and reflection (Falchikov and Macleod, 1996); critical reasoning and thinking (Atwater, 1991; Shepelak *et al.*, 1992); critical feedback (Falchikov, 1996); oral communication and team working (Devine *et al.*, 1994); library skills (Madge, 1995); listening skills (Falchikov, 1995a and 1995b); keyboard competence, time management, group interaction and personal presentation (Hall, 1995). Specialist modules, courses or areas used as 'vehicles' for the development of generic skills include: business studies (Smith and Wilson, 1992); dental education (Joshi and Douglass, 1992); geography (Healey, 1992; Madge, 1995); health studies (Falchikov, 1996); introductory classes in government (Atwater, 1991); psychology (Falchikov, 1995a and 1995b); Russian (Hall, 1995); sociology (Shepelak *et al.*, 1992); soil science (Mellor, 1991). Unsurprisingly, several of these reports expressed the view that embedding generic skills development was preferable to developing these skills in stand-alone modules.

The single most frequently encountered area of generic skills development is in the area of IT. For example, a recent edition of *Active Learning* was devoted to this topic (Martin and Beetham, 1997). In it, Watson (1997) argued that the use of IT is more 'naturally embedded' throughout the curriculum than many skills. Watson acknowledges the role of recent programmes such as the Teaching and Learning Technology programme (TLTP) and the Teaching and Learning Initiatives Fund (TLIF) in promoting IT skills development. In addition, Stainfield (1997) argued that skills development in this area may also be aided by the gradual embedding throughout the teaching environment of technology to support learning. As with other generic skills, IT skills are being developed in a variety of contexts, and, as with other skills, there appears to be no evaluation of the relative effectiveness of different modes of delivery. However, Martin (1997) reported that, in his university, some departments had required students to demonstrate the use of IT in other course assignments. However, there are potential problems in linking subject assessment with generic skills assessment. Were the students to whom Martin refers marked on the content of their work, on the excellence of their argument, on its structure or on their use of IT skills?

Within the area of IT skills, there seems to be a consensus that embedding of skills development within a course is preferable to the stand alone mode. There is even a meagre amount of evidence to support this view (e.g. Bull and Zakrzewski, 1997).

At Cape Technikon, in Cape Town, an across the board approach to integration of generic skills development is being attempted – *The Integrated First Year Experience* (IFYE) (1996–97). The importance of the first year of higher education is acknowledged, first-year teaching is carried out by the 'best teachers' and the development of necessary academic skills is systematically integrated into the curriculum. Modules for the use of teaching staff are written by educational experts in the institution and contain information relating to the aims of the exercise, the skills that are to be developed, the recommended time allocations and format of presentation, as well as background information and references. Ready-made transparencies, worksheets and handouts are provided. When and how the programmes are implemented is 'in the hands of the subject specialist (the teacher)' (p. 4), though advice and support are offered by the Teaching Development Unit. It is to be hoped that this initiative will be monitored and evaluated.

17.7.2   Stand-alone initiatives

The most frequently mentioned American initiative to support students is the *Freshman Seminar* or *Freshman Orientation Seminar* (FOS) (e.g. Cuseo, 1991). Cuseo reported the benefits of a full semester stand-alone programme, in which links are made with the requirements of other courses, so as to make the FOS immediately relevant and useful.

Only one stand-alone initiative was located in a search of the literature (Whittemore, 1995). In this paper, the researcher describes a one-hour-per-week course designed to develop oral communication, listening and team working skills, which also involved peer evaluation. The course was offered to students of animal science on a voluntary basis. Evaluations of the course by those who chose to take it were positive.

17.7.3   Which mode of delivery is most effective?

While evaluations of IT skills initiatives have suggested that embedded delivery is most likely to meet with success, some problems and questions remain. For example, few, if any direct comparisons of stand alone and embedded or integrated deliveries are to be found. We do no know whether development of other generic skills resembles development of IT skills. Moreover, in some studies the mode of delivery variable is confused with the variable relating to voluntary or compulsory take up. Further evaluative research is needed.

17.8 The need to assess the effectiveness of different approaches: the Napier University 'Toolkit' evaluation

The need to carry out a rigorous evaluation of different modes of delivery of generic skills development has been identified and a recent initiative at Napier University relating to student support through generic skills development provides the opportunity to do this.

17.8.1 Policy background

Guidelines prepared to assist academic staff in the development of 'Toolkit' skills provision recommended one of the following modes of delivery:

1. a stand-alone module with appropriate learning outcomes;

2. specific learning outcomes addressing the appropriate range of skills incorporated into a range of level 1 core and option modules.

A third option, a combination of the two, is also possible, with individual initiatives being offered in addition to a stand-alone module.

Students are required to provide evidence of achievement of outcomes in the form of a portfolio, which must normally be completed (and deemed satisfactory) before entry to the second year of study. Students will be encouraged to seek evidence for their portfolio from the full range of modules they are studying.

17.8.2 Theoretical background

Controversies concerning the 'best way' in which to provide opportunities for generic skills development, identified above, are being addressed by this research. Specifically, issues concerning the question of whether it is more beneficial to embed such training within specialist modules or to provide purpose-built modules will be investigated. As there is a wide variety of solutions to this challenge across the university, it is important that each be evaluated. Both stand-alone and embedded methods of delivery carry pedagogic and practical advantages and disadvantages. For example, the stand-alone version is easier to develop, implement and monitor than its embedded equivalent. However, as we have seen, some (e.g. Bochner *et al.*, 1995; Bull and Zakrzewski, 1997) argue that incorporating generic skills within a module is more likely to be effective in developing skills than delivery through free-standing modules. As we have seen, this topic has raised much debate, but relatively little hard evidence.

In addition, as the context is deemed to be influential in a wide variety of situations within higher education (Ramsden, 1997; Laurillard, 1997), skills development programmes are likely to be differentially effective according to the particular context in which they occur. Thus, explorations of effects across a range of first-year undergraduate programmes of study is an important part of this research.

17.8.3   Research project

The 'Toolkit' evaluation involves the following:

1. *before measures* of skills levels;

2. *survey of strategies* selected by each department within the university;

3. *questionnaire survey of all staff* involved in the design and delivery of Toolkit skills modules (or Toolkit outcomes within other parts of the curriculum);

4. *focus group interviews* with staff;

5. *focus group interviews* with random samples of year 1 students from a range of departments;

6. *questionnaire survey of all staff involved in teaching year 1 students*;

7. *questionnaire survey of all year 1 students*;

8. *after measures* of skills levels.

Finally, a report, identifying perceived strengths and weaknesses of different modes of delivery in different contexts will be produced, and recommendations for future delivery of Toolkit skills made.

17.9   Conclusion

This paper has raised a number of important questions and issues relating to generic skills development:

- is this a good way to support students in their first year?

- is there a 'best' mode of delivery?

- should take up be voluntary or compulsory?

- how should such skills be assessed?

- is transfer possible?

- what are the effects of the context?

The results of the evaluation study should provide some useful information to move us nearer to some answers, though being mindful of the importance of the context, we shall exert caution before we generalize our results too widely.

17.10   References

Atlay, M. (1997) Letter to the *Times Higher Education Supplement*, 9 May, 15.

Atwater, T. (1991) Critical thinking in basic U.S. government classes, *PS: Political Science and Politics*, **24**(2), June, 209–11.

Bloom, B.S. (1956) *Taxonomy of Educational Objectives. Handbook I: Cognitive Domain*, New York: Longmans Green.

Bocher, D., Gibbs, G. and Wisker, G. (1995) *Teaching More Students. Supporting More Students*, Oxford: Oxford Centre for Staff Development.

Bull, J. and Zakrzewski, S. (1997) Implementing learning technologies: a university-wide approach. In Martin and Beetham (eds), *Active Learning, No. 6, Embedding Technology into Teaching: Achieving Institutional Change*, July.

Carter, D. (1993) Critical thinking for writers: transferable skills or discipline specific strategies?, *Composition Studies/Freshman English News*, **21**(1), 86–93.

Cooper C.L., Cooper, R.D. and Eaker, L.H. (1988) *Living with Stress*, Penguin Books: London.

Cuseo, J.B. (1991) *The Freshman Orientation Seminar: a research-based rationale for its value, delivery and content*. Monograph. National Resource Centre for the Freshman Year Experience, Columbia: University of South Carolina.

Devine, M. *et al.* (1994) *School for Skills: A National Survey of the Development through TVEI of Personal and Transferable Skills*, Technical and Vocational Initiative, Edinburgh: Scottish Council for Research in Education.

Earwaker, J. (1992) *Helping and Supporting Students: Rethinking the Issues*, The Society for Research into Higher Education and Open University Press: Buckingham.

Falchikov, N. (1996) Improving learning through critical peer feedback and reflection, *Higher Education Research and Development*, **19**, 214–18.

Falchikov, N. (1995a) Peer feedback marking: developing peer assessment, *Innovations in Education and Training International*, **32**(2), 175–87.

Falchikov, N. (1995b) Improving feedback to and from students. In Peter Knight (ed.), *Assessment for Learning in Higher Education*, London: Kogan Page.

Falchikov, N. and Macleod, L. (1996) Using psychology in the community: developing transferable skills, *Psychology Teaching Review*, **5**(2), 63–74.

Fisher, S. (1994) *Stress in Academic Life: The Mental Assembly Line*, The Society for Research into Higher Education and Open University Press: Buckingham.

Hall, T. (1995) Birmingham's prelim project: transferable skills in foreign language teaching, *Language Learning Journal*, **11**, March, 43–6.

Healey, M. (1992) Curriculum development and 'Enterprise' group work, resource based learning and the incorporation of transferable skills into a first year practical course, *Journal of Geography in Higher Education*, **16**(1), 7–19.

Heskin, K. *et al.* (1994) Generic skills requirement for stakeholders: and Australian case study. Paper presented at the *34th Annual Forum of the Association for Institutional Research*, New Orleans, LA, 29 May–1 June.

Hyland, T. (1997) The skills that fail to travel, *Times Higher Educational Supplement*, 2 May, 12.

Integrated First Year Experience (IFYE) (1996–97) Manual, Cape Technikon, Cape Town, South Africa.

Johnson, V. (1996a) Raising progression rates at Napier: and analysis of a course leader survey. Internal report to Academic Standards Committee and Quality Assurance Unit, Napier University, Edinburgh.

Johnson, V. (1996b) Progression of Napier students through the first year of the modular course 1994–95. Internal Report, Edinburgh: Napier University.

Joshi, A. and Douglass, C.W. (1992) An introductory course in dental computing and research methods, *Journal of Dental Education*, **56**(11), Nov., 757–61.

Laurillard, D. (1997) Styles and approaches in problem-solving. In F. Marton, D. Hounsell and N. Entwistle (1997) *The Experience of Learning*, 2nd edn, Edinburgh: Scottish Academic Press, 126–44.

Macleod, L. and Falchikov, N. (1997) Student development through structured voluntary work in the community. Paper presented at the *Conference on the Student Experience in the 1990s*, Napier University, 26 May.

Madge, C. (1995) 'More than books': use of a problem-solving exercise to explore university library resources, *Journal of Geography in Higher Education*, 19(1), 69–82.

Martin, A. (1997) Student IT induction: an evolving requirement. In Martin and Beetham (eds), *Active Learning, No. 6, Embedding Technology into Teaching: Achieving Institutional Change*, July.

Mellor, A. (1991) Experiential learning through integrated project work: an example from soil science, *Journal of Geography in Higher Education*, 15(2), 135–49.

Pickering, J.W., Calliotte, J.A. and McAuliffe, G.J. (1992) The effect of noncognitive factors on freshman academic performance and retention, *Journal of the Freshman Year Experience*, 4(2), 7–30.

Raab, G. (1995) Progression of Napier students through the first year of the modular course, 1993–94. Internal report, Edinburgh: Napier University.

Ramsden, P. (1997) The context of learning in academic departments. In F. Marton, D. Hounsell and N. Entwistle (1997) *The Experience of Learning*, 2nd edn, Edinburgh: Scottish Academic Press.

Shepelak, N.J. *et al*, (1992) Critical thinking in introductory sociology classes: a program of implementation and evaluation, *Teaching Sociology*, 20(1), Jan., 18–27.

Smith, D. and Wilson, H. (1992) The development and assessment of personal transferable skills during work-based placements, *Assessment and Evaluation in Higher Education*, 17(3), 195–205.

Stainfield, J. (1997) Using IT to manage a third year module. In Martin and Beetham (eds), *Active Learning, No. 6, Embedding Technology into Teaching: Achieving Institutional Change*, July.

Taylor, N. (1997) Survey of paid employment undertaken by full-time undergraduates at an established Scottish University. Unpublished research.

Thomson, K. and Falchikov, N. (1997) 'Full on until the sun comes out': the effects of assessment on student approaches to studying. Paper presented at the *2nd Northumbria Assessment Conference, Encouraging Partnership in Assessing Learning*, 3–5 Sept. 1997.

Tinto, V. (1975) Dropouts from higher education: a theoretical synthesis of recent research, *Review of Educational Research*, 45, 89–125.

Watson, B. (1997) Supporting the integration of IT into the curriculum at the University of Durham. In Martin and Beetham (eds), *Active Learning, No. 6, Embedding Technology into Teaching: Achieving Institutional Change*, July.

Weitzman, D. (1997) Letter to the *Times Higher Education Supplement*, 9 May, 15.

Whittemore, C.T. (1995) Teaching interpersonal and transferable skills to students of agriculture: a case study, *European Journal of Agricultural Education and Extension*, 1(4), March, 87–105.

18 Biology students' and tutors' understanding of 'a good essay'

Stephen Merry, Paul Orsmond and Kevin Reiling
School of Sciences, Staffordshire University, Stoke-on-Trent, UK

18.1 Introduction

There are conflicting views as to the worth of essays with Gibbs (1992a) advocating 'a total moratorium on student essays' and Bradley (1993) advocating 'more student essays'. It is acknowledged that there is a trend towards more innovative approaches of assessment in higher education (Mowl and Pain, 1995), but essays, and other forms of creative writing, are likely to continue to contribute to both formative and summative assessment for the foreseeable future. This is because they have traditionally been used within final examinations forming the basis of degree classifications and universities may be reluctant to discard this standard for untried methods. The use of essays is defended because essays can be a useful vehicle to enable students to synthesize and evaluate ideas (Pain and Mowl, 1996) and, furthermore, skills learnt during essay writing can form the basis for other types of professional presentations such as practical or fieldwork reports, reviews and project dissertations.

In a pilot study an essay self-assessment form (modified from Gibbs, 1992b) was used to gather information concerning second-year Biology degree students' perception of their own performance in a time-constrained essay. Analysis of these forms showed that students were more concerned with factual content and less concerned with structural aspects (such as the development of logical arguments) than their tutor (Orsmond et al., 1997). This dichotomy of views between tutor and student is important because providing relevant feedback to students is central to helping them improve as learners (Brew, 1995). The results of this pilot study suggest that students may not be receiving the feedback they expect and so currently have little basis on which to develop their essay-writing skills. Students need to understand the feedback they receive and this often requires specific discussion between tutor and students.

This pilot study has now been extended by a more detailed programme of structured interviews involving both tutors and students at all levels of our Applied Biology programme. This further study was designed to determine if the results of the pilot study were generally applicable to Biology students. The ultimate aim of the programme is the development of meaningful student guidance methods to aid development and success in this important aspect of assessment.

18.2 Methods

Ten level 1, 12 level 2 and 15 level 3 Applied Biology students were randomly selected using the university's student record system. The different numbers of students selected at each level reflect different total numbers in the cohorts. All 19 Biology tutors were also included in the study. All participants were invited to take part in structured interviews and interviews were carried out with 8 level 1 students, 12 level 2 students, 13 level 3 students and 17 tutors. Written notes of the subject's responses were made during all interviews and their accuracy was confirmed by the subject before the end of the process.

As a central part of the interview subjects were asked to visualize 'a good essay' that they had recently written or read, to suggest the factors that had made this 'a good essay' and then to rank these factors in order of importance. Tutors were asked to state their expectations from student essays at each level of study whereas students were asked to state their current opinions. In the analysis of the interview responses commonly stated factors were first identified. Then an overall ranking for each of these factors at each level was obtained using student and staff responses by comparing average rank for each factor. In another section of the interview interviewees were also questioned regarding their approach to essay writing or, in the case of tutors, their approach to essay marking.

18.3   Results

Table 18.1 shows our preliminary analysis of the results obtained. Both students at all levels and tutors ranked logical structure highly. In addition, when directly asked about their preferred essay structures, both tutors and students gave identical responses. There was disagreement between tutors and students regarding the importance of the essay being factually complete. This was especially true at levels 1 and 2. Finally, there was some disagreement between tutors and students regarding the importance of good presentation at level 3 and, to a lesser extent, at level 1.

A trend that was noted from responses to specific questions was that students relied heavily on pre-university guidance regarding their approach to essay writing. They felt that they lacked the ability to change their established approach.

Table 1:
Average ranking of tutor and student perceptions of factors which contribute to "a good essay" . 1= most important; 6= least important.

	Tutor/student Ranking					
	Level 1		Level 2		Level 3	
	tut.	st.	tut.	st.	tut.	st.
1. Logical Structure	1	2	1	1	1	2
2. Relevant content	2	3	2	3	4	1
3. Good presentation	2	4	3	3	1	5
4. Evidence of background reading	4	5	3	3	1	3
5. Evidence of independent thought	5	6	5	6	4	6
6. Factually complete	6	1	6	1	6	4

Table 18.1

18.4 Discussion

18.4.1 Interview outcomes

Any analysis of the data in Table 18.1 must take into consideration that some of the categories appear to overlap. Notable examples of these are (a) 'relevant content' and 'factually complete' and (b) 'logical structure' and 'good presentation'. Nevertheless, an important dichotomy is revealed by these data. The high importance placed by students, especially at levels 1 and 2, on the inclusion of all relevant factual material relative to tutors is evident. Similar findings have been previously reported (Jackson, 1991; Orsmond *et al.*, 1997; Pain and Mowl, 1996).

Our data builds on the previous reports in that levels of study are considered. It is notable that at level 3 the discrepancy between tutors and students regarding the importance of the essay being factually complete is much reduced. A single reason for this reduced discrepancy was not apparent from the interview data. There is certainly a notable increase in motivation between levels 2 and 3 which seems to come from the realization that final degree classification is largely based on their level 3 performance. Furthermore, in response to direct questions, level 3 students often reported that they felt that their approach to essay writing had 'matured' or 'developed' during their university careers, but was still based on pre-university guidance. The impression given was that a change had taken place in the absence of any conscious effort to change.

It is also interesting to note that tutors will often emphasize the factual content of their teaching, but give low importance to factual completeness when marking essays. Perhaps it is correct to place low emphasis on factual completeness in essay assessment, but these different emphases between teaching and assessment may be confusing to students. Tutors are potential role models and strong emphasis on factual content during teaching may be the underlying cause of students placing similar emphasis when writing essays.

Table 18.1 also shows a general trend (despite the agreement at level 2) for tutors to attach a greater importance to good presentation than students. Greater dialogue, involving the use of examples, between tutor and student will help to address this discrepancy.

18.4.2 Changing approaches to essay writing

Why must we wait until level 3 for students to 'mature' in their approach to essay writing? Should not tutors consider methods of changing student approaches to essay writing at levels 1 and 2? Two factors are important in this context. The first is that students need to develop the ability to change and the second is that students need to know what is expected of them. We have previously reported on the importance of dialogue with students to ensure a common understanding of marking criteria (Orsmond *et al.*, 1996). While the first of the above factors has been identified definitely as a skill that students lack the second factor may be more complex.

Students perceptions of good essay structure might serve as a useful example. Students are generally able to clearly state a preferred essay structure that is identical to that suggested by tutors. They also regard structure as important. This contrasts with the observations by tutors that student essays often lack structure (Orsmond *et al.*, 1997). Students know how they should structure essays, but are unable to put this into practice.

A further study is currently being undertaken which involves both peer, self and tutor review of essays together with the opportunity for students to revise their initial draft in the light of the comments received prior to final submission for assessment. This study is designed to require students to read and evaluate essays of different styles and merits and to reflect upon their own work. Jackson (1991) has reported that 'strong' writing strategies adopted by students require a critical approach in which the draft is continuously revised on the light creative thinking and further reading. Self, peer and tutor review directs students towards such strategies. Requiring students to reflect on their essays is a necessary precursor to any change.

This is a work-in-progress report and our analysis of the interview data is as yet incomplete. Analysis in respect of student level of study has generated the interesting results described above. Further analysis of the same data in terms of students' overall academic performance, age and previous academic experience is ongoing.

18.5   Conclusion

Tutors and student differ in their perceptions of 'a good essay' and the discrepancies are most marked at levels 1 and 2. Students attach more importance to factual completeness and less importance to presentation than tutors. Greater dialogue between tutors and students is required to address these differences. Exposure of students to other students' work and the requirement to reflect upon their own work imposed by peer and self assessment exercises may be a useful vehicle to generate such dialogue.

18.6   References

Bradley, G. (1993) Improving the quality of students' writing, *The New Academic*, 2(3), 4–6.

Brew, A. (1995) What is learner self assessment? In D. Boud (ed.), *Enhancing Learning through Self Assessment*, 11–23.

Gibbs, G. (1992a) Down with essays!, *The New Academic*, 1(2), 18–19.

Gibbs, G. (1992b) *Assessing More Students*, Teaching More Students Series, No. 4, Oxford: Oxford Centre for Staff Development, 21.

Jackson, M.W. (1991) Writing as learning: reflections on developing students' writing strategies, *Higher Education Research and Development*, 10(1), 41–52.

Mowl, G. and Pain, R. (1995) Using peer and self assessment to improve students' essay writing: a case study from geography, *Innovations in Education and Training International*, 32(4), 324–35.

Orsmond, P, Merry, S and Reiling, K. (1996) The importance of marking criteria in the use of peer assessment, *Assessment and Evaluation in Higher Education*, 21(3), 239–50.

Orsmond, P., Merry, S. and Reiling, K. (1997) Students' and tutors' perceptions of 'a good essay', *Research in Education*, (58), 81-84.

Pain, R. and Mowl, G. (1996) Improving geography essay writing using innovative assessment, *Journal of Geography in Higher Education*, 20(1), 19–31.

19 Supporting students' frameworks for conceptual understanding: knowledge objects and their implications

Noel Entwistle
Centre for Research on Learning and Instruction, University of Edinburgh

19.1   Introduction

In the recent literature on student learning, the distinctions between deep, surface, and strategic approaches to learning and studying have guided a good deal of the thinking about ways of improving university teaching and supporting high-quality learning. The very popularity of these ideas has, perhaps inevitably, also attracted criticism both of the categories themselves and of the methodology on which they depend (phenomenography) (see, for example, Webb, 1997; *Higher Education Research and Development*, 1997). The contrast between deep and surface approaches certainly provides a straightforward conceptual basis for explaining the essence of effective teaching and learning (Entwistle, 1997a); nevertheless, this appealing simplicity has also led to confusions and misapprehensions.

19.2   Memorizing and understanding

One of the main problems has come from linking the deep approach to *conceptual understanding*, and the surface approach to *memorization*, with the implication that there is no place within a deep approach for rote learning, or even the learning of facts. In defining contrasting categories, inevitably differences are emphasized and qualifications played down. But the crucial difference between deep and surface approaches is the *intention* of the learner – whether to achieve a personal understanding of the topic or to satisfy the teacher in a minimal way. In many subject areas, personal understanding depends on acquiring basic knowledge and may involve a certain amount of rote learning of technical terms, particularly in the early stages. It is consequently not memorization itself which characterizes a surface approach, but the routine and inappropriate uses of rote learning which lead to impoverished understanding.

Even the meaning of the term *memorization* has itself been questioned (Biggs, 1991; Marton and Booth, 1997), as a result of research with Asian students. Experience suggests that such students rely on memorization in studying, and yet they often achieve outstandingly good grades. This was initially seen as a paradox, but interviews with Chinese students in Hong Kong have shown that they typically try to understand the material for themselves before committing that understanding to memory. They call that process 'memorization', but it is very different from the accepted meaning of a surface approach – rote learning material without personal engagement.

The meaning of the term *understanding* was initially rather taken for granted in the research on student learning. But an interview study we carried out in Edinburgh helped to clarify this meaning within a university setting (Entwistle, A. and Entwistle, N., 1992). Students who had just taken Finals were asked to describe, and reflect on, the process of understanding. At first sight, their descriptions seemed to be very similar. They all said they had tried to make sense of the material they were revising for Finals, and indicated that understanding involved bringing it together into a coherent whole, linked to what they already knew.

> In school you've got to learn facts, but understanding [is different] – knowing what an issue's about, being able to reorganise it in different ways, manipulate it, form argument if need be . . . [Understanding is] the feeling that you understand how the whole thing is connected up, the way it all hangs together – you can make sense of it internally . . . It is as though one's mind has finally 'locked in' to the pattern . . . And you know you understand [when you can] construct an argument from scratch . . . by yourself – can explain it so that you feel satisfied with the explanation.
>
> (edited from Entwistle, A. and Entwistle, N., 1992, p. 10; Entwistle, N. and
> Entwistle, A., 1997, p. 148)

Conceptual understanding at university, or in any formal educational setting, is not just a matter, though, of feeling satisfied with the coherence reached. There is also a *target understanding* (Entwistle and Smith, 1997), presented by the teachers and examiners who decide what will count as an appropriate and adequate form of understanding. Students are judged against *those* requirements rather than the students' own experiences of *personal understanding*. Until recently, however, the target was largely invisible, or at least shrouded in the mist of brief and vague syllabuses. Increasingly, precisely stated objectives or learning outcomes are presented to students, making the target easier to discern, at least up to a point. But the whole target in higher education cannot ever be fully revealed. In assessments, the adequacy of students' explanations is judged in relation to the teachers' knowledge of the discipline as a whole. Most areas of study depend on an academic discourse which students acquire only by being thoroughly immersed in the discipline, and by becoming skilled in presenting explanations in disciplinarily acceptable ways. Few students actually hit, or even clearly perceive, the 'bull's eye', even if they have used their own understanding to the best of their ability.

Although most students described 'understanding' as their goal, the interviews showed that the term was being used in importantly different ways. Five contrasting *forms of understanding* were found, with differences in breadth (how much material students had brought together in forming their understanding), depth (how much effort had been used in forming and elaborating connections between the component aspects) and structure (the extent to which the student had relied on the structure provided by the teacher or sought an individual interpretation) – see Table 19.1.

The five categories also reflected contrasts in the balance between deep, surface and strategic approaches to studying. Too ready acceptance of the lecture notes (category B) leaves the student over-reliant on the lecturer's own way of understanding the topic, and remains a surface ploy. Categories C, D and E all show strategic awareness of the specific assessment demands combined with a deep approach, but to differing degrees. Only in the final category (F) had immersion in the discipline, and personal engagement with the topics, allowed the students fully to perceive the target understanding, and so provide explanations within the required academic discourse.

Forms of understanding in relation to approaches to studying and revising

A. Absorbing facts, details, and procedures, without consideration of structure

B. Accepting and using the logical structures provided in the lecture notes

C. Developing own summary structures from notes solely to answer exam questions

D. Developing structures to represent own understanding and to control exam answers

E. Developing structures relating own understanding to the nature of the discipline

Conceptual analysis of the categories of forms of understanding

Breadth of understanding

Depth or level of understanding

Structure used to organise the material being learned

    a. little or no structure being imposed on the facts learned

    b. relying exclusively on the lecturer's structures

    c. producing prepared answers to previous years' questions

    d. adapting own understanding to expected question types

    e. relying on an individual conception of the topic

Table 19.1   Contrasting forms of understanding in revising for Finals
(from Entwistle & Entwistle, 1997)

19.3   Revising – committing to memory and memorizing

Looking now at the ways in which deep, strategic students went about revising for Finals, a fairly consistent, logical approach can be discerned (see Figure 19.1). The starting point was an attempt to achieve an outline understanding of all the notes. Students then embarked on a process of 'concising', by writing successive summaries in decreasing levels of detail until, typically, there was just a page of notes for each main topic. This final summary note was always intended to emphasize key aspects, but the actual form of this structured mnemonic differed widely. Some students used well-organized 'mind maps' (Entwistle and Napuk, 1997), some had written numbered summaries in different areas of the page, while others preferred a linear listing of headings and brief summaries. Once they were confident of their understanding, the students then committed it to memory in ways similar to those described by Asian students. The firmly established understanding was then sometimes visualized as an entity in its own right: the *structure* of it could be 'seen' (although not the details), and its overall meaning reviewed. Moreover, focusing on one aspect of it 'pulled in' additional related information and ideas.

> I can see that virtually as a picture. I can review it, and bring in more facts about each part . . . Looking at a particular part of the diagram sort of triggers off other thoughts. I find schematics, in flow diagrams and the like, very useful because a schematic acts a bit like a syllabus; it tells you what you should know, without actually telling you what it is. I think the facts are stored separately . . . and the schematic is like an index, I suppose.

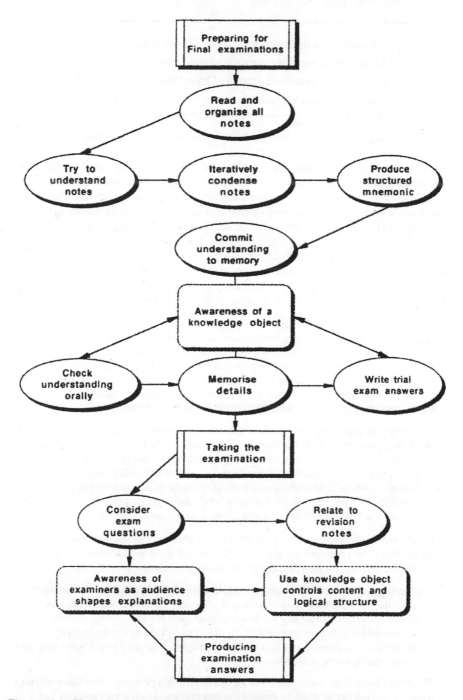

Figure 19.1 Flow diagram of procedures involved in revising for Finals

---

Awareness of a tightly integrated body of knowledge

Visualisation and 'quasi-sensory' experiences

Awareness of unfocused aspects of knowledge

Use in controlling explanations

Table 19.2   Defining features of 'knowledge objects' (from Entwistle, in press)

This phenomenon came to be described as a *knowledge object* (Entwistle and Marton, 1994), with the defining features shown in Table 19.2. As students who had established elaborated and well-defined knowledge objects described their experiences of taking Finals, the function of the knowledge object became clearer. It seemed to provide flexibility in gearing the explanation to the specific question set, and also to guide the emerging answer through well-rehearsed pathways of thinking about the topic. The answers produced are necessarily unique, as the evolving explanation draws in a chance selection of illustrative material which affects the specifics of the evolving argument. Yet, the structural properties of the knowledge object mean that the generic form of explanations given on different occasions can be expected to have a similar shape, as these two quotes imply.

> I had tried to structure my revision so that I could understand what was going on . . . So, although I had this structure when I went into the exam, I still wanted it to be flexible, so that I could approach the question [itself] . . . At the time, as I was writing, I was just using anything that came into my mind [and fitted in]. I had learned a good deal of detail, and yet I could use [only] a small percentage of it . . . [As I wrote], it was almost as though I could see it all fitting into an overall picture. I think you're almost developing what you know, and are playing it in a slightly different way.

> Following that logic through, it pulls in pictures and facts as it needs them... Each time I describe (a particular topic), it's likely to be different . . . Well, you start with evolution, say . . . and suddenly you know where you're going next. Then, you might have a choice . . . to go in that direction or that direction . . . and follow it through various options it's offering . . . Hopefully, you'll make the right choice, and so this goes to this, goes to this – and you've explained it to the level you've got to. Then, it says 'Okay, you can go on to talk about further criticisms in the time you've got left.'

Not only did some students show an awareness of their own structured understanding, they were also strategically conscious of the need to present their explanations to a specific audience – the examiners. As two of these more strategic students commented:

> In an exam, you have to have background knowledge of the subject, and an ability to interpret the information in your own way . . . You don't sit down and think 'How much can I remember about this particular subject'; you try and explain your ideas, using examples which come to mind . . . You can't use all the information for a particular line of argument, and you don't need to; you only need to use what you think is going to convince the examiner.

> The more I have done exams, the more I'd liken them to a performance – like being on a stage; . . . having not so much to present the fact that you know a vast amount, but

having to perform well with what you do know . . . Sort of, playing to the gallery . . . I was very conscious of being outside what I was writing.

After the first round of interviews, the phenomenon of knowledge objects had been adequately described, but questions were still left unanswered. For example, was it simply a product of the artificial conditions produced particularly by final examinations, with all their associated stress? And, again, was it no more than an ephemeral phenomenon, fading rapidly from memory after having served its purpose?

Further interviews, focusing on course work, suggested that knowledge objects are sometimes experienced in essay writing, but only when students have engaged personally with the topics (Entwistle, 1995). Course work does not generally seem to create the firmly structured understandings which are possible from thorough revision, and very recent interviews with students in a department which relied heavily on course-work assessment produced only one rather unconvincing instance of a knowledge object.

Most people find it difficult to describe their experiences of understanding and the thought processes associated with them. Our attempts to explore the nature of knowledge objects have thus relied disproportionately on a few particularly articulate and reflective respondents, and recently on individuals who were already aware of the concept. The initial conceptualization (Entwistle and Marton, 1994) was seeded by the comments of one student who explained:

> [In exams], I just clear my mind and something comes . . . You know it's visual in some ways, but it's also just there without necessarily being visual . . . [It's not as if] you remember a page, and the page is locked in your memory. What I'm saying is that the ideas are locked in your memory and they display as a page when you're thinking about it, but not necessarily when you're putting it down . . . You can sort of by-pass the conscious perception of your memory: it may not be a visual memory, but [sometimes] it may have to be perceived as a visual memory . . . I think, in a stress situation like an examination, you don't actually [have to] reach for it, it comes out automatically. That may show that it's not actually a visual memory, as such, but a visual expression of 'central memory'.

This student subsequently became involved in discussions about knowledge objects and was asked to comment on some advice about revising. In doing so, she accidentally triggered a memory which she recognized as a knowledge object, experienced initially as vivid visual images. Interrogation of these images enabled the student to recreate the structure of an answer she had given in Finals five years previously (Entwistle, 1998b).

> The first image was that of a bird flying over a landscape of hills; the second portrayed a bird in a cage. These unexpected images provoked reflection which soon produced a connecting link, and a recognisable knowledge object . . . [Then] I sort of questioned it: what was the caged bird? It wasn't active, as in searching [your memory] for something . . . I stalked it, if you like, and said 'What's that?'. Then it, sort of, told me that these things . . . were the different avenues that could possibly explain . . . [the apparently] 'magical' navigation of birds. It was basically by stopping there and pausing, these other things were sort of pulled in . . . almost as a set of sub-headings . . .
> At that stage, I . . . defocused on the caged bird . . . and switched again to a picture of a bird in flight. But [then] this was more like a bird's eye view picture, of dark hills . . And this knowledge – of the fact that you could use hills [for navigation] – then brought back the structure of the essay as a whole. I'd got these experiments on the one hand [the bird in the cage], and this local [navigation] knowledge on the other, and putting

> those together created a whole . . . When I actually stopped and looked at . . . the picture of the bird in the cage . . . a door seemed to open and the information came out . . . [Eventually I felt] 'There's potentially specific knowledge [still there], but I can't get at it.' You get to a point where you know there is knowledge that you have come across in the past, but you can't find the way into it.

This memory of a knowledge object, remembered after five years without having used it in the intervening period, shows its longevity, in this instance. However, the student could not recall any other knowledge objects related to the Final examination questions she had answered, indicating the crucial importance of the initial trigger linked to strong imagery.

Another instance of a knowledge object was reported by David Perkins, an educational psychologist at Harvard University. He had been asked to give a presentation on facilitating group discussions, of which he had considerable practical experience. He had, however, not given a formal presentation on that topic previously. The initial activity of bringing together rather loosely related ideas and experiences seemed to him like forming a knowledge object. Working out a framework for the talk gave him access to the whole topic in a more organized and complete way. Perkins described his knowledge object as a feeling of having 'a highly coherent, easily surveyable representation' which he considered to be 'important in communicating coherently and effectively about a strong competence, even if it isn't necessary for exercising that competence' (personal communication). The framework which was chosen for his presentation (Perkins, 1994) had a logical structure, a flow (time sequence), and it was based on an elaborate and sustained metaphor – space exploration – which inevitably evokes strong visualization and so has the characteristics of a memorable knowledge object.

Recent interviews with academic staff are beginning to suggest that some of the more experienced lecturers may well be relying on knowledge objects, cued by overheads, to develop a flexible dialogue in explaining their ideas to students – as a challenging conversation rather than a formal lecture (Entwistle, 1998c). So far, however, the existence of knowledge objects can only be inferred from a number of rather disparate comments, such as the following.

> Lectures provide a presence that a book doesn't, and you can utilize that in the lecture by a directly engaging question. The lecturer can actually engage [the student] in that question, in a much more interactive mode. Teaching also has a theatrical element to it. I suppose I'm saying that the function of the lecture is to bring inquiry to life, the inquiry that learning is . . . I'm constantly challenging the students in the lecture to think something through for themselves. I think that generates a certain sense of – I think intrigue is a good word, but wonderment is another one, appreciation is another one, and understanding is related to that. [And] in my preparation *I actually have to create this [situation] every time*, rather than just remember [the content]. [The lecture] is a conversation in which there's active listening involved.

19.4   Discussion

It seems that well-developed knowledge objects are necessarily somewhat idiosyncratic; they are the product of the student's own attempts to create an explanatory structure for him or herself. In some people at least, they may well be stored in memory through powerful visual images which trigger the whole form of the prior understanding. The example from Perkins, with its structure based on a striking metaphor, suggests that some teachers may be able to offer frameworks for understanding which 'seed' the student's own knowledge objects in peculiarly effective ways. Of course, the idea of *advance organizers* is already well established in the educational psychology literature. They are frameworks designed to help students anticipate the logical relationships which lead up to an important principle or theory (Ausubel, Novak and Hanesian, 1978). But the seeding of a knowledge object may require something more – a metaphor or imagery which stimulates students to build up their own understanding around it. And the quote above from a lecturer indicates how students can be challenged through questions and lively debate, even within a lecture, to carry on the active thinking necessary to discover personal meaning in the topic.

No attempts have yet been made to present the idea of knowledge objects to undergraduate students, and so its potential in raising study awareness has still to be explored. Nevertheless, mind maps do seem to parallel the integrative function of a knowledge object and also provide a way of exteriorizing and supporting its development. Some students certainly find the production of mind maps to be very helpful, and a case study of one student who had developed elaborate mind maps for revision has recently been reported (Entwistle and Napuk, 1997). She likened understanding to jigsaw pieces coming together to create a recognizable whole, with mind maps aiding that process. In the report, we commented:

> The mind map was used in two ways. First, it displayed the component parts – the jigsaw pieces, as it were. It allowed the process of sorting and connecting to be carried out on paper, but it also provoked more thinking and connecting in the mind. The second way the mind map helped was by offering a reassuring mnemonic – a representation of the way the connections had been made which could be used either in the process of writing an essay to be discussed in a tutorial, or during an exam. It seems as if the mind map offered a two-dimensional representation of the understanding which had been developed both in researching the essay and in revising for the exam. It is tempting to see it also as a representation of . . . what we have called a knowledge object.
>
> (Entwistle and Napuk, 1997, p. 24)

The systematic use of mind maps may well prove to be an important way of encouraging students to think more deeply, and independently, about important academic topics, and to help them become aware of knowledge objects and the way they aid explanations. Even students who initially feel uncomfortable with their use may grow into them. If, as seems likely, one of the strengths of a mind map is to mimic the kinds of interconnections which take place in the mind during the process of developing understanding, then most students should benefit from exploring their potential value.

The use of knowledge objects in lecturing also seems to have potential in educational development work. One of the characteristics of an effective lecture is the way the explanation develops 'naturally' and takes account of feedback from the audience. Many lecturers use overheads, and could well be using them in conjunction with knowledge objects, to evoke well-structured explanations adapted to the specific needs of the audience. Becoming more consciously aware of how knowledge objects are formed may help in gaining the confidence and facility to lecture in a more 'natural' mode.

The use of final examinations has come under increasing criticism in recent years. Yet the evidence from our interviews has been that thorough revision fosters the development of knowledge objects. If the examinations are seen to test understanding, students will generally revise in ways which integrate the content of the topics covered. And an extensive and intensive period of revision is more likely to produce coherent and well-constructed forms of understanding. A similar intensity of focus can, of course, be achieved in some other types of assessment – for example, in well designed project work – but the skill of integrating and committing an understanding to memory, and creating convincing explanations under time pressure is a valuable transferable skill. Such advantages will, however, only emerge where students are actively encouraged to develop personal understanding and a sense of the academic discourse within the discipline.

In considering assessment policies, therefore, the value of examinations should not be too readily dismissed. Certain forms of examinations, used within a well-designed set of assessment procedures, may well be crucial in maintaining those academic skills which depend on intensive engagement and critical analysis.

19.5 References

Ausubel, D.P., Novak, J.S. and Hanesian, H. (1978) *Educational Psychology: A Cognitive View*, New York: Holt, Rinehart & Winston.

Biggs, J.B. (1991) Approaches to learning in secondary and tertiary students in Hong Kong: some comparative studies, *Educational Research Journal*, **6**, 27–39.

Entwistle, A.C. and Entwistle, N.J. (1992) Experiences of understanding in revising for degree examinations, *Learning and Instruction*, **2**, 1–22.

Entwistle, N.J. (1995) Frameworks for understanding as experienced in essay writing and in preparing for examinations, *Educational Psychologist*, **30**, 47–54.

Entwistle, N.J. (1998a) Improving teaching through research on student learning. In J.J.F. Forest (ed.), *University Teaching: International Perspectives*, New York: Garland (in press).

Entwistle, N.J. (1998b) Approaches to learning and forms of understanding. In B. Dart and G. Boulton-Lewis (eds), *Teaching and Learning in Higher Education: From Theory to Practice*, Hawthorn, Melbourne: Australian Council for Educational Research.

Entwistle, N.J. (1998c) Motivation and approaches to learning: motivating and conceptions of teaching. In G. Thompson, S. Armstrong, & S. Brown (eds) *Motivating Students*. London: Kogan Page.

Entwistle, N.J. and Entwistle, A. C. (1997) Revision and the experience of understanding. In F. Marton, D.J. Hounsell and N.J. Entwistle (eds), *The Experience of Learning*, 2nd edn., Edinburgh: Scottish Academic Press.

Entwistle, N.J. and Marton, F. (1994) Knowledge objects: understandings constituted through intensive academic study, *British Journal of Educational Psychology*, **64**, 161–78.

Entwistle, N.J. and Napuk, S. (1997) *Mind Maps and Knowledge Objects. Research report, University of Edinburgh: Centre for Research on Learning and Instruction*.

Entwistle, N.J. and Smith, C.A. (1997) Personal understanding and target understanding: a question of match (article under consideration).

Higher Education Research and Development (1997) **16**, 2. Whole issue

Marton, F. and Booth, S. (1997) *Learning and Awareness*, Mahwah, NJ: Lawrence Erlbaum.

Perkins, D. (1994) Missions in possibility space (internal paper). Boston, Mass.: Harvard University Graduate School of Education.

Webb, G. (1997) Deconstructing deep and surface: towards a critique of phenomenography, *Higher Education*, **33**, 195–212.

20 Student strategies when reading expository text

Effie Maclellan
Department of Educational Studies,
Faculty of Education,University of Strathclyde

20.1 Overview

The purpose of the study was to describe students' strategic behaviour when reading expository text. The cognitive strategies framework developed by Weinstein and Mayer (1986) was used to generate a taxonomy of (20) reading behaviours. This taxonomy was the basis of a survey instrument in which 120 undergraduate students rated the frequency of their engagement with the specified behaviours on a three-point scale. Endorsement of the behaviours varied widely but their analysis in terms of the cognitive processing which each was alleged to promote suggests that students were engaging with their reading in a limited and limiting way. It is suggested that students should be enabled, and required, to summarize their reading material so that they can be autonomous in their learning.

20.2 Introduction

An important medium of instruction in higher education is reading (Guthrie, 1982). In recent times some disturbing evidence has emerged to suggest that students in higher education are not proficient readers. For example, Baker (1985), found that students did not check that ideas expressed in expository text were either consistent with each other or consistent with what the students themselves already knew. Guthrie (1988) found that adults were quite inefficient in reading documents to locate specific information. Pressley *et al.* (1992) found that students were poor at monitoring whether they had understood the main points in a piece of text, so much so that they gave equal confidence ratings to their responses to comprehension questions, regardless of whether their responses were right or wrong. Schnotz (1993) found that undergraduates with extensive prior knowledge processed text more intensively (with the consequence of achieving superior recall and comprehension scores) while students with limited prior knowledge processed text 'relatively quickly and superficially'. Zabrucky and Commander (1993) found that while all students would reread text to resolve a comprehension problem, rereading was more selective and problem focused among good readers than it was among poorer readers who reread 'everything'. Booth and Hall (1994) found that among college undergraduates, cognitive word knowledge (hypothesized as an essential pre-requisite for high level text understanding) was not significantly better than that of secondary school 15-year-olds and indeed the undergraduates had a slightly less refined grasp of the cognitive word 'know' than had the school pupils. Bell and Perfetti (1994) found that college students trying to read text which they found difficult showed a pattern of component reading skills typically found in children. These are worrying findings which challenge the commonly held assumption that most educated adults read effectively.

Students' approaches to learning can be characterized in a variety of ways. Typically these approaches identify the cognitive strategic processing which influences academic performance. In other words, these approaches identify what the individual does to change the structure of his/her extant knowledge base intentionally, and is therefore able to learn. Weinstein and Mayer's (1986) framework for describing cognitive strategic processing (or learning strategies) was the framework selected for this study. Reasons for this choice were twofold. First, the Weinstein and Mayer framework is theoretically driven. It is based on a constructivist view of learning which holds that learning is an active process that occurs within the learner and can be influenced by the learner. What is learned depends not only on what information is presented to the learner but also on how the learner processes that information. A second reason for choosing the Weinstein and Mayer framework is that there is some statistical evidence (Christensen *et al.*, 1991) that the framework is more discriminating of differing cognitive strategies than is the well-established Study Process Questionnaire (SPQ) devised by Biggs (1987).

In their framework, Weinstein and Mayer identify three cognitive strategies (rehearsal, organization and elaboration) and the metacognitive strategy of comprehension monitoring.

Rehearsal includes behaviours such as repeating the material aloud, copying the material, taking selective verbatim notes and underlining the important parts of the material. In rehearsal behaviours the learner is actively saying, writing or pointing to parts of the text with the purpose of remembering specific information.

Organization is reported as the translation of information in the text into an alternative form such that it will be easier to understand. Examples would include reclassifying lists of information according to another criterion, representing a piece of prose diagrammatically, carving up a very long piece of text into particular sub-sections and creating an outline of, say, a chapter in a book. The declared purpose is to allow the learner to construct what, for the learner, are new connections between ideas, and thereby make sense of new, incoming information.

Elaboration includes activities such as paraphrasing, summarizing, creating analogies, generative note-taking and generating/answering questions in relation to the text. Here the purpose is to make connections between what the learner already knows and what he/she is trying to understand; in other words, to integrate prior knowledge with new learning.

The metacognitive strategy of comprehension monitoring is concerned with the learner's monitoring and management of his/her own learning so that comprehension failure would be recognized and remedial action would be instituted if and when understanding had not taken place.

In short, the cognitive strategies as outlined by Weinstein and Mayer represent three kinds of resource which are potentially available for the active and autonomous learner while the metacognitive strategy is one of managing the effective use of the available resources. The task then was to find out the extent to which these strategies were used by higher education students while reading to learn.

20.3   Method

One hundred and twenty second-year B.Ed. students were surveyed in connection with a psychology module which was a core element of their teacher-education. At the end of the module in which the reading of a dedicated expository text had been an integral activity, students were asked to reflect on their reading behaviour and to rate the extent to which they had engaged in 20 listed behaviours. A three-point rating scale was used: I did this often/I did this occasionally/I never did this.

The items listed were generated to reflect the Weinstein and Mayer classification, but with modification. Weinstein and Mayer are quite explicit in the examples of behaviour which they consider to indicate both Rehearsal and Elaboration. Hence it was a fairly straightforward matter to generate ecologically valid items for each of these strategies. However, examples of Organization were much more difficult to discern. Take 'creating an outline' which Weinstein and Mayer cite as an example of this strategy. In order to do this the reader would need to judge which ideas are the central ones of the text. The reader would then need to apply condensation rules to the text, and finally the reader would need to generate a new and skeletal version of the original text. This type of behaviour seems not to be qualitatively different from that involved in summarizing, which is an example of Elaboration. Because it was not possible to decide, through the survey instrument alone, whether a particular behaviour was for the purpose of Elaboration or for the purpose of Organisation, a distinction between the two categories was not made. Behaviours which might arguably be in one or other of these categories were considered to be examples of Elaboration. The 20 listed behaviours were in three categories: the cognitive strategy of Rehearsal (4), the cognitive strategy of Elaboration (8) and the metacognitive strategy of Comprehension Monitoring (8).

20.4   Results

Inspection of the results suggests a depressing picture. It is not surprising to observe that highlighting/underlining was a frequently used study behaviour. Such a finding is heavily reported in the literature, and however useful it might be in drawing attention to potentially important textual information, it does not enable the reader to integrate what is being read with prior knowledge nor does it enable the reader to construct any kind of coherence out of a range of sources. Indeed evidence for regular engagement in behaviour which might actually enable students to make meaning and construct new knowledge was sparse, with paraphrasing or summarizing being regularly adopted by less than a quarter of the students. On the other hand, it was heartening to note that selective re-reading of the text was a common behaviour when comprehension was recognized as not taking place, since this is considered to be preferable to total re-reading which suggests a lack of sensitivity to the reading task. However, the proportion of students who seemed to have confidence in peers, and in the substance/content of the associated lectures to resolve difficulties experienced with reading, was perhaps rather high and may say something about how

Reading Behaviour	Percentage Ratings		
	I did this often	I did this occasionally	I never did this
I read and repeated the material aloud	12	42	46
I copied out sections of the text	8	31	61
I copied out what I thought were important details	28	36	36
I underlined/ highlighted important points	·68	27	5

Table 20.1   Rehearsal Strategy

Reading Behaviour	Percentage Ratings		
	I did this often	I did this occasionally	I never did this
I wrote summaries of the text in my own words	17	27	56
I focused on the study tasks as a means of making sense of the text	35	57	8
I created pictures and images in my mind of what I was reading	26	48	26
I wrote out real life examples of ideas which were in the text	4	21	75
I made notes in my own words of main points and supporting details	24	45	31
I made mental connections between information in the text and what I already knew	38	54	8
I mentally combined information from different parts of the text together	26	57	17
I mentally organised the text information into a new order which made sense to me	13	38	49

Table 20.2   Elaboration Strategy

Reading Behaviour	Percentage Ratings		
	I did this often	I did this occasionally	I never did this
I reread the entire text several times	15	36	49
I reread portions of the text which I did not understand well	73	26	1
I carried on reading in the hope that later reading would clarify what I did not understand	32	52	16
I consulted other texts in the hope of clarification	4	27	69
I consulted my peers/ friends to see what their understandings were	59	38	3
I sought clarification from a tutor	12	69	19
I mentally asked myself questions about what I was reading	41	48	11
I made a lot of use of the lecture input to help me to understand the text	69	30	1

Table 20.3   Comprehension Monitoring

students themselves conceive of the notion of learning (Marton, 1988). In summary the results suggest that only a small proportion of the students were engaging comprehensively in the cognitive strategic processing which is thought to influence learning. A larger number engaged with learning either sporadically or only partially. What sense can be made of this?

20.5   Discussion

The purpose of having students read expository text is that they might learn. But in order to learn from text, students need to approach the reading task strategically. If the goal is just to remember information from the text then rehearsal strategies will suffice. Rehearsal behaviours facilitate the amount of material which is learned although the time which is needed for rehearsal is lengthy. While Rehearsal may define part of what is involved in learning in higher education, it should not represent it completely. A more demanding but nevertheless more desirable goal (in the context of higher education) is to integrate new information in the text with that which is already known. Students can then derive new insights into their subject matter, accept that there are alternative perspectives on most phenomena or make coherent sense out of incomplete or even conflicting evidence. To achieve such ends requires strategies in which students elaborate their extant knowledge base. And yet this is precisely what most of the students did not do: they did not regularly summarize their reading; they did not routinely make their own notes from what they were reading; they did not systematically make links within what they were reading or with what they already knew. Essentially the students did not reflect on their reading. And yet summarizing has been emphasized by Scardamalia and Bereiter (1984), Pressley *et al.* (1992) and Mayer (1995) as being what distinguishes skilled from less skilled readers. What is not clear from this study is whether students appreciated what summarizing could actually do for them or whether they simply lacked the tactical skill required to summarize.

For summarizing to be realized as a powerful learning tool, students need to engage in metacognitive monitoring. An indication to students of what has been learned and of what progress is being made is their attempts to transform the information in the text into their own words. Being unable to summarize the text should alert students to the need for further action. However, if students are unaware that they are not learning, they are unlikely to invoke remedial action. Poor monitoring is not uncommon and is affected by aspects of the learning context (Garner, 1990). When the task is perceived as unimportant, when there is no need to act on the reading, or when effortful activity is neither valued nor rewarded, monitoring is unlikely.

As well as appreciating the power of monitoring, students need to develop skill in summarizing. The components of summarizing develop slowly, and proficiency cannot be assumed even in adult readers (Hidi and Anderson, 1986). First there must be a conscious evaluation of what parts of the text are/not important; secondly, condensation rules must be applied; and thirdly the essence of the original is shaped into a form which itself is a coherent and accurate representation.

However, there are two main factors which make it more or less difficult to develop skill in summarizing. One factor is whether the student is summarizing text for his or her own perusal or for the perusal of others, and the other factor which makes the task of summarizing less than straightforward is the physical availability of the original text when summarizing.

A writer-based summary is primarily constructed to monitor and facilitate the writer's own understanding of the text. A reader-based summary, on the other hand, is primarily constructed to demonstrate the writer's skill in accurately representing the original text. The very different purposes served by the two types of summaries have fairly obvious pedagogical implications. If students are quite unpractised in routinely summarizing their reading they should gain experience in constructing accurate records of what they are reading and such experience may need to be structured both in terms of the length and complexity of the reading which is to be summarized. When students are proficient in writer-based summaries they can progress to reader-based summaries where the writer needs to be familiar with the material being summarized in order to construct a polished account.

In text-present summarizing the original is available for repeated perusal while in text-absent summarizing, the writer must retrieve all information from memory. Hidi and Anderson (1986) suggest that text-absent summarizing promotes a more active type of processing than does text-present summarizing but Kirby and Woodhouse (1994) argue that text-absent summarizing encourages deep processing of the text only in those students who are actively engaged with the material. In other words, requiring students to summarize in text-absent conditions will not of itself promote a deep approach to learning. Again there is developmental progression implied by the issue of whether or not the text is available. If the reader is unskilled or if the material is new and initially difficult there seems nothing to be lost and much to be gained from summarizing in text-present conditions. However, with increasing practice and increasing mastery of the substantive domain, students should be encouraged to move towards text-absent summarizing since habitual reliance on text-present summarizing might encourage surface approaches to learning.

The paucity of students' strategic behaviour clearly demands some attention and from the evidence here it seems obvious that students should be enabled to develop and refine both cognitive and metacognitive strategies (Paris *et al.*, 1983; Dole *et al.*, 1991; Butler and Winne, 1995; Simons, 1995). However, it is probably important to remind ourselves that the strategies will be effective only to the extent that they are perceived by the student to facilitate learning (Marton, 1988). Students who conceive of learning only as 'more things to know or remember' are going to treat the text as though it were a repository of facts to be raided, and so may well be satisfied with Rehearsal. On the other hand, students who are open to the possibility that a text might radically affect the way they think about aspects of reality are going to engage with the line of reasoning expounded and evaluate it in terms of a range of criteria. This in turn requires them to review extant learning, ask questions of the text (and of themselves), compare what they are reading with other sources, hypothesize and extrapolate from the text, and remedy or extend their understanding when it is in error or incomplete. In other words, students who recognize that reading is both an effortful task and one which is perfectly within their own control to manage are going to engage in Elaboration and Comprehension Monitoring Strategies.

In enabling students to value the power of reading expository text, it is important that we, as teachers, subscribe to the view that reading is effortful and can be problematic. This is not to say that the learning from text need necessarily be painful or difficult, but since it is not guaranteed, the reading demands which we make of students must be consistent with the intention that students learn to think (with increasing sophistication) for themselves. If students are only required to learn what has already been processed for them by others, they learn to believe that this is what learning means. If the teacher is the one who summarizes the text and defines the important terms, students are not required to think for themselves and are, in effect, being encouraged to adopt a surface approach to learning (Entwistle, cited in Vermunt and Van Rijswijk, 1988; Entwistle and Entwistle, 1991). As an aid to, and manifestation of, their learning from text students should routinely and intentionally incorporate summarizing into their reading activities. It is when students are effective in their summarizing that they have control over their own learning.

For a variety of reasons (Ramsden, 1992) students may be initially reluctant to think for themselves. However, the consequence of believing that learning is only the accretion of information is to prevent any essential change in the person because such a view of learning does not include the possibility that conceptual boundaries could shift to form new perspectives. It is, therefore, of critical importance that students progressively and explicitly focus on enriching and revising their understanding (Bereiter and Scardamalia, 1989; Dart and Clarke, 1991; Dall'Alba, 1993; Baillie *et al.*, 1996) rather than focus on accumulating and reproducing a near verbatim account of what has been read.

20.6 Conclusion

The study aimed to describe the self-reported learning strategies which students adopt when reading expository text. Notwithstanding the difficulties of any methodology which attempts to gather data through self-report techniques, the results were disappointing though not altogether surprising. To the extent that most of the students seemed not to engage regularly in the strategies of Elaboration and Comprehension Monitoring, they were not engaging in learning in any real sense. This is viewed as a serious lack if students are to be independent and autonomous learners. Because the majority of the students focused almost exclusively on the strategy of Rehearsal (where selecting the appropriate information to attend to is the prime purpose) they were denying themselves the opportunity of learning in a way which would both support the recall of information and allow application of the information in the widest possible way. If students are to learn from their reading of expository text, they must have a repertoire of strategic behaviour from which to make conditional and considered choice. One way of supporting students in their development of strategies is to have them regularly summarize their reading. However, summarizing will only have value if it is sincerely recognized by students and teachers as a useful and powerful means of making explicit and extending one's own understanding. In this respect it has to be recognized that reading expository text is effortful and requires intention on the part of the student. Teachers' understandings of what it means to 'help' students may thus be in need of revision. Some appreciation of what this might mean in both conceptual and operational terms would be useful.

20.7 References

Baillie, A., Porter, N. and Corrie, S. (1996) Encouraging a deep approach to the undergraduate psychology curriculum: an example and some lessons from a third year course, *Psychology Teaching Review*, 5(1), 14–24.

Baker, L. (1985) Differences in the standards used by college students to evaluate their comprehension of expository prose, *Reading Research Quarterly*, 20(3), 297–313.

Bell, L. and Perfetti, C. (1994) Reading skill: some adult comparisons, *Journal of Educational Psychology*, 86(2), 244–55.

Bereiter, C. and Scardamalia, M. (1989) Intentional learning as a goal of instruction. In L. Resnick (ed.), *Knowing, Learning and Instruction*, Hillsdale, New Jersey, Lawrence Erlbaum Associates.

Biggs, J. (1987) *Student Approaches to Learning and Studying*, Melbourne: Australian Council for Educational Research.

Booth, J. and Hall, W. (1994) Role of the cognitive internal state lexicon in reading comprehension, *Journal of Educational Psychology*, 86(3), 413–22.

Butler, D. and Winne, P. (1995) Feedback and self-regulated learning: a theoretical synthesis, *Review of Educational Research*, 65(3), 245–81.

Christensen, C., Massey, D. and Isaacs, P. (1991) Cognitive strategies and study habits, *British Journal of Educational Psychology*, **61**, 290–9.

Dall'Alba, G. (1993) The role of teaching in higher education: enabling students to enter a field of study and practice, *Learning and Instruction*, **3**, 299–313.

Dart, B. and Clarke, J. (1991) Helping students to become better learners: a case study in teacher education, *Higher Education*, **22**, 317–35.

Dole, J., Duffy, G., Roehler, L. and Pearson, P. (1991) Moving from the old to the new: research on reading comprehension instruction, *Review of Educational Research*, **61**(2), 239–64.

Entwistle, N. and Entwistle, A. (1991) Contrasting forms of understanding for degree examinations: the student experience and its implications, *Higher Education*, **22**, 205–27.

Garner, R. (1990) When children and adults do not use learning strategies, *Review of Educational Research*, **60**(4), 517–29.

Guthrie, J. (1982) Aims and features of text. In W. Otto and S. White (eds), *Reading Expository Material*, London, Academic Press, 185–8.

Guthrie, J. (1988) Locating information in documents: examination of a cognitive model, *Reading Research Quarterly*, **23**, 178–99.

Hidi, S. and Anderson, V. (1986) Producing written summaries: task demands, cognitive operations and implications for instruction, *Review of Educational Research*, **56**(4), 473–93.

Kirby, J. and Woodhouse, R. (1994) Measuring and predicting depth of processing in learning, *The Alberta Journal of Educational Research*, **40**(2), 147–61.

Marton, F. (1988) *Describing and improving learning. In R. Schmeck (ed.),* Learning Styles and Learning Strategies, *New York: Plenum, 53–82.*

Mayer, R. (1995) Study habits and strategies. In L. Anderson (ed.), *International Encyclopaedia of Teaching and Teacher Education*, Oxford, Elsevier Science Ltd, 434–6.

Paris, S., Lipson, M. and Wixson, K. (1983) Becoming a strategic reader, *Contemporary Educational Psychology*, **8**, 293–316.

Pressley, M., El-Dinary, P. and Brown, R. (1992) Skilled and not-so-skilled reading. In M. Pressley, (ed.), *Promoting Academic Competence and Literacy in School*, New York: Academic Press.

Ramsden, P. (1992) *Learning to Teach in Higher Education*, London, Routledge.

Scardamalia, M. and Bereiter, C. (1984) Development of strategies in text processing. In H. Mandl, N. Stein and T. Trabasso (eds), *Learning and Comprehension of Text*, Hillsdale, New Jersey, Lawrence Erlbaum Associates, 379–406.

Schnotz, W. (1993) Adaptive construction of mental representations in understanding expository texts, *Contemporary Educational Psychology*, **18**, 114–20.

Simons, P. (1995) Metacognitive strategies: teaching and assessing in: L. Anderson (Ed.) International Encyclopaedia of Teaching and Teacher Education, pp. 481-485 Oxford, Elsevier Science Ltd.

Vermunt, J. and Van Rijswijk, F. (1988) Analysis and development of students' skill in self-regulated learning, *Higher Education*, **17**, 647–82.

Weinstein, C. and Mayer, R. (1986) The teaching of learning strategies. In M. Wittrock (ed.), *Handbook of Research on Teaching*, New York: Macmillan, 315–27.

Zabrucky, K. and Commander, N. (1993) Rereading to understand: the role of text coherence and reader proficiency, *Contemporary Educational Psychology*, **18**, 442–54.

21 Involving the personal tutor in supporting student learning

Rosalind Crouch, Amanda Jefferies and Andrew Fitzharris
Faculty of Engineering and Information Sciences,
University of Hertfordshire

21.1   Overview

With the recent general increase in student numbers, first-year students need to cope not only with the pressures of the transition to university, but also with the effect of larger classes with less personal contact. Concern about students' study skills on a technological degree led to a review of the personal tutoring scheme on the premise that many students seemed not to be aware that they were at risk of failure and/or were not able to take responsibility for their own learning. All first-year students on an undergraduate course were given early feedback on academic performance and offered a limited amount of individual support particularly with self-management and task-related skills in the form of an individual personal tutor interview. Seventy per cent of students attended the interviews and data was collected about student performance on the early tests and at a later point in the year, and on types of problem brought to tutors. Students attending the interviews tended to improve their performance more than those not attending. Students perceived at interview as reporting they had no problems (whether or not they failed the early tests), tended to improve more than those reporting study problems, who in turn tended to improve more than those reporting external problems affecting their ability to concentrate on their studies. Tutors appeared to be generally successful in identifying which of the students interviewed needed further support.

21.2   Introduction

This is an account of the implementation of a practical proposal aimed at improving student study skills on an undergraduate course. The need for such a proposal became evident as the number of students on the course increased (reflecting the general rise in student numbers in higher education) leading to concern that more undergraduates seemed to be finding it difficult to study successfully in their first year. Fisher (1994) has highlighted the difficulties many students face on entering university, experiencing stress in coping with the demands of the new environment and in adapting to new study patterns, perhaps experiencing a sense of loss of control and loss of previous support. First-year students now not only have to cope with this transition to university, but also often with increased student numbers in class and possibly less staff-student contact than in their previous educational institutions.

The course concerned is an undergraduate technological degree where each part builds on the one before, so failure to understand earlier parts of the course can cause considerable difficulties later on. Staff formed the strong impression that some students seemed to be finding it difficult to take responsibility for their own learning, possibly feeling that it is better to fail through lack of effort than risk the inference of lack of ability (Covington and Omelich, 1979, de Jong *et al.*, 1988). As Covington and Omelich point out, simple exhortations to put in more effort may increase students' feelings that their ability is inadequate to the task. Instead, students need to acknowledge their perceptions of their own ability and effort, but then restructure the situation, redefining success in terms of achieving their own standards. They then need to increase a sense of control by developing their own realistic goals (identifying a need to develop appropriate self-management and task-related skills). It was decided to introduce two preliminary measures we hoped might foster this: a study skills programme and the restructuring and retiming of coursework in order to make more realistic feedback available to students on their progress throughout the year.

We describe here a three-year study-skills programme which was modified in the second year. In the first year of the programme, all students were timetabled fortnightly throughout the year for (unassessed) group seminars aiming to foster study and self-management skills. The emphasis was on small-group discussion with the tutor introducing appropriate exercises and materials and acting as facilitator. Attendance started off well, reducing after the first few weeks and then dwindling in the second half of the year, although a steady band of students persevered throughout. Whether as a result of these measures or not, student progression increased by 2 per cent at the end of the year, and it was decided to continue with the programme in an enhanced form to try and reach more students. Earlier and more structured coursework and tests were introduced giving early feedback to the students on their progress combined with study skills input in the form of one-to-one interviews.

The second year of the programme is described in this chapter. It was decided to collapse the previous study skills course for first year students into a few group sessions at the beginning of the year. After six weeks of the autumn term, early tests were held in the four subjects being studied on the degree and the results communicated to students and personal tutors. We expected that many students would not perform particularly well on the tests, although they were not felt to be difficult if students had kept up with the required work. Some courses also introduced random small tests throughout the year with quick feedback, in addition to coursework. Marks for coursework and tests were communicated to students and to personal tutors as they became available.

Following these early tests, a personal tutor was to meet with each student for a half-hour one-to-one interview. It was felt important that students not doing well on the early tests were offered autumn interviews, and those achieving a satisfactory level in all subjects were then seen immediately after Christmas due to time constraints. Students could request an earlier interview at any time, and some did. Progression increased again in this second year of the programme, though by a modest amount (1%), largely due to a higher than usual number of withdrawals during the year, which may have been due to variations in student intake, to the programme itself (e.g. allowing students to make earlier decisions about their suitability for the course) or to unknown factors. However, in the third year of the programme, which took approximately the same form as in the second year (with a slightly increased amount of coursework), progression increased by a further 7 per cent, and withdrawals fell to their usual level. Following the introduction of the individual interviews in the second and third years of the programme, staff perception was that first-year students who withdrew or failed to progress at the end of the year tended to appear more focused, having thought through their future plans more. This view may gain some support in that many more of these students than before were successful in continuing their studies (either within the university or elsewhere), with the proportion applying successfully to change course for the new academic term being 52 per cent in the second year of the programme compared with only 5 per cent in the previous year (before the introduction of the interviews). This was maintained in the third year of the programme with 62 per cent of these students continuing in higher education (though not necessarily at degree level).

21.3   The study skills programme

The students for the second year of the study skills programme numbered 154 (135 male, 19 female: 136 aged 18–25, 18 aged over 25) and were on the first year of an undergraduate degree in a technological subject. All students, except three who were absent, sat the early tests in all four subjects being studied during the year. Results on these tests were compared with the accumulated course marks in the four subjects at a point just before Easter. Information was also collected from the personal tutors, who recorded the number of students interviewed; whether students were seen more than once; how many appeared worried; how many students seemed to the tutors to feel that they had no problem with their work and how many felt they did have a problem and, if so, whether students considered it a study problem (with no apparent external problem) or an external problem affecting their work (e.g. health, relationship, family or financial problems).

The one-to-one interview with the personal tutor generally lasted for half an hour. There were four personal tutors involved (two male and two female), all lecturers in the department with some aptitude for the role. Students were sent a personal message inviting them to see a particular tutor at a predetermined time and place in the near future with the opportunity to rearrange the time if necessary. It was explained during the early group study skills sessions that the interviews were voluntary and were for tutors and students to work side by side in as non-judgmental a way as possible in order to consider what the student wanted from the course and the best way of achieving this. Interviews were structured but open-ended in that tutors wanted to find out how students felt about their test results and progress on the degree, what their goals were and their methods for achieving them. (Goals tended to be to pass the first year, pass the degree, become a professional or similar, but could also be, for instance, to change course, to leave and get a job, and occasionally to live up to, or subvert, family expectations. Some students had never considered what their goals were before, and were surprised by them.) Generally, the student's views were invited first with the tutor clarifying and supporting, and sometimes tactfully confronting when necessary. Tutors then facilitated students' formulation and review of goals and of appropriate methods of achieving them, given the constraints of reality.

The aim was to maintain a supportive but adult-to-adult atmosphere, with tutors seeking to avoid the role of teacher and allow students to take the initiative as much as possible. Later in the interview, students and tutors might explore methods for improving study habits where appropriate and might agree to meet again. If students did not attend the first or subsequent interviews, only one more offer of a new time was usually made. However if an interview was subsequently requested, this was arranged. Seventy per cent students attended for a first interview (108), most coming at the time originally set.

21.4   Findings

We wanted to know, as far as possible, if the programme appeared to benefit students and whether we appeared to be applying our limited resources in the right areas. Among the issues we wished to clarify were whether the individual interviews seemed an appropriate strategy for improving student performance and whether our perceptions of what students were telling us were useful indicators, i.e. whether we could trust our judgement as to who needed further support. For instance, were we right not to follow up further those students whom we perceived as saying they had no problems (even those who had failed on the early tests), or to concentrate our resources on following up students we perceived as reporting problems or who seemed worried?

21.4.1   Student progress and attendance at interview

We expected that many students would not do well in the early tests and in fact just under half the students did not reach a satisfactory level in all subjects (49%). It was not possible to set further tests later on for purposes of comparison, so we compared results on the early tests with accumulated student marks in each subject at Easter. Results of the early tests were compared with the marks at the later assessment point in terms of the number of students achieving a satisfactory level in all subjects ('Pass all'), students not achieving a satisfactory level in one or more subjects ('Not pass all') and students who had withdrawn or changed course ('Other'). We also looked at progress made, in terms of those students who continued to pass all subjects or improved the number of subjects passed between the early tests and Easter ('Pass/improve'), and those who failed at least one subject in the early tests and had not increased the number of subjects passed by Easter ('Not improve').

One hundred and eight students (91 aged 18–25, 17 over 25) took up the offer of an interview with a personal tutor (70 per cent of the total number) and 46 did not. One might expect an improvement over time as a natural progression for most students, but students attending the interviews with the tutor were more likely to improve compared with those not attending (Tables 21.1 and 21.2). Of those seeing the tutor, 29 per cent more passed in all subjects at Easter than did in the early tests and a further 10 per cent improved, compared with 9 per cent fewer passing (and no improvers) for those not attending for interview.

Considering only those students who did not pass all subjects in the early tests (though numbers are small for those not seeing the tutor), 68 per cent of interviewed students passed or improved at Easter as against 31 per cent of students not interviewed (Table 21.4), despite percentage results on the early tests being roughly comparable (if those absent on the early tests can be considered for this purpose to have failed in all subjects (Table 21.4a)). Of those passing the early tests, even here the non-interviewed group had a somewhat lower pass rate at Easter than those interviewed (Table 21.3). One could speculate whether this is the effect of coming for interview and thus acknowledging and engaging with the situation and receiving support from the tutor, or whether there is some other factor common to the group of non-interview-attending students which also makes it somewhat less likely that they will improve.

21.4.2   Perception of the need for improving study skills

Of the 108 students interviewed, 42 per cent had reached a satisfactory level in all subjects in the early tests, and 58 per cent had not reached a satisfactory level in one or more subjects. Just over half of the students interviewed were reported as considering their study skills to

Key: Pass all   The number of students achieving a satisfactory level in all four subjects.
Not pass all   The number of students not achieving a satisfactory level in one or more subjects.
Absent   Number of students not submitting work.
Pass/improve   The number of students achieving a satisfactory level in all subjects at Easter or
otherwise improving the number of subjects passed since the early tests.
Not improve   The number of students who did not achieve a satisfactory level in all subjects at Easter and
did not improve on the number of subjects passed.
Other   The number of students who had withdrawn or changed course since the early tests.

Table 21.1 Progress of all students attending study skills interview (108) between early tests and later assessment point at Easter (92 male, 16 female)

	Early tests	Easter		Progress made
Pass all	45 (42%)	77 (71%)	Pass/improve	88 (81.5%)
Not pass all	63 (58%)	18 (17%)	Not improve	7 (6.5%)
Absent	0	13 (12%)	Other	13 (12%)

Table 21.2 Progress of all students not attending study skills interview (46) between early tests and later assessment point at Easter (43 male, 3 female)

	Early tests	Easter		Progress made
Pass all	30 (65%)	26 (56%)	Pass/improve	26 (56%)
Not pass all	13 (28%)	16 (35%)	Not improve	16 (35%)
Absent	3 (7%)*	4 (9%)	Other	4 (9%)

*all 3 absent students in the early tests were present but not passing in all subjects at Easter

Table 21.3 Results at Easter of students passing all subjects in early tests and seeing tutor (45) compared with those not seeing tutor (30)

Easter	Students Interviewed (45)	Students not interviewed (30)
Pass all	41 (91%)	21 (70%)
Not pass all	2 (4%)	7 (23%)
Other	2 (4%)	2 (7%)

Table 21.4 Result at Easter and progress of students not passing all subjects or absent in early tests and seeing tutor (63) compared with those not seeing tutor (16)

Easter	Students Interviewed (63)	Students not interviewed (16)	Progress made	Students Interviewed (63)	Students not interviewed (16)
Pass all	36 (57%)	5 (31%)	Pass/improve	43 (68%)	5 (31%)
Not pass all	16 (25%)	9 (56%)	Not improve	9 (14%)	9 (56%)
Other	11 (18%)	2 (12%)	Other	11 (18%)	2 (12%)

Table 21.4a Students not passing in one or more subjects in early tests: number of subjects failed

Early tests	Seeing tutor (63)	Not seeing tutor (16)
Fail 1 or 2 subjects	43 (68%)	11 (69%)
Fail 3 or 4 subjects	20 (32%)	2 (12%)
Absent	0	3 (19%)

be adequate to the task of passing the course (defined as 'no problem'), the rest were either reported as feeling that they had problems with studying itself (defined as a 'study-related problem') or that some outside problem, e.g. a health, relationship, family or financial problem, was affecting their ability to work (defined as a 'non-study-related problem').

Those students reporting no problems (53 per cent of those interviewed) seem the most likely either to pass or improve at Easter, despite under half of them not doing well initially. Ninety-seven per cent improved and 91 per cent passed in all subjects (Table 21.5). It could be argued that those not attending for interview (Table 21.2) might also be taken to be signalling that there is no problem and therefore no need to see the tutor. If so, then the interviewees seem to have a greater tendency to be realistic in their assessment of the academic situation as only 56 per cent of non-attenders passed or improved at Easter .

Students perceived as reporting study-related problems alone (29 per cent of those interviewed) tended to improve their academic performance over the year (Tables 21.6 and 21.7) as compared with those with non-study-related problems (18%), who also had a greater tendency to withdraw from the course. This might be expected, given the nature of many non-study-related problems and their obvious impact on students' ability to work. Those reporting problems were usually seen more than once by the same tutor and a few were seen intermittently for most of the year.

Table 21.5 Progress of students with no problems (58) between early tests and later assessment points

	Early tests	Easter		Progress made
Pass all	34 (59%)	53 (91%)	Pass/improve	56 (96%)
Not pass all	24 (41%)	4 (7%)	Not improve	1 (2%)
Absent	0	1 (2%)	Other	1 (2%)

Table 21.6 Progress of students with study-related problems (31) between early tests and later assessment point

	Early tests	Easter		Progress made
Pass all	8 (26%)	20 (65%)	Pass/improve	23 (74%)
Not pass all	23 (74.%)	6 (19%)	Not improve	3 (10%)
Absent	0	5 (16%)	Other	5 (16%)

Table 21.7 Progress of students with non-study related problems (19) between early tests and later assessment

	Early tests	Easter		Progress made
Pass all	3 (16%)	4 (21%)	Pass/improve	9 (47%)
Not pass all	16 (84%)	8 (42%)	Not improve	3 (16%)
Absent	0	7 (37%)	Other	7 (37%)

Table 2 is repeated for purposes of comparison.

Table 21.2 Progress of all students not attending study skills interview (46) between early tests and later assessment point at Easter (43 male, 3 female)

	Early tests	Easter		Progress made
Pass all	30 (65%)	26 (56%)	Pass/improve	26 (56%)
Not pass all	13 (28%)	16 (35%)	Not improve	16 (35%)
Absent	3 (7%)	4 (9%)	Other	4 (9%)

21.4.3   Amount of work and attendance

We had expected to find that many students were not attending or working hard enough. Unfortunately we have no data on this point for students not interviewed. Looking at the amount of work and attendance at classes reported to tutors, it appears there is a tendency for those with non-study-related problems to work and attend less than those with study-related problems (who in turn work and attend less than those with no problems). A third of students with study-related problems are reported to feel they have not been working enough, compared with over a half of those with non-study-related problems. Insufficient attendance is more likely to be associated with a non-study-related problem often combined with insufficient work, reflecting, in our view, the impact of the external problem on students' ability to concentrate on their studies.

Table 21.8 Reported work and attendance of students with no problems, study-related problems and non-study-related problems

Work/attendance	No problems (58)	Study-related problems (31)	Non-study-related problems (19)
Insufficient work only	2 (3%)	8 (26%)	2 (11%)
Insufficient attendance only	5 (9%)	0	0
Insufficient work & attendance	1 (2%)	2 (6%)	9 (47%)
Total insuffic. wk/attendance	8 (14%)	10 (32%)	11 (58%)
Sufficient work/attend.	50 (86%)	21 (68%)	8 (42%)

21.4.4   Perceived worry

We also considered that worry or stress might be affecting student performance. Of the 108 students interviewed, 31 (29%) seemed to the tutors to be worried, particularly those reporting non-study-related problems of whom 84 per cent seemed worried. Despite this, worried students tended to make some progress, though not as much as those who were not worried (Tables 21.9 and 21.10), with the exception of a small group of students (7) reporting study-related problems who passed the early tests and were still doing well at the later assessment point (Table 21.11).

Table 21.9 Progress of students appearing worried (31)

	Early tests	Easter		Progress made
Pass all	9 (29%)	16 (52%)	Pass/improve	21 (68%)
Not pass all	22 (71%)	10 (32%)	Not improve	5 (16%)
Absent	0	5 (16%)	Other	5 (16%)

Table 21.10 Progress of students not appearing worried (77)

	Early tests	Easter		Progress made
Pass all	36 (47%)	61 (79%)	Pass/improve	67 (87%)
Not pass all	41 (53%)	8 (10%)	Not improve	2 (3%)
Absent	0	8 (10%)	Other	8 (10%)

Seventy-one per cent of those appearing worried had failed on the early tests, comprising roughly one-third of all failing students interviewed. All except one of the worried students reported having a problem. For those not passing in the early tests, this was more likely to be a non-study-related problem (Table 21.12) and the reasons for concern were usually related to the nature of the problem and its capacity to interfere with study and concentration. However, among those who passed the early tests, all except one of those appearing worried reported a study-related problem (Table 21.11).

Table 21.11 Those passing early tests (45): reported problems and perceived worry

	Not worried	Worried	Total
No problems	34	0	34
Study-related problems	1	7	8
Non-study-related problems	1	2	3
Total	36 (80%)	9 (20%)	45 (100%)

Table 21.12 Those failing early tests (63): reported problems and perceived worry

	Not worried	Worried	Total
No problems	23	1	24
Study-related problems	16	7	23
Non-study-related problems	2	14	16
Total	41 (65%)	22 (34%)	63 (100%)

There are only a small number of students (8) who pass the early tests but report study-related problems (Table 21.6). Nearly all of them seem worried (7), nearly all report excellent study-habits (7) and all report good attendance. Tutors were happy with their approach to study and the students were all continuing to do well at Easter, but nevertheless seemed to benefit from feedback and encouragement. Though numbers are small, this contrasts with students not passing all subjects in the early tests and reporting study-related problems (23), less than a third of whom appear worried. It is possible that this small group of students were successfully employing a strategy of defensive pessimism (Cantor and Norem, 1987), confronting anxieties in advance of stressful tasks as a means of gaining control.

21.4.5   Follow-up interviews

We followed up those students who seemed to tutors to need, or to request, more support (a small number of whom had more than one interview if necessary), mainly those who felt they had problems or who seemed worried. We wished to see if allocating our resources in this way was useful. Just over half of the students interviewed (57%) were seen only once. Most of those seen once (46 (74%)) felt they had no problem and did not appear worried. In fact, 88 per cent (51) of the total number of students reporting no problem were seen once only, and 91 per cent were passing at Easter and 96 per cent passing or improved (Table 21.5). Only five students appearing worried were seen just once and they all passed at Easter. Five of the students with study-related problems were only seen once, and four passed at Easter, whereas only one student with a non-study related problem was seen once, due to withdrawal from the course. Numbers are small in some cases, but tutors' judgement here seems reasonably good. Table 21.13 further supports the view that tutors could generally judge who would manage well without further support as 93 per cent of students seen only once passed at Easter and 95 per cent improve.

Table 21.13 Progess of students seen for one interview by tutors (62)

	Early tests	Easter		Progress made
Pass all	36 (58%)	58 (93%)	Pass/improve	59 (95%)
Not pass all	26 (42%)	3 (5%)	Not improve	2 (3%)
Absent	0	1 (2%)	Other	1 (2%)

Table 21.14 Progress of students seen for more than one interview by tutors (46)

	Early tests	Easter		Progress made
Pass all	9 (20%)	19 (41%)	Pass/improve	29 (63%)
Not pass all	37 (80%)	15 (33%)	Not improve	5 (11%)
Absent	0	12 (26%)	Other	12 ((26%)

Students seen again were generally those reporting problems, especially if they seemed worried. Though it could be argued that they appear to have benefited from the interviews (Table 21.14), the number making progress is considerably larger (63%) than the number passing at Easter in all subjects (41%). Whether more could be done here needs further exploration. Some students seen more than once (26%) may also have considered that withdrawal from the course was more appropriate in terms of their perceived goals and considered this option with the tutor.

21.5   Discussion

It is a matter for speculation why a higher proportion of students who came for interview passed or improved at Easter as compared with the group who did not attend (though numbers in this group are small) and this is something that needs further investigation. It may be that students coming to interview tended in any case to be more ready to be involved with the course and this may itself have motivated academic performance. It is also possible that, without a facilitating environment such as the tutor interview, it may have been more difficult for students to feel they had some control in a new situation (by attributing academic success to things that they could put right, such as self-management and task-analysis skills), and so non-interviewed students may have been less able to engage with the demands of the course. A further consideration is that the interviews may simply have provided support and interpersonal contact at a time when it was needed. Students may need to feel borne in mind by tutors and appreciate their difficulties being noticed in the upheaval of settling in to a new environment. Cottrell *et al.* (1994) note that first-year personal tutees on a medical course seemed particularly to appreciate the tutor's making the initial contact and taking a personal interest in them. This seemed more so for first-year students than for tutees on later years of the course. Whatever the factors involved, it seems important to explore ways of successfully approaching more of the students who did not respond to the invitation to attend the study skills interview. It cannot be assumed that they will necessarily do well on their own.

We concentrated most of our resources on offering further support to those students interviewed whom we perceived as indicating they were having problems. If tutors' perceptions can be taken to be reasonably accurate reflections of what students are telling them, it appears that those students attending the interviews were able to judge fairly well whether they were in a good position academically or whether they had a problem which would interfere with future performance. Those who felt they had no problem in studying, whether or not they passed in the early tests, were likely to be right.

In the case of study-related problems, students seemed able to recognize that there was a problem and to give some thought as to how to improve the situation. After discussing study skills with the tutor and in two-thirds of cases having further interviews, most considerably improved their academic performance, though not necessarily always enough to pass in all subjects. Some decided the most appropriate way forward was to withdraw or change course. There are a small group of high-achieving students reported as feeling they had a study-related problem, who were likely to be worried, but nevertheless continued to do well. It is in the group acknowledging study-related problems (with the exception of the high-achieving students), and even more particularly in the group of students with non-study-related problems, that lack of study and attendance is evident. For the former group of students, this may be a matter of acknowledging the problem and taking steps to set personal goals and work on self-management and study skills, but for the latter group it seems likely to be a sign of an external problem interfering with concentration and academic performance. Students in this latter group were likely to perform less well. This is probably due to the effect of the problem on concentration, but there may be a knock-on effect on academic progress even if the problem itself is resolved. Our impression is, however, that such students may do better in the longer term if adequate support is available, though some may need to withdraw and return later.

We are encouraged by the findings reported in this chapter, tentative though some of them are, to feel that the system of study-skills interviews with personal tutors can be useful to students. For the future, we are exploring ways of involving even more students and of expanding study-skills support. It also seems important to consider the general question of quantity and quality of staff-student contact as student numbers increase, particularly for first-year students as they enter a new academic environment.

21.6   References

Cantor, N., Norem, J.K. *et al.* (1987) Life tasks, self-concept ideals, and cognitive strategies in a life transition, *Journal of Personality and Social Psychology*, **53**(6), 1178–91.

Cottrell, D.J., McCrorie P. and Perrin, F. (1994) The personal tutor system: an evaluation, *Medical Education*, **28**, 544–9.

Covington, M.V. and Omelich, C.L. (1979) Effort, the double-edged sword in school achievement, *Journal of Educational Psychology*, **71**, 169–82.

Fisher, S. (1994) *Stress in Academic Life: The Mental Assembly Line*, The Society for Research into Education and Open University Press.

de Jong, P.F., Koomen, W. and Mellenbergh, G.J. (1988) Structure of causes for success and failure: a multidimensional scaling analysis of preference judgments, *Journal of Personality and Social Psychology*, **55**(5), 718–25.

22 Four good reasons for cheating and plagiarism

Phil Bannister and Peter Ashworth
Learning and Teaching Institute, Sheffield Hallam University

22.1 Introduction: the research context

The phenomenon of student cheating is by no means a new one, yet in recent years it has become the subject of increasing concern for academic staff within higher education in the UK. Fears of its becoming more widespread have been prompted (in part) by certain of the far-reaching changes which higher education has undergone in the current decade and continues to experience. The move towards a system of mass participation in higher education has meant a wider range of student ability on entry, an increasingly disproportionate student–tutor ratio and reduced direct contact time. This has been concurrent with a gradual shift away from relatively 'tried and tested' forms of student assessment (whose validity have been maybe naïvely taken for granted by staff and students) such as the formal examination, towards more continuous, coursework-based assessment, with an increased emphasis on collaborative student learning. Communication and information technologies are assuming an increasingly integral role in student learning, with a simultaneous proliferation of electronic information sources (e.g. full text journals available across the Internet).

Such changes in the learning environment provide increased scope for students to cheat, and make the task of regulating student behaviour less straightforward. At the same time, in a climate of increased accountability, academics are also under pressure to deal with instances of cheating through formal institutional-level processes, rather than through exercising their own personal judgement and discretion.

22.2 Research aims and objectives

Although considerable, predominantly North American research into this subject area exists, previous studies have tended to assume that the meaning of cheating is unequivocal and straightforward, shared by all of the research subjects (usually students, but on occasion academic staff as well). The intention of such research has been largely on estimating the prevalence of cheating in higher education, and/or the perceived seriousness of different behaviours which are classed as cheating. Questionnaires and attitude scales are characteristically used to collect data (e.g. Roberts and Tooms, 1993; Franklyn-Stokes and Newstead, 1995).

Our belief is that before such research approaches can yield meaningful information, which can usefully assist academics in the task of minimizing cheating and plagiarism among students, it is necessary to acquire an understanding of the place and possible meanings of cheating within the student lifeworld. Key areas of inquiry include the specific practices classed as cheating; the hierarchies and typologies into which they are organized; the processes of moral evaluation involved when someone is caught cheating; and how the context in which cheating occurs influences its interpretation (e.g. circumstances which mitigate the seriousness of certain prohibited behaviours).

The intention of the study reported here was to attend to the meaning of cheating within the student experience as closely as possible, without imposing any external conceptual framework. No attempt was made to judge perceptions against a yardstick of truth or morality, or to defend a position with which the researcher identifies from criticism that might be regarded as unjust. The aim was to ascertain the place of cheating and plagiarism within the lived experience of the students interviewed, whether their perceptions were wise or foolish. This form of qualitative research may be termed 'phenomenologically based' in that it draws on the implications for empirical research of that philosophical approach (Giorgi, 1985).

Nineteen interviews were carried out by the course members towards the end of a semester-long Master's degree unit in qualitative research interviewing. Each interviewed one student, and competed a full analysis and report on that interview – this constituted the unit assessment. The interviewers are acknowledged as co-authors of this chapter. The interviewees were not undertaking the interviewing unit, they were of both sexes, from a number of universities, at all stages in their courses, and from the whole range of discipline areas (see Table 22.1). Further analysis on the set of interviews as a whole was carried out by two of the authors.

Intervie w-ee	Gender	Mature[1]	Discipl- ine[2]	Full-time / Part- time	Level[3]	SHU[4]	Intervie w-er gender
1	f	✓	a	f	g	✓	f
2	m	✓	a	p	3	✓	m
3	f		b	f	g		f
4	m		a	f	1	✓	f
5	m	✓	b	f	3	✓	f
6	m	✓	a	f	1	✓	f
7	f		a	f	2		m
8	f		c	f	2	✓	f
9	f		a	f	3	✓	f
10	f		a	f	2		m
11	f		b	f	3		f
12	f	✓	a	f	3		f
13	m	✓	b	p	3	✓	f
14	f	✓	b	p	g		f
15	m	✓	b	f	3	✓	f
16	m	✓	a	p	3	✓	f
17	f	✓	c	f	g	✓	m
18	f	✓	a	f	2		f
19	m	✓	a	f	g		m

Key

1 The interview entered the course described in the interview as a mature student

2 Referring to a course which was mainly (a) Arts, Humanities or Social Science
   (b) Business, Science or Technology or Engineering (c) Mixed

3 In year or level 1, 2 or 3 or graduated (g) at time of the interview

4 Referring to a course at Sheffield Hallam University or elsewhere

Table 22.1   Research Participants

As the area of investigation of this study is a potentially contentious and emotive one, a number of issues concerning the research technique employed are worthy of note. The acceptability of the interviewers is felt to be significant. Each of the students was interviewed by someone known to them, and with whom there was some form of social relationship; a condition of trust existed. The interviewers were of an equal status to the research subjects in terms of the fact that all were higher education students or recent graduates. The interviewers were not the representatives of any form of authority, institutional or otherwise. (Indeed, the researchers and their subjects were not always within in the same higher education establishment.) This provided the conditions for candidness of response and potentially lessened the possibility of interviewees attempting to second-guess the researcher's agenda in their responses. The openness of the technique of interviewing and analysis to student perceptions is of importance. The focus of the research was limited only to the student viewpoint; this involved researchers setting aside presuppositions, especially moral ones, and not attempting to challenge the views of the research subjects. Interviews were semi-structured to allow instances and situations to be described, rather than just the eliciting of opinions (as is the case with questionnaires) – so permitting any complexities around the issue of academic cheating to emerge (e.g. the possibility that the meaning of cheating varies according to the specific context in which it occurs). Important issues of safety and confidentiality were addressed within the research method: the anonymity of the interviewees was maintained throughout the process of analysis, with only details of their gender, academic discipline etc. being made available to the tutor who assessed the assignment within which the interviews were carried out.

Analysis of the set of interviews as a whole indicate to us that students believe there are a number of 'good reasons' for cheating. These are grouped into four areas – the ethics of peer loyalty and fellow-feeling, and of learning; opportunities and excuses; symbolic ambiguity – the reduction of fatefulness in assessment; and alienation and cheating. The italicized quotes in each of these sections are taken verbatim from the student interviews, and exemplify themes prevalent within the whole research sample.

22.2.1   The ethics of peer loyalty and fellow-feeling, and of learning

Students typically have strong moral beliefs related to cheating. All of the interviewees considered cheating within a framework of personal morality, including those who admitted to having cheated at university (of whom there were several). What is problematic is that there is a difference between these values and the official academic ones. A highly pervasive student ethic is that of fellow-feeling and peer loyalty. Potentially questionable practices are evaluated primarily in terms of the effect they have on the student peer group, with a strong consensus that the least acceptable forms of cheating are those which actively disadvantage other students. Yet at the same time, this ethical principle of peer loyalty can imply that copying and collusion are allowable where a fellow student is in genuine difficulties.

> I think allowing someone to look at your work is teaching – you are just doing the job of the teacher, which the teacher may have done badly or may have done well. If you are willing to do it, which is a decision for you to make, then I don't think it is cheating. (5)

Adherence to this ethical principle can also legitimate, or lessen the perceived seriousness of forms of cheating which do not have a direct effect on the student's peer group – for example, plagiarism from a textbook:

> You can plagiarise someone who's written a book, because they're not on the same level as you. If you copied your friend's work, when you get marked for it you'd be getting her mark, but you're not getting someone else's who's way above you. (11)

Another widely acknowledged ethical principle is the centrality of learning. Several interviewees drew a distinction between forms of cheating which entirely circumvent the learning process, and those which can be seen as 'shortcuts to learning'. Behaviours in the former category – for example, word-for-word copying of another student's work – were seen as reprehensible, offensive to those who have completed the work through honest means. By contrast, practices which reduce the need for personal graft, but which still demand a modicum of understanding – such as the unacknowledged paraphrasing of material in a textbook, or taking material into an exam to jog one's memory – are merely 'shortcuts to learning' which can be justified to oneself.

> 'I'd actually done the work on it, it's just that I needed some sort of trigger, because I'd got the information in my head – it wasn't as if I'd gone in there with quotes and things written up my arms, just a mnemonic [denoting a precise sequence of items]. I suppose that is a cheat, having a little memory aid, but I had done the work, I would justify myself.' (12)

Similarly, cheating that is occasional and brought on by necessity can be justified if, in the greater scheme of things, one is working hard. This perspective is evident in the following quote from a student who admitted to taking more than the allowed amount of material into a seen examination:

> 'Some people can just do brilliant on some parts of the course but not quite make the grade on other parts, and just cause you cheat doesn't necessarily mean that you don't work hard either. I mean certainly in my case I've never worked so hard in my life as I did on my course. [. . .] You know, why ruin somebody's whole career just because they couldn't get through, say, the computing side of it, when they were getting in the seventies and eighties in other subjects: there's no point, is there? (17)

A value for some students is the centrality of learning those things which are seen as being significant. Here it is perceived as entirely justifiable to get through those elements of one's course which are regarded as unimportant or merely hurdles to be jumped, by whatever means are available, in order to concentrate on more significant work.

> It's not relevant to what you're going to do, you're never, probably, going to use it ever again, so why just 'clog' your memory – store it up with something you're not going to use? (12)

22.2.2   Opportunities and excuses

Some methods of assessment are seen as affording much greater opportunities for cheating than others. The informal context in which coursework assignments are completed means there is ample scope to cheat through collusion, plagiarism and so forth, in contrast to the controlled, invigilated environment of formal examinations.

> The unit I mentioned before is probably quite easy to cheat in . . . It would be easy to copy [someone else's work] as it is only a side of A4, not like a full written essay. I think with the essays, the lecturers are more likely to see that you have copied your essay off someone else. So, I think the courses with coursework spread throughout are probably easier to cheat in, because you are not writing as much. (8)

The incidence of some forms of cheating is felt to be related to the likelihood of getting away with it undetected:

> It is easier to cheat at university in a way. Because you can plagiarise and they can't chase it up. There's so many of you. (11)

The excuses and justifications for cheating given by interviewees frequently involved the direction of blame towards the institution for various shortcomings and hypocrisies which lead, directly or indirectly, to student cheating. The university is held culpable for causing students to cheat for a variety of reasons, including the imposition of an unsustainable amount of assessment; failing to take adequate measures to prevent cheating; using flawed forms of assessment.

> I think it stupid for people having to remember chunks of formulae and I can't really see why someone shouldn't take information in [to exams]. (5)

In some instances, work is seen to be assessed in a manner that almost invites cheating. For example, with group-based work, awarding all students in the group an undifferentiated mark makes it highly unlikely that all group members will make an equal contribution. The university was also charged with giving contradictory messages to students: collaboration is punishable, while groupwork is actively encouraged.

> I think I have cheated on practicals in that I've collaborated with other people, but then you're encouraged to collaborate. If you're expecting people not to collude or not to copy each other's ideas, you're a bit stupid to ask them to work together, because it's just a natural thing to do. Why should they penalise you for it if the situation they put you in means you do it? (11)

A particularly important criticism directed towards the university concerned the inadequacy of guidance on the regulations governing cheating and plagiarism. From the interview responses, cheating seems to be simultaneously a high- and low-priority issue for the university: the potential penalties are severe, but the information detailing which types of behaviour fall into this category is given in an unco-ordinated fashion and may not be very enlightening.

> It's not laid down exactly what does count as cheating . . . So in the absence of any clear guidelines you've got to put your interpretation on what you think is right. (1)

Plagiarism in particular appeared to generate a host of difficulties for the students interviewed – both in terms of what exactly it is, and why it is of significance. Although all interviewees were conscious of the need to reference the source of material cited, the positive reasons for adopting this practice – other than to avoid punishment – were not universally apparent. While some did share the 'official' view of its significance, others were perplexed as to why academic staff tend to be so uptight about this issue, especially in relation to undergraduate level studies where students are generally not involved in producing original work but rather engaging with well-established ideas. Although the notion of plagiarism as a form of intellectual theft did have some currency among the interviewees, the tendency was actually to see correct referencing rather in terms of academic etiquette and polite behaviour. In addition, certain students appeared to conceive of plagiarism only in a very literal, concrete sense: the verbatim use of another author's words obviously counts as plagiarism, but to paraphrase their argument in one's own words renders the offence in some way different, lesser. In general, plagiarism is a far less meaningful concept for students than it is for staff, and ranks relatively low in the student system of values.

22.2.3 Symbolic ambiguity – the reduction of fatefulness in assessment

The informal context in which coursework exercises are completed contrasts with the controlled, invigilated environment of unseen examinations. There is a notable reverence for this most traditional form of assessment. Students appear to view examinations as powerfully symbolic, with those occurring at the end of a period of study necessarily carrying a sense of dramatic climax. The perceived formality of the examination as an Occasion lends it gravity, as does its atypical and staged nature.

> There is more of an aura of formality in that situation, when you are all there and it's quiet and you've got an invigilator . . . the rules are very clear – you know that it's just you and your table and your pen and paper – nothing else. (5)

The regulations governing examinations are seen by students as almost self-evident, perceived through signifiers such as the visible presence of institutional authority and the physical exclusion of certain materials from the examination hall. By contrast, the rules governing coursework are much less apparent and clear-cut. Cheating in an exam is a deliberate and flagrant contravention of self-apparent rules – and is possibly premeditated rather than merely opportunistic – and so is thus worthy of particular censure. The symbolism and the fatefulness perceived in the end-of-session examination is seen by students as watered down in other forms of assessment, which are given less credence. As a consequence, cheating in course assignments is of a lesser moral magnitude.

> You can see why people copy things in coursework assignments, it's not a big moral issue but actually cheating in an exam, I mean, I wouldn't be able to do that. (11)

Some of the significance attributed to exams – and the corresponding reduced significance of coursework – appears connected to the precise social context in which the assessment takes place.

> There's something about an exam, isn't there? You're all sat there in the same boat, it's more like you'd be betraying the other people with you rather than just yourself, whereas with an essay you just think, 'I'm cheating myself so who cares?' (7)

Formative assessment appeared to be very devalued in the eyes of many students: several interviewees admitted to having cheated within non-assessed assignments without having experienced any particular guilt.

22.2.4 Alienation and cheating

Cheating is sometimes a symptom of a more general malaise. The interviewees expressed some general discontent with the situation of the university undergraduate student, which was at least partially related to how the students perceived themselves to be regarded by academic staff. The experience of being a degree student was frequently described as anonymous, particularly in comparison to school study or further education where contact with staff is more prolonged. The movement from an intensively taught style of education to one in which the emphasis is on independent learning, classes are larger, and academic staff have a role not confined to teaching, may result in students feeling neglected by the system.

However, student discontent was not simply due to large classes and the lack of staff contact with students. Assessment tasks which did not engage the student symbolized the gap between students and staff, and implied disrespect. A complaint made by a number of interviewees was that the work did not demand original thought, but the rather the re-iteration of well-established ideas and concepts. Within such a perspective, the need to observe official regulations – particularly with regard to the citation of information sources – was not universally recognized.

> Academia does depend on everything being acknowledged, especially if it's actual research, something that is intended to be of value – then I think it's very important that things are referenced, if it's leading edge stuff. If it's an undergraduate essay on a subject that's been discussed and looked over for donkey's years, then it doesn't really matter. (5)

In some cases, students felt that the subject had been comprehensively exhausted – it was just not possible to say anything that had not been stated many times previously. One interviewee spoke critically of an assignment that had been set in virtually unchanged form year after year. The devaluation of undergraduate work in the eyes of the students, the lack of its perceived intrinsic value, has the net effect of lessening student commitment to work and opens the way to cheating.

22.3　Significance

In the light of increasing concern about cheating and plagiarism in higher education, we argue that an understanding of the students' perspective on cheating and plagiarism can significantly assist academics in their efforts to communicate appropriate norms.

- The research study indicates that there is a strong moral basis to students' views, which focuses on such values as friendship, interpersonal trust and good learning. This means that some punishable behaviour can be regarded as justifiable (and that some officially approved behaviour can be felt to be dubious). It is unnecessary to undermine what are, in principle, laudable values – but, in addition, academic values need to be instilled. The basis of the official rules in the values and practices of scholarship must be explained.

- The meaning of plagiarism must be communicated clearly, with examples of good practice presented for students to follow. Also, the positive values of scholarship must again be emphasized, rather than leaving students with the impression that plagiarism is merely an impolite lack of acknowledgement of other's work. Stressing the dire consequences of failing to observe official guidelines, in the absence of positive and constructive guidance, may have a counter-productive, 'crippling' effect on the academic confidence of students.

- Factors such as alienation from the university due to lack of contact with staff; the impact of large classes; and the greater emphasis on group learning are perceived by students themselves as facilitating and sometimes excusing cheating. The attempt to deal with cheating and plagiarism by greater bureaucratization of the assessment process – for example, through making students sign declarations of academic honesty for every piece of work that they submit – itself falls prey to the same pathology of impersonality.

Acknowledgement

Full details of the research method used in the research on which this chapter is based can be found in 'Guilty in whose eyes? University students' perception of cheating and plagiarism in academic work and assessment', *Studies in Higher Education* (1997), **22**, 185–201 (by P. Ashworth, P. Bannister, P. Thorne and 18 members of MA Methods of Social Research, qualitative interviewing unit, 1996).

22.4   References

Franklyn-Stokes, A. and Newstead, S.E. (1995) Cheating: who does what and why?, *Studies in Higher Education*, **20**, 159–72.

Giorgi, A. (ed.) (1985) *Phenomenology and Psychological Research*, Pittsburgh: Duquesne University Press.

Roberts, D.M. and Toombs, R. (1993) A scale to assess perceptions of cheating in examination-related situations, *Educational and Psychological Measurement*, **53**, 755–62.

23 Thinking women

Helen Peters
Centre for Higher Education and Access Development,
University of North London

23.1 Introduction

This chapter looks at the experience of a small group of mature women students at university in the light of research carried out by Belenky *et al.* (1986) and Baxter-Magolda (1992) in the United States. The work of these researchers looks at how students develop ways of approaching knowledge in the course of their studies. They focus particularly on young people starting university after leaving school, and in the case of Belenky *et al.* (1986), on young women. Because of the large number of women returners in many universities in the UK at the present time, I felt it would be interesting to investigate whether they approach learning in a similar way to the younger students studied by Belenky *et al.* (1986) and Baxter-Magolda (1992). No comparison is made either between mature men and mature women students, or between mature women and young women students, since the limited study described here involved only mature women. However it does produce some interesting insights into these particular women's perceptions of study at one university, and their own positions and reactions in relation to teaching and learning, the teachers, and their fellow students.

23.2 'Women's ways of knowing'

Belenky *et al.* (1986) carried out a study of women at college, taking as their starting point William Perry's (1970) four positions. Perry had described young white male students as typically going through four stages starting from basic dualism: seeing the world in polarities. From there, he suggested, they move through a stage of multiplicity, where they believe that 'everyone has a right to his opinion', to relativism subordinate, a more analytical and evaluative approach. The final stage is relativism, where the student completely understands that truth is relative.

After interviewing 135 women from nine different institutions, Belenky *et al.* (1986) went beyond Perry's stages to formulate five epistemological perspectives from which women know and view the world, starting from a position which they ascribe particularly to women: that of silence. This concept of silence encompasses factors such as:

- the small number of women's voices in literature;
- the common everyday devaluation of 'women's talk';
- the fact that women tend to speak less in mixed groups and be interrupted more frequently.

From the position of silence women might progress to one of received knowledge, where they perceive themselves as capable of receiving but not of creating knowledge. This is superseded by subjective knowledge, where truth and knowledge are conceived of as private and personal, subjectively known or intuited. Subjective knowledge gives way to procedural knowledge, where women apply objective procedures for obtaining and communicating knowledge. The final perspective is constructed knowledge, where women view knowledge as contextual, experience themselves as creators of knowledge and value both subjective and objective strategies for knowing.

Belenky *et al.* (1986) suggest that women in a male dominated academic world particularly may experience themselves as voiceless. They suggest that all women, and especially mature women returners, approach knowledge in a very different way from men, and that this should be taken into account in both content and teaching methods in higher education. Baxter-Magolda (1992) however views this lack of voice as something which is experienced by any student, male or female, finding themselves in a position of subordination, but particularly women and students from minority ethnic groups who may feel doubly or triply subordinated, and therefore feel that their voice has less value. Both Baxter-Magolda and Belenky *et al.* emphasize the importance of a connected model of education along the lines of Freire's, where students and teacher think together, as most appropriate for all students who feel silenced, and particularly for women 'Because so many [...] are consumed with self doubt' (Belenky *et al.*, p. 228). These concepts and ideas were the starting point for this study, which aimed to question their relevance in a context fairly far removed from those in which Belenky *et al.* (1986) and Baxter-Magolda (1992) carried out their research.

23.3   Background to the research

The study was carried out in a large, inner city, new university with a student body comprising 75% mature students and 55% women. Participation was entirely voluntary. I discussed the aims of the project with colleagues in the Women's Development Unit and the Interfaculty Office who passed on information to students. I also talked about it with other women students with whom I came into contact. As a result of this, several women volunteered and eventually eight were interviewed.

The women interviewed were aged between 31 and 55 and on courses in Architecture, History, Business Studies, Health Studies, French/English, Film/Irish Studies, Film/Critical Theory, History/English (six full-time and two part-time). Five were in their first year of study, one in her second year and two in their third year . All but one of them had children.

Two women had come into the university via a Women's Development programme aimed at building confidence. Both of these were in their thirties and had young children. One woman was an evening student with a full-time job and two pre-school age children. At 31 she was the youngest of the interviewees. I had met her previously on a 12-week pre-entry programme to the Business School which she had dropped out of the first time around because of her second pregnancy. After the birth of the child she had returned to the programme, completed it and has now completed the first year of an HNC. One woman had applied for an Access course and been told she did not need one and had proceeded directly to a degree. The other four were direct-entry students living locally, three full-time and one part-time.

Two of the women were of African Caribbean origin, one educated in the Caribbean and the other coming to the UK as a very young child. Two of the women were Irish, one having come to the UK as an adult. The others were English from different parts of the country. Only two of the women were known to me prior to the investigation.

The interviews were semi-structured. A list of questions based on Belenky *et al.* (1986) (see Appendix 23.1) had been drawn up and each interview followed the same pattern, but varied depending on how interviewees interpreted the questions and how much they wanted to say about each topic. The questions were grouped under three general headings: 'background', 'the university experience' and 'learning'. Under 'background' I intended to focus on the interviewee's past education and life experience, with a particular emphasis on her experience as a woman, and her reasons for returning to education as a mature student. Under 'the university experience' the focus was on the structures and systems encountered by the students at the university, their feelings about these, about their courses, and about themselves as mature women students and in relation to their fellow students. Under 'learning' the interviewees were asked to consider their experience of learning at the university, and their feelings about knowledge, the transmission and exchange of knowledge and their own role and that of tutors and fellow students in this process. I hoped, through interviews and discussion with this small but varied sample, to gain some insight into the experience of what now constitutes a significant group in higher education. At the same time I hoped the women in the sample would, through this opportunity to consider and reflect on their own experience, gain insight and awareness of their own and others' position and feel empowered by the experience.

23.4   Findings

As a means of analysing the material gathered in the interviews I have examined the women's responses in the light of Belenky *et al.*'s (1986) epistemological perspectives.

23.4.1   The position of silence

When describing the position of silence Belenky *et al.* (1986) suggest that while women are as awed by authority as men, they do not identify themselves with it – authority is outside them, resides in men or in bodies controlled or dominated by men such as the military, the judiciary or big business, and it is this that renders them voiceless.

Several of the women in the study mentioned the different status of men in society. V. (aged 35, Year 2) came from a family where only males were qualified, she was the only female to go to university and her mother ignored the fact that she was studying and would not discuss it. She said: 'I always felt like a second class citizen,' and said she was terrified of political units because 'men do politics'. V. described her subject, History, as a male-dominated arena where 'they sometimes find it difficult to appreciate a woman's view'. Her feelings about her family background become transposed into her subject of study where she perceives attitudes which confirm what she has already observed in her own life.

J. (aged 48, Year 1), explaining why she hadn't done a degree before, said 'it was tied up with the feeling of fear of a masculine power that I could never quite rise to, and I was always afraid'. While (F. aged 55, Year 1) said, 'Women of my generation remain in some sort of confusion about their gender, it's years of growing up with supposing that the world actually belongs to men.'

These last two, who were among the older of the interviewees and had both worked for years in demanding contexts, also described their lack of confidence: 'We are terribly lacking in personal confidence and reassure each other like girls do. I think it is very much a women thing from our generation' (F.) and 'I was appalled at my own timidity' (J. describing her relationship with her tutor).

However while acknowledging their timidity and awe of male authority these same women, by their own account, were far from silent in the academic context, a fact which they attributed specifically to their maturity and experience. One after another they described their experiences in seminars:

> We (the three older women) tend to sit together and we tend to be the ones that talk in the seminar situations. We find there are a few others too but we were all disappointed at the sort of lack of interest of a general level.
>
> (M. aged 49, Year 1)

> I found that also in the group sessions I had a lot to offer, having left school and college a long time ago, when we had discussions and so on we mature students had just as much to offer as the younger students.
>
> (A. aged 54, Year 1)

> But there are a lot of people here who don't talk unless asked, they don't feel competent to speak, yet because I am older than most of the tutors and I feel sorry for them when they throw out a question or when they want someone to respond to something, and because I have lived 55 years I have thoughts. I should have. They are not profound, they are quite hard earned some of them, but I have things to say, so I say them.
>
> (F.)

> I am intimidated, I mean I am not always sure that I can explain but I am surer than others, that's all I can say, and I mean God if I've got to 48 and I haven't a clear feeling about some things then you know, and that's the thing, I am older so in a sense it is easier.
>
> (J.)

One woman even described how she had leapt to the defence of a younger student who she said was being browbeaten by the tutor:

> She couldn't hold her own. He threw ten or fifteen questions at her and she was nearly in tears. I stood up and told him off.
>
> (V.)

So while recognizing that other students are often silent, and one woman said that specifically students whose first language is not English tended to keep quiet in her group, these mature women demonstrated clearly that silence is not a position they are comfortable with.

23.4.2   The position of received knowledge

This position is described by Belenky *et al.* (1986) as one where women perceive themselves as capable of receiving but not creating knowledge. The women in the study in many cases regarded their lecturers as authoritative voices and providers of information, and had a great confidence in and admiration for them. In this sense they seemed to perceive themselves as receivers of knowledge, although some of them felt the lecturers were not always very good at communicating. I asked them if they ever disagreed with their lecturers and some of them seemed to feel this was not appropriate:

K. (aged 31, Year 1) said:

> I think in general the lecturers all have a great expertise in what they do but it's just sometimes the level of communication or how they communicate or maybe it's their assumption that people should know certain things already . . . I don't think I've ever disagreed with what the lecturers say.

and J. said:

> In Political History, I trusted his judgement because it seemed to be a pretty good and balanced judgement and I really didn't feel I had enough knowledge to disagree with him.

Others, while acknowledging the strong influence of lecturers, seemed to have an awareness that this was a stage in their intellectual development which they would eventually transcend. The following two quotes suggest that while the students perceived themselves as receiving knowledge they were already starting to question the process:

> At university I rely on being pointed in the right direction . . . my mind has been opened by ideas. I've been widened I think by some of them.

(M.)

> With the tutor it's all homogenized facts, not related to the world outside . . . tutors tend to mould students to their way of thinking, their personal view rubs off, especially if you like them.

(V.)

F. is more explicit about what she wants to achieve by studying but has not yet attained:

> I tend to think my opinion is less valid than the other person's. What I would like to gain from being here is that I don't question my own judgement.

This suggests that these women were already aspiring to Belenky *et al.*'s (1986) third stage of subjective knowledge.

23.4.3   The position of subjective knowledge

In the stage of subjective knowledge, according to Belenky *et al.* (1986), students begin to recognize their own private and personal way of knowing as having some validity. Some of the women in the study were already questioning the knowledge of the lecturers, and one said that she had heard it said that lecturers think they have to be on their toes when there are mature students in the group, that they '. . . can't just fob them off with any old stuff.' This student (P. aged 38, Year 1), a qualified nurse, said:

> . . . it was in psychology and I felt able to question. I said, 'You know what you just said, don't you think . . .?' and he just said, 'No this is what the book says and this is what it is.' It's like this is a fact and this is the only way and there's no other way of thinking about it.

She clearly felt critical of this attitude and had a certain confidence in her own knowledge, stemming from her extensive professional experience, which enabled her to express this.

Likewise C. (aged 37 Year 3), at a more advanced stage of her course than many of the others, was able to say:

> A lot of college is brainwashing . . . it's like telling you that this is the good way to do it. You have to pick and choose, to be quite astute. I think there are experts but I would like to make my own judgement about who they are or aren't. I am constantly amazed by what other people think is good.

She expresses a concept of knowledge as subjective and intuitive in that she adds: 'You get to know whether you agree if you've got any experience. It's not by anybody saying anything or reading any books.' and M. likewise feels that 'Sometimes you know that something is good, it's difficult to put your finger on it but it's like cooking.'

Contrast this with K. who gives the impression that knowledge is out there to be found and verified rather than something that can be intuited or judged on the basis of experience, so that:

> Some things you never find any right answers basically because nobody's gone out to research and get the information, but if you're going to leave it open then you have to go and do some more work I guess and find the right answer.

Although she doesn't rule out using her own judgement in that:

> I'd follow what my instincts tell me or what I've read or what my facts are I wouldn't just take people's word for what they've said.

23.5   The position of procedural knowledge

Viewing knowledge as procedural implies a recognition of certain ways of obtaining knowledge and communicating it. Some of the women expressed an awareness of the learning procedures that form part of study in the university, and were conscious of acquiring the ability to follow these procedures in the pursuit of knowledge. This was in some cases what the women found most valuable. They felt they were learning to learn. M. does not express this explicitly, nevertheless an awareness of the learning process is implicit when she says:

> People can often get to see things from a different point of view and that's one of the very nice things about university education, that you do get other people who have thought about things and you can have some really lively discussions.

J. on the other hand is quite clear about what is happening:

> I really liked the learning. I really found it was exciting to have access to these ideas and it was very satisfying to put them in historical context and understand things that I never understood before . . . it did supply me with a kind of language of understanding ideas.

23.5.1   The position of constructed knowledge

Belenky *et al.* (1986) describe this position as one where subjective and objective strategies are valued in the acquisition and creation of knowledge, which is viewed as contextual. Many of the women in the study expressed an awareness of the contextuality of knowledge, especially those who were in their second or third year of study:

> It broadened my perception in that for example you could get three or four writers approaching a topic from a different angle and then realise that there wasn't one set answer to something.

(A.)

I question facts all the time, a lot of people take what they read as cut and dried.

(V.)

A critical judgement is how people tend to assess stuff – a kind of vetting procedure. There is no right answer.

(C.)

However few of them seemed to perceive themselves as creators of knowledge. One (M.) said:

> I don't think I can create, I don't think I'm a creator or a creative person but I'm very good at analysing and I can often have insights into something that someone else has created that somebody else hasn't had but I don't think I could ever do something totally original from nowhere. Once it's there I'm quite confident that I can attack it or mould it or look into it and find something in it but I could never invent something.

This raises the question of how creativity is defined, and how it relates to the concept of originality of thought. It is an issue which gives rise to much discussion, as students are aware that the latter is generally the defining criterion for an A grade. One of the women in the study had been told by a lecturer that he never gives A grades to first-year students. Should this be interpreted as indicating that first-year students are not expected to show originality of thought? Chandler (1995) quotes Dewey as stressing that the role an individual is assigned in an environment – what he (*sic*) is permitted to do – is what the individual learns. Many of the women in this study were working hard at achieving a view of knowledge as contextual, and certainly those in their first year did not feel confident about expressing original thoughts and found it difficult to reconcile this with the requirements of academic rigour.

23.5.2   Developing voices

While expressing their difficulties and the needs they were experiencing in their studies, the women interviewed also demonstrated considerable resourcefulness in getting those needs met. They found essay writing difficult. J. a creative writer in her own right said:

> It was a very painful experience to learn, I mean it still is, writing an essay. Learning how to write an essay is a very difficult experience.

A. described her experience in similar terms:

> At the beginning I felt like I was floundering. I mean I knew how to write an essay but the point is was it the type of essay that was needed for the assignments. I learned my lesson the hard way.

Perhaps the requirements of the essay genre were what stultified the women's creativity. However what they felt they needed but didn't get was more one to one contact with tutors:

> I really do miss some sort of tutorial. I miss talking about it.

(J.)

> I think they should have more tutorials or smaller seminars. They never have any time for you. For the first assignment you have a ten minute tutorial and that's it. That's the only time you ever get to speak to anyone one to one and it's not enough.

(M.)

Their solution to this was to turn to each other for support. They formed groups with other 'mothers, wives, women with partners' or 'women in a similar position with children' because 'people tend to identify with like'. Baxter-Magolda (1992) has mentioned how belonging to a group that differs from others 'heightens the need for strong identification with a shared social identity'. These women are boldly entering new territory at a stage in their lives when they have already acquired a wealth of experience, and overcoming their timidity to express their hard won thoughts and knowledge. At the same time as they are deeply appreciative of the learning on offer and eager to learn, the shortcomings of the learning environment are starkly clear to them, and they are drawing on their own resources to compensate for this.

> We supported each other, it just happened.
>
> (A.)

> We help each other a lot. I quickly sorted out the few people that know what they're doing and I just hooked on them really.
>
> (K.)

This tendency to want to work with people of similar background and experience also bears out Weiler's (1996) feminist critique of Freire where she points out that a connected model of learning is not enough. If the different status of the participants in the learning is not recognized, the model may not prove useful in that women may feel intimidated by men even if they are both in a subordinate position, and people from different ethnic groups may also feel themselves to be in a position of disadvantage. One of the interviewees expressed the view that being put into groups by lecturers could be counter-productive, whereas all agreed that their self-selected support groups were lifesavers.

23.6   Conclusions

Belenky *et al.*'s (1986) epistemological perspectives have proved a useful tool for examining this small group of women's approaches to learning and a number of interesting observations can be made. With such a small sample it is not possible to make generalizations; however these women, from a range of different backgrounds and spanning more than twenty years in age, nevertheless have one thing in common: they are manifestly not voiceless. Several of them put this down to their maturity and mentioned the reluctance of many younger students to speak out in discussions. This is interesting particularly as several of them did acknowledge the influence of perceptions of the world as male dominated on their own experience.

The women seemed to represent the various positions of received, subjective, procedural and constructed knowledge, to a certain extent depending on the stage they had reached in their studies but perhaps also depending on their age and previous experience. Where they had previous experience relevant to the field of study, as in the case of the nurse, this could lead to a position of procedural and constructed knowledge. Although several of the women described themselves as receivers of knowledge, this position did not exclude the use of their subjective intuitions as a resource, and they all seemed to be somewhere along the road to constructed knowledge through the perceived application of objective procedures for obtaining that knowledge. In other words, although it is possible to distinguish the epistemological perspectives there is overlap and contradiction in the progression from one stage to the next, with a number of factors influencing the process.

Perhaps the most important of these is the women's perception of the teaching and learning process as not including enough talking, of the lack of time of the lecturers and the need for smaller groups and more tutorials. These women clearly are looking for a more connected model of education, as Baxter-Magolda (1992) suggests, and the way they have compensated for its lack is to turn to each other for support, in time honoured fashion.

23.7   Bibliography

Belenky, M.F., Clinchy, B.M., Goldberger, N.R. and Tarule, J.M. (1986) *Women's Ways of Knowing*, USA: Basic Books.

Baxter-Magolda, M.B. (1992) *Knowing and Reasoning in College*, San Francisco: Jossey-Bass.

Chandler, D. (1996) *The Act of Writing*, Aberystwyth: University of Wales.

Perry, W.G. (1970) *Forms of Intellectual and Ethical Development in the College Years*, New York: Holt, Rinehart & Winston.

Weiler, K. (1996) Freire and a feminist pedagogy of difference. In R. Edwards, A. Hanson and P. Raggatt (eds), *Boundaries of Adult Learning*, Routledge: London.

24 Developing students' essay-writing skills: implications of case studies in essay writing of undergraduate students in an education faculty

David Smith, Jennifer Campbell and Ross Brooker
Queensland University of Technology, Brisbane, Australia

Despite the challenges posed by increasing demands for 'authentic assessment' (Wiggins, 1993) and performance-based assessment, literature-based essays continue to play an important role in assessing university students. Yet there has been surprisingly little research into students' understanding of and approach to the construction of such essays. This chapter uses two case studies, drawn from a funded research project which focussed on the essay writing approaches of 53 first and second year education students at Queensland University of Technology. The two case studies have been selected to illustrate a number of the qualitative findings which emerged from the study.

24.1   Review of the literature

Although the essay has long been regarded as both a useful tool of assessment in tertiary education and as a valuable means of promoting higher-order thinking (Hounsell, 1984; Entwistle, Entwistle and Tait, 1991; Biggs, 1988; Nightingale, 1988), it is only comparatively recently that researchers have begun to examine the kinds of learning and thinking involved in producing an essay, particularly in the light of evidence that deficiencies in undergraduate essay writing are not so much related to problems with mechanics and basic skills as they are to higher-order thought processes and the ability to analyse information critically and develop arguments (Nightingale, 1988). The importance of this approach to understanding student essay writing is also emphasized by evidence concerning the impact of assessment procedures on students' learning. While short-answer or multiple choice questions requiring mainly factual recall tend to elicit surface approaches, essays are more likely to encourage a deep approach and hence to promote desired forms of student learning (Entwistle et al., 1991). There are, however, substantial variations between students in the depth of understanding achieved when writing essays (Entwistle, 1995), and the form of understanding developed appears to be related to underlying conceptions of learning and beliefs about knowledge. Research on students' essay writing from these theoretical perspectives remains, nevertheless, limited, with most research focusing on more traditional linguistic analyses and quantitative comparisons of essay features, students' characteristics and grades.

Branthwaite, Trueman & Hartley (1980) Norton (1990) & Mahalski (1992) provide examples of recent research which has focused on quantitative descriptions of essay-writing processes and outcomes. In both studies students were interviewed about their essay-preparation strategies, such as making a plan and the number of drafts developed. Specific aspects of students' essays were analysed, such as length, number of references and number of main points. Preparation strategies and essay characteristics were then related to essay marks. While these results can be interpreted in terms of the advice that can be given to students to improve essay writing, such as making a plan and leaving time for refection between reading and successive drafts of the essay, they tend not to further theoretical analysis of students' underlying conceptual understandings of the essay writing process. Similarly, while Taylor and Nightingale's (1990) linguistic analysis of undergraduates' essays indicated that grammatical errors may reflect problems with meaning, the students' understanding of those meanings were not ascertained.

In contrast, work by Hounsell (1984) focused more directly on underlying meanings. He identified three qualitatively different conceptions of an essay among history undergraduates: the essay as an argument, viewpoint or arrangement. When the essay is conceived as an argument it is seen as 'an ordered presentation of an argument well-supported by evidence' (1984, p. 109), ideas are 'moulded' into a logical, integrated whole. Students who conceive of an essay as a viewpoint are also concerned with presenting a distinctive point of view, but tend not to focus on the role of data in supporting their interpretation. Finally, for students viewing essays as arrangements, the focus is on marshalling 'an ordered presentation embracing facts and ideas' (1984, p. 111), where the concern is not with presenting a unified position but rather with assembling discrete thoughts and information.

These conceptions of an essay are clearly related to students' broader conceptions of learning, understanding and knowledge. Thus students with a constructivist orientation are more likely to conceive of the essay as a process of developing a thesis or building an argument whereas students who view knowledge and learning as involving accumulating and reproducing information are more likely to adopt essay-writing strategies characterized by reproduction as opposed to its transformation and reconstruction.

More recently Entwistle (1995) and Prosser and Webb (1994) have also investigated students' conceptual understandings of the essay-writing process. Prosser and Webb (1994) interviewed students about their experiences writing essays and used the SOLO Taxonomy (Biggs and Collis, 1982) to differentiate between university undergraduate students who had a multistructural or a relational conception of an essay. Students with a multistructural conception tended to view it as an ordered arrrangement of relatively discrete chunks of information whereas students with a relational concept viewed it as a coherent thesis to which all sections of the paper contributed. Clearly, these conceptions are analogous to the conceptions of essay as argument and the essay as ordered arrangement of ideas, respectively. Students were classified according to whether they adopted a deep or surface approach to essay writing and systemic functional linguistic analysis of each essay's structure indicated relationships between the process of essay writing and the final structure of the essay such that students who had a relational conception of their essay, and adopted a deep approach to writing it, tended to have well-structured essays focusing on the relationships between semantic fields rather than on their serial listing. This research is unusual in that it not only analyses students' experiences of the essay-writing process in terms of the theoretical distinction made above, contrasting the serial reproduction of discrete items of information with their transformation and integration into a coherent unified structure, but it also relates these to measures of the conceptual structure of the essay itself.

The study underpinning the present chapter was also designed to relate the conceptual structure of the actual essay to students' understanding of essay writing processes. In addition it attempted to relate students' use of particular essay-writing procedures, such as those described by Mahalski (1992), to their underlying conceptualization about these procedures.

Method

24.2.1   Sample

The case studies reported in the present chapter were selected from 21 third-year students who volunteered to be part of an investigation relating to essay writing in first- and third-year students drawn from the Bachelor of Education degree course at Queensland University of Technology. The essay-writing task related to a third-year core subject, Psychology of Teaching and Learning, and involved a 1500-word literature review which formed part of a larger field study investigating teaching children with special needs. Students were given considerable scope as to their precise topic and how they would approach it.

24.2.2   Procedure

Students were asked to complete a log of their essay-writing procedures and to bring it to an interview which occurred after they had submitted their essay, but before its return. Interviews were semi-structured and included four 5-point rating scales, viz: perceived success in locating references; satisfaction with their written paper; effort expended on the assignment; and level of understanding of the topic. In addition, interviews explored the way in which students understood and engaged in the different activities involved in writing their essay, particularly finding references; reading and extracting information; moving from reading to writing and the way in which they conceptualized the information and ideas they were writing about; and the drafting and revision processes involved in arriving at the finished product. Students were also asked whether they had consulted the assessment criteria, and to explain two criteria which were used to assess their essays, namely (1) organization and synthesis of information; and (2) critical evaluation of the literature. The interviews, which were all tape-recorded and transcribed, varied in length from 20 to 45 minutes.

With students' permission, copies of their marked essays were obtained from their tutors, and the SOLO Taxonomy (Biggs and Collis, 1982; Biggs, 1988) was used to analyse their essays' conceptual structure. The interview data were separately analysed to ascertain the way in which students undertook and conceptualized the different components of the essay writing task.

24.3   Results and discussion: two case studies

The students featured in the following two case studies serve to exemplify the range of understandings and essay writing approaches evident across the whole sample. One of these students produced a relatively sophisticated essay while the other produced a cognitively simple essay at a unistructural level.

Case study 24.1   Mary

Mary's self-chosen title, 'How Does Technology Impact on the Motivation of Children with Special Needs?', reflected her intent to develop a relational paper addressing a problematic issue. In her conceptually sophisticated paper Mary developed a humanistic theoretical framework relating to student motivation which embraced and integrated expectancy x value theory, self-efficacy theory and the concept of self-actualization. The potential impact of technology on special-needs students was evaluated through constant reference to this integrated theoretical perspective. Thus, for example, having developed her theoretical perspective Mary proceeded to consider the potential of technology to promote autonomy and self efficacy in students with learning disabilities as evidenced in the following extracts from her paper:

Having greater control over their environment through the use of speech devices, electric wheelchairs, computer programs and more (Freedman, 1991; Hannaford, 1983; Williams, 1987) enables children to determine for themselves what, how and when they learn (Computers in Learning Policy). This control can create feelings of safety, security and acceptance for the children and produce motivation to participate and set goals for their learning (Kolesnik, 1978; Woolfolk, 1995).

Technology which allows children to succeed helps them to develop an expectation of success which is so important in the expectancy *x* value theory of motivation (Biggs and Moore, 1993; Kolesnik, 1978; Woolfolk, 1995). This expectation of success not only increases motivation when using technology but increases children's motivation on activities away from computers (Heward and Olansky, 1984; Kolesnik, 1978; Williams, 1987).

For the second part of her assignment Mary undertook three case studies of teachers working in special schools. Her linking of these case studies with her literature review was exemplary, reflected in her citing 17 of her 25 references in the 'Discussion' section of her paper.

Mary's understanding of and approach to the essay-writing task

As previously indicated, even the title of Mary's paper indicated that she conceived of the task as one which involved relational thinking. The interview with Mary and her essay-writing log indicated that she saw the need to develop a coherent theoretical framework as an important aspect of the task.

Like 23 of the 25 third-year students participating in the research study, Mary indicated that she had consulted the assessment criteria for the paper and in common with all seven third-year students whose essays were categorized as relational, Mary displayed a clear grasp of what was implied by the criteria 'organization' and 'synthesis'.

That's the structure, the layout of the thing. How the information goes together, how it flows. The synthesis would be the same idea or subject area from a range of books.

In common with all students except another third-year student who had also written a relational paper, Mary's understanding of the criterion 'critical evaluation of literature' was incomplete.

That would be looking at the information that literature provides and looking at it critically. I mean looking at it, it need not necessarily be right . . . looking at different situations that it might work in or like, if it's a teaching strategy, well that might be well and fine there but it's not going to work over here. It's analysing it, looking at what's good and what's bad about it.

Mary's research efforts reflected her understanding that the kind of paper she intended to construct would require extensive reading and she cast her net widely in an attempt to locate pertinent references. Her search for references embraced keyword searches using the library catalogue, browsing through computer journals and special education journals and the use of CD-ROM. Like most students who produced high-quality essays, Mary rated herself as very successful (4.5 on a 5-point self-rating scale) in locating appropriate references and in fact her paper included 25 references (of which 10 were journal articles).

Mary moved from her sources to recording information both by summarizing and by typing some quotations directly on to her computer, at the same time including full bibliographic details. Thereafter, she read through each entry and organized them systematically.

I read through them and I try and sort out some sorts of categories, some themes that run through the groups of information that I might have and I label them, like with humanistic periods are obviously 'H' and motivation is an 'M' and you put H and M in, and all that sort of thing, all beside every single point. Or good quotes . . . you put an asterisk next to a really good one. Then depending on how big the assignment is, for one assignment I did last year there was so much on each area that I had to go through another stage of putting all the areas together before I could write it, but most assignments aren't that huge, so as you're writing it you just flick through your pages and find anything that relates to motivation or whatever you are talking about at the time, and pick those points out, and because they are already referenced under the author and the year you just whack the reference in and it's not a problem. Referencing is done.

Mary's approach to organizing her notes in terms of themes was typical of that adopted by students who had produced complex multistructural or relational essays but Mary was somewhat atypical in that she did not have an initial plan or overview of the paper as a whole. Yet this lack of an overview was compensated for by Mary's iterative approach to structuring the paper:

I sit down and I write it and then I look at it and go, okay that needs to go there, and that needs to go there and this fits in there and that will go down there, and move it around when it's actually some sort of resemblance of a written paper. All the points, there might be two or three paragraphs on one thing or whatever, but it's all written and · it's just a matter of editing and moving, sort of adjusting from there.

A significant feature of Mary's approach to the task was her approach to drafting and editing. Mary's drafting and editing were not discrete events; rather her paper evolved from a number of drafts, each of which involved a restructuring of material to achieve a coherent paper underpinned by an integrating theme. Feedback from others was actively sought and utilized in this progressive restructuring process.

I spoke to my sister a lot. Just clarifying things, clarifying terms . . . we spent a couple of hours just simply going through the terms of like, what 'disability' is, what 'handicap' is, things like that that just help the whole understanding of it . . .

. . . She [my tutor] clarified a few things and some of the theoretical side of it and said, 'why don't you try doing this' and 'why don't you try doing that' or 'is this what you are after?' And we had a really good discussion about it because I knew what I was talking about so anything she said wasn't over my head or anything . . .

And then when I think it [the essay draft] is pretty good, I get my boyfriend to read it and he just rips it apart. He is very good. We have major arguments because he rips it apart . . . he doesn't actually do anything, he just rips it apart and goes 'that's crap' or 'fix that'. 'What the hell are you trying to say here?' which is very disheartening. You think you've got this really good and he's going to rewrite it. So I did, this literature review I completely rewrote, restructured, re-ordered everything.

Not surprisingly, Mary rated the effort which she had put into her assignment as extensive, indicated that she felt very satisfied with the assignment, had a deep level of understanding of the topic and expected to obtain a high grade 'If I get any less than a 6 [on a 7-point scale] I want to know why. I'm expecting a 7 but let's be conservative.'

Case study 24.2   Jane

Jane, had chosen attention deficit disorder as her assignment topic. Her paper represented a stark contrast to Mary's. While even the title of Mary's paper reflected her attempts to grapple with an issue she considered problematic, Jane's bland title, 'Attention Deficit Disorder', reflected the unsophisticated structure of the paper which essentially represented a serial reproduction of factual material as illustrated by the following introductory paragraphs:

Classroom teachers must develop a better understanding of this complex disorder before they can meet the needs of A.D.D. children. If teachers are not prepared to become knowledgeable about this disorder and learn how to best deal with it children diagnosed with this will be virtually out of control and this only leads to more classroom difficulties.

Green (1994: 35) states that Attention Deficit Disorder today is referred to as a troublesome cluster of behaviours that cause a child to behave poorly, despite having a good intellect and receiving quality parenting.

Hyperactivity is commonly associated with it, hence it is often referred to as Attention Deficit Hyperactivity Disorder.

Children with A.D.D. usually exhibit the three core behaviours that is inattentiveness, impulsiveness and overactivity. Reduced attention is the common characteristic. A.D.D. is a medical problem that affects the whole person in all areas of development, that is social, emotional, physical, moral behaviour and cognitive. A.D.D. is a barrier to learning and in terms of education it is identified as a specific learning disorder.

The cause of A.D.D. is still unknown, though many professionals attribute it to a biochemical abnormality in the brain (Intersoil: 1988).

Barkley (1981: 51) states statistics [sic] indicate that 3 to 5 percent of children of school age have A.D.D. Boys are six to nine times more likely to be affected than girls. Even though 60 to 70% of A.D.D. children show symptoms of the disorder during infancy it is commonly not recognised until the child actually starts school.

The above extract demonstrates the essentially unistructural character of Jane's essay. Jane reproduces, in staccato fashion, predigested information in a series of discrete points. There is no attempt to synthesize information from diverse sources within particular paragraphs and the paper lacks any integrating thesis. As might be expected from the bland title, information is presented in an unproblematic fashion with the only effort at critically evaluating her sources being the disingenuously bold and misleading claim that:

With having experience in the field of teaching, Barkley's statements ring true as you find in the majority of classes the boys have ADD and usually you find you have no girls with it.

Jane's understanding of and approach to constructing the essay

At every stage in the preparation for and construction of her paper, Jane's approach was markedly different from that of Mary.

Jane's location of references and acquisition of reference material was far less extensive (she listed seven references including five journal articles compared with Mary's 25), less deliberate and altogether less sophisticated than that of Mary.

J: I went to the library and went to the computer and found some books and found some articles.

I: *What sorts of things did you type in?*

J: First of all I just went to the titles and just wrote in Attention Deficit Disorder, and found some books and then I found articles, I just went up and had a look and got some articles.

I: *Do you mean in the journals?*

J: Yes, in the journals.

I: *What, did you just scan the shelves?*

J: Yes, someone said they knew where they were, so instead of looking it up it was the easy way out.

I: *Right, anything else?*

J: No not until I went, and actually I got some information faxed to me from the school that I enquired about, and that's where I did my case study. And they sent me some really good information and another journal that they had, that was more up to date, and I used that.

Jane rated herself precisely at the midpoint between 'very unsuccessful' and 'very successful' in relation to her perceived success in locating appropriate references. She used a combination of note-taking and highlighting to identify and record material which she planned to use in her paper.

I scribbled notes down and underlined and that was mainly it, mainly points, and then highlighted on the journal articles what I thought was important.

While Jane's literature search and her subsequent recording of information was to some extent directed by specific information which she planned to use, this information was at a factual, unproblematic level:

I: *So how did you decide what to highlight or what to take notes about?*

J: The most important things that stood out.

I: *What were you looking for?*

J: What actually ADD was, the effects, the medication involved, the strategies people used I think that's about all.

Jane described moving from reading to drafting as the 'hardest part of the assignment' and when asked how she structured information she described a relatively mechanical, uncritical process:

> I read back through all my notes and the way I started I think was just mainly to start off with a definition of what Attention Deficit Disorder was and gave a quote and then structured it and tried to structure it, the effects and sort of followed on.

> I jotted down what I wanted, like the introduction, the main sort of part of it, and mainly information to back it up and sort of just the conclusion to round it all up to show that I understood.

Like Mary, Jane stated that she had consulted the assessment criteria for the assignment but her inadequate understanding of some of these was reflected in her confounding of 'synthesis' and 'organization'.

I: *Organization and synthesis of information. What did that mean to you?*

J: How I structured my essay and was the information appropriate.

Jane stated that she found difficulty in conceptualizing how her personal opinions could find a place in her literature review.

> I find literature reviews are hard sometimes because you always want to put your own opinion in but you're not supposed to.

This somewhat naive dichotomizing of what she apparently viewed as relatively objective *knowledge out there* as opposed to subjective opinions was also reflected in her inadequate understanding of *critical evaluation* of literature which for her was based exclusively on personal judgments.

J: [Critical evaluation of literature] means you have to critique the literature. You have to be critical of what they say. I find that quite hard sometimes.

I: *Okay, so did you try and do it in this one?*

J: Yes.

I: *What did you do?*

J: What different authors had said or psychologists had said, I either agreed or disagreed with their literature . . . for the information that I had read and what I knew about it.

Like Mary, Jane submitted a draft of her paper to her tutor prior to submitting her final paper. Jane reported that her tutor had described her writing style as too 'chatty' and her redrafting based on this feedback centred upon stylistic changes in an attempt to use a more academic genre:

> I had little comments of saying that it was too chatty and I like changed all that wording around and made it more formal and cut out most of the chat, in my own opinion, out.

In performing the second part of her assignment, a case study of a student with Attention Deficit Disorder, Jane spoke with a teacher whom she found to be a useful source of information:

> She gave me a set of guidelines that she follows and the support that you need, so . . . it enhanced and helped my learning.

However, her conversations with the teacher did not lead to any changes in her literature review. She viewed the case study and literature review as two discrete tasks:

I: *Did that* [information derived from the teacher and the print material supplied by the teacher] *come to be incorporated into your literature review?*

J: No, not from the information she gave me. In the case study it did but in the literature review mainly just the journal article that I received.

Jane's assignment reflected her apparent difficulty in linking the two sections of her paper. The case study and related discussion included no citations within the text and made no links with the previous literature review.

Jane rated herself as reasonably satisfied with her paper (approximately 3.7 on a 5-point scale) and rated herself precisely at the midpoint on the scale representing how much effort she herself perceived as having put into the assignment. Jane rated herself as 4 on the 5point scale representing her perceived understanding of the topic and indicated that she expected a grade of 5 for the assignment on the 7point rating scale.

When asked what she had learned from the tasks, Jane responded:

That you should never leave a big assignment like this to the end. I've done that a few times before and it's better to do it in parts . . .

24.4 Discussion

The essays submitted by Mary and Jane differed markedly from one another with respect to all assessment criteria from appropriateness of literature reviewed to clarity of expression but it was in the area of underlying conceptual structure that the most significant differences were observed. Essentially, Jane's essay was unistructural in its enumeration of a series of discrete points in serial fashion. Information was structured in terms of simple, obvious categories explicitly mentioned in the literature and there was little evidence of active processing of information and building of arguments. Jane's essay may therefore be viewed as representative of the category of essays which Hounsell (1984, p. 111) describes as an 'ordered arrangement of facts and ideas'.

By contrast, Mary's paper was conceptually far more sophisticated, being at a relational level. Unlike Jane, Mary had developed a coherent conceptual framework which she then used as a basis for selecting and critically evaluating the literature. In essence, her paper represented an attempt to develop and sustain a central thesis relating technology to the motivation of special needs students. Thus Mary's paper exemplifies the essay as 'an ordered presentation of an argument well supported by evidence' (Hounsell, 1984, p. 109).

The contrasting end-products represented by the two essays appear to be related to very different conceptions of, and approaches to, the essay at every stage of the assignment, thus supporting studies by Entwistle (1995), Hounsell (1984), Prosser and Webb (1994), showing how students' essays are related to their conceptual model of the essay. These may be summarized with respect to three broad phases of the task, the students' conceptions of the task; notetaking and organization of information; and drafting and editing.

24.4.1 Conception of the task

Mary's choice of title, her discussions with her sister and her reference search all reflected her concept of the task which she intended to perform as one requiring relational thinking.

In contrast, Jane's bland unproblematic essay title and relatively narrow literature search reflected her concept of the essay as involving nothing more than selection and presentation of information in a logical sequence.

These differing conceptions of the task are also reflected in differences in their understanding of the assessment criteria. While Jane claimed to have attempted to address the assessment criteria, her inadequate understanding of the terms 'synthesis' and 'critical evaluation' suggests she had not recognized the importance of synthesizing information. Mary, on the other hand, recognized clearly what was implied by the term 'synthesis' and to a lesser extent 'critical evaluation of literature'.

24.4.2 Notetaking and organization of information

Like the other students who produced relational essays, Mary devised a system for categorizing information based on themes which she had herself selected. Each of these themes was, in turn, related to the central thesis of her paper. In contrast, Jane's recording and organization centred upon highlighting what she viewed as pertinent information. Unlike Mary, Jane did not use an organizational system for synthesizing material by theme across sources.

24.4.3 Drafting and editing

Even although Mary did not produce a written plan for her paper, the paper was structured in accordance with a well-developed schema. Her development of a theoretical framework relating to motivation served as an overarching integrating structure for the entire paper and helped her achieve coherence. By contrast Jane, although structuring her paper in terms of a written plan, lacked an integrating schema which would underpin the entire paper. The organizational categories she used were at a simple, obvious, factual level and were derived entirely from the literature.

With respect to editing and/or redrafting of the essay, marked differences between the two students were again obvious. For Jane, editing was at the level of changing wording and attempting to adopt a more academic genre whereas for Mary editing was a far more radical process involving restructuring of ideas and information to strengthen arguments and achieve greater coherence. Jane's response to feedback from her tutor was at a relatively low conceptual level of eliminating the 'chattiness' and using more 'academic' language. By comparison, Mary's response to feedback from her tutor and her boyfriend was at the conceptual level of critically evaluating structure and coherence and ensuring that her central thesis was adequately supported by appropriate evidence and clear arguments.

24.5 Conclusion

The case studies featured in this paper encapsulate a number of the findings emerging from the research project of which they are a part. They suggest that the understanding of and approach to the task of producing a literature-based essay differs greatly between students producing high-quality relational essays and those producing relatively unsophisticated unistructural and multistructural essays. These differences exist at both a quantitative and a qualitative level. At a quantitative level they include such variables as number of references used and cited, number of journal references cited, level of satisfaction with reference search, perceived level of understanding of topic and expected grade. At a qualitative level differences emerged with respect to understanding of assessment criteria, notetaking, organization of information derived from the literature search, drafting and editing.

Perhaps the most significant outcome of this study is the implication that students' conceptualization of the task governs their approach at every stage of the essay construction procedure from identifying references to final editing. This in turn implies that tertiary educators aiming to promote the essay writing competence of their students need to address the issue of how students conceive of the task. Prescriptive essay writing guides focussing on surface features of the essay or even on such features as structuring of information are of themselves unlikely to promote more sophisticated approaches to writing. It would appear that lecturer student dialogue focussing on students' and lecturers' conceptions of the task and the meaning of particular assessment criteria has an important role to play in preparing students for essay writing. The case studies and the investigation as a whole suggest that feedback from lecturers and/or other critical readers can play the useful role of prompting students to evaluate critically and, if necessary, to restructure their essays. The case studies suggest, however, that the conceptual level at which students respond to such feedback is itself moderated by the student's understanding of the subject matter and the task requirement. Thus Jane's response to feedback focussed exclusively on style while Mary, with her greater understanding of the topic an understanding which may have approached the status of a *knowledge object* (Entwistle, 1995) and her more sophisticated conception of the essay, responded at the level of evaluating the structuring of her paper and the cogency of her arguments.

At a more general level, findings in the present study reinforce the view developed by Nightingale (1988) that when considering how to improve students' essay writing skills, there needs to be a shift from a focus on discrete skills to an emphasis on the relationship between students' understanding of the content and their ability to write about it. Understanding needs to be taught as part of the writing process, and students need help with building understandings representing the body of knowledge they are working with prior to the final construction of their essay (Entwistle, 1995; Taylor and Nightingale, 1990). For instance, the processes of synthesizing and critically evaluating differing information and perspectives need to be modelled for students and practised prior to writing. Such help does, however, need to take into account students' current developmental status. Students who are currently writing unistructural essays and who have the conceptualizations that accompany that level of operation are unlikely to make the leap straight into a relational level of operation. The processes involved in constructing multistructural essays first need to be explained and practised. In contrast, those who are currently writing multistructural essays could be extended to relational concepts and ways of operating.

24.6   References

Biggs, J.B. (1988) Approaches to learning and essay writing. In R.R. Schmeck (ed.) *Learning Strategies and Learning Styles*, New York: Plenum Press.

Biggs, J.B. and Collis, K.F. (1982) *Evaluating the Quality of Learning: The SOLO Taxonomy*, New York: Academic Press.

Branthwaite, A., Trueman, M and Hartley, J. (1980) Writing essays: the actions and strategies of students. In J. Hartley (ed.) *The Psychology of Written Communication*. London: Kogan Page

Entwistle, N. (1995) Frameworks for understanding as experienced in essay writing and in preparing for examinations, *Educational Psychologist*, 30(1), 47-54.

Entwistle, N., Entwistle, A. and Tait, H. (1991) Academic understanding and contexts to enhance it: a perspective from research on student learning. In T.M. Duffy, J. Lowych and D.H. Jonassen (eds), *Designing Environments for Constructive Learning*, Berlin: Springer-Verlag.

Hounsell, D. J. (1984a) Learning and essay writing. In F. Marton, D. Hounsell and N. Entwistle (eds), The Experience of Learning, Edinburgh, Scottish Academic Press.

Mahalski, P.A. (1992) Essay writing: do study manuals give relevant advice? Higher Education, 24, 113-132.

Nightingale, P. (1988) Understanding the processes and problems in student writing, Studies in Higher Education, 13(3), 263-283.

Norton, L.S. (1990) Essay writing: what really counts?, Higher Education, 20, 411-442.

Prosser, M. and Webb, C. (1994) Relating the process of undergraduate writing to the finished product, Studies in Higher Education, 19(2), 125-138.

Taylor, G. and Nightingale, P. (1990) Not mechanics but meaning: error in tertiary students' writing, Higher Education Research and Development, 9(2), 161-175.

Wiggins, G. (1993) Assessing Student Performance, San Francisco: Jossey-Bass.

25 ASSIST: a reconceptualization of the *Approaches to Studying Inventory*

Hilary Tait[i], Noel Entwistle[ii] and Velda McCune[ii]
(i) Napier University, Edinburgh; (ii) University of Edinburgh

25.1   Introduction

The original *Approaches to Studying Inventory* (ASI) (Entwistle and Ramsden, 1983) was developed as a research instrument and had twin aims. First, it aimed to investigate the interrelationships between study habits and the new constructs relating to student learning which had recently appeared in the literature. These new constructs included deep, surface and strategic approaches to studying (Marton and Säljö, 1976, Entwistle and Ramsden, 1983); holist and serialist styles of learning and their respective associated pathologies of globetrotting and improvidence (Pask, 1976); and different forms of motivation (Entwistle, Thompson and Wilson, 1974). Secondly, the *Approaches to Studying Inventory* was to be used to describe the different ways in which students carry out academic tasks. It was never intended to be, nor indeed designed to be, a commercially available or widely used instrument, and the interest that it has continued to evoke internationally has surprised the original authors and those involved in its subsequent development.

Leaving aside translation into foreign languages and adaptation for different educational environments (see for example, Entwistle, Kozeki and Tait, 1989), this development work has broadly been of two types. On the one hand, the ASI has been modified to produce variants suitable for specific research projects (see *inter alia*, Entwistle *et al.*, 1989; Wall *et al.*, 1991, Newble *et al*, 1988). On the other hand, researchers attempting to replicate the factor patterns shown in the seminal literature have suggested either changes to the phraseology of individual items, or more commonly and seriously, to the composition of main scales sometimes to the extent of the removal of several items or even one or more subscales. But many of these suggested 'improvements' have been based on rather limited samples, sometimes taken from a single department in one institution, and with a sample size inappropriately small for multivariate analysis which is nonetheless performed. To suggest refinement of the ASI based on a single study anyway fails to acknowledge that there is bound to be variation in factor patterns produced due to the influence of the learning environment. Even where the methodology does seem adequate, there has been a growing concern that these more recent versions, by the cumulative effects of their slight modifications, are corrupting the defining features of the original constructs of the ASI.

Consequently, it seemed timely to revise the ASI substantially to take these observations on board. It was proposed that the new inventory would be incorporated within a longer questionnaire named *ASSIST – Approaches and Study Skills Inventory for Students –* which would also contain sections relating to other aspects of studying in higher education.

25.2 Proposed differences between ASSIST and the ASI

The literature, and copious personal communication, indicated that the ASI has been widely used by teaching staff in higher education to try to identify students who are experiencing difficulty with the ways they go about studying; to monitor the success of teaching innovations using a pre-test/post-test design; or to explore the effects of their routine teaching practices on students' approaches to studying. The original ASI was, however, not designed for such purposes, but it was clear that there was a perceived need for an instrument capable of being used in these ways and it was intended that a revised inventory should try to meet at least some of these requirements.

It seems unlikely that an inventory of this type will ever be fully capable of monitoring changes in student learning as a result of teaching innovations for three reasons. First, the ASI is based on the principles of attitude measurement, and this suggests that, just by completing the inventory, a student's approach to learning might be expected to change because the issues contained in it will have been thought about and possibly even discussed with peers. Secondly, the inventory is designed to be appropriate for the majority of courses in higher education and is consequently not sufficiently fine-grained to pick up slight changes in students' approaches to studying in a particular course. Thirdly, deep approach is known to have a developmental aspect to it, so even if students had much higher deep-approach scores at the end of a course, this increase could not be solely attributed to a change in teaching.

It was also intended that the new inventory would be trialled to an extent that would render endless repetitive item analyses redundant, and that instead it could be used at subscale or main scale level with some confidence.

25.3 Revising the inventory

A 60-item *Revised Approaches to Studying Inventory* (RASI) was developed in 1992. Its composition was influenced by several factors. First, an examination of four comparable inventories was carried out (the *Study Processes Questionnaire* (Biggs, 1987), the *Inventory of Learning Processes* (Schmeck, Ribich and Ramanaiah, 1977), the *Learning and Study Strategies Inventory* (Weinstein, Schulte and Palmer, 1987) and a study strategies inventory developed by Janssen (1992)). Secondly, recent staff development literature (Denicolo, Entwistle and Hounsell, 1992) had been stressing the importance of teaching for active learning and this influenced the decision to include new scales on active and passive learning in the RASI. Thirdly, Meyer had suggested that both fragmentation and memorization should be captured within a surface approach and that reflection should be incorporated within a deep approach (Meyer, 1991; Meyer and Watson, 1991). Fourthly, the authors wanted to produce an inventory which was aesthetically pleasing by including comparable subscales in each main scale – an intention, a study process and a motivation. To achieve comparability among the main scales, the composition of deep approach had to be re-evaluated, since with the inclusion of a new active learning subscale and items on reflecting, the scale was now lengthy. It was decided that Pask's constructs of holism and serialism could be subsumed in relating ideas and use of evidence respectively, and it consequently made sense to discard the related pathologies.

After considerable trialling with a large pool of items, several items were discarded, leaving a 60-item version of RASI containing 15 subscales each of four items. These subscales formed four main scales (deep, surface, strategic and apathetic), with academic self-confidence existing as a separate scale. RASI was completed by 640 first-year students from four contrasting disciplines. Maximum likelihood factor analysis produced a clear four-factor solution which explained 62 per cent of the variance. This is shown in Table 25.1 along with estimates of the scales and subscales internal reliabilities (measured by Cronbach's Alpha).

Scale	Fac 1	Fac 2	Fac 3	Fac 4	Alpha
Deep approach					*.83*
Intention to understand	.71				.51
Active interest	.53				.64
Relating ideas	.80				.60
Use of evidence	.64				.59
Surface approach					*.79*
Intention to reproduce		.58			.28
Passive learning	-.42	.67			.41
Unrelated memorising		.44			.60
Fear of failure		.68			.79
Strategic approach					*.77*
Intention to excel			.28		.57
Alertness to assessment demands			.38		.44
Study organisation			.72		.55
Time management			.77		.77
Apathetic approach					*.79*
Lack of direction				.47	.66
Lack of interest				.99	.68
Academic aptitude					
Academic self-confidence		-.56			.73

Loadings less than .3 have been omitted.

Table 25.1   Factor analysis of the 60-item RASI, and associated Cronbach's alpha values

While the resultant factor pattern was exactly what would have been expected conceptually, and all four main scales had acceptable internal reliabilities ranging from 0.77 to 0.83, two of the surface subscales, intention to reproduce and passive learning, fell below the value which is generally regarded as an acceptable minimum for scales of that length and type (0.5). Alertness to assessment, from strategic approach, also had a low alpha value, but this was not considered to be particularly worrying because the inventory had been completed by first-year students before they had had much, if any, experience of being assessed.

Shorter forms of this 60-item version were subsequently produced for use in a specific project (Tait and Entwistle, 1996). These versions contained 44 and 38 items respectively, and when analysed, produced consistently impressively clear factor patterns at item level. The reduction in length was achieved by removing the one or two 'poorest' items from each subscale (those which had not loaded as strongly as anticipated in the 60-item item level factor analysis or which were detrimentally affecting the Cronbach's alpha value). These new short subscales (containing just two or three items) could no longer be treated justifiably as stable units of analysis, and the four main scales, having acceptable levels of internal reliability, were used as the units of analysis for the purposes of the project.

On a second inspection of the analysis of the 60-item RASI, it was observed that it was the *defining feature* of surface approach, 'intention to reproduce' which had had an unacceptably low internal reliability, and that the *defining feature* of deep approach, 'intention to understand', was barely acceptable at 0.51. On reflection, it was admitted that the 38- and 44-item versions had been produced as a result of iteratively manipulating the 60-item version until the remaining items and main scales could be empirically justified, and that in doing so, the conceptual integrity of the shorter versions had been sacrificed. This pointed up the importance of using several guiding principles, not just statistics, when involved in development work of this type.

25.4 Reconceptualization

Many different data sets have been gathered by the authors over the past ten years, and those, along with their resulting analyses, helped to indicate which items and subscales were reasonably stable across different disciplines and institutions, and which were more sensitive to the learning environment. A review of these studies was carried out, supported by the current relevant literature, as a first step in determining the content of ASSIST.

In the latter stages of the development of RASI, Gustafsson from Sweden offered to carry out a form of confirmatory factor analysis on the RASI data using his STREAMS program (Structural Equation Modelling Made Simple)(1996). This confirmed the existence of deep and strategic approaches to learning which combined in a single 'study effectiveness' dimension and which was consistent with what Janssen had described as the 'studax' (1996). While most of the other scales made convincing, if small, contributions to the variance, the surface approach as it stood proved to be an exception. This was not entirely unexpected, since surface approach has had a long history of problematically low internal reliability. Instead though, a combination of items which could be collectively described as a surface apathetic approach seemed necessary.

The literature was indicating that collaboration in learning and metacognitive awareness were important, and it was decided to develop scales for these constructs, at least for trialling. Metacognitive awareness was broadened slightly to become 'monitoring effectiveness'.

Using the STREAMS analysis in conjunction with the literature and previous analysis, a lengthy pilot inventory of 99 items was developed. It was intended from the outset that the items would be purged only after both conceptual and empirical analyses had been undertaken. Exploratory analysis suggested that the new 'collaboration' subscale was only related to the deep approach for some students, so it was decided to retain it as a separate subscale to allow variation to emerge rather than incorporate its items within an existing scale. Monitoring effectiveness appeared to fall within both the deep and strategic approaches.

Several items for which there was no empirical justification, and others which appeared to duplicate ideas, were discarded, and the new inventory finally contained just 52 items constituting 13 subscales and three main scales. Other sections were included in a surrounding questionnaire on preparedness for higher education, orientations to learning, study skills, preferences for different types of teaching, influences on successful studying, and a single item which asked for a self-rating of performance to date. All of these additional sections had been trialled previously.

25.5   Method

25.5.1   Sample

Analysis was carried out on a sample of 1231 university students, the majority of whom were in their first year of study. The sample was drawn from six institutions which reflected the range of types of universities in the UK (ancient, post-Robbins, technological and new). Some 16 disciplines were included, most of which came from the arts and social sciences or from science and engineering.

25.5.2   Analyses

Initially, Cronbach's alpha was computed to measure the degree of internal reliability of each of the 13 subscales and of the main scales both including and excluding the associated motives. The main scales ranged from .80 to .87, and the subscales from .54 to .76 with a median value of .62, so all scales and subscales exceeded the minimum acceptable value of 0.5.

Factor analysis was carried out using maximum likelihood extraction, and the matrices were rotated to oblique simple structure. Various numbers of factors were extracted to study the behaviour of individual items during conditions of fragmentation or compression. The data set was then partitioned in various ways to investigate the stability of the factor

	Fac 1	Fac 2	Fac 3	Alpha
Deep (exc/inc motives)				.79/.83
Seeking meaning		.68		.57
Relating ideas		.80		.60
Use of evidence		.74		.54
Associated motives				
Interest in ideas		.65		.76
Collaboration				.75
Strategic (exc/inc motive)				.83/.87
Organised study	.80			.58
Time management	.93			.76
Monitoring effectiveness	.46	.39		.55
Associated motive				
Achieving	.77			.69
Surface apathetic (exc/inc motives)				.75/.80
Unrelated memorising			.79	.55
Lack of purpose			.45	.68
Syllabus boundness			.38	.62
Associated motive				
Fear of failure			.66	.76

Loadings less than .3 have been omitted.

Table 25.2   Factor analysis of the 52-item ASSIST, and associated Cronbach's alpha values

	Fac 1	Fac 2	Fac 3	Fac 4
Approaches to learning				
Deep approach				
Seeking meaning	.69			
Relating ideas	.75			
Use of evidence	.71			
Interest in ideas	.69			
Strategic approach				
Organised study		.77		
Time management		.94		
Monitoring effectiveness	.43	.43		
Achieving		.75		
Surface apathetic approach				
Unrelated memorising			.65	
Lack of purpose			.42	
Syllabus boundness				.34
Fear of failure			.69	
Preparation for higher education				
Ability to study independently		.37		
Prior knowledge			-.42	
Study skills		.41		
Ability to organise own life		.41		
Orientations to learning				
Intrinsic orientation	.55			
Personal extrinsic				
Academic extrinsic				
No clear goals				
Preferences for teaching				
Deep lectures	.46			
Deep books	.56			
Deep exams	.38			
Deep courses	.40			
Surface lectures				.48
Surface books				.45
Surface exams				.57
Surface courses				.50

Loadings less than .3 have been omitted.

Table 25.3   Factor analysis of the inventory subscales and selected questionnaire variables

patterns produced. The three factor pattern obtained for the overall sample and explaining 60 per cent variance, reflects the most consistent and conceptually interpretable factor pattern. It is shown in Table 25.2 along with the estimated levels of internal reliability for the scales and subscales.

The factor analyses indicated that there was empirical justification for the substantial majority of the subscales. The 99-item pilot version had indicated that the collaboration subscale did not load on the deep factor consistently, and this was again found when exploring the main data set. Interviews carried out with a subset of these students revealed that collaboration was used by students in contrasting ways. For well-motivated, interested students, who were keen to understand course material and do well, talking to other students about course content or course work was a routine part of their lives. But for the students who were struggling with course content or course work, collaboration was used as a last resort, in an attempt to 'get the right answers' or to share the burden of work.

In some previous versions of the inventory, fear of failure had tended to dominate apathetic approach, but in this version, where it was associated with the new surface apathetic approach, this was much less apparent. Nonetheless, because of its past history, and of the uncertain behaviour of the collaboration motive associated with the deep approach, it was concluded that it is best to keep the motives as separate subscales in cases where analysis is being carried out at main scale level.

Factor analysis of the inventory subscales along with other variables from the questionnaire was then carried out. These other variables included orientations to learning, preparedness for higher education and preferences for different types of teaching and course. Again, many analyses were carried out with different combinations of variables and for each of the 16 participating departments, and various factor extractions were attempted on each occasion. An indicative four factor solution, explaining 44 per cent of the variance, is shown in Table 25.3.

In general, it was found that deep approach was associated with an intrinsic orientation to the course and with preferences for types of teaching and courses that would support a deep approach. Strategic approach was associated with feeling well-prepared for higher education in terms of being able to work independently, having good prior knowledge, having good study skills and being able to organize one's own life generally. Surface apathetic approach was associated with feeling that prior relevant knowledge was inadequate (and also, in broader analyses, feeling that 'other factors', such as personal relationships, doing paid work and daily travelling time, were adversely affecting the ability to study effectively). Preferences for types of teaching and courses that would support a surface approach were associated with syllabus-boundness.

Inventory scales and subscales were correlated with average performance taken over completed modules. Assessment methods differed among modules, but invariably included both coursework and examinations. Regrettably, this performance data was only available for about half of the sample ($n = 649$), but a self-rating of performance, which previous studies have suggested correlates at about 0.6 with 'real' performance, was available for the whole sample. Table 25.4 shows the correlations between scales and subscales and these two performance indicators.

At subscale level, organized study, time management and achieving all correlated positively with performance at the 0.01 significance level, and unrelated memorizing, lack of purpose, syllabus boundness and fear of failure all correlated negatively. At main scale level, strategic approach correlated positively at the 0.01 level, surface apathetic approach correlated negatively and deep approach did not correlate at all. For the self-rating of

	Av. module mark (n=649)	Self-rating (n=1231)
Deep	.07	.22**
Seeking meaning	.05	.18**
Relating ideas	-.02	.15**
Use of evidence	.06	.17**
Associated motives		
Interest in ideas	.12*	.19**
Collaboration	.03	.08**
Strategic	.22**	.49**
Organised study	.17**	.36**
Time management	.23**	.43**
Monitoring effectiveness	.06	.29**
Associated motive		
Achieving	.24**	.55**
Surface apathetic	-.27**	-.43**
Unrelated memorising	-.23**	-.43**
Lack of purpose	-.19**	-.35**
Syllabus boundness	-.20**	-.28**
Associated motive		
Fear of failure	-.17**	-.28**

Table 25.4   Correlations between ASSIST scales and subscales and performance indicators

performance, all subscales and scales correlated in the expected directions at the 0.01 significance level, but since the overall sample size was moderately large ($n = 1231$), some of these significant correlations were in fact quite small. Again though, it was the subscales from strategic and surface apathetic approaches which correlated most strongly and, not surprisingly, these same two scales at main scale level.

25.6   Concluding remarks

ASSIST is the product of many years of inventory development work which has taken on board current literature on student learning in higher education. The overall questionnaire aims to meet the needs of teaching staff who want to use it to try to identify students who are experiencing difficulty with their studies, or who want to investigate the ways in which their teaching is influencing their students' learning. It does not seem possible though at this stage that it could be used with much confidence in a pre-test/post-test design to assess the success of a teaching or course innovation.

Forerunners to ASSIST have tended to be used equally often at either separate subscale level, or at main scale level where the subscales within that scale are summed together. The analysis carried out on ASSIST, however, suggested that indiscriminate summing of motives and their associated scales was inappropriate, since some of these motives formed part of their associated main scale for some students only. It was also noted that in the old apathetic approach, fear of failure had tended to dominate, suggesting that when fear of failure is summed with other subscales, it may give a misleading impression of the strength of the overall scale. As a consequence, it is now suggested that subscale level factor analysis be routinely conducted in the first instance to investigate how the motives behave in relation to their associated scales to guide the decision on whether it is justifiable summing them in with their associated scales. Because of the newness of ASSIST and the relatively small sample on which it is based, it is also necessary to confirm (using a test of internal reliability such as Cronbach's alpha) that the items form coherent groupings and that the subscales are thus empirically justified for the particular sample being studied. If one or two subscales have unacceptably low alpha values, then any subsequent analysis using them needs to be interpreted with extreme caution. If several subscales cannot be empirically justified, but the main scales do have acceptable alpha values, then subsequent analysis should be carried out at main scale level, subject to the caveats above.

In psychometric terms, the data set on which ASSIST has been piloted is relatively small, numbering just 1231 students. Although it is heterogeneous, and the many partitions of the data that were made suggested a remarkable degree of stability of the factor structure, it is highly likely that future data collection and conceptual analysis will suggest further modifications that should be made. Already it would seem sensible to rethink the apparently ambiguous 'collaboration' subscale (and probably remove it altogether) and to reinstate 'alertness to assessment' thereby moving strategic approach closer to its original definition where good study habits were combined with attempting to maximize performance in assignments and examinations.

25.7   References

Biggs, J.B. (1987) *Student Approaches to Learning and Studying*, Melbourne: Australian Council for Educational Research.

Denicolo, P., Entwistle, N.J. and Hounsell, D.J. (1992) What is active learning? Module 1 in the series *Effective Learning and Teaching in Higher Education*, Sheffield: Universities' and Colleges' Staff Development Agency.

Entwistle, N.J., Hounsell, D.J., Macaulay, C., Situnayake, G. and Tait, H. (1989) *The Performance of Electrical Engineering Students in Scottish Higher Education*. Final report to the Scottish Education Department. University of Edinburgh: Centre for Research on Learning and Instruction.

Entwistle, N.J., Kozeki, B. and Tait, H. (1989) Pupils' perceptions of school and teachers (Parts I and II), *British Journal of Educational Psychology*, 59, 326–48.

Entwistle, N.J. and Ramsden, P. (1983) *Understanding Student Learning*, London: Croom Helm.

Entwistle, N.J., Thompson, J. and Wilson, J.D. (1974) Motivation and study habits, *Higher Education*, 3, 379–96.

Gustafsson, J-E. and Stahl, P.A. (1996) *STREAMS User's Guide*, University of Gothenburg: Department of Education and Educational Research.

Janssen, P.J. (1992) On the construct and nomological validity of student descriptions of studying and lecturing by means of Likert-type questionnaires: a 3 x 3 matrix of nine common 'primary' factors'. In M. Carretero, M Pope, R-J. Simons and J.I. Pozo, J.I. (eds), *Learning and Instruction: European Research in an International Perspective*, Vol. 3, Oxford: Pergamon Press.

Marton, F. and Säljö, R. (1976) On qualitative differences in learning. I – Outcome and process, *British Journal of Educational Psychology*, **46**, 4–11.

Meyer, J.H.F. (1991) Study orchestration: the manifestation, interpretation and consequences of contextualised approaches to learning, *Higher Education*, **22**, 297–316.

Meyer, J.H.F. and Watson, R.M. (1991) Evaluating the quality of student learning. II – Study orchestration and the curriculum, *Studies in Higher Education*, **16**, 251–75.

Newble, D.I., Entwistle, N.J., Hejka, E.J., Jolly, B.C. and Whelan, G. (1988) *Medical Education*, **22**, 518–26.

Pask, G. (1976) Styles and strategies of learning, *British Journal of Educational Psychology*, **46**, 128–48.

Schmeck, R.R., Ribich, F.D. and Ramanaiah, N. (1977) Development of a self-report inventory for assessing individual differences in learning processes, *Applied Psychological Measurement*, **1**, 413–31.

Tait, H. and Entwistle, N.J. (1996) Identifying students at risk through ineffective study strategies, *Higher Education*, **31**, 97–116.

Wall, D., Macaulay, C., Tait, H., Entwistle, D. and Entwistle, N.J. (1991) *The Transition from School to Higher Education in Scotland. Final report to the Scottish Office Education Department*, University of Edinburgh: Centre for Research on Learning and Instruction.

Weinstein, C-E., Schulte, A. and Palmer, D. (1987) *Learning and Study Strategies Inventory (LASSI)*, Clearwater, Flor.: H. & H. Publications.

26 Fostering collaborative learning during student transition to tertiary education: an evaluation of academic and social benefits

James Dalziel and Mary Peat
The University of Sydney, Australia

26.1 Overview

Recent research has highlighted the importance of the first-year experience in satisfaction with academic and social aspects of university life (McInnis, James and McNaught, 1995; Tinto, 1989). While orientation programmes for new tertiary students are common, many of these fail to integrate social and academic adjustment to university life with collaborative learning in a productive way, especially in large and diverse degree programmes. In 1997 we offered a 'transition workshop' to new first-year science students prior to the commencement of university classes. Student timetables were manipulated prior to the workshop to ensure that attending students would be members of small 'peer study groups' (8–15 students) who shared similar subjects and career aspirations, and that these groups would share at least two tutorial classes per week. During the workshop peer study groups spent time getting to know each other, discussing expectations and considering possibilities for collaborative learning. The workshop also included a tour of local facilities to make students aware of locations where they could meet and work together, and talks from staff and previous first-year students on making the transition.

An end of workshop evaluation indicated enthusiastic support for the programme, with the most popular aspect being the formation of peer study groups. A follow-up survey at the end of the first semester included measures of academic and social adjustment, together with the Approaches to Study Questionnaire. Surveys were sent to three categories of students: those attending the workshop; those offered the workshop but who did not attend; and students from a different faculty (with no transition workshop). Transition workshop attenders scored significantly higher on almost all measures that indicated better adjustment to university life. The pedagogical and social benefits to students of this transition workshop are reviewed in the light of current research and theory on the first-year experience.

26.2 Introduction

The experiences of university students during their first year of study appear to be crucial to their academic performance and personal adjustment. For many students, the first year is a significant time of transition and change, particularly for those entering tertiary education following the end of secondary studies. During recent years there has been increasing interest in the 'first-year experience', and various attempts have been made to aid students in making a successful transition to university studies.

For example, in his keynote address to the Inaugural Pan Pacific First Year Experience Conference in 1995, Professor Vince Tinto stressed the importance of the initial experiences of students in their overall university progression. Adjustment problems during the early stages of university are the primary reason for students dropping out or deferring studies not just in the first twelve months, but throughout their degree programme. One of the solutions suggested for the problem of student adjustment is the formation of collaborative study groups, where students with similar academic interests work together as a regular part of their university life. Not only do such groups allow students to assist each other in academic study, but they also provide a cohesive peer group that helps to buffer the difficulties of the initial period of transition to university life (Tinto, 1975, 1989, 1995).

Collaborative learning is important not just for coping with academic study and first-year difficulties (accruing from the social benefits of a peer group), but also due to its inherent educational qualities. Students working together in an (initially) unstructured group without direction from a tutor or lecturer must learn to organize their time and priorities if the group is to be successful. Further, students learn from each other in a non-hierarchical learning environment, and the kind of teamwork, cooperation and communication skills that this requires are applicable far beyond first-year university study – indeed, many of the skills learnt from such an experience are important in fostering life-long learning. In an age where generic skills are increasingly valuable to university graduates, due to the flexibility of careers and the workplace, collaborative learning is a tool that has much to offer students and educators.

However, the traditional concept of collaborative learning as a 'peer study group' meeting regularly to work together highlights only one type of collaboration between students regarding their learning. While it is probably one of the most effective examples of this idea, there are many other less intensive activities that can be subsumed under a broader definition of collaborative learning. Activities such as seeking assistance from a more senior student, sharing the tasks of collecting and understanding reference articles, swapping lecture notes, using classroom 'free time' to work on student studies rather than social discussions, and even spontaneous discussion of academic work in social settings can all be considered examples of collaborative learning. Viewed in this more general sense, collaborative learning is probably a common experience of many students, regardless of any attempt by a university to foster such activities. However, there may also be ways in which university programmes can increase the likelihood of collaboration and support this type of learning. One example of this is the pre-university 'transition workshop'.

Workshops for assisting students with adjustment to university life are not new. Within the Australian context, they are common for residential university colleges where many students are from rural areas. They are also reasonably prevalent among small, specialized courses of study where limited student numbers and shared weekly classes make it feasible and valuable to provide transition workshops for students. While these workshops may not make use of findings concerning the transition period, or encourage collaborative study, the high level of contact between a small number of students may in many cases be sufficient to create cohesive peer groups that buffer the academic and social difficulties of early university life, and hence increase progression rates and improve student adjustment. Due to the combination of the above factors, it is possible for staff in these situations to develop brief workshops that do not require enormous amounts of time, energy and funding in order to be successful, but which can have lasting benefits.

The same cannot be so easily said for large, diverse degree programmes. In large generalist faculties where hundreds or thousands of students study, the difficulties of fostering collaborative learning and aiding students in the transition to university life appear to increase exponentially with size. As student numbers increase, lecture classes grow, subject selection becomes more varied and timetabling becomes increasingly complex. This may result in individual students having few if any other students that share with them more than a few classes per week. The personal isolation and lack of shared subjects resulting from such large and diverse degree programmes can be formidable barriers to student adjustment to university life.

Hence, the existing difficulties of the transition period, the problems of adjustment to tertiary study, the benefits of collaborative learning, the size and diversity of large degree programmes and the need for realistic and cost-effective methods of student support are all issues that are applicable to the first-year experience of students. This chapter describes an innovative transition workshop programme and subsequent follow-up evaluation of student adjustment developed by the Faculty of Science at the University of Sydney, Australia. By addressing the issues mentioned above, it provides a model for other universities that wish to assist students in their first year of university study.

26.3   The transition workshop

During 1996, the Faculty of Science implemented a pilot transition programme, in which 150 students were invited to a half-day workshop on making the transition to university life prior to the commencement of studies (see Peat and Jelks, 1996). The 68 students who attended were presented with various activities, including a number of talks on surviving the early stages of university life and adjusting to academic studies. Students received a showbag of pamphlets and other resources, and at the conclusion of the morning attended a lunch provided by the Faculty of Science at which staff associated with first-year studies met informally with students. The most important aspect of the morning programme was the creation of peer groups and time for these groups of students to get to know one another. These groups of 10–20 students had been identified before the workshop, and their university timetables were manipulated so that they would share at least two tutorial/practical classes per week (amounting to approximately six hours/week), in addition to shared lectures in many cases. The prior manipulation of the timetables of those responding to the workshop (possible due to students returning a reply letter) was important as first-year science courses at the University of Sydney have many practical/tutorial classes (from 20 to over 60 per week), and hence students would almost certainly not have shared classes if left to random allocation. After the initial workshop, students were invited to several follow-up meetings during the first semester, and a core group of interested students formed a focus group in which issues were discussed, and materials for the 1997 workshop were developed.

In 1997, all new first year Bachelor of Science (680) students were invited to attend a one day transition workshop during a weekend just prior to commencement of studies (see Peat, 1997). Students returned a letter indicating their interest to attend, and noting their general career aspirations. Prior to the workshop, the students who returned a letter or otherwise indicated they would attend had their timetables manipulated so that they would spend at least 2 weekly tutorial/practical classes together (in the same way as the 1996 workshop, and in addition to lectures), and these groupings were based on students who had similar subjects choices and career aspirations. Also prior to the workshop, a showbag of resources was compiled which included a special 'Student Orientation Manual' that had been developed by the student focus group from the 1996 workshop, based on information that the 1996 students wished they had received during their first weeks at university.

The transition workshop began with a registration period where students were allocated to one of three groups for the morning sessions and received their showbags. Each of the three groups was based on different broad career aspirations (physical/mathematical/computing sciences, biological/chemical sciences, and psychology and related fields), and a coordinator of first-year studies within each of these general areas led the morning sessions. Approximately 230 students attended, with about 80 students in each large group. These sessions included general introductory talks, 'survival tips', and an introduction to the showbag resources. They also included briefs talks from previous first-year students on their experiences of early university life and how they adjusted. All students were given blank 'business cards' on which they were encouraged to write their name and contact details, so that these could be given to other members of their allocated peer group. As in 1996, the central aspect of the morning was the formation of peer groups (based on previous timetable manipulation), in which groups of 8–15 students met, got to know each other, discussed expectations, swapped 'business cards', and considered future possibilities for collaborative learning. The morning also included a brief tour of local facilities to make students familiar with the buildings most associated with Faculty of Science programmes.

As in 1996, students were then provided with lunch, this time in front of the main university quadrangle, followed by a formal welcome by the Dean of the Faculty of Science and other senior members of staff in the University's Great Hall. In addition to the students themselves, parents of students were invited to attend this formal welcome and also to attend a separate parents workshop during the afternoon concerning the ways in which parents could assist students in making the transition. After the formal welcome, students left for a longer and more comprehensive tour of the university campus, while the parents programme consisted of talks on current understanding of the transition process, advice for parents from the director of the university counselling service, and reflections on the first-year experience from a senior undergraduate student. Following this, parents were able to ask questions of a panel of people involved in the workshop and the transition process.

Evaluation of the student and parent workshops by a brief end-of-session questionnaire indicated an enthusiastic response to the programme, with students particularly appreciating the formation of peer groups and the advice of past first-year students. Parents appreciated advice concerning the transition process, and the general commitment of the university to provide assistance to new students during the transition period. Many unsolicited comments of thanks and congratulations were given to the workshop team for the high quality of the overall programme.

26.4   The follow-up evaluation

To assess the potential benefits of the transition workshop, a survey was developed which examined academic and social dimensions of students' initial experiences of university life. Survey questions included: demographics and prior schooling, qualitative-answer questions concerning positive and negative aspects of early university life, questions about specific aspects of adjustment (such as experiences of collaborative learning), and a number of relevant scales. Academic adjustment was assessed using the 'First Year Experience Questionnaire' (FYEQ) developed by McInnis *et al.* (1995) in their comprehensive study of Australian students' experiences of the early stages of university life. This measure contains seven subscales: academic orientation (e.g. 'I enjoy the intellectual challenge of subjects I am studying'), sense of identity (e.g. 'I really like being a university student'), sense of purpose (e.g. 'I am clear about the reasons I came to university'), academic application (e.g. 'I worked consistently throughout first semester'), teaching (e.g. 'The teaching staff are good at explaining things'), course (e.g. 'Overall I am really enjoying my course'), and workload (e.g. 'My course workload is too heavy'). In addition, the 'Approaches to Study Questionnaire' (ASQ) as presented by Gibbs (1992) was included to examine differences in student approaches to learning, as demonstrated by the three subscales of achieving (e.g. 'When I'm doing a piece of work, I try to bear in mind exactly what that lecturer seems to want'), reproducing (e.g. 'When I'm reading I try to memorize important facts which may come in useful later'), and meaning (e.g. 'I usually set out to understand thoroughly the meaning of what I am asked to read'). Both of these scales are scored on 5-point agree/disagree Likert scales, with the middle value indicating a neutral view.

Social adjustment was examined using the college student version of the Interpersonal Support Evaluation List (ISEL), developed by Cohen and Hoberman (1983), which includes four subscales of: tangible support (e.g. 'I know someone who would loan me $50 so I could go away for the weekend'), belonging (e.g. 'There are people at university who I regularly run with, exercise with, or play sport with'), appraisal (e.g. 'I know someone who I see or talk to often with whom I would feel perfectly comfortable talking about problems I might have budgeting my time between university and my social life'), and self-esteem (e.g. 'Most people who know me well think highly of me'). Each ISEL statement is answered as either 'probably true' or 'probably false'. Finally, as a control for the personality trait of extroversion, the six-item extroversion subscale of the EPQR-A (Francis, Brown, and Philipchalk, 1992) was included within the ISEL questions (some items were reworded slightly to suit the ISEL style and answer format – 'I am a talkative person: probably true/probably false' – rather than 'Are you a talkative person? yes/no').

To study the effects of the transition workshop, three groups of first-year students were surveyed at the end of the first semester of 1997. These three groups were (1) first-year Faculty of Science students who were invited to, and attended, the transition workshop, (2) first-year Faculty of Science students who were invited to, but did not attend, the transition workshop, and (3) first-year students from other faculties (which do not have transition workshops). Group 3 students were predominantly Bachelor of Arts students, but also included some from the Bachelor of Economics and Bachelor of Education programmes, as well a few students from many other programmes.

The reason for two 'control' groups for this study was to provide different comparison groups – one for those who chose not to attend the workshop, and another of students who were not offered the possibility of attending a workshop (due to being in different faculties), as there are potential problems with simple comparisons between those who attended and those who did not. From a methodological perspective, the ideal experimental design for the follow-up section of the transition project would have been to randomly allocate some students to the transition workshop programme, and others to a control group. This procedure could attempt to account for differences between attenders and non-attenders that existed prior to the workshop (indeed, differences that could affect self-selection for the workshop in the first place, such as the motivation to do well at university). If there are pre-existing differences between attenders and non-attenders, these could confound the findings of observed differences between survey groups 1 and 2 (findings that would otherwise have been attributed to the transition workshop).

However, a random allocation experimental design encounters ethical problems in allocating some, but not all students to a potentially beneficial programme. Further, as the primary motivation for the transition workshop project was pastoral rather than scientific, all students were offered the opportunity to attend. Thus, comparisons between attenders and non-attenders need to take this methodological problem into account. An alternative comparison that may help answer this difficulty is using students from other degree programmes (group 3), where these students did not have the any opportunity to attend a transition programme. This group (3) do not necessarily encounter the same problems of selection bias as for the comparisons between group 1 and 2. For this reason, comparisons between group 1 and 2, and 1 and 3 are both of value.

The hypotheses for the current study were that students who attended the transition workshop, as a result of the benefits of this programme, would score higher values on the FYEQ scales, higher values on the ISEL scale, and the higher values on the ASQ scales of achieving and meaning, but lower values on the ASQ scale of reproducing. Also, workshop participants were expected to consider deferring or dropping out of university studies less than other groups. Finally, due to the emphasis on collaborative learning and peer groups, workshop participants were expected to engage in more collaborative learning activities and to meet outside university for social activities more than the other groups. By way of control, the groups were not expected to differ on measures of personality (extroversion), previous school performance (as measured by the 'TER'), or relative preference for collaborative learning (as compared to working individually).

26.5   Method

Students in group 1 and 2 were sent the survey by mail, and those who did not return it within several weeks were sent a reminder letter. Students from these groups who were also first-year psychology students were able to gain credit for involvement in research by returning the survey. The students for group 3 were all non-Science students who chose to participate in the survey as part of the research participation component of first-year psychology studies, and students either collected surveys to complete in their own time, or completed them during lunchtime sessions. On return of the survey, these students were given credit for research participation. For all discussion that follows, group 1 refers to those who attended the workshop, group 2 those who were invited but did not attend (both group 1 and 2 are Faculty of Science students only), and group 3 is made up of students from other faculties which did not have transition programmes. Appendix 26.1 contains the individual questions asked in the survey which are not from previously reported scales.

26.6   Results

Using university enrolment records, 181 Faculty of Science students who attended the transition workshop were sent surveys, and 72 of these were returned (40% – group 1). Five hundred and sixty-six (566) Faculty of Science students who did not attend the workshop were sent surveys, of which 131 (24% – group 2) returned surveys. Each of these response rates, particularly the second, should be viewed as minimum rates, as some students remain on the university records despite withdrawing from studies, and some students would have had incorrect postal addresses (these problems are estimated to account for 10–30 per cent of the total sample). Seventy-six (76) students from other faculties were surveyed (group 3), brought the total sample size to 286.

Students were asked to indicate whether they had considered deferring or dropping out of university studies (Appendix 26.1, Q1). Figure 26.1 indicates relative percentages across the three groups. If these categories are treated as a scale with values 1 (none), 2 (occasional) and 3 (serious), then group 1 students are significantly less likely to consider deferring/dropping out than group 2 (gr 1 mean = 1.5, gr 2 mean = 1.8, t = -2.2, p < .05), or group 3 (gr 1 mean = 1.5, gr 3 mean = 1.9, t = -3.5, p < .001).

To examine participation in a variety of potential collaborative learning activities, percentages for each group were calculated for nine different activities (Appendix 26.1, Q2). Figure 26.2 indicates the patterns across each activities for the three groups studied. When taken as a whole, group 1 students were involved in significantly greater number of collaborative learning activities than group 2 (gr 1 average number of activities = 4.8, gr 2 = 4.1, t = 2.5, p < .01) or group 3 (gr 1 = 4.8, gr 2 = 3.9, t = 2.9, p < .01). These differences did not appear to be due to differences in personal preferences for collaborative/individual study (Appendix 26.1, Q3) across the three groups (see Table 26.1). Regarding social events outside of university (with other newly met university students – Appendix 26.1, Q4), a higher percentage of students from group 1 (68%) had participated in this kind of activity than those from group 2 (55%) or group 3 (62%).

Table 26.1 presents the results for the three scales used (FYEQ, ISEL and ASQ), together with the three control variables (introversion/extroversion, overall school performance – TER score, and individual/collaborative learning preference). The means for each group are

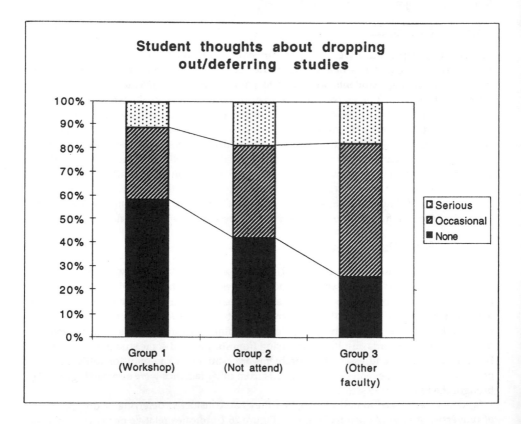

Figure 26.1   Percentage of students considering deferring/dropping out of university studies across the three groups studied

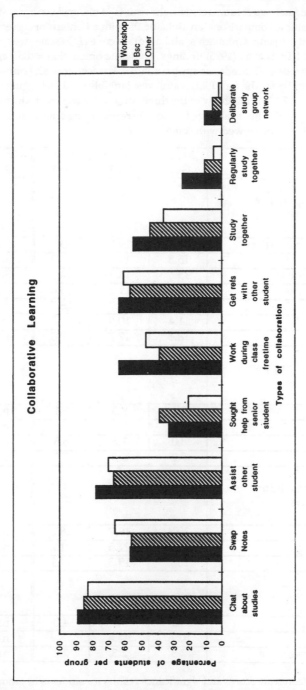

Figure 26.2   Percentage of students involved in various collaborative learning activities across the three groups studied.

shown, and the final two columns contain the results of planned contrasts statistical tests. To account for multiple comparisons, an alpha of .05 with a Bonferroni correction was used.

The reliability (using Cronbach's alpha) of each FYEQ scale was satisfactory and equivalent to McInnis *et al.* (1995) findings: academic orientation = .85, sense of identity = .85, sense of purpose, .71, academic application = .64, teaching = .82, course = .78, workload = .80. The reliability for the four ISEL scales was: tangible = .75, belonging = .64, appraisal = .89, self esteem = .70. The reliability of the three ASQ scales was: reproducing = .40, meaning = .71, achieving = .59. The reliability of .40 for the reproducing scale indicates that the values for this scale should be viewed with some caution.

Scale	Mean Gr 1	Mean Gr 2	Mean Gr 3	Gr 1 vs Gr 2	Gr 1 vs Gr 3
First Year Experience Questionnaire					
Academic Orientation	21.3	19.3	20.3	Sig	ns
Sense of Identity	15.8	14.1	14.2	Sig	Sig
Sense of Purpose	15.8	14.7	14.8	Sig	ns
Academic Application	12.2	11.2	10.6	Sig	Sig
Teaching	29.1	27.7	28.7	ns	ns
Course	11.4	10.0	10.5	Sig	Sig
Workload	18.1	17.7	17.0	ns	ns
Interpersonal Support Evaluation List					
Tangible	8.4	8.3	9.1	ns	ns
Belonging	5.4	5.3	5.6	ns	ns
Appraisal	8.0	7.6	8.3	ns	ns
Self Esteem	7.2	6.6	7.3	ns	ns
Approaches to Study Questionnaire					
Achieving	20.3	19.7	18.6	ns	Sig
Reproducing	21.0	21.5	21.7	ns	ns
Meaning	20.7	19.3	19.1	Sig	Sig
Controls					
Extroversion	3.5	3.7	4.0	ns	ns
TER	81.6	84.8	78.9	ns	ns
Learning Preference	2.3	2.3	2.2	ns	ns

Table 26.3   Mean scale scores and significance results for students in group 1 (transition workshop), group 2 (non-transition workshop BSc), and group 3 (other faculty).

26.7 Discussion

In general, the results presented here support the contention that students who attended the transition workshop are making a more successful transition to university life than students who did not, both in academic and social spheres. As the results indicate, workshop attenders think less about deferring/dropping out of university studies, are more likely to have been involved in collaborative learning activities and are more likely to have met in social settings outside of university. They are more academically motivated, have a greater sense of purpose and identity, and rate their courses more highly. They are also more likely to have adopted a 'meaning' or 'deep' approach to their learning. All of this adds up to a very positive picture for students who chose to attend the transition workshop, and suggests strongly in favour of the workshop programme's beneficial nature.

As noted earlier, one qualifier of these findings is the possibility of differences prior to the beginning of university between students who attended the workshop and students who did not, for example, perhaps only those students who are already motivated to do well at university and to work hard would attend a workshop of this kind. While this is possible, the evidence presented here argues against this interpretation. The pattern of differences between group 1 and group 2 was the same in most instances for group 1 and group 3, the only major exception to this being the results for some of ISEL measures, which are probably due to the differences between Faculty of Science programmes and other faculty programmes. That is, Faculty of Science programmes are generally very demanding, and require a large number of contact hours per week in first year, thus reducing the potential time available for social activities outside of classtime. Students from other faculties with less demanding programmes may have more time for social contact, and hence the benefits this provides (as demonstrated in the higher ISEL scores for group 3).

The lack of significance of past school performance and extroversion also argue in favour of the beneficial effects of the workshop, as workshop attenders are not more extroverted or higher achieving than those who did not attend – indeed, in each case the value for workshop attenders was lower than for non-attenders. Further, all three groups were equivalent in preferences for collaborative learning, and hence the differences observed for collaborative learning activities are not due simply to a selection effect of those who enjoy collaborative learning choosing to attend the workshop. It should be noted that the results presented here regarding collaborative learning have been based on a broader view of this concept, and this approach appears to have been valuable in the current context.

While the results to date are positive, further development of this programme would be of additional value. It would be useful to find more ways of encouraging additional peer group contact during the first semester beyond the confines of the classroom, such as through lunchtime barbeques and other social activities. Also, a staff development programme aimed at educating first-year staff in the nature of the transition period and the special needs of new first-year students could be of potential value. Due to the fact that students surveyed here provided extensive qualitative data regarding their early experiences of university life, further work on this project may consider the relationship of these comments to the scale scores of the present study. Finally, as most students gave permission for the current research project to examine the relationship between the variables discussed here and overall course marks, follow-up studies will examine the relationship between adjustment to university life and academic performance.

Acknowledgements

The authors gratefully acknowledge the help of the many people who assisted with the workshop, including Professor Robert Hewitt (Dean), Tony Greening, Graham Mosely, Bronwen Parry, Michael Young, Sue Franklin, Claudia Morales, Piers Ettinger-Epstein, Kirsten Morley, Simone Boulding, Tessa Boyd-Caine, Steve Rawling, Tim Nicholson, Gina Sartore and the members of the 1996 workshop focus group. This study was funded by a Faculty of Science Teaching Development Fund grant.

26.8   References

Cohen, S., and Hoberman, H. (1983) Positive events and social supports as buffers of life change stress, *Journal of Applied Social Psychology*, **13**, 99–125.

Francis, L. J., Brown, L. B. and Philipchalk, R. (1992) The development of an abbreviated form of the Revised Eysenck Personality Questionnaire (EPQR-A): Its use among students in England, Canada, the U.S.A. and Australia, *Personality and Individual Differences*, **13**, 443–449.

Gibbs, G. (1992) *Improving the Quality of Student Learning*, Bristol: Technical and Educational Services Ltd.

McInnis, C., James, R. and McNaught, C. (1995) *First Year on Campus*, Canberra: Australian Government Printing Service.

Peat, M. (1997) *Report of the Student Transition Workshop and Parents Program, 1997*, Faculty of Science, University of Sydney.

Peat, M. and Jelks, B. (1996) Helping to make the transition: Faculty of Science style. Presentation to the *2nd Pan Pacific First Year Experience Conference*, Melbourne, Australia.

Tinto, V. (1975) Dropout from higher education: A theoretical synthesis of recent research, *Review of Educational Research*, **45**, 89–125.

Tinto, V. (1989) *Leaving College: Rethinking the Causes and Cures of Student Attrition*, Chicago: University of Chicago Press.

Tinto, V. (1995) Keynote address to the *Inaugural Pan Pacific First Year Experience Conference*, Brisbane, Australia.

Appendix 26.1   Individual survey questions

Q1.   The following question asks about deferring your studies/dropping out of university. Please circle the statement that best represents your view on this.

(1) I have not thought at all about deferring/dropping out

(2) I have occasionally thought of deferring/dropping out, but I have not seriously considered it

(3) I have seriously considered deferring/dropping out

(4) I have seriously considered deferring/dropping out and am reasonably certain I will not complete this year

Q2.   During your first semester of university, have you done (or are you about to do) any of the following? Please circle ALL that apply to you.

(1) Spontaneously discussed aspects of your studies with friends while having lunch, coffee, drinks, etc.

(2) Swapped notes with a fellow student to help get a better understanding of a subject

(3) Helped another student to catch up on missed material by going over content with them

(4) Sought the help of an advanced/higher year student to explain difficult material to you

(5) Used free time during class to talk with fellow students about subject content (rather than social discussions)

(6) Worked together with another student(s) to collect readings and references

(7) Met with at least one other student to study material together

(8) Regularly (e.g. weekly) meet together with at least one other student to study together

(9) Formed a deliberate, organized network of students who regularly meet together and assist each other in study, collecting references, and other aspects of university studies

Q3.   Which of the following statements best describes your personal learning preference?

(1) I prefer to study entirely on my own

(2) I mainly prefer to study on my own, but I sometimes like to study with fellow students

(3) I equally prefer studying on my own and studying with fellow students

(4) I mainly prefer to study with fellow students, but I sometimes like to study on my own

(5) I prefer to study entirely with fellow students

Q4.   Have you gone to any social occasions with other students from this university (who you did not know before you came here) outside of university hours?

(1) Yes

(2) No

27 Improving students as learners in groups: an evaluation of the impact of peer assessment on the 'social loafing' phenomenon and on student perception of equity and fairness

Diane Garland
Plymouth Business School, University of Plymouth

27.1   Introduction

There are many benefits associated with working effectively in small groups which are well documented in the literature. However, effective group working is very difficult to achieve. In practice, actual group productivity often falls short of potential productivity (Steiner, 1972). In higher education, little evidence exits as to the effectiveness of student learning in small groups and to ways in which the student learning may be improved. Research conducted at Plymouth Business School, University of Plymouth (Garland, 1996) involving both staff and 875 undergraduates identified the 'free rider' (or social loafing) as a 'real problem' in group work, with 64 per cent of student respondents finding it 'unusual for all members to fully cooperate in group work'.

This chapter discusses the findings of further research, conducted within Plymouth Business School, with two groups of students comprising part-time management students and full-time final year undergraduates, to evaluate the impact of peer assessment on the social-loafing phenomenon and on student perception of equity and fairness, with a view to improving students as learners in small groups.

The research strategy adopted with both groups of students is documented, together with the form of assessment, the assessment process, the criteria used for assessment and the judgment of the student's assessment performance. Overall, there is evidence to suggest that peer assessment, properly introduced and employed as part of a coherent assessment strategy, can contribute to improving students as learners in small groups.

27.2   Literature review

One explanation for the fact that actual productivity may fall short of potential productivity in group work is the tendency for individuals to work less hard when their efforts are combined with those of others, than when they are considered individually (West, 1994). This is not a newly discovered phenomenon, but was studied by Ringelmann, a French agricultural engineer more than 100 years ago (Kravitz and Martin, 1986) and has since been termed 'social loafing' by Latane, Williams and Harkins (1979) when they found that individuals working alone shouted and clapped harder than those performing in groups (Latane et al., 1979, p. 823) define social loafing as 'a decrease in individual effort due to the social presence of other persons'. Social loafing effects have since been replicated on tasks requiring physical and perceptual effort in laboratory settings.

One cause of social loafing may be that individual effort or contributions are often perceived as unidentifiable. Evidence exists which suggests that when individuals in a group believe that their efforts or contributions will be identifiable to others and there is potential for evaluation of those efforts, social loafing is effectively eliminated (e.g. Harkins and Jackson, 1985, Kerr and Bruun, 1981).

Why should identifiability deter social loafing? Jones (1984) provides one explanation for this finding. When individual contributions are unidentifiable, the perceived link between individual effort and rewards and punishment is low, and this results in decreased motivation. Conversely, when individual effort is perceived to be identifiable, individuals are accountable for their own behaviour and the resulting positive or negative consequences can be expected. According to Lateen *et al.* (1979, p. 830) 'since individual scores are unidentifiable when groups perform together, people can receive neither precise credit nor appropriate blame for their performance'. Lateen *et al.* (1979) and Jones (1984) conclude that one reason individuals engage in social loafing is because they believe their individual efforts will go unrecorded and/or a lack of effort will not be punished.

Social loafing is not just a problem in terms of lost productivity of the individual group member(s) who engage in social loafing. Rather, if some group members engage in social loafing, other group members may reduce their own effort levels so as not to be 'suckers' (Kerr, 1983). Research by Jackson and Harkins (1985) suggests that when groups members expect others to engage in social loafing they may reduce their own efforts to approximate the effort levels of the social loafers. Group members may loaf because they desire to preserve equity by not having others gain from their efforts without expending effort themselves (Adams, 1965). The evidence points to the fact that social loafing may also cause others in the group to lower their own contributions.

Earlier research conducted at Plymouth Business School, University of Plymouth (Garland, 1996) involving both staff and 875 undergraduates also identifies the 'free rider' (or social loafing) as a 'real problem' in group work, with 64 per cent of student respondents finding it 'unusual for all members to fully cooperate in group work'.

In higher education, although alternative methods of assessment are available, student group work is often assessed by the tutor alone, who marks the tangible output submitted and commonly allocates the same mark to all group members. A major concern with this approach is that the tutor cannot know the extent of individual contribution to the group task and therefore no allowance is made in the marking procedure in respect of individual effort. Under such circumstances, if students believe their individual efforts will go unrecorded and/or a lack of effort will not be punished, social loafing may occur. One way of lessening the effects of the social loafing phenomenon may be to involve student group members in identifying and acknowledging their individual contribution to a group project via peer assessment. This may have the effect of enhancing their perception of equity and fairness in the assessment process and also have the desired positive impact on student contribution and learning.

As a result of the literature review and the findings of the earlier research within Plymouth Business School, the author decided to evaluate the impact of peer assessment on the social loafing phenomenon and on student perception of equity and fairness, with a view to improving students as learners in small groups.

27.3　Research strategy

The subjects consisted of two groups of students:

1. 38 final-year full-time business undergraduates;

2. 17 first-year part-time (day release) management students.

Quantitative data was obtained from questionnaires collated from eight male and 30 female students from group (1), and from nine male and eight female students from group (2). Qualitative data in the form of semi-structured interviews of approximately 30 minutes duration were conducted with individual students from both groups in order to illuminate the quantitative data.

27.4   Form of assessment

The peer assessment forms utilized in the research can be found at Appendix 27.A. These forms are a derivation of the work of Gibbs (1995).

27.5   Assessment process

In both instances, students were required to work in groups on an assignment which formed part of the assessment process for the module. Each group had to submit a written report on a topic area. The undergraduates also had to present orally their findings to their class. Each student received the peer assessment form attached to the assignment instructions and an oral explanation as to criterion utilized, the method of completion, the date by which the written report and the peer assessment form should be submitted and the weighting the peer assessed marks would carry in relation to their individual overall module mark. Room on the peer assessment form was also left for the students to explain further their individual role in the completion of the assignment.

Minutes of group meetings were to be taken and submitted. The students were required to hold a final group meeting prior to submitting the report to discuss their *relative* rather than *absolute* contributions to the assignment and to award marks according to the instructions given. The tutor marked the assignment and allocated one overall group mark to the work prior to looking at the peer assessment forms. This mark was later amended by the tutor, as required, according to the peer assessed marks.

27.6   Criteria used for assessment

The criteria used for the peer assessment (see Appendix 27.A) was derived from the components of the group assignments.

27.7   Results

27.7.1   Undergraduate students

Students worked in groups consisting mostly of either four or five members. As final-year students, many (29) reported that they had worked with others taking the module prior to this assignment. The decision to work in their chosen group was influenced both by social relationships already formed with group members and by prior experience of working with the group members. Twenty-five students reported that choice of topic area had *no* influence upon their decision to work in a particular group.

27.7.2   Management students

Students mostly worked in groups of three for this assignment. In contrast to the undergraduates, as this was their first group assignment, none of the students had worked together before, reporting they had chosen their group members mainly on the basis of proximity to others in the classroom.

27.7.3   Similarities and differences in research outcomes

An analysis of the questionnaire data is presented in Appendix 27.B.

27.7.3.1   *Student perception of equity and fairness*

It can be seen that there was a high level of agreement that peer assessment is a fairer method of assessment than one mark for all group members regardless of individual contribution for both the business studies (52%) and management (62%) respondents. A similar number of students, business studies (52%) and management (64%) believe peer assessment helps in identifying strengths of individual members. Both sets of students, business studies (52%) and management (76%) agreed that peer assessment encouraged everyone to participate and share the workload.

Of those who did differentiate between members with regard to the overall group mark, both business (85%) and management (54%) students reported that one/more than one group member did not participate as fully as they might have done, and both business (85%) and management (81%) students agreed it seemed appropriate to give more marks to those who contributed more towards the project.

Of those who did not differentiate marks, the business (86%) and management (74%) students agreed that they all worked together, with similar amounts of effort, and so they all deserved the same mark. Both groups of students were equally divided over whether they were prepared to upset other group members by haggling over marks. Forty-eight per cent of business studies students agreed it was the lecturer's responsibility to allocate marks, not the students, while 28 per cent disagreed. None of the management students agreed with this statement and 24 per cent disagreed. It seems that the management students were more amenable to being involved in the assessment process and having the opportunity to influence marks than the business studies students.

27.7.3.2   *Alternative methods of recording individual contribution*

Sixty-five per cent of business studies students did not agree that keeping minutes helped to keep the group on schedule and found having to do so excessively time-consuming. This is in contrast with the finding for the management students where 47 per cent agreed that keeping minutes did help to keep the group on schedule. One explanation for this finding might be that the management students have seen minutes as helpful in ensuring projects in the workplace are kept on schedule and are used to minutes being kept. Some business students (31%) found the keeping of individual logs useful to recognize the extent of their contribution, but more (42%) disagreed. Training in the recording of minutes and log books may help business students improve their skills and learn more from using these methods.

27.8   Judgment of the students' assessment process

A number of difficulties can be identified with student peer assessment :

1.   Student loyalty

Evidence from interviews reveals that unless students are really aggrieved at the way in which another member(s) of their assignment group has not contributed to the work in the same proportion as they perceive themselves to have contributed, student loyalty will usually outweigh individual desire to have their own individual efforts recognized and duly rewarded by amendment to their marks. Students do not wish to be perceived as someone who has 'split' upon other(s) in the group to the tutor and 'labelled' as such.

2. Confidentiality

During the interviews, three students reported they would have preferred to have given their views confidentially to the tutor rather than holding a group meeting to allocate marks. There are two issues here: one of avoiding confrontation and unpleasantness with a group member(s), and secondly of avoiding student responsibility for amendment to marks. These issues are linked with (1) above.

3. Practical difficulties in completion of the peer assessment form.

Some students were found to be unclear and asked for clarification on the following points.

(a) Weighting of the peer assessed mark in relation to the assignment.

(b) Range of marks that could be used.

(c) Some students did not like the negative association of awarding minus points to other group members.

In the light of these comments, the author has modified the peer assessment form in an attempt to make it more clear (see Appendix 27.C).

27.9   Benefits of the peer assessment process

There is evidence from both the questionnaires and interview data that many of the students associate the idea of fairness and equity with peer assessment. Fifteen respondents used the word 'fairness' on the questionnaires, with many elaborating on this during the interview. Some positive student comments regarding peer assessment in this regard are given below:

> Peer assessment makes people contribute — we all made sure we did our fair share!

> At first I thought — bit of a bind. There had been no problem before, everyone contributed equally — but actually I was really glad that peer assessment was being used when I was writing the report !

> I'd like to see peer assessment on all modules as part of the course work. It would then be accepted — you know, not seen as telling tales. The more people do, the more they're prepared to do.

> My first thoughts were, unfamiliar — can't do that! A model of how to complete the form would be useful.

> Makes people take responsibility for their input. They realise they can't just free ride!

> Parallels the real world of work.

> Should be introduced at induction, perhaps with an exercise before to practice.

> There should be a standardised form for the Faculty which is widely available, so everyone's aware of it and can use it if necessary.

27.10   Negative comments

Not everyone was in favour. Other comments included :

> Waste of time!
>
> Should not be compulsory — individuals should complain to their tutor if they are dissatisfied with other(s) contribution.
>
> Should be completely confidential because of bad feeling and later conflict.
>
> It is not the job of the student to mark others. The tutor should do this. There should be more individual work rather than peer assessment.

27.11   Conclusions

Although more research is necessary with a larger sample of students to see if similar results are found and for further statistical analysis to be employed, the evidence to date suggests that peer assessment can be a useful tool, both in (1) encouraging students to contribute to group work, and (2) contributing to their perception of equity and fairness, lessening the desire for social loafing. The evidence to date further suggests that peer assessment properly introduced and employed as part of a coherent assessment strategy can contribute to improving students as learners in small groups.

27.12   Recommendations

1. The concept of peer assessment needs to be taken on board by the Faculty/Department, so that it becomes accepted by both staff and students as a normal part of the assessment process where appropriate.

2. Introduce peer assessment at induction with a simple exercise as part of a general introduction to working in groups.

3. An oral explanation of the aim of using peer assessment should be given, together with an example of a completed peer assessment form.

4. Criterion categories need to have face validity for the students in relation to the learning objectives and content of the exercise.

5. Method of completion of the peer appraisal form needs to be clearly explained, together with the mode and date of submission.

6. The issue of 'confidentiality 'needs to be considered.

7. Consideration should also be given to the use of log books and the taking of minutes of meetings, in addition to peer assessment, as aids to individual feedback and motivation. If a decision is made to include such aids, skills training in these areas should be provided.

8. Whether students should be given the option to use the form should be considered by tutors

9. Peer assessment need not be used in every module nor on every group assignment, but should be employed as part of a coherent, overall assessment strategy.

27.13 References

Adams, J.S. (1965) Inequity in social exchange. In L. Berkowitz (ed.), *Advances in Experimental Social Psychology*, 2, New York: Academic Press, 267—99.

Garland, D.Y. (1996) Using research to improve student learning in small groups. In G. Gibbs (ed.), *Improving Student Learning: Using Research to Improve Student Learning*, Oxford: OCSD, Oxford Brookes University.

Gibbs, G. (1995) *Learning in Teams: A Tutor Guide*, Oxford: OCSD, Oxford Brookes University.

Harkins, S. and Jackson, J. (1985) The role of evaluation in eliminating social loafing, *Personality and Social Psychology Bulletin*, 11, 457—65.

Kerr, N.L. (1983) Motivation losses in small groups: a social dilemma analysis, *Journal of Personality and Social Psychology*, 45, 819—828.

Kerr, N.L. and Bruun, S.E. (1981) Ringelmann revisited: alternative explanations for the social loafing effect, *Personality and Social Psychology Bulletin*, 7, 224—31.

Kravitz, D.A. and Martin, B. (1986) Ringelmann rediscovered: the original article, *Journal of Personality and Social Psychology*, 50, 936—41.

Latane, B., Williams, K.D. and Harkins, S. (1979) Many hands make light the work: the causes and consequences of social loafing, *Journal of Personality and Social Psychology*, 37, 822—32.

Steiner, I. (1972) *Group Processes and Productivity*, San Diego, CA: Academic Press.

West, M.A. (1994) *Effective Teamwork*, London: British Psychological Society and Routledge.

Appendix 27.A

Women in the Business World (BUS 492)

Assessment 1:	Tutor Mark for Group Project	30%	(Oral presentation & written report)
	Individual Mark	20%	(Peer assessment)
		50%	of total module mark

Group Project:

Student Name:

Please state your individual contribution to the group.

For each group member in turn, discuss and note their *relative* contribution to the completion of each component of the group project. Did they contribute above or below average within the group? You can't all have contributed above average, so make sure your individual marks average the same as the group mark.

Extent of Individual Contribution:

Component of group project	*Well below average*	*Below average*	*Average*	*Above average*	*Well above average*
Ideas for project	-2	-1	0	+1	+2
Collection of data	-2	-1	0	+1	+2
Analysis of data	-2	-1	0	+1	+2
Writing of report	-2	-1	0	+1	+2
Oral presentation	-2	-1	0	+1	+2

Tutor mark for group: ....

Sum of moderation mark (range -10%:+10%): ....

Individual mark: ....

Signatures of group members:

....

....

Appendix 27.A

People & Organisations

Assessment 1: Tutor Mark for Group 30%

Individual Mark 20%

‾‾‾‾

50%

Group Project:

Student Name:

Please state your individual contribution to the group.

For each group member in turn, discuss and note their *relative* contribution to the completion of each component of the group project. Did they contribute above or below average within the group? You can't all have contributed above average, so make sure your individual marks average the same as the group mark.

Extent of Individual Contribution:

Component of group project	*Well below average*	*Below average*	*Average*	*Above average*	*Well above average*
Group Learning Contract	-2	-1	0	+1	+2
Research of reading material	-2	-1	0	+1	+2
Contribution to organisational/personal data	-2	-1	0	+1	+2
Integration of theoretical/practical data	-2	-1	0	+1	+2
Writing of report	-2	-1	0	+1	+2

Tutor mark for group: ....

Sum of moderation mark (range -10%:+10%): ....

Individual mark: ....

Signatures of group members: ....

....

....

Appendix 27.B

Results from Peer Assessment Questionnaires

	Business students %					Management students %				
1 = strongly agree, through to 5 = strongly disagree, with 3 being neutral	1	2	3	4	5	1	2	3	4	5

Describe your reactions to the following statements regarding peer assessment

• Fairer assessment method than one mark for all group members regardless of individual contribution	21	31	26	13	8	31	31	19	12	6
• Helped to identify strengths of individual members	10	42	23	21	2	17	47	23	12	-
• Keeping minutes of meetings helped to keep the group on schedule	2	16	16	34	31	12	35	30	12	12
• Encouraged everyone to participate, workload shared	18	34	16	18	13	35	41	12	-	12
• Keeping individual logs helped me to recognise the extent of my contribution	10	21	26	26	16	6	17	65	6	6

Which of the following operational difficulties did you experience with peer assessment?

• Inappropriate categories of performance used	8	18	42	26	5	6	35	29	29	-
• Inappropriate rating scale used	21	26	34	16	2	-	12	65	23	-
• Keeping minutes of meetings was excessively time consuming	26	34	23	8	8	6	23	29	29	12
• Keeping an individual log was excessively time consuming	16	23	37	16	8	6	12	64	18	-
• It was difficult to arrange meetings so all group members could attend	18	31	18	26	5	53	23	-	23	-

Did your group differentiate between members with regard to the overall group mark?

• Seemed appropriate to give more marks to those who contributed more towards the project	57	28	14	-	-	54	27	18	-	-
• One/more than one group member did not participate as fully as they might have done	71	14	14	-	-	27	27	18	9	18
• Differentiation makes little difference to overall individual mark for the project	14	14	43	14	14	-	18	54	9	18
• Differentiation makes little difference to overall individual mark for the module	14	14	57	-	14	18	27	36	18	-

Why did you not differentiate marks?

• We all worked together, with similar amounts of effort, we all deserved the same mark	80	6	3	-	9	62	12	12	12	-
• Didn't want to upset other group members by haggling over marks	19	9	38	3	29	12	37	-	-	50
• Differentiation makes little difference to overall individual mark for the project	6	20	43	20	10	14	14	43	14	14
• Differentiation makes little difference to overall individual mark for the module	6	16	48	19	9	14	28	28	14	14
• It is the lecturer's responsibility to allocate marks, not the students	19	29	22	19	9	-	-	-	75	12	12

Appendix 27.C
Human Behaviour in Organisations (BUS 126)

		Module weighting	
Assessment 1:	Tutor Mark for Group Project	20%	(Written report)
	Individual Mark	10%	(Peer assessment)
		30%	of total module mark

Group Project:
Student Name:

Please state your individual contribution to the group (may be continued on reverse side).

For each group member in turn, discuss and note their *relative* rather than *absolute* contribution to the completion of each component of the group project. Did they contribute above or below average within the group? You can't all have contributed above average, so make sure your individual marks average the same as the group mark.

Extent of Individual Contribution:

Component of group project	Well below average	Below average	Average	Above average	Well above average
Developing learning contract	-2	-1	0	+1	+2
Ideas for case study	-2	-1	0	+1	+2
Collection of information	-2	-1	0	+1	+2
Analysis of information	-2	-1	0	+1	+2
Writing of report	-2	-1	0	+1	+2

Tutor mark for group: ....

Sum of moderation mark (**range -10%:+10%**):   ....

Individual mark: ....   ← (sum of mod.mark)

Signatures of group members:

....

....

....

28 Encouraging students' academic 'engagement' to promote lifelong learning

Peter Radloff

Behavioural Health Science, Curtin University of Technology

28.1　Overview

Successful learning is determined by many factors, with in-class activities contributing only about a quarter of the total variance. But universities focus on summative student ratings of teaching rather than on whether 'value adding' has occurred, or if lifelong learning has been encouraged. Improving instruction is a laudable aim, but it requires formative approaches and a supportive institutional environment. However excellent the teaching may be, limiting one's commitment to teaching, without a focus on student learning, will yield only small gains in outcome, since three-quarters of the variance would remain unaddressed. Three questions need to be addressed. First, do current evaluation of teaching tools have a role in supporting students' development of appropriate skills for lifelong learning? Second, does the way they are currently being used support and promote a collegial learning environment? And third, can strategies be devised to provide individualised feedback on teaching and learning to promote the acquisition of positive attitudes to lifelong learning?

28.2　Introduction

The increases in numbers, and in the diversity of students coming to universities following the Australian Federal government's 'free university education' policy from 1973 necessitated a too rapid increase in staff numbers. And no-one seemed to ponder whether the then existing educational approach was appropriate even for 'elite' students who were attending universities before the expansion. This highly selected cohort could probably do well without help from academics, so almost no value adding may have been occurring in those 'good old days'. Instead of doing some analysis of what was going on, the newly appointed staff were left to emulate what had been done up till then, and a chorus of 'more means worse' was heard. More *students*, it was argued, would mean that the less able would be entering university and would cause problems. Instead of considering how to manage the larger number and wider variety of students, it was 'blame the student, the schools, the society' time. One message notable for its absence was that more means worse applies also, and perhaps more appropriately, to staff. But problem-solving or innovation was forgotten once expansion started. There was more funding, but much of it was also used to increase the number and diversity of administrative middle managers, while instructors soon found themselves treated to a phased in, part-time, or contract based supplementation of staff to meet seemingly short-term needs, which ended up being permanent. During the time of plenty, no-one was too concerned, but now that the lean years have arrived, the pain may not be doled out appropriately.

The point has been made for California by Gumport and Pusser's (1995) analysis of 25 years of data of the University of California during a time which covers years of plenty, and the more recent lean years of retrenchment and difficulty. Their situation involved an expansion where proportionally more growth of administrative positions and structures occurred than seemed warranted at the time, and their current retrenchment is aimed, in many cases, at the reduction of academic resources, with administrative resources being conserved. Gumport and Pusser (1995) put it thus: 'as the context has changed, one unanticipated consequence of administrative growth may be that administrative units have become, not only managers and co-ordinators of the educational enterprise, but consumers of significant core resources as well'.

The dissatisfaction, anger and sometimes helplessness being experienced in Australia may be, in part, due to the feeling that it is precisely the failure of administrators to manage core functions both during the earlier growth and the later decline, which lies at the heart of the current malaise. If one were to take the quality agenda seriously, the focus should move to establishing what the students, academics and administrative staff actually needed. 'Managing upwards' (Gower, 1994) would lead to a determination as to what essential functions had to be preserved. A layer of middle management may be found redundant to requirements. In a real sense, 'retrenchment is reform', but quality upwards management seems needed to determine what gets done.

But the journey may not be easy. Guskin (1994) has presented a 'case study' of Antioch University where it became necessary to close the existing administration and start up a completely new one for costs to be brought under control and for essential structural changes to be introduced, and for these changes to be maintained, i.e. to survive. His story provides a very helpful message from the really tough reality of working for change, and the even tougher task of having whatever changes are made survive into the future. He notes the paradox 'where hierarchy was needed to produce collaboration' and where 'a centralized decision was required to decentralize; and the decentralization of the university administrative structure led to the increased integration of the university' (Gusking, 1994, p. 29). But for now we will leave the bitter realities of administrative resilience, and return to students and their need to be noticed and listened to.

Whenever students have reacted or objected to their situation, their protests were either not heard, or not taken seriously. Yet, in retrospect, students in the 1960s were right, and more attention should have been given to their concerns then. And we need to listen more carefully now. Overcrowding is one problem voiced here and internationally. Lack of contact with staff, another. 'Many undergraduate students are increasingly dissatisfied', and 'Big Universities seek smaller classes, more contact with Professors' are headlines found in the Chronicle of Higher Education in early 1991 (Collison, 1991). 'I am graduating from one of the best economics departments in the country and I've never had a Professor. I don't know what I've been missing' – a quote from the same coverage.

In the United States one big issue for students involves discretionary time where prestigious staff (i.e. those with a good research background) are hired not just with a good salary but with the promise of time off (off teaching that is) so that they can spend more time on research or other activities. The staff unions pursue this discretionary time quite vigorously, attempting to ensure benefits obtained by the few will flow to all staff. The student unions have opposed this since there is a direct link to fees. If staff salaries increase, students have to pay more. Does this relationship, although partly hidden, apply also in Australia? On the surface a mutual admiration society seems to apply to academic staff and student unions, but in reality there is no mutuality of support, and students are kept well away from any effective role or influence in this sphere, as well as being neutralized and prevented from having any real influence over general university administration. This is one of the most serious mistakes in the administrative arrangements of most universities in Australia. The enormous enthusiasm and talent of this cohort of gifted students is being frittered away.

In Australia, the AVCC (Australian Vice-Chancellors Committee) has recognized the importance of students within the University community, and has moved to have a National Code of Ethics adopted to protect students. This is a worthy aim, but is this tactic appropriate? Academics are the group being approached to attempt to arrange for students to be treated in a more ethical manner! It would seem more appropriate to arrange for students to be empowered to operate within universities in their own interests, by having a better appreciation of their own role. They need social and negotiation skills training to be available, and to experience a supportive context which would enable them to contribute to the administration of the university. A mutual recognition of their rights and responsibilities would be the result, and the students and university community generally would both benefit. Having students integrated into the university administrative structure is what I wish to argue for, and to do this in a way which will be of benefit. But first we should examine areas of university functioning to see why such a move could benefit universities. Since so much reforming zeal has gone towards teaching, its assessment, improvement, and its role in learning, we will do that last. Instead we will start with the physical (spatial and temporal) environment.

28.3   The physical environment

University expansion has meant more staff and students, but also more buildings, cars and car parks. Where a single building addition can destroy a campus's atmosphere, and affect the whole community, we are having many buildings, and seeing the gutting and refurbishment of existing facilities. An analysis of campus architectural design by Griffith (1994) emphasizes that the preservation of open space is vital to the maintenance of a quality university environment and thus a campus must arrange for spaces between the buildings to be preserved, so that the site can function well, and reflect the image, mission and goals of the university. One can call for the 'unstuffing of the curriculum', and there are now many joining in this important process. But there are far fewer who are proposing unstuffing university sites. The tendency is to welcome additions, and to interpret them as necessary progress, and not to call for surveys of university 'plant and facilities'.

The increasing importance given to recreation and exercise also reminds one that the original academy supported, and may even have been designed around, peripatetic instruction. Now that we can document the value of exercise not just for relaxation, reflection, endorphin release and the maintenance and enhancement of health and wellness, we can argue for vistas not just to add to the aesthetic enjoyment experienced on journeys through the campus, but also because it will encourage many and regular future journeys. Also important is the linking of the campus to the surrounding community. Walking and cycling paths need to relate the university to the suburbs, or city, to embrace the whole community, develop neighbourliness supporting an awareness, which because of good design, will also counter vandalism, and crimes against persons. To my knowledge, environmental psychologists have not attended to the requirements of campus design. But it does seem to be essential.

What about the buildings themselves as instructional spaces? Architects and designers refer to building codes to arrive at their allocation of floor space to office and teaching areas, common areas, passage and access spaces. In following formulae they may not meet the real needs of different academic areas. The 10 metres of office shelving, room for three *foolscap* filing cabinets (Australia went metric 34 years ago, and four A4 units would fit the same space), a desk, and at most two chairs to accommodate visitors, may not be universally suited to all areas. And teaching spaces, designed according to historically based criteria, may no longer be suitable for their purpose. Some of these issues have been addressed by Babey (1991) and by Owu (1991) in his survey of classroom allocation and use at MIT. Owu's conclusion was that too few small teaching spaces, and too many large lecture halls (which covered 7 per cent of course hours taught but had 31 per cent of availability) were provided. Lecture halls also had inadequately maintained audio-visual technology. At MIT upgrading one lecture room and installing the latest technology reduced seat numbers, but increased comfort, and led to this space being in continuous high demand when it had formerly been shunned. Regular surveys, including questions included in teaching evaluation forms, would locate unsuitable teaching facilities quite easily. A staff survey of large lecture theatres was carried out at Curtin University in 1994. The results allowed a number of problems which needed to be remedied, and some design issues to be addressed, and for all the main large lecturing spaces to be equipped with basic audio-visual and computer based teaching aids. It would be very useful, however, also to have students' views on teaching spaces, but obtaining such information is even less common than having academic input into the design.

Should one wish to use a large lecture space to support punctuated lectures, or even buzz and pyramid groups, an immediate problem becomes evident. Most of these spaces are designed to have sound travel one way – from the front to the furthest corners. They are designed so that one cannot hear anyone speaking across the space, or from the rear. So carrying out what higher education instructional experts are recommending is not feasible because the physical space does not support it.

Students have complained that other facilities for meetings or discussion are not available even though these are very important and would support their academic development. Classrooms may be overcrowded and in continuous use but 'common rooms remain quite uncommon', as Palmer (1992) points out. Such spaces are often absent from university building codes, even though they may be most important to foster student support in the teaching areas. Of course provision of such spaces assumes that time is available for their use by students (and staff). This may not be the case.

28.4   The temporal environment

The campus plan may be important, but the timetable probably exerts more influence on the quality of teaching and learning. Green spaces, gardens, trees and vistas between buildings are important, but gaps in the timetable may be vital. A community of learning has to have occasions available for social, and serious discussion outside the classroom. So timetable scheduling should not fill all available time. There must be spaces between classes. Forty-five minute classes are preferable to 50-minute ones, and two separate 45-minute periods better than a two-hour lecture. These are obvious changes, and would be seen as essential to anyone with the slightest understanding of learning and memory – that the real work goes on during the gaps between supposedly 'active' learning. There also has to be time for a community to meet for lunch or tea. This can only happen if the university recognizes the importance of such social occasions. If occasions are provided by having a common hour for lunch through the week, this becomes 'prime time' and it becomes possible for a range of activities to be taken up by students and staff.

Collison (1990) points out that many colleges and universities are now encouraging students to get involved in outside activities, and are considering out of class time as very important to enable better integration into the community, to enhance academic performance, and to increase completion rates. But how may this be achieved so as to have students actively engaged and involved, while yet contributing also to the administrative well-being of the institution? Peterson (1994) finds it puzzling that organizations devoted to fostering student learning pay no attention to which components of their practices actually do promote learning. Almost no research examines the relationship between organizational variables and learning outcomes treated as dependent variables. Correlations between, for example, research climates and outcomes, are important but how about documenting what forms of administrative structures promote learning? Or whether a common room, or lunch or tea break, enhances completion and continuation rates. Students are important, and what they have to say, and how they can inform the university of their needs, has to be addressed.

So the quality initiative should assign *students* a foundational role in setting and supporting the mission and purposes of the institution. They and the academics need to be supported to plan for the present and future health of universities. Is it possible, through appropriate organizational change to encourage a stable and enduring influence from students. During the 1960s one was told almost continuously that students were transients and could not really be expected to make an enduring contribution to the functioning of universities. This is based on a mistaken premiss. We are not talking about individual students on their own. Through appropriate structures one can ensure continuity across student cohorts. Working groups, or committees, provided they are linked to the really important components of an institution, can guarantee continuity. What has to be done is to arrange for student activity to be directed towards academic and achievement goals. A more general political activity can still go on, to the overall benefit of students and the community, but at present there is no real continuing input from students into the academic life of universities. A possible means to promote academic input from students could direct their activity in a way which could benefit their course work. How could one recruit students to contribute to their own and the institutions benefit

28.5 How could students be recruited into the quality improvement agenda?

Currently Australian universities have Student Representative Councils, sometimes called Guild Councils, which are elected from the student body as a whole. They in turn nominate or appoint a range of other representatives without further elections taking place. The resultant hierarchy resembles, in terms of its ambience, the main university administrative body, the Council. The Student Council would remain, but devolution of the academic representatives would allow each department, for example, to have each course (unit) with a representative from each of the instructional areas involved. Each tutorial, laboratory, or clinical unit of instruction would have a representative elected, and they in turn, as a departmental committee, would nominate two departmental (school) members to serve on a faculty (divisional) committee. The representatives from all the faculties (divisions) would constitute the Student *Senate* (Guild Senate) and would elect a chairperson and a deputy both to be on the Student Representative Council (Guild). This structure would replace the two (or more) centrally appointed, or co-opted, representatives from each faculty (division).

This approach could yield an academically relevant representative structure empowered to work with academic staff, with the departmental and faculty structures, and through representation on general university committees, could contribute to the university generally. Adopting such an administrative structure would empower students to make a significant contribution, since their perspective would enhance the administrative process in a way to benefit its academic mission. It is likely also to benefit the general organizational climate of the institution. This arrangement would also be in line with quality principles since the (numerically) largest group would be contributing to its own advancement.

We need to make such changes in order to have students experience the university in the same way faculty were found by Rice and Austin (1990) to respond to high morale colleges where participative leadership, a flat administrative structure, shared authority to empower others, respect and a sense of trust existed, and where decisions were, and hopefully are still, taken in open fora. As a result, faculty felt that the institution is theirs. So too would students if treated in a similar fashion, within a structure that supported such processes. Under such conditions student involvement and engagement is supported, and it is these variables which have been demonstrated to be vital to student success. Such strategies may also yield a more committed alumni cohort interested in advancing their alma mater in more material ways.

28.6   The teaching initiative

'Teaching better with less' is perhaps an apt summary of the last decade, although the daily reality of the phrase is to be found in the lack of support, and increased isolation of academic instructors. There is no doubt that teaching quality has improved, and congratulations are due almost universally, including to HERDSA (Higher Education and Research Development Society of Australasia) for their *Checklist on Valuing Teaching* and *Challenging Conceptions of Teaching: Some Prompts for Good Practice*. On the other hand, the attention to teaching has meant increasing stress levels among staff. Things have become too serious. All the emphasis upon improved techniques, classroom assessment, group process, co-operative and collaborative learning fails to recognize the tensions already present, the prevailing student culture, and above all, whether the context can support the learning structures being promoted. The pressure is fully on staff who are expected to write and produce and perform in each separate act of a production lasting a whole semester. The present context is suggesting that in-class activities are crucial – the evidence shows this view to be mistaken.

There is at present a climate which accepts that things can be improved, but should teaching and instructors be the main target? Duffy and Jones (1995) have written an engaging book in which they spell out many of the imponderables in teaching, making very clear their point that there are so many vital, yet seemingly almost unnoticeable factors playing a role in determining a successful outcome for a course, that only eternal vigilance would have any hope of tracking down what needs to be done, left undone, or done differently. Their point is that it is a very complex process, and that it needs to embrace the total learning environment, and that one can still end up ignorant as to the factors operating!

The assumption that teaching staff can contribute a great deal to the success or failure of students is also questionable. Riesman (1971) quotes America's Coleman report to support his statement that 'the home and the street' are dominant influences upon success in the high-school system. We can answer the question for tertiary education authoritatively following the research done by Pascarella and Terenzini (1991), who report on twenty years of data and by Astin (1993) who started accumulating data from the early Sixties. Astin emphasizes the importance of involvement, of activity, of joining in, since this supports academic and general development. His other specific finding is that the peer group (and its values, self-concept and socio-economic status) is the *single most important contributor to a student's development*. Faculty research orientation, on the other hand, has a negative influence on outcomes, while faculty student orientation has positive effects. Generally a research orientation in a department or institution as a whole, negatively weights student outcome variables. This finding goes against Lowe's (1994) suggestion that strengthening the research component of universities will necessarily improve teaching and learning. Both teaching, *as well as* research excellence, need to be separately pursued: exceptional individuals combine excellence in both spheres, but each component needs to be valued, each supported, and each required of candidates for appointment to (academic) teaching positions.

To underline this point, Terenzini and Pascarella (1994) have as one of their myths about tertiary teaching: 'The good teachers are good researchers.' They quote Feldman (1987) who carried out a meta-analysis of 40 studies relating research productivity to student assessments of instructional effectiveness. The correlations ranged between 0.10 and 0.16 with an average of 0.12, so that at *best*, less than 2 per cent of the variance is accounted for by research productivity, *and over 98 per cent by other factors*. This work has been taken further by Volkwein and Carbone (1994) using more developed measures of research climate, student outcome and evaluation of instruction. They conclude that 'research variables are not significantly correlated with the teaching variables, neither individually nor collectively' with correlations ranging between -0.22 and 0.17. This study of over 600 students thus shows that teaching and research climates are independent. The finding neutralizes the polemicists on both sides of the research-teaching controversy. We need to pay greater attention to the 98%: those other influences which do make a difference, such as the peer group and the overall climate of intellectual inquiry within a university.

28.7 Student evaluation of instruction

The work of Astin (1993) and of Terenzine and Pascarella (1994) and Pascarella and Terenzine (1991) together with other papers from these authors suggests that in class activities contribute about 25 per cent, and out-of-class activities the other 75 per cent of the variance of achievement, or success. It is the engagement of students in the activities of the peer group, involvement in and with other students across subject and year differences, and also in on-campus employment (Wilkie, 1994) that promotes success. It is only when the number of hours of work becomes too great that performance suffers. This has been explored by Marchese (1996) who while pointing to the absolute need for students to work in order for them to remain in university, deplores the fact that 'Gone everywhere, it seems, is the old understanding that college takes three hours outside class for every one in.' When students have outside work loads or 20 or 30 hours, it seriously compromises their ability to benefit from, and to contribute to, their courses.

28.8 Student evaluation of teaching

There is rarely any attempt to examine the affective or feeling side of teaching and learning. It is obviously important and, in a sense, all teachers use therapeutic techniques, in the context of their discipline, in order to enable students to cope with the demands of the material. The issue is how to 'trap' students into spending the same level of energy, the same time, on achieving excellence in an advanced aspect of their major, as they may dedicate to developing a new interactive visual basic, object orientated computer game program. Should we be more concerned with the affective side of teaching and learning? Obviously, the answer is yes. There are numerous studies to show this to be true, such as McLeod's (1992) research on affect in mathematics. Centra (1987) would be sympathetic to this view, since he wishes evaluation to be inclusive and not to be strictly by numbers. But the real problem with evaluation measures may be that they are vaganotic, i.e. one measures something associated with a descriptive phrase, and then on giving it to students, finds that some lecturers have more of it than others. But this is an evaluative noun, and not related to any real theory of instruction, nor tied to effectiveness. If one assumes an additive model for learning and instruction, then one has to use pre-tests, and find out how much has been added by a particular course. This has not yet been done.

Ramsden (1991, p. 129) has produced the Course Experience Questionnaire (CEQ) which offers 'a reliable verifiable and useful means of determining the perceived teaching quality of academic units in systems of higher education'. The CEQ has been used nationally in Australia so that there are databases available of all students across probably, most universities. The problem is that the CEQ remains a preference scale which is not tied in to value added, or even to examination performance. The aim is not to denigrate attempts to use measures of this type since they are useful and provide one source of information about teaching. However, they may not have as much to say about learning. In most applications the CEQ, or alternative, is not able to be related to student performance over the year. Were this to be done, the effect of different aspects upon performance would be useful indeed. I have just one example where this was the case. In a unit (course) with six separate workshops, each with about 16 students, one of the three tutors had students achieving consistently lower marks over the semester than the other two. Examining the more detailed feedback forms used revealed that a number of students commented on problems with feedback. Enquiries soon revealed that this instructor kept assessments for presentations for a week, whereas the other two handed them back immediately. This appeared to be the single most important difference, confirming the role of feedback in learning. It had a large effect size, and it was easily remedied so the differences should disappear. This is an example of evidence based teaching and done more systematically, should probably be what is aimed at for improving instruction (learning) and staff development.

There is one further difficulty about relying on the CEQ. It seems to be unstable across courses, and produces different factor patterns where different forms of teachings are in use so that scoring should be specific to each course! These very preliminary observations need to be followed up since they could prove of some importance.

If we wish to promote lifelong learning, we first must address the issues raised in this chapter, namely the disproportionate power wielded by the administration in the life of the university; the apparent disregard for those research studies which clearly link the environment; physical, temporal and social to student engagement and learning outcomes; and the current attempts to improve the quality of teaching through the use of what could be insuffiently targeted, or inappropriate ways of measuring student satisfaction while neglecting value adding. Instead of viewing students, as some do, as 'the problem' it would be better to see them as part of the solution.

28.9 References

Astin, A. W. (1993) *What Matters in College: Four Critical Years Revisited*, San Francisco, CA: Jossey Bass.

Babey, E.R. (1991) The classroom: physical environments that enhance teaching and learning. Paper presented at the *Annual Meeting of the American Association for Higher Education*, Washington, DC, 26 March.

Centra, J.A. (1987) Formative and summative evaluation: parody or paradox? In L.A. Aleamoni (ed.), *Techniques for Evaluating and Improving Instruction*, San Francisco, CA: Jossey Bass, 47–55.

Coates, J. (1994) *Managing Upwards*, Aldershot: Gower.

Collison, M.N-K. (1990) Many colleges begin to pay attention to the time their students spend outside the classroom, *Chronicle of Higher Education*, 36(28), 28 Mar., A37.

Collison, M.N-K. (1991) Big universities seek smaller classes, more contact with professors, *Chronicle of Higher Education*, 37(1), 9 Jan., A37.

Davis, T.M. and Murrell, P.H. (1993) Turning teaching into learning: the role of student responsibility in the collegiate experience, *ASHE-ERIC Higher Education Report*, No. 8, Association for the Study of Higher Education, Washington, DC.

Duffy, D.K. and Jones, J.W. (1995) *Teaching within the Rhythms of the Semester*, San Francisco, CA: Jossey-Bass.

Griffith, J. C. (1994) Open space preservation: an imperative for quality campus environments, *Journal of Higher Education*, 65(6).

Gumport, P.J. and Pusser, B. (1995) A case of bureaucratic accretion: context and consequences, *Journal of Higher Education*, 66(5).

Guskin, A.E. (1994) Reducing the costs and enhancing student learning: the university challenge of the 1990s. Part I: Restructuring the administration, *Change*, July/Aug., 23–9.

Owu, M.K. (1991) The classroom: physical environments that enhance teaching and learning. Paper presented to the *AAHE 1991 National Conference on Higher Education*, 26 Mar., Washington, DC.

Palmer, M. (1992) Common rooms remain quite uncommon, *Grok*, 19 Aug.

Pascarella, E.T. and Terenzini, P.T. (1991) *How College Affects Students: Findings and Insights from Twenty Years of Research*, Jossey Bass, San Francisco, CA.

Peterson, M.W. (1988) The organizational environment for student learning. In J.S. Stark and I.A. Metz (eds), *Teaching and Learning through Research: New Directions for Institutional Research*, no. 57, San Francisco, CA: Jossey-Bass.

Riesman, D. (1971) Notes on educational reform, *The Journal of General Education*, 23, (2), 81–110.

Rice, R.E. and Austin, A.E. (1990) Organizational impacts on faculty morale and motivation to teach. In P. Seldin (ed.), *How Administrators Can Improve Teaching: Moving from Talk to Action in Higher Education*, San Francisco, CA: Oxford.

Terenzini, P.T. and Pascarella, E.T. (1994) Living with myths: undergraduate education in America, *Change*, Jan./Feb., 28–32.

Volkwein, J.F. and Carbone, D.A. (1994) The impact of departmental research and teaching climates on undergraduate growth and satisfaction, *Journal of Higher Education*, 65(2) 147–67.

29 Dilemmas in using student feedback to improve tutoring at a distance

Robert Fox, Anna Boyd and Allan Herrmann
Teaching Learning Group, Curtin University

29.1 Overview

The current emphasis on quality assurance across all universities has lead to the widespread use of questionnaires asking students for feedback on various aspects of teaching effectiveness. Marsh and Roche confirm the view that many universities are increasingly relying on students' evaluations of teaching effectiveness as feedback to lecturers, in the hope that information obtained will lead to improvements in tutoring and assessment, student course selection and research on teaching and learning (1992, p. 278). In institutions with a distance education profile, questionnaires on teaching effectiveness are provided alongside, or included in, questionnaires on distance study materials and management and administrative support services.

In this chapter, evaluating distance teaching and learning is considered problematic in the sense that much of the distance 'teaching' is developed well before individual students are known and that the 'teaching' is embedded in the study materials. Secondly, staff who develop the teaching materials may not be teaching the unit. And further, those teaching may not be the same as the staff who are marking the assignments. There may be more than one tutor and more than one marker per unit and individual staff roles within the teaching of one unit may not be clear. Thirdly, if the study materials were mailed late or the materials were below par, the students' responses may not truly reflect the quality of the tutor's performance. Therefore distance education should be seen as a method of mediated teaching and learning that requires particular and careful evaluation processes and instruments; as Cresswell and Hobson state: 'with distance education, problems are compounded because there is less opportunity for discussion to clear up possible misunderstandings' (1996).

This chapter highlights the dilemmas and complexities created in using standardized feedback questionnaires used to improve tutoring to distance students and outlines some of the difficulties created in the teaching and learning environments where students never meet face-to-face with their tutors.

29.2 Introduction

Distance education and open learning is under pressure from a wide number of sources to expand and diversify, at the same time as shaking off the image of being the 'poor-cousin' to face-to-face teaching (Marsden, 1996; Chambers, 1995). With cuts in funding for higher and further education, university hierarchy, business managers and some staff developers, are advocating the concept of 'teaching better with less' (Fox and Radloff, 1997). In addition, the advent of 'user-pays' education means there is a demand from the clients/students themselves for the production of quality courseware that is well administered and well taught. If an institution cannot cater to specific needs, students may go elsewhere. It is essential, therefore, that distance education institutions provide courses of quality and more importantly, that they provide evidence that they are doing so (Chambers, 1995; Bates, 1997). This evidence can be provided through various evaluations of course materials, teaching, student support and administrative procedures.

Traditional evaluation in distance education revolved around simple data gathering using instruments and variables easy to manage in the face of large numbers, and the evaluations tended to be managed by those external to the course, being devised, administered and interpreted by other than the authors and/or tutors (Altrichter *et al.*, 1991). In deference to the 'mass market' of distance education, postal surveys have been widely used as a form of basic quality control (Altrichter *et al.*, 1991). This necessity of coping with large numbers of students is probably more of an issue in the large open universities of the UK, India and Asia compared with institutions in Australia although this same mentality still remains here. Altrichter notes that the indiscriminate use of postal surveys can 'lead to a hegemony of survey methods, in the sense that the data collection procedures established within an organization can be used repeatedly in a somewhat uncritical manner' (Altrichter *et al.*, 1991, p 9). There needs to be illuminative evaluation and phenomenological research to gain a holistic view of how and why students study, and students need to be given the opportunity to express their opinions and perceptions about their course material and their teaching (Altrichter *et al.*, 1991; Chambers, 1995).

One of the major difficulties in distance education evaluation is determining who is the 'teacher' and what constitutes the 'teaching' (Altrichter *et al.*, 1991). In some way, the writer of the course material, the editor or instructional designer, the graphic artist, the tutor and the support staff may all influence how a student perceives and evaluates a particular course (Marsden, 1996). Despite these difficulties, a recent survey of distance education students at the University of Southern Queensland found that 95 per cent of students believed it was important to evaluate distance education courses, although ironically only 29 per cent of this same group had ever returned an evaluation form (Jegede *et al.*, 1995) – an issue that we have also raised in an earlier paper (Boyd *et al.*, 1996). Another difficulty arises in the design of the evaluation forms themselves. In a survey assessing a MBA programme delivered through distance education, Cook and Armstrong (1995) found that up to 72 per cent of the students responded to questions about lectures and lecturing with an answer of 'not applicable', even though they attended weekend schools and were provided with audiotaped lectures. This indicates that internal evaluations cannot simply be adopted for distance education students, but that they must be specifically designed, developed and administered for a particular purpose, be it the evaluation of distance education materials, teaching or systems.

29.3 Distance Education Students' Unit Evaluation or DESUE

Since 1980, teaching staff at Curtin have had access to the Student Appraisal of Teaching or SAT instrument, designed to provide diagnostic feedback that will be useful for the improvement of teaching and to measure teaching effectiveness to be used in administrative decision-making – in the latter case, to support applications for promotion and incremental progression. The use of SAT has always been voluntary and, apart from its use for promotion and incremental progression, it is confidential. SAT has, however, only been available for use with on-campus classes and with the growing number of distance courses and distance students, increasing by over 15 per cent each year (University Statistician's Report, 1996), a mechanism to provide staff with such an instrument for use in the distance mode became an essential task.

In a commissioned report, *Valuing University Teaching*, though staff indicated they supported the regular use of student evaluations of teaching, they were critical of the SAT questionnaire, observing that it did not meet their needs and was 'outdated' (Baker, 1993). This view is supported by Gibbs, Habeshaw and Habeshaw (1989, p. 15) in their review of Curtin's SAT survey of six factors stating that it 'is very difficult for any brief set of teaching rating scales not to embody particular values or assumptions about how teaching ought to be conducted'. As a result of an investigation into evaluating and revising Curtin's appraisal of teaching systems, the university decided to pilot the Student Evaluation Of Educational Quality or SEEQ. SEEQ was developed:

> by Professor Herbert Marsh of the University of Western Sydney (Macarthur), an
> internationally recognized expert in this area of psychometrics. It was established that
> SEEQ had been exhaustively evaluated in many universities, in many different teaching
> and learning contexts, and over a considerable period of time. SEEQ had also been the
> subject of a DEET Evaluations and Investigations Program.
>
> (Marsh and Roche, 1994; Latchem, 1995, p. 3)

SEEQ was designed for use in the conventional face-to-face teaching contexts. However, it was envisaged that it might be adapted for student evaluation of other forms of teaching and learning – for example, clinical supervision, laboratory work, teaching supervision, interactive multimedia, self-directed learning, computer managed learning, postgraduate supervision and distance learning.

SEEQ operates as a quality cycle in which:

1.   The lecturer reflects upon what it means for them to be 'a good teacher' and what attributes they wish to be appraised by the students. They can use the 9 factors on the front of SEEQ which translate into 31 questions and their own lecturer-supplied questions on the reverse of the form to self-rate themselves before inviting the students to appraise their teaching and learning. This enables them to compare their perceptions with those of the students.

2.   The lecturer invites the students to rate his/her performance using the SEEQ instrument which provides valid/reliable questions and feedback in regard to the 9 factors, answers to the lecturer-supplied questions and open-ended comments, all of which are contextualized by the background subject/class characteristics data.

3.   The lecturer receives the students' evaluations in the form of mean and percentile data which can be used for the purposes of bench-marking and comparison with the self-rating survey.

4.   Equipped with this feedback, the lecturer may then engage in action research or reflective practice to enquire further into the nature of his/her performance . . . And/or, the lecturer may ask for Targeted Teaching Strategy Booklets which basically provide 'hints and tips' on improving practice in the areas covered by the 9 factors.

(Harrison, 1996).

The quality cycle outlined by Harrison (1996) was considered desirable for application in distance teaching and learning contexts. However, for the purposes of SEEQ's use in distance education, a number of important issues needed to be addressed.

Evaluating distance teaching and learning is problematic in the sense that, first, much of the 'teaching' is developed well before individual students are known and that the 'teaching' is embedded in the study materials. Secondly, staff who develop the teaching materials may not be teaching the unit. And further, those teaching may not be the same people as the staff who are marking the assignments. Also, there may be more than one tutor and more than one marker per unit and individual staff roles within the teaching of one unit may not be clear. Thirdly, if the unit's study materials were mailed late or the materials were below par, the students' responses may not truly reflect the quality of the tutor's performance. Therefore distance education should be seen as a method of mediated teaching and learning that requires particular and careful evaluation processes and instruments, as Cresswell and Hobson state: 'with distance education, problems are compounded because there is less opportunity for discussion to clear up possible misunderstandings' (1996).

The SEEQ instrument has a set front page, with nine factors and 31 questions which cannot be altered in any way. Staff involved in reviewing SEEQ for distance purposes encountered many areas leading to ambiguity when applied to distance teaching settings. The review team therefore decided to create a separate, yet equivalent, instrument to SEEQ for distance education.

In developing the Distance Education Students' Unit Evaluation or DESUE, sample evaluation processes and questionnaires from six universities offering distance education also were reviewed, along with SEEQ supplied supplementary questions that had been gathered from multiple sources (Marsh and Roche, 1994, p. 7). In designing DESUE, attention was given to the components of teaching effectiveness to be measured and distinctions between teaching, teaching materials and the assessment were made.

DESUE focuses on five factors, namely, the Unit, Organization, Clarity; Teaching, Learning Materials; Assessment, Examinations, Grading; Teaching; and Workload, Difficulty. These factors translate into 28 questions to which the students have to indicate the extent of their agreement/disagreement by circling numbers on a nine-point scale (Strongly Disagree; Disagree; Neutral; Agree; Strongly Agree).

The SEEQ quality cycle outlined by Harrison (1996) was considered as pivotal to the DESUE. DESUE, like SEEQ is seen not simply as an appraisal instrument but a self-development package comprising:

- a Tutor Self-Rating Survey which staff members can complete before using DESUE with their students;

- the DESUE survey form which asks questions about teaching effectiveness, study materials, study processes and background/unit characteristics and allows for additional tutor-supplied questions and open-ended comments by students;

- administration instructions for students;

- a guide to interpreting the students' evaluations summary reports;

- a Summary Report which uses an SPSS scoring programme and provides data which can be used for comparison or benchmarking purposes and compared against the Tutor Self-Rating Survey;

- the SEEQ Targeted Teaching Strategy Booklets containing simple advice to help staff improve in areas where the feedback suggests improvement or the staff may wish to strengthen their knowledge and skills.

29.4 The DESUE pilot

Seven teaching staff electing to pilot DESUE in second semester 1996 were sent a copy of the DESUE form and a copy of the Tutor Self-Rating Survey. This self-assessment is seen as an important component of the reflective practice and self-development approach embodied in DESUE. Tutors were advised that they could devise their own rating items by developing the 'Tutor Supplied Items' section of the form. If tutors decided to develop their own 'Tutor Supplied Items', these were printed on a separate sheet and copies sent to each student.

The surveys were processed through Teaching Learning Group using SPSS and Summary Reports and a guide to interpreting the students' evaluations summary report were forwarded to staff. Targeted Teaching Strategy Booklets were made available to tutors on request.

29.5 DESUE as a tool for reflection

The special feature of DESUE is that staff are able to compare how they rated their own teaching with their students' ratings. Where discrepancies in opinions between the tutor and the students exist, the tutor is provided with an opportunity for further reflection. In some situations students may identify outcomes that are not those anticipated by the lecturer, in which case changes are possible. If appropriate, the tutor may decide to modify the teaching materials and/or their teaching practice. Alternatively, the students' opinions may indicate that they are very happy with the way in which a course has been taught, which can provide support and encouragement to those new to teaching or for those trying out new ideas or technologies.

29.6 Conclusion

Distance education teachers at Curtin now have a confidential mechanism to evaluate their teaching effectiveness and that of the study materials and study processes within a distance unit. As DESUE is itself evaluated and validated, distance teachers will be able to include the results of the student evaluations in their teaching portfolios for promotion purposes and in general for appraisal purposes.

DESUE is intended to be used as part of a self-development package, providing tutors with the opportunity to consider their own teaching and then to be able to compare their opinions with those of their students'. Upon reflection, tutors can then decide if they need to modify any element of the course and/or their teaching. This quality cycle is seen as both valuable and unique and the encouragement of scholarly activities such as action research and reflective practice, will potentially set DESUE apart from more traditional mechanisms of evaluation in distance education. However, it is important to note that DESUE is only one form of collecting and analysing feedback from students and it will be important to continue to collect data from the routine DESSE survey (Boyd, Fox and Herrmann, 1996), as well as to encourage individual communications between teachers and students to help to construct a fuller and more useful picture of our distance students' views and needs.

29.7 References

Altrichter, H., Evans, T. and Morgan, A. (1991) *Windows: Research and Evaluation on a Distance Education Course*, Geelong: Deakin University.

Baker, R.G. (1993) *Valuing University Teaching and Learning: Academic Staff Perceptions*. A report prepared for the University Academic Board: Teaching and Learning Advisory Committee, Perth: Faculty of Education, Curtin University of Technology.

Bates, A.W. (1997) The impact of technological change on open and distance learning, *Distance Education*, **18**(1), 93–109.

Boyd, A., Fox, R. and Herrmann, A. (1996) An investigation: using student feedback for staff development. In S. Leong and D. Kirkpatrick (eds), *Different Approaches: Theory and Practice in Higher Education*. *Proceedings of the 1996 Annual Conference of Higher Education and Research Development Society of Australasia (HERDSA)*, Perth: HERDSA, 58–60.

Chambers, E. (1995) Course evaluation and academic quality. In F. Lockwood, *Open and Distance Learning Today*, London: Routledge.

Cook, M. and Armstrong, B. (1995) An analysis of student evaluations and student results of an MBA economics unit. In F. Nouwens (ed.), *Distance Education: Crossing Frontiers*. *Proceedings of the 12th Biennial Forum of the Open and Distance Learning Association of Australia (ODLAA)*, Rockhampton: Central Queensland University, 36–40.

Cresswell, R. and Hobson, P. (1996) Fallacies and assumptions in the use of student evaluation of distance education teaching materials, *Distance Education*, **17**(1), 132–44.

Fox, R., Boyd, A. and Herrmann, A. (1995) Attitudes and access to technology in distance education. In L. Summers (ed.), *A Focus on Learning. Proceedings of the Teaching Learning Forum '95*, Perth: W.A., Edith Cowan, 89–93.

Fox, R. and Radloff, A. (1997) How can we 'unstuff' the curriculum? In *Learning through Teaching. Proceedings of the Teaching Learning Forum '97*, Perth: W.A., Murdoch, 118–23.

Gibbs, G., Habeshaw, S. and Habeshaw, T. (1989) *53 Interesting Ways to Appraise Your Teaching*, 2nd edn, Bristol: Technological and Educational Services.

Harrison, A. (1996) Enhancing the student evaluation of educational quality (SEEQ). A memo prepared for staff involved in stage 2 pilot of the SEEQ at Curtin, July, Perth: Teaching Learning Group, Curtin University.

Herrmann, A. and Fox, R. (1992) Gender differences in the perceptions of distance education students. In *Research Forum '92*, Perth: Western Australian Institute of Educational Research.

Jegede, O. J., Walkington, J. and Carter, G. (1995) Enhancing students' participation in external unit evaluation: USQ students' opinion. In F. Nouwens (ed.), *Distance Education: Crossing Frontiers. Proceedings of the 12th Biennial Forum of the Open and Distance Learning Association of Australia (ODLAA)*, Rockhampton: Central Queensland University, 115–21.

Latchem, C.R. (1996) *Student Evaluation of Teaching at Curtin University: Piloting the Student Evaluation of Educational Quality (SEEQ)*. A report to the Promotions Review Committee, The Teaching and Learning Advisory Committee and University Academic Board, Perth: Teaching Learning Group, Curtin University.

Marsden, R. (1996) Time, space and distance education, *Distance Education*, **17**(2), 222–46.

Marsh, H.W. and Roche, L.A. (1992) The use of student evaluations of university teaching in different settings: the applicability paradigm, *Australian Journal of Education*, **36**, 278–300.

Marsh, H.W. and Roche, L.A. (1994) *The Use of Students' Evaluations of University Teaching to Improve Teaching Effectiveness*, Higher Education Division Evaluations Program, Department of Education, Employment and Training (DEET), Canberra: ACT, Australian Government Printing Service.

Sochacki, R. (1996) *Enrolment Monitor of External Load by Course and Unit Base*. A report to the Teaching Learning Group, November, Perth: University Planning and Statistics, Curtin University.

30   The *Collegium Invisibile*

Beata Kasperczuk
Collegium Invisibile, Warsaw, Poland

30.1   Introduction

The *Collegium Invisibile* was established in 1995.[1] It is the Polish counterpart of the educational initiative designed to revive the tradition of élite education in the countries of Central and Eastern Europe.

The idea of establishing the *Collegium Invisibile* came from Hungary, where in 1992 the Lathatatlan Kollegium (Invisible College) was founded.

The name of the College was borrowed from the British 'Invisible College', a name which refers to informal meetings of scholars organized in the 1640s in London and Oxford, which resulted in the creation of the Royal Society.

The Latin name of the Polish college draws on the native tradition, namely the educational tradition of the 'Collegium Nobilium' established in 1740 in Warsaw by a Priarist Stanislaw Konarski.

The *Collegium Invisibile* enables highly gifted Polish university students of the humanities and social and economic sciences to broaden their intellectual horizons through organizing tutorial education run by distinguished scholars, both Polish and foreign.

30.2   Aims of the *Collegium Invisibile*

- assuring quality improvement of teaching/learning with some involvement in research;

- continuing the highest possible commitment to academic excellence, the guardians of which are the outstanding professors serving as: tutors, lecturers and members of the supervising bodies of the *Collegium Invisibile*;

- initiating changes in higher education; re-introducing a master-pupil method of education;

- encouraging participation in cross-disciplinary education and inter- as well as multi-disciplinary discussions through seminars and guest lectures.

30.3   Admission procedures

Admission[2] to the *Collegium Invisibile* is based on an open competition.

30.3.1   Qualifying proceedings

The qualifying proceedings consist of:

1. submission by the candidates of biographic questionnaires and respective enclosures which certify achievements made so far (in primary and secondary schools and during the current studies) and present scientific and professional plans, examples of individual scientific or artistic works and social work, together with references from professors under whose direction they have studied;

2. the initial selection of candidates carried out on the basis of the questionnaires and enclosures;

3. passing an entry oral examination before the Examination Commission.

Up to twenty students are selected each year.

Upon admission, students become members of the *Collegium Invisibile* retaining their regular full-time student status at the university where they are enrolled. Education in the *Collegium* is parallel to the students' university studies. Students spend three or four years as members of the *Collegium* until they receive their MA or equivalent diploma from their respective universities. Some of them may spend further years in the *Collegium* as PhD students.

30.4 Tutorial

The main form of the *Collegium Invisibile*'s academic activities are regular meetings between students and their tutors. Each student works under the supervision of a head tutor in a chosen scientific speciality.

The branch of learning the student concentrates on, and the programme of studies, is decided between the tutor and the student each semester. It may be a subject that originates from work carried out in a classical, long-established field of research, or a multi-disciplinary or interdisciplinary field, covering fields that are not so obviously linked.

In the 1996–97 academic year, the students of the first and second years of the *Collegium Invisibile* studied:

- Social Psychology
- Social Policy
- European Integration; European Law
- Rhetoric of Advertising
- Social and Political Philosophy
- Sociology of Politics
- Public Law; Constitutional and Administrative Law
- Sociology of Culture
- Economics
- Theory of Finance and Econometrics
- Business Ethics and Praxiology
- History; Recent History
- History and Anthropology of Tourism

- Modern Philosophy; History of Philosophy
- Ontology
- Philosophy of Art; Theory of Art
- Psychology of Art; Psychology of Literature
- Theory and Criticism of Literary Translations
- History of Polish Literature
- Theory of Literature
- Theatre Sociology
- Classical Philology
- Biblical Studies

The specific methods of study depend upon the subject. The most common methods used by students are the following:

- analysis of literary texts;
- comparison of critics', theorists' and artists' texts;
- context analysis;
- analysis of philosophical texts;
- analysis of historical sources;
- research in state archives;
- analysis of empirical data, for example:
  - data concerning social security in Poland,
  - public opinion polls,
  - data from the Central Statistic Office,
  - Polish and European community regulations;
- empirical research, for example:
  - interviews,
  - survey research,
  - participation in theatre festivals and events;
- statistical analysis;
- case studies;
- computer simulations.

The results of the students' activities are presented in the form of essays, papers and reports, many of which are published or are to be published in professional journals.

Since tutorial work constitutes the backbone of the academic experience of *Collegium*'s students, special attention is paid to the selection of tutors. The guiding principle is that tutors must be among the best in their fields, with high academic standards, and must be willing to deal with individual students on a weekly basis.

The tutors supervise the students' work during regular meetings and consultations and at the end of each semester submit a report on each student's progress.

The *Collegium Invisibile* now takes care of 60 students altogether (44 men and 16 women). They come from 33 cities and towns in 18 provinces (voivodeships) and are studying at 14 different universities located in 8 cities (among them 41 study in Warsaw, 7 in Cracow, 3 in Wroclaw, 3 in Katowice, 3 in Gdansk and 1 in Lodz, Lublin and Poznan).

These figures go to prove that the *Collegium*, although élite in terms of students' abilities and aspirations and the curricula offered, is democratic both geographically and financially, not only with regard to candidates who applied, but also those who have been enrolled.

30.5   Other activities

30.5.1   Seminars

The *Collegium Invisibile* organizes monthly seminars for the members of the college.

During these seminars lectures on various subjects are given by guests speakers, tutors or students of the *Collegium Invisibile*.

This is an opportunity for members of the College to meet scholars specializing in disciplines or subjects different from their own.

30.5.2   Conferences

Once a year the *Collegium* organizes a two-day conference. These conferences allow students not only to learn but also to get to know one another more closely.

30.5.3   International camps

In July 1996 students of the *Collegium* attended the Summer Camp organized by the Hungarian Invisible College.

In June/July 1997 the Summer Camp was organized by the *Collegium Invisibile* in Poland. Students from Hungary, Lithuania, Moldova, Slovakia and Poland participated in the Camp.

These international meetings allow students from different countries of Central and Eastern Europe to exchange ideas and information and develop an international network of intellectual élite, which is important for integrating Europe.

30.6   Publications

In order to provide an insight into the activities of the *Collegium Invisibile*, publication of the series 'Acta – *Collegium Invisibile*' was initiated in 1996. The series is devoted to the presentation of lectures delivered at the Collegium's seminars and selected papers by the members of the *Collegium*, students and tutors.

30.7   Evaluation

The idea of the *Collegium Invisibile* is much appreciated by members of the college. The students are happy that they are able to work with the 'the professors of their dreams', while the tutors enjoy the challenges offered by their younger colleagues. Both students and tutors alike stress that this specific form of co-operation is exceptionally creative. It is a genuine meeting between two sets of individuals who respect each other.

A testimony to, and acknowledgement of, the good results achieved by the *Collegium Invisibile* was a nomination for the 1997 Hannah Arendt Prize established by the Institute for Human Sciences (IWM) in Vienna, Austria and Körber Foundation in Hamburg, Germany for outstanding self-initiated reform efforts in higher education and research in East Central Europe.[3]

In March 1997 the *Collegium Invisibile* was invited to attend the 'European Centres of Excellence' Conference held in Budapest, initiating an international programme (connected with European integration) concerning new developments in higher education and scientific research in the countries of Central and Eastern Europe.

Notes

1. The umbrella organization for the CI is the Tadeusz Kotarbinski and Ludwig von Mises 'Knowledge and Action' Foundation, established in 1991. The Foundation is a legal entity. The competent supervisory organ in respect to the goals of the Foundation is the Polish Academy of Sciences. Operating the CI is the main task of the Foundation which emanates from its statutory goals.

2. Admission is announced via: newspaper advertisement; letters to deans of the humanities and social sciences faculties at all Polish universities; letters addressed directly to the home addresses of the most gifted students taken care of earlier by the special Polish Fund for Children and to the finalists of the school contests called School Olympiads. Those who applied receive a Biographical Questionnaire to complete. In the 1995/96 academic year 469, and in 1996/97 academic year 369, students applied for admission to the college.

3. The prize was awarded to the Invisible College in Budapest, Hungary.

31 Simulated professional practice as a means of improving the ability to learn from experience

Della Freeth
City University

31.1   Introduction

This chapter is concerned with simulated professional practice within higher education as a means of assisting students to learn more effectively from experiences in workplace settings. It considers the uses of simulation in professional development and in higher education. The drivers behind the use of simulated professional practice in the education of nursing and medical students are identified and the Clinical Skills Centre at St Bartholomew's is described. Seven ways in which simulated professional practice aids student's ability to learn from supervised clinical practice are discussed.

31.2   Simulation

There is extensive discussion within the literature which attempts to define simulation and to distinguish it from other teaching and learning strategies, often with elaborate outcomes (e.g. Gredler, 1992). However, for this chapter it is sufficient to adopt a simple definition:

> The essence of a simulation is that it is a working representation of reality . . . a dynamic representation of a system, process or task.
>
> (Rediffusion Simulation, 1986, p. 3)

Simulation is employed for a variety of interrelated reasons, most frequently:

- *Cost* – for example, London Underground train drivers commence their training in groups in a simulated train shell, where they can acquire elementary skills and awareness. This is less costly than providing one-to-one tuition and supervision on real trains, which would also incur the costs of delays in service, and additional wear and tear on the equipment in service.

- *Safety* – for example, the risk of costly accidents is reduced by the simulated experience gained by aircrew and air traffic controllers as an integral part of their training.

- *Improved learning* – during simulations learners are actively engaged in the task; they can safely make and learn from mistakes; and they can have repeated experience of normally infrequent but important events. In addition, experiences can be carefully structured and controlled. Time can be slowed to simplify the task, or accelerated to provide swifter feedback on the consequences of decisions. These aspects of simulation should lead to deeper, more integrated learning. The repetition permitted by simulation may allow skills to become automatic in response to particular stimuli. This may be very important where the actual experience presents a high level of risk or requires a swift response.

- *Unavailability of actual experience* – disasters such as plane crashes and chemical spillages are simulated to train people who would be called to respond, because (thankfully) these events are too infrequent to ensure the preparedness of personnel. In addition, they are generally unsuitable for basic training on grounds of safety.

- *Assessment and selection* – simulations of work activities have considerable face validity as a means of assessing or selecting trainees. Examples include the OSCE (Objective Structured Clinical Examination) in medicine, leadership exercises for aspiring management trainees and 'life'-saving tests for swimming pool attendants. These have greater reliability than assessments of actual practice by establishing more consistency both in demands made of candidates and the rewarding of their efforts. The validity of such assessments hinges on the implied transfer of skills from the simulated experience to the practice.

The degree of fidelity chosen for a simulation depends upon its objectives, assessments of the learning gain and degree of transfer obtained and upon balancing these against constraints such as cost. It is not usually necessary (even if possible) to replicate all physical and dynamic aspects of an experience, but just those instruments, cues and responses which are essential to the particular learning task. Arguably, it is never possible to replicate all the psychological aspects of the real experience. However, this may be a considerable advantage for complex tasks and those associated with a high level of stress. Simulation can simplify these tasks, slow the passage of time and reduce stress to a level where learning is more effective. Carefully graded simulated practice can then allow the development of fluent skills or responses: competencies which can transfer to the real environment. (Gredler, 1992; Horn and Cleaves, 1980; Taylor and Walford, 1978)

Abt (1980) suggested that simulations should be evaluated with reference to: the degree of active involvement of participants, realism, clarity, feasibility, repeatability and reliability. He argued that all participants should be actively involved and stimulated, and that there should be sufficient realism to convey the essential truths of the simulated situation. This can be assessed by the degree to which the choices produced by the simulation and their consequences and interactions mirror reality. Consequences and causes need to be clear, resulting from participant decisions more than from random factors.

31.3 Simulation in higher education and professional education/training

Simulation as part of professional education has been known and practised for centuries. For example, it is thought that chess developed as an instructional war game, and Second World War RAF pilots benefited from experiencing the consequences of their decisions and mistakes from the safety of the Link Trainer. In the post-war years simulations became more sophisticated and increasingly popular. The use of simulation as a teaching strategy in higher education expanded rapidly in the 1960s and SAGSET (the Society for the Advancement of Games and Simulations in Education and Training) was established in 1969.

Today, many professionally related courses in higher education employ simulated professional practice. Law students are given opportunities to participate in Moot Courts.

Students of Journalism participate in 'disaster training' for the emergency services, becoming the 'reporters' of simulated emergencies. Business schools employ sophisticated management games to develop decision-making skills. Simulated Professional Practice sits happily with the ideologies of andragogy (Knowles, 1984, 1990), experiential learning (Kolb, 1984), problem-based learning (e.g. Boud and Felletti, 1991) and reflective practice (Schön, 1983, 1987). In recent years, continued interest in simulated professional practice has been ensured by the attention given to developing competencies (Barnett, 1994) and changes in society, particularly increased litigation and the Citizens' Charter (HMSO, 1991).

31.4 Simulated professional practice in nursing and medicine

Traditionally, medical and nursing students learnt their clinical skills through observation of experienced practitioners, ward-based instruction in the presence of patients and supervised practice. Essentially, they served an apprenticeship. In recent years many changes have rendered this an untenable pattern for the future.

- Scientific advances and greater recognition of psychosocial elements in health care have contributed to curriculum overload and concerns about fragmentation.

- Changes in the delivery of health care, with more being located in primary care settings and the trend towards far shorter hospital stays, have made hospital-based professional education less appropriate. The range of patients and conditions experienced by students in hospitals can be too narrow (O'Driscoll *et al.*, 1997) and inpatients are often too sick for it to be appropriate for them to be involved in the education of students. There are ethical difficulties with the ability to give informed consent and further, the multiple problems of very sick patients can overwhelm students.

- The *Patients' Charter* (DoH, 1995) emphasized the right of individuals to decline to participate in the education of students. It also stressed the expectation of open communication with patients/clients, and where appropriate with their carers. It accelerated the trends towards a more holistic view of the consumers of healthcare and greater attention to alternative perspectives. This has hastened curriculum development, particularly in the field of communication skills.

- The 'internal market' and drive towards greater efficiency in the NHS has increased the workloads of practitioners and hence, decreased the amount of close supervision and mentoring available to students. The purchasing arrangements within the new NHS are likely to influence the provision of clinical experience for nursing and medical students who are based in higher education.

For all these reasons Simulated Professional Practice has become a growth area.

Heath (1984) noted an increase in the use of simulation within nurse education and related this to changes in: the role of the nurse, the delivery of healthcare and accountability to other professionals, patients and carers. The types of simulation which her survey identified were role play, use of case studies, structured discussion, problem-solving exercises and communication skill exercises. More recently, Neary (1997) stressed the importance of Simulated Professional Practice within the education of nurses, concentrating upon safety, confidence, professional socialization and developing competence.

31.5   The Clinical Skills initiative at St Bartholomew's

The empirical work for this chapter was conducted in a Clinical Skills Centre for medical and nursing students. The facilities include two skills laboratories (one arranged as a ward) equipped with up-to-date equipment of the type students will encounter in clinical areas, sophisticated mannequins and video-recording facilities. There is also a communication skills suite with a small 'consulting room', closed-circuit TV facilities and seminar rooms connected by a two-way mirror. Students can develop dexterity with real equipment and practise techniques on mannequins or non-invasive techniques on each other. Simulated patients are employed for the development of communication and consulting skills, and for assessment of students' skills. Self-directed learning facilities are available, including hands-on practice with real equipment, and computer or video-based simulations. The Skills Centre encompasses a large subset of Simulated Professional Practice as it is employed within medical and nursing education.

The motivation for developing a centre to support Simulated Professional Practice was multifaceted:

- There was a desire to raise the profile of clinical skills within the curriculum and hence, influence student learning. This was a reaction to concerns that the preparation for these practice-based professions were too theory-laden, with undue emphasis on atomistic knowledge and insufficient integration or focus upon clinical realities (Jolly and Macdonald, 1989; Studdy *et al.*, 1994a).

- Safety – the Skills Centre was intended to provide a safe (physical and emotional) learning environment in which students can practise clinical skills without fear of harm to themselves or patients (Studdy *et al.*, 1994a,b).

- The Skills Centre offers the opportunity to improve the quality of student learning through the use of structured simplification and guided reflection, and by providing an environment in which students can be allowed to make and learn from mistakes: something which cannot be allowed in clinical areas (Studdy *et al.*, 1994b).

- Traditional, ward-based apprenticeship training now needs to be augmented with other forms of education to reflect changed roles and powers of professionals and service users; to reflect the moves towards a primary-care-led health service; and in response to the pressures of the 'internal market' in health care (Dacre *et al.*, 1996; Leathard, 1994; Owens *et al.*, 1995; Soothill *et al.*, 1995).

31.6   Improving the ability to learn from experience

The simulation of professional practice within the Skills Centre falls into the categories of role-play and machine/computer simulation. Students use sophisticated mannequins; interactive video and CD-ROM simulations; they handle real clinical equipment and may practice non-invasive techniques on each other; they interact with trained simulated patients.

Simulated professional practice within the Skills Centre does not simply replace supervised practice in clinical areas. Rather, it improves students' ability to learn from practice in clinical areas, so making best possible use of increasingly scarce clinical placements. There are various aspects to this, seven of which will be outlined.

31.6.1   Space for guided reflection

The Skills Centre provides physical and emotional space for guided reflection upon past clinical experience, without the high levels of conflicting demands that characterise practice areas. Students consistently rate this as one of the most important features of the Skills Centre.

> An opportunity to clear up all those unanswered 'daft' questions, in a friendly environment!
>
> (medical student)

> Nice to get a break from the sometimes too manic or too stern atmosphere of the wards.
>
> (medical student)

31.6.2   Permitting experiential learning

There are two aspects to this. First, permitting students to make and learn from mistakes, safely. For example, in a simulated setting video recordings of a student's sterile dressing technique can be video-recorded, including mistakes such as running their hands through their hair. Students can then view their tapes and identify their strengths and weaknesses, if necessary with help. In a clinical area, the tutor would have to intervene to prevent infection, unsettling the patient and the student and interrupting the flow of the performance. Secondly, there is very limited scope within clinical areas for students to experience being in receipt of care. Within a Skills Centre students can experience such things as being lifted in a hoist, having their teeth brushed by another, and being fed. This is very valuable, rapidly producing deep leaning (Marton and Säljö, 1976) which is retained for a long period.

31.6.3   Carefully structured learning experiences

More community-based care and shorter hospital stays have made it difficult to give students experience with 'straightforward' cases before encountering very sick patients with multiple problems. In these circumstances students can feel overwhelmed and unable to participate as a member of the healthcare team (Freeth and Nicol, in press; Jones and Rafferty, 1996). They are likely to learn very little as helpless spectators. Simulated professional practice allows the creation of a carefully structured of learning experiences which gradually introduce complexity and unpredictability. Further, it is not necessary for each student to progress through the learning experiences at the same pace, nor perhaps always in the same sequence.

31.6.4   Integration of theory and practice

The balance between and integration of theory and practice has generated much debate in the health care professions (e.g. Chastonay, 1996; Hickey, 1996; MacLeod and Farrell, 1994). Simulated professional practice provides a bridge between these aspects of professional development. It allows students both to set skills and knowledge in the context of holistic care, and to reflect upon past experiences such that new knowledge and theory can be generated.

31.6.5   Vicarious experience

Simulated professional practice exposes students to the experiences of others and situations which they would not otherwise encounter. This provides the potential for them to develop knowledge of and strategies for responding to a greater range of professional experiences than each individual could experience through supervised practice in placements.

31.6.6   Base-line competencies

Simulated professional practice permits the development of certain base-line competencies prior to patient or client contact. These might include manual dexterity with certain instruments, appropriate and accurate recording, or awareness of roles, responsibilities and their own limitations. This helps to ensure the safety of students and patients, thus reducing costs. The basic competencies allow students to make a real contribution to the teams in which they are placed for clinical experience. They are, thus, better able to take advantage of the learning opportunities afforded in each placement.

31.6.7   Strategic approach to subsequent experience

The assessment of clinical skills and reflection upon past experience which occur within the Skills Centre enable students to identify their strengths and weaknesses and gaps in their knowledge or experiences to date. This permits them to plan strategically when entering a new clinical placement. They will be more able to identify to mentors and managers what they can already offer and which facets of professional practice they need to practise rather more, or have yet to experience.

31.7   Conclusions

Simulated professional practice improves students' ability to learn from experience in several ways.

- Past experience is drawn into the execution of simulated practice.

- The simulated setting exposes students to experiences which they could not otherwise acquire.

- Reflection and assessment during simulated practice provides students with knowledge that encourages the strategic planning of subsequent experience.

- Simulated professional practice develops skills which enable students to contribute positively to the work of the practice teams to which they are attached on placement.

31.8   References

Abt, C. (1980) *Serious Games*, New York: Viking Press; cited in Redifussion Simulation Ltd (1986) *Simulation in Training: A Guide for Trainers and Managers*, Sheffield: Manpower Services Commission.

Barnett, R. (1994) *The Limits of Competence: Knowledge, Higher Education and Society*, Buckingham: SRHE and The Open University Press.

Boud, D. and Felletti, G. (1991) *The Challenge of Problem Based Learning*, London: Croom Helm.

Chastonay, P. (1996) Editorial: The need for more efficacy and relevance in medical education, *Medical Education*, **30**, 235–8.

Dacre, J., Nicol, M.J., Holroyd, D. and Ingram, D. (1996) The development of a clinical skills centre, *Journal of the Royal College of Physicians of London*, **30**, 318–24.

DoH (1995) *The Patients' Charter and You*, London: Department of Health.

Freeth, D.S. and Nicol, M.J. (in press) Shared learning for advanced clinical skills, *Nurse Education Today*.

Gredler, M. (1992) *Designing and Evaluating Games and Simulations: A Process Approach*, London: Kogan Page.

Heath, J. (1984) Gaming/simulation in nurse education. In D. Thatcher and J. Robinson (eds), *Perspectives on Gaming and Simulation, Vol 8: Business, Health and Nursing Education. The Proceedings of the 1982 Conference at SAGSET at Portsmouth Polytechnic*, Loughborough: Society for the Advancement of Games and Simulation in Education and Training, 59–65.

Hickey, G. (1996) The challenge of change in nurse education: traditionally trained nurses' perceptions of Project 2000, *Nurse Education Today*, 16, 389–96.

Horn, R. and Cleaves, A. (1980) *A Guide for Simulation Games for Education and Training*, Beverley Hills: CA: Sage.

HMSO (1991) *The Citizens' Charter: Raising the Standard*, London: HMSO.

Jolly, B.C. and Macdonald, M.M. (1989) Education for practice: the role of practical experience in undergraduate and general clinical training, *Medical Education*, 23, 189–95.

Jones, S. and Rafferty, M. (1996) Practical matters, *Nursing Times*, 92(35), 47–9, 52.

Knolwes, M.S. *et al.* (1984) *Andragogy in Action*, San Francisco, CA: Jossey Bass.

Knowles, M.S. (1990) *The Adult Learner: A Neglected Species*, 4th edn, Houston, TX: Gulf.

Kolb, D.A. (1984) *Experiential Learning*, Englewood Cliffs, NJ: Prentice Hall.

Leathard, A (ed.) (1994) *Going Inter-Professional: Working Together for Health and Welfare*, London: Routledge.

Macleod, M.L.P. and Farrell, P. (1994) The need for significant reform: a practice-driven approach to curriculum, *Journal of Nursing Education*, 33(5), 208–14.

Marton, F. and Säljö, R. (1976) On qualitative differences in learning: II. Outcome and process, *British Journal of Educational Psychology*, 46, 115–27.

O'Driscoll, M.C.E., Rudkin, G.E., Carty, V.M. and Maddern, G.J. (1997) New horizons in surgical teaching: undergraduate medical teaching in day surgery. In *Advances in Medical Education. Proceedings of the Seventh Ottawa Conference on Medical Education and Assessment*, Dordrecht, The Netherlands: Kluwer, 787–9.

Owens, P., Carrier, J. and Horder, J. (eds) (1995) *Interprofessional Issues in Community and Primary Health Care*, Basingstoke: Macmillan.

Rediffusion Simulation Ltd (1986) *Simulation in Training: A Guide for Trainers and Managers*, Sheffield: Manpower Services Commission.

Schön, D.A.(1983) *The Reflective Practitioner: How Professionals Think in Action*, London: Temple Smith.

Schön, D.A. (1987) *Educating the Reflective Practitioner: Toward a New Design of Teaching and Learning in the Professions*, San Francisco, CA: Jossey Bass.

Soothill, K., Mackay, L. and Webb, C. (eds) (1995) *Interprofessional Relations in Health Care*, London: Edward Arnold.

Studdy, S.J., Nicol, M.J. and Fox-Hiley, A. (1994a) Teaching and learning clinical skills. Part 1 – Development of a multidisciplinary skills centre, *Nurse Education Today*, 14, 177–85.

Studdy, S.J., Nicol, M.J. and Fox-Hiley, A. (1994b) Teaching and learning clinical skills. Part 2 – Development of a teaching model and schedule of skills development, *Nurse Education Today*, 14, 186–93.

Taylor, J.L. and Walford, R. (1978) *Learning and the Simulation Game*, Milton Keynes: The Open University Press.

32 Perceptions of justice in assessment: a neglected factor in improving students as learners

Jo Brunas-Wagstaff and Lin Norton
Department of Psychology, Liverpool Hope University College

Since Marton and Säljö's (1976) original distinction between deep and surface approaches to learning, research has shown that the way a student is assessed is one of the most powerful ways of either encouraging or inhibiting a deep approach (Biggs, 1996; Boud, 1990; Brown 1997; Entwistle, 1995; Ramsden, 1992). This has led to recent trends in higher education to assess students by rewarding them for taking a deep approach in their coursework and in their examinations (e.g. McDowell, 1995). In spite of such developments, many students still do not appear to learn from experience and persist in taking a surface approach (see, for example, Cuthbert, 1995; Solomonides and Swannell, 1995). Why should this be so?

One explanation which draws on the justice literature is that perhaps students do not believe that the assessment system is fair, particularly when it comes to rewarding effort. Studies of public perceptions of justice have demonstrated that people believe that a system which rewards individuals for the amount of effort they put in is fairer than a system which rewards them according to their ability (e.g. Lamm et al., 1983). Applying this research paradigm to student learning could mean that students who believe tutors assess them by giving them higher marks for ability rather than for the amount of effort they have put into a piece of work may feel disaffected and powerless. This might explain why they tend to adopt a surface approach. It might also explain why they sometimes turn to other widespread strategies such as cheating (Franklyn-Stokes and Newstead, 1995) and 'rules of the game' – essay-writing strategems designed to impress tutors (Norton, Dickins and McLaughlin Cook, 1996a,b).

To our knowledge, there is little in the literature about the effects of students' perceptions of the fairness of the assessment system and no one has yet asked the question as to what part this might play in determining which approach to learning they take. Nevertheless there is evidence in the literature that some students do believe that the amount of effort they put into their work should be reflected in the mark they receive. In a study on the effects of tutor feedback on students' essays Norton (1997) found that students did expect, or at least hoped, that the amount of effort they had put into their essays would be taken into account in the essay grade that they were given. Supporting evidence comes from some research by Longhurst and Norton (1997) looking at how accurately students can assess their own essays. They found that students who had put a lot of effort into their essays and were highly motivated expected to get good grades, but the authors concluded this might distort the accuracy with which students can judge their own work. This point is illustrated by some student comments in a study by Davies (1995) evaluating a self- and peer-assessment project. Davies asked the students how they felt about assessing themselves. Some of the answers he quotes shows that there is a complexity of understanding shown by students about how much effort should be rewarded:

It is important to judge your work on what is presented rather than to think of all the hard work you have done and reward yourself for that.

Making the marks appropriate to all the hours of hard work, and setting aside how hard I knew I worked – to marking what I had actually achieved.

I found this quite difficult as I didn't want to mark myself too high, but also wanted to make sure I got a good mark due to the amount of effort I knew I put into my work.

(Davies, 1995, p. 120)

The current position from the empirical evidence suggests that the question of how much weight assessors should give to effort as opposed to the quality of the work, which is a demonstration of the student's ability, is not clear. The balance of evidence would seem to suggest that many students do believe that effort should be rewarded but whether they would prefer tutors actually to credit effort more than ability when assessing a piece of work has not yet been tested.

The study reported here was designed to address this question directly as well as to find out how students' perceptions of the fairness of their assessment affected their approaches to learning as well as their self-reported cheating and 'rules of the game' behaviours.

32.1   Method

Tutors in the psychology department of a university college were asked to distribute a pack of four questionnaires to all students who attended their third year option courses. Tutors asked students if they would help n the research by completing all four questionnaires in their own time and returning them to either the tutor concerned or to one of the two researchers. Eighty-two students responded (about 50 per cent of the total number of third-year psychology students), but one of the pack of questionnaires was not fully completed, leaving a total of 81 usable responses for data analysis.

The pack consisted of the following four questionnaires:

1. The *Approaches to Studying Inventory* (ASI) devised by Entwistle and his colleagues (Entwistle, Hanley and Hounsell, 1979; Entwistle and Ramsden, 1983: Ramsden and Entwistle, 1981). This has appeared in many versions and is still being developed. For this study, the 32-item version recommended by Richardson (1990) has been used, which has two main factors measuring meaning orientation (similar to a deep approach) and reproducing orientation (similar to a surface approach). Both factors consist of 16 items to which students are invited to respond by ticking one of the following categories: 'definitely agree, agree with reservations, item not applicable, disagree with reservations, definitely disagree' which respectively score from 4 to 0. The maximum score obtainable for both factors is therefore 64 and the minimum is 0.

2. The *Rules of the Game* (ROG) questionnaire devised by Norton, Dickins and McLaughlin Cook (1996a). This asks students if they have ever used any of the 25 essay-writing strategies that are listed. All 'yes' responses score 1 and 'no' responses score 0, therefore the maximum possible score is 25 and the minimum is 0.

3. The *Cheating questionnaire* devised by Franklyn-Stokes and Newstead (1995) is similar to the *Rules of the Game* questionnaire in that it asks students if they have ever used any of the 21 cheating behaviours listed. Again 'yes' responses score 1

and 'no' responses score 0, therefore the maximum score is 21 and the minimum is 0.

4. The *Perceptions of Fairness in Assessment* questionnaire was designed by the first author specifically for this study (see Appendix 32.1 below). It consists of a range of different questions regarding students' beliefs about how fair they think the system of assessment is at their college as well as items to measure whether they believe that the system rewards mostly student effort or mostly student ability for coursework and examinations. The questionnaire is thus in three parts as follows.

32.1.1 Perceptions of the fairness of the assessment system

Students' responses are scored on a 10-point scale where a score from:

1–4   indicates a belief that the system is fair;

5–6   indicates that students are undecided or neutral about the fairness of the system;

7–10   indicates a belief that the system is unfair.

32.1.2 The ability versus effort dichotomy

Students' responses are scored on a 10-point scale where a score from:

1–4   indicates a belief that the system rewards mainly ability;

5–6   indicates that students are undecided or believe that effort and ability are equally rewarded;

7–10   indicates a belief that the system rewards mainly effort.

32.1.3 Judging the fairness of hypothetical outcomes using the ability versus effort dichotomy

Hypothetical vignettes were presented to which students were asked to judge the fairness of marking outcomes for an exam and a piece of coursework based on alternative outcomes: one in which effort was rewarded over ability and the other in which ability was rewarded over effort. Students were given the following response options: 'fair', 'quite fair', 'not sure', 'quite unfair' and 'unfair', and their responses were coded quantitatively from 5 to 1 respectively, when the outcome rewarded ability. When the outcome rewarded effort, the coding was reversed. Thus students who thought that outcomes which rewarded ability were fair had a high score overall and those who thought that outcomes which rewarded effort were fair had a low score overall.

32.2 Results

Students were split into groups according to their responses to each question on the 'Perceptions of Fairness in Assessment' questionnaire.

32.2.1 Students' overall attitudes to the assessment system

Table 32.1 gives the percentages of students within the 'fair/unfair' and 'not sure' categories for the question: 'How fair do you think the present system of assessment at Liverpool Hope is?' and the percentage of students who believed that the assessment system measures ability, effort or both. The proportions of students whose responses to the vignettes indicated that they preferred an outcome based on ability or effort are presented in Table 32.2.

Question	Fair	Unfair	Not sure
1.How fair do you think the present system of assessment at Liverpool Hope is?	47%	32%	21%

Question	Ability	Effort	Both
2. How much do you think the assessment system at Liverpool Hope takes into account student ability and/or student effort?	60.5%	26%	13.5%
3. How much do you think tutors at Liverpool Hope take into account student ability and/or effort when marking coursework?	60.5%	26%	13.5%
4. How much do you think tutors at Liverpool Hope take into account student ability and/or effort when marking exams?	67%	16.5%	16.5%

Table 32.1   Percentages of students within each response category for questions 1-4 of the Approaches to Fairness in Assessment questionnaire (N = 81)

	Outcome based on **effort** is fair	Outcome based on **ability** is fair	Not sure
Coursework assessment	11%	65.5%	23.5%
Examination assessment	74%	7.5%	18.5%

Table 32.2   Percentage of students who preferred an outcome based on effort or ability when judging the fairness of fictional assessment outcomes presented in vignettes. (N = 81)

The results suggest that 47 per cent of the students rated the overall assessment system as fair. However, although many students expressed satisfaction with the assessment system, just over half of the students still felt that the system was unfair or were undecided (53%). The majority of the students sampled believed that the assessment system at their college did reward ability more than effort, and this was the case for both coursework and examinations. However, students' ratings of fairness in relation to the fictional assessment outcomes in the vignettes suggested that, although most students rated an outcome based on ability as fair for coursework, they preferred an outcome based on effort for examinations. There appeared to be a mismatch, therefore, between students' beliefs that their tutors reward ability for examinations and their own 'gut-feelings' that an examination outcome based on effort is fairer. This suggests that students as a whole may perceive examinations as unfair forms of assessment.

32.2.2 Relationship between students' perceptions of fairness, cheating behaviours, rules of the game and approaches to learning

Students' scores on the ASI, ROG and Cheating questionnaires were compared for each of the groups of students in Tables 32.1 and 32.2 using a series of one-way analyses of variance. Students' scores on the ROG and Cheating questionnaires did not differ significantly in any of the comparisons. Thus, whether students considered the assessment system to be fair or unfair, whether they believed that the system rewards effort or ability and whether they preferred an outcome based on effort or ability (measured in the vignettes) bore no relationship to their tendency to cheat or to use 'Rules of the Game'. Students' scores on the ASI were also unrelated to whether students perceived the assessment system as fair or unfair, and to how they rated the outcomes of the vignettes. However, ASI scores did differ significantly according to students' perceptions of whether the assessment system rewards mostly ability or effort (see Table 32.3). Using one-way analyses of variance and planned LSD comparisons, the ASI scores were compared between the groups who believed either that: (1) ability was rewarded over effort or (2) both were equally rewarded or (3) effort was rewarded over ability.

System as a whole	Ability (N= 49)		Both (N = 11)		Effort (N = 21)		Statistical significance
	Mean	SD	Mean	SD	Mean	SD	
Meaning orientation	40.69	8.59	37.66	9.48	33.73	8.35	$p<0.02$
Reproducing orientation	37.20	8.76	40.90	7.91	44.18	8.24	$p<0.03$
Coursework	Ability (N = 49)		Both (N = 11)		Effort (N = 21)		Statistical significance
	Mean	SD	Mean	SD	Mean	SD	
Meaning orientation	40.22	8.32	38.24	10.59	34.73	8.21	NS
Reproducing orientation	37.20	8.76	40.90	7.91	44.18	8.24	$p<0.03$
Examinations	Ability (N = 53)		Both (N = 13)		Effort (N=13)		Statistical significance
	Mean	SD	Mean	SD	Mean	SD	
Meaning orientation	40.07	8.57	36.38	9.89	36.61	10.31	NS
Reproducing orientation	38.79	9.03	36.31	6.92	44.46	7.33	$p<.04$

Table 32.3   Comparison of ASI mean scores according to students' perceptions of whether effort or ability or both are rewarded in assessment

Students who believed that the assessment system mostly rewards ability were significantly more likely to adopt a meaning orientated (or deep) approach to their studies, according to their scores on the ASI (F = 3.12, df = 2, 78, p < 0.02), whereas students who believed that the assessment system mostly rewards effort were significantly more likely to adopt a reproducing orientated (or surface) approach (F = 3.25, df = 2, 78, p < 0.03). The pattern of results was broadly similar for coursework, where students who believed that coursework was mostly rewarded for ability were more likely to take a meaning-orientated approach (although the difference in this case was not statistically significant, the means were in the same direction), whereas students who believed that effort was rewarded more than ability were significantly more likely to take a reproducing orientation (F = 3.67, df =2,78, p < 0.03). The results for examinations were less clear-cut. Students who believed that examination assessment rewarded ability were more likely to take a meaning-orientated approach (again the means were in the expected direction, but were not statistically different), but students believing that examinations assessment rewarded effort were significantly more likely to take a reproducing orientation than students who believed examination assessment rewarded both effort and ability, (F = 3.31, df = 2, 76, p < 0.04) but there were no significant differences from those who believed that ability was rewarded. Overall, these findings suggest that there is an association between students' perceptions of what their tutors look for when assessing students (evidence of student effort or student ability) and students' approaches to learning.

32.3 Conclusions

It is possible to summarize the results as follows:

1. Although many students rated the assessment system overall as being fair, there was still a considerable proportion of this particular sample who rated the system as unfair. This is an interesting finding given Newstead's (1997) observations about the unreliability of marking standards. It also confirms McDowell's (1995) view that one of the major concerns that students have about assessment is its fairness.

2. The majority of students believed that their tutors reward ability rather than effort on coursework, examinations and overall. However, the majority indicated by their responses to the vignettes that, while an outcome based on ability was fair for coursework, they preferred an outcome based on effort for examinations. This may offer an explanation as to why so many students fear examinations and perform badly, compared to their performance on coursework assignments (see for example, Covington and Omelich, 1987; Zeidner, 1995). If an examination paper is unseen, there is little they can do to control the outcome, because they cannot know what questions they will be asked. All they can do in such a situation is to work hard. It seems logical, therefore, that many students believe that effort should be rewarded as they feel an examination is not a true reflection of their ability.

3. Students who believed that the system of assessment rewards ability were more likely to adopt a meaning-orientation approach whereas students who believed that the system rewards effort were more likely to adopt a reproducing-orientation approach to studying. Approaches to learning were therefore related to beliefs in whether the system measures effort or ability. This is a particularly important finding and lends support to the growing body of educationalists who are advocating more innovative forms of assessment, many of which are reported in

Gibbs (1995). Increasingly, researchers are finding that students need to see that assessment tasks are meaningful activities, that they are tasks in which the students themselves have some control and that they reward the amount of effort put into the task as well as the quality of the final product.

4.   Approaches to learning were not related to students' overall conceptions of fairness of the assessment system in this study. One possible explanation is that students accept the system as a *fait accompli* – it is not relevant whether the system is fair or unfair: it is as it is. This suggests that 'fairness' itself may not be all that important in determining study styles; rather students' perceptions of what examiners are looking for is what matters to them. Ramsden (1992) graphically illustrates this point by quoting some of the comments from students whom he has interviewed about assessment. One such quote is reproduced here:

Techniques [are] involved in learning how to cut down on the understanding and just aim at the marks. How quickly you adapt to the techniques involved in passing exams, in getting assignments in with good marks.

(p. 71).

This would seem to be characteristic of a student whom Entwistle (1987) describes as a strategic student – one who finds out how the assessment system works and then adapts his or her learning styles accordingly. On the other hand, the fact that there was a mismatch between students' beliefs that their tutors reward ability for exams and their 'gut feelings' (measured by the vignettes) that people should be rewarded for effort (not ability) in an examination suggests that most students may, after all, believe that examinations are unfair. What consequences this may have for exam performance specifically remains to be established. One factor which we did not measure in our study was student motivation. Our findings therefore suggest that it may be fruitful to examine the combined effects of conceptions of fairness in relation to examinations and student motivation on exam performance and anxiety.

32.4   General discussion

More generally, this research poses a number of interesting questions regarding students perceptions' of the assessment system and student learning in general.

1.   What is the nature of the relationship between students' approaches to learning and their perception that the system of assessment rewards either effort or ability?

As most students in this study appeared to agree that the assessment system measures ability more than effort, it is surprising that more of them did not also score higher on the meaning-orientation factor in the ASI if we assume that the approach they take is a strategy based on their perception of the requirements of the system. Are students' choices of approach to learning based on their understandings or misunderstandings of what their tutors are trying to measure (ability or effort), or is there a sort of self-fulfilling prophecy operating whereby students believe that the system measures whatever it is that they do? The essay-writing literature has some evidence to support this latter interpretation (e.g. Norton 1990, 1997) where students seem to believe that effort on its own should be rewarded (a surface approach) regardless of whether or not they have answered the question (a deep approach).

2.   What is it that tutors are actually rewarding? Ability or effort?

Most tutors would probably agree with the students that the system rewards ability (a deep approach) more than effort (a surface approach), although the research literature is divided on this point. Boud (1990) in reviewing the literature on assessment practices in higher education found that students were still being assessed 'on those matters on which it is relatively easy to assess them' – the emphasis being on covering the material and demonstrating knowledge so students typically regurgitate lecture notes, textbook material and pass – all of which is typical of a surface approach. There is, however, some more recent evidence to suggest that practices may be changing. Longhurst and Norton (1997) looked at whether tutors did actually reward students for taking a deep approach. They found a significant correlation between marks on identified deep criteria and the overall grade awarded. If then it can be assumed that assessment systems are changing and do take account of a deep approach, how do tutors get this message across to their students? Most tutors would like to think that they at least appreciate student effort, and clearly ability and effort are related – without some evidence of effort even the most able student is unlikely to get a high grade. Perhaps, though, the feedback that might be given to students in acknowledging their effort misleads them about the importance of taking a deep approach. Hounsell (1987) suggested that one of the reasons that feedback sometimes fails to have an impact on students is because they have different perceptions of what the marking criteria mean. It may be that in attempting to give positive feedback tutors may unintentionally be encouraging some students to believe that effort is valued more than ability in assessing students' work.

3. Why do the students appear to be happy with an outcome which rewards ability on an essay, but prefer an outcome which rewards effort on an examination?

One possibility is that students regard examinations as more 'out of their control' than an essay and thus feel that the only thing they can be certain of in an exam situation is the amount of work they put in when revising. If this is true, then it would be interesting to see whether this operates for a 'seen exam paper' where students are given the exam questions in advance. McDowell (1997) comments that non-conventional examinations such as open book exams are becoming increasingly common in the United Kingdom. Certainly, the indications from this study would suggest that more innovative and authentic ways of assessing students may help to communicate an unambiguous message to students that taking a deep approach is at the heart of the learning experience.

4. Is the perception of the fairness of assessment an explanation as to why students do not always take note of tutor guidance and improve as learners?

In the title of this chapter, we posited that the notion of fairness has been largely neglected in the research on improving student learning and, to our knowledge, this appears to be the case. What this study has shown is that fairness itself does not appear to be the real issue; students appear to accept the status quo in that there is no evidence that it affects either their approaches to learning or their tendency to cheat or use rules of the game. What has emerged though is the effect of the dichotomy between ability and effort which has come from the public perceptions of justice literature. The implication is that those who take more of a deep approach also tend to believe that assessment rewards ability whereas those who take more of a surface approach believe that it is effort which is mainly rewarded. What this study cannot show is cause and effect. Is it the belief that ability is rewarded that causes students to take a deep approach or is it because they do take such an approach that they believe that ability is rewarded? Falchikov (1997) has suggested that Entwistle's (1987) original assertion that learning styles were relatively consistent individual differences does not appear to be the case and there is research evidence to show that students can and do change (for example, Duckwell *et al.*, 1991). If this is so, tutors need to make explicit to students the relative weighting they give in assessment to ability and to effort. Only then might it be a real possibility that students can be encouraged to move away from a surface approach and thus improve the whole of their learning experience.

32.5 References

Biggs, J. (1996) Enhancing teaching through constructive alignment, *Higher Education*, **32**, 347–64.

Boud, D. (1990) Assessment and the promotion of academic values, *Studies in Higher Education*, **15**(1), 101–11.

Brown, G. (1997) Teaching psychology: a Vade Mecum, *Psychology Teaching Review*, **6**(2), 112–26.

Covington, M. and Omelich, C. (1987) 'I knew it cold before the exam!' – a test of the Anxiety Blockage Hypothesis, *Journal of Educational Psychology*, **79**(4), 393–400.

Cuthbert, K. (1995) Student project work in relation to a meaning oriented approach to learning. In G. Gibbs (ed.), *Improving Student Learning: through Assessment and Evaluation*, Oxford: The Oxford Centre for Staff Development.

Davies, A. (1995) Evaluating a deep approach to assessment. In G. Gibbs (ed.), Improving Student Learning: through Assessment and Evaluation, *Oxford: The Oxford Centre for Staff Development.*

Duckwall, J.M., Arnold, L. and Hayes, J. (1991) Approaches to learning by undergraduate students: a longitudinal study, Research in Higher Education, *32(1), 1–13.*

Entwistle, N., Hanley, M. and Hounsell, D. (1979) Identifying distinctive approaches to studying, Higher Education, *8, 365–80.*

Entwistle, N. (1987) A model of the teaching-learning process. In J.T.E. Richardson, M.W. Eysenck and D. Warren Piper (eds), Student Learning: Research in Education and Cognitive Psychology, *Milton Keynes: Open University Press and SRHE.*

Entwistle, N. (1995) The use of research on student learning in quality assessment. In G. Gibbs (ed.), Improving Student Learning: through Assessment and Evaluation, *Oxford: The Oxford Centre for Staff Development.*

Entwistle, N.J. and Ramsden, P.(1983) Understanding Student Learning, *London: Croom Helm.*

Falchikov, N. (1997) Living in the realities of today's higher education: certainties and uncertainties, Psychology Teaching Review, *6(2), 142–4.*

Franklyn-Stokes, A. and Newstead, S.E. (1995) Undergraduate cheating; who does what and why?, Studies in Higher Education, *20(2), 39–52.*

Gibbs, G. (ed.) (1995) Improving Student Learning: through Assessment and Evaluation, *Oxford: The Oxford Centre for Staff Development.*

Hounsell, D. (1987) Essay writing and the quality of feedback. In J.T.E. Richardson, M. Eysenck and D.Warren Piper (eds), Student Learning: Research in Education and Cognitive Psychology, *Milton Keynes: SRHE and Open University Press.*

Lamm, H., Kayser, E. and Schanz, V. (1983) An attributional analysis of interpersonal justice: ability and effort as inputs in the alllocation of gain and loss, Journal of Social Psychology, **119**, *269–81.*

Longhurst, N. and Norton, L.S. (1997) Self-assessment in coursework essays. To appear in Studies in Educational Evaluation *(in press).*

McDowell, L. (1995) *The impact of innovative assessment on student learning,* Innovations in Education and Training International, *32(4),* 302–13.

McDowell, L. (1997) *Assessment, meaning and learning: a response to issues raised by George Brown,* Psychology Teaching Review, *6(2), 137–9.*

Marton, F. and Säljö, R. (1976) *On qualitative differences in learning: 1. Outcome and process,* British Journal of Educational Psychology, *46, 4–11.*

Newstead, S.E. (1997) *The psychology of student assessment,* The Psychologist, *9, 543–7.*

Norton, L.S. (1990) *Essay writing: what really counts?,* Higher Education, *20(4), 411–42.*

Norton, L.S. (1997) *The effects of tutor feedback on student motivation in essay writing. Seminar paper presented at the* SEDA Spring Conference on Encouraging Student Motivation, University of Plymouth, 8–10 April.

Norton, L.S., Dickins, T.E. and McLaughlin Cook, A.N. (1996a) *Rules of the Game in essay writing,* Psychology Teaching Review, *1–14.*

Norton, L.S., Dickins, T.E. and McLaughlin Cook, N. (1996b) *Coursework assessment: what are tutors really looking for? In G. Gibbs (ed.),* Improving Student Learning: Using Research to Improve Student Learning, *Oxford: The Oxford Centre for Staff Development.*

Ramsden, P. (1992) *Learning to Teach in Higher Education,* London: Routledge.

Ramsden, P. and Entwistle, N.J. (1981) *Effects of academic departments on students' approaches to studying,* British Journal of Educational Psychology, *51, 368–83.*

Richardson, J.T.E. (1990) *Reliability and replicability of the Approaches to Studying Questionnaire,* Studies in Higher Education, *15, 155–68.*

Solomonides, I. and Swannell, M. (1995) *Can students learn to change their approach to study? In G. Gibbs (ed.),* Improving Student Learning: through Assessment and Evaluation, *Oxford: The Oxford Centre for Staff Development.*

Zeidner, M. (1995) *Adaptive coping with test situations – a review of the literature,* Educational Psychologist, *30(3), 123–33.*

Appendix 32.1   Student Perceptions of Fairness questionnaire

A   **Please indicate your opinion of the system of student assessment at Liverpool Hope by circling the appropriate response.**

Q1. How fair do you think the present system of assessment at Liverpool Hope is?

Very fair							Very unfair		
1	2	3	4	5	6	7	8	9	10

	Marks are based entirely on evidence of ability			Marks are based equally on evidence of ability and effort			Marks are based entirely on evidence of effort		
Q2. How much do you think the assessment system at Liverpool Hope takes into account student ability and/or student effort	1	2	3	4	5	6	7	8	9	10
Q3. How much do you think tutors at Liverpool Hope take into account student ability and/or effort when marking coursework?	1	2	3	4	5	6	7	8	9	10
Q4. How much do you think tutors at Liverpool Hope take into account ability and/or effort when marking examinations?	1	2	3	4	5	6	7	8	9	10

B   **The following hypothetical situations describe various alternative outcomes of an examination or piece of coursework for fictional students. Please rate the outcomes according to how fair you think each outcome is by circling the appropriate response below each statement.**

1.   Frank did a lot of revision for his exam but he is not good at taking exams.

      John did not do much revision for his exam, but he is good at taking exams.

(a)   John got a good mark and Frank got a poor mark.

      Fair   quite fair   not sure   quite unfair   unfair

(b)   Frank got a good mark and John got a poor mark.

      Fair   quite fair   not sure   quite unfair   unfair

2.   Mary did a lot of work for her essay, but she is not good at writing essays.

      Carol did not do much work for her essay, but she is good at writing essays.

(a)   Mary got a good mark and Carol got a poor mark.

      Fair   quite fair   not sure   quite unfair   unfair

(b)   Carol got a good mark and Mary got a poor mark.

      Fair   quite fair   not sure   quite unfair   unfair

33 Developing students' meta-cognitive awareness through self-evaluation: a South African perspective

Lee Sutherland
Academic Development, University of Zululand

33.1 Introduction

My work is grounded in a first-year course in Historical Studies at the University of Zululand. Many students come to this university from educationally disadvantaged backgrounds, where passive rote learning has resulted in a surface approach to learning. For most, English is a second, if not third, language, although it is the language of learning at the University of Zululand. My research attempts to gain entry into the meta-cognitive world of the students through their self-evaluations. Using this the programme aims at promoting greater meta-cognitive awareness with a view to developing students' capacity to learn more efficiently.

South Africa just recently emerged from an oppressive political and educational system and many students who have been educationally disadvantaged by the previous system are entering the field of higher education. Academic support programmes were introduced in South Africa in order to meet the needs of these students. However, the concept of Academic Support has evolved into one of Academic Development, where it is acknowledged that institutions of higher learning need to adapt to the new profile of our student populations. One of the results of the changes taking place, is that the specific focus of education has now been overtly stated as being 'to produce life-long learners'.

33.2 Theoretical framework

If tertiary institutions in South Africa hope to produce life-long learners, students need to acquire the ability to assess the value of their own work. Self-assessment can then become a vehicle for self-directed learning. Such thinking on assessment is in line with the emergent paradigm of assessment which Broadfoot (1993, cited in Klenowski, 1995, p. 145) describes as a paradigm in which 'it is learning itself, rather than simply the measurement of that learning, which is its central purpose'. In keeping with international trends, higher education in South Africa is starting to recognize, that 'one of the main goals of professional higher education is to help students develop into "reflective practitioners" who are able to reflect critically over their own professional practice' (Kwan and Leung, 1996, p. 205).

The notion of reflecting upon one's experiences and practices with a view to improving them is a well-documented one. (Schön (1987) has done ground-breaking work in this regard.) The reflection referred to here is characterized by Boud as one pursued with intent, rather than undirected, indulgent day-dreaming (1988, p. 11). It is also one in which the affective component has a role to play: positive feelings and emotions can greatly enhance the learning process (ibid.).

Up to now, many of the assessment practices have been grounded in a traditional paradigm educational theory and have rewarded rote learning and the regurgitation of facts. As assessment is a perspective of the curriculum, assessment practices will also change: Orsmond *et al.* points out that traditional assessment practices have limited scope for developing student responsibility and autonomy (1996, p. 240). He continues, saying that 'it is becoming apparent that in order for students to become more self-reliant with regard to their academic development, changes in staff assessment practices will have to be made in that some power will have to be handed over to students' (ibid.).

Boud *et al.* (1988b) have developed a model of reflection that is symbiotic with self-assessment. They argue that 'reflection is the context of learning is a generic term for those intellectual and affective activities in which individuals engage to explore their experiences in order to lead to new understandings and appreciations' (p. 19). Furthermore, if more teachers and learners understand this reflective aspect of learning, the more effective learning can be (ibid., p. 20).

Various researchers have emphasized both the role that self-evaluation plays in learning and the educational merits of using self-assessment as part of the learning process. As Boud (1989) points out, it is now well-accepted that the ability to assess one's own work is an important element of learning. Brown and Dove (1991 in Kwan and Leung 1996) suggest that self- (and peer-) assessment, if handled successfully, can (among other things):

- foster students' feelings of ownership for their learning;
- encourage their active participation in learning;
- make assessment a shared activity rather than a lone one;
- lead to more effective and directed learning;
- signal to students that their experiences are valued and their judgement respected;
- produce a community of learning in which students feel they have influence and involvement (p. 206).

The use of student-derived marks for formal grading purposes is a controversial one and is under debate. (To pursue this debate, see for example Kwan and Leung, 1996). In this research, student self-evaluations were conducted as a learning tool (formative assessment) rather than a grading process (summative assessment).

33.3   Research methodology

Students participate in a Writing Respondent Programme (WRP) which is integrated into the course material of the first-year History course. This programme is theoretically grounded upon the understanding that researchers in the field of literacy development have arrived at, that writing can be used as a tool for learning. In other words, students are encouraged to write to learn, rather than to learn to write. In addition, it is based on the assumption that students learn by being actively engaged in the learning process. A process-oriented approach to writing is adopted by the close integration of writing task with course content (see Boughey (1994) for a more full theoretical explanation of this approach).

Students are required to write a response to a question at various intervals during the course. They are subsequently provided with a response to their work, in which the writing respondent engages the student in a written dialogue. This takes the form of questioning and challenging the student in areas where there is vagueness or unsubstantiated conclusions, for example.

At the end of six such writing sessions, students submit a portfolio of writing, for which they receive marks. The students are also asked to submit a self-assessment sheet (see Appendix 33.1) together with their portfolios, without which their portfolios are considered incomplete. The self-assessment sheets are intended to encourage students to be more self-critical and consist largely of open-ended headings and questions. It aimed at providing students with the opportunity to express their self development. A broader aim of the research is to evaluate the extent to which the self-evaluative exercise had developed students' meta-cognitive awareness.

33.4 Discussion

33.4.1 Self-evaluation

The data obtained from this questionnaire shows that the students do not start off with sophisticated and reliable judgements about their own work; as Gibbs (1995) observed in a similar study, they need practice and training in order to develop this judgement. They also need to be convinced of the value and validity of the self-assessment process (ibid.). In addition, research shows that students who come to the University of Zululand have very little understanding of what will be expected of them in a university. They demonstrated a lack of insight into their own work and a poor understanding of the 'standards' which staff thought were being applied.

The 'inability' to judge their own worth effectively is often particularly characteristic of second-language learners, who prefer to measure their worth through the reflections of others. This is illustrated by the following kind of comments:

> I did not see any improvement because no marks were allocated.

This dissatisfaction is compounded by the notion that, as Boud (1989) points out, students do not have a well-defined sense of the criteria which should be used to judge their work, and that they may find it difficult to interpret criteria with which they have been provided. What emerges is a picture similar to the one painted by Main (1988) when he says that students 'seem to be unable to predict confidently the consequences of different study methods or learning styles. It is as if they believe that success or failure is determined by external agents – using inscrutable criteria' (p. 97).

Many students revealed that the portfolio and its self-evaluation had been cathartic in gaining a perspective of self-value. These comments support this notion:

> If I compare assignment no 1 to other assignment I felt that my performance was better.

> I thought I understood what I were asked but I was surprised to see a lot of questions being asked.

> Piece No 3 I am not happy with it because I failed to express precisely what I want to say.

> For the first time I was able to stick on the point of argument, but now I can understand the topic clearly and follow it in context.

> I didn't do well in assignment no. 4 because I was not able to focus directly on the topic.

However, there remained a group of students who demonstrated an inability to measure their own self-worth, which is often characteristic of ESL (English as Second Language) learners. Such students could only measure or judge their worth through the reflections of others:

What does your portfolio show that you can do?

> My portfolio doesn't show how I can do because there is no mark and indicates how marks I obtained, but there is a lot of questions . . .

> I do not see any improvement because no marks were allocated.

> I selected this piece [1] because I performed very well in my first test.

33.4.2   Approaches to learning

A variety of different frameworks have been developed in order to investigate approaches to learning and the most recurrent of these is one that makes the distinction between deep learning, where the learner attempts to understand and interact vigorously with the content, and surface learning, where there is a reliance on memorization and an uncritical, passive acceptance of the content. In addition to these two broad categories, are the non-academic approach to learning (where the motivation for improvement is extrinsic rather than intrinsic) and the strategic approach (where the learner manipulates the learning environment in order to achieve success). (For further discussion of this model, see Entwistle 1987.)

In addition, Entwistle and Ramsden (1983) describe the deep approach as being characterized by, among other things, an integration of formal learning with personal experience and as one associated with a reflective approach. Alternately, the surface approach is characterized by an attitude of unreflectiveness. Boud however states that these approaches are not consistent in any one student, but depend on the specific circumstances and intentions (1988, p. 24). My research bore testimony to this.

Main sums up the thinking of Gibbs with regard to the relationship between study habits and academic success and states that there is little evidence to suggest a clear relations between the two. This is of great significance to our university, in that there is an ever-increasing demand for programmes on study methods which give advice in a generalized way that Gibbs and others argue against (1988, p. 91).

Students' responses were however revealing with regard to the underlying assumptions that they make about learning and the approaches they take to learning. In response to the question: *Which pieces of writing are you unhappy with and why?*, one student said:

> All of them because I do not exactly know what was required from me to do. To me, this assignment shows no improvement. Instead I'm extremely offended because the test book said Free Burghers. It does not go into detail explaining to me who they are as you ask in of my assignment so really I'm sad.

This kind of response is fairly typical of both the cognitive and affective components of our students' learning experience. Many students want to be told precisely what to do in essays and other work. This would suggest that many students assume what Entwistle (1988) refers to as a 'reproducing orientation' to learning. In keeping with this orientation to learning, this student is fairly typical of many students who tend to read very little beyond what is required for completing assignments.

Some students revealed a notion of an entirely teacher-directed education where students are simply passive recipients of information. These students prefer not to be challenged in any kind of way. The following comments are revealing of this approach to learning:

I would like to see mistakes being corrected not be asked questions to something which I've never understood, for example DEIC [Dutch East India Company]. How can I explain what was it.

The one who marked my assignment I will be happy if he/she can make corrections in my assignment not ask questions to what I wrote.

I would like to be asked a question and the marker should tell me what am I supposed to do if I correct my mistake because it seems as if I make one and the same fault.

33.4.3   Meta-cognitive awareness

Although students are universally reluctant to take part in activities which are not awarded formal marks that will influence their success in a particular course (see, for example, Boud, 1989), my research shows that student had achieved greater meta-cognitive awareness. For example, in response to the question: *In what ways have you improved?*, one student said:

I understood the question clearly and I feel I provided enough information. I had enough time to prepare for it, redrafting it. I tried with effort to correct the mistakes of past assignments.

This suggests that the student is reflecting on a process that would prove to be academically successful.

There is further evidence of such student awareness:

It shows me that I must write the assignment with my own understanding.

I have just took the text and read through out the relevant topics and close it up and bring about my own understanding.

It [my portfolio] showed that I must read with understanding and ask myself questions while I'm reading.

These are some of the specific areas in which students achieved greater meta-cognitive awareness:

33.4.4   What 'good writing' means

Some students showed an awareness to read as an intelligent reader, to engage with the content and to attach personal meaning to reality – which is essentially a constructivist view of learning. These responses also reveal an approach to learning which Entwistle (1988) refers to as 'meaning orientation' (essentially associated with a deep approach to learning) where students look for personal meaning and have academic motivation.

The Writing Respondent Programme allowed students to find their 'voice' of which Cleary (1991) talks, rather than aping an academic style without understanding it. These are some of the comments that students made about the writing that they were required to do:

If people can be given freedom to write whatever they like as long as it is relevant to the question and it is true. Not to be asked where did you get this.

I selected this piece because I revealed all the information that was needed and I didn't relay [sic] on a book only but I wrote with my own ideas.

33.4.5 Moving away from plagiarism

Many students saw the need to move away from plagiarism in an attempt to develop both their skills as a writer and their own 'voice':

> I selected this piece because I write my assignment with my own words, even the marker appreciate it.

Angelil-Carter (1995) argues however that, at first year level, plagiarism in student writing is rarely intentional, but a far more complex problem. As a lengthy discussion of plagiarism is beyond the scope of this chapter, it must suffice to say that many researchers, Angelil-Carter included, feel that imitation is an important part of the learning process and should not be 'criminalized'.

33.4.6 Awareness of discourse ...

One student demonstrated a rudimentary sense of awareness of the discourse of the discipline: in response to the question: *Which pieces are you unhappy with and why?*, one student said: @extract1:Piece no 1. I did not write in any form that was expected to me as a history student.

33.4.7 Awareness of audience ...

Cleary (1991) reports that second-language learners often have less sense of 'appropriate' purpose and audience (p. 125). However while this was evident in some students' responses, the WRP proved to be successful in creating an awareness of audience within others students without deliberate or overt attempts to do so. The follows comments provide evidence of this:

> It also show that I must explain and elaborate some words or terms. It also show that I must write as if one who is marking don't know the story.

However, an inappropriate awareness of audience could be detrimental if students develop what Cleary calls a 'please-the-teacher mentality' (1991, p. 161). Furthermore, she sees this as part of the submission/dominance power structure set up in classrooms. Such a mentality might be associated with the strategic learning approach that Entwistle (1987) and others talk about. In this research, there was a strong inclination on the part of some students to find out 'what the teacher/lecturer wants'. A number of students made comments similar to this:

> I would like the lecturer to tell me the way he / she like me to answer the question and show me the corrections.

33/4/8 Contextualization

Students also came to realize the need to contextualize their writing for the reader:

> It [the portfolio] shows that I must answer the question accurately and avoid to write things that may lead the marker to ask why, when, what.

33.4.9 Affective component

Boud, Keogh and Walker (1988a) argue that the reflective process is a complex one in which feelings and cognition are closely interrelated and interactive (p. 11). Furthermore, negative feelings can form a barrier to learning, distort perceptions and lead to false interpretations. Positive feelings on the other hand can greatly enhance the learning process (ibid.).

The self-evaluation exercise in this research showed the importance of the affective component to the writing process of which Cleary (1991) and Boud *et al* (1988a) speak. In answer to the question: *What does your portfolio show that you can do?*, one student simply said:

> I can write an assignment.

Another student put this point more directly:

> I would like to see positive comments in my work. I want to feel happy when I read my own writing knowing that what I have written makes sound sense.

Cleary (1991) also argues that when students see grading as a form of criticism or praise, as a mirror by which to view themselves or as a means of comparing themselves to peers, it had more effect on their writing confidence than on the development of writing ability (p. 156).

33.5   Recommendations

Gibbs (1981, cited in Main, 1988, p. 92) suggests the following six ways in which to facilitate students' learning development, which this research corroborates:

1. take a student-centred approach;

2. give responsibility to the student for his or her own learning;

3. make changes of methods and approaches a safe activity;

4. emphasize the students' purpose not technique;

5. emphasize the reconceptualization of study tasks;

6. emphasize the student's awareness of his or her own learning.

33.6   Conclusion

However, students demonstrated that they had gained heightened awareness in following areas:

*   how writing can be used as a tool for learning;

*   what 'good writing' means;

*   the need to engage with the text and attach personal meaning;

*   awareness of audience in writing;

*   the need to adopt a deep approach to learning.

As other research has shown, this awareness was not consistent in all ways of any one student's approach to learning.

While students showed many traits and problems that have come to be known as being synonymous with ESL learners, many students, however, found the Writing Respondent Programme and the self-evaluative exercises empowering. It allowed them to find their 'voice' of which Cleary (1991) talks, rather than aping an academic style without understanding it.

This chapter might appear to be judgemental of the students' abilities, but it must be emphasized that, for a number of students, the opportunity to critique their own work was both a new and cathartic experience. Given the educational background from which they come to the university, much needs to be done to foster their self-development. Students need to be convinced of the need to take control of their own learning (Boud, 1988b). In the light of these findings, I agree with Boud when he says that 'there needs to be a greater emphasis on the relationship between learning and self-assessment' (1989, p. 28). Teachers need to find ways of incorporating some forms of reflection into their courses (Boud, 1988b, p. 8).

33.7   References

Angelil-Carter, S. (1995) *Uncovering Plagiarism in Academic Writing: Developing Authorial Voice within Multivoiced Text*, M.Ed. thesis, Rhodes University.

Boud, D., Keogh, R. and Walker, D. (ed.) (1988a) *Reflection: Turning Experience into Learning*, New York: Kogan Page.

Boud, D., Keogh, R. and Walker, D. (1988b) Promoting reflection in learning: a model. In D. Boud, R. Keogh and D. Walker, D. (eds), *Reflection: Turning Experience into Learning*, New York: Kogan Page.

Boud, D. (1989) The role of self-assessment in student grading, *Assessment and Evaluation in Higher Education*, **14**(1), 20–9.

Boughey, C. (1994) *Towards a Model of 'Writing to Learn': Reflections on Two Years' Work at UWC*, Bellville: UWC.

Cleary, L.M. (1991) *From the Other Side of the Desk: Students Speak out about Writing*, Portsmouth: Heinemann.

Entwistle, N. (1987) *Understanding Classroom Learning*, London: Hodder & Stoughton Educational.

Entwistle, N. (1988) *Styles of Learning and Teaching: An Integrated Outline of Educational Psychology*, London: David Fulton Publishers.

Entwistle, N. and Ramsden, P. (1983) *Understanding Student Learning*, London: Croom Helm.

Gibbs, G. (1995) *Assessing Student Centred Courses*, Oxford: Oxford Brookes University.

Klenowski, V. (1995) Student self-evaluation processes in student-centred teaching and learning context of Australia and England, *Assessment in Education*, **2**(2), 145–63.

Kwan, K-P. and Leung, R. (1996) Tutor versus peer group assessment of student performance in a simulation training exercise, *Assessment and Evaluation in Higher Education*, **21**(3), 205–14.

Main, A. (1988)   Reflection and the development of learning skills. In D. Boud, R. Keogh and D. Walker, D. (eds), *Reflection: Turning Experience into Learning*, New York: Kogan Page.

Orsmond, P., Merry, S. and Reiling (1996) The importance of marking criteria in the use of peer assessment, *Assessment and Evaluation in Higher Education*, **21**(3), 239–50.

Schön, D.A. (1989) *Educating the Reflective Practitioner*, San Francisco: Jossey-Bass Publishers.

Sutherland, L. (1996) Student perceptions of assessment at the University of Zululand. Working paper.

Walker, D. (1988) Writing and reflection. In D. Boud, R. Keogh and D. Walker, D. (eds), *Reflection: Turning Experience into Learning*, New York: Kogan Page.

Appendix 33.1

HISTORY DEPARTMENT

TUTORIAL PROGRAMME

Research has shown that students benefit from assessing their own performance. Students performance improves as a result of such self-evaluation. The following questions will help you to evaluate your own performance.

(Complete this sheet and attach to your portfolio.)

1. <u>Best piece selection</u>

1.1   I feel that I performed the best in assignment no

☐

1.2   I selected this piece because ...

_____

2.   What does your portfolio show that you can do?

_____

_____

3.   Which pieces of writing show that you have made improvements?

☐   ☐   ☐

In what ways have you improved?

_____

4.   Which pieces are you unhappy with and why?

_____

5.   What changes would you like to see in your portfolio?

_____

file: history\self496

34 An investigation of students' changing perceptions of professional studies provision for Fine Art, focusing on student experience of work placements and enterprise projects[1]

Heather MacLennan
Cheltenham and Gloucester College of Higher Education

34.1 Introduction

The focus of this case study is the learning experience of students and their self-reflection, set against the wider background of designing appropriate higher educational experience for future art graduates. A central theme of the research is to test whether subject-based studies can successfully incorporate generic skills experience without a conflict forming in the mind of the student.[2] Thus it responds to a philosophy which seeks to defend a liberal arts education and yet is supportive of the provision of useful experience for the world of work. The research findings presented here arise from the particular context of a professional studies module delivered at level two of a Fine Art degree (defined route). The module consists of an assessed work-study project, undertaken as part of the normal academic curriculum but outside the usual college environment.

The aim of the research was to provide information to enable students to become better focused while learning from experience, through an overall understanding of the educative process and its effect on the individual. In order to assess the situation and the student's response it was clear that there was a need to understand motivation and anxiety more fully in relation to work projects built as enterprise challenges.[3] Some students in an earlier study showed an ambivalent attitude towards professional studies, viewing this part of the curriculum as significantly different from their main subject of aesthetic studies.[4] The perceived conflict led to tensions which affected students' normally positive outlook and also raised a question about the nature and purpose of esoteric study in relation to other demands, following Dearing, for the curriculum to more directly address graduate outcomes.[5] While there was a view among students that professional studies was necessary, some thought that their performance in this area should not affect the assessment of the degree, which they liked to think principally reflected their achievement in the studio. Students in previous interviews had shown very poor ideas of skills development and awareness, were vague about graduate outcomes, confused over non-traditional modes of assessment, needed much encouragement, yet showed that they were very capable when they tackled quite ambitious projects. These students, coming from a range of backgrounds and life experiences and with an extreme variety of skills and abilities, demonstrated that they had much to offer; but they were in need of a more focused attitude towards themselves and their potential careers.

Research focused on the first assessed modular cohort of the compulsory work placement programme in Fine Art, Professional Studies, a programme in which students are encouraged to become reflective learners in professional studies by:

1. 'owning' the aims and objectives of their projects;

2. having control over modes of assessment, negotiated in relation to learning outcomes that are linked to generic skills;

3. reflecting on their experience and evaluating its outcome through self-assessment and feedback interviews.[6]

Projects are set up on an enterprise model, few being delivered as a package to the student; rather the terms and conditions have to be negotiated and set up by the student, whether working independently or as part of a team, and making considerable demands on the individual's initiative and tenacity to see a project through.[7] Support and advice is given and all projects have to be sanctioned by the college. Projects are set up using learning contracts (called study agreements) which, while appearing strange at first to students unused to such regulation and form filling, do seem to work efficiently. From the study it became evident that time needs to be given to advising students when selecting and framing projects and when negotiating assessment.

34.2   Aims of the research

The research set out to discover whether anxiety and poor awareness, revealed in a pilot study to include ambivalent motivation and negative attitudes about the compulsory nature of professional studies, would be positively changed by experience. Consideration was given to the value of relaying other students' experiences through mentoring (to allay student anxiety). Students were asked to reflect on whether they felt they had benefited as a consequence of the work placement and whether they thought their levels of confidence had increased.

Further to this, the research aimed to discover whether the relative depth of understanding in students of their skills development altered in any way as a consequence of the professional studies programme.

In addition information was needed to help educators plan effective ways of giving strategic support (to whom, when, how); disseminating information (how, when, in what format); carrying out assessment; and providing feedback.

There was an expectation that there would be some deviation in responses to enterprise work projects. While setting out to obtain an idea of the consensus within the group on a number of issues, the questionnaire and interviews were designed to elicit any significant differentiation according to age, previous experience and gender, in student attitudes to professional studies, its role and relationship to main study, the delivery of the programme, and to the issue of skills acquisition and students' perception of their own abilities. It was expected that students coming to higher education from previous careers would have different outlooks from the normal student age-group as far as work projects and graduate outcomes were concerned, and that their motivation would be different. A proportion of mature students come from well-established careers, for example, nursing, state employment (civil service, fire service), the public sector (British Telecom) and the armed services. Explanations were sought for known student anxieties about assessment and ambivalence towards professional studies. And new information was sought on attitudes to mentoring and awareness of graduate destinations.

34.3   Were expectations fulfilled?

The full study revealed how the student body coped in a new set of circumstances following modularization. Two factors were different from the pilot: (1) professional studies and work placement were no longer optional and (2) assessment had become a fixed requirement.

Students whose attitudes were studied in the pilot had been distinguished by their high degree of motivation to do work placement (this was voluntary and outside their normal college curriculum); also they could opt to be assessed through an independent study module. By contrast, students in the full study were the first cohort of the mandatory module. Delivery of the professional studies programme was more mechanistic (61 had to do enterprise and work-placement projects compared with about 20 in the previous year), while before, projects happened in an ad hoc way, agreed by one or two consenting individuals. Also staff teaching on the degree course were required to deliver their part of professional studies alongside their usual teaching duties, as part of the official programme, which meant a change from their former work schedule. They had to approve many more learning contracts, monitor a wide variety of projects happening at different times, and ensure parity of assessment.

Expectation that students gained from the experience was largely met, and that their understanding of transferable skills and the importance of these was increased. Also their deeper awareness of career development and their maturing self-reflection were evident in interviews. Students also seemed to develop their critical skills through their interaction with the delivery and evaluation of the programme. They seemed critically engaged in the whole process. A number revealed deep anxieties and clearly felt stress.

One surprise was the differentiation according to gender noted in students' self-perception of generic skills. While a case study can only provide an enriched picture of a particular situation, the findings may well be significant for what is revealed about gender and confidence. Such factors may well be significant taking into consideration the ways in which each individual responds to new situations.

The delivery of enterprise projects (adapted to suit) is a feasible alternative for all subject areas and this approach may be worth considering applied to other curricula.

34.4   Analysis of survey data and short summaries of findings

Two sets of interviews were held, the first at an early stage in the delivery of the programme when only a few students had chosen projects, the second towards the end of the semester. Interviews were structured, the participants being broadly acquainted with the underlying agenda. These students are now part of a longitudinal study which will track them beyond first destination graduate outcomes.[8]

A group of ten students were interviewed at first stage, eight at second stage, in small focus groups. All interviews were tape-recorded and transcribed.

A questionnaire was distributed to students and 25 completed questionnaires were returned. Participation in interviews was voluntary and depended on availability of students. The cohort studied consisted of 61 full-time students (enrolled 1995/96) now in their second year of the Fine Art course. Of the present group, 33 are female, 28 male. At enrolment, 28 of the original group of 70 were aged 21 and over on entry, 63 white, 1 other, 3 disabled.[9]

34.5   First stage interviews

Questions were directed at understanding students' views about:

- the Fine Art degree;

- their previous educational experience;

- post-graduate aims;

- the inclusion of professional studies in the degree and its value as a compulsory element;

- their understanding of what is involved in professional studies and their attitudes to skills and understanding of these;

- their understanding of the process of assessment in professional studies.

34.5.1   Findings

Very few students felt dissatisfied with their Fine Art Degree. There was a high level of satisfaction with the direction of their undergraduate studies.

Professional studies was thought to be important and useful for post-graduate careers, although post-graduate ambitions seemed vague and unformed.

Professional studies was not seen to be directly related to the content of the main study and were even regarded as unrelated. Students were more highly motivated about the aesthetic and self-developmental thrust of the main subject, Fine Art, seeing this as a fundamental and positive, if esoteric experience.

Some students interviewed were confused about how professional studies projects should be set up and some were shocked that they had to take so much initiative. They did not feel they knew where to start and had a poor idea of what the available options were. There was a feeling that they had not been given enough information about deadlines and timing; and they were worried that they did not have the skills to cope.

Students valued the mentoring (a level-3-run Student Symposium on the experience of work placements).

Those already engaged in projects seemed highly satisfied with content and aims.

34.5.2   Students perceptions of the value of Professional Studies in relation to the acquisition of skills

Students readily identified the following skills as useful outcomes from their anticipated projects:

- bargaining;

- diplomacy;

- making arrangements according to a schedule;

- being organized, managing people, resources, time;

- taking responsibility;

- using their initiative;

- learning to be flexible, to adapt;

- being firm, making decisions;
- making contacts;
- meeting professionals;
- encountering difficulties;
- meeting deadlines.

34.5.2.1   *Examples of responses (early in project)*

What kind of skills are being used in the project?

> It depends on bargaining and being diplomatic. Trying to sort out exactly what was wanted for my project. Sorting out, arranging meeting times, things like that, which I wouldn't have done anyway and I've now probably got more confidence for when I leave . . . to be able to go and present myself.

What is the point of professional studies for Fine Art students?

> It makes it more like an old apprenticeship. You don't get the job at the end, but you get the taste of work experience, like school, but its heavier in the sense that you're running it and it's your responsibility.

> When I finish my Degree I've to be doing it myself, if I do it now while I'm still in College it gives you a bit of protection I suppose against it all going wrong.

Describing their experience

> So it's very much this kind of going through hoops for administrative reasons rather than for something which you see as important for [your] own artistic development.

> Yeah. It's causing quite a bit of friction with what we're trying to do to get a space for it [the exhibition] and people like they want this and they want that and I can't do that because I'm trying to get this done and I can't make any more time available to get it done because I've got a time limit as well. Which is good because it is hard in the business world and that's how it's going to be, there's going to be deadlines and people wanting this and you can't get your own way and all that sort of thing . . .

While cognisant of the value of generic skills and their particular need to develop them, students do not necessarily relate these skills to their main subject of their degree; they do not necessarily see these skills in the same context as others they value such as artistic invention and creativity, mastery over technique, handling of media, achieving aesthetic merit or being well regarded for aesthetic achievement in the field of Fine Art.

This division does interestingly reflect a similar distance in the rhetoric about art encountered in much twentieth-century art discourse.

34.6   Questionnaire analysis and interpretation

Questionnaires were distributed at the time of the second set of interviews. Questions were set up to elicit student perceptions about their degree, about their abilities in relation to skills areas (attributes) and about their responses to the various aspects of the delivery of professional studies, in other words to correspond with the direction of interview questions. Of the 25 completed questionnaires analysed, 17 were by women and 8 by men, 11 age 21 and under, 14 age 22 and over, of which 4 were aged 30 plus.

34.6.1   View of Fine Art degree as a whole

92%   satisfied

8%   less satisfied/dissatisfied

This matches interview evidence.

34.6.2   What sort of job on graduation?

About 48 per cent of the group (male and female) identified with artistic or creative work after graduation rather than with jobs related to art such as arts administration or art teaching; 20 per cent identified with jobs in applied art or arts administration (all women); 24 per cent elected for teaching or teaching related jobs (mostly women); 8 per cent for jobs not related directly to art (male and female).

The male students in this sample identified readily with artistic or creative work.

The results confirm the perception staff had that students are unclear about the reality of graduate destinations and are not fully cognisant of career opportunities in areas related to the arts, or indeed in business and self-enterprise.

34.6.3   Feelings about skills and abilities/confidence rating (on a scale 1 to 6; 1 = excellent, 6 = very poor)

While most of the group's responses placed them in the middle category there are some interesting and significant differences at the higher and lower ends of the scale. Accordingly, the findings are presented to illustrate the marked difference of responses according to gender.

Women's perceptions of their abilities in skills areas seem under-confident in relation to known performance abilities and they mostly scored lower than the men. For example, 37.5 per cent of men described themselves as having a very good level of confidence; by contrast, only 11.76 per cent of women regarded themselves as being very confident; 87.5 per cent of men rated themselves as fairly confident, none regarded their level of confidence as poor; 58.82 per cent of women rated themselves as fairly confident and as many as 23.53 per cent as poor.

These seem to be very significant differences which are reflected in other questions about skills, with two notable exceptions (see (8) and (10) below). Skills responses were as follows:

1. *Communication skills*   Most of the group had a modest-to-good view of their abilities but a larger proportion of women self-scored lower than the men (17.65 per cent of women scored as poor, no men placed themselves in the lowest categories). Most men had greater confidence in their communication skills (50%) compared with women in the same higher categories (just under 30%).

2. *People skills*   Here men appeared much more confident.

3. *Motivation*   Men scored highly with 67.5 per cent indicating they regarded themselves as well motivated and by contrast women scored 41.17 per cent. Few men placed themselves in the poor category (12.5%) while of the women, 58.82 per cent were in the poor category.

4. *Organization*	No men placed themselves in the poor category, although 17.64 per cent of the women placed themselves in categories 5/6 (very low). A few women placed themselves in category 1 (high): 5.88 per cent, but no men.
5. *Creative skills*	Men scored more highly (62.50 per cent men in categories 1and 2), in comparison to women: 35.29 per cent in the same categories.
6. *Problem-solving*	Men scored more highly – 50 per cent men in categories 1 and 2 – in comparison to women who scored 23.53 per cent in the same categories. Of the women as many as 41.17 per cent had a poor view of their abilities while only 25 per cent of men rated themselves in the same low categories (5 and 6).
7. *Planning*	Men scored slightly higher than women in category 2 (high) but broadly they scored similar results.
8. *Community-spirited*	Women self-scored more highly than men (41.17 per cent in the top two categories, while men scored 0 per cent).
9. *High achiever*	More men placed themselves in the higher category.
10.*Team-player*	Apart from the top category where equal numbers of men and women scored, most men (75%) thought less well of their team skills

To conclude, women scored less well than men in all categories except team skills and being community spirited. Students' appreciation in interview that the acquisition of skills is important is interesting in relation to this brief self-assessment guide.

This small study suggests that there may be a difference in levels of confidence according to gender, and that some individuals evidently feel that they perform less well in some skills areas. However, these subjective views need to be measured in relation to an objective assessment of student achievement. The findings are significant because of the role self-confidence plays in motivation and self awareness in reflective learning. Clearly further study is needed following up student's views of themselves in relation to skills one year on.

The enterprise projects seem well designed from the point of view of skills acquisition through the emphasis on learning outcomes and are geared to be a pro-active part of students' self-developmental process.

34.6.4   Students' opinions on the running of professional studies

Students' views were as expected. They showed quite high levels of anxiety about grading student performance in line with the modular system, yet there was a consensus that an assessed mandatory programme was needed:

- A large proportion of the cohort interviewed had a good understanding of the programme's aims and the role of the placement.

- Most agreed with the planned length of the projects and the timing (76%).

- Most agreed that projects should be assessed (72%) and that assessment should be by staff, students and professionals actually involved in the project.

- Most felt that assessment should not count towards the degree (65.38%); more women objected than men (70.59 per cent women and 55.56 per cent of men objected), while 30.77 per cent of the whole group were content with this.

- Most thought that the project programme should be a compulsory element (over 57%) while 38.46 per cent did not.

- Within the sample, 32 per cent did the programme and placement because it was compulsory, while 56 per cent said they would have done it anyway (both sexes equally).

There may be a correlation between women's lack of confidence and their negative views about assessment counting towards the classification of the degree.

There might be some advantage in investigating a pass/fail assessment rather than grades and percentages. Clearly students do need full feedback on their performance in relation to specific skills and goals. Self-assessment is an important element in their self-growth.

34.7   Second stage interviews

These took place towards the end of Semester Two. Questions were framed to discover:

- how the project had fared and what the students' experience had been;
- what the students' reflections were on the skills they had used;
- the students' view of the value of the project;
- their view of its compulsory nature;
- any reflections on former anxieties and whether their views had changed;
- their attitude to assessment and its process, whether the projects should be assessed.

Students related positive and negative experiences in relation to the projects. Some resented the stress that arose from initiating projects. In many cases it had been hard work, but all had been determined to see their project through and had not given up. They had a critical view of the relative value of different types of projects and felt on reflection that projects had to be selected carefully. Students seemed critically aware of the educative process and were assertive and confident in putting their views across in interview. Students seemed clearer than before as to outcomes and values of skills and talked more coherently about these.

Students talked positively about skills gained as a consequence of professional studies, and showed awareness of self-improvement in spite of some difficult experiences en route. They stated that they had:

- gained social confidence, using communication skills and social skills;
- used their initiative;
- seen a project through;
- solved health and safety problems and tackled resourcing;
- dealt with problems of timing;
- got on with management;
- shown the ability to be flexible and to adapt ideas.

34.7.1 Examples of responses

And what was your experience?

I was the 2nd year rep on the Gloucester Docks Exhibition and I just had to oversee the exhibition really, get people together with paintings, get them over there, out them up, go to different meetings with other reps, lecturers, tutors and council people. And then the day before it opened. I had to go to a buffet lunch with council reps and the Mayor and things . . .

Did that develop your social skills in that situation?

Yeah, because they were all officials and stuff . . . It's one thing I've got to do anyway. My social skills aren't that brilliant anyway, meeting people . . . It got me out there, shaking a few hands.

Do you think in principle, that it's a good idea that you should be going out and doing work outside the College as part of your Degree?

I think we should because art is all about getting people to see it and getting involved with people out there.

If the module hadn't been compulsory, would you have wanted to do some kind of work outside college?

Yes . . . It helps us really, at the end of the day. It gives you so much more experience once you leave the college. Once you leave, you can come back but it's not the same. You're not in that environment. If you do well with professional Studies. then you get contacts outside and you've also got the confidence to go up to other people as well and actually ask them things.

Students felt the projects had value; also they appreciated the opportunity to gain useful contacts for when they leave college.

Most felt that professional studies should be available within the curriculum and the majority thought it should be compulsory in order to spur them into action. They thought. that it was a good idea to be able to do such projects while a support system was available, in order to gain experience for when they leave college. They thought that professional studies gave an appropriate focus on 'graduate skills' – they perceived these as useful.

Students were still anxious about parity of assessment in relation to perceived differences in project size and degree of challenge; indeed, they showed considerable anxiety about assessment and wanted further clarification on how it was done. Students were positive about self-assessment, but not all felt that Professional Studies should be formally assessed or that the grade should count towards the degree. One view was that there was a clear difference in criteria and philosophy used in assessing the main subject of the degree and that of Professional Studies. They were keen to have feedback from experts in the field on their performance.

Most students had realized their capabilities, and had gained in confidence.

34.8 Comments and conclusion

Clearly students see a necessity for professional studies but this is not looked on by many students as part and parcel of their degree; it is in their view, a useful add-on. Students' idea of the purpose of the Fine Art degree (seen to be esoteric and self-developmental in the area of aesthetics through the main study – art practice) does not easily match with their initial understanding of the real world of opportunities (jobs) outside college.

Many of the generic skills highlighted in professional studies projects are at first perceived by undergraduates to be unrelated to the theme of the main degree; yet, while seen apart, these skills are nevertheless recognized as important.

Professional Studies is seen as supplying a necessary missing element (the practical application of art to the wider world) but these students would not elect to study in this way for 100 per cent of the curriculum. Research suggests that the present balance between professional studies (about 12%) and main studies (about 88 %) works for them, that is, it fits with their motivation.

Subject-based studies can successfully incorporate graduate skills through assessed projects undertaken in tandem with main studies as long as tensions within the curriculum are skilfully managed in terms of timing and delivery.

Student worries about projects usually subside after the event. Other studies have shown that level 3 students have much more positive feelings in retrospect, valuing their work experience immensely.[10] But enterprise project work is very demanding on staff and students and can be stressful on the individual and on staffing resources.

The findings of the study suggest that there is a need to further consider student anxiety over assessment, to reconsider whether work experience should be graded, with the grade counting towards the classified degree result, although student anxieties about assessment revealed in the study may be modified when they come to be interviewed post-assessment.

Student awareness of skills increases through the kind of practical focus that occurs in work projects where they are expected to address skills specifically as specific learning outcomes and through feedback focused critically on relative strengths and weaknesses.

Strategic support should be given in the form of small self-help groups at regular intervals during the delivery of the programme. The role of students and recent graduates as mentors is invaluable. Information should be delivered on a need-to-know basis, particularly on learning contracts, coping with glitches as they arise and in relation to assessment.

The expected heavier proportion of negative attitudes was not in evidence, even though professional studies was mandatory. However there are some notable extreme and contrasting views about the programme and about individual's experiences, suggesting that some personalities thrive in such situations where others clearly struggle, this is interesting in comparison with the figures on gender and confidence levels.

As far as the interpretation of the perceptions of students according to gender is concerned, it would seem that women are either more candid or more modest about their abilities or have far less self-confidence. The extent to which this is a significant factor in the way they respond to and seize hold of opportunities remains to be discussed and may be a topic for further investigation.

Many women students tend to perform well in modes of assessment geared to written reports, so they do not necessarily under-perform in the academic curriculum in the same way that they perceive their ability to perform. Achievement and assessment are not necessarily matched by the findings on perception, but these findings may have other significance in relation to motivation and preparation. Anxiety levels vary according to each individual but also seem to differ according to gender. While some women displayed a high degree of anxiety during the projects, some men appeared to be more relaxed over issues of preparation.

Maturity in age and previous life experience are not significant factors in relation to anxiety, ability to cope or perform well in work-based projects. Since students choose their project and adapt the aims and objectives to meet their own needs, they are all in a similar pressured situation, whatever their age or previous experience.

Nearly all the students have shown that they are immensely capable of running enterprise projects, that when encouraged and challenged they can overcome reticence about their abilities, and hesitation about taking on challenges.

The investigation suggests that a level of anxiety about new situations is inevitable and not necessarily a bad thing. Yet support is clearly necessary for some students.

Focus on generic skills and self-development is advantageous. While the meta-cognition of Level Two students might not be very sophisticated, this kind of reflective learning on a negotiated basis within the academic curriculum can be immensely helpful to the individual's growth and awareness, leading to higher pro-active levels of self-management as part of the educational process and improved career planning.

The world of work is fully integrated within the curriculum and students have the opportunity to reflect on their experience in the non-vocational environment of the college.

Notes

1. The research material was prepared by Dr Karen Ross.

2. See Walker (1994).

3. The types of projects undertaken are normally short-term, of a few weeks' duration and include working with local art gallery and museum staff providing projects for the under-fives and print workshops; painting commissioned murals; artist residencies in schools; coordinating visual arts displays for department stores and businesses; helping to plan and run a local arts festival with open-air exhibits, group exhibitions. These work projects differ from those that cater exclusively for professional qualifications in industry; the latter, while introducing undergraduates to a real work force, do not necessarily offer initiative tests nor enterprise challenges useful to future art and design graduates.

4. MacLennan (1997).

5. The National Committee of Enquiry into Higher Education (1997); see also THES (1997) and Winter (1997).

6. This is best described as 'controlled' independent learning, reflecting on an excellent group discussion following the paper given by Evans and Morgan (1997) at the *5th Improving Student Learning Symposium: Improving Students as Learners*, Glasgow 1997.

7. This is a different approach from that of other work schemes. Compare with Industrial Placement for Catering Management, Hotel Management, Leisure and Tourism Management. See 1996 Module Guide, C&GCHE, Peter Christensen.

8. The Department of Art, C&GCHE is participating in *Destinations and Reflections: The National Survey of British Art, Craft and Design Graduate Education*, led by Birmingham Institute of Art and Design, 1998–2000.

9. See CGCHE Faculty Summary Field Statistics of Annual Review 1995/96; 1996/97.

10. Unpublished data from informal interviews with third-year undergraduates at C&GCHE, held during 1995–97. For a comparative study see papers relating to the ESRC Learning Society Programme: The Acquisition of Core Skills in Education and Employment,

Centre for Research on Teaching and Learning, University of Exeter, especially: Moira Fraser (1997) Students' experiences of compulsory core skills modules in vocational and non-vocational degree programmes: three case Studies, conference paper given at *5th Improving Student Learning Symposium: Improving Students as Learners*, Glasgow 1997.

34.9   References

Evans, T. and Morgan, A. (1997) Independent learning confronts globalisation: facilitating students' development as learners. Conference paper given at the *5th Improving Student Learning Symposium: Improving Students as Learners*, Glasgow.

Fraser, M. (1997) Students' experiences of compulsory core skills modules in vocational and non-vocational degree programmes: three case studies, Conference paper given at the *5th Improving Student Learning Symposium: Improving Students as Learners*, Glasgow 1997.

MacLennan, H.M. (1997) Using action research to develop a resource based Professional Studies programme for B.A. Hons. Fine Art students, *Using Research to Improve Student Learning through Course Design*, Oxford : OCSD.

The National Committee of Enquiry into Higher Education (1997) *Higher Education in the Learning Society* (The Dearing Report).

Times Higher Education Supplement (1997) 'What Dearing says' and 'Summary' *Times Higher Education Supplement*, 25 July.

Walker, L. (ed.) (1994) *Institutional Change towards an Ability-Based Curriculum in Higher Education*, Oxford Brooks University.

Winter, J. (1997) *Skills for Graduates in the 21st Century*, Whiteway Research, The Association of Graduate Recruiters.

35 Academic development during the first year at university

Velda McCune
Centre for Research on Learning and Instruction, University of Edinburgh

35.1 Introduction

Although there has been considerable research in recent years into the ways in which first year students learn and study in higher education, very few studies have considered how students' learning develops throughout these early experiences. This chapter describes progress in a longitudinal study of the ways in which first year students carry out, and think about, their academic tasks. The main research focus is the nature and extent of this development, also of interest are factors which influence development, and relationships between development and outcomes. Following students' progress throughout the year in this way allows in depth exploration of students' experiences as they happen, and lets the researcher consider the order in which events and changes occur. This gives greater potential for understanding how and why students' learning develops during the first year.

Data collection for the study is being carried out in two phases. In the 1995/96 academic year three semi-structured interviews were carried out with a group of 18 students taking Psychology 1. The first of these interviews was conducted as early as possible in the first term. The second and third interviews were timed so as to coincide with events likely to influence students' development, such as essay-writing and examinations. A matched group of students was interviewed only at time three, in order to explore the effects of the repeated interviews on students. Finally, the Approaches and Study Skills Inventory for Students (ASSIST, Tait, Entwistle and McCune, 1997) was presented to the entire psychology first-year group midway through the year. The second phase of the main study data collection is in progress at present, it will mirror the first phase except that the ASSIST inventory will be presented twice, to allow development to be explored in both quantitative and qualitative data.

To date only initial analysis of one-third of the repeat interview data can be described. One purpose of this analysis was to explore how concepts identified from the literature were represented in this data. A range of concepts are relevant in this context, but the present chapter will discuss only a subset of these. In their course work the first-year psychology students are expected to write essays which show their understanding of a topic; to gain high marks students are expected to be able to relate disparate material and show that they have thought about the topic for themselves. This being the case, it seems likely that a deep approach to studying will be important in this context. The defining features of a deep approach are an intention to understand for oneself and an active interest in course content, coupled with methods of processing that content. These forms of processing include:

relating ideas to previous knowledge and experience; looking for patterns and underlying principles; checking evidence and relating it to conclusions; and critically examining logic and argument (see, for example, Entwistle, 1997).

Although this general description of a deep approach is well established, the exact nature of a deep approach will vary depending on context (Marton and Säljö, 1997). It is therefore important to establish what a deep approach to learning in first-year psychology might be before one can consider how that approach develops. The initial analysis suggests the aspects described in the following section, but these categories may shift when additional interviews are incorporated into the analysis.

35.2   Aspects of a deep approach

An intention to understand course content appears in the analyses, although the emphasis is often more towards understanding what a lecturer means, or what a section of a textbook means, rather than on understanding for oneself. The interview analyses also picked out the interest aspect of a deep approach. Looking at deep processes, students related ideas to their previous knowledge, although they tended to be relating ideas only within topics in psychology, rather than between topics or subject areas. Students also thought critically about materials, often doing this by considering the strengths and weaknesses of evidence, and how this evidence was related to conclusions.

These categories map clearly onto previous descriptions of a deep approach. Two additional categories describing action on content were also identified which seemed to fit within a deep approach: *selecting important ideas* and *organizing* material. Selecting important ideas describes students choosing what to include in their notes, rather than copying everything down. Important ideas may be what students see as the main points in a topic, but material may also be selected based on interest or novelty.

> [If] I've really not heard about it before or . . . it's something that just I don't know anything about I'll listen carefully to what he's saying and write it all down. If he's talking more in general, I'll maybe write down the odd piece of information but just the key things . . . We're talking at the moment about chimps and . . . I don't write down all the names of the various chimps or what they can do themselves, just the basic conclusions and disagreements about what chimps can and cannot do.

Organizing describes students arranging materials for themselves by drawing diagrams or maps, writing plans or drawing together related materials from different sources.

> I get my categories and use maybe a highlighter pen and sometimes I'll even number [concepts] . . . I'll decide what links onto what and I'll have them all sitting in front of me, you have to have a huge desk for this, and I'll have the categories highlighted and then I'll have a note of what colour I'm going to do first, maybe four different highlighted sections.

It seems conceptually justifiable to see *selecting important ideas* and organization as processes that would be associated with an intention to understand. Selecting important ideas maps fairly closely onto the scale selecting main ideas, described by Weinstein, Palmer and Schulte (1987), which has previously been linked to a deep approach (Tait and Entwistle, 1996). A similar category to organization is described in the Motivated Strategies For Learning Questionnaire, analyses of which link organization to subscales whose items clearly overlap items previously used to describe a deep approach (Pintrich, Smith, Garcia, and McKeachie, 1991).

35.3   Aspects of metacognition and self-regulation

As well as processing content, students must take decisions about the ways in which they process content. This in turn implies awareness and monitoring in relation to that content. These themes of monitoring in relation to content and directing processing of content are implied by a deep approach, but more explicitly describe aspects of self-regulation and metacognition. Metacognition is most often defined in terms of knowledge of one's cognition and monitoring and regulation of one's cognitive activities (Vermunt, 1998; McKeachie, 1990; Brown, 1987; Weinert, 1987). In the context of student learning, self-regulation refers to individuals monitoring, controlling and directing aspects of their learning for themselves. Self-regulation therefore overlaps metacognition but is broader, taking into account monitoring and regulation of aspects of learning other than cognition, such as mood, goals, and resources (Pintrich, 1995). Self-regulation or metacognition in relation to content might involve, for example, being aware when material is not understood, trying to discern why there are difficulties in understanding, changing one's study processes to enhance understanding, and selecting content material for oneself (Pintrich, Smith, Garcia and McKeachie, 1991; Vermunt, 1998).

For students in this study, these aspects of metacognition and self-regulation are emerging in several categories. *Self-regulation of content* involves students selecting the reading they do based on their own interests, rather than simply reading all of what they are told to read. Students may select reading from within the syllabus or go beyond it. *Monitoring understanding and related regulation* describes students modifying their studying where they are having difficulties understanding, for example, by doing further reading in that area or by working on their notes in that area.

Awareness of content and related regulation refers to students monitoring the content material being collected or used during a study task, based on awareness of what content is required to complete the task. Students then regulate based on that monitoring. For example, they may monitor and regulate the material they are noting for an essay in relation to their essay plan and the content of the notes they have already made. The previous two categories refer to 'on-line' monitoring and regulation. *Reflecting on success* describes students considering the success of their processing or regulation of content. This may occur some time after a task is completed. For example, students may decide subsequently that mind maps are better for relating ideas, or that gaining an overview is helpful in selecting content for an essay.

> One book I read . . . it didn't really give any of the other story, and if I'd had that and maybe one of the others that was like that, then I wouldn't have got a full picture of what the debate was really about . . . I think you've got to know, maybe from one of the general psychology books like Gleitman, who the main theorists are . . . then go and find their work in books in the library . . . If you have something like that for your essay, it gives a good overview of what you are going to be covering, and then you can just go on in more detail.

35.4   Developmental aspects of studying

In addition to these more developed categorizations, it is possible to give some further, tentative, suggestions based on the interview analysis. It seems that, in general, the students did not make great changes in the ways they carried out and thought about academic tasks. They might modify some details but clear development of approaches, self-regulation or metacognition was rare. Where students had changed, it was typically by working things out for themselves or through advice from friends or tutors; students rarely took advantage of study skills materials or courses. The following quote comes from one student who had show development, in that she began to think critically using evidence, which she had not done previously. This change seemed to have been caused by detailed advice from a tutor, on how to think critically when reading.

> I think I question things more and also the tutorials that I've had, we always have an article or a chapter of a book to read before the tutorial, and then we go in and discuss it. We've been questioning a lot more how the writer goes about (it). From the introduction whether they actually cover the points that they've said they'd cover, and questioning whether the author is biased, and I found that that's really made me think a lot more about what I'm actually reading . . . I have to keep remembering with Psychology that they're only ideas, and psychologists' views on something, and it's not actually dead set. Whereas before with my A levels most of what I've been reading is actually fact, so yeah I think that's helped me. . .In a way, it makes me less trustworthy of what I'm reading, but in a way it makes me feel more independent in my work, it makes me feel less like I'm being taken in by what they're writing. If I actually think well, why (are they saying) what they are saying.

Some possible reasons have emerged to suggest why this sort of development is unusual, and why there is a low uptake of study skills materials. Students often held negative attitudes to materials giving advice, believing that such materials would not add to what they already knew about studying. They often felt that their current methods were working well enough, and therefore did not see any need to make the effort required to change them. Some students saw themselves as fixed in their methods, unable to change even should they wish to do so.

35.5   Future directions

The categories established suggest that recognizable aspects of a deep approach to studying, of self-regulation and of metacognition have been identified during the interviews. These and other categories will be developed further using the full set of interview data. Given this basis, later analyses will describe in detail how these aspects of students' learning develop, or do not develop, during the first year. Once development has been described, the analysis can focus on influences on development, systematically exploring their effects.

Acknowledgements

The research described in this chapter is supported by an Economic and Social Research Council Postgraduate Training Award.

35.6   References

Brown, A. (1987) Metacognition, executive control, self-regulation and other more mysterious mechanisms. In F. E. Weinert and R. H. Kluwe (eds), *Metacognition, Motivation and Understanding*, Hillsdale, NJ: Erlbaum.

Entwistle, N.J. (1997) Contrasting perspectives on learning. In F. Marton, D.J. Hounsell and N.J. Entwistle (eds), *The Experience of Learning*, 2nd edn, Edinburgh: Scottish Academic Press.

Marton, F. and Säljö, R. (1997) Approaches to learning. In F. Marton, D.J. Hounsell and N.J. Entwistle (eds), *The Experience of Learning*, 2nd edn, Edinburgh: Scottish Academic Press.

McKeachie, W.J. (1990) Research on college teaching: the historical background, *Journal of Educational Psychology*, **82**(2), 189–200.

Pintrich, P.R. (1995) Understanding self-regulated learning. In P.R. Pintrich (ed.), *New Directions for Teaching and Learning: Understanding Self-Regulated Learning*, California: Jossey-Bass.

Pintrich, P.R., Smith, D.A.F., Garcia, T. and McKeachie, W.J. (1991) *A Manual for the Use of the Motivated Strategies for Learning Questionnaire (MSLQ)*, Ann Arbor, Mich: National Centre for Research to Improve Postsecondary Teaching and Learning.

Tait, H. and Entwistle, N.J. (1996) Identifying students at risk through ineffective study strategies, *Higher Education*, **31**(1), 97–116.

Tait, H. Entwistle, N.J. and McCune, V. (1997) ASSIST: a reconceptualisation of the approaches to studying inventory. Paper presented at the *5th International Improving Student Learning Symposium*, University of Strathclyde, 1997.

Vermunt, J.D. (1998) The regulation of constructive learning processes, *British Journal of Educational Psychology*, in press.

Weinert, F.E. (1987) Introduction and overview: metacognition and motivation as determinants of effective learning and understanding. In F.E. Weinert and R.H. Kluwe (eds), *Metacognition, Motivation and Understanding*, Hillsdale, NJ: Erlbaum.

Weinstein, C.E., Palmer, D.R. and Schulte, A.C. (1987) *LASSI: Learning and Study Strategies Inventory*, Florida: H & H Publishing Company.

36 Researching business: delivering a research module using learning sets and the World Wide Web

Alistair Mutch
The Nottingham Trent University

36.1   Introduction

The concern of this chapter is the exploration of and reflection upon the delivery of an undergraduate module on research in a business school. This module is designed to be an introduction to both research methods and to issues surrounding the selection and development of research topics. As such it raises a whole range of issues, but the principal focus of this chapter is on the use of learning sets, with a subsidiary focus being the use of a Web-based mailing list to support the process. It is, of course, impossible to wrench these issues out of their context and the chapter will touch upon the impact of modularization, the place of research modules in business education and the design of the assessment process.

The research that underlies the chapter has three principal dimensions. One is a reflection on five years of experience in teaching on such modules, an experience mediated by a lasting commitment to research and informed by current research interests in the area of information management.[1] The perspective taken is that of the centrality of an understanding of the place of theory in research, a keen appreciation of the need to connect with the student experience and an interest in the role of information technology (IT) in both education and the workplace. One influence on the latter has been the use of the notion of the 'electronic text' as outlined by Zuboff. She observed the contradictory impacts of the ways in which 'electronic communication provided a documentary record of formal communication' and similar impacts might be found in an educational context (Zuboff, 1988, p. 384). However, for research purposes the archive of material generated during the course of the module forms a rich source of material.[2]

A further source of material has been the reflections of the students themselves, captured at two group evaluation sessions towards the end of the module and transcribed. The tone of the chapter is avowedly exploratory, reflective and tentative; this is an evolving, dynamic area and the experiences recorded here are a stage in a process, not an end point.

The chapter commences with some brief comments on the place of research in business programmes which are intended to point out some key contradictions. In this context it goes on to reflect on the experience of four years of participating in research modules. This experience and the dissatisfaction with it forms the backdrop to an outline of the current module. The issues behind its design are explored before undertaking an evaluation of the experience with a primary focus on the learning sets. The conclusion is that the model used is a useful one but that it raises some interesting questions. The chapter concludes with some speculations on the role and purpose of groupwork in higher education and on the problems of embedding new delivery methods in the fabric of existing courses.

36.2 Uncomfortable bedfellows: research and business studies

Business and Management is now the largest single area of British higher education. Its massive growth and 'success' conceals a range of concerns and tensions, centring principally on the 'identity' of the subject (Mutch, 1997). In truth, Business degrees (which I will use as a convenient shorthand for the entire range of undergraduate offerings in this area) vary widely in content and discipline base. The central tension here might be between those who see Business degrees as firmly in the vocational area and those who are anxious to stress origins in more traditional disciplines, notably social science. This tension is not one which can be written out, and it can be a source of creativity, but its impact as far as research is concerned might be to split staff into two broad camps. Those in the 'vocational' wing, particularly those who have been recruited as much for their practical experience as their academic background, may well view research and a research module as being primarily about method. One thinks here in particular of the affiliation of marketing with large scale surveys. Students are affected by this influence of subject content and, reinforced by the powerful quantitative tradition in some business research (notably as displayed in many American journals), come to see research as involving problems of sample selection, probability etc. In the other camp are those who have a primarily academic research background, often powerfully influenced by ethnographic traditions. There is often a tendency here to defend the 'academic tradition', a tradition which, in connection with student learning in particular, is often seen, one might argue, through a rose-tinted lens (Macfarlane, 1997). The result can be a failure to connect with students' concerns at what is perceived as very difficult subject matter.

These tensions, contradictions and uncertainties are reflected in student perceptions, often over-determined by 'instrumentality'. By this term I refer initially to the motivation behind students choosing this as an area of study, which is more influenced by considerations of employability than other areas of study. This means that students are often unaware of what Business as an area of study might involve before they join their courses, a lack of awareness which might take some time to resolve. This primary focus on the degree as an entry to the job market tends towards a focus on education as a process of information transmission and assessment as the key motivation. In this context, subjects which are not seen to possess an immediate 'relevance' are open to question and hostility. This can be reinforced by the large minority of students for whom higher education would not have in the past been a natural progression and by the growth in access to higher education, especially through qualifications which stress their vocational nature. These tensions form the background to the development of the current module, but this also has to be seen in the context of lessons learnt from several years of change and development of research modules.

36.3 Researching IT in Business: context and development

Nottingham Business School has a portfolio of seven full-time undergraduate degrees with an annual intake of some 500 students.[3] This is therefore a substantial programme and has been organized as such since the early 1990s, with core modules taken by all students and a wide variety of options. The School adopted a modular scheme in 1991 and moved to semesters two years later. The introduction of modules saw the opportunity for the introduction of a module aimed at all of the students bar those on European Business called Exploring Business Research. This module went through a series of metamorphoses from which a series of lessons were learned. These were of the desirability of student choice in the assessment process and of the need to connect material with where students were at, as opposed to where staff might like them to be.

These lessons converged with a parallel interest in the possibilities offered by IT to overcome some of the problems previously encountered. This convergence was sparked by two factors: firstly, the author's research and practical interests in the impact of IT in both education and the workplace; and secondly, the growing support infrastructure within the School. In the first regard, the author was involved in a number of successful attempts to embed the use of spreadsheets in an accounting module (Mutch, 1993).. These attempts then led to some use of the World Wide Web in the support of seminar activity (Mutch, 1996) The lessons drawn from this experience were the need to embed technology as part of the learning process and the need to place it in the context of the development of student abilities in what are regarded as 'traditional' areas, such as the ability to outline key parts of an argument. The author was, then, sceptical about the claims made for technologies such as multimedia (Hamilton, 1996) but alert to the possibilities in other directions. This awareness was stimulated by other attempts in the school to use IT such as conferencing and also by the growing ability of the infrastructure, both physical (i.e. the spread of Windows PCs with the ability to support Web browsers) and human, notably the appointment of a learning-focused Internet co-ordinator. These factors meant that an additional resource was available to help solve the conundrum of how to give a degree of individuality to learning in a mass programme.

It had become clear that the new module would have to start from the basis of allowing students to choose their own topic for the research proposal. This was to be tied in much more closely to the final-year dissertation, about which there was widespread concern among staff. Performance was seen to be below the levels achieved in other areas and, while there were a number of potential reasons for this, one contributory factor was seen to be students' inability to select and research a topic early enough. From this perspective, and given the concerns highlighted above, it seemed clear that the lecture programme would have to be structured round the process students were going through. As such, it was totally restructured so that it started from the process of selecting a topic and rose gradually from the concrete to the abstract. In doing this, it was hoped that it would mirror the student's own developmental process. The testing of the more theoretical areas was incorporated by the construction of much more explicit assessment criteria[4]. The problem remained, however, of how to support students in their learning, given the inadequacy of the previous seminar programme and the numbers involved.[5] The answer was sought in the combination of learning sets and the use of the Web.

Learning sets are used successfully in the School's postgraduate provision, but their success might seem to rest in particular on the motivation and self-discipline of students in that area. There was some experience of the use of learning sets to support the dissertation in the final year, but there was some indication that tutors tended to dominate these. In addition, tutor attendance would not be feasible in the tight resource constraints obtaining. The decision was therefore taken to use the features of the Web to both control and enhance the use of learning sets. Students were set specific outcomes for each week and these outcomes were to be reported each week via electronic mail. As these were IS students and the technology was simple and readily available this was not though to impose any significant barrier. The mail would be archived in a Web-based list, which was simple to manipulate into different views – topic, date and author. The list was not explicitly designed to act as a conferencing mechanism, but it was explicitly tied into the lecture programme. This was done by amending the content of the lectures to reflect problems highlighted in the postings. Each week these were reviewed and issues identified. One such issue which was explored was the production of working titles, when one student's topic was selected and various potential titles explored. The learning sets ran for five weeks and culminated in a learning set which the module tutor attended at which informal presentations were given of progress on research proposals to date. This was to act in some form as formative feedback and a chance to air issues. The design of the module was intended to afford the maximum student choice and flexibility of delivery within very tight resource constraints: to what extent can it be said to have succeeded?

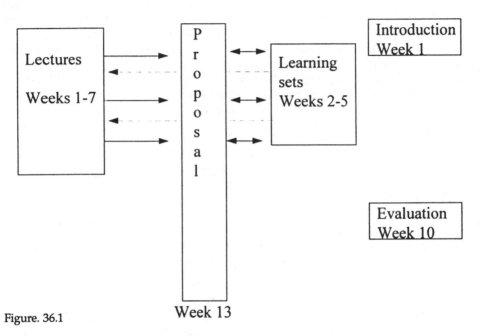

Figure. 36.1

36.4   The module in practice

The following account is structured around Laurillard's four elements of a principled teaching strategy: that it should be discursive, adaptive, interactive and reflective (Laurillard, 1993, pp. 94–5). The use of this framework seems appropriate not only because it is presented in the context of the assessment of the place of different types of educational technology, but also because it allows for an account which can reflect the interdependent nature of the methods used in a way which would be harder if the methods were discussed individually. The discussion will examine the characteristics which Laurillard draws out as characterizing each element, inter-weaving evidence from the evaluation sessions, the electronic text and tutor reflections. It will then seek to draw out some key issues for further debate and research.

Discursive: teachers and students conceptions should each be accessible to the other; teacher and students must agree learning goals for the topic, and task goals; the teacher must provide an environment within which students can act on, generate and receive feedback on descriptions appropriate to the topic goal

One conflict between conceptions which became apparent during group sessions was that over the nature and purpose of learning sets. In part, we can relate this to the orthodox conception of group work within business programmes. The students are used to working within groups in work that draws on parallels of the use of teams within business. That is, the group has to produce (generally) a piece of work owned collectively. This generally produces a reasonable amount of debate about levels of contribution and makes students very sensitive to the 'free rider' problem. A vehicle which uses groups to support individual effort is alien to this concept, and students found it difficult to adapt to. In particular, they questioned the value to themselves of participation in groups where other members knew little about their own topic:

> I don't think learning sets worked at all. I don't see how a system can work that by people with different ideas can be expected to comment on your ideas because the fact is with a module as in, say a choice of essay titles, you choose one, you're not expected to choose 4 and basically you've got to like home in on your own thing and not everybody else, I just don't think it really worked at all. The learning set idea, that you're going to learn from other people.

The feeling was among this group of students that the learning sets had descended to the level of ritual and that, in so far as they existed, they were to meet the demands of the mailing list: 'with our group I know that we mailed you out of obligation because we knew that we had to mail you that week and we didn't really put much though into what we were mailing'. This was compared by this student explicitly to the experience on other modules: 'It didn't seem as though it was a group thing, the others are, we know they're group work and we did them together.' There is then a problem of existing expectations setting up a clash of conceptions. However, it was noticeable that other students did not experience this clash:

> Our group actually worked quite well. We did get a lot out of it. James just said, you don't know what everybody's doing, I mean I did the learning and Andrew did OLAP, I didn't actually know anything about OLAP but once Andrew had explained what he was doing and where he was going its easy just to say well what about this angle or what about that angle and that's what we thought the aim of the learning set was, and so we actually took it down that way. We gave everybody a chance to speak at what they was looking at and what problems they had got and we just brainstormed together. So you don't have to be an expert on somebody's field of study you can just help them out.

While this might point to a need to explore conceptions earlier in the module, it also has to be seen in a further aspect on the learning context that was a persistent feature of discussions during the module as well as in evaluation sessions, that of student competitiveness. In the words of one student: 'basically our course is very competitive anyway. There is a lot of competition on the course and inherently there's going to be competition within groups.' The source of such competitiveness is open to speculation: contributory causes could be the general social environment, the specificity of business courses, the gender balance on the course. However, the impact is clear: in the words of one (male) student:

> I think the thing is at the end of the day we all want to get good grades and if it helps our assessment we'll try and do something towards getting a better grade. But if that's not how it works then we're not so inclined [female student interrupts] Stuff everybody else.

An observation on this would be that the mature students (of either gender) and female students were more inclined to argue that learning sets could work and to have appeared to have made more of a conscious effort to get them to work. However, all the students were generally supportive of the degree of choice given them in selecting their own topic for research. However, this did add another layer of anxiety to that of grappling with an unfamiliar assessment vehicle. We will look at this further below, but it does point to a dilemma for teachers in designing balanced assessment strategies, particularly in a modular scheme. (Mutch, 1996b) The problem is that a wide range of assessment types might be considered desirable, but that it causes students problems in adapting to what is required.

We have already seen that for some students the use of the mailing list took on a ritual character, and indeed tutor disappointment with this was expressed at one point on the website. However, some students argued that this was partly a matter of organization and partly a question of timing. They didn't use the list, they argued, to search out material on others doing similar topics, because searching through it was too complex. There is a clear role for the teacher here in providing clear signposts as to how the list might be used in this way. However, some students also felt that the mailing list and the sets stopped just when they might be getting to be useful:

> I think its only really worked from when we stopped the learning sets, its only then that people have been getting in to what they really need to do. If you get something out of a learning set you will put something in, because you know how important it is for you. So its not something that you can really give much effort to earlier on . . . Because it hasn't been thoroughly important for your project until then, its difficult to suddenly jump in and say ah yes its going to be really important now.

The notion is that the pacing of a semester from a student's point of view and that of the teacher may be very different, and that this pacing differs between groups of students. While timing is heavily constrained by modular schemes, this might point to the need to see the learning process as running over the boundaries of modules, a point which will be returned to. However, to what extent was the module successful in adapting to the development of student conceptions?

Adaptive: the teacher has the responsibility to use the relationship between their own and the students conception to determine the focus of the continuing dialogue

This element could be seen to relate to two components of the module: the aim of modifying lectures to adapt to student concerns as raised in the output from learning sets and the level of debate which took place on the mailing list itself. The principle of running a partially flexible lecture programme was welcomed:

> It showed a degree of flexibility on your part, that it wasn't just set up at the start and you had to follow it, regardless of what our interests were, so it did show that you were prepared to be flexible in the things we wanted to know about.

However, in terms of learning it was clear that students put much more value on the presentation session in week 8. The problems with getting the learning sets going in many cases meant that few direct questions were raised on the mailing list, although some students did use the facility to raise questions which seemed to indicate a 'deep' approach to the topics on the module:

> A quick(!) question though . . . in sociological research, the researcher obviously has to make decisions about what data/info. they are to collect. Will their political stance (and the fact that they cannot be objective) affect the validity of their findings – won't there always be an element of uncertainty in the results? Also, couldn't another researcher who is studying the same organization (or whatever) come up with an entirely different result? It seems that because it is impossible to be neutral, the integrity of our findings could suffer as a result . . .

This was rare, though, and there was certainly no sense of a student to student discussion. However, such a discussion was not expected or planned for: there is a question mark over the realism of using conferencing technologies for students present in one location. If we accept the argument that there is a 'need to weave the groupware system into the daily workflow, so that it does not stand there as an obstacle to the flow, but rather as an embedded step of a complex task' then we will have doubts about the extent to which conferencing systems can be so embedded in the daily student context (Ciborra, 1996, p. 203).

Interactive: the students must act to achieve the task goal; the teacher must provide meaningful intrinsic feedback on the actions that relates to the nature of the task goal

Once again, the lack of familiarity with both the form of learning in the module and with the assessment vehicle meant that many students found it difficult to get going.

> I think it's a strange piece of work to actually have to write, well I personally, I can't speak for the rest of us, I've never done anything like that before. I know its a hybrid between an essay and a report but I've never written anything like that before. So I found it difficult at first to get into it.

However, the relation of the learning sets and the mailing list to the assessment was seen as supplying a useful set of prompts:

> I think the mailing list had a very beneficial effect. It got you thinking every week about what your proposal was and when something's got to be in you think oh yeah, I'd better get on with that and it gets you thinking about it all the time so it's not left to the last minute. Which is quite easy with other modules where nobody even talks about it at all

What was seen to be of real value was the presentation session in Week 8. The opportunity to get direct feedback on where individual proposals were going was seen to be an enormous help, to the extent that students wished they had had an additional session in week 4. There was seen to be little substitute for direct contact, even though the pressure of resources was appreciated.

Reflective: the teacher must support the process in which students link the feedback on their actions to the topic goal for every level of description within the topic structure

One of the problems in measuring the success of this module is that its impact will only be partially revealed in the assessments done specifically for it. However, there was evidence that for some, at least, valuable lessons had been learned:

what I've really learnt from this module, the quality of the information is important, and like a lot more ways that you can get your information rather than just your normal sort of bog standard, your trade papers. It wakes you up a little bit. It opens your eyes, I reckon, personally.

Its true success will come in the quality of the dissertations completed in the final year and in the learning exhibited during the production of that document. The evaluation sessions, however, clearly reflected the importance of dialogue at all stages in a module, in that it helped to have an in-depth discussion which was self-consciously reflective about the design and delivery of the module. In this sense, evaluation is a powerful learning tool for not only staff, but also for students. In too many modules students feel that nobody talks to and with them, only at them, and that module evaluation questionnaires are just another way to avoid a real engagement. If this module has been able to help students in the process of reflection, this may have been its greatest achievement. Certainly, it had measurable success in that at least half a dozen students had developed topics which they could carry forward to their placement year. In this, it had given them a much clearer sense of direction about the degree as a whole. The value of this module, then, needs to be set in the context of a broader and longer process of development.

36.5 Conclusions

The perception of the author is that learning sets can be used with a degree of success in this environment and that, further, the use of Web mailing lists is a useful adjunct to the process. However, the experience raises many issues. Central here is the nature of the context in which such uses are made. There are clearly issues which can be tackled at the modular level, relating to better matching of student and lecturer conceptions. But these may well founder on factors in the broader context. Two issues for further exploration suggest themselves. One is the nature of the models of group work used within business courses. While these are used to give students experience of team work in an explicit desire to match practice at work and prepare students with transferable skills, do they adequately reflect the full nature of the way in which individuals and teams interact? Might not the mutual support offered by groups to individuals actually match more elements of practice, and ought we not to be striving to make more use of this model? The second is the problem of embedding the use of technological support media in the fabric of educational activities. This is extraordinarily difficult to do, given resource constraints, but it is suggested that the type of 'background' use of tools like Web lists is a more useful model than, for example, multimedia. Such use has implications for the development of teacher skills but the more fundamental challenges are for us to be continually returning to basic questions about the learning process.

Notes

1. Recognizing that one's own research agenda has a powerful influence on the way one approaches the whole subject of the teaching of research theory and methods, it is only fair to reveal the major influences on my own approach. My own research was initially in history and emerged from the tradition of the British Marxist historians. After a period in industry I returned to academia in the field of business information systems. I found the debate between adherents of quantitative and qualitative methods singularly un-enlightening and would prefer to base my approach on the notions of critical realism as elaborated by Margaret Archer (1995).

2. The electronic material referred to is available via my Home Page

http://www.nbs.ntu.ac.uk/staff/mutchaf/grm215/grm215.htm

3. The full time undergraduate degrees are BAs in Business Studies, Accounting and Finance, European Business, Business Information Systems, Financial Services, Business and Quality Management, and International Hospitality Management. There are also part time degrees, HNDs and 'top up' provision, delivered by an academic staff of over 100.

4. The criteria, and a sample proposal, are included in the Web archive.

5. 34 students in two seminar groups.

36.6   References

Archer, M. (1995) *Realist Social Theory: The Morphogenetic Approach*, Cambridge: Cambridge University Press.

Ciborra, C. and Suetens, N.T. (1996) Groupware for an emerging virtual organization. In Ciborra (1996), 185–210.

Ciborra, C. (ed.) (1996) *Groupware and Teamwork: Invisible Aid or Technical Hindrance?*, Chichester: Wiley.

Galliers, R. (1992) *Information Systems Research*, Oxford: Blackwell Scientific.

Hamilton, R. (1996) We have a product, but do we have a market?, *Account*, 8(3), 23–6.

Laurillard, D. (1993) *Rethinking University Teaching: A Framework for the Effective Use of Educational Technology*, London: Routledge.

Macfarlane, B. (1997) The business studies first degree: institutional trends and the pedagogic context, *Teaching in Higher Education*, 2(1), 45–57.

Mutch, A. (1993) Student response to a spreadsheet-based assessment, *Account*, Summer, 19–24.

Mutch, A. (1996a) H_ML_T: a Tragedy in Three Acts, *Proceedings of the 21st Improving University Teaching Conference*, Nottingham, July, 547–58

Mutch, A. (1996b) Assessing the undergraduate programme in NBS, *Innovation*, July, 37–42.

Mutch, A. (1997) Rethinking undergraduate business education: a critical perspective, *Management Learning*, 28(3), 301–12.

Zuboff, S. (1988) *In the Age of the Smart Machine: The Future of Work and Power*, London: Heinemann.

37 Using action learning sets for undergraduate dissertation support: a business school experience

Len Hand
Department of Accounting, Nottingham Business School,
Nottingham Trent University

37.1   Overview

The action enquiry is set within a business school which had experienced a long period of: rising student numbers; larger seminar and lecture groups; and reduced staff/student contact time – and these trends seemed likely to continue. At the same time, and not coincidentally, increasing attention was being given within the business school to the development of student-centred learning.

The enquiry stemmed from the author's dissatisfaction with the one-to-one process which was in place to support final-year students through their dissertations. A change to practice was implemented: action learning sets were introduced as a means of improving the level of support for students. Following an action enquiry method, evidence was gathered about the change, including: a reflective diary, audio-taped group meetings, questionnaire feedback from the students and audio-taped interviews with colleagues who were also using learning sets.

The Action Learning Set model derives from management development programmes where managers work in autonomous sets to help each other in formulating and solving organizational problems. The learning set offers a powerful mechanism both for mutual support and for problem-solving; and there are many similarities between groups of problem-solving managers and undergraduates who are writing dissertations.

The learning sets were (generally) well received by the students, and many of the supposed benefits appeared to be achieved. However, a major concern is raised regarding the low level of engagement of the students in the learning set process. The chapter concludes by reflecting on three possible reasons for this problem: (1) student perceptions of the tutor as expert, (2) tutor attitudes which may discourage student engagement, and (3) perceived levels of competitiveness between undergraduate peers.

37.2   Keywords

- undergraduate
- action learning
- learning sets
- final-year students
- dissertations

37.3   Introduction

This enquiry is concerned with the use of action learning sets with final-year undergraduates as a support for their dissertations.[1] I carried out this exploratory study because, while I was convinced of the value of final-year dissertations, I was dissatisfied with the performance of many of my own students. I had previously supervised my dissertation[2] students by one-to-one contact on a student-demand basis (i.e. when they asked for help, I gave it). This approach was problematic in a number of ways. First, students could remain out of contact for long periods of time, and their progress was uncertain. Second, the weaker students often made poor progress in the early weeks and this lack of progress did not become evident until far too late in the process. Thirdly, there was the practical difficulty of the students meeting up with me and arranging mutually convenient times. Finally, it seemed that many of the queries which students had were common process problems (as opposed to technical content problems) and I found myself responding to the same question from each student in turn (for example, questions about research methods, referencing, and structure).

I considered a change to my practice and chose the action learning set as an alternative learning model following some personal experience as a learning set member, and after witnessing a colleague's use of sets with undergraduates. My enquiry sought to discover whether learning sets could enhance the supervision process for me and the learning process for the students.

37.4   Action learning and learning sets

Group work is common in higher education as in the workplace. But what is it about learning sets that distinguishes them from other forms of groups? According to McGill and Beaty (1995, pp. 21, 25):

> Action Learning involves a group of people (called a set) working together for a concentrated period of time . . . the essence of an action learning set is its focus on the individual and their future action . . . the set [uses] a one-at-a-time rule which makes it a very different experience from working in other types of groups . . . their rationale for being together is to work on the future action of each individual set member.

The learning set movement appears to have its roots in management development programmes (see, for example, Revans, 1982a, 1982b). In a managerial setting each group member is aiming to solve an organizational problem and gains support from colleagues who help him/her to identify problems and to seek solutions. My own experience as a set member (when undertaking a masters course) certainly echoed the notion of individual tasks within a shared support group.

Another important feature of the action learning set 'is based on the relationship between reflection and action' (McGill and Beaty, 1995, p. 21). By working in a structured group time is available for reflection on actions taken and those being contemplated. Thus the learning set encourages a fuller approach to learning through a balance between action and reflection.

If a learning set is to be successful a number of conditions need to apply, the most important of which seem to be that members of the set:

- are capable of helping each other – that each has the necessary interpersonal skills (listening, presenting, time management and so on) which are demanded in a learning set;

- are motivated to learn – to engage with the problems presented, and to learn about themselves as well as their problems;

- are capable of empathizing with other members;

- can operate in an unselfish co-operative manner, giving time to her/his peers' projects as well as her/his own;

- are clear and agreed about the purposes of the learning set;

- each have a real problem to be addressed.

This may appear to be an idealistic shopping list for a successful set, though these criteria are certainly implied by McGill and Beaty (1995) and Revans (1982a, 1982b, 1983). Though such perfect conditions will rarely exist the above criteria may provide a benchmark for judging the quality of learning sets in action.

37.5   Undergraduates and action learning

To what extent, then, could I argue that my final-year undergraduates could benefit from using an action learning set?

First, the notion of the set helping each of its individual members with their own actions appeared to be relevant; each of my students was completing a different dissertation though all members shared a similar learning challenge. Without doubt my undergraduates were certainly operating in a world of 'common ignorance' to use Revans' words (1982b, p. 21) – for each came to the project in a state of anxiety and ignorance. The dissertation represented uncharted territory for all of them, fertile ground for learning set activity where there are few available prescribed solutions. Secondly, mutual support would be important, for listening skills and empathy would be important if the sets were to be effective. Third: the ability to criticize in a constructive manner and to engage with the problems of others seemed relevant to the development of high quality dissertations. Finally, working in a learning set implied a commitment to action – in order to make progress with their own dissertations, the set allowed for each member to make this commitment in a public forum. Articulating this commitment, and reporting back to the set on progress appeared to offer a stimulus for the students which would not be available were they to be working in isolation.

Thus my students do appear to have much in common with the managers in action learning situations: there is a problem which is a new problem – there is no agreed solution; there is a requirement to articulate the problem through a series of questions (e.g. what am I trying to understand? what is problematic? how can I discover? what is my next step? what obstacles do I have to overcome?). However, there are two *apparent* differences between managers solving problems through sets and my undergraduates tackling their dissertations through sets. Notably:

- My undergraduates are not (usually) making recommendations for change via problem-solving – but are extending their understanding. A minority of undergraduate dissertations based on industrial placement experiences do feed back to an organizational problem and lead to action by managers. Most, however, do not carry this weight. However, for the student, actually *producing* the dissertation is a major problem! So maybe my definition of 'problem' is unnecessarily restricted.

- The undergraduate will often be younger, less mature and possibly less independent, than the professional manager. Certainly the undergraduate may be inexperienced at problem solving merely through age and lack of experience. But again the difference may be illusory – independence is not necessarily related to age alone. As one critical friend remarked: 'I sometimes think that nursery age children show more independence in their learning than at almost any other stage of their school life!'

In conclusion: action learning sets appeared to offer a way forward for undergraduate dissertation work, where small group support may be appropriate and where each student may have different tasks within a shared process.

37.6   Research method – an action research approach

My research was in the action enquiry tradition in which the practitioner enquires and reflects on his/her own practice. My research process has been: (1) to consider changes which may improve the quality of my practice, (2) to gather evidence about the changes, (3) to reflect on that evidence, and finally (4) to reconsider my future practice. This is the 'teacher as researcher' model as promoted by (for example) Elliott (1991) and Kincheloe (1991) which 'involves the cultivation of restless, curious attitudes that lead to more systematic inquiries' (Kincheloe, 1991, p. 16).

My personal compelling purpose for this research stemmed from my beliefs about the potential for the quality of the learning process when the importance of human interaction in the learning process is recognized. Many of the learning experiences, which I had either personally undergone or witnessed as a tutor of others, informed me that isolation could often stifle learning while communication and contact could enhance and enrich learning. Thus I wanted to know whether the human interaction encouraged by learning sets could improve the quality of the learning experience for my final-year undergraduates. The evidence which I gathered was aimed at shedding light on that issue.

37.7   The nature of my evidence

* I kept a *reflective diary* throughout the period in which the learning sets met. My diary was written up at any time when significant points had arisen and in particular immediately after the close of set meetings. This evidence provided insights into how I saw the development of the sets.

* Two full *set meetings were taped and transcribed*. The evidence from these tapes provided a record of learning sets in action. Key events during the set meetings could be identified and analysed from the tapes.

* In order to gain understanding of how the students received and perceived the learning sets, I used short *feedback questionnaires which provided for both structured and open-ended responses*. Clearly, the questionnaire evidence is limited in a number of ways. The questions were chosen by me (although there was an opportunity, through open-ended questions, for the student to respond to other than my own agenda). Furthermore, the students knew that I would be looking at their responses (which were *not* anonymous) and that I was to mark their projects. However, it seemed important at that time to register (however imperfectly) the recorded perceptions of the students. After all, the change to my practice (of establishing learning sets) was affecting them in some way – I felt a strong need to know how they were perceiving the process. The broad-brush feel of these responses could be significant in confirming or questioning my own assumptions.

- Finally, I held *semi-structured discussions and interviews* with three other colleagues who were engaged in a similar process at a point towards the end of the set process. The discussions were taped and transcribed and provided me with a record for identifying and contrasting my experiences with those of other tutors.

37.8   What happened with the learning sets?

At the beginning of the academic year, along with three colleagues, I began working with my (ten) dissertation students in two action learning sets of five students each (plus myself as facilitator). Though this chapter is concerned with my own learning sets, the experiences of my colleagues provided me with a wider view on the process than would have been possible had I been working in isolation.

The set meetings began at the end of September, at the beginning of the academic year. Each set meeting lasted for around two hours, at two or three week intervals. In the first meeting we spent some time agreeing the way in which we would operate and I explained what I saw as the benefits of the learning set approach for supporting dissertation work. The students appeared enthusiastic and committed to the idea. Several expressed the view that the set would have a valuable support function and also that the meetings would provide a focus for their work to be completed.

After we had established a pattern and agreed the objectives of the sets we began to work on the students' own dissertations. At the beginning of each meeting we spent a short time in reviewing the progress of each student since the last meeting. We then devoted around 20/25 minutes to each of the students. The students, in turn, acted as 'presenter' by explaining their current progress (or lack of it!), by identifying any problems which they were encountering, and by explaining what they wanted from this particular meeting. Other members of the set were then encouraged to focus on the presenter's dissertation and to help by asking questions which would enable the presenter to move forward or to overcome obstacles. At the end of the student's time slot a series of action points would be agreed by the student as achievable targets for the next meeting. These targets were recorded by the student and by me as facilitator. This one-at-a-time focus is central to the learning set; set members can provide a powerful resource if they focus on each individual's problems in turn. Acting in this way, as an 'enabler' of the work of others is also an important learning experience in its own right; the evaluation of another student's efforts helps in the development of critical faculties. Further, the problems of one student frequently overlap with others (particularly where research method and process issues are involved). Thus, discussion of one student's dissertation frequently seemed relevant to the problems being encountered by others.

By the middle of February each set had met on five or six occasions, by which time the dissertations were at an advanced stage. The demise of the set meetings seemed to occur quite naturally at this time as students needed to focus on final completion and detailed writing up.

37.9   Students' reactions to the learning sets

In both structured and anecdotal feedback, the students were generally, and unanimously, positive about the learning set experience and felt that it had provided them with better support than the one-to-one supervision which they had been expecting. Their comments included:

the value of regular contact with my tutor . . . an insight into what other students were doing . . . a chance to clarify methodology and other common problem areas . . . an opportunity to solve any problem . . . regular meetings as targets, pressure and motivation . . . the set as a comforter and support group . . . solace for the troubled mind – a bit like Alcoholics Anonymous! . . . having to explain to others helped me to clarify what I was doing.

The students appeared to value the opportunity for meeting with their tutor and peers on a structured and regular basis. The meetings were felt to be of the right length and students were comfortable with the two/three week break between. In fact the two-hour slot was chosen because of timetable constraints – I would have preferred more time; learning set meetings often last for a whole or half day (see, for example, McGill and Beaty, 1995, p. 250).

Students generally found the discussion of their own dissertations within the sets to be most valuable, but were also positive about the times when they were focusing on the work of other students (i.e. acting in the enabling role).

Student feedback was not unanimous, however. One student questioned whether meeting with other students was valuable

because feedback tended to come from tutor.

And students were at different stages in their dissertations; one who was further ahead than others felt frustration with later meetings when

I had got further than others.

Another negative comment was about

other members [having] little to offer . . . some members did not seem to care.

Yet another student asked if set membership could be voluntary after a certain stage, and whether there could be individual meetings as well as the set

because some things cannot be discussed in the group.

Though the critical comments were not made by many of the students, a number of them tie in with the major concern which I had about the set meetings – namely the lack of student engagement. It is to this that I now turn.

37.10 The (in)ability of my students to participate fully in the learning sets

My main concern about the learning sets, from my own study, is the low level of engagement with, and commitment to, the set process by the students. In particular many of the group discussions (when a fully active set would have been engaged in 'enabling' the dissertation of the presenting student) became dialogues between me, the tutor/facilitator) and the presenting student. The questioning and enabling seemed to come almost exclusively from me. My own diary, personal recollections and the set meeting transcripts are full of instances where the students would be looking to me for guidance rather than becoming involved in helping each other. There were exceptions to this and some valid student-to-student engagement did take place; but it was quite rare.

This apparent failure of the students to engage as set members is a major obstacle which will prevent sets from becoming good quality learning experiences. I would like to offer reflections on this phenomenon to help myself and any other practitioners who may be considering the use of learning sets with undergraduates. There appear (to me) to be three possible explanations for this problem, and I will here explore each one: (1) that they were seeing me (the tutor) as the main source of guidance and knowledge; (2) that I somehow disallowed student contributions by dominating the meetings; and (3) that students felt competitive about their dissertations.

37.9.1 Perhaps the students thought I was the only one who knew anything!

The students had spent two years at university by the time that our sets began. In that time they had become accustomed to a tutor–student relationship in which the tutor appeared to be the 'expert'. Lectures, and to a lesser extent seminars, would almost always be lead by the tutors – hence, despite the language of student-centred learning, the real relationships which students encountered have implied that the tutor 'knows' and the student is here to 'find out'. To ask students suddenly to behave differently is probably asking too much. What is needed, surely, is a gradual development of the student as an independent learner throughout her/his university life such that, by the final year, s/he has gained enough confidence to use the tutor/facilitator of a learning set as a learning partner and supporter rather than as some kind of all-knowing expert. The development of 'learning-to-learn' modules, now common in my own and many other universities is one sign that this may be happening. Such modules, if my study is typical, are long overdue – but must be (1) integrated into the whole curriculum and not be seen as bolt-on extras (2) followed up throughout all years of the course to encourage continuous development of independent learning skills.

37.9.2 Did my own style encourage dependence?

In a successful learning set members should be equal partners (see, for example, Beaty *et al.*, 1993). If one member dominates, as in any group situation, then the cohesion and working of the structure may be undermined. As self-appointed facilitator and tutor I was, of course, in a very powerful position vis-á-vis the students. I needed to work very hard at diminishing that power difference – the reason for the students' apparent lack of independence may, therefore, have been that I did not allow it. None of the students, it has to be said, made this criticism of me (but then perhaps they would be reluctant to say so, even though they felt it?). My own recollections (evidenced by diary entries and transcripts) are that I did allow space and time for the students to develop their own contributions to debate – but that they often failed to respond. I was conscious of trying to allow student contributions before making my own, but of having to step in to prevent the set discussion from drying up or from becoming very superficial. Maybe I have to work harder at this, and be prepared for the debate to dry up; for if the students know that I will step in as a kind of 'talker of last resort' they may take the easy way out and wait for my interventions.

37.11 Competition not co-operation – Elsa's experience

Elsa,[3] one of my learning set students came to see me privately between set meetings. Elsa had made reasonable progress with her project compared to other students and complained about having to

> *bring in [to the sets] extracts from my project.*

I explained why this could be helpful to everybody but she felt that her efforts could be used by other students who were less advanced to '*piggy-back*' on her ideas and approach. Elsa related bad experiences from the past with other students (as she put it) '*ripping me off*'; she had helped others with courseworks and then received lower marks than the people she had helped! Elsa said that she saw the marking of dissertations as quite competitive, and believed that the marking would be 'norm-referenced' (my interpretation of her words) despite my assurances that we used strict criteria for dissertation marking and that '*if everyone gets a first or two-one we are quite happy*'. So Elsa saw the course as a competitive environment, and I'm sure that she is not alone in that view – only that she expressed her thoughts more strongly than most! Action learning sets are based on concepts of co-operation, mutual support, and empathy; if students feel and act competitively they will become protective of their own ideas and unsupportive of others.

Two of my colleagues Patrick[4] and Dawn did not have similar experiences and felt that their students appeared to be quite co-operative. The third colleague (Adam), however thought that

> *the context of undergraduate studies is seen as very competitive . . . you keep your cards close to your chest in case someone else gains a competitive advantage from your contributions.*

Adam's learning set experience had demonstrated the dangers of competitiveness quite dramatically. He recalled:

> *some individuals were quite ambitious . . . they interpreted the word 'critical' [i.e. as in critical friend] very liberally . . . in a negative way . . . destructive criticisms of other's projects . . . this caused a huge sense of panic in the less confident students . . . thus sometimes people were reluctant to open up and [there was] a tendency to be overcritical . . . what we got after the first meeting was a real problem . . . from being quite confident in what they had done some students felt really quite shattered . . . by what their peers had said.*

Adam's experience, though alien to the other sets which we were running, is salutary. At the very least it shows the need for awareness of the potential problems of competitiveness within what is assumed (by tutors) to be a co-operative venture. Setting ground rules and trying to reach common understandings about the nature and purposes of the sets early in the process becomes important.

37.12 Final reflections

Given the continuing reduction of resources into HE, it is likely that undergraduates will have to be less reliant upon tutors for their learning. In such a scenario, researching skills, self-study skills and the ability to learn from and with peers rather than from tutors become crucially important.

Learning sets are one way in which students can be encouraged to become self-reliant and in which peer support can be fostered to enrich the learning experience. The learning set model may be taken up by HE managers who see the possibility of squaring the circle: achieving cost reductions while improving learning quality. Certainly learning sets may offer an exciting way forward for undergraduate education and can save time and costs (depending on the alternative models to which it is compared). I personally feel committed to the ideals embodied within the learning set, but must sound a note of caution. Without the requisite skills of both students and tutors alike to take advantage of the opportunities of set life then we may only achieve a superficial level of self-reliance in our students.

Furthermore, the action learning set should not, in my view, be grafted *ad hoc* into the curriculum. Rather it should be part of a truly student-centred curriculum which fosters students' self-reliance in all subjects and at all levels of study. The responsibility for development of the students' study skills is a shared responsibility within the academic community. But the move towards independent, student-centred learning sometimes puts too much emphasis on the supply side of the equation with reference to resource-based learning, IT support and the like. This enquiry informs me that the demand side is equally important – the best resources and learning opportunities can be wasted if students have not developed the skills to use them.

Notes

1. The study formed part of a Master's programme by Action Inquiry. A full account, including transcripts of meetings and interviews is available from the author.

2. The students were all taking a BA (Hons) in Accounting and Finance and each of their dissertations were in related areas.

3. Students' names have been changed.

4. Staff names have been changed.

39.13   References and bibliography

Beaty, L., Bourner, T. and Frost, P. (1993) Action learning: reflections on becoming a set member, *Management Education and Development*, **24**(4), 350–67.

Elliott, J. (1991) *Action Research for Educational Change*, Developing Teachers and Teaching Series, Buckingham: Open University Press.

Kincheloe, J. (1991) *Teachers as Researchers: Qualitative Inquiry as a Path to Empowerment*, Basingstoke: Falmer Press.

McGill and Beaty (1995) *Action Learning: A Practitioner's Guide*, London: Kogan Page.

Revans, R.W. (1982a) What is action learning? Action Learning Trust, *Journal of Management Development*, **1**(3), 64–75.

Revans, R.W. (1982b) Action learning: its origins and nature, *Higher Education Review*, **15**(1), Autumn, 20–8.

Revans, R.W. (1983) *The ABC of Action Learning*, Bromley: Chartwell-Bratt.

38 Research as independent learning: emerging issues in 'supervising' postgraduate researchers in their professional contexts

Terry Evans
Faculty of Education, Deakin University, Australia

38.1 Introduction

Australian universities are embracing professional doctorates enthusiastically, with most of the nation's 37 universities offering such awards in 1997. However, there are many issues and challenges stemming from these developments, ranging from concerns over: the status of doctoral degrees; fostering research which is useful for professions, industry, commerce and government; developing and sustaining appropriate research and dissemination skills in students; developing and sustaining appropriate supervision qualities in staff, and appropriate examining qualities in others; and balancing coursework and research.

Behind each of these concerns lay many issues which are important to those working in higher education; not just academics, but rather everyone involved in the support (especially libraries and information technology services) and administration (especially recruitment, enrolment and examination) of such doctoral programmes. This chapter is based on previous and forthcoming work by the author (Evans and Green, 1995; Evans, 1995; Evans, 1996; Evans and Pearson, 1997, in press) and draws on current Australian research to illuminate the issues, and refers to work based on the Doctor of Education (EdD) programme at Deakin University, to analyse and discuss some of the key points involved. The experience and research based on this programme – including its use of computer-mediated communications to construct virtual research and learning communities – is used to outline ways in which some possibilities for improving postgraduate pedagogy, supervision, learning or research are being pursued.

The focus of the chapter is on the unfolding 'supervisory' relationships and characteristics which are required of organizations and their staff as they provide and facilitate doctoral learning and research for professional or workplace contexts. In particular, the significance is discussed of these changing relationships for both students' research and their learning about research, and for universities relationships with professions and workplaces.

38.2 New universities: the place of research

In comparison with other educational institutions, research is commonly regarded as the distinguishing feature of the twentieth-century university. Research is viewed, not as a discreet entity, but rather as something which pervades university life. It is understood as the engine of the production of knowledge which universities are expected to achieve. Universities are said to have 'research cultures' which value research in terms of its activities and products, and which encompass a commitment to scholarship, that is to critique, debate, inquiry and impartiality.

However, these expectations of universities are being shifted or challenged by both external and internal forces. Outside the universities there has always been a number of competing organizations – some with links to universities – which have contributed to the production of knowledge: research institutes, government research and scientific organizations, charitable organizations etc. However, with the increasing commercial exploitation of 'intellectual property', it appears that there is a commensurate increase in commercially funded, controlled and exploited knowledge production. Inside contemporary universities in 'developed' nations – Australian universities may be a paramount case – there have been amalgamations with other tertiary institutions which increase their size and diversity, but which also 'dilute' their research profiles. Additionally, universities are required to: increase enrolments with less than commensurate increases in resources; seek other sources of revenue, especially from commercial, fee-paying and international sources; demonstrate that quality assurance procedures and other performance and accountability measures are being employed; and relate their courses and research closer to the needs of business (even their own 'business') and government.

Taken together, the above challenges ensure a fierce competition ensues inside and outside universities around research. The pressures on staff to teach more students, to pursue 'entrepreneurial' activities, and to ensure their quality and accountability measures are exercised, create a consequential diminution of their capacities to undertake research. It is not always recognized that a large proportion of the research conducted in universities is undertaken by research students, rather than staff. It is here that a further twist to the competition 'screw' emerges.

38.3   The twist: teaching the research student

Part of the 'teaching' expansion of universities is focused on increasing 'higher degree by research' students so, in this respect, research in universities is being required to expand. The 'professional doctorates' – which in Australia range from 17% to 100% research work, with the balance being 'coursework' (Trigwell, Shannon and Maurizi, 1997, 6–7) are a related and increasingly significant part of this expansion. However, the 'supervision' of such students constitutes an additional load on 'active research' staff who are required to undertake the supervision which, consequentially, threatens their own capacity for research. Hence, it can be argued that, by focusing attention and development on research degree supervision, pedagogy and learning, especially in terms of the particular circumstances of professional doctorates, there may be substantial benefits to be made to both university research and teaching; although the capacity for staff research may be diminished as a consequence, which may eventually affect the capacity to supervise.

In many respects, the PhD degree represents the pinnacle for the interrelatedness between teaching and research. As with all 'research' degrees, ostensibly there is no curriculum or teaching: it could be seen as a high form of independent learning, especially outside of the physical sciences where students tend to have their own individual projects, rather than team ones. 'Supervisors' are teachers in some respects, and the curriculum can be seen as research (methodology and practice) together with the substantive field of enquiry. In Australia, administratively, research students count as 'teaching load' and are funded accordingly (indeed, they are funded at a higher rate than coursework in any given discipline area). In other respects, the 'products' of doctoral work (theses, articles, conference papers etc.) are counted as 'research' in measures of research performance for the calculation of government and institutional research quanta.

Australian 'traditional' doctoral students are generally on-campus, full-time, and have recently graduated with honours. In more recent times – over the past two decades – from a small base there has been an accelerating expansion of the opportunities for part-time doctoral study, alongside a steadier expansion for full-time students. In total, these opportunities have been pursued to such an extent that enrolments have expanded by over two-and-a-half times in eight years: from 8744 doctoral students in 1988 (James and Beattie, 1996, p. 10) to 22,696 (36% part-time) in 1996 (Pearson and Ford, 1997, p. 8).

38.4 New types of research student, new types of research degree

Despite the selection filters which apply to postgraduate research students entering universities, this broadening of the student enrolment – especially in part-time students, and on professional doctorate courses – means that a greater diversity of student needs, interests and contexts now prevails. This is heightened by more 'open' forms of entry for students with a broader range of qualifications (often requiring professional experience). Whereas traditionally supervisors worked almost exclusively with young students on scholarships, nowadays they can also expect students as old or older than themselves, who balance senior work responsibilities and family commitments alongside their research, and who may well earn more than their supervisors! This requires a substantial change in the way supervisors deal with their (older, professional) students. It also means dealing with some different student-orientations to doctoral research, and also adapting to the potential of drawing on the richness of their professional contexts, and of addressing research questions and issues related to those contexts.

In general, the professional doctorate has been adopted in Australia as a means to achieve a different – some would even say better – type of research degree which is designed to produce useful or significant knowledge, but where the usefulness or significance is determined more by its application, relevance and pertinence to a professional or workplace context, rather than to a body of knowledge within an academic discipline. Of course, the boundaries between usefulness or significance to an academic discipline and a professional or workplace context can overlap considerably; however, at the extremes, a thesis or dissertation which might satisfy the examiners for a PhD might not satisfy them for a professional doctorate, and vice versa. However, this distinction is not just one of examination: the emergence of professional doctorates has raised, even excited, many debates and discussions about the nature of doctoral awards, programmes and, rather crucially here, about postgraduate learning more generally (Jongeling, 1996; Trigwell, Shannon and Maurizi, 1997). Traditionalists are finding that their criticisms of professional doctorates have been met with even more vigorous criticism of their tradition: the PhD! As a result of such critical scrutiny, it is just possible that real improvements will be made for students of both types of programme, especially as universities move to enhance their profiles in the postgraduate 'marketplace'.

An important source of useful theory and practice for the enhancement of postgraduate research resides in the literature on adult learning, independent learning, and open and distance education. Likewise a good deal of the resources for enabling such enhancement rests on the new communications and information technologies, especially when harnessed with what might be called the established equivalent communication and information technologies in universities: seminars, workshops, laboratories, conferences and, perhaps most of all, libraries. Approaches to 'supervising' postgraduate research, especially professional doctoral research, which draw on the work of adult and independent learning theorists and practitioners – such as Brookfield or Candy –are likely to yield significant benefits for the postgraduate programme involved by shaping them as critically reflective, action-oriented, and student-focused programmes. This seems every bit as important for postgraduate research, if not more so, as it is for postgraduate or undergraduate coursework, for example. The need for postgraduate students to construct critically reflective, theoretically grounded and useful research seems essential if it is to address the contemporary challenges in their professional contexts.

38.5 New 'supervision'

Previously it was noted that the emergence and establishment of professional doctorates has been accompanied by an increase in the diversity of the types of students who pursue those awards in comparison with those who pursue the PhD full-time, on-campus before they embark on their careers. The broader range of experience, resources and responsibilities (work, family, community) which apply means that supervisors need to go beyond the narrow focus of the research to be conducted, and rather be 'open' to the needs, problems, possibilities and potentials of the students and their professional contexts. For example, the 'traditional' full-time PhD student's topic may well stem directly from their immediately previous honours work and/or may be part of a team project which the supervisor has established. In this case, the supervision focus is generally well-defined and the task is to ensure that the student completes safely, satisfactorily and on schedule, usually within the confines of the university itself. However, professional doctorate students (and, to a lesser extent, part-time research students generally) are almost invariably intending to do research which is based, both physically and intellectually, within their professional worlds, rather than within the university.

The physical and intellectual placement of professional doctorate research within the students' professional worlds represents a profoundly important difference for the 'supervision' which is conducted by both the university – in the sense of its role as the formal authority attesting to the quality and standards of the research and its 'products' – and the individual staff member (or staff members) appointed as 'supervisor'. There are risks and benefits, or positives and negatives, as a result of this difference. For example, the legal and ethical liabilities of the university are confounded by those of the workplace; the costs of the research are borne less by the university and more by the workplace. Setting aside these aspects, perhaps the most difficult area to address concerns constructing a balance between 'doctoral' standard research, and professionally relevant and applicable research. It is here that 'supervision' appears to be something of a misnomer.

If one sees 'supervision', perhaps rather too literally, as 'overseeing' students' research – as if peering over the student's shoulder in the lab, in the field, at the desk or in the library – then this is hardly possible or appropriate for a professional doctorate student. 'Supervision' is perhaps more a matter of being an 'adviser' (a term often used instead of 'supervisor' in North American universities) or a 'mentor', than an 'overseer'. However, the point is not about nomenclature, but rather about practice. Supervision practice needs to change significantly in comparison with the 'traditional' young, full-time, on-campus PhD student, with respect to professional doctorates, because both the nature and purpose of the research are different to 'traditional' doctoral degrees, and the capacities, responsibilities and experience of the students are different to 'traditional' students. It is substantially for these reasons, that the 'coursework' components of professional doctorates can be so problematic – what course can be designed by outsiders to teach people who already know so much about what they are doing inside their professional contexts? What these 'learners' require is the opportunity, guidance and support to explore and to research, problems and issues which are related to their professional practice. This means that, at the outset, the supervisor is required to adopt a role which is less to do with supervising, and more to do with clarifying needs, aims and goals, helping to identify resources and literature, and supporting the student in their research, as they endeavour to sustain their professional, family and community responsibilities. This is not to deny that some remnants of supervision remain. Clearly, there are 'gate-keeping' and 'rule-bounding' roles which help the student achieve an examinable outcome which earns them the degree for which they are striving.

The task becomes one of structuring research and learning tasks-students' research and learning are interrelated here – in ways which enable the students to complete the doctoral requirements. In some instances, these tasks could be directly related to research being conducted in the workplace as part of the student's responsibilities, or they could be more broadly related to a professional field. The supervisor may need to negotiate with the parties concerned to ensure that the university's, the student's and the employer's interests were met. For example, matters concerning ethics, commercial confidentiality, intellectual property, time and resources may need to be negotiated appropriately. Although this may seem to be a difficult task, often these may be conducted by the student in consultation with the supervisor, and the potential for useful research and good university–industry partnerships appears high. It is worth considering the structure of the Deakin EdD programme at this point as one model for professional doctorates which might be worth adapting for other professional contexts.

38.6   The Deakin EdD

It is useful to commence by drawing on a previous paper (Evans and Green, 1995) to help delineate the key features of the Deakin EdD which has been distinguished since its inception in 1993 from other similarly designated doctoral programmes by its distinctive character as a research degree, rather than research and coursework degree. It combines a structured sequence of units (Phase 1) designed to culminate in the presentation of a substantial and well-articulated proposal at a formally constituted examination panel (called the 'colloquium'). When this is completed successfully then the student develops a research folio (Phase 2). The folio is a related collection of original products, including a dissertation-the latter of which is required to articulate and link the contents of the folio. The EdD involves an understanding of research, its nature and purpose(s), which contributes to, and enhances, both knowledge and practice in regard to the professional (in this case, education or training) contexts of the candidates. The nature of the research 'project' is generally tied to a specific place or site of educational-institutional work, together with its associated needs or problems.

A recent review of 'research-coursework' doctorates in Australia led the authors to exclude the Deakin EdD from their deliberations because it was understood as a research (only) degree and thus outside their 'research-coursework' brief. However, they made the following observation:

> This highly structured approach to the professional doctorate is to be applauded . . . It is . . . best practice example . . . and we recommend that the model adopted by Deakin University in this degree be explored as exemplary (Trigwell, Shannon and Maurizi, 1997, p. 7).

Brennan and Walker (1994) have discussed the origins of the EdD programme and discussed the implications for matters such as supervision of the new programme and its students.

Subsequently, there has been a considerable amount of development, refinement and elaboration of the program as the experience unfolds, and this is continuing (Evans, 1996; Evans and Green, 1995; Green, 1996; Jeans, 1995; Reid, Stacey and Henry, 1995; Walker and Henry, 1995). A significant part of this elaboration has concerned the nature of the research, and its relationship to the candidate's professional practice. One aspect of the work has involved thinking about the nature of supervision in this new type of research degree. For example, Evans and Green have pointed to the centrality of debates about supervision within the EdD.

> A central claim in developing and defending the EdD has been that it serves to 'challenge understandings of supervision' in postgraduate studies (Brennan and Walker, 1994: 226). There are several aspects of this. Firstly it is highly significant that the focus of the work done towards the degree is on the specific albeit changing nature of the educational workplace, essentially one's own, at least professionally. That is to say, the emphasis is on educational *practice*, both as (and within) an organisation and as (and within) a form of work. This means, further, that it is likely to be much more communal and collaborative than is the usual case with higher degree research, which tends to occur away from the worksite as such, or indeed the research site. By definition, students are likely to have more knowledge and experience regarding their own site(s) of work/research than is the usual case for postgraduate students, as well as in relation to their supervisors. Finally, given the differentiated nature of the Folio it may well be that a student works with several minor (or 'local') supervisors in the course of completing the degree, albeit under the general coordination of a major (or 'global') supervisor. What this means is that the relationship between student and supervisor(s) needs to be understood and indeed reconceptualised more in terms of 'negotiation' rather than 'direction', and moreover as less 'private and privatised' than is the usual case in postgraduate studies, with a less hierarchical and more reciprocal structure of authority (Brennan & Walker, 1994: 227) (Evans and Green, 1995, pp. 5–6).

Although the EdD has no coursework in the pedagogical sense, there is a considerable volume of resource material on research which is provided in print, audio and electronic forms. The course also supports the students, both individually and in groups, using computer-mediated communications (CMC) – principally conferencing and email. The CMC facility – which is not compulsory, but which is used by many students – not only mediates academic staff support for the students, but also allows students to discuss, debate and inform each other. There has developed a stronger sense of (virtual) community among the students than exists with the part-time PhD students. The EdD students do have the opportunity, as do all doctoral students, of attending the annual postgraduate summer school – again not compulsory, but attended by many students. The summer school, and increasingly the CMC facilities, provide for 'scholarly' (and not so scholarly!) discussions.

In the above respects, it can be seen that the absence of 'coursework' does not mean that that there is not what might be called research or supervision pedagogy. Those working in on-line or CMC teaching environments will note some obvious similarities. However, the pedagogical intention is not to teach disciplinary or professional knowledge, skills or values, but rather to facilitate a (beginning) researcher community, a community which is drawn from the members of various education-related professional or workplace contexts.

38.7   Concluding comment

I have argued rather gently here – and more strongly elsewhere (Evans, 1995) – that postgraduate research can be seen to be 'opening-up' many possibilities for the future of universities. As noted previously, a fundamental distinction between universities and other educational institutions is their involvement in research, and teaching about research – often called 'research training' – is an important aspect. Professional doctorates offer the possibilities for learning about, and practising, research, not only by contributing to research and research training itself in the ways that PhDs do, but rather in ways which also prove to be beneficial to professions, enterprises, governments and industries. The Deakin EdD programme provides an example of one such venture where a new kind of research degree is unfolding which has the potential benefits. The development of other research-based professional doctorates has the potential to enhance professional knowledge and practice in ways which seem more powerful and appropriately doctoral, than the 'advanced' coursework path.

38.8   References

Brennan, M. and Walker, R. (1994) Educational research in the workplace: developing a professional doctorate. In R. Burgess and M. Schratz, (eds), *International Perspectives in Postgraduate Education and Training*, Innsbruck: Austrian Academic Press, 220–33.

Evans, T.D. (1995) Postgraduate research supervision in the emerging 'open' universities, *Australian Universities Review*, 38(2), 23–7.

Evans, T.D. (1996) Realising a new kind of research degree: the EdD as a structured professional doctorate, *2nd Quality in Postgraduate Education Conference*, April, Adelaide.

Evans, T.D. and Green, W.C. (1995) Dancing at a distance? Postgraduate studies, 'supervision', and distance education, *Australian Association for Research in Education Conference*, November, Hobart.

Evans, T.D. and Pearson, M. (1997) Off-campus doctoral research in Australia: emerging issues and practices. In A. Holbrook and S. Johnston (eds), *Supervision of Postgraduate Research in Education*, Australian Association for Research in Education (in press).

Green, W.C. (1996) E-quality, postgraduate supervision and the Education doctorate: the Deakin experience, *Quality in Postgraduate Education Conference*, April, Adelaide.

James, R. and Beattie, K. (1996) *Expanding Options: Delivery Technologies and Postgraduate Coursework*, Department of Employment, Education, Training and Youth Affairs, Canberra.

Jeans, B. (1995) The professional doctorate: exporting best practice?, *Australian Association for Research in Education Conference*, November, Hobart.

Jongeling, S.B. (1996) Professional doctorates in Australian universities, *Second Seminar of Deans and Directors of Graduate Studies in Australian Universities*, April, Adelaide.

Pearson, M. and Ford, L . (1997) *Open and Flexible PhD Study and Research*, Department of Employment, Education, Training and Youth Affairs, Australian Government Publishing Service, Canberra (in press).

Reid, J., Stacey, E. and Henry, C. (1995) The getting of information: integrating CMC and postgraduate education, *Australian Association for Research in Education Conference*, November, Hobart.

Trigwell, K., Shannon, T. and Maurizi, R. (1997) *Research-coursework Doctoral Programs in Australian Universities,* Department of Employment, Education, Training and Youth Affairs, Canberra.

Walker, R. and Henry, C. (1995) Reconstituting the concept of 'taught courses' in the context of doctoral studies, *Australian Association for Research in Education Conference,* November, Hobart.

39 Challenging assumptions: problematizing the practice of improving students as learners

Sarah J. Mann
The University of Western Australia

In recent years there has been an increasing emphasis in higher education on the teaching and learning of generic and transferable skills, and on lifelong and self-directed learning, an emphasis on the 'production' of employable students, suited to a modern, flexible workforce able to update itself through continuous learning. Concomitant with this focus have been greater demands for efficiency and the speeding up of the circulation of knowledge through the Internet and information technology. Lyotard has described this as a shift from truth or justice as criteria of value in the production and dissemination of knowledge to 'performativity' as the key criteria. This greater focus on performativity, rather than on truth or justice, provides the context to the goal of improving students as learners.

The aim of this chapter is to problematize this current move in higher education towards improving students as learners and in particular towards integrating such 'skills development' into the curriculum with the consequence that it becomes assessable. In doing this, I wish neither to examine whether student learning can be improved or not when integrated into the curriculum, nor do I wish to focus on how to do this better. My aim is to raise questions about a practice that is undertaken and discussed in most higher education forums nowadays as though it were self-evidently a good thing.

I shall approach the issue from two perspectives, an experiential and a theoretical one. First, I shall present the voices of four students describing their experience of studying. I do this in order to reveal the complexity of the student's engagement with learning and thus of the task of improving students as learners. Secondly, I shall describe what I see as some of the key assumptions underlying the attempt to improve students as learners, and then draw on the work of Freud, Lacan, Derrida and Foucault in order to offer a counter-perspective.

39.1 The experiential perspective

While reading the four student voices below,[1] consider the question of how one would help each of these students to improve their learning, and what the impact on each of these students would be of engaging in a series of tasks for the purposes of improving their learning, where the outcomes of these tasks are assessed in some way.

39.1.1 Sheila's voice

> For the first five to ten minutes I don't absorb much of what I read. It takes a while to get concentrating, at least with set texts, then there comes the middle period where my concentration and absorption is at its greatest, lasting about half an hour, then concentration and interest ebb and I have to do something else for a short while. This cycle is then repeated.

I know that I'm going to have to think about it. It's not just going to float above my head. I'll have to really get into the text.

I love reading. I read loads and loads as a kid. I am an only child, so I used to hibernate with books. They were the biggest part of my life.

University is a protective outer garment that will protect you and look after you while allowing you to be yourself. It may give gentle hints as to the right direction but it is somewhere you can go and be yourself in an intellectual atmosphere, an atmosphere of thought. It's home from home really. It's a comforting place.

39.1.2   Judith's voice

I don't enjoy it so much. Not for the fact of what it is but because it is work. If I've got to do it, told to do it, then I sit down and time myself and count it as work. Whereas if something might be part of a course but it's just for interest, it's different. I think because it's work I feel I have to take it all in and therefore read more slowly and with more concentration. I just sit down and do it, but if I'm not taking it in, I'll put it down and come back to it later. I like to get it out of the way as soon as possible after it's given me. To be free again. I read slowly if it needs concentration. How I read depends on what I'm reading. It depends on my interest and on whether I need it in the future.

I usually have a book on the go for pleasure. I read novels to get involved with the story, which is pleasurable.

I came here because I wanted a decent career. I like the idea of three or more years' education and to give me independence from home. I'm not aiming particularly high but I would want to get a 2:2.

39.1.3   Monica's voice

I just do what I have to do and then do something else. I don't mind if it's easy, but I don't push myself hard. I don't like the concentration needed.

For seminars I pick out main points because I know what I'm going to be asked. They will say 'can you sum this up' and then I'll think about the deeper implications because I know I will be asked and I link to the theme being done at the time.

I don't like reading much. It's a bit of a waste of time. A lot of the time I'm reading through and I'm thinking I can't think of anyone who would just read this for fun.

Socially it [being at university] makes you higher status or whatever. It's good to have something like that behind you.

Academic should be more important, perhaps I haven't analysed what I've actually learnt, it's not so obvious, but socially I know where I stand and so it strikes me that I've learnt more socially.

39.1.4   Sally's voice

I probably go into too much detail, into it too thoroughly, and can't see the wood for the trees. I used to take notes but now because it takes so long and I end up not finishing the task and then I'd have to come back to it and it's rather depressing because it is half finished.

I'm totally lazy, partly because I'm nervous because I put things off. When I know I ought to be doing something I put it off, nearer the time I get panicky and therefore more nervous. It's a vicious circle. I know I do that.

There's pressure on you now. Everything you have to read you have to concentrate more on. Here I don't read much for pleasure as I feel I ought to concentrate on academic work.

If there is no pressure to do something with a text then I can read it more and I'm less worried of the consequences of reading it.

As it was my second start I was worried whether I would stick it out. I was conscious of having to prove myself a lot. Before I had taken it for granted I was intelligent, I would go through the system but when I found I had nothing to identify with, no academic status at all I felt as if I had lost all my brainpower. Now I'm back I feel on a par with everyone else and it's in perspective more.

My aim in presenting these four voices is simply to reveal the complexity of the student's engagement with learning and thus the complexity attendant on any attempt to work with students to improve their learning. This complexity seems to be related to the current significance to the student of being a student at university, to the way the student's life history up to now impacts on her experience and interpretation of where she now finds herself. Being at university provides each of the students with a different experience of their emerging sense of self, confirming, enhancing or threatening their intellectual and social being. And this sense of self, and what the students take to be meaningful activity, seems to be significantly bound up with their approach to academic work, to 'learning'. Furthermore, it seems that this sense of self and the sense of what is meaningful is intimately connected, at least most obviously for Sally, with assessment. In many ways, it is the assessment process and its outcomes, which inevitably crystallizes the point at which her sense of self will be confirmed or disconfirmed. To intervene, in order to improve student learning, by introducing into the curriculum assessable units or components on 'learning to learn' thus has the potential to simply compound the problem. The intervention becomes yet one more task for the student to negotiate.

39.2 The theoretical perspective

A number of assumptions underlie the move to improve students as learners through curricular intervention. These can be said to relate to ideas about the self, individuality, language, power and the role of education. I consider these assumptions below, first identifying those associated with the self and language, and secondly those associated with power, individuality and the role of education. I do this in a necessarily stereotypical way in order to highlight the main 'themes'. In each case, I counterpose these assumptions with a different set of assumptions arising from the work of Freud, Lacan, Derrida and Foucault.

My aim is not to denigrate the attempt to improve students as learners. I myself am involved in similar practices in my own field of work. Rather my aim is to question the basis of such practices so as to reveal some of the complex threads and tensions implicit in them.

39.2.1 Assumptions about the nature of the self and language

In the move to improve students as learners through the introduction of courses on learning into the curriculum, the self is seen as self-conscious and rational. It is a unitary self whose identity is fixed and known. From this perspective, a person can be said to have a true, essential, and natural self, which exists prior to language. Language is seen as a 'neutral' tool, which can be used to represent and thus communicate one's inner world and the shared outer world. In this way it is possible to be transparent to oneself, and self-presence and mastery of self are possible.

This rational self-conscious self is brought famously into being by Descartes' 'I think therefore I am.'

> in doubting, Descartes thinks and thereby confirms the certainty of his existence, thus vanquishing the deceiver. Descartes thought therefore that he had found presence, a certainty based on the essential rationality of himself as a knowing conscious subject, with an innate rationality, immune to deception. The knowing subject not only knows but also knows it knows; consciousness implies self-consciousness. Ultimately the fact of self-consciousness, of being master of oneself, is the guarantee of knowledge.
>
> (Usher and Edwards, 1994, p. 57)

A straightforward capacity for self-reflection on an inner process is assumed, allowing for the possibility of self-knowledge, including knowledge about one's learning processes.

In this way, learning is given an 'objective' status, i.e. a status as something rather like an object or an entity that can be observed, described, communicated and thus known. Once known, learning can then be broken down into its component parts, for example as a set of skills, which can thus be taught and the learner's achievement assessed according to its approximation to the original 'object' or model.

Language, the means by which learning is made 'concrete', is seen as an unproblematic tool for the representation and transmission of 'objects' in the real world, including the inner 'psychological' world.

39.2.2   Alternative assumptions – Freud, Lacan and Derrida

> I think where I am not, therefore I am where I do not think.
>
> (Freud)
>
> (quoted by Usher and Edwards, 1994)

My thinking, rational self is not where 'I' am, for 'I' am to be found in the unconscious where I cannot be known.

Since consciousness is always in process, partly obscure to itself, there can therefore never be a subject of self-certainty.

> an incompleteness which can never become completed . . . the subject is always in the middle of this movement, caught in a dialectical and changing relationship between itself and that which it knows.
>
> (Usher and Edwards, 1994, p. 58)

I desire toand believe I can master myself, and in so doing I thus repress the unconscious, and fall further into 'untruth'. This lack, this gap between myself and my unknown self, leads to a desire for certainty or mastery through knowledge, which can never be satisfied. Thus, the rational, self-conscious self described above, is, according to Freud, a self-deceiving self.

From a Lacanian perspective, the point is not so much that the self can never know itself, implying the goal at least of potential knowledge of one's essential self. Rather it is the idea that the self and the sense of self is a construction, derived from the Imaginary (images, projections, and visual identifications) and from the Symbolic (language and culture).

The ego (*moi*/me) arises from seeing itself in the mirror or in the eyes of the Other. The image in the mirror allows the infant to construct him or herself as object (me), thus giving a sense of unity, autonomy, and coherence. But this unity is based on an alienating self-deception since one's sense of self arises from the constant play of mirrors, of how others see one. The ego self (the self-conscious self) can only understand itself from a position of otherness.

The 'I', the subject self, arises out of the insertion of the individual into language and culture. The 'I' speaks, and is spoken, is named and placed within his or her particular social order. Through the symbolic, the 'I' gains its identity and thus its continuity. From this Lacanian view, language is prior to the self, positioning the subjective self in its place in society. Self and agency are thus no longer psychological concepts, but social and linguistic ones arising within the play of intersubjectivity and language.

Language, seen to serve as a neutral tool for the direct representation and communication of inner and outer worlds in the previous perspective, not only, from a Lacanian perspective, positions the self through language's prior existence to the 'self', but, from a Derridean perspective, language is that which mediates reality, or rather language is reality. From this perspective, there is nothing outside the text, nothing except acts of interpretation. Meaning does not derive from the relationship between a particular linguistic sign and its referent in the outside world, requiring an act of decoding, rather meaning derives from the relationship between signs, requiring acts of interpretation. Thus, the listing of skills that might constitute learning is not seen from this perspective as the listing of objects that exist and can be known and expressed through language, rather lists of skills constitute constructs brought into being through the discoursal possibilities of particular disciplines, in this case psychology or education.

39.2.3 Assumptions about power, the individual and the role of education

From within the perspective of helping students become better learners, education is seen as an emancipatory and improving practice, contributing to the good of the individual and of society.

It is learners who are seen as needing improving and not, for example, the education system itself. A neutrality or transparency is assumed to characterize the education system, such that it is not seen as significant in its effect on the learner's problematic experience of learning.

The idea of teaching learners to be self-directed and autonomous is seen as straightforward. The paradox of asking learners to undertake activities designed by others to help them become autonomous learners is rarely made explicit, such that it is seen to be quite logical to assess learners on their progress towards self-direction as learners.

39.2.4 Alternative assumptions – Foucault

Foucault argues that there has been a shift in the way power is exercised over the past two to three centuries. Rather than power being manifested in physical coercion, power is now wielded through 'disciplinary practices', such as education. 'Disciplinary practices' bring into existence the idea of the individual, whose position in society can be mapped according to his/her aptitudes and capabilities. Through this process individuals are both given substance through the measurement of their 'achievements', at the same time as they are placed in a position of subjection through what they 'lack', i.e. what they have been measured to have not 'achieved'. The examination is seen by Foucault to be an archetypal expression of such disciplinary practices, exemplifying the use of two key processes – hierarchical observation and normalizing judgement.

> Traditionally power was what was seen, what was shown, and what was manifested . . . Disciplinary power, on the other hand, is exercised through its invisibility; at the same time it imposes on those whom it subjects a principle of compulsory visibility. In discipline, it is the subjects who have to be seen. Their visibility assures the hold of the power that is exercised over them. It is the fact of being constantly seen, of being able

always to be seen, that maintains the disciplined individual in his subjection. And the examination is the technique by which power, instead of emitting the signs of its potency, instead of imposing its mark on its subjects, holds them in a mechanism of objectification. In this space of domination, disciplinary power manifests its potency, essentially, by arranging objects. The examination is, as it were, the ceremony of this objectification.

(Foucault, 1991, p. 187)

The examination constitutes individuality by on the one hand providing substance, a place in the scheme of things, and at the same time, through the normalized hierarchy it is based on, marks, finds gaps and thus renders the individual less than others. It both provides substance and takes it away.

[Exam] as the fixing, at once ritual and 'scientific', of individual differences, as the pinning down of each individual in his own particularity ... clearly indicates the appearance of a new modality of power in which each individual receives as his status his own individuality, and in which he is linked by his status to the features, the measurements, the gaps, the 'marks' that characterize him and make him a 'case'.

(Foucault, 1991, p. 192)

These disciplinary practices are made more potent according to Foucault by the constitution of the individual, through discursive and material practices, as a confessing individual, where confession is taken to be the route to truth. Self-confession becomes self-regulation, and individuals become self-disciplining.

Confession therefore results in regulation through self-regulation, discipline through self-discipline. Instead of being monitored, we monitor ourselves.

(Usher and Edwards, 1994, p. 95)

Learning journals, learning contracts, portfolios and profiles are all examples of practices that engage the learner as a self-disciplining learner.

39.3   Concluding remarks

In this chapter I have tried to problematize through both an experiential and a theoretical perspective the practice of attempting to improve students as learners, especially where this practice involves the integration of such aims into the curriculum, where students' work becomes assessable.

I have tried to show how complex the undertaking is – both from the perspective of lived experience and from the perspective of a set of assumptions that challenges the rational, modernist approach to such an undertaking.

In conclusion, I summarize below the double-binds and paradoxes I see as implicit in the practice of improving students as learners.

Teaching learners how to learn places the responsibility for the difficulties learners experience with the learners, and exonerates the education system.

It poses the learner with a significant double-bind. The need to improve as a learner is likely to have arisen as a result of previous educational experiences and yet it is from within that very educational system that 'help' is at hand.

A further double bind faces the learner. On the one hand, the aim is to improve the learner towards being a more autonomous, self-managing, independent, lifelong learner, and yet the initiative to do this comes from government, the institution, the department and the teacher.

Furthermore, the learner is confronted with the fact that their 'improvement' towards autonomy is to be assessed, i.e. the 'autonomous' process of learning is to be embedded in a power relationship where the teacher will have the ultimate power to judge the learner's achievement of autonomy.

There is a subtlety in the move to improving students as learners – not only does this practice contribute to creating self-directing lifelong learning individuals able to contribute efficiently to the workforce. Foucault would argue that it is also implicitly coercive and oppressive in the sense that the energy entailed in maintaining self-direction and self-management is diverted from the energy for struggle and revolt. Paradoxically, though emancipatory in its intent, the practice of taking upon ourselves the responsibility for improving students as learners, may itself be oppressive.

Note

1. The student voices presented here are from a study (Mann, 1987) I undertook into the reader's experience of reading, where seven of the informants were first-year humanities undergraduates at a UK university.

39.4   References and bibliography

Derrida, J. (1978) *Writing and Difference* (tr. A. Bass), London: Routledge & Kegan Paul.

Felman, S. (1987) *Jacques Lacan and the Adventure of Insight*, Cambridge, MA: Harvard University Press.

Foucault, M. (1975) *Discipline and Punish – The Birth of the Prison* (tr. A. Sheridan), Harmondsworth: Penguin.

Foucault, M (1982) The subject and power. In H. Dreyfus and P. Rabinow , *Michel Foucault: Beyond Structuralism and Hermeneutics*, Chicago: Chicago University Press.

Lacan, J. (1977)The mirror stage as formative of the function of the I as revealed in psychoanalytic experience. In *Ecrits, A Selection* (tr.A. Sheridan), Tavistock Publications, ch. 1.

Lyotard, J.F. (1984) *The Postmodern Condition: A Report on Knowledge*, Manchester: Manchester University Press.

Mann, S.J. (1987) *Revealing and Understanding Reading: An Investigation with Eighteen Readers*, PhD thesis, University of Lancaster.

Miller, J-A (ed.) (1988) *The Seminar of Jacques Lacan, Book I, Freud's Papers on Technique 1953–1954* (tr. J. Forrester), Cambridge: Cambridge University Press.

Rabinow, P. (ed.) (1984) *The Foucault Reader*, Harmondsworth: Penguin.

Usher, R. and Edwards, R. (1994) *Postmodernism and Education*, London: Routledge.

40 Getting a grasp of studying computer science and engineering: on the experience of learning in groups

Shirley Booth[i] and Jenny Petersson[ii]
Chalmers University of Technology, Göteborg; (i) Center for Educational Development; (ii) Office of the School of Electrical and Computer Engineering

40.1 Background

This chapter is based on a study carried out in the academic year 1995/96 in connection with the first year of a reformed programme in Computer Science and Computer Engineering at Chalmers University of Technology in Göteborg, Sweden. A more complete report is available, and this report is based on further interpretation of certain aspects of the data (Booth, Petersson and Bayati).[1]

40.1.1 Some aspects of the Computer Science and Engineering (CSE) programme

Since the autumn of 1995 the four-and-a-half-year masters degree programme in Computer Science and Engineering at Chalmers has been given in a radically revised form, funded by the Swedish Council for the Renewal of Undergraduate Education as one of five projects with the overriding goal of attracting more women into natural sciences and engineering. Inherent in all these projects is a turn to new pedagogical measures for meeting the goal (Wistedt, 1996). The programme and its reform are reported elsewhere (Svensson, 1996; Jansson, 1996).

In 1994 a national evaluation of all Swedish degree courses leading to a Masters degree in Computer Engineering and related fields was published.[2] The Chalmers D-programme, although found to be of very high class with respect to its disciplinary area, was criticized for being (1) fragmented, (2) narrow and specialized, (3) insufficiently oriented towards computers in society and (4) having too few women students. The programme leader took on the challenge of reforming the programme as a whole and made a successful application for funding (Svensson and Thomas, 1993). This challenge, after debate among the teachers concerned, led to the following statement of goals (our translation):

> The principle goal of the project is to reform the educational programme so that it becomes more attractive, with special regard to women students. The programme will be changed towards considering an increased holistic view of both the computer engineer's role in society and professional role, as well as the potential for and consequences of computer engineering. By changing the structure of the programme and increasing the degree of autonomy, the students' interest and commitment should be increased, with the resultant possibility of deepening the educational programme.

The content of the programme and approaches to working should favour personal development and not only give the 'raw knowledge' that a computer engineer needs. This is justified, not least, by the significant role that the master of engineering (civilingenjör) has in society. At the same time as the students' own responsibility for their education is emphasized, the interaction between students and teachers will be highlighted (Svensson and Thomas, 1993)

For most purposes the students worked in groups of 8, formed before the start of term. The most important principle applied to group formation was that the gender distribution should be such that groups were either evenly mixed or all male. These groups remained together throughout the term, either in eights or in fours, or pairs, for all their studies. In a new building, each group had its own room with two computers and storage space, and there were communal office tools.

40.1.2   The goals of Computer Science and Engineering in Context (CSEC)

This chapter deals exclusively with a course intended to support the induction of the students into the programme of education and their future professional roles, called Computer Science and Engineering in Context (CSEC). It runs throughout the first semester, is intended to make up about 20 per cent of the students full-time study, parallel with courses in mathematics, programming techniques and digital engineering.

Its purpose is to put the students into situations from the outset that will support the ways of working expected of them throughout large slices of the programme. Working in groups on a limited project, exploring the project subject not only from technical perspectives but also from societal perspectives, finding information from a variety of sources, holding discussions within the group and with a tutor,[3] writing a collective technical report and presenting it to the rest of the class were all aspects of CSEC that were intended to foreshadow the programme as a whole.

Note that it is not an isolated course charged with the induction, but one of several in which groups will work together in different constellations and with varying learning goals. However, special emphasis was put on it, placing it at the start of the programme and investing in development for the graduate students who acted as tutors (Booth and Christmansson, Chapter 53 of this volume).

There are two main learning goals. First, there is a *computer science and engineering content* intended to link forward to the disciplinary knowledge that will be the subject of coming studies and to a future professional life, and to an awareness of the computer's role in society. Second there is a *ways of working content*, intended to lay the grounds for investigative approaches to study, informed use of the tools of the engineer's trade and successful collaboration and project work during the programme. Note that the goals of CSEC make no mention of attracting and supporting women students; while this is a goal of the programme reform as a whole, this course is intended to improve it for all.

For the CSEC course each group was assigned a tutor, a graduate student from a subject related to the degree programme (computer science, computer engineering, mathematics, electrical engineering, physics etc.). The group met the tutor at the outset of the course and they worked together on choosing a project from a list of vaguely worded projects, developing a more precise focus and writing an application to be allowed to take on that project. Thereafter, the group met the tutor formally for two hours a week and informally when need arose. The main focus of the meetings was the details of and schedule for the project and, later, the status of the emerging report. The tutors had been given a course on the process of writing reports, and they met weekly with one of the staff responsible for the course to discuss difficulties.

The evaluation that was carried out during the first year of the course has led to a problematization of the nature of *working in groups, learning to work in groups* and *learning by working in groups*, which will be the subject of the rest of this chapter.

40.2 The evaluation study: a phenomenographic approach

CSEC was chosen as a focus for evaluation because it was seen by the project leadership (which included one of the authors, Booth) as central to the success of the programme, in pedagogical terms. Two interview studies were carried out and a questionnaire was used at the end of the course. The approach chosen for the study was informed by the phenomenographic research tradition, in that it was the ways in which the tutors and students experienced certain aspects of the course that were the object of study.

Phenomenographic research has experience as its object of study – the ways in which people experience phenomena in their worlds – and it aims to describe the variation found therein in units of qualitatively distinct ways of experiencing (see e.g. Marton and Booth, 1997, for a more complete description of the tradition). Material is collected that can reveal fragments of a collective experience of the people involved in the situation under study. This is generally in the form of semi-structured interviews with a theoretical sample of the people, chosen to represent the variation to be found there in significant dimensions. In this study, interviews were held with all ten tutors and with two students from each of eight of the 14 groups. The groups were chosen so that four were mixed-gender and four all-men, and of which four were considered by their tutor to have been a successful group while the other four were seen as having had difficulties. One man and one woman were chosen from each mixed-gender group. The interviews thematized the individual goals of the course, being sufficiently open to explore each theme until a sense of mutual understanding was reached.

The collected material in a phenomenographic study, characterized as a *pool of meaning*, is analysed by seeking similarities and distinct differences in it, in an interpretative process of contextualization (whole transcripts), decontextualization (isolated units of meaning) and recontextualization (with like meanings) until structure in the data becomes apparent. In this way an understanding of the whole in terms of a descriptive structure of categories is sought. Each category, abstracted from the empirical material as it is, can be interpreted as a particular way of experiencing the phenomenon in question. That is *not* to say that each individual in the study can be allocated to a category, but rather that they have expressed *aspects* of the phenomenon, or shown a capability for a way of experiencing the phenomenon, that go to make up one category or another. Categories can, in general and ideally, be analyzed into a succession or hierarchy in which particular aspects are more focal or less focal, the *outcome space*.

In an educational context there might be a normative understanding of the phenomenon which the researcher has as reference, whether it is an understanding preferred within a discipline, or an experience desired by the educational goals of the situation under study. That is not to say that the researcher raises that norm to a standard against which the results are measured, but rather that the aspects revealed in ways of experiencing the phenomenon can be seen as more or less constituting, or more or less conducive to arriving at, the desired norm. Nor is it to say that the norms are exclusive; they rather refer to the *capability* for seeing or experiencing the phenomenon in particular ways and for the individual student those particular ways can be complementary to idiosyncratic ways of experiencing the phenomenon. A phenomenographic study also reveals ways in which the object of study is experienced which do not conform to norms and are thus quite unexpected.

In an *educational development* context, it is precisely these ways of experiencing a phenomenon that do not conform to norms – whether inconducive to the desired norm or idiosyncratic deviation from the norm – that are interesting and important when they are revealed, because they can serve to open a dimension of variation for those students and teachers who have not questioned the goals or the nature of the phenomena but have taken them for granted.

In the interviews with students the theme of working and learning in groups formed a substantial part. Learning as such was taken up in other contexts as well, both in general terms and related to something that the interviewee considered important. The planned questions in the interview scheme included: 'What was the most important thing you learned, would you say?' (let us call it X), 'How did that come about?', 'How did you work together as a group?', 'Did any changes take place?', 'How did your tutor work with you?', 'Was there anyone else who played a significant role?', 'Would you say there is anything special about working in a group, when you learned X for instance?', 'What does it mean, to learn, would you say in general?', 'How was it to work in a mixed/all man group?' 'Might it have been different to work in an all man/ mixed group, do you suppose?' These questions were neither planned nor executed as part of a spoken questionnaire, but they served rather to lead the interview to important aspects of the theme and were open for extension as well as diversion.

It is this section of the interviews that form the basis for the analysis that will be described in the next section.

40.3 The experience of learning in groups in the CSEC course: an empirical outcome space

Learning as a psychological act is necessarily directed towards something beyond the act itself: a student is never learning, but is always learning *something*. This leads us to speak of the 'what' of learning – the content that is learned – and the 'how' of learning – the nature of the learning act. Further, the act of learning is also directed to some notion of what learning is, which has been called the *indirect object* of learning in contrast to the content as direct object (Marton and Booth, 1997). Of course, these three aspects of the act of learning are inextricably interwoven and they are only separated out for analytical purposes. Here they serve as a descriptive model of learning.

If the model is applied in the context of learning in CSEC, we can suggest the following questions as starting points (Figure 40.1):

- *Direct object*: What was experienced as the outcome of learning?

- *Indirect object*: How was learning in groups experienced? and

- *Act*: How was the group as learning group experienced?

Each of these aspects of the experience of learning in groups can be described in terms of an outcome space of categories of description which describes the essential variation. The indirect object, which embodies the experience of learning in groups, will be described in some detail while the other constituents of learning will be given only as summary diagrams. Further details are given elsewhere (Booth, in preparation).

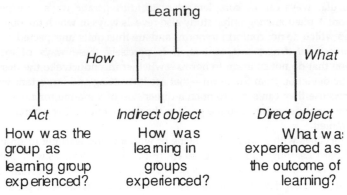

Fig. 40.1   The organisation of this paper, relating specific aspects of the students' experience of learning to the direct object, the indirect object and the act of learning

40.3.1   What was experienced as the outcome of learning?

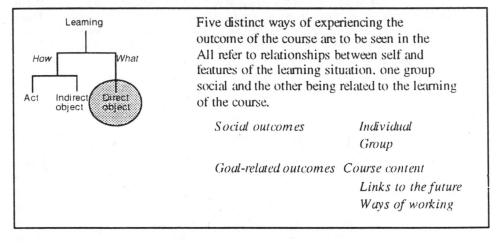

Five distinct ways of experiencing the outcome of the course are to be seen in the All refer to relationships between self and features of the learning situation, one group social and the other being related to the learning of the course.

Social outcomes   Individual
                         Group

Goal-related outcomes   Course content
                         Links to the future
                         Ways of working

Fig. 40.2   The outcome of learning, five categories described by the students

40.3.2   How was learning in groups experienced?

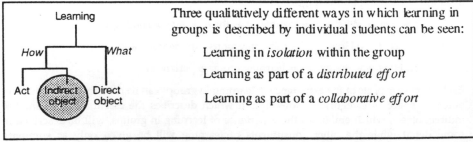

Three qualitatively different ways in which learning in groups is described by individual students can be seen:

Learning in *isolation* within the group

Learning as part of a *distributed effort*

Learning as part of a *collaborative effort*

Fig. 40.3   Learning in groups, three categories described by the students

40.3.2.1 *Learning in isolation within the group*

In this category the group is experienced above all as an organizational expedience, a negligible factor in the course, or in the programme of studies, and even as a hindrance in getting on with 'real' learning. S5 describes his experience of learning in groups thus:

> I want there to be somebody there who knows, a teacher, who knows how things are, *and then me.* Then I can take the information he can give me and think about it myself and work at it. I can't work in the way we've got it now, where there are several of us who don't know anything, and we read a bit and try to figure out *what* it's about, not how it *is*, because we don't *know* how it is. We know how it might be and we try to build up a picture of how it is . . . we don't really know what is right.

This completely recognizable and rather sad lament points to a mismatch between how beginning students view knowledge and learning and the way teachers both think themselves and want their students to think. It is well researched and well documented, as well as being part of every observant teacher's experience, that young or inexperienced students tend to see the world they are entering in absolutes (Perry, 1970; Baxter Magolda, 1992). Knowledge is experienced as having a true–false or a right–wrong or a correct–incorrect dualism; teachers and textbooks are seen as the sources of the true knowledge and the student's own role as one of acquiring the right knowledge from the sources in a correct form.

40.3.2.2 *Learning as part of a distributed effort*

The second category sees the learning in groups in terms of the members of the group contributing to it, as S1 expresses:

> There are different ways of learning. You can learn by heart and you can learn to understand. *Learning in a group means that you don't need to understand it, you don't have to learn it for yourself, somebody else can do it . . .*
>
> (S1)

When asked if you have actually learned it then, she replies:

> Yes, you have. Then whether it's right or wrong, you don't know that, because nobody tells you.
>
> (S1)

This still indicates a state of right-wrong dualism and learning in a group is seen as each member contributing parts of the true knowledge that is needed by the group. This contribution is then distributed to the other members who thus, it is felt, work more efficiently, in this case it is implied by using individual talents or interests.

The same notion is expressed by S2 in connection with writing a report:

> I wrote a chapter [of the report] with X, and *we had a bit of a problem in discussing how we should organise it and such like. We weren't talking on the same wavelength really, so in the end we wrote a half-chapter each.*
>
> (S2)

Instead of negotiating an agreement with his writing partner S2 chose to act independently and then bring the two independent contributions together. Again, the rationale is that it saved the effort of finding 'the same wavelength'.

40.3.2.3   *Learning as part of a collaborative effort*

The third category experiences learning in a group as being supportive of learning through various forms of collaboration. S9 relates that talking to another student about a problem is often more productive than asking the teacher:

> well it's good if you come across a problem, *you can often get it explained by somebody who is pretty much like you, thinks in the same way. It's a bit different if you ask a teacher or tutor, for they often take you directly to the answer. But if you sit in a group and get a problem then you can make sure that you solve it together. I don't know, maybe you grapple with it a bit more. Maybe you learn by doing it as well.*
>
> (S9)

Referring once again to the work on epistemological development at university, we see here a manifestation of coming to see knowledge as relative, multi-faceted or contextual; one can have opinions that one can uphold against the opinions of others.

S3 also expresses this way of experiencing learning in groups, going beyond the value in situations where one has a problem, to using the possibility to discuss in order to address overriding questions of goals of learning:

> It's actually to do with understanding (talking with other members of the group). If you get stuck on something, for example, and try to solve it, then you've got to understand what it's all about if you're going to get any further, otherwise you won't get so far. *Then you might sort of tell a friend what it's about, so you try to discuss your way towards and answer to 'What is it we're actually trying to do here?'*
>
> (S3)

This points to a further stage according to Perry. Despite your knowing something, holding an opinion, or holding something to be good and true, you realize that in other circumstances, or for other people, there are other norms or reasons for other beliefs. Then you start to become able to see the world from other perspectives and stand up for your own way of knowing something against a background of others' equally legitimate ways of knowing that thing.

If working in a group is to be a learning experience, the group members must be at least in the process of shifting from a desire for absolute knowledge to an admittance of perspectival knowledge, as S9 might be alluding to at the end of the quote above: 'maybe you grapple with it a bit more. Maybe you learn by doing it [discussing with peers] as well'.

S2 describes working in a group thus:

> One thing that is great is when you get stuck. When you are reading something in a text-book then you find things that are complicated, that you don't really understand. *But when you are working in a group and that happens then there is always somebody else who has a completely different perspective on the same problem, and that's really good. It's really good to find out that different people can see the same problem in so many different ways, it is invaluable.* Otherwise, if you have to study something by yourself, then you sit there with your reference book and don't understand anything, and there's nothing to do about it.
>
> (S2)

S2 indicates a pleasure in finding such different perspectives in contrast with the single track one tends to stick to when working alone, and a willingness to draw on the experience and insights of others.

At the same time, working at a limited project in a group can be a medium for bringing about such a shift, and that puts demands on the sort of project and the way in which the tutor works with the group. S3 voices a query that many students and teachers voice when faced with project- and problem-focused courses:

> and you can also wonder, if you're going to have a course based on project work, then you can't go into everything that's necessary for the course during the project. I really wonder if you can.
>
> (S3)

To understand that the knowledge one gains in a course of any kind is just one way of experiencing the subject or content of the course, and that there are others; to realize that learning about any concept or principle or way of working or whatever, is something that can proceed throughout one's working life and that the institutional education of the university is intended to lay the foundations for such learning goes along with the sort of development we have described earlier.

40.3.2.4   Discussion: What is learning?

It is a common observation that people find it difficult to speak of their learning. When asked what they learn, how they learn, and what learning actually is, students often find it difficult to distinguish aspects of learning and studying, and teachers find it difficult to distinguish their students' learning from their own teaching. Thus it was particularly interesting to ask the students what learning actually was, when something they had learned had previously been discussed.

Marton, Beaty and dall'Alba (1993) have identified six conceptions of learning among students from the Open University (Figure 40.4). Alongside each of the OU conceptions is an illustrative quote from this study – all six are to be found there too. Note that a quote by no means implies an exclusive perspective on the nature of learning – it is like all else dependent on context. S5, for instance, implies that nothing has been learned if no new knowledge has been acquired (A), but goes on to say that learning involves understanding and visualizing (D).

There is a significant division of these six conceptions of learning, which comes between (C) and (D), namely that the first three are devoid of 'meaning' – no demand is made for finding any sense in what one is learning. These students might actually seek meaning, but it is taken for granted in what they recount for the interviewer, in contrast to what the next two students say, which is essentially relating that which is learned to everyday life or the 'real world'. S3 draws an interesting line between learning in the context of the sort of thing he learns and what he imagines students of other subjects to learn:

> Do you mean the process? Well, it might be that you have a particular problem and you learn to cope with it, in general. There is a general problem, and you learn – now I'm talking a bit mathematically, like an engineer – and then you learn to solve the problem in a general way, so you can solve special cases of the problem as well. [. . .] It's different, of course, to learn maths from learning from texts, history and social sciences because that's mostly a question of cramming in a lot of facts. That's not as hard, it just means sitting down and reading a lot of times. But then, there are two aspects to learning, reading in a mass of facts and understanding what you read. That's the difference, knowledge and understanding.
>
> (S3)

Learning as		
(A) *increasing one's knowledge*	S5	I can't say I've learned anything because when I learn something I learn concrete things. This has been of an experience, something I've done.
(B) *memorizing and reproducing*	S11	It's something that you remember. Something you've read or heard or talked about and that you remember. Something that you can use again later I
(C) *applying knowledge*	S12	I've got some knowledge of something and I remember that knowledge as well. Yes, something you can use then afterwards. maybe even teach it to somebody
(D) *understanding*	S5	Now that I'm here I learn things I want to learn, almost everything. It's only the subjects I think fun that I want to learn. To learn something, it's to understand it, maybe not know it by heart - though I often do anyway - but if I've understood something so I understand it, I understand the context. I can visualise it in my head quite easily, certain mostly if it's been well explained.
(E) *seeing something in a different way*	S2	It's hard to explain. You realise how things work, simply seeing new angles on old well-known problems and situations. It might be in with everyday life or with mathematical problems. The more you learn, the more new angles you see on the old problems you have met before.
(F) *changing as a person*	S4	A philosophical question! Everything is actually, everything that you remember. It's hard to point to anything that isn't learning, I think you use of everything you've experienced actually. It doesn't need to be - It's easy to sort of think "Oh, if I read this book I'll learn much more than if I go into town", but it's not necessarily so, it's more a question of having all the aspects there I

Fig. 40.4   Conceptions of learning as identified by Marton et al. (left-hand column) and illustrative quotes from the CSEC study (right-hand column)

When S3 speaks of mathematics or engineering he shows an understanding of learning which generalizes and relates one problem to another, in line with an (E) conception of learning, whereas he attributes students of humanities and social sciences with a much more trivial sort of learning, of type (A). He 'understands' while they merely 'know'.

This important distinction is associated with students' approaches to their studies and the outcomes of their learning, as has been developed in, for example, Marton and Booth, 1996. Students who see learning as acquiring facts (A), even if they see recalling them (B) and applying them (C) as being part of learning, might not find much satisfaction in the learning in such a course as CSEC. These are ways of experiencing learning that are typical for school studies and the traditional university course in which a short and intensive period of study is followed by a stiff examination in which arbitrary parts of the content of the course, and no more, have to be reproduced. CSEC intends students to learn ways of working and to develop approaches to studying that will serve them well in future, as well as giving them a start in moulding the subject matter they will meet in later courses into a whole, and relating it to a wider world of computer engineering in practice and in society.

40.3.3   How was the group as a learning group experienced?

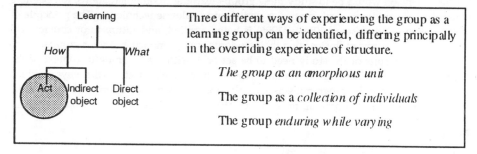

Three different ways of experiencing the group as a learning group can be identified, differing principally in the overriding experience of structure.

The group as an amorphous unit

The group as a *collection of individuals*

The group *enduring while varying*

Fig. 40.5   The group as a learning group, three categories described by the students

40.4   Summary

The variation in ways of experiencing learning in groups is summarized in Figure 40.6, following Figure 40.1.

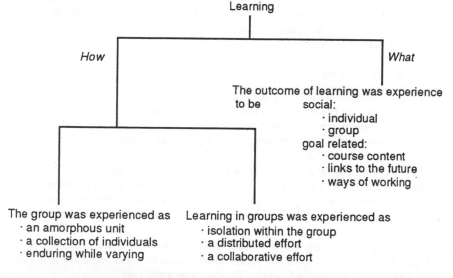

Fig. 40.6   A summary of the results of the analysis of the experience of learning in groups

If we take a normative perspective, we can say that while all of the learning outcomes are desirable, and in line with the hopes of the course, achieving the social outcomes without the goal-related outcomes would be wasting the course. It is the goal-related outcomes that are qualitatively unique for the course, and which imply the best grounding for the coming years in school and work. The next question to be addressed, elsewhere, is, 'What does it demand of the how of learning in groups that this outcome should be achieved?' (Booth, in preparation).

40.5 Conclusion

More work is needed to fill in the gaps seen here. The outcomes of learning, for instance, could be elaborated in qualitative terms; and the ways in which different individuals in the groups describe their experience could be brought together to an integrated description. A further extension would be to study these groups learning in other situations, for example when they are studying mathematics or digital and analogue techniques. The principle of collaborative action research (Beaty, 1996) is being applied, and future tutor courses will examine other aspects of the learning their students are experiencing in their groups.

Finally, the results of the study need to be set back within a meaningful context of the CSEC course, tutors' interaction with their groups, the course's effects on the ways in which students experience the programme as a whole, and the learning outcomes as they follow the students through the programme and out into the workplace.

Notes

1. Starting from the Table of Contents at http://www.pedu.chalmers.se/shirley/CSECTOC.html.

2. For details see, http://www.dtek.chalmers.se/Dpp/Publikationer/utdrag.html.

3. The name 'tutor' has been chosen here as the English designation for the doctoral student who worked with the group. This does not imply the traditional role of a tutor, however, as a person with an overall view of and interest in the student's progress, but is restricted to work with the group and its project. The Swedish 'handledare' implies a more proactive role than was intended, and in any case the tutors were able to mould their own roles according to how they saw their groups.

40.6 References

Baxter Magolda, M.B. (1992) *Knowing and Reasoning in College: Gender-related Patterns in Students' Intellectual Development*, San Francisco: Jossey-Bass.

Beaty, E. (1996) Consultancy style action research: an approach to educational development. Paper presented at the *4th International Improving Student Learning Symposium*, held in Bath, 9–11 September 1996.

Booth, S.A. (no date) On the experience of learning in groups. Manuscript

Booth, S.A., Bayati, Z. and Petersson, J. (1996) Getting a grasp on Computer Science and Engineering: the reception and learning effects of a project-related course in the first term. Paper presented at *3rd East-West Congress on Engineering Education*, Poland, September 1996.

Jansson, P. (1996) Encouraging female students of Computer Science and Engineering programme: the psychological and socio-cultural grounds, Paper presented at *3rd East-West Congress on Engineering Education*, Poland, September 1996.

Marton, F., Beaty, E. and dall'Alba, G. (1993) Conceptions of learning, *International Journal of Educational Research*, **19**, 277–300.

Marton, F. and Booth, S. (1996) The learner's experience of learning. In D. Olson and N. Torrance (eds), *Handbook of Education and Human Development: New Models of Learning, Teaching and Schooling*, Oxford: Blackwell, 534–64.

Marton, F. and Booth, S. (1997) *Learning and Awareness*, Mahwah NJ: Lawrence Erlbaum Inc.

Perry, W.G. (1970) *Forms of Intellectual and Ethical Development in the College Years: A Scheme.*,

New York: Holt, Rinehart & Winston.

Svensson, B, and Thomas, B. (1993) *Ansökan om projektstöd för att reformera D-utbildningen på Chalmers* (Application for project support to reform the D-programme at Chalmers).

Svensson, B. (1996) Reforming a Computer Science and Engineering degree programme: operative goals and learning-related strategies, Paper presented at *3rd East-West Congress on Engineering Education*, Poland, September 1996.

Wistedt, I (1996), *Gender-inclusive Higher Education in Mathematics, Physics and Technology:. Five Swedish Development Projects*, Högskoleverket 1996, 5 S.

41 Disciplinary thinking: the case of environmental planning

Dory Reeves[(i)] and David J. Nicol[(ii)]
(i) Department of Environmental Planning; (ii) Centre for Academic Practice, University of Strathclyde

41.1 Overview

This study is an exploration of thinking within a specific discipline – Environmental Planning. Two teachers from an MSc/Diploma in Urban and Regional Planning were interviewed to find out what thinking skills they expected to develop in students through the classes they teach. Differences were found in how the teachers conceived of thinking, and how they taught and assessed thinking. These interviews on teaching practices were interpreted in relation to the research literature on thinking. This dialogue between practice and research-based theory highlighted some crucial issues that should be addressed in further studies of thinking.

41.2 Introduction

This pilot study was a first attempt to explore how teachers responsible for teaching classes in an MSc./Diploma in Urban and Regional Planning think about thinking skills in relation to their students and to their teaching. Do they have systematic views about thinking? Do teachers of planning make conscious efforts to teach their students thinking skills? How do they assess thinking skills?

The Royal Town Planning Institute (RTPI) in its guidelines to Planning Schools (1996) sets out the skills to be developed through accredited courses. A number of these are 'thinking' skills in a general sense:

- problem definition and collaborative problem-solving;
- research skills and data collection;
- quantitative analysis;
- synthesis and application of knowledge.

Other skills specified by the Institute relate to the way planners are assumed to think within the workplace. For example, according to the institute students are expected to develop 'aesthetic and design awareness' or to develop 'the ability to see the strategic and synoptic implications' of an issue (synoptic here means having a comprehensive view). Some skills defined by the Institute concern modes of expressing or articulating thinking, for example, written, oral and graphic communication.

The study reported here was carried out by Dr Dory Reeves (DR), a relatively new teacher to higher education. Having come from professional practice she was concerned that thinking skills in university courses were invariably tacit rather than made explicit to students, even though such skills are specified in RTPI documents. This concern led her to carry out some initial 'grounded' research on teaching practice within her discipline using phenomenological methods. She was thus following in the established tradition of the 'teacher-researcher'. The other author, Dr David Nicol (DN), is an educationalist employed by the university to work in partnership with teaching staff on initiatives aimed at improving the quality of student learning. With regard to the study reported here his role was to act as a consultant and resource providing advice to support the teacher's research and guidance through the research literature. Although each author had a specific role, what is reported in this paper is the outcome of a collaborative relationship.

41.3   Method

The pilot study involved semi-structured interviews with two university teachers from the MSc/Diploma in Urban and Regional Planning. The course offered at the University of Strathclyde is accredited by the RTPI and provides a training in professional planning. Each interview lasted one hour and was tape-recorded and then transcribed.

The interviews were intended to provide an opportunity to explore the way in which thinking skills were made explicit in the teaching of the course either in lectures or tutorials or in the organization of projects. Three key questions guided the semi-structured interviews:

Q1   What do you understand by thinking skills?

Q2   Do you develop thinking skills in your class? (how?)

Q3   How does the assessment for the class relate to these skills?

Supplementary questions were used to keep the interview focused on these three issues.

The interview data were analysed by DR who looked for key themes in the transcripts (illustrated in the results section) in relation to the three questions above. This involved some discussion with DN. DR then wrote a commentary on each interview. After this, DN linked the interviews and DR's commentary to issues in the research literature on thinking.

41.4   Results of interviews

41.4.1   Interview 1

Interview 1 took place with a lecturer with six years' university teaching experience. He is responsible for the delivery of a class called 'Theory of Planning' on the MSc/Diploma. Students take this class in the first year of the postgraduate course. It involves 12 lectures and two tutorials. The class is assessed by means of two essay assignments and an essay-based examination.

41.4.1.1   *Teacher's conceptions of thinking*

In the context of the Planning Theory class, the lecturer explained that students' thinking must be understood in terms of the conceptual nature of the subject:

> The aim of this class is to examine the concepts and ideas which underpin planning and to set them in a historical context but without dwelling too much on the history. [thinking] . . . is the ability to abstract from reality . . . to understand the ideas which help explain things . . . to think about the concepts behind planning.

> In order to achieve the learning objectives [for this class] . . . [the students] . . . have to think . . . to understand the concepts and articulate these ideas in their own words rather than copying things out of books.

When asked what 'specific' thinking skills are developed in students the tutor said that what he is trying to do is:

> to get students to look around at the world in which they live and to get an understanding of how it came to be (90 per cent of what you see has been developed in the last 160 years) . . .

41.4.1.2 Fostering thinking in students

In answer to the question 'How do you get the students to develop this understanding [of how the world came to be]?' the lecturer said he used story telling.

> I'll tell a story around this, for instance, the planner as a scientific expert . . . rational, comprehensive . . . I'll show what contrasting approaches can bring about . . . for example, Corbousier and Howard . . . My aim in the end is for the students to see things in a different way – to change the perceptions of the students . . . I talk about issues to do with ethics, social justice and environment, utilitarianism.

Later in the interview the relationship between teaching and learning was clarified further:

> what I try to get across to students is the range of ideas, and the kinds of ideas which come up again and again. I hope that they will be able to make the links. I try to direct students through the lectures and in the tutorials. I am trying to get the students to read and to evaluate. I want the students to make contrasts and comparisons. I try to direct students through the lectures and in the tutorials, to read and to evaluate. I want the students to make contrasts and comparisons.

41.4.1.3 Assessment and thinking

When asked how thinking skills are assessed the lecturer gave two examples of what was expected of students in answering an essay question in the final examination. Here is one example from the two:

> the question on the 1997 paper 'Examine Lindbolm's argument that there is no place for rational decision making in planning' requires the students to explain rational decision-making ideas and then look at the criticism of this by Lindbolm and having contrasted these two approaches these should now address the question of whether rational decision-making is possible.

41.4.1.4 DR's interpretation of interview 1

When asked to talk about thinking skills the teacher seems to emphasize subject content but how should thinking skills be related to the content? If the course is meant to develop thinking shouldn't the thinking 'goals' be made more explicit to the students?

This teacher also seems to view thinking in relation to what he does – the stories or historical tales which he uses to illustrate changes in concepts over time. It sounds very much like telling the students what the key points are. This 'telling' seems to contradict what I've read in current research which argues that student should be active in learning (Ramsden, 1994: Nicol, 1997). Is the teacher getting the students to think actively by themselves?

In relation to assessment, the tutor wants the students to use their understanding of underlying ideas and concepts to make and evaluate arguments in writing. Thinking skills are involved in answering the essay questions although it is not clear how the skills for the essay relate to the skills being developed in the course.

41.4.2   Interview 2

Interview 2 was with the tutor responsible for the last project (of five) on the postgraduate course. She has over 20 years' university teaching experience. This particular project involves students in groups producing a tender for a Scottish Office research project on the topic 'Environmental Sustainability'.

The tutor discussed thinking in relation to the stages of the project. The tutor identified five stages in the project:

Stage 1   The students in the groups gather information in relation to the topic.

Stage 2   Students define their own 'brief' or approach to the project and its organization

Stage 3   Students implement their own brief.

Stage 4   Students present their projects and submit a written report on the project.

Stage 5   Students write a reflective report on the competencies involved in carrying out the project.

41.4.2.1   Teacher's conceptions of thinking

According to the tutor the aims of the project are:

> to extend capacities and to develop professional competencies which include familiarity with contemporary material, to get students to think about the competencies which are necessary . . . [and] . . . to encourage creativity . . .

The tutor related thinking skills to professional competencies and referred to these in the context of the project stages. Each stage required specific competencies (or thinking skills), for example, task management, team management, contingency management, making decisions about presentations, reflecting.

In gathering information in stage 1 the students were expected to make a critical interpretation of sources. Contingency planning was the thinking skill needed for stage 3 , time management was an important thinking skill required for stage 4 and 'reflection' is a key skill in stage 5.

The tutor felt that reflection was important to enhance learning and students awareness of the competencies of planners:

> they were asked to reflect on the learning experience and were given a set of articles to look at including the Simon Divodi article on skills for planners.

In addition, the tutor believed that creativity was important to all stages of the project work:

> accessing, finding out information working out the value of information, analysing information, critical thinking . . . they all involve creativity . . .

41.4.2.2 Fostering thinking in students

In addressing the issue how the course developed thinking skills the tutor first mentioned that the students were on a postgraduate course and that:

> a number of skills have been developed and . . . [this project] . . . would not be run in this way for first year undergraduates.

The subsequent discussion focused on the environmental conditions necessary for the expression and development of creativity in project work.

> there are certain conditions necessary for creativity . . . [it] . . . develops in a non-stressful situation . . . for example, limited assessment initially building in to later stages so that they feel relaxed and able to contribute . . .

41.4.2.3 Assessment and thinking

This project is assessed by an oral presentation and an individual and group report. Students also submit a reflective report on the process of undertaking the project. The tutor felt that these methods tested students' ability to think.

41.4.2.4 DR's interpretation of interview 2

The thinking skills (competencies) developed through this project relate to the guidelines of the Royal Town Planning Institute (e.g. problem definition and collaborative problem-solving). The tutor simulates a 'real-life' planning situation and encourages students towards a structured way of working by setting out explicitly the stages they should reach week by week. Creativity is also seen as an important thinking skill and the tutor emphasizes the conditions she feels are necessary for successful creative thinking.

The tutor plays a facilitating role by making the learning environment for creativity non-stressful. There might, however, be a tension between the desire to encourage creativity and the way in which the project has been prescribed and structured. How is creativity defined and does she make this explicit to the students?

The reflective reports in the assessment required students to relate their experience and the way they think to how professional practitioners work and think and students were given some material to help them do this. Are the students coached in these reflective skills?

41.5   Discussion

41.5.1   Links with the research literature on thinking

DR began with a concern about how to make thinking goals explicit to students. The pilot study, and the interpretation of this study by DR raise a number of issues that resonate with the research literature on thinking.

41.5.2   Interview 1

41.5.2.1   *Thinking, content and skills transfer*

How should thinking be related to content and made explicit to students? This question, raised by DR, is important in the research literature on thinking (see Bonnett, 1995). It has implications for the learners' ability to 'transfer' their thinking skills to new contexts. If thinking comprises general skills (processes) which can be applied to any subject content (or context) then transfer is easy. However if thinking is bound up with (and contextualized within) the subject content being taught then teaching for transfer is more difficult. It would require the 'active decontextualization . . .the deliberate mindful abstraction of a principle . . . and its application to a different context' (Perkins and Saloman, 1989).

41.5.2.2   Developing thinking through metacognition

The last sentence highlights the main strategy – 'metacognition' – advocated by researchers and practitioners to develop critical thinking (Biggs, 1985: McGuinness, 1993). The emphasis with metacognition is on encouraging students to explore their own thinking and knowledge construction so that they learn how to self-regulate their cognitive processes (see Resnick, 1987, 1989). Metacognition is developed when teachers make explicit the ways in which they think (e.g. through think-aloud modelling) and when they help students themselves to make explicit, reflect on, self-assess and analyse how they think and solve problems.

41.5.2.3   Thinking as an active process

This discussion of metacognition is relevant to another aspect of interview 1. Was the lecturer merely 'telling' students what the key points are, as DR suggests, or was he actually modelling through his lectures how an expert thinks? This would be a good thing to do but it is difficult to tell from the interview data if this is indeed happening. Moreover, even if the teacher does model thinking this should be followed up with opportunities for students to practice thinking *actively* by themselves (Nicol, 1997: Ramsden, 1992), as suggested by DR: e.g. by having them carry out analyses of planning situations in tutorials using the disciplinary thinking modelled in the lectures. Activities like these would make thinking processes more explicit. Perhaps the lecturer does this in his tutorials. It would be necessary to sit in on both lectures and tutorials to confirm how thinking is exemplified and practised.

41.5.2.4   Assessing professional thinking abilities

DR raises a final issue with regard to interview 1: how are the skills being used to produce an essay related to the skills being developed in the class? On the face of it the essay is a good test of the thinking skills he is teaching. The lecturer asks the students *to explain, to make contrasts and comparisons* and *to evaluate* in their essays. These processes parallel his conceptions (earlier in the interview) of the thinking of planners. However, if he was interested in how planners think in 'authentic planning situations' he might require alternative assessment methods.

41.5.3   Interview 2

41.5.3.1   Teacher's conceptions of thinking

This teacher seems to possess a more general view of thinking skills than the teacher in interview 1. She relates the skills to the general problem-solving processes needed for the project. However, it is difficult to know from the interview exactly how she thinks about subject content, or as DR suggests, how she views creative thinking and makes her views explicit to students. This is important because teachers' conceptualizations of thinking undoubtedly have an important influence on how they go about helping students to think (e.g. Prosser, Trigwell and Taylor, 1994). For this reason, it is essential that each teacher develops insight into her own conception of effective thinking before she communicates this conception to students (or teaches in relation to her conception).

41.5.3.2 *Thinking as more than a cognitive process*

This teacher's concern that creativity be developed in a non-stressful context is congruent with recent literature that views learning as not just being about cognition (Nicol, 1997, Perkins *et al.*, 1993). In addition, her use of reflective processes in the assessment where students think and write about their own thinking in relation to the project and the skills of professional planners is highly consistent with the research cited earlier on metacognition.

41.6 Conclusion

This pilot study on thinking skills in planning has helped clarify the questions that should be asked about thinking and about how to make thinking explicit to students. One outcome of this study will be the submission of this paper as a discussion document to the UK Discipline Network for Planning. The paper will also act as a platform for follow-up research in the Department of Environmental Planning at the University of Strathclyde.

Acknowledgements

The authors wish to thank the two teachers from the department of environmental planning who provided input to this research.

41.7 References

Biggs, J. (1995) The role of metalearning in study processes, *British Journal of Educational Psychology*, **55**, 185–212.

Bonnett, M. (1995) Teaching thinking and the sanctity of content, *Journal of Philosophy of Education*, 29(3), 295–309.

McGuinness, C. (1993) Teaching thinking: new signs for theories of cognition, *British Journal of Educational Psychology*, 13, 305–16.

Nicol, D. (1997) *Research on Learning and Higher Education Teaching*, UCoSDA Briefing Paper Forty Five, Sheffield.

Perkins, D.N., Jay, E. and Trishman, S. (1993) Beyond abilities: a dispositional theory of thinking, *Merril Palmer Quarterly*, 39(1), 1–21.

Perkins, D.N. and Salamon, G. (1989) Are cognitive skills context-bound?, Educational Researcher, *18*(1), 16–25.

Perkins, D.N. and Salamon, G. (1988) Teaching for transfer? Educational Leadership, Sept., 22–32.

Prosser, M., Trigwell, K. and Taylor, P. (1994) A phenomenographic study of academics conceptions of science teaching and learning, *Learning and Instruction*, 4, 217–31.

Ramsden, P. (1992) *Learning to Teach in Higher Education*, Routledge.

Resnick, L.B. (1987) *Education and Learning to Think*, Washington, National Academy Press.

Resnick, L.B. (1989) *Cognitive Instruction: Issues and Agendas*, Hillsdale N.J, Erlbaum.

RTPI (1996) *Accreditation Guide-lines*, London, RTPI.

42 Building skill development into the undergraduate mathematics curriculum

Peter Kahn
Department of Mathematics, Liverpool Hope University College

42.1 Introduction

With mass higher education and a broader school curriculum, it can no longer be assumed that many students entering higher education in the UK have fully grasped the cognitive skills needed to study their chosen discipline(s), particularly in the case of mathematics.1 Identifying the relevant skills needed for the study of a specific discipline and developing them in the students is thus important.

Mass higher education also ensures that students enter with more varied aspirations. In order to attract and retain students, undergraduate programmes therefore need to meet a wide set of aims. Focusing on skills is one way of ensuring that this occurs, by aiding personal development and preparation for employment. While the skills that this chapter considers are initially proposed as subject specific, scope is present for a measure of transfer, as is considered below.

Specialist skill development in first-year mathematics courses in the UK has so far concentrated on the understanding of mathematical proof,[2] and at a more basic level on skills of manipulating algebraic expressions, although a notable exception is the Open University.[3] This chapter considers a project that seeks to develop a variety of advanced skills needed for the specialist study of mathematics, with teaching and learning beginning in September 1997. The first-year students involved are on degree programmes in mathematics and another subject, and the skills are developed alongside the teaching of pure mathematics.

42.2 The project

The pattern of the project is first to introduce standard content, from abstract algebra, and to follow this with the teaching and learning of a particular skill – while also making use of, and thus reinforcing the learning of, the earlier mathematical content.

It is important to observe that such help should not be administered on a haphazard or single issue basis. Given the complexity of advanced mathematical thinking, it is unlikely that simply focusing on one cognitive skill will be sufficient; such as simply concentrating on the understanding of proof. After all, advanced mathematical thinking is characterized by complex interactions between its constituent elements. It is also important to address the existing cognitive development of the students and target those areas which are most at odds with the processes of advanced mathematical thinking.

Initial research has identified the following skills as critical to the study of undergraduate mathematics: writing mathematical text; logical thinking and the understanding of proof;

problem solving; learning mathematics; and connected or global understanding. Running throughout the development of these skills is an emphasis on the underlying skills of analysis and synthesis.

Work in the first semester concentrates on the first three of these skills. The ability to write coherent mathematical text is fostered by considering both the meaning of particular symbols and concepts, and the underlying structure of mathematics. Understanding of proof requires mastery of the basic elements of logical thinking but also of a variety of standard forms and procedures. Finally, it is well established that a structured approach enhances problem solving. Reflection on the solution of problems is an important way of developing such skill.

The remaining skills are covered in the second semester. In developing the ability to learn advanced mathematics, it is important to realize that new concepts involve interactions between more basic concepts, requiring the mastery of each underlying concept and interaction. The role of examples, asking questions, obstacles to understanding (and the clash between intuitive and formal approaches in particular), and a systematic approach are also relevant. Given a tendency in advanced mathematics to concentrate on procedural knowledge, global or connected understanding is particularly important.[4] This involves an overview of mathematics as a whole, and how individual concepts relate to that whole, understanding mathematical principles of wide application – such as space, abstraction and relationship – and examples of interactions between mathematical topics.

A variety of learning and teaching strategies are employed during the project. In addition to more traditional methods these include the following: small group work, group presentations, students completing partial lecture notes, and reflection in a variety of forms on the processes of advanced mathematical thinking. Continuous assessment will form an integral part of the skill development. For instance, an assignment will consist of the solution of a problem and the requirement that the students describe the strategies that led to the solution. Students will be asked to submit a plan as to how to learn a specific topic, to describe any difficulties encountered carrying it out and finally to solve associated problems. Self-assessment and multiple-choice tests also feature.

Whether, and why, such an approach is effective will be considered. A standard instrument developed at City University will determine changes in levels of confidence and motivation for the study of mathematics, and examination results will be analysed with the previous intake for comparison. Changes in approaches to learning and perceptions of the discipline as a whole will also be considered. Finally, regular feedback will be sought from the students, who will each complete two detailed course evaluation schedules, followed by selective interviews.

42.3 Conclusion

The project primarily seeks to meet the needs that have arisen as a result of mass higher education and changes in schools, by developing the skills that are essential for learning advanced mathematics.

However, given the need to meet a wide variety of student aspirations, it is interesting to consider the transfer of such cognitive skills. This transfer is generally more difficult for theoretical aspects of a subject, which are harder to relate, say, to employment – certainly in the case of mathematics. While applications of mathematics have obvious relevance, skills associated with the study of pure mathematics are still important. For instance, a recent study[5] found that one of the two distinguishing qualities of mathematicians in industry was the 'highly developed skills in abstraction, analysis of underlying structures, and logical thinking'. Since many problems are of a logical/analytical nature it is not surprising that such skills are valued by employers.

To enhance their transfer, it would be important to increase the variety of situations in which these skills are applied. Students who take a general module on critical thinking are also likely to increase such transfer. Sophisticated cognitive skills are the hallmark of a graduate and with mass higher education their development needs to be explicitly fostered.

42.4   References

1. London Mathematical Society (1995) *Tackling the Mathematics Problem*, London: LMS.
2. Kahn, P.E. and Hoyles, C. (1997) The changing undergraduate experience: a case study of single honours mathematics in England and Wales, *Studies in Higher Education*, **22**(3) (in press).
3. Ekins, J. (1997) Embedding core skills in OU Mathematics courses, *Math Skills Newsletter*, **3**.
4. Tall, D. (ed.) (1991) *Advanced Mathematical Thinking*, London, Kluwer.
5. The Society for Industrial and Applied Mathematics (1997) *Report on Mathematics in Industry*, http://www.siam.org/mii/miihome.htm.

43 Improving graduate outcomes: curriculum approaches to building communication skills

Christine Ingleton[i], Barbara Wake[ii] and Alison Southwick[iii]
(i) Senior Lecturer, Advisory Centre for University Education, University of Adelaide; (ii) Lecturer, Advisory Centre for University Education, University of Adelaide; (iii) Associate Lecturer, University of South Australia, Adelaide

43.1 Overview

Australian graduates are frequently criticized by employers and in the press for their lack of communication and critical thinking skills. During the course of a two year literacy and communication skills project, different approaches were developed for identifying the required skills, and including them in the curriculum in four contrasting discipline areas. These were Agricultural and Natural Resource Sciences, Maths, Labour Studies and Commerce. The most comprehensive changes were introduced in a Commerce Department, and these are used as a case study in this chapter.

Data from structured interviews of Year 12 teachers, first- and third-year Commerce students, and employers, and an analysis of students' examination papers and assignments, show some of the reasons why Commerce graduates lack appropriate communication skills. Through staff development, preparation of discipline-specific materials, tutor training and student workshops, changes were made not only in assessment practices, teaching strategies and marking, but also in the teaching culture of the department.

This chapter focuses specifically on the teaching and learning of critical thinking, and shows how changes in a Commerce Department have improved the development of critical thinking and communication skills.

43.2 Improving graduate outcomes: curriculum approaches to building communication skills

To assist Commerce students in becoming adept communicators, the Department of Commerce at the University of Adelaide has introduced innovations into the curriculum which take account of, and teach explicitly, the specialized ways that students need to think and communicate in Commerce subjects. Such an approach bypasses the notion that the communication and intellectual skills required by students at university are prelearned or generic, or that they are solely to blame when tertiary students are criticized for poor literacy skills. Rather, the approach makes explicit the different ways that each subject constructs and communicates knowledge (Bakhtin, 1986). These innovations, begun as part of a Literacy Project in 1994, have provided the groundwork for the teaching of communication skills in core subjects throughout a three-year Commerce degree programme. A language specialist and an educational developer from the Advisory Centre for University Education (ACUE) at the University have collaborated with Commerce teachers to integrate these skills into a range of subjects.

This greater emphasis on thinking skills within a vocationally oriented discipline aims for a closer partnership between schools, universities and the profession in a coherent progression towards students becoming professional accountants. The Joint Accreditation Review Task Force (October, 1995:1) call for graduates to be competent professional initiates has meant that many tertiary teachers are re-evaluating the focus of their curriculum in accordance with the Task Force Guidelines (p. 5):

> Emphasis should be placed on the development of critical thinking, analytical reasoning, problem-solving skills and research techniques which support the ability for continued lifetime self-learning ... Concept issues should be appropriately related to practical applications in an intellectually challenging manner, with a minimum of emphasis on formal technical procedures.

Research undertaken as part of the Literacy Project confirmed that skills of critical thinking and effective communication are stated as desired learning outcomes by Commerce teachers both in schools and the university, and by employers of Commerce graduates. However, any assumption that each educational sector is interlinked, and therefore provides the next developmental stage, was contradicted by the research. Interviews with senior secondary Commerce teachers revealed that while their educational aims were to assist students develop greater critical thinking skills, such aims were stifled, on the one hand, by the diverse educational needs of a broad cohort of students, many of whom are not intending to study at university, and by a public examination system which they felt encouraged the reproduction of factual, rote-learned information.

In order to enhance the communication and intellectual skills of first year Commerce students, and so meet university and employer expectations of graduates' skills, the primary aim of the project was to assist students move beyond the mere presentation of facts to being able to critically interpret, apply and communicate knowledge.

43.3 Defining literacy, communication skills and critical thinking

In this chapter, we have used the term 'literacy' interchangeably with 'communication skills' to refer to students' abilities to read, write, speak, listen and to utilize a range of critical thinking skills. The definition used to guide the project emphasizes the integral relationship between language and context:

> Literacy is the ability to read and use written information and to write appropriately in a range of contexts. Literacy involves the integration of speaking, listening, and critical thinking with reading and writing.
>
> (Department of Education, Employment and Training 1991: 9)

'Critical thinking' is often used as a generic term in the literature and by educators for the application of intellectual skills, such as analysis, interpretation and evaluation. However, the term is rarely filled with any precise meaning as to how 'critical thinking' appropriately applies knowledge within its context. For the purposes of the project, Lipman's (1991) definition provided a description of the essential elements of critical thinking as 'thinking that (1) facilitates judgment because it (2) relies on criteria (3) is self-correcting, and (4) is sensitive to context'.

A key approach taken to assist students become 'critical thinkers' was the explicit modelling of the function of each written text. In this way, the processes involved in critical thinking, and their representation in writing, were revealed and commonly understood by both students and assessors. By demonstrating the particular structure and function of each text, that is, its 'sensitivity to context', and by linking these to specific descriptors making up the assessment criteria, students also had a clear understanding of the link between written texts and how their texts are assessed. This common understanding of the criteria by which assignments are assessed largely overcomes subjective marking. Students are not second guessing when they undertake their assignment tasks, and the ratings between different assessors are more reliable.

43.4   Expectations and criticisms of students' skills

An investigation into the expectations of the 'stakeholders' in the Commerce degree was conducted by way of interviews over the two-year period of the Literacy Project, with employers of Commerce graduates, university lecturers who teach Commerce subjects to first-year students, first-year and third-year university students studying for a Bachelor of Commerce degree, and senior secondary-school teachers of Commerce-related subjects.

Analysis of the data from the interviews revealed that three of the groups – employers, university staff and senior secondary teachers – had similar expectations of students' skills in the areas of critical thinking, written and oral communication, and the application of theory to practice (see Table 43.1).

Employers n=4	Lecturers n=14	Senior secondary teachers n=16
critical thinking	critical thinking	critical thinking
high level of communication skills, written and spoken	communication skills - written and spoken	communicating information clearly, using formal English
analytical/ problem solving	think for themselves	exam preparation
practical knowledge and skills	use initiative	confidence/ self esteem
teamwork	learn independently	independent learning
people related skills	motivation, discipline	time management

Table 43.1   Expectations of students' skills

Each group was critical of the fact that students often do not possess these skills. Employers criticized students in relation to communication skills, critical thinking skills and the ability to apply theory to practice. All the employers confirmed it is essential that graduates have highly developed critical thinking skills, identified as skills of analysis, the evaluation and construction of arguments, the ability to analyse a problem, construct a solution and plan implementation, as well as the ability to present arguments and defend views. Employers also required that graduates' written skills be appropriate for the business environment. Commerce Department lecturers were concerned that students, while able to describe concepts or issues reasonably well, lacked skills of analysis, demonstrated in their written assignments by not being able to explain effects or apply concepts to problems, or theory to case situations. In addition, students often displayed difficulties with developing a logical argument and expressing it succinctly and coherently.

43.5 Students' rating of importance of critical thinking skills

Two hundred and sixty-nine first-year and 48 third-year students, interviewed prior to the implementation of the project, indicated that they placed greater value on the acquisition and application of practical skills than they did on the development of critical thinking skills. First-year students were primarily concerned with time management and organizational skills, the ability to study independently, possessing a responsible attitude, and communication skills, as shown in Table 43.2.

Third-year students, however, indicated that they considered oral and written skills to be the most important skills that should be developed.

64	Time Management / Organisational skills	10	Coping - with stress, time pressures, understanding expectations
64	Independent work, without teacher watching & controlling	9	Ambition - Goal setting
61	Attitude - motivation, discipline, responsibility	8	Adaptability, flexibility, open minded, willing to learn new things
52	Communication skills - reading, listening, verbal & written	8	Showing initiative.
40	Lecture and tutorial system	6	Computer Literacy - skills and typing
16	Assignments - structures & practice	6	Balanced Lifestyle between study and leisure
14	Private study skills	4	Attendance at lectures & tutorials, and preparation skills
14	Teamwork	2	Innovation
13	Subjects - choice of right subjects	2	Conformity
12	Confidence & self esteem	2	Understanding - teach students not to memorise but to understand
11	Exam techniques and skills		

Table 43.2   First-year students' perceptions ranked by the number of references made to that skill

43.6 Explicit teaching of critical thinking and communication skills in core first-year subjects

Early in 1995, a Literacy Committee was established in the Commerce Department to guide the Project. Members agreed that three first-year subjects would be involved in the project: Financial Accounting 1A, 1B and Information Systems 1. Over 400 students were enrolled in these courses. The first two subjects would focus on developing students' skills in short answer assignments, short essay assignments and report writing, and the third on oral presentations. This chapter focuses on the changes made in the first two subjects. The language specialist was employed to determine the structure and language of assignments and texts, and invite the writing of model texts by the lecturers and professional accountants. Subsequently, the collaborative revision of assignment and assessment tasks was negotiated, including assessment criteria for both content and literacy. Aligning teaching and assessment is essential for improved outcomes (Ramsden, 1992).

Analysis of 1994 examination answers indicated that students were often unable to analyse, evaluate and interpret information, or apply what they had learned to new situations. They frequently presented no point of view or logical discussion, and only one student had written the first report assignment in an acceptable format. Staff also complained that students copied from each other and regurgitated information. Significantly, there was little interaction in tutorials; the student charged with the presentation, or the tutor, was expected to do all the work.

The following discussion shows how students were encouraged to move from descriptive to interpretive writing, from *ad hoc* structures for reports to appropriately formatted texts, and how assessment was changed to bring about more desirable outcomes. Tutors were also trained to use methods to increase student interaction in tutorials. Financial Accounting 1A required students to complete short answer questions in both assignments and exams. The major written assignments in Financial Accounting 1B were three financial accounting reports (see Table 43.3).

Aims of Financial Accounting 1A
Short answer questions

- to meet the needs of future business executives, administrators and others who use accounting information frequently for decision-making and who therefore need to understand the basis on which this information is prepared
- to meet the needs of those who intend to pursue a professional career in accounting and for whom this subject serves as a preparation for studies in accounting and related areas later in their course.

Aims of Financial Accounting 1B
Reports

- to use appropriate accounting procedures for recording transactions
- to critically evaluate the concepts underlying those procedures
- to analyse the effects of transactions on financial statements
- to interpret available financial information.

Table 43.3   Aims of Financial Accounting 1

43.6.1 From descriptive to interpretive writing: Financial Accounting 1A

The different types of texts in each course mean that each has a distinctive way of constructing meaning according to the epistemological framework – the logical reasoning – of the subject. For short answer assignments in Financial Accounting 1A, students need to understand a concept, its application and the effect or outcome of its application. For example, the question 'Why is a multicolumn journal used?' requires students to understand the reason for the use of a multicolumn journal, the effect, and examples of its use (see Figure 43.1).

A multicolumn journal is used for cash receipts and cash payments	Topic
because *there may be repetitive transactions, cash payments and cash receipts from many sources.*	Reason
Therefore *for posting efficiency, time saving and cost saving, multicolumns are needed for the many sources of these repetitive transactions involving cash*	Effect
eg. Cash receipts - payment of accounts receivable, discount allowed on timely payment of account, interest revenue, cash sales, inventory etc.	Examples
Cash payments - payments of accounts payable, expenses (eg. wages etc) discount received for timely payment of account, cash purchase of inventory, equipment etc.	

Figure 43.1   1994 Successful student examination text

Analysis of a random selection of 19 first-year examination texts in Financial Accounting 1A in 1994 revealed that the majority of students were unable to answer interpretive questions. In response to the question, 'Why is a multicolumn journal used?', many students wrote short answers describing multicolumn journals, often in note form or points, rather than explaining their use (see, e.g. Figure 43.2).

43.6.2 Moving towards interpretive writing in short answers

To determine if students' communication and critical thinking skills had in fact improved as a result of the more explicit teaching approaches, a selection of 1995 student exam texts was compared with the 19 exam texts of 1994. The 1995 corpus comprised 17 texts. Only interpretive questions were posed in the 1995 exam in order to focus on the development of students' analytical skills. Table 43.4 indicates that all students in the 1995 sample were able to answer the two interpretive questions (Q1: Explain the derivation of the accounting equation; Q2: Explain the relationship between the Accounting Equation and double-entry accounting). The changes indicate that students were able to structure their short-answer texts to demonstrate their understanding of the concept, the reason underlying its application and the effect or outcome of that application, as in Figure 43.3.

Student A

The totals of cash received or payed [sic] from the Cash Receipts and Cash Payments journal.

Student B

Postings from special journals to cash at bank are:-

Cash Receipt Journal - end of day balance - debit to CAB

Cash Payment Journal - end of day balance - credit to CAB

where CAB = Cash at Bank

Figure 43.2   Examples of descriptive answers from 1994 texts

Total exam mark % 1994 and 1995	Factual question % 1994	Interpretive question % 1994	Interpretive question % 1995 Q1	Interpretive question % 1995 Q2
36.5	0	0	100	62.5
40	50	0	100	75
46.5	100	50	50	87.5
47.5	100	0	100	75
52	100	0	100	87.5
55	50	25	100	75
55	100	50	100	50
63.5	100	0	33.3	100
63.5	100	0	50	75
70.5	100	0	100	100
75.5	100	0	100	100
76	100	0	100	87.5
78.5	100	75	100	75
78.5	100	100	100	75
79.5	100	75	100	87.5
84.5	100	50	100	62.5
89	100	100	n/a	n/a
89.5	75	75	100	100
90	100	100	n/a	n/a

In 1994 higher percentages were achieved by students for factual answers compared with interpretive answers. In 1995 interpretive answers showed greater improvement.

Table 43.4   Sample of 1994 and 1995 examination results

1995 exam question: *Explain the relationship between the Accounting Equation and double-entry accounting.*

Student answer:

Double-entry accounting is a means of book-keeping where there are at least tow entries for every transaction. These two entries must be comprised of an equal debit and an equal credit entry.	Establishes topic
The Accounting Equation states: $\Delta A = \Delta L + \Delta OE$. *So for every ΔA there must be an equal ΔL or ΔOE. This means whenever one part of the equation changes, there must be another equal change to another component of the equation (ie either ΔA, ΔL or ΔOE), so that the Accounting Equation must always hold.*	Provides a reason
Because double-entry accounting involves an equal debit and equal credit entry whenever a transaction occurs this produces an equal change.	States the effect
An example is, if you bought \$330 worth of...	Gives an example

Figure 43.3 Interpretive answer excerpted from 1995 student exam text

Figure 43.3 is typical of a 1995 exam short answer which shows a clear logical structuring of the text.

43.6.3   Financial Accounting 1B

The purpose of writing reports in Financial Accounting 1B is for students to provide 'management' with simple accounting reports. Students develop skills both to critically evaluate, analyse and interpret financial information, and to construct reports with an understanding of the function of its various parts. Authentic reports from a firm of practising accountants provided valuable models for how to construct and communicate the writer's understanding of the subject (see Figure 43.4).

Stage of report: Body of Report	Function of stage
3. REPORT DETAILS	
3.1 General Information	
Audited information statements are available for the	
last three years for both companies. Both	Background Information
companies...	
The companies are offered for sale at approximately	
the same price.	
3.2 Earnings Analysis	
Before tax profits for the last three years are greater	
for Bay Ltd than for Cove Ltd...	
3.3 Balance Sheet Analysis	
Both companies have invested capital of $400,000,	Analysis of Information
but because dividends have been approximately the	
same for the two companies in the last three years,	
Bay Ltd has slightly greater Retained Profits because	
of its greater pre-tax profits...	
Generally a stronger cash and working capital	Advantages
position is seen as desirable. A weak working	
capital position increases the risk...	Disadvantages
3.4 Recommendations	
We recommend that Samela Sydney purchase the	Recommendations
company Cove Ltd for the following reasons:...	

Figure 43.4   Report provided by Lock LHS, Accountants. (Excerpt taken from student notes: *Financial Accounting Report Writing*)

43.6.4   Problems with report writing

A diagnostic report writing task was given to students at the beginning of Course B, again revealing that the majority of students did not have the necessary skills to complete reports appropriate for the specific function of the task successfully. Without a clear understanding of how to complete the exercise, interestingly, many students relied on the approaches learned in first semester from their short-answer assignments and tried to apply notions of cause and effect. Reports were submitted in various formats such as short essays, notes, or letters to the client (see, e.g, Figure, 43.5).

43.6.5   Student outcomes: representing critical thought in report writing

Figure 43.6 is an excerpt of a report written by the same student who produced the 'letter report' in Figure 43.5. The following text was written following the teaching of the

Dear Samela Sydney,

The following report illustrates the operation of both Bay Ltd. and Cove Ltd., and my recommendation as to which company you should look at purchasing.

Both Bay Ltd and Cove Ltd. are reasonably new companies, each began operations three years ago with invested capital of $400,000 and machinery costing $200,000 ...

Hope I shed some light as to which company to purchase.

Yours sincerely,

Figure 43.5 Excerpt from a student's 'report' written in the form of a letter

communications component of Financial Accounting 1B which focused on the explicit modelling of the purpose, the function, the structure and the assessment criteria of financial reports. In the excerpt, the student demonstrates critical thinking and communication skills in several ways:

- by the accurate structuring of the report according to the appropriate functions of each part of the report;
- by the integration of evidence into the discussion of the report; overwhelmingly, in students' diagnostic reports figures and graphs had not been referred to in the discussion;
- by logically linking the recommendations to the analysis in the main discussion in the report.

3.1 Operating Profit Analysis *In order to compare these three plans, it is necessary to look at the operating profit per share.* *Operating profit per share is at its greatest using Plan A, that is borrowing (refer to appendices [sic] 4). Operating profit per share is $5.44. This is $1.44 greater than existing operations. One factor contributing to this result is the company's prediction that operating profit before tax and interest will increase by $1,500,000. That is an additional $960,000 after tax and before the interest payment is deducted (refer to appendices [sic] 4.4). Although Plan B also shows an increase in operating profit of $960,000 (refer to appendices [sic] 4.7), this increase is divided over 100,000 more shares etc.*	**Evidence integrated into analysis**
3.4 Recommendations *It is recommended that BPI systems Ltd. adopt Plan A, that is to borrow at 12. This recommendation is based on the following reasons ...*	**Recommendations linked to analysis in body of report**

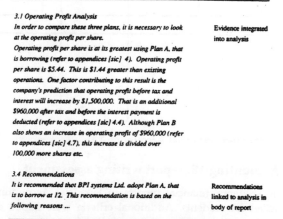

Figure 43.6 Excerpt taken from student's second report

43.7   Making assessment criteria explicit

A significant innovation in the Commerce Department was the collaborative development of a set of assessment criteria by teachers and project staff. Additional descriptors referring to the specific content of each assignment could be added to the criteria, but importantly the basic set of criteria was known and understood by both students and assessors prior to students undertaking each assignment. In Lipman's terms, students are able to self-assess, having an understanding of each descriptor within the set of criteria. In terms of marking, the criteria aim for closer rating which is both objective and replicable.

43.7.1   Financial Accounting 1A: short answer assessment

Criteria for assessing short-answer assignments were categorized under three headings: content, structure and grammar as shown in Figure 43.7.

<u>Short Answer Assignment 2</u>

1. *A business omits to do a bank reconciliation at the end of the month. Explain the implications of this omission.*

CONTENT	10	20	30	40	50	60
• purpose of bank reconciliation • could be incorrect figures in financial report • from errors in books • from bank initiated transactions • but not from outstanding cheques & deposits						
STRUCTURE & LANGUAGE		10	20	30		40
• topic is clearly established • reasons are clearly stated • clear statement of effect/s • examples provided • clear expression of ideas						
GRAMMAR						
• appropriate tense • correct spelling • subject/verb agreement • correct use of articles						

Figure 43.7   Assessment criteria Financial Accounting 1A

43.7.2 Financial Accounting 1B: report writing assessment

Criteria for assessing students' financial reports in Financial Accounting 1B were also explained and modelled for students. Additional criteria were added according to the demands of the particular assignment report – see the brief notes to students below the set of criteria shown in Figure 43.8.

43.8   Implementing change

The dynamic interaction between teaching and learning means that any one change affects a number of factors in the curriculum. Changed objectives mean changes in teaching, assessment, tutor training, departmental planning, time given to 'covering the content' and time given to new teaching processes and skills development. Successful change needs leadership and support from the Head of Department, commitment by a core of staff to specific learning objectives, and resources of time and money. In this Project, an approach to professional development that embraces both academic staff and student support enabled close collaboration in both staff and student development between the Advisory Centre and the Commerce Department.

The objectives and assessment criteria agreed on by staff early in the year were communicated to tutors and students during four tutor training sessions. The 14 tutors were also shown how to use the materials, including model answers, with students. The resources required to train casual tutors, who are generally postgraduate students, are significant. With new tutors continually being employed, the investment is short-lived. However, if teaching is seen as essential to postgraduates' experience, tutor training is essential. Generally, postgraduate students recreate the tutorials of their own experience with little insight into student-centred learning, and, as with most new teachers, their anxiety about their grasp of content overrides their focus on learning processes. Increasing competition for tutoring positions sometimes means that a new batch of tutors is appointed each semester, making the training option even more expensive.

Prior to the project, the tutorials themselves were marked by a very low level of student interaction. Students were silent and frequently unprepared, expecting the tutors to give the answers to the questions with little discussion. With such expectations, discussion itself was seen by some students as a waste of time, and so the necessity for training in small group processes arose. One half-day session was held for all staff, and included presentations by Commerce staff skilled in group process. In this way, departmental staff became resources within the department, and staff outside the core group involved in the project became involved in discussions on the use of tutorials and student interaction.

By the middle of first semester, the project had brought about changes in the following areas: course objectives, the way questions were asked in examinations and tutorials, methods of marking and giving feedback, restructuring of tutorials to increase student interaction, and use of materials written to focus students on the structure and logic of their assignments. As the first semester progressed, the cycle of consultation and identification of objectives for the second semester continued, with further changes to assessment and marking criteria. In the mean time, the project officer had begun work on a handbook for students providing information and a style guide for Commerce assignments, and a discussion of spelling and grammatical errors commonly appearing in first-year assignments.

Assignment and examination results have shown clearly the improved control over short answers and the writing of reports. Critical thinking skills have been developed through the requirement for and assessment of analysis, interpretation and application of material. A critical mass of staff was convinced that the changes were working and worth extending. At the final meeting of the Literacy Committee, augmented by a number of interested staff, the extent of the department's commitment to the project in the following year (1996) was considered. The meeting focused on the qualities the department was aiming to develop in graduates, and where (indeed whether) these were taught and assessed. Simultaneously,

Prepare a Report to Samela Sydney	Mark out of...	Assessed mark
• The Table of Contents accurately lists all the sections included in the report	5	
• There is a clear Statement of Purpose or Aim in the Introduction and/or Executive Summary	10	
• The discussion in the report consistently and logically relates to the Statement of Purpose or Aim	15	
• There is a clear Outline, Methods and/or Scope	10	
• The Summary/Executive Summary outlines the main issues and the recommendations contained in the report	10	
• The Body of the report provides background information to the issue	5	
• The Body of the report contains adequate analysis of the issue/s:		
Earnings Analysis	10	
Balance Sheet Analysis	10	
Appendices	5	
• The Body of the report and/or Conclusion provides recommendations if appropriate	10	
• Writing is appropriately formal	5	
• Spelling is correct	5	
• Grammar is accurate		
Total	100	
Assessor's Comments:		

Note to students on criteria sheet: These Assessment Criteria relate specifically to the Report to Samela Sydney. The Assessment Criteria for each Report assignment during the semester will change in relation to the type/s of analysis that is expected in the body of the report.

Figure 43.8   Assessment criteria Financial Accounting 1B

the Institute of Chartered Accountants in Australia had published the Exposure Draft of Guidelines for Joint Administration of Accreditation of Tertiary Courses by the Professional Accounting Bodies. Their outline of a Core Curriculum in Generic skills Areas (App. B: 16) proved to be a strong ally as the department was required to report on the implementation of generic skills teaching, and the project provided much of that data.

In order to identify what skills students should be learning, all staff were surveyed to enable the Committee to draw up a map of the flow of communications skills taught throughout the degree, and [to] help us respond to the Exposure Draft of the joint accounting bodies' (Memorandum to staff, Deparment of Commerce, December 1995). Responsibility for the development of literacy was then taken on by the department as a whole, making it possible for consulting staff to reduce their involvement. From the survey, a map of skills identified in subjects throughout the degree programme was drawn up and discussed by the whole department. As a result, the map was included in the 1997 Course Handbook, which is distributed to all staff and students, to draw attention to the value given to the development of such skills, and to keep staff committed to that value. In 1997, the department committed funds to further training and materials development, and maintained the role of the Literacy Coordinator to ensure the process will continue.

43.9   Conclusion

In this chapter we have focused on how the logic and knowledge of the discipline is communicated, and in that context, how assessment is essential to ensuring that students are able to develop and apply communication and intellectual skills. This approach (Ingleton and Wake, 1997) to developing literacy and communication skills is based on a curriculum model, showing how, at tertiary level, the key to changing student outcomes in literacy and critical thinking lies in curriculum management.

43.10   References

Bakhtin, M.M. (1986) *Speech Genres and Other Late Essays*, trans. V. B. McGee; ed. C.Emerson and M. Holquist, University of Texas Press, Austin.

Department of Education, Employment and Training (1991) *Australia's Language: The Australian Language and Literacy Policy*, companion volume to the Policy Paper, Australian Government Printing Service, Canberra.

Guidelines for the Joint Administration of Tertiary Courses by the Professional Accounting Bodies, Exposure Draft, The Institute of Chartered Accountants, October 1995, Sydney.

Ingleton, C. and Wake, B. (1997) *Literacy Matters*. ACUE, The University of Adelaide.

Ramsden, P. (1992) *Learning to Teach in Higher Education*, Routledge, London.

44 Helping science students become better communicators: development and evaluation of a student-centred 'communication-in-context' course

Alex Radloff,[i] **Barbara de la Harpe,**[i] **and Marjan Zadnik**[ii]
Curtin University of Technology, Perth, Western Australia:
(i) Centre for Educational Advancement (ii) Department of
Applied Physics

44.1 Overview

The development of effective communication skills is now widely recognized as an important goal of university education. The ability to communicate well is valued by employers and needed for professional advancement. It is also important for effective learning. Unfortunately, students, especially science students, often view communication skills courses as peripheral to their main study and largely irrelevant to their learning, particularly when taught by staff from another discipline area. In order to address these negative perceptions and to increase student involvement in developing their communication skills, we have changed a standard communications course into a discipline-specific 'communication-in-context' course, emphasizing student-centred learning and the development of generic transferable life skills. Students, rather than being passive recipients of information, are given ownership and responsibility for their own learning through organizing and participating in a student scientific conference and preparing and publishing the Conference Proceedings. Throughout the three years the course has been offered, we have monitored student reactions and communication skills development by means of questionnaires, classroom observation, group discussion and student written reports. Overall, feedback indicates very high student acceptance of the course. Students appear to be interested and involved in the course, judge that their oral and written communication skills have improved and enjoy the team-work, networking and problem-solving activities. A booklet, video and teaching materials based on the course have been developed to assist colleagues interested in using a similar approach in their courses.

44.2 Introduction

Communication skills are becoming increasingly recognized as critical for student learning and for professional development. Good communication skills – oral and writing – help students to learn. Speaking and writing, as part of learning, allow the learner to think about and make sense of new knowledge and ideas and to share new insights with others. Students who have well-developed oral and writing skills can engage actively in learning through peer and group discussion, asking and answering questions, and debating, through note-making, summarizing, expository writing, journalling, keeping a learning log etc. On the other hand, students with poorly developed communication skills are at a disadvantage in mastering the subject content and in demonstrating their knowledge and skills.

Effective communication skills are also important for professional development and advancement. Employer and professional groups place communication skills, especially oral and written skills, high on the list of graduate attributes which they seek (Beare and Millikan, 1988). However, recent reports on employer satisfaction with graduate employees in Australia and Britain reveal a serious gap between what employers want and what they judge that they are getting from graduates in terms of communication skills (Australian Association of Graduate Employers, 1993; Harvey, 1993).

44.3   Communication skills and learning at university

University lecturers regularly complain about students' communication skills, especially oral and writing skills. Such complaints are voiced about students at both undergraduate (Bate and Sharpe, 1990; Cowen, 1993) and post-graduate levels and are growing with the increased diversity of the student body which now includes more students from non-traditional backgrounds including, especially, students from Non English Speaking Backgrounds (NESB). Although there is an ongoing debate in Australia as to whether the 'literacy' skills of school leavers are improving, declining or remaining static, there is general agreement that the expectations for high levels of these skills are growing in university courses and as professional and career demands change and become more complex (Radloff and Samson, 1990; Wickert, 1989).

University students enrolled in science courses are often perceived to have poorer communication skills than students enrolled in other non-technical disciplines. This is not surprising as the high-school science curriculum generally emphasizes analytical and problem-solving skills rather than speaking and writing skills. At university, the poor communication skills of science students are a problem since the level of communication skills needed for successful science study at the tertiary level is higher than that needed for learning science in high school.

Science students therefore, need explicit help to develop and use their communication skills throughout their study. Typically such help, when it is available, has been most commonly offered as an extra 'add on' or adjunct to regular coursework rather than as an integral part of learning science (Latchem, Parker and Weir, 1994). As a result, students and many teaching staff have perceived communication courses as less relevant or important than the major discipline study area and sometimes even as 'remedial', and only for students who are 'deficient' and need to be 'fixed up'. There is also evidence that 'generic' communication courses because of their very nature (decontextualized and general), may not help students to develop discipline-specific communication skills (Colomb, 1988; Radloff and Zadnik, 1995).

If students' communication skills are to be improved, lecturers need to devote more time to developing these skills in the context of teaching and learning science (Holliday, 1992). Russell (1990) suggests that lecturers, instead of blaming students for their poor communication skills, should support them to develop communication skills in particular, writing, by setting content-specific writing tasks for them to complete. Science lecturers are best placed to introduce students to the language, format and conventions of their discipline. They should recognize that students need 'to practice writing about science beyond filling in blanks and writing a paragraph or two on texts and in lab manuals using simple-minded knowledge telling strategies, typically unacceptable at good colleges' (Holliday, 1992, p. 59).

44.4 Making the initial changes to the communication course

In view of the importance of communication skills and the gap between science students' needs and typical course offerings, we describe an alternative approach we have used to help undergraduate Physics students develop their communication skills based on teaching communication skills in the context of the undergraduate science curriculum. The original communication course for Physics second-year students was taught by staff from the departments of English and Physics. The English component covered 'generic' written and verbal communication skills and the Physics component involved a weekly presentation on research activities by Physics staff. The two sections were taught and assessed independently from each other with no effort made to integrate them. Feedback from students indicated that they did not rate the course highly or believed that either the English or the Physics sections were helping them develop their communication skills adequately. Furthermore, the science lecturers did not see much improvement in students' ability to communicate scientifically. Thus, despite completing a semester-long course in communication skills, Physics students did not appear to be developing their communication skills to any great extent.

The Physics lecturer in charge of the course (Zadnik), therefore, decided to try a new approach. In 1994, working with a colleague from the Teaching Learning Group at Curtin University of Technology (Radloff), he changed the Physics section of the course into a student-run Physics conference. The English component remained largely unchanged. A conference was chosen as the context for developing relevant communication skills since conferences form an important part of the professional life of scientists and provide a vehicle for developing a wide range of important communication and life skills. The student conference proved to be very successful based on both student feedback and staff reflections. Details of the initial changes to the course and the outcomes are described in Radloff and Zadnik (1995). The innovation was also formally evaluated for the Department of Applied Physics (Radloff, 1994).

Based on the feedback from the students and the evaluation report recommendations, the Department of Applied Physics decided that from 1995, the communication course would be taught entirely by Physics and moved to the second semester of the first-year programme. This decision was in line with Curtin University's Communication-in-Context policy (Latchem, Parker and Weir, 1994) which recognizes that communication skills are best taught in the context of each discipline and encourages university departments to take responsibility for identifying the communication skills appropriate to their discipline and providing opportunities for their development as an integral part of their courses. How the course was developed and run in 1995 and 1996 and student and staff reactions to it are described in the rest of this chapter.

44.5 The communication course in 1995

Colleagues from Applied Physics, Education and the Teaching Learning Group developed a team teaching approach to run the course in 1995. The 1994 course was further refined so that students could develop oral and written communication skills using the content of Physics as a basis. The Physics lecturer co-ordinated the course, acted as facilitator and student resource person. The other two lecturers provided advice on curriculum planning, developed instructional materials, acted as facilitators for the team-taught sessions, and evaluated the course using both formative and summative methods.

The course aimed to develop a range of communication skills, not only written and oral skills, but also other lifelong learning skills such as problem-solving, team work, organization and negotiation skills. The course comprised a weekly two-hour workshop followed by a one-hour student-run group meeting, leading up to a conference which took place in the tenth week (the week free from class contact) of the 14-week semester. In 1995, 35 students, 10 first- and 25 second-years, enrolled in the communication course.

A student-centred instructional approach was adopted which required students to become active partners with the lecturers in their own learning, taking charge of the learning task and accepting responsibility for their own learning. Students were encouraged to make decisions collectively and individually about how they would accomplish the set task – organizing and presenting a two-day student Physics conference. The instructional principles on which this approach was based included active student involvement in learning, an emphasis on socially mediated learning and lecturers taking on the role of facilitators and scaffolds, all of which have been shown to encourage meaningful, 'quality' learning (Ramsden, 1992; Meyers and Jones, 1993; Walberg, 1990).

In line with the student-centred approach, students were given the opportunity to take charge of the course. Each student had to choose a topic, write a scientific paper for peer review and publication in the Conference Proceedings, and prepare a ten-minute presentation based on the paper for the Physics conference. The class as a whole was responsible for planning, organizing and running the conference. Specifically, they formed committees including publicity, catering, facilities and publishing, to carry out the necessary work required to organize and run a conference and put together and publish the proceedings. Students had to decide on issues such as the theme of the conference, keynote speaker, publicity, sponsorship, venue, equipment, and publication of the conference proceedings. Although students had a considerable degree of freedom, as skill development is gradual, the course was very carefully structured to ensure that support was provided at the appropriate time. Students were 'scaffolded' to assist them to develop their communication skills and other related life skills, and the timetable was flexible, taking into consideration students' time commitments and study load.

The workshop sessions consisted of a mix of student-centred and teacher-led learning activities. Session activities were carefully planned to be appropriately timed to meet student learning needs. Sessions included opportunities for students to develop a range of communication skills, including speaking up in class, negotiating, questioning, working in small groups, and problem-solving, as well as discussing career options and writing a resumé. Students were encouraged and supported to identify and work on the skills they wanted to improve. At the beginning of each session, a few minutes were devoted to general items of interest such as possible part-time job opportunities, current news items relevant to the students' learning and how physics was being used in world events. Students also contributed their own items from time to time. Although usually at least two of the lecturers were present at the sessions, the emphasis was on the students determining the agenda and making decisions. Sometimes this approach created difficulties as students expressed frustration at being left 'to do it themselves' or struggled to work cooperatively within their groups. We as lecturers were tempted from time to time to revert to the more traditional role of managing and telling but overall, by supporting one another, succeeded in maintaining the student-centred focus.

The conference itself provided a real-life context in which students could demonstrate what they had learned in the course. The conference was held over two days. The audience comprised Year 11 (5th Form) Science students and their teachers from local high schools who had accepted the students' invitation to attend and provide an authentic audience, Physics staff and other students. Two keynote speakers were invited to present. The conference presentations were grouped into themes, with each presenter allocated ten minutes for the presentation (typically using overhead transparencies or a computer PowerPoint presentation) and five minutes for questions and discussion. Students took turns to chair sessions. The paper abstracts were collated into a booklet which was distributed to the audience at the start of the conference. Presentations were assessed by a panel of judges comprising the authors and two other Physics staff. The conference ended with a conference dinner at which best presenters were acknowledged and received certificates of merit.

44.6   Further development of the course in 1996

In 1996, as Zadnik was on sabbatical, the course was co-ordinated and run by Dr R. Loss, another member of staff from Applied Physics assisted by a senior student who had participated in the course in 1994. The course format and materials developed in 1995 were used in the 1996 course. There were 28 students enrolled in the 1996 course of whom 20 were first years and 8 were more senior students who had not as yet completed the course but who needed to do so in order to graduate. Staff running the course reported that the combination of inexperienced first-year students together with a small group of less than enthusiastic more senior students created problems with motivation and the group took some time to get going on the task. The new lecturer experienced some doubts about the viability of the student-centred approach to the course and was tempted on a number of occasions to step in and take over but resisted doing so.

Despite some setbacks along the way including students' failure to secure outside funding for the conference because of poor timing in approaching possible donors, the conference took place successfully. Since the conference took place during school holidays, no school students were able to attend. Instead, the audience consisted of students and staff from Physics together with science students from one of the other local universities. An innovation to the 1996 conference was the inclusion of a poster session in addition to the paper presentations. It was decided to include posters so that all presentations could be fitted into one day and also because a number of students preferred the less threatening format of speaking informally in a one-to-one situation. Incidentally, the poster session proved very popular and the 10 students who had chosen to present posters found that they talked as much, if not more, than those who did a formal presentation. Another change from 1995 was the decision to publish the conference papers electronically on a website. Unfortunately, this proved to be too difficult and time consuming and in the end was abandoned.

44.7   Student reactions to the communication course

The 1995 and 1996 courses were closely monitored. Student feedback, both formal and informal, was collected during and at the end of each course. Students completed a Student Feedback questionnaire at the end of each semester, had a debriefing session after each conference, and wrote a conference report in which they reflected on what they had learned and its impact on their personal development.

Students were very positive about the course in both 1995 and 1996. Indeed, even though the two groups of students differed from each other and the two courses were co-ordinated by different staff, student feedback from both courses was almost identical. Of the 30 students who completed the end of semester Student Feedback questionnaire in 1995, 25 students (83%) believed that the course had met their needs and said that they would recommend it to other students. A further four students were not sure, either of what their needs were, or whether they had been met. Only one student believed that his or her needs had not been met by the course. In 1996, of the 22 students who completed the Student Feedback questionnaire, 17 students (77%) believed that the course had met their needs. One student believed that the course had partly met his or her needs and only one student believed that the course had not met his or her needs (three students did not respond to the question).

The reasons students gave for believing that the course had met their needs were similar across the two years and included comments such as the ones below.

> It covered many aspects of professional communication [for example] papers, meetings, presentations and group work.

> Gave me confidence in producing real life scientific material suitable to be published [and] presented.

> It helped me understand the organisation and format of a conference meeting [and] also improved my skills in research and also my writing ability.

> It has helped build up my confidence in giving ideas and speaking in a group.

Students were asked to list the three most useful aspects of the course. The responses from students in the 1995 and 1996 courses are summarized in Table 44.1.

Most useful aspects	Number of times mentioned
Oral presentation skills	34
Paper writing skills	34
Resume writing skills	17
Group work skills	16
Organisational skills	15
Miscellaneous doing own research meeting deadlines increasing self knowledge	18

Table 44.1   Most useful aspects of the course and how often mentioned

Students also compared the communication course with other courses they were doing in terms of its value for their professional development. Their responses showed that for both years over 80% of students rated the course very high, using adjectives such as 'useful', 'very useful', 'very good', 'excellent' 'highly valuable', 'higher than all the others' and 'top 10%'. Students were asked to list three adjectives that in their opinion described the course. The examples given below are representative of the adjectives which students used.

- relevant; fun; useful;
- exciting; fun; hard work;
- innovative; different; involving;
- dynamic; hands-on; professional;
- interesting; challenging; daunting;
- scary; enjoyable; stressful.

Students' comments indicated that they particularly enjoyed the opportunity to get to know other students better and work collaboratively in groups, and to take responsibility for their own learning things which they did not typically experience in their other courses. The quotes overleaf provide examples of such comments.

> The way in which we were allowed to organize the detail was good, since we learned to organize ourselves and to trust others.

> The class discussion and the feeling of unity were very impressive.

> Working with others I became better friends with people I previously did not know very well.

> Working as a team – it is good to build a network with other students, especially for the years to come.

> I found this unit to be one of the best units this year because it has taught me to work as part of a team and how to present my efforts to a group of people.

> People that do the largest amount of work and put in max effort, get rewarded for their efforts, this is good.

Students also developed additional skills not originally anticipated. For example, students responsible for publishing the conference proceedings in 1995 developed high-level desktop publishing skills; students involved in fundraising learned about negotiation and persuasion skills and how to write proposals for funding; and those responsible for conference publicity were interviewed by the press and on the university radio.

The students' conference reports revealed many examples of how the course had contributed to their personal development. The extract below from one student's report is typical of student reflections.

> I feel that for me, the conference was very beneficial in terms of increasing my awareness of what Physics is. I was excited by the great diversity of fields that are covered and their relevance to everyday life. I was also glad to see the diverse and interesting fields in which Physicists can gain employment – changing my previous notion that a Physics degree provides little scope for employment.
>
> For my part, in the organisation of the conference and in the presentation of my paper, I have benefited enormously. The experience in public speaking was invaluable as I now feel more confident in my ability to put on a presentation to a group of alert

and informed people. It was also beneficial to help in the organisation and running of the conference as I gained an insight into the work involved in such an undertaking. I am sure, given this experience, I could do the same again – even better!

In watching all the presentations I picked up on a number of things which make a presentation exceptional. All the good presentations were highly visual with interesting slides and overheads and even including the audience. I am resolved to include such techniques in my future presentations so as to make them even more interesting and engaging.

44.8   Student reactions to the instructional approach

Since the communication course involved innovative teaching and learning strategies, we were interested to find out what students thought of these changes. Students in both the 1995 and 1996 courses responded to a series of statements about the teaching/learning processes used indicating whether they strongly disagreed, disagreed, were neutral, agreed or strongly agreed. Responses were collated combining the strongly disagree and disagree, and strongly agree and agree categories and are presented in Table 44.2.

	Teaching/learning processes	D	N	A
1	I had the opportunity to plan, implement and evaluate aspects of this unit	6	17	77
2	Having more than one lecturer worked well	2	38	60
3	The support materials eg. handouts, videos, were useful for my learning	6	25	69
4	Having an opportunity to read and respond to other students' draft papers helped me with my own writing	10	13	77
5	The feedback I received on my draft paper helped me to improve the final version	13	10	77
6	The assessment activities were clearly related to the unit objectives	4	10	86
7	The assessment criteria were clear to me	5	10	85
8	My ideas and opinions were valued by other students	13	21	66
9	This unit helped me develop leadership skills	17	37	46
10	Participating in this unit has increased my confidence as a learner	13	17	70
11	The unit helped reduce my feelings of isolation	17	33	50
12	The activities and assignments I did in this unit encouraged me to think about my learning	15	23	62
13	The group activities provided me with the opportunity to work with and learn from other students	10	19	71
14	This unit helped me to develop professional skills and attitudes	2	19	79
15	Participation in this unit has increased my interest in Physics	13	33	54
16	The effort I put into this unit was worthwhile in terms of what I learned	10	10	80

Table 44.2   Percentage of students responding to statements about the teaching/learning processes (D = disagree; N = not sure and A =agree) (N=52)

Responses show that 70% or more of the students believed that they had input into the way the course was planned and run, that the course materials were useful, and that the feedback they received helped them improve their writing. Over 80% judged the assessment to be appropriate and assessment criteria, clear. About 70% judged that the course had provided them with opportunities to learn with and from other students and increased their confidence as learners while almost 80% found that the course helped them to develop professional skills and attitudes. Finally, 80% believed that the effort they put into the course was worth while in terms of what they had learned.

44.9   Impact on students' communication skills

The students who completed the 1995 course rated on a seven-point scale at the beginning and again at the end of the course, their perceived level of skill in writing papers, giving oral presentations and working in groups, the three areas of communication skills which the course aimed to address. Student responses were analysed using the SPSS software package. The analysis showed that student self-ratings of their skills were higher at the end of the course in comparison to the beginning of the course. The statements for which changes in self-ratings were statistically significant (significance levels ranged from .000 to .05) are presented in Table 44.3.

Statement	Pre course means	Post course means
Writing a paper		
I can adjust my style of writing to suit the needs of any audience, including the lecturer	4.75	5.21
I can rewrite my wordy and confusing sentences easily	4.88	4.92
I can explain abstract ideas clearly in writing	4.50	5.08
I can locate and use appropriate reference sources	5.21	5.67
When I write on a lengthy topic, I can make outlines for the main sections	5.04	5.67
I can revise a first draft of my paper so that it is shorter and better organised	4.88	5.33
When I edit my paper, I can find and correct my grammatical errors	5.17	5.50
I can find people who will give critical feedback on early drafts of my paper	5.00	5.79
Giving presentations		
I can turn a written paper into a good oral presentation	4.42	5.29
I can alter my presentations to suit different audiences	4.54	5.38
I feel at ease when talking in front of an audience	3.46	4.42
I am able to use presentation aids such as overhead transparencies, white board and slides, effectively	4.00	5.04
I have good presentation skills eg clear voice, eye contact, appropriate body language	3.88	4.88
Working in groups		
I can communicate my ideas clearly to others in a group	4.33	5.42
I can handle other people's opinions without getting upset even if they differ from mine	5.21	5.38

Table 44.3   Statistically significant changes in student self-ratings of writing, presentation and group work skills (N=26)

Student self-ratings of improvements in their oral and writing skills have been supported independently and informally by lecturers who have taught them subsequently. In particular, the interest in working in groups appears to have persisted beyond the course with many of the students continuing to work in informal groups. A number of the students have also become involved in providing mentoring for first-year science students. Thus, it would appear that a more collaborative group oriented approach to learning can work successfully with science students despite the traditional view that learning in the sciences is basically individualistic and competitive in nature.

44.10 Some vital advice

From our experiences in developing, implementing and evaluating the communication skills course, we have identified some key instructional principles which we offer as VITAL advice (V – valuing, I – integrating, T – teaching, A – assessing, and L – listening).

44.10.1 Valuing communication skills

When presenting the course aimed at developing students' communication skills, we ensured that it was accepted by staff and students as a legitimate part of the curriculum. The course was developed in line with the university's communication policy and in 1995 the Department showed its commitment to it by embedding it in its degree structure. A communication course should not be seen as a 'soft option' or as an add-on to core 'content' courses. We also carefully introduced the idea of a communication course to the students and used input from employers, professional bodies and senior students to reinforce the importance and value of communication skills for academic success and professional advancement. If students can see the inherent value and usefulness of the communication skills being developed, both to their learning at university and to their future careers, they are more likely to embrace the skills and thus become more committed to the course objectives. If the lecturers are also able to see the value they are more likely to experience a greater sense of purpose, commitment and satisfaction in teaching the course.

44.10.2 Integrating communication skills into course content

In order to teach communication skills in context, we considered and selected objectives carefully so that they matched the communication skills needed by Physics students and graduates. The communication skills to be developed should come from, and be embedded in, the discipline rather than be presented in isolation and out of context.

44.10.3 Teaching communication skills

In order to help students develop their communication skills, we made explicit the match between course objectives, material presented and work assessed. We created an environment which provided an appropriate mix of challenge and support. While it is recognized that there is no ready formula for the appropriate level of cognitive challenge, providing a challenge requires judgements based on clearly defined goals for higher education, and an understanding of the motives, skills and abilities which students bring with them to their study (McInnis, James and McNaught, 1995). We also encouraged active independent learning. If students are encouraged to be active learners, they are more likely to become aware of how they learn, and to assume control of their learning through planning learning tasks, monitoring progress, and evaluating their work.

44.10.4 Assessing communication skills appropriately

When planning how student learning was to be assessed, we selected 'authentic' assessment tasks and avoided 'busy work'. Students are motivated to complete activities which they perceive as relating to the real world and are likely to enjoy doing such activities. We ensured that assessment tasks were arranged throughout the semester so that students had to work consistently to fulfil the assessment requirements. We also provided many opportunities for teacher, peer- and self- assessment making sure that it was timely and meaningful, since communication skills are best developed in an environment which allows for plenty of practice with feedback.

44.10.5 Listening to students

Throughout the course, we took into account students' background knowledge and experiences when planning learning activities and providing support. We sought and valued students' views and opinions and acted on them. Students should be able to see that their opinions are genuinely considered and are used to inform practice. We were also prepared to make changes to traditional teaching practices, especially in terms of giving students autonomy and choice, as well as responsibility for their own learning.

44.11 Conclusions

The key to developing students' communication skills in the context of their discipline is careful planning and preparation of teaching and learning activities. In addition, emphasizing the value of communication skills, and providing challenge and support, increases student interest, motivation and ability to communicate effectively in their discipline.

Our experiences in developing and teaching the communication course for Physics students over the last three years show that it is possible to integrate successfully communication skills into a course in the undergraduate science programme. Students believed that the course met their needs, had many useful and enjoyable aspects, and contributed to their personal development. They also indicated that the course had had a positive impact on their writing, presentation and group work skills. Students also made positive comments about the way the course was structured, taught and assessed.

From our perspective, the success of the course has reinforced our belief that it is possible to help science students to learn worthwhile communication skills and life in a challenging, supportive and enjoyable environment. However, despite the consistently positive feedback from students and the effort and work put into refining the course and developing a course booklet and accompanying video to assist interested lecturers to offer similar courses, budgetary and programme review decisions have led in 1997 to the communication course being downgraded from a compulsory core course in the undergraduate programme to one of a number of options which students may select to do as part of their undergraduate study. It remains to be seen how many will take up the opportunity.

Acknowledgement

We thank Dr R.D. Loss, Department of Applied Physics, Curtin University of Technology, for teaching and evaluating the 1996 course.

44.12   References

Australian Association of Graduate Employers (1993) *National Survey of Graduate Employers*, Sydney: Author.

Bate, D. and Sharpe, P. (1990) *Student Writer's Handbook*, Sydney: Harcourt Brace Jovanovich.

Beare, H. and Millikan, R.H. (eds) (1988) *Skilling the Australian Community: Futures for public education: What users want from Australian schools in the nineteen nineties.* A report of the project sponsored by the Australian Teachers Federation and the Commission for the Future. Parkerville, Victoria: University of Melbourne, Faculty of Education.

Colomb, G.G. (1988) Where should students start writing in the disciplines? Paper presented at the *Annual Meeting of the Conference on College Composition and Communication*, St Louis, Missouri. 17–19 March.

Cowen, K. (1993) Responding to the writing crisis in universities: writing across the curriculum. Paper presented at the *Queensland Branch of the Higher Education Research and Development Association of Australasia Annual Conference*, Brisbane, 15–16 April.

Harvey, L. (1993) *Employer Satisfaction*. Interim report, Quality in Higher Education, University of Warwick.

Holliday, W.G. (1992) Helping college science students read and write, *Journal of College Science Teaching*, September/October, 58–60.

Latchem, C., Parker, L. and Weir, J. in association with staff from the Teaching Learning Group, School of Communication and Cultural Studies, Centre for International English, University Counselling Services, Centre for Aboriginal Education and Faculty of Education (1994). *Communication in Context*. A report on communication skills development for the Teaching and Learning Advisory Committee, Curtin University of Technology, Western Australia.

Meyers, C. and Jones, T.B. (1993) *Promoting Active Learning: Strategies for the College Classroom*, San Francisco: Jossey-Bass.

McInnis, C., James, R. and McNaught, C. (1995) *First Year on Campus*. A commissioned project of the committee for the advancement of university teaching, Canberra: Australian Government Publishing Service.

Radloff, A. (1994) *Scientific Communication 202: Feedback and preliminary evaluation of innovations to this unit in 1994 and recommendations for 1995.* Internal report to the Dept of Applied Physics, Curtin University of Technology.

Radloff, A. and Samson, J. (1990). Literacy and open learning. In R. Atkinson and C. McBeath (eds), *Opening Learning and New Technology, Perth, WA: Australian Society for Educational Technology, WA Chapter, pp. 283–9.*

Radloff, A. and Zadnik, M.G. (1995) A student-organised conference: student-centred learning of communication-in-context. Paper presented at the *20th Conference on Improving University Teaching*, Hong Kong.

Ramsden, P. (1992) *Learning to Teach in Higher Education*, London: Routledge.

Russell, D.R. (1990) Writing across the curriculum in historical perspective: toward a social interpretation, *College English*, **52**(1), 52–73.

Walberg, H.J. (1990) Productive teaching and instruction: assessing the knowledge base, *Phi Delta Kappan*, February, 470–8.

Wickert, R. (1989) No Single Measure: a survey of Australian adult literacy. Summary report. Canberra, ACT: Commonwealth Department of Employment, Education and Training.

45 Embedding skills in a university-wide modular credit scheme

Mark Atlay (Head of Staff Development and Quality Enhancement), Richard Harris (Dean of Quality Assurance) and Jeremy White (Assistant Academic Registrar)
University of Luton

45.1 Summary

The University of Luton is committed to developing a vocationally relevant undergraduate curriculum to meet the career aspirations of its students and the employment needs of the community it serves. All undergraduate courses are fully modularized and the University's Modular Credit Scheme (MCS) currently embraces over 1000 validated modules leading to 120 approved awards across a wide and diverse range of disciplines.

The development of skills is a fundamental component of this curriculum. A skills template has been agreed and the skills developed and practised have been explicitly identified for every module. Furthermore, within the flexibility of the MCS, the university has attempted to ensure that all students are assessed in all the skills by identifying, for each programme leading to a named award, a module at level 2 and 3 which together will enable students to practise all of the skills. The first cohort of students with a full experience of a curriculum which encompasses the core skills template will graduate in the summer of 1999.

All students receive a Career Management Portfolio which explains the importance of skills and the University's approach to their delivery and support. The University is currently working on the development of a 'skills profile' which will enable both students and their prospective employers to gain a better understanding of the student's capabilities.

This chapter is in two parts, the first deals with the background to the implementation of the University's policy on skills and the second presents some initial research findings.

45.2 Background

45.2.1 Core skills

The University debated at length and in detail how it could integrate generic core skills into the academic curriculum to create a distinctive Luton experience for its students. By core skills, the University means fundamental transferable attributes which arise authentically from the higher education process, such as for example written expression, familiarity with mathematical techniques, competence in the use of information technology, awareness of equal opportunities, and oral presentation. They are non-subject-specific features of a higher education experience which are important to the formation of competent professionals.

The desirability of enhancing students' prospects on the labour market by giving prominence to core skills was not a matter of contention among staff of the University. A much lengthier debate (lasting the better part of two years) was, however, required to agree the identity of the specific core skills and to establish a structure within which they could be practised and tested. At an early stage of the debate, the University determined some key parameters within which the debate should be conducted. Among the institutional principles adopted were:

- that subject syllabuses should form the vehicle for developing the requisite core skills, and that the introduction of discrete skills modules, with the implied dilution of the subject content of degree programmes, did not represent an appropriate way forward for the University

- that the University should have a single set of core skills which would be introduced to students across all programmes, albeit with the acknowledgement that the interpretation of the core skills would necessarily vary between subjects and professional areas

- that, notwithstanding the corporate commitment to student choice and flexibility through the Modular Credit Scheme, the delivery of core skills should be managed so that all students are given the opportunity to follow a curriculum which introduces them to all the skills determined by the University

- that the impact of core skills on the workloads of academic staff should be minimized consistent with a real enhancement of the vocational attributes and career management skills of students.

Institutional debate during the planning period centred on the following key issues.

First, agreement was needed on the exact core skills which would form the common thread of students' experience irrespective of their particular degree programme. Sites of the debate included the extent of numerical competence expected of graduates, whether competence in a foreign language should be promoted, the place of what might broadly be termed attributes of 'good citizenship', and the varying expectations of English language skills between different subjects and professional areas. After extensive discussion both institutionally and within departments, embracing consultations with the University's employer partners as well as staff and students, the whole community agreed to subscribe to the skills template included in appendix 1.

Secondly, the mechanism for assessing core skills needed resolution. One approach suggested that none was necessary: that the most the University could say was that students had been exposed to certain skills during the delivery of their programmes, and that in any case it was asking academic staff to exceed their authority to expect them to grade students' competence across the range of core skills. At the opposite end of the spectrum, it was argued that graduates and employers would be content with nothing less than a full graded profile, although it was also acknowledged that any variation between an employer's and the University's assessment of a student's competence could potentially adversely affect the reputation of the University. The end result of the debate was the adoption of a middle way in the first instance: that the module grades awarded students would also reflect their performance in the core skills, but that a corporate programme of staff development and record systems development would in due course enable a valid and reliable grading structure to be introduced.

Thirdly, concern was expressed that, in a modular scheme, students might choose modules which would enable them to avoid experiencing certain core skills. A solution favoured early on in the debate was that all the core skills should be contained within the core modules for programmes (i.e. the modules which all students must take in order to qualify for a particular named award), but it became clear that the varying numbers of core modules between programmes made such a suggestion impractical. A two-phase solution was reached. First, once the skills template had been agreed, staff were able to map the skills onto existing learning and assessment requirements within the modules for which they were responsible, and they found that only fairly minor adjustments were needed to pedagogical strategies and learning outcomes to embed at least one core skill in most modules. Second, it was decided that each programme should designate two existing core modules (one at level 2 and one at level 3) as opportunities for students to rehearse skills already acquired and to practise skills not previously encountered: the modules selected have tended to be a research methodology module at level 2, and the double project module at level 3. Originally it was hoped that at least one of the modules would be specially designed for the purpose, offering students the opportunity to reflect critically on their subject and skills development up to that point, and to make informed choices about their future programmes of study in the light of an assessment of their academic strengths and interests, gaps in their vocational skills profile, and their career aspirations as refracted through an understanding of the labour market in their particular professional area. This option was not, however, generally favoured due to concern about overcrowding subject content in the remainder of the syllabus, although interest in an integrated module along these lines has been elicited from certain departments. Nevertheless, the scheme now adopted will enable students to manage their own career development by synthesizing their core skills in the context of their subject specialisms, and to demonstrate proficiency in the application of subject knowledge in a variety of analytical, organizational and presentational contexts. It will also facilitate the generation of a skills profile.

Fourthly, colleagues were concerned about levels of skills competence through the Modular Credit Scheme. Initially, the skills template was designed with three levels, corresponding with the three academic levels of an undergraduate programme. The fineness of the distinctions was likely to make the proposal too difficult to manage and monitor, however, so it was agreed that the number of levels should be reduced to two.

All modules were redrafted to make more explicit the core skills embedded in them. The faculty academic standards committees were asked to take responsibility for confirming that programme teams had undertaken the re-presentation exercise in a manner consistent with University policy. The whole re-presentation process was scheduled over two academic years, with first-level modules being redrafted and approved during 1995–6 for implementation with effect from the 1996–7 academic year, and second- and third-level modules being redesigned during 1996–7.

During induction students are issued individually with handbooks (the *Career Management Portfolio* a revised version of the previous *Personal Development Portfolio*) explaining the aims of the core skills initiative, describing how core skills are identified on individual modules, and encouraging them to develop and maintain a portfolio of evidence of skills acquisition and to monitor their own practice. Introductory sessions on the University's core skills initiative are held during induction week, strengthened by contributions from employers. Students will be expected to use their portfolios to support their reflection on their educational and vocational formation during the specially designated modules at levels 2 and 3. The Career Management Portfolio will be aligned with the revised, national, Profile.

45.2.2   Student records

The complexity of the Modular Credit Scheme, the University's commitment continuously to improve the service it offers to its students, and the resource imperative that requires all staff to work smarter, are all factors that have led the University to a student administration system that is operationally reliant on computerized systems. Its strategy is to link all facets of student administration, from admission and registration through to assessment and the production of award certificates, so that the time of academic and professional support staff is released for personal interaction with students.

Related both to the drive for automated administration and to the core skills initiative recorded above, the University has reached agreement on a new standard form for describing modules. The module information form requests programme teams to set out in some detail the aims, objectives, teaching and assessment methods and learning outcomes of individual modules. More importantly, however, the form also links to the student record system on the one hand, and on the other into the core skills initiative by asking programme teams to identify the particular core skills developed through each module. A project is currently in hand to hold the module information forms on the University's internal web site, fully accessible to staff and students, which will in turn be linked to the process for registering students on modules.

As a parallel exercise, developments are being initiated in the reports that can be printed from the student record system. A project is in hand to capture the details of the core skills embedded in individual modules, so that a list of the skills encountered by individual students can be created on a central data base to guide students in their selection of modules and to enable them to monitor their own progress. Achievement in the specially designated modules at levels 2 and 3 will enable the University to print individualized transcripts upon graduation. The facility will also allow the University to confirm that students have attained a minimum threshold competence in the skills integral to the modules they have passed. University mark sheets will be modified to show the corporate template of skills and, once the programme of staff development is completed, examiners will be asked to record students' attainments against the corporate skills template as an integral part of the marking process.

From these developments, it is only a short step to designing a record of achievement for students, covering performance in both academic and core skills areas, although significant progress will be dependent on three factors: the priority that can be given to it in terms of software development; the success of national negotiations about a record of achievement covering all phases of education; and agreement within the higher education sector as a whole that records of achievement in competences and skills are a more useful instrument for graduates and employers than the honours degree classifications currently in use.

45.3   Initial research findings

The institutional model is being used as the basis for action research. At present the University is at the early stages of defining the parameters within which this research will be conducted. This section outlines the strategy being adopted and the initial findings.

There will be three main mechanisms for this research; institutional, programme (through the annual course monitoring procedures) and skills oriented through the establishment of working groups in each of the broad skills areas. The intention will be to evaluate the impact of the skills initiative on all parties: students, academic staff and employers.

45.3.1 Annual monitoring

The university requires all programme areas to write an annual report. For this year, field managers have been asked to comment specifically on the implementation of the skills initiative in their area. Reports are analysed at the faculty level and themes identified. These reports are currently being written.

45.3.2 Student evaluation

The university canvasses student opinion on each of the modules which it offers through a questionnaire. This student perception of module (SPOM) data is collected and externally processed. One format is used for all modules across all disciplines and levels.

For 1996/7 the questionnaire was amended to include four questions directly related to the four broad skills areas (see Figure 45.1).

Transferable Skills

Given what you understand this module is trying to achieve, has this module improved your ability to:

13	Retrieve and use information correctly
14	Communicate and/or present information effectively
15	Effectively apply given methods to solve problems
16	Work well with other people

Figure 45.1

Options were; 'yes', 'no' or 'not relevant to module'.

45.3.3 Analysis

Preliminary analysis of the data from semester 1 has been undertaken on a faculty basis; this will be refined to provide information at the programme level. Initial results, based on a total sample size of over 13 000, are summarized in Table 45.1.

	Sci & Comp	Des & Tech	HC&SS	Bus	Mgt	Hum
Sample Size	2032	1746	2789		482	2696
Retrieve and use information correctly		+		+	+	-
Communicate and/or present information effectively	--	+		-	+	+
Effectively apply given methods to solve problems		++	-	++	-	---
Work well with other people	--	-	+	-	+	

Notes

+   *indicates students perceive modules as contributing to the development of the appropriate skill*

-     *indicates that modules not perceived as developing the skill.*

Comparison is relative to the university average.

Table 45.1

For Access programmes at level 0, the student perception was strongly positive in all areas.

These initial findings are generally in line with stereotypical images of student characteristics; however, there are some results which require further consideration. For example:

- the differences between Science and Computing, and Design and Technology

- the differences between Business and Management

It is not clear whether these factors are student or discipline related. Work is also underway to establish discipline specific characteristics and rankings of these skills.

While the use of questionnaires is an invaluable research tool, its use in this setting must be considered against the danger of 'questionnaire overload' and its resource demands.

45.3.4   Staff evaluation

Academic staff were questioned on the implementation of the skills initiative at level 1.

1   *Template*

Broadly they felt that the range of skills in the template were appropriate although some felt that there were too many skills (19) at this level.

> It seems a good idea but difficult to implement and interpret.

> Languages are usually skills oriented so once the template was clear, it was not difficult to adapt it. Subject nature places emphasis on communication.

> I believe the skills template to be too simplistic as to provide little information about the genuine complexity and sophistication of most of our students' achievements.

2   *Implementation*

Seventy per cent reported that they had had to make little or no changes to their established delivery practice at this level.

> Students need to be sold the idea, most seemed quite unaware of transferable skills and were not sure of what use they would be to them.

3   *Assessment*

Fifty per cent were assessing skills separately from content (not a requirement); 90% believed that their assessment techniques were effective in assessing skills; 71% thought that they were able to objectively test skills.

> Clear criteria should be agreed that are common to all disciplines. E.g. what standards of communication skills are required, how many spelling errors should you allow in one essay?

4   *Staff development*

Two areas were highlighted: the need for a set of clear and objective guidelines on the standards required, and the opportunity for discussion with peers.

Appendix 45.1   Modular Credit Scheme – Level 1 Generic Descriptors & Core Skills

MODULAR CREDIT SCHEME - LEVEL 1 GENERIC DESCRIPTORS & CORE SKILLS

	CHARACTERISTIC OF CONTEXT	RESPONSIBILITY
	At Level 1 the Learner:	
1. Operational Contexts	Should be working within defined contexts demanding the use of a specified range of standard techniques.	Should be learning in an environment where the work is directed, with limited autonomy, and within defined guidelines.

	KNOWLEDGE & UNDERSTANDING	ANALYSIS
	By the end of Level 1 the Learner:	
2. Cognitive Descriptors	Should have a given factual and/or conceptual knowledge base with emphasis on the nature of the field of study and appropriate terminology.	Should be able to analyse with guidance using given classifications/principles.

	INFO. RETRIEVAL & HANDLING		COMMUNICATION & PRESENTATION	
	By the end of Level 1 the Learner:			
3. Core Skills Descriptors	Should be able to seek, describe and interpret information. In particular:		Should be able to communicate effectively in context, both orally and on paper. In particular:	
	- identify and use a wide variety of primary sources, including electronic and print based indices, citing sources appropriately	I1-1	- distinguish between ideas, opinions and judgment in his/her own writing	C1-1
	- describe, interpret and organise data establishing relevant information as necessary	I2.1	- identify key themes from written work and oral presentations	C2.1
	- scan information under a time constraint for specific purposes	I3.1	- express key themes in written work, recognising the style, structure and level of written material in relation to its target audience	C3.1
	- use appropriate IT hardware (particularly microcomputer systems) safely, including power up, login/logout, protecting against accidental loss of data and obtaining hard copy	I4.1	- write reports, notes and assessment material according to an approved standard, correcting grammar, spelling and syntax as necessary	C4.1
	- select and use appropriate packages (including word processors) making use of on-line help facilities	I5.1	- give a short presentation using methods suitable for the target audience.	C5.1
	- use a spreadsheet package to handle data tables.	I6.1		

ETHICAL UNDERSTANDING

Should be aware of social and cultural diversity and ethical issues and be able to discuss these in relation to personal beliefs and values.
In particular:
- be sensitive to language and imagery
- understand ethical issues relevant to the subject(s) of study
- be aware of personal responsibilities and professional codes of conduct
- work within the University guidelines on ethics.

SYNTHESIS/CREATIVITY

Should be able to collect and characterise ideas and information in a predictable and standard format (e.g. in essay form, as a report etc.).

EVALUATION

Should be able to evaluate the reliability of data using defined techniques and tutor guidance (where appropriate).

PLANNING & PROBLEM SOLVING

Should be able to apply given tools/methods accurately and carefully to a well defined problem and draw appropriate conclusions.
In particular:

- anlayse problem situations, identifying and describing the nature of the problem	P1.1
- break a problem down into manageable parts, allocate priorities and identify suitable solution/draw appropriate conclusions	P2.1
- implement and evaluate solutions/conclusions	P3.1
- understand and apply numerical conventions, interpreting trends and data	P4.1
- communicate quantitative information effectively to the audience using an appropriate format (including charts, tabular data as necessary).	P5.1

SOCIAL DEV. & INTERACTION

Should be able to work with an meet obligations to others (tutors and/or other students) In particular:

- demonstrate self reliance by relating personal goals to planning and performance measurement, including completing work on time	S1.1
- relate to and co-operate with others in contributing to a group's achieving a defined goal	S2.1
- recognise own strengths and weaknesses and give and receive constructive feedback.	S3.1

Appendix 45.2   Modular Credit Scheme – Level 3 Generic Descriptors & Core Skills

MODULAR CREDIT SCHEME - LEVEL 3 GENERIC DESCRIPTORS & CORE SKILLS

	CHARACTERISTIC OF CONTEXT	RESPONSIBILITY
	At Level 3 the Learner:	
1. Operational Contexts	Should be working within complex and unpredictable contexts demanding selection and application from a wide range of innovative or standard techniques.	Should be autonomous in planning and managing the learning process within broad ??

	KNOWLEDGE & UNDERSTANDING	ANALYSIS
	By the end of Level 3 the Learner:	
2. Cognitive Descriptors	Should be able to demonstrate confident familiarity with the core knowledge base of his/her discipline(s) and an awareness of the provisional nature of knowledge.	Should be able to anlayse new and/or abstract data and situations without guidance, using a wide rang e of techniques appropriate to the discipline(s).

	INFO. RETRIEVAL & HANDLING		COMMUNICATION & PRESENTATION	
	By the end of Level 2 the Learner:			
	Should be able to seek, describe and interpret information within the context of the discipline(s). In particular:		Should be able to communicate effectively in context, both orally and on paper. In particular:	
	- identify own information needs to support complex problem requirements	I1.3	- produce a complex piece of work which demonstrates a grasp of vocabulary of the subject and deploys a range of skills of written expression appropriate to the subject	C1.3
3. Core Skills Descriptors	- complete an information search using a range of appropriate primary and secondary sources. Draw accurate conclusions independently using the subject methodology	I2.3	- assess the quality of his or her own oral communication and identify areas for improvement	C2.3
	- analyse data, using appropriate techniques	I3.3	- deliver a paper or presentation which succeeds in communicating a series of points effectively.	C3.3
	- use appropriate IT resources independently to support previously identified areas.	I4.3		

ETHICAL UNDERSTANDING

Should be aware of personal responsibility and professional codes of conduct and be able to incorporate a critical ethical dimension into a major piece of work.

SYNTHESIS/CREATIVITY	EVALUATION
With minimum guidance, should be able to transform abstract data and concepts towards a given purpose and be able to design novel solutions.	Should be able to critically review evidence supporting conclusions/recommendations, including its reliability, validity and significance, and investigate contradictory information and/or identify reasons for the contradictions.

PLANNING & PROBLEM SOLVING		SOCIAL DEV. & INTERACTION	
Should be able to apply given tools/methods accurately and carefully to a well defined problem and draw appropriate conclusions. In particular:		Should be able to work with and meet obligations to others (tutors and/or other students). In particular:	
- decide on action plans and implement then effectively	P1.3	- formulate effective strategies for achieving goals when working with others	S1.3
- manage time effectively in order to achieve intended goals	P2.3	- participate effectively in the operation of a team an collaborate with members of the team	S2.3
- clearly identify criteria for success and evaluate his or her own performance against those criteria	P3.3		
- produce creative and realistic solutions to complex problems	P4.3		

5   *Other points*

- Difficult in some cases to make students realize their responsibility to the other members of the group.

- Skills need to be taught as well as assessed.

- Skills can detract from content.

- Students found individual class presentations very stressful at level 1.

- Remedial English is required for some students especially in written skills.

- Difficult to get students to take responsibility for their own development.

45.4   Summary

Initial findings on the evaluation of the university-wide skills template are beginning to show interesting differences between the emphases given to different skills by the different subject disciplines. Further work will be undertaken on the precise nature of these differences and how they vary through the levels of the undergraduate programme. Furthermore, an investigation of the differences pre and post the implementation of the template at levels 2 and 3 is also being undertaken.

46 Using the principles of standards-based assessment to improve assessment practice across a large tertiary institution

Shona Little and Jim Lester
Centre for Staff and Educational Development, Auckland Institute of Technology

46.1 Overview

This chapter discusses the experience of the Auckland Institute of Technology (AIT), the largest polytechnic in New Zealand, where the principles of standards based assessment have been used to improve student assessment across the Institute. Key reasons for implementing standards-based assessment include the acknowledgement of the stakeholding interests of students, employers, industry organizations and professional bodies, as well as the need to prepare students for the richness, complexity and constant change of today's workplace. The implementation process has raised a number of issues in the areas of staff development and administrative systems as well as that of curriculum change. AIT has provided a range of mechanisms for supporting staff in the developmental process. Key curriculum issues concern whether to use competence or achievement-based assessment or both, and the use of integrated holistic assessment to minimize a tendency towards over-assessment and more accurately reflect workplace reality. The AIT experience has been that addressing these issues has been worthwhile, resulting not only in better programme documentation and assessment practice, but also a greater degree of understanding and commitment on the part of staff.

46.2 Background

Many writers and theorists have commented on the way in which what has variously been described as 'outcomes based', 'competence based', and 'standards based' education has impacted on the English-speaking world since the mid 1980s. In an address to an Auckland Institute of Technology staff development conference in 1995, Andrew Gonczi stated his belief that the impact of this had perhaps been more intensely felt in New Zealand than it had anywhere else in the world. Government policy since 1988 together with the development of the New Zealand Qualifications Authority have ensured that, apart from the traditional university sector, our education system nation-wide is now at least oriented towards, if not already using, some form of standards-based assessment.

The vocational focus of the polytechnic sector in New Zealand has resulted in a history of awareness of students' learning needs. This led in the early 1980s to developments in a number of areas, including student-centred curricula, initiatives to improve the reliability and validity of assessment procedures, an overall focus on greater transparency and accountability in the educational process, and an acknowledgment of students as primary stakeholders in their own education.

Although there has been an ongoing debate in New Zealand about the desirability of applying to tertiary education the pure competency approach which is used in much workplace training (and which is evident in some aspects of the New Zealand Qualifications Framework), nonetheless there are aspects of standards-based assessment and general principles which the AIT believes can be used to not only provide clarity and transparency of curriculum, but also to improve assessment practice across the Institute . Accordingly, in 1996, AIT decided to use standards based assessment for these purposes, and this was written into the General Academic Statute for 1997.

46.3   Influences on this decision

Educational decisions concerning ways of improving assessment practice across the Institute have been influenced by a range of theorists and writers on the assessment of higher education and adult learning in general, including Boud (1996, 1987), Entwistle, Thompson and Tait (1992), Fletcher (1992), Gonczi (1995a, 1995b), Crooks (1988). In addition to this educational thrust there are also more pragmatic issues which influenced the decision. One of these was the pervading political climate and its expression in the New Zealand Qualifications Authority and the National Qualifications Framework (which is modelled in part on the SCOTVEC system). Industry is indisputably a key stakeholder in the education that polytechnics provide, at all levels from short-course certificates to degrees. Their orientation is one of inputs, outputs, transparency and accountability, and systems have been established to guarantee and maintain their input at a national level.

In addition to employer groups, professional bodies and related organizations are also key stakeholders. Their stake in this process extends to acting as gatekeepers for their professions. To fulfil this role they are outcomes focused. This role is acknowledged by both the polytechnics and the students themselves.

There are many other reasons for moving towards a standards-based assessment system. A key reason is the expectations of students. The impact of the New Zealand Qualifications Framework at secondary level has meant that students are likely to enter tertiary education with prior experience of standards based assessment and consequently they are increasingly expecting that clearly communicated learning outcomes and assessment criteria will be provided for them well in advance of any assessment event. Students have always been very focused on assessment and the fact that they are now paying increasingly high fees means that that focus is becoming more and more intense. With New Zealand's Consumer Guarantees Act covering the field of education, lecturers now have legal as well as educational responsibilities.

The workplace for which polytechnic students are preparing themselves, whether it be in the traditional professions, in industry or in commerce, is commonly assessing its workers using systems which include learning outcomes, standards and criteria against which performance can be measured. It is important therefore, if our graduates are to compete effectively in such a workplace, for them to be skilled in managing such systems before they graduate, and consequently our assessment systems must mirror that reality. And for our graduates to compete effectively in a world marked by frequent change, the skills of identifying their own learning needs, framing their own learning objectives, deciding on the criteria against which they and others can effectively measure their performance, and evaluating the outcome, are invaluable. These skills are also essential for the development of self-directed and independent learning.

Standards-based assessment is the only assessment approach which can realistically provide for learning completed elsewhere to be assessed and recognized for academic credit within another programme. Tertiary students in New Zealand are increasingly expecting their prior learning will be appropriately recognized and that they will be able to acquire credit for it.

46.4   What is standards-based assessment?

AIT has developed a range of Curriculum Development Guidelines which have been printed for staff in booklet form. In Guidebook 2: Writing Module Descriptors (Ker and Reid *et al.*, 1995), the two forms of standards-based assessment, competency-based and achievement-based assessment have been described thus:

> Competency based assessment judges the learner's performance against a pass/fail criterion. There are no grades or ranking associated with the learner performance, although merit may be acknowledged.
>
> Achievement based assessment measures a learner's performance against a predetermined set of grade-related criteria, that is, one set of criteria which if satisfied will result in the student being granted an A; a different set of   criteria which will result in a B; another set of criteria which will result in a C, etc.

Standards based assessment itself has been defined as:

> a method of assessment whereby a learner's performance is measured against pre-determined standards of achievement or competence.
>
> (Ker and Reid *et al.*, 1995)

46.5   Issues in the implementation of standards-based assessment

These occur in three key areas: staff education and support; institutional reporting systems and administrative structures; and curriculum.

First, the issue of staff education and support. It is not possible to push staff beyond their comfort level, nor is it sensible or ethical to put them in situations in which they risk being viewed by their students, their colleagues, or themselves, as ineffective practitioners. AIT has recognized that individuals, departments, discipline groups and programme teams are at various stages along a developmental path to implementing standards based assessment. They need not only knowledge and understanding of both the principles and the practice, but also an acceptance of the rationale underlying its implementation. This acceptance takes time to develop. Staff must come to terms with the changes that may need to be made to their own practice or programmes. Over and above all this however, they need support throughout the developmental process, including practical help with writing documentation, implementing the curriculum, and designing appropriate assessment events.

Secondly, AITs institutional reporting systems and administrative structures were designed to meet the needs of a different assessment regime, one based on a numerical model of percentages, weightings and aggregation. These have been progressively refined to better suit this end. This system represents a significant investment for the Institute, which cannot afford to dismantle it. Such a system places considerable barriers, both real and perceived, in the path of innovation and curriculum change.

Thirdly, the introduction of standards based assessment inevitably generates a range of curriculum issues. Standards based assessment should not be seen as an 'add-on' or an 'overlay' to existing curriculum documentation. In almost all cases curricula need to be reconsidered in the light of the philosophy and requirements of standards based assessment. At the very least curriculum documentation must be written in terms of outcome statements. Standards-based assessment may have critical implications for the way in which a programme is delivered, such as for example timing, communications with students, and even the teaching and learning process itself.

A fundamental decision regarding the introduction of standards-based assessment concerns whether to use competence or achievement based assessment or a combination of both. Designing and administering achievement based assessments is more complex. Identifying the essential criteria which will separate one grade from another, can be a difficult process. Potential benefits of achievement based assessment include the provision of information to potential employers about a student's level of attainment and the incentive for learners to perform to their full potential (see Clayton, 1995, p. 169). Students tend to be unhappy with the opportunity only to pass or fail.

When staff attempt to specify learning outcomes and the associated assessment tasks, their desire for transparency and accountability can often lead them to become too specific and reductionist. The consequence of this can be a 'dumbing down' of the curriculum. Rowntree (1987) describes this as making the measurable important rather than the important measurable.

Over assessment can also be a problem. The understandable desire to be '100% certain' as to the level of student achievement in every aspect of every outcome can lead to an excessive number of assessment events, which may be repetitive (to guard against any result being a 'one-off' occurrence) and/or reductionist.

A key issue for any tertiary institute is how to undo the habits and expectations of both staff and students with respect to the perceived value of fine grade and/or percentage distinctions. In addition to the questionable validity of such fine distinctions in terms of the margin of error in any assessment, within an achievement-based model there is a need to express grade distinctions (grade related criteria) explicitly in writing.

46.6 Responding to issues of staff development and support

A range of strategies have been used to address the developmental needs of staff. An Institute needs to encourage professional debate and the communication of useful ideas. At AIT, several one-hour seminars, open to all staff, were held. These seminars focused on the rationale behind the implementation of standards based assessment, key principles, issues which staff would need to consider, and some models of existing best practice which staff could use or adapt. The content of the seminar was backed up with a Guidebook (Lester and Little, 1997) – a 'takeaway' resource which staff could refer to and action when the need arose. This resource was also provided free to module and programme teams. It enlarged on all the material addressed in the seminar as well as providing suggestions and guidelines for curriculum development, frameworks, flowcharts, and sequences of steps on which staff could base their work if they wished (see Lester and Little, 1997, pp. 49–53). The Guidebook also provided a range of models of standards-based assessment already being used within the Institute and examples of the relevant documentation. This Guidebook was the third in a series of Learning and Teaching Development Guidelines designed to encourage staff to further develop their curriculum, to write the appropriate documentation as required by the Institute and to support them in this process.

Staff facing the task of implementing standards-based assessment will naturally be focused within their own programme context. However, our experience has underlined the importance of a multidisciplinary perspective in developing curriculum assessments. Staff activities, or forums at which staff from across the Institute contribute, provide valuable opportunities to learn from other disciplines and avoid 'tunnel vision'.

As well as the Guidebooks and seminars, the Institute staff developers worked closely with programme and module teams, at times running workshops focusing on the specific needs of particular groups or disciplines, and at other times being closely and actively involved in the developmental process, acting simultaneously as group facilitator, consultant, and co-developer.

There are other ways of supporting staff. Some key innovators in their own programmes within the Institute have been used as 'catalysts' to encourage staff and support the development of new or improved programmes in other areas.

46.7   Addressing system constraints

As far as reporting systems are concerned, change is inevitably a long-term process. At AIT, initial discussions were held with Academic Registry to explain the philosophy of standards-based assessment and the difficulties in implementing it within the existing system. An interesting pilot project was undertaken using one of the most innovative programmes in the Institute. The project's aim was to find ways to adapt the centralized assessment reporting system to fit a non-numerical, non-aggregating standards based model. Progress to date is encouraging.

46.8   Dealing with curriculum issues

In providing advice and support to staff in the development process, a number of strategies for dealing with the curriculum issues have emerged as being useful across the broad spectrum of the Institute's programmes.

Not all programmes within AIT have developed their curricula and documentation to the same extent. Some programmes and/or modules are not yet written in terms of learning outcomes. For staff teaching on these programmes, the implementation of standards-based assessment must begin by tackling this task. In writing learning outcomes, staff need to identify important, meaningful, achievable, assessable and reasonably generic skills. Advice on this process is included in the Guidebook. (Lester and Little, 1997, pp. 50–3).

In deciding whether to use competence or achievement based assessment or both, a most useful approach has been to begin with the consideration of the nature of the learning outcomes themselves. Do they lend themselves to a pass/fail criterion, that is competent or not competent, or are they in fact better measured on a continuum using an achievement based model with grade related criteria?

If an achievement-based model is deemed appropriate, the next issue to be addressed is the generation of the grade-related criteria. These criteria might include such parameters as breadth or depth of treatment, time taken to complete a task or speed of production, and precision of result. However, parameters of this type may well be seen as too mechanistic or low level for degree or diploma programmes. A key element in this decision process relates to the relative criticality of the learning outcomes, that is, the grade schema must be seen to reward the most important outcomes or attributes.

At AIT, documentation for most higher level programmes includes a statement of the 'graduate profile'. This profile is effectively the set of capabilities which staff and other stakeholders agree make up the essence of that profession. The debate among programme teams which leads to the generation of the graduate profile, has proven to be a very beneficial exercise in terms of team building, values clarification, and commitment to their students' development and achievement of those capabilities.

Once agreement has been reached on the graduate profile, each module team considers which of the capabilities apply to their module (not all capabilities would necessarily be applicable to every module e.g. some modules by their nature might not emphasize the development of say, reflective practice). This discussion needs to consider not only which capabilities it is reasonable to say may be being developed, but also which we may expect to see evidence of and to what degree or level. The overall programme then needs to be revisited to ensure that in total the agreed set of capabilities are indeed being addressed.

A minimum condition for a pass in individual modules would be demonstration of the competencies. For some modules, especially those at higher levels, evidence of a minimum standard of achievement of some capabilities might also be part of the pass (or C grade) criteria. Beyond this basic requirement, the award of higher grades is tagged to the degree of development of the capabilities appropriate to that module.

For example, at lower levels it might be appropriate that the actual demonstration of certain skills constitutes a pass, but that the reflective application of those skills is rewarded by a higher grade - 'can do' versus 'knows when and why to do'.

Integrated, holistic assessment events can be used to help overcome a tendency towards over-assessment, as well as addressing the critical issue of accurately reflecting the richness and complexity of real world professional behaviour by assessing whole-task application. Professional competence (Gonczi, 1995a) is based in the attributes that underlie professional performance. That is, for example, the ethical, problem-solving and communicative capabilities which are required in the real-life professional context. In order to assess these capabilities we need to create assessment events which match the real-world context wherever possible. And professional capabilities do not exist in isolation – they are normally demonstrated in situations which also require expertise in terms of both knowledge and skills.

Thus we may need to construct whole task assessment events which may include any of the skills shown in Figure 46.1.

One approach to developing an integrated assessment event is to construct a task or situation which reflects the real-world context as closely as possible. A training restaurant is an obvious example of a suitable venue for such an event. A simulation could be another example.

In some instances it may not be feasible to set up simulated or real-world whole task events as outlined above. Where the opportunities for assessment may be limited to, for example, a written product, a simpler approach needs to be found.

Ways of developing written integrated assessment events could be the creation of a project, research, or portfolio task, where knowledge, technical skills, research skills, self appraisal, and so on, are integral to the creation of the final assessable product

Professional competence is often inferred from a student's ability to simultaneously exercise professional judgement, demonstrate the relevant technical skills and behave in an ethically appropriate manner in context. Although, for example, individual knowledge outcomes may not be 'seen' as part of that assessment event, they may be legitimately inferred from the professional performance in context.

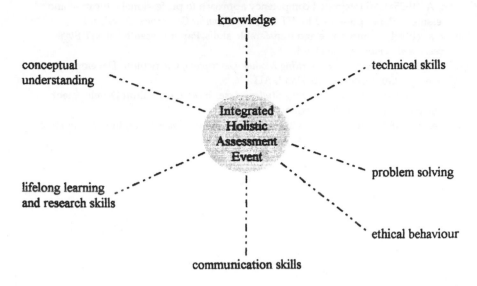

(Adapted from Gonczi 1995a)

Figure 46.1

46.9   Concluding comments

Standards-based assessment provides the opportunity for considerable improvement in assessment practices overall. It can also be a valuable means of meeting the current needs of a variety of stakeholders for transparency and accountability in both curriculum documentation and assessment procedures. However there are a number of barriers to its implementation. At AIT we have attempted to be as realistic as possible. We have remained focused on our ultimate goal, that is, to improve assessment across the Institute by using the principles of standards-based assessment (rather than getting 'locked in' to too much detailed theory). Where necessary we have adapted the theory to suit our reality, while at the same time ensuring that we adhered to sound educational principles. We believe that the benefits of implementing standards based assessment outweigh the difficulties. Staff tend to understand the assessment process better and are frequently more committed to achieving programme goals as a result of working through the developmental process.

46.10   References

Boud, D. (1996) The new agenda for assessment: maximising opportunities for learning. Keynote address given to *Partnerships in the Assessment of Student Achievement* conference, Auckland, AIT.

Boud, D. (1987) *Implementing Student Assessment*, HERDSA Green Guide No 6.

Clayton, B. (1995) *Focusing on Assessment*, Adelaide, NCVER.

Crooks, T. (1988) *Assessing Student Performance*, HERDSA Green Guide No 8.

Entwistle, N., Thompson, S. and Tait, H. (1992) *Guidelines for Promoting Effective Learning*, Edinburgh, University of Edinburgh.

Fletcher, S. (1992) *Competence-Based Assessment Techniques*, London, Kogan Page.

Gonczi, A. (1995a) An integrated competency approach to professional education and assessment. Paper presented to *AIT Staff Development Conference*, Auckland

Gonczi, A. (1995b) Competence and transferable skills. Paper presented at *AIT Staff Development Seminars*, Auckland.

Ker, P. and Reid, M. *et al.* (1995) *Writing Module Descriptors*, Curriculum Development Guidelines, Guidebook 2, Auckland, AIT.

Lester, J. and Little, S. (1997) *Improving Student Assessment*, Curriculum Development Guidelines, Guidebook 3, Auckland, AIT.

Rowntree, D (1987) *Assessing Students: How Shall We Know Them?*, London, Kogan Page.

47 Using records of achievement to improve learning in higher education

Hugh Somervell
University of Wolverhampton

47.1 Overview

Records of Achievement (RoAs) have been introduced at the University of Wolverhampton in an attempt to involve undergraduate students in both the process and product of the educational system. Combining a formative system using a 'development planner' with a summative record, students are able to optimize their learning by selecting appropriate modules and keeping a profile of their development while building up a record of their achievement. The RoA is linked to the development of learning outcomes and students are encouraged to analyse their own development through the achievement of these as they progress. This chapter examines research being carried out analysing the extent to which the process of development planning through the RoA helps students to reflect upon their learning and leads them to a better understanding of the process. This, it is claimed, should involve students in a deeper approach to learning and help them get the most of their undergraduate studies.

47.2 Background

The development of Records of Achievement (RoAs) in the 1980s, according to Broadfoot (1986), started in Scotland with the 'Pupil Profiles' project. From there it very quickly mushroomed into a national system in England that Broadfoot suggests has been quite alarming in its growth. Yet this growth has largely bypassed higher education where their use is not as clear or as well- defined as it is in other sectors.

Much of the development of RoAs during the expansion of the 1980s was on either an individual or regional basis. However, as Pole (1993, p. 4) explains, in 1991 the process was given the official endorsement by central government when the two Secretaries of State for Employment and Education 'in launching a National Pilot Record of Achievement, tied together the outcomes of the emerging National Curriculum and the needs of industry'. The NRA was clearly seen as a vehicle for producing a summative document. The extent to which it is also useful as a formative process is not elaborated which raises an important issue that echoes Broadfoot's (1986) anxiety. She wondered to what extent the system will provide not just 'a plethora of new record cards, but a fundamental change in educational priorities of a depth and intensity not seen since the institution of universal secondary education in 1944/5'(Broadfoot, 1986, p. 21)

When originally introduced the NRA was intended to be optional, although schools and colleges were strongly advised to use it, and it was supposed to 'evolve and develop over time in the light of users' own practical experience of it' (DES quoted in Pole, 1993, p. 4). The evolution of the NRA over the six years following its launch, however, has not been smooth. The take-off experienced in the 1980s would appear to have slowed:

> It has strong advocates in schools and colleges, but commitment to it varies. Many small - and medium-sized firms and employers have little knowledge of it. Students often have insufficient understanding of how to use it effectively in preparing a job application or at an interview.
>
> (Dearing, 1996, p.15)

In his 'Review of Qualifications for 16–19 Year Olds' Dearing suggests that it has 'the potential to be much more than a summary of achievement' (p. 15) and that it should be used in a formative way by being 'an important instrument through which young people develop the practice of managing and taking responsibility for their own learning, as a skill they need for life, continuing through college, university and into work'. In this sense Dearing sees a wider role for the NRA than was intended at its launch. The recommendations made by Dearing (1996) suggest a review and relaunch of the NRA. He argues that such processes as 'learning agreements' could be introduced in colleges to help students plan and manage their own learning and that this process itself could be assessed in some way (although formal assessment should remain optional).

The problem would seem to be that while RoAs may function as 'summaries' of achievement, their potential as a formative tool and as a means of involving students in the 'process' of education is either overlooked or has not yet been properly developed.

Within higher education there has not been a similar trend. Although not much attention seems to have been paid to the role of the NRA (the discussion being restricted to the recruitment system and the 'summative' aspect of the process) the debate here seems to have concentrated more upon 'student profiling' and the process of the system rather than the product itself. Although the term RoA may imply the summative aspect of the system, Trowler and Hinett (1994, p. 54) suggest that within HE there seems to be a view that 'the process that leads to that record' is, if anything, more important than the product. They conclude that

> given realistic goals and appropriate implementation strategies it can lead to improvements in student selection, assessment and placement while at the same time raising important questions about curriculum content and delivery.
>
> (Trowler and Hinett, 1994, p. 61)

From their interviews with participants it was clear that both aspects are seen as part of the overall system. What seems to have emerged, therefore, is a view that the summative element, and the formative process, are equally important:

> The formative process is, then, at the heart of development, but many would see the production of an end document or summative record as equally important to students, employers and other 'end users' of such documents in that they provide a more rounded picture of an individual than a narrow list of examination results. A narrowly-defined RoA might describe only certain aspects of the process, rather than acknowledge that 'process' and 'product' dimensions operate simultaneously.
>
> (Assiter and Shaw, 1993, p .20)

47.3   Transferable skills and learning outcomes

Within higher education there is a link between the development of RoAs and the growing interest in 'transferable skills' (Holmes, 1995). This is largely due to the influence of the Enterprise in Higher Education Initiative which raised the profile of transferable skills and has helped in understanding the development of these skills in our students (Kemp and Seagraves, 1995). The introduction of these skills, and the need to be clear about what we mean by such terms, has driven those working on RoAs, and on the development of Teaching and Learning at Wolverhampton to articulate our own definitions not only of the concept of 'transferable skills' but also what we mean by 'learning outcomes'.

In trying to overcome the confusion that surrounds such terms as 'objectives', and the many other words used to describe what we expect students to learn or be able to do when they complete their courses of study, a working group within the University of Wolverhampton has produced a classification of learning outcomes which is based on three broad categories (Allan, 1996). These can be summarized as:

1. *subject specific outcomes* – these refer to the subject being studied and the knowledge component. They 'subsume learning objectives and are complex discipline-based outcomes which are capable of being assessed' (Allan, 1996, p. 107);

2. *generic academic outcomes* – referring here to outcomes that we would expect students to achieve which relate to academic study in higher education: making use of information; thinking critically; analysing; and synthesizing ideas and information;

3. *personal transferable outcomes* – which involve: communicating effectively; organizing; gathering information; using information technology; acting independently; working in teams; and numeracy.

A student would be expected to achieve all of these outcomes during their study towards a first degree. The extent and depth will vary between programmes, however all graduates should be able to demonstrate some competence in all the specified learning outcomes. This raises issues with regards to planning of students' programmes to achieve these outcomes, their assessment and the recording of the process. How much information, for example, are students given about the modules available to them? What outcomes are being assessed in each module and can students demonstrate their achievement of these at the end? How are these outcomes linked to form a coherent programme? It was in order to answer these sorts of questions that the RoA has been devised and implemented within the university of Wolverhampton.

47.4   The University of Wolverhampton Record of Achievement

In designing a RoA a similar approach has been used to that adopted by the Scottish Higher Education Record of Achievement. The RoA consists of a 'Development Planner' and a summative document. Like the Scottish example it is student-owned and concentrates on the initial identification and later development of defined learning outcomes.

The initial bid for the project included a rationale which outlines the main ideas the team was hoping to develop as follows.

1. A commitment by the University that: 'by the academic year 1995/6 records of achievement will be available to all University of Wolverhampton students'.

2. The use of RoAs is perceived as an essential tool in helping students to take responsibility for their own learning and becoming effective and autonomous learners.

3. The project is closely linked to the specification of modules in learning outcomes form.

4. RoAs help students to track the development of transferable personal skills. Students can thus make a choice of modules which are appropriate for the enhancement of their personal portfolio of skills.

5. RoAs are perceived as a process as much as a product. They do not necessarily require endorsement by academic staff.

The 'Personal Development Planner' was produced by the project team and has been put onto the Internet. The team has also produced a series of title pages for the summative RoA document which are also on the Internet but may be downloaded as 'Word' documents.

47.4.1 The Personal Development Planner

A large part of the group's time was spent in devising the Personal Development Planner.This is the formative aspect of the process. So that all students can gain access to the planner, without having to pay for expensive hard copy, it was decided to put the planner on to the Internet within the University. The planner consists of a number of pages of information and exercises that students complete in order to start thinking about their own development and the programme of study they will follow. Students are introduced to the different categories of learning outcomes and also at this early stage the career they may wish to pursue. The idea of putting the planner onto a computer network was to provide as wide an access as possible, to help develop students' IT skills and to enable students to interact with the software as a learning resource. All students have access to the network within the University and are expected to develop IT skills.

Within the Personal Development Planner there is also a section on CV writing and this is linked to the University's Careers Guidance Scheme. The CV and other parts which require students to produce documents formally are included in a word-processed format that can be downloaded onto students' individual disks. Title pages for the finished document are included and so, as the students progress through their course, they can build up a disk copy of their own RoA. At a suitable time this can be printed off and included in the students' folders. Thus the summative record is produced as a consequence of having completed aspects of the 'formative' development planner.

47.5   Research

The working group were conscious that throughout the construction of the Development Planner it was important to work with students and produce something that was useable. Students were co-opted onto the project team from two subject areas and were asked to use what was being developed. As a result changes were made to the system and the process refined in the light of comments made by the students.

Apart from this on-going evaluation, the group also commissioned an evaluation from an external researcher. This was carried out in the summer of 1995 towards the end of the development phase. The main findings of this evaluation would suggest that the project was seen as being 'worthwhile and that the deistinction between the Personal Development Planner and the RoA was both valid and useful' (Harrison, 1995, p. 3). While raising some basic questions about the concept of a RoA as a part of the assessment process in HE, the research found that the students were very positive about the process and their criticism was constructive and designed to make the documents more effective. In its conclusion the evaluation states that the students' 'positive attitude should encourage further development of something which has the potential to maximise the students' use of their time at University. Any real problems would seem to lie with the concept of RoAs in general rather than with this example in particular' (Harrison, 1995, p. 4).

Following this initial evaluation into the RoA there have been two small-scale surveys of students' opinions using a questionnaire. Both these have been carried out with first-year students using the RoA and in both cases the results reflect those given by students in the initial evaluation where practical problems in accessing and using the system were seen as the main ones. Following on from this, although students saw the value of the scheme and were happy to be involved initially, very few questioned had actually continued to use the RoA after their induction session (13 of the 15 respondents in one of the surveys said they were not still using the facility half way through the first year). Combining these small-scale surveys with other anecdotal evidence of the problems faced by students, a fuller research programme has been introduced to try to examine, in greater depth, the value of the process and whether it does improve student learning by involving students in a more reflective approach to their studies.

The research currently being carried out has been designed in three stages. Initially the project has consisted of a series of focus group meetings designed to gather information and 'obtain perceptions on a defined area of interest in a permissive, non-threatening environment' (Krueger, 1994, p. 6). The second stage will involve a series of questionnaires and interviews with students and staff across the University. By this time the first group will have completed their undergraduate programme and the first cycle of involvement will be complete. The third stage of the research will involve a further series of focus group meetings to examine changes made at each of the previous stages and analysing the effects in more detail. In this sense an 'Action Research' (Elliott, 1991) approach is being taken where it is hoped to improve the RoA as well as explore its value as an aid to deeper learning.

47.6   Results

Work already carried out by Allan (1996) has demonstrated that using learning outcomes, and being made aware of them, improves student learning and involves them in deeper rather than surface approaches. The results of the focus group interviews already conducted would tend to support this point and suggest that students are more aware of what is expected of them and what they hope to achieve. One group of six students have met on three occasions and on each occasion have made positive comments about the use of learning outcomes:

> I think it is clear having learning outcomes in your modules because you know what they want you to do and they are linked to assessment, aren't they?

> I found it useful to look at them and the lecturer went through them and explained them to us . . . it helps to know what we have to do at the beginning and you can focus your reading better.

> I have a better understanding of the subject because I know what it's on about, it's better than some modules. I have learnt more in [name of module] than in my other ones.

> We all agree that they [learning outcomes] help us to understand what the module's about and what is expected of us in the essay and in the presentation.

When discussing the Development Planner the students have again been positive in their comments about the use of the Internet and the exercises and information given in the planner. With certain reservations they can see the value of a development planner and of the recognition of personal strengths and weaknesses:

> It's a good idea, I mean it helps me to understand what I need to do and how I can achieve it . . . the exercises are good and fun but they would take time if we did them properly, I mean not just when we were being shown how it works.

> The development planner could be really helpful. It is good for the assignment for Learning for Success [a study skills module in the first year where the RoA is used], especially the C.V. but the RoA pages didn't work properly.

On the negative side, however, students have found it difficult to find the time to use the development planner as intended and feel that is an 'addition' which, when under pressure to complete assignments and revise for examinations, tends to be ignored and sacrificed for the sake of more immediate concerns:

> It was alright at first, I had all these good intentions but when it comes down to it I guess you have to prioritise and it felt like a bit of a waste of time so I guess I concentrated on other more immediate things . . . I guess it's my own fault really, if I'd done what it was trying to get me to do. I mean time planning, then I guess I should have had time for it.

> I don't think it's a waste of time, I mean not if we had time to do it properly, if it was assessed everyone would do it, wouldn't they, like the C.V. in Learning for Success, I found it useful for that.

When questioned as to the possible solutions to this problem it was clear that where, as in one module, the RoA was incorporated into the module the students used it, and they therefore suggested that if it were 'somehow linked to the assessment of modules' it would have more use. Although students were aware of the long-term benefits of the system, they tended to sacrifice this for the more immediate issue of completing assessment.

47.7 Conclusion

In situations where students are made aware of the learning outcomes, and are encouraged to reflect upon what these are and how to achieve them, then a deeper approach to learning can be achieved. The RoA would seem to have the potential to act s a vehicle for this process and through the use of the 'formative' development planner, encourage greater reflection.

The research discussed here is only the start of a fuller project which, when complete, should give us a clearer understanding of the potential of this process and how it can be refined. Initial findings suggest that although there are problems with the design of the system, the concept of a formative Personal Development Planner linked to a summative RoA could be of benefit to the students. The success, at this stage, is hard to gauge and it must be remembered that as Trowler and Hinett (1994) suggest there are a number of careful considerations that need to be heeded, not least of which is its inclusion in the assessment and accreditation system of the University.

47.8   References

Allan, J. (1996) Learning outcomes in higher education, *Studies in Higher Education*, **21**(1), 93–108.

Assiter, A. and Shaw, E. (1993) Records of achievement: background, definitions and uses. In Assiter, A. and Shaw, E.(eds), *Using Records of Achievement in Higher Education*, London: Kogan Page.

Broadfoot, P. (1986) Sowing the seed: pupil profiles, research and policy in Scotland. In P. Broadfoot (ed.), *Profiles and Records of Achievement: A Review of Issues and Practice*, London: Rinehart & Winston.

Dearing, R. (1996) *Review of Qualifications for 16–19 Year Olds: Summary Report*, Hayes: SCAA Publications.

Elliott, J. (1991) *Action Research for Educational Change*, Milton Keynes: Open University Press.

Harrison, R. (1995) Evaluation of the Pilot Record of Achievement Project, unpublished paper, University of Wolverhampton.

Holmes, L. (1995) Skills: a social perspective. In A. Assiter (ed.), *Transferable Skills in Higher Education*, London: Kogan Page.

Krueger, R. (1994) *Focus Groups*, London: Sage.

Pole, C. (1993) *Assessing and Recording Achievement: Implementing a New Approach in Schools*, Buckingham: Open University Press.

Trowler, P. and Hinett, K. (1994) Implementing The Recording of Achievement in Higher Education Project, *Capability*, **1**(1), 53–61.

48 Changes in first-year university students' learning strategies following a semester long in-context learning support programme

Barbara de la Harpe,[1] Alex Radloff and Lesley Parker
Curtin University of Technology, Perth, Western Australia

48.1 Overview

This chapter reports research focused on the implementation and evaluation of a support programme aimed at developing first-year university students' repertoire of learning strategies and metacognitive skills. The program was provided for a group of first-year Education students ($n = 43$), and was presented by the discipline teacher as an integral part of the first semester Educational Psychology core course. It included an emphasis on goal-setting and time management, reading and writing strategies, preparing for tests and examinations, and managing test anxiety. At the beginning of the semester, data on all ($N = 128$) first-year students' reported use of learning strategies in high school was gathered using the Pintrich et al. (1991) Motivated Strategies for Learning Questionnaire (MSLQ). At the end of the semester, all students again completed the MSLQ and a sample of 21 were interviewed. Analysis of the data revealed that, in comparison to studying at high school, students in the learning support class reported using more cognitive learning strategies (rehearsal, organization and elaboration), especially rehearsal, and more metacognitive control strategies (planning, monitoring and evaluating), by the end of the first semester at university. In contrast, students in the regular Educational Psychology class reported using fewer organization and elaboration strategies and fewer metacognitive control strategies, in comparison to studying at high school. The implications of these findings for improving students' ability to be effective learners are discussed with specific reference to the role of rehearsal in learning, the tension between content and process in the curriculum, and the instructor's role in facilitating first-year students' learning at university in the current context of higher education.

48.2 Background

Academic studying is often characterized as an isolated and individual activity that takes place in a relatively ill-defined environment. Students are rarely given either directions for, or instruction in, what or how to study (Pressley, Woloshyn, Lysynchuk, Martin, Wood and Willoughby, 1990; Tait and Entwistle, 1996). Thus, self-initiated, self-defined and self-regulated effort is required (Thomas and Rohwer, 1986).

Weinstein (1987), among others, argues that, for students to perform successfully in this environment they need to have an organized knowledge base, knowledge about cognition, the ability to exercise control over learning and thinking, and fluency and flexibility of thought – in short, a well-developed set of learning strategies. Weinstein suggests that

> "autonomous learners need the strategies required for effective management of learning. Without them students cannot take responsibility for their own learning or their role in the teaching-learning act."

> (Weinstein, 1987, p. 595)

Overall, there are indications that possessing a repertoire of learning strategies and being metacognitive about learning enables students to develop the appropriate strategies to assist their learning, and therefore, to become more effective learners (Baird and White, 1984; Dart and Clarke, 1991; Kirkpatrick, Fuller and Chalmers, 1993; Pintrich, De Groot and Garcia, 1992; Pintrich and Johnson, 1990; Volet, 1991; Weinstein, 1988; Zimmerman and Pons, 1986). Furthermore, the evidence overwhelmingly favours the conclusion that many strategies that improve academic performance can be taught to students (Borkowski, Carr, Rellinger and Pressley, 1990; McKeachie, Pintrich, Lin and Smith, 1986). However, such help is rarely given (Applebee, 1986; Durkin, 1979; Goodlad, 1984; May, 1986; Moely, Hart, Santulli, Leal, Johnson, Rao and Burney, 1986; Schneider and Pressley, 1989). If it is agreed that helping students to become effective learners is an important educational goal, then helping them develop the competencies and attitudes needed for self-directed learning is imperative (Weinstein, 1987). In fact, Mckeachie, Pintrich, Lin and Smith (1986) state that

> "every course should help students become aware of strategies for learning and problem solving. An explicit goal of education throughout the curriculum should be to facilitate the development both of learning strategies and problem solving skills and of effective strategies for their use."

> (McKeachie *et al.*, 1986, p. 1)

A small number of learning support programmes have been used successfully to develop students' learning strategies and metacognitive skills. These have focused on the implementation of strategies within the context of students' disciplinary learning (Biggs, 1985; Dart and Clarke, 1991; Fuller, Chalmers and Kirkpatrick, 1994; Volet, 1991; Weinstein, 1987; Zimmerman and Bandura, 1994). Weinstein (1987) refers to this approach as implementing a metacurriculum which involves the teaching of learning strategies while teaching the content area of the discipline. Hadwin and Winne (1996) suggest that an effective context for learning study tactics and strategies, in contrast to stand-alone study skills or developmental reading courses, is one where students are able to determine the utility of the tactics and strategies in relation to their own learning goals and the course content. Further, they believe that a more comprehensive view of teaching study strategies includes teaching learners about setting learning goals as well as a range of alternative strategies that may be strategically used in order for them to reach their goals. They suggest integrating students' work in their regular courses with instruction about study strategies. They state that to learn and hone study tactics and strategies students must work with real academic content and

> "that higher education should not merely teach students knowledge in curricular subjects . . . Institutions should also provide means for students to develop adaptable strategies with which to pursue knowledge and solve problems during and after postsecondary experiences."

> Hadwin & Winne, 1996, (p. 1).

Furthermore, Tait and Entwistle (1996) suggest that, for study advice to have maximum impact, it needs to be included as an essential part of the course and provided as soon as the need becomes apparent. Hattie, Biggs and Purdie (1996) recommend that learning strategy training other than for simple memorisation, should:

- take place in the context of subject teaching rather than in counselling or remedial centres;

- take place in the context of subject teaching rather than in counselling or remedial centres;

- use tasks related to the content being learned emphasising the conditions under which the strategy works best; and

- encourage learners to be active and metacognitively aware.

Learning support programmes should, therefore, be designed to assist learners to become effective and realistic managers of their learning in the context of the subjects they are studying. Moreover, for reasons pertaining to fairness and equity, all students should be assisted in their endeavours to understand the material presented. Weinstein (1987) believes that, contrary to some teachers' opinions, teachers have many opportunities to teach learning strategies while simultaneously teaching the subject content.

The study reported here outlines the impact of a one semester in-context learning support programme on first-year students' learning strategy use. The findings presented form part of a larger study focusing on increasing theoretical and practical understanding of student learning at the tertiary level. The larger study involved implementing a year long programme to assist first-year university students to be effective learners in the context instructor's and students' perspectives, the outcomes of the programme.

48.3   Method

Participants in the study were first-year Education students undertaking either Early Childhood, Primary or Secondary programmes. Students were enrolled in an Educational Psychology course, Ed 101, Growth and Development, a compulsory first-semester, first-year subject. The course involved three hours of contact time per week – a one-hour lecture and two-hour tutorial. Lectures focused on the main topics relating to human development. Tutorial sessions were used for activities dealing with the designated topic set for the week which normally expanded on the ideas presented in the lecture and were supported by the prescribed readings from the set textbook. Assessment comprised two written project reports together worth 40 marks, three short answer tests worth 10 marks each, and a final multiple choice examination worth 30 marks.

At the beginning of the semester students were randomly assigned into six tutorial groups with approximately 20–25 students per group. Students' ages ranged from 17 to 45 years (M = 20.42, SD = 5.85), with 80.5% being less than 21 years of age. Eighty-eight percent of the group were female and approximately 80% were school leavers. Permission was obtained to implement a learning support programme with two classes which were taught by the first author as part of her normal teaching responsibilities. The remaining four classes were taught in the conventional way and are referred to as the regular group.

Students in the learning support group were informed in the first tutorial that the instructor was integrating learning support in their tutorial classes, and that, based on the literature, the method should be at least as effective if not better than the more traditional methods of teaching content only. Students were given the opportunity to change to another class if they did not wish to participate in the learning support programme. All however, agreed to be involved in the programme.

The learning support programme was based on an integrated cognitive, behavioural and social learning theoretical approach. It aimed to increase students' repertoire of learning strategies, and to develop their metacognitive skills in the context of their discipline. Underlying both the approach adopted and the strategies selected was the view that the learners are active participants in learning and that learning involves a change in the way learners think, feel and behave. Further, the instructor adopted an eclectic and pragmatic approach. Thus, while it was considered essential for both the strategies selected and the approach adopted to be theoretically validated and located in an accepted theoretical perspective, the overriding imperative was to select strategies which research has shown have the greatest likelihood of being successful.

The learning support programme focused on the role of goals for learning, reinforcement, self-management, modelling, practice with feedback, resource management, group work, cognitive learning strategies (rehearsal, elaboration, organization), and metacognitive learning strategies (planning, monitoring, evaluating and reflecting). The instructor endeavoured to ensure that students were informed and active participants in their own learning. Further, the selection of the learning support strategies and the approach adopted to teach them all encouraged group interaction, open discussion, personal reflection and self-reinforcement.

In order to evaluate the effectiveness of the learning support programme, data were gathered using both quantitative and qualitative methodologies. Quantitative data were gathered by means of the Motivated Strategies for Learning Questionnaire (MSLQ) administered at the beginning and at the end of the semester. The MSLQ, a standardized instrument comprising two sections namely, a motivation section and a learning strategies section, is an 81-item self-report questionnaire designed to assess university students' motivational orientations and their use of different learning strategies (Pintrich, Smith, Garcia and McKeachie, 1991; Pintrich, Smith, Garcia and McKeachie, 1993). A summary of the MSLQ scales relating to the learning strategies section and an example item for each subscale are shown in Table 48.1.

Results of statistical analyses suggest that the MSLQ scales represent a coherent, conceptual and empirically validated framework for assessing student motivation and use of learning strategies in the tertiary classroom (Pintrich, Smith, Garcia and McKeachie, 1993).

Data from those participants who completed the MSLQ at the beginning and end of the semester ($n = 128$, F = 113 and M = 15) were analysed using SPSS. In presenting the quantitative data, estimates of effect sizes were used following Carver (1996) who believes that standard errors and effect sizes should be used in place of tests of statistical significance. Therefore, in line with this currently favoured approach (Hattie, Biggs and Purdie, 1996; Tatsuoka, 1993), effect sizes were calculated by dividing the difference between the pretest and posttest mean scores by the common within-group standard deviation. Furthermore, to ensure that the sample size did not bias the effect size calculated, a correction factor was used to produce an unbiased effect size estimator. The correction factor was a multiplier J, which depended on the degrees of freedom for the standard deviation in the denominator of the effect size (Hedges, Shymansky and Woodworth, 1989).

Learning strategies		
Cognitive		
	rehearsal	When studying for this class, I practice saying the material to myself over and over.
	elaboration	When I study for this class, I pull together information from different sources, eg. lectures, readings, discussions.
	organisation	When I study the readings for this course I outline the material to help me organise my thoughts.
	critical thinking	I often find myself questioning things I hear or read in this course to decide if I find them convincing.
Metacognitive		
	metacognitive self-regulation	before I study new material thoroughly I often skim it to see how it is organised (planning).
		I ask myself questions to make sure I understand the material I have been studying in this class (monitoring).
		If course materials are difficult to understand I change the way I read the material (adapting).
Resource management		
	time and study	I make good use of my study time for this course.
	effort regulation	Even when course materials are dull and uninteresting, I manage to keep working until I finish.
	peer learning	When studying for this course, I often try to explain the material to a classmate or a friend.
	help-seeking	I ask the instructor to classify concepts I don't understand well.

Table 48.1   Examples of the scales, subscales and items in the learning strategies section of the Motivated Strategies for Learning Questionnaire (MSLQ)

Qualitative data gathering involved interviewing a sample of students ($n = 21$, F = 17, M = 4) at the end of the semester. The interviews, which were conducted by the first author, were semi-structured and sought students' perceptions of the teaching context and the method they used when doing their set tasks for the course. Questions included: 'In Ed. 101, for project One (remember Piaget) you were asked to conduct an experiment and then to write a report out of class time. Can you explain the particular method you used to plan and write the report?'; 'In Ed 101, you had to complete three short answer tests. Please explain the method you used for preparing for the these tests.'; and 'Please think back to the final exam in Ed 101. Please explain how you went about preparing for the exam.' With the permission of the interviewee, interviews were taped, with each interview taking approximately 45 minutes. Findings relating to the strategies students used when learning for their tests and examinations only are reported in this chapter.

Interviews were transcribed and then coded and analysed using QSR NUD•IST (Non-numerical Unstructured Data Indexing, Searching and Theorizing), a software package designed to facilitate analysis of unstructured data (such as interviews) according to the researcher's theoretical and conceptual needs (Richards and Richards, 1991). NUD•IST is considered to be one of the best programs available for qualitative data analysis and "ranks as one of the top two or three programs available for coding-oriented data analysis" (Weitzman and Miles, 1995 p. 256). A theory-driven approach was used when coding the responses. Categories were derived from the conceptual framework underpinning the MSLQ (Pintrich, Smith, Garcia and McKeachie, 1991) and the literature on student learning. These are summarized in Table 48.2.

strategy	description for tests and examination
rehearsal	repeating, underlining, highlighting, verbatim note taking
elaboration	paraphrasing, summarising, creating analogies, generative note taking
organisation	selecting main idea, clustering, outlining, ordering, diagramming
planning	goal setting, analysing task, activating prior knowledge, skimming, generating questions
monitoring	self-testing, self-questioning, tracking attention
evaluating	re-reading, reviewing, fine tuning and adjusting cognitive activities
time appropriate	scheduling, timetabling, effective use of study time
time inappropriate	lack of scheduling, leaving study to last minute,
effort regulation	effort attribution, self-talk, self-reinforcement, persistence
peer learning	collaborating, discussing, sharing ideas
help seeking	seeking assistance from teacher, peers, or others

Table 48.2   Description of the learning strategies used by students when studying for the tests and the examination

48.4   Findings

Outcomes of the analysis of the MSLQ and interview data are presented below.

48.4.1   MSLQ

Students' responses to the MSLQ related specifically to the learning strategies they used at high school (pre-questionnaire) or during their first semester at university in their Educational Psychology course (post-questionnaire). Figures 48.1 and 48.2 show the mean responses for students in the learning support and regular groups, respectively.

Differences in learning strategy use by students in the learning support and regular groups, as reported in the pre-questionnaire and the post-questionnaire, are shown as effect sizes in Table 48.3 and Figure 48.3.

As can be seen, effect sizes were more positive for the learning support group than for the regular group for all strategies except critical thinking. Exceptionally large differences for students' reported use of organization, metacognitive self-regulation, and effort regulation strategies and very small differences for their use of help seeking strategies are also shown.

For students in the learning support group, small positive effect sizes were found for their use of rehearsal ($g = 0.31$) and metacognitive self-regulation strategies ($g = 0.32$), while small negative effect sizes were found for their use of time and study environment ($g = -0.23$)

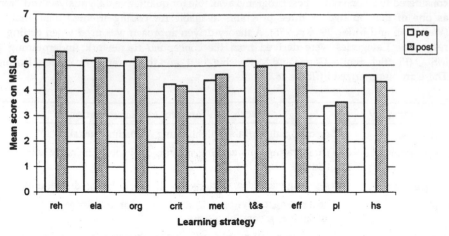

Figure 48.1 Mean MSLQ scores for learning strategy use by learning support group at beginning and end of the semester

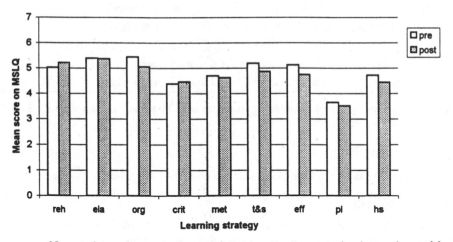

Note. reh = rehearsal, ela = elaboration, org = organisation, crit = critical thinking, met = metacognitive self-regulation, t&s = time and study environment, eff = effort regulation, pl = peer learning, and hs = help seeking.

Figure 48.2 Mean MSLQ scores for learning strategy use by regular group at beginning and end of the semester

Measure	means (*M*)		within *SD*	Effect Size
	pre	post		
rehearsal				
learning support	5.20	5.53	1.08	0.31
regular	5.02	5.21	1.04	0.18
elaboration				
learning support	5.19	5.29	0.88	0.11
regular	5.39	5.37	0.85	-0.02
organisation				
learning support	5.17	5.35	1.13	0.16
regular	5.44	5.06	0.94	-0.40
critical thinking				
learning support	4.28	4.21	0.94	-0.07
regular	4.39	4.47	1.17	0.07
metacognitive self-reg				
learning support	4.42	4.64	0.69	0.32
regular	4.70	4.62	0.73	-0.11
time & study environ				
learning support	5.17	4.95	0.94	-0.23
regular	5.19	4.87	0.89	-0.36
effort regulation				
learning support	4.98	5.06	1.07	0.07
regular	5.12	4.75	1.17	-0.32
peer learning				
learning support	3.40	3.55	1.27	0.12
regular	3.64	3.51	1.23	-0.11
help seeking				
learning support	4.60	4.34	1.18	-0.22
regular	4.72	4.44	1.14	-0.25

Note. learning support $n = 43$; regular group $n = 85$. Positive values indicate higher post than pre values.

Table 48.3   "Pre – Post" Effect Sizes for Learning Strategy use by Students

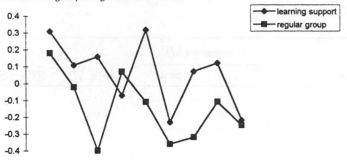

rh ela org crit met t&s effrt pl hs

Note. rh = rehearsal, ela = elaboration, org = organisation, crit = critical thinking, met = metacognitive self-regulation, t&s = time and study environment, effrt = effort regulation, pl = peer learning, and hs = help seeking.

Figure 48.3 "Pre – Post" effect sizes for learning strategy use by learning support and regular groups

and help seeking strategies (g = -0.22). For the regular group however, while no educationally significant[2] positive effect sizes were found, there were small negative effect sizes for students' reported use of organization (g = -0.40), time and study environment (g = -0.36), effort regulation (g = -0.32) and help seeking strategies (g = -0.25).

Overall, therefore, the learning support programme appeared to be associated with an increase in students' use of rehearsal strategies and metacognitive self-regulation strategies (planning, monitoring and evaluating) when studying at university in comparison to when studying at high school. In contrast, being in the regular group did not appear to be associated with any educationally significant increase in students' reported use of learning strategies. While being in either group appeared to be associated with a decrease in students' use of strategies to manage their time and study environments and to seek help, only being in the regular group was also associated with a decrease in students' use of organization and effort regulation strategies.

48.4.2 Interviews

Analysis of student responses to the interview questions relating to the strategies used when learning for the tests and for the examination supported the MSLQ data findings. Overall, in terms of cognitive and metacognitive learning strategies, students in both the learning support and regular groups reported using rehearsal strategies the most. Further, a greater percentage of students in the learning support group reported using elaboration, organization and metacognitive self-regulation strategies. In terms of resource strategies, students from both groups reported using fewer strategies to manage their time and effort, while more students from the learning support group reported using peer learning and help seeking strategies. However, in comparison to the use of cognitive and metacognitive strategies, resource management strategies were mentioned the least.

48.5 Discussion

Based on student responses to the questionnaire and interview, it appears that providing in-context learning support can contribute to first-year students' use of learning strategies and metacognitive skills. Both the MSLQ and interview data suggest that students who participated in the learning support programme showed an increase in the use of the majority of learning strategies, with significant increases in their use of rehearsal and metacognitive self-regulation strategies. These findings suggest that first-year students can increase their use of learning strategies when learning support is provided. While the gains are small, they do indicate that it is possible to get a shift in the way first-year students learn. These findings are especially encouraging given that, as reported by McInnis, James and McNaught (1995), school-leavers (who were the majority of students in the study reported here) are a particularly problematic group of first-year students across the university system who are found to be "relatively less certain of their roles than older students, less diligent in their study habits, and less academically oriented" (p. xi).

An increase in the use of rehearsal strategies could be interpreted as indicating that students adopted a more surface approach to learning, a finding that has been widely reported (see for example Gow and Kember, 1990; Ramsden, Beswick and Bowden, 1986). An alternative explanation, however, may be that, when students have to master a large body of new knowledge in a short space for time, they initially focus on remembering, and, only later, when they have mastered the basic ideas of the new subject, are they able to aim for understanding (Shuell, 1990). Further, according to Biggs, not all students who use rehearsal to ensure recall of information have the same intentions. Some students may use rehearsal strategies to achieve surface learning outcomes while others may intend to acquire the factual knowledge as a basis for achieving deep learning (Biggs, 1993).

The finding that the learning support group students' use of time management and help seeking strategies was lower at university, when compared to high school, was disappointing. It would suggest that more support is needed to encourage students to establish effective time and study patterns and to seek help when needed. In terms of time management, the findings may suggest that students did not need to use effective time management strategies in order to meet the learning demands of the course. Further, students' poor use of time may reflect the difficulties they experience when required to manage their own time at university after being used to a structured school environment.

The findings reported here were based on a learning-support programme provided in one course across a single semester. It could be argued that participating in a one-off programme is not sufficient for most students to develop effective learning strategies and metacognitive skills. Students may benefit more from experiencing learning support in a variety of contexts and over a longer period, which includes enough time to prompt the use of learning strategies and to provide corrective feedback (Weinstein, 1982).

One reason more time is not devoted to providing system-wide support for the development of learning strategies is the resistance which subject specialists may have to the inclusion of learning strategy instruction at the perceived expense of regular course content. Furthermore, many tertiary teachers believe that it is not their duty to teach students how to learn and that, if such support is needed, it should be provided somewhere else. They, therefore, may have little interest or motivation to teach learning skills and processes (Miles, 1988; Wilson, 1988). Students also have expectations that courses will provide them with content knowledge and thus may express concern at what they perceive to be an emphasis on process rather than on content. While it is true that, when including learning strategy instruction, some class time will be diverted from teaching content, teaching learning strategies will improve student' abilities to manage the content. Thus, providing students with a good start in learning will pay dividends as they progress through their courses (Weinstein, 1982). Although the rewards in higher education may not be in devoting time and energy to helping students learn, tertiary teachers and those in leadership positions in management and administration should recognize the benefits to students, staff and the institution of adopting an approach which focuses on teaching both the content and processes of learning. In addition, tertiary teachers, if required, should be given appropriate encouragement and assistance to develop curricular and instructional skills which enable them to focus on both content and the process in their teaching.

The findings of this study suggest that tertiary teachers need to provide more structure in the first semester of study, since, if the learning environment is too ill-defined, students may find it more difficult to be self-directed. Further, students may not know what they are meant to do when asked to study. Students therefore, need to have set tasks and structured activities to complete out of class, as well as prompts in class, in order to scaffold them in the transition phase. Furthermore, the academic context should demand that students use appropriate learning strategies and offer assistance to help them develop these in the context of their discipline. Thus, courses should be designed to provide sufficient levels of cognitive challenge to require students to use effective learning strategies and metacognitive skills, as well as the learning support which they need.

An encouraging finding of the present study is that students are able to change the way they learn provided that the teachers and the context make this "possible, appealing, and/or unavoidable" (Miles, 1988, p. 335), as the quotes below, from students who participated in the learning support programme illustrate.

> Ed101's contribution to my method was the explosion chart [concept map] . . . introduced the explosion charts, because I just used to write them all on study cards but I think the explosion chart is probably easier. [S107]

> That's good actually [reflecting on learning], . . . because that makes us say exactly what we learnt. I like that actually . . . I really like that, I really do because we never had that before...when you sit there and say 'what did you learn today?' you've actually got to think, well did I learn something today? I learnt this and you can tell them and then you think, yes I did lean that today and once you've said it, and once you've told everyone that's what I learnt today, then you believe it yourself . . . [S101]

> Ed101 helped, it made me do it [make a summary]. Sort of if I was doing it myself and you didn't say to do it that way and bring it in that week I probably would have done it kinda two days before the test or something, but because it was in your mind before it was easier to study for it. It was kinda already there from doing it beforehand. [S106]

We believe that putting energy into assisting first-year students to develop their learning strategies, while not always easy, is a worth-while investment. Providing students with learning support can be rewarding for students and their teachers, since, as McInnis, James and McNaught (1995) point out, students are "generally positive, they want to learn and most appreciate the challenge of independence" (p. 125). It is now up to tertiary teachers to ensure that first year students have an appropriate context in which to be effective learners.

Notes

1. Please address correspondence to the first author at delaharpe@educ.curtin.edu.au

2. Effect sizes greater than 0.20 were deemed educationally significant.

48.6   References

Applebee, A.N. (1986) Problems in process approaches: toward a reconceptualisation of process instruction. In A.R. Petrosky and D. Bartholomae (eds), *The Teaching of Writing: Eighty-fifth Yearbook of the National Society for the Study of Education*, Chicago, Illinois: University of Chicago Press, 95–113.

Baird, J.R. and White, R.T. (1984) Improving learning through enhanced metacognition: a classroom study. Paper presented at the meeting of the American Educational Research Association, New Orleans.

Biggs, J. (1993) What do inventories of students' learning processes really measure? a theoretical review and clarification, *British Journal of Educational Psychology*, **63**, 3–19.

Biggs, J.B. (1985) The role of metalearning in study processes, *British Journal of Educational Psychology*, **55**, 185–212.

Borkowski, J.G., Carr, M., Rellinger, E. and Pressley, M. (1990) Self-regulated cognition: interdependence of metacognition, attributions, and self-esteem. In B.F. Jones and L. Idol (eds), *Dimensions of Thinking: Review of Research*, Hillsdale, New Jersey: Erlbaum.

Carver, R.P. (1996) The case against statistical significance testing, revisited, *Journal of Experimental Education*, **61**(4), 287–92.

Dart, B.C. and Clarke, J.A. (1991) Helping students become better learners: a case study in teacher education, *Higher Education*, **22**, 317–35.

Durkin, D. (1979). What classroom observations reveal about reading comprehension instruction, *Reading Research Quarterly*, **14**, 481–538.

Fuller, R., Chalmers, D. and Kirkpatrick, D. (1994) Teaching university students learning and study strategies in context: an experimental study. Paper presented at the HERDSA Annual Conference, Canberra, July.

Goodlad, J.I. (1984) *A Place Called School*, New York: McGraw-Hill.

Gow, L. and Kember, D. (1990) Does higher education promote independent learning? *Higher Education*, **19**, 307–22.

Hadwin, A.F. and Winne, P.H. (1996) Study strategies have meager support: a review with recommendations for implementation, *Journal of Higher Education*, **67**(6), 1–17.

Hattie, J., Biggs, J. and Purdie, N. (1996) Effects of learning skills interventions on student learning: a meta-analysis, *Review of Educational Research*, **66**(2), 99–136.

Hedges, L., Shymansky, J.A. and Woodworth, G. (1989) *Modern Methods of Meta-analysis*, Washington: National Science Teachers Association.

Kirkpatrick, D., Fuller, R. and Chalmers, D. (1993) But it's harder this way. Paper presented at the *Australian Association for Research in Education*, November, Fremantle, Western Australia.

May, W.T. (1986) Teaching students how to plan: the dominant models and alternatives, *Journal of Teacher Education*, **37**, 6–12.

McInnis, C., James, R. and McNaught, C. (1995) *First Year on Campus: A Commissioned Project of the Committee for the Advancement of University Teaching*, Canberra: Australian Government Publishing Service.

McKeachie, W.J., Pintrich, P.R., Lin, Y. and Smith, D.A.F. (1986) *Teaching and Learning in the College Classroom: A Review of the Research Literature* (Technical report No. 86-B-001.0), National Center for Research to Improve Postsecondary Teaching and Learning, University of Michigan.

Miles, C. (1988) Cognitive learning strategies: implications for college practice. In C.E. Weinstein, E.T. Goetz and P.A. Alexander (eds), *Learning and Study Strategies: Issues in Assessment, Instruction, and Evauation*, San Diego: Academic Press, 333–47.

Moely, B.E., Hart, S.S., Santulli, K., Leal, L., Johnson, T., Rao, N. and Burney, L. (1986) How do teachers teach memory skills? *Educational Psychologist*, **21**, 55–72.

Pintrich, P.R., De Groot, E.V. and Garcia, T. (1992) Student motivation and self-regulated learning in different classroom contexts. Paper presented at the *XXV International Congress of Psychology*, August 1992, Brussels, Belgium.

Pintrich, P.R. and Johnson, G.R. (1990) Assessing and improving students' learning strategies. In M.D. Svinicki (eds), *New Directions for Teaching and Learning: The Changing Face of College Teaching*, San Francisco: Jossey-Bass, 83–91.

Pressley, P., Woloshyn, V., Lysynchuk, L.M., Martin, V., Wood, E. and Willoughby, T. (1990) A primer for research on cognitive strategy instruction: the important issues and how to address them, *Educational Psychology Review*, **2**, 1–58.

Ramsden, P., Beswick, D. and Bowden, J. (1986) Effects of learning skills interventions on first year university students' learning, *Human Learning*, **5**(15), 151–64.

Richards, T. and Richards, A. (1991) *Data Base Organisation for Qualitative Analysis: The NUDIST System*, Technical Report No. 18/91, Melbourne, Australia: La Trobe University.

Schneider, W. and Pressley, M. (1989) *Memory Development between 2 and 20*, New York: Springer Verlag.

Shuell, T.J. (1990) Phases of meaningful learning, *Review of Educational Research*, **60**(4), 531–47.

Tait, H. and Entwistle, N. (1996) Identifying students at risk through ineffective study strategies, *Higher Education*, **31**, 97–116.

Tatsuoka, M. (1993) Effect size. In G. Keren and C. Lewis (eds), *A Handbook for Data Analysis in the Behavioral Sciences: Methodological Issues*, Hillsdale, New Jersey: Lawrence Erlbaum Associates, 461–79.

Thomas, P.R. and Rohwer, W.D.J. (1986) Academic studying: the role of learning strategies, *Educational Psychologist*, **21**(1 and 2), 19–41.

Volet, S.E. (1991) Modelling and coaching of relevant metacognitive strategies for enhancing university students' learning, *Learning and Instruction*, **1**, 319–36.

Weinstein, C. (1982) Learning strategies: the metacurriculum, *Journal of Developmental and Remedial Education*, **5**, 6–10.

Weinstein, C. (1987) Fostering learning autonomy through the use of learning strategies, *Journal of Reading*, **30**(7), 590–5.

Weinstein, C.E. (1988) Assessment and training of student learning strategies. In R.R. Schmeck (eds), Learning Strategies and Learning Styles, *New York: Plenum Press, 291–315.*

Weitzman, E.A. and Miles, M.B. (1995) *Computer Programs for Qualitative Data Analysis*, London: Sage Publications.

Wilson, J.E. (1988) Implications of learning strategy research and training: what it has to say to the practitioner. In C.E. Weinstein, E.T. Goetz and P.A. Alexander (eds), *Learning and Study Strategies: Issues in Assessment, Instruction, and Evaluation*, San Diego: Academic Press, 323–31.

Zimmerman, B.J. and Bandura, A. (1994) Impact of self-regulatory influences on writing course attainment, *American Educational Research Journal*, **31**(4), 845–62.

Zimmerman, B.J. and Pons, M.M. (1986) Development of a structured interview for assessing student use of self-regulated learning strategies, *American Educational Research Journal*, **23**, 614–28.

49 Improving the teaching and learning experiences of overseas students

Susan Hughes and Gina Wisker
Anglia Polytechnic University

49.1 Overview

In the current higher education funding situation in the UK, overseas students can provide valuable income for resource constrained universities. In addition the development of franchising and partnership arrangements between home universities and overseas higher education providers has enabled an increasing number of international students to study in the UK or to follow a UK accredited course within their home institution. There have been a number of consequences of such policies, from increased competition between universities vying to attract these students, to individual tutors being faced with much larger groups of overseas students than previously encountered and experiencing any additional challenges that this represents. Previous research has suggested students studying in a foreign country can appear to underperform in relation to their ability, e.g. Church (1982) suggested that the functioning of 15-20% of international students might be impaired.

The concept that students studying in a foreign country may encounter problems is not new, neither is the idea that these international students may present problems or challenges to their host institutions and teachers. This is shown in the use of the negative term 'foreign student syndrome' coined by Ward in 1967. With the increasing importance of overseas students in a UK higher education system where greater emphasis is being placed on quality, it is now time for universities to review their approaches to and provision for overseas students, to better enable these students to achieve quality outcomes in their studies. A study carried out at Anglia Polytechnic University (APU) 1996-97 took the researchers' own experiences with international students and, in the light of established research, attempted to discover relationships between students' learning, teaching and learning strategies and institutional practices.

49.2 Research background

Previous reseach involving overseas students has tended to fall into two categories, i.e. research into culture shock and associated problems, e.g. Furnham (1993), Sandhu (1994) and research into the learning styles or approaches to study adopted by these students e.g. Biggs (1991), Kember and Gow (1991). Of the first type emphasis has been placed on the problems that students experience, e.g. Dyal and Chan (1985) and Ebbin and Blackenship (1986) found that international students, especially females, were at greater risk of self-reported stress-related symptoms than home students and the most frequently reported health problems of international students were: insomnia; anxiety and depression. Students from a variety of ethnic backgrounds have reported racism or at least racially orientated awkwardness (Harris, 1995). Sandhu (1994) has suggested that there are two main types of factor that cause problems for international students, firstly, intrapersonal factors, i.e. factors within the individual such as a profound sense of loss, sense of inferiority, threats to cultural identity and perceived hatred and discrimination. Secondly interpersonal factors, i.e. involving other people, such as communication problems due to lack of language and social skills, culture shock as they experience new expectations and social norms and the loss of their normal social support systems.

Of the second type of research emphasis has been placed on determining the styles of learning or the approaches to study adopted by overseas students. Attention has been paid in particular to non-western, often Asian students. Of research undertaken on Asian students, e.g. Biggs (1991) and Samuelowicz (1987), the evidence suggests that their approach to learning is characterized by rote memory learning rather than by learning to understand and that they tend to adopt a reproducing orientation and surface approach to understanding. In Samuelowicz's study the academic staff involved saw the lack of poor development of analytical, integrating, problem-solving skills as a consequence of the adoption, by the students of a reproducing, atomistic, surface approach to learning. However this view of the Asian learner has been challenged. Kember and Gow (1991) have suggested that anecdotal observations of rote learning in Asian students may be explained more by the nature of the curriculum and the teaching environment they experience rather than an inherent characteristic of the students themselves.

Samuelowicz believes that the behaviour of Asian students can be explained by educational practices in their home countries. In support of this Harris (1995) has stated that the education systems in many pacific rim countries value a highly deferential approach to teachers and place considerable emphasis on rote learning and that this promotes surface or reproductive learning. It would therefore appear that the previous educational experiences of students can have a profound effect on their learning style and approaches to study.

It could also be argued that overseas students, who have been used to adopting a surface approach to learning find it very difficult to change due to the very pressures they suffer when studying in a foreign country. Harris (1995) suggests that 'The financial investment which their stay in the UK represents will not increase the likelihood of risky educational behaviour on their part.' Therefore the students do not dare to reject an approach that has served them well in the past but persevere in the hope that the use of these methods will result in success. Harris also suggests 'It is . . . probable that the experience of being an overseas student itself encourages a cautious serialist approach to learning.' Individuals who are trying to cope with all the new and unfamiliar aspects of living and studying in a foreign country may be forced to take an approach that aids survival but does not allow for a more integrative view of their studies. This is, of course, exacerbated in modular systems. Harris has suggested that it is possible to encourage students to adapt to more participative forms of teaching and learning but that it requires the use of carefully planned training programmes and additional support.

49.3   The study

The experiences of academic staff within Anglia Polytechnic University (APU) have mirrored the experiences reported in Samuelowicz's study. Concerns expressed by tutors, and often by the students themselves, have been cultural and language difficulties, approaches to learning and assessment, level of class participation and skills of criticism and analysis. Students often appear to adopt a surface approach to learning and have difficulty becoming independent learners. In addition students are sometimes disappointed by their performance which does not always appear to match their expectations. As a result a research project was established within APU the main aims of which were: to investigate the approaches to study adopted by overseas students on their arrival in the UK; to involve these students actively in monitoring both any changes taking place in these approaches and their overall progress; to investigate cultural factors that may influence their experiences at APU and finally as a result of the research, devise a number of support and training strategies to be adopted for both current and future overseas students and to suggest changes and developments in teaching, learning, assessment and institutional practices to better enable the quality learning of these students.

49.4 Context and design of research

APU is a multi-site institution which operates an undergraduate modular scheme. Currently 4.5% of the full-time student population are overseas students. Many other international students study on franchised degrees in their home countries while others attend at APU for relatively small parts of their courses. Due to the split site and the interests of the researchers concerned the project, which is the start of a much more comprehensive study, was carried out in two parts. The first part was a single school study, concentrating on the experiences of undergraduate students, from one country, Malaysia and in one particular academic subject area, Business Studies, based at the Chelmsford Campus. The second was more widely based, was a pilot study looking at students from a range of academic areas and cultures and concentrated primarily on their learning experiences.

49.5 Part I

The Business Studies department has always recruited a significant number of overseas students and being aware of their needs has instituted and developed, over a number of years, a specifically targeted induction programme. However in the last three years there has been a marked increase in the number of Malaysian students entering directly into the final year of the undergraduate degree programme from two in 1994/5 to 86 in 1996/97. This group of Malaysian students constitute 45% of the final year. They are an important source of income for both the department and the university and it is expected that similar cohorts will continue to join the degree programme for the next few years. These students are not a homogenous group, they currently come from two higher education institutions (Institutions A and B) which appear to have differing approaches to HE. They also come from the three main Malaysian ethnic groups, i.e. Malay, Chinese and Indian, have different religious backgrounds and have experienced an educational and social system that favours the Bumiputra or ethnic Malays. In addition these students have only eight months of study in the UK, they need therefore to settle in and become effective learners in their new educational environment as quickly as possible. This project was set up to find ways of helping the students achieve this goal.

A range of both quantitative and qualitative research methods were used. This included the administration of Entwistle's 64 item Approaches to Study Inventory (ASI) to both Malaysian students on their arrival and final-year home students for comparison purposes. A series of focus group discussions with the students were carried out throughout the year. Interviews and discussions were held with teaching staff. Students' results were reviewed and a research log kept. As a result of this research a wealth of material was obtained.

The results of the ASI were interesting and, to some extent, unexpected. Of particular interest was that both groups of Malaysian students achieved mean scores for 'Deep Approach to Learning' that were higher than those achieved by home students. This suggested that the Malaysian students were more inclined to take a deep approach to study. In support of this Malaysian students from Institution A had a lower mean score for 'Surface Aproach' than the home students. However the Malaysian students did exhibit the highest scores for 'Strategic' and 'Reproducing Orientation' although the standard deviation for the latter was very wide as it was also for the 'Meaning Orientation' score where the home students once again produced the lowest scores.

Interestingly these results did not support the experiences of the teaching staff as reported earlier. However it should be noted that teaching staff felt that the students from Institution A were better prepared and more able to adapt to teaching and learning in the UK, this may reflect a history of close cooperation with APU. Further research is being undertaken on these figures, however they do appear to suggest that these particular Malaysian students are more likely to adopt a deep approach to learning than some previous research would suggest, although these results would support Kember and Gow's position.

The focus groups also produced interesting results, some of which reflected previous research. The topics that were raised by the students most frequently in the early discussions were: the physical and cultural shock of being in a different environment; the weather; the feeling of disorientation; the awareness of gender differences; their high levels of motivation; their previous educational experiences; housing; finances; food; shopping and differences in religious practice. They were also very concerned over aspects of personal safety, e.g. dark, early winter evenings. They were also very keen to establish relationships with other students but were encountering problems of acceptance. With respect to their studies they were very aware of the differences between their previous and current educational experiences and were concerned that tutors should take this into account. It was very clear that they did not separate their experiences in the college environment from those outside but felt that all factors played a part in how well they were adapting.

Focus groups held later in the year showed clear evidence of students adapting to life in the UK and in APU. They reported that they felt much happier now they 'knew the system'. Many tutors were now more aware of their situation and as a result had adapted their style and or pace of presentation and management of learning situations. This show of concern had helped the students. They reported feeling much more at ease concerning participation in tutorial and seminar sessions. However they still expressed concern about the difficulties they had making friends outside their own group and the continued problems with the seeming inability or unwillingness of some home students to accept them as full group members in a group work situation.

As a result of these findings and those obtained from the other qualitative methods, five main issues on which action was required were identified. These were: the preparation for study in the UK and APU; the use of language; the socialisation of students; guidance on study in a specific academic area, in this case Business Studies; and finally issues relating to staff and staff development.

Preparation for study appeared to fall into two parts, i.e. academic preparation and the preparation or orientation for the study context. However each appeared to have a profound influence on the other. The previous educational experience of the students, especially those from Institution B appeared not to prepare them for the approach to their studies that they are expected to take within APU. Despite the results of the ASI, it appeared to teaching staff that these students take a surface approach to studying and have difficulty in thinking critically and effectively analysing and evaluating information and argument. It would appear that the students feel that they also need to be prepared more effectively for the physical or contextual aspects of their study.

In spite of the provision of language classes, the use of language also proved to be a major area of concern, in particular one raised by staff. Studying in a second language is a daunting prospect for most students but entering directly into the final-year compounds any language problems. Both students and staff mentioned problems with spoken English. The students said that although they could follow formal teaching sessions well, it was sometimes difficult for them to follow interactions between teachers and home students. Therefore tutorials and other interactive sessions could cause problems for them, this supports previous findings by Bilbow (1989). Teaching staff also expressed concern over the standard of written English, however, the students themselves did not necessarily agree with this!

Socialization was an issue raised by all students. They were very appreciative of the help they had been given, especially in the induction period, but felt that they needed more assistance in this area and that if they could settle more easily into student life at APU, this would have a direct, positive, influence on their studies. They reported particular problems attempting to form friendships with other students as most final-year home students were part of well-established friendship groups. They reported finding other overseas students and mature home students more approachable. One important point, mentioned earlier, was the rejection they sometimes experienced when working in groups.

An area of prime importance is that concerning guidance on studying in the Business Studies area. It is expected that final-year students will understand the nature and forms of assessment used in Business Studies and an understanding of the theoretical approaches to the subject area is also required. This understanding was lacking in some of the Malaysian students and they needed assistance in this area.

Several issues relating to staff were raised by both the students and the staff themselves although interestingly they tended to be two distinct sets of issues. The students stated that they would like to get to know their teachers more and to meet and establish a relationship with them before teaching starts. They would also like to see more understanding, by their teachers, of their situation, taking into account aspects such as the pace of presentation and the use of inappropriate examples. Staff, on the other hand, had other concerns, these ranged from a concern for the maintenance of standards to the advisability of providing extra tuition and support for the students. They also expressed concern over their lack of understanding of the culture to which these students belong, the acknowledgement that culture and gender issues exist but an ignorance of what these issues might be.

During the academic year a number of support strategies and structures were developed to address some of these issues, e.g. the appointment of a Malaysian Liaison Officer. In the process of developing these strategies some additional issues were raised, e.g. extra language sessions were offered but students often had to be encouraged to recognize their problems in this area. Open access study sessions were made available but this highlighted student problems with time management and the cultural difficulty of approaching a tutor direct and asking questions that could result in either the tutor or student 'losing face'.

As a result of this study a number of key issues involving overseas students in the Business Studies degree programme have been identified and a new induction and year long development programme has been created for those Malaysian students joining the final year of the degree in September 1997. In addition further staff development is envisaged, building upon successful sessions held in the current academic year.

49.6   Part II

The second part of the study was university-wide and concentrated on the learning experiences of overseas students in different subject areas, and on the perceptions of and strategies used by staff to enable students' learning achievements. The ASI was administered to a third-year group of Malaysian undergraduates on English and Education programmes, first-year Greek Cypriots on a Music programme and Malaysian students on a nursing programme validated and taught by APU staff in Malaysia. Results of the ASI, although not statistically significant matched those of Part I, in that students emerged as taking a largely Deep Approach and having both a Meaning and Reproducing orientation. This result surprised staff working with them who frequently perceived Malaysian students in particular to be surface learners whose reproducing orientation rather precluded complex, imaginative, reflective, analytical and original work.

Two sets of focus group discussions were held with Malaysian and Cypriot students followed by in-depth interviews with individual Malaysian students over a period of time. Discussions concentrated upon: their approaches to study; perceptions of study demands on APU courses; awareness of how students had to change to fit in and finally an awareness of what could be put in place in teaching, learning and contextual terms to aid mutual understanding and the achievement of graduate learning outcomes. In addition assignments completed by Cypriot, Malaysian and Brunei students were studied and then discussed in focus group and individual interviews.

Early work produced in the new cultural context uniformly showed varieties of confusion over what was demanded by the task set. For both Cypriot and Malaysian students there was a tendency to repeat authoritative materials rather than analyse, critique and provide their own discussions based on critical reading and thinking. In worst cases this was perceived by staff as plagiarism, and in others as lack of engagement with the topic. The students unanimously said that they were unused to debating critically with authorities, needed initial guidance and clarification as to what was expected in their study, in particular in written assignments, and in fact worked very hard, often with a burning interest in the subject.

Students said that they would find models of expected academic essay work useful and explanations about how the academic essay is constructed as a dialogue and argument with authorities and references etc. Strategies for taking useful notes from fast lecture delivery and enormous reading lists were also requested. The tendency of many students interviewed was to take too many unfocussed notes, encouraging regurgitation. Some commented upon the need for structured small group work and advice on working in groups with home students. This reflects findings in Part I. The reticence of some students could mean non-involvement in exploratory talk also limiting intellectual ownership and the ability to work with argument and knowledge which precedes transfer into essays and oral presentations. This does not in itself indicate lack of potential for such skills. Relaxed in focus groups, or over time in individual interviews these students proved themselves articulate, able to take a problem-solving approach, well able to synthesize primary and secondary reading and to argue their own case. This suggests that conditions of trust and a developmental approach might aid student performance.

Like the early assignments of the Malaysian students, the Cypriot student assignments analysed showed problems based on a misunderstanding of what was required. Careful wording of assignment tasks and assessment criteria are necessary.

> Sometimes, for example, they say to make a critic for something, and we didn't know what they wanted just our ideas and we made essay about it and then they say no it's not that we want.

> (Cypriot student)

> Some of them tell us clearly what they want for the next lesson, and its difficult for us because sometimes we don't do things, not because we don't want to but because we didn't understand.

> (Cypriot student)

Other issues concern the language register students need to adopt in written and oral responses, which would also be aided by modelling, lecturers speaking more slowly, and initial explanations of technical terms and subject discourse.

All students reported the usefulness of working in groups with their peers who spoke the same language so that they could process in their mother tongue. Asked whether there were others in their language group and if working with them aids understanding, students agreed that the subject discussion helped enormously. However staff are torn between the need to mix students up so that they can learn to work together and add a social element to study which helps learning (Lewis, 1984), and the need to encourage students to work in their own language groups to aid mutual translation, interpretation and processing at a deeper level.

Students reported the usefulness of initial and ongoing induction and orientation, both academic and emotional and cultural once again reflecting the findings in Part I. Such induction reduces the waste of emotional energy produced by culture shock and helps them concentrate on study (Makepeace, 1989; Oberg, 1960). Students reported the importance of having a personal tutor or someone specifically allocated to work with them to whom they could go for support.

As mentioned earlier, students' previous educational experiences affect their expectations of what will be demanded of them in higher education in the UK and the culture shock of very different expectations and demands can lead to underachievement. The students commented on the differences and lack of guidance:

> Well first of all there was culture shock . . . the style of studying and everything . . . it was like a big leap because it was spoon fed and then suddenly you have to do everything. On my first day when I first came to class I thought they would give us notes or something, but it was like - OK, you have to do this for the next class.

> (Malaysian student)

Reflection, use of secondary sources in a large library, the ways in which students are expected to take lecture notes, work between classes, discuss critically in seminars and then compose written responses are all new.

> I think the reading just left me exhausted and drained . . . I just kept on saying to myself, when is it going to end? Because we never did any research or background reading in Brunei, we never do that. I mean we don't have sufficient books . . . we do have but not the kind that we get here. It's not like - it is really great we have lots to say on this - it's just that we read it, we consume it, and that's it.
>
> I haven't used my High School's library, never, but here I use it all the time, because . . . in high school . . . the teacher's guide us as what we're going to do, but here we

have to do everything for ourselves . . . and about taking notes, in our country all the things that we have to take note were written on the blackboard but here we have to follow the speech of the teacher, and sometimes they speak too fast for us.

(Malaysian student)

The students were in favour of allowing extra time for processing when translating is taking place in their head.

I had some problems with the theory because I read in Greek but I didn't know it in English. I had to translate it and knew something but I didn't couldn't say it.

Cypriot student

This is true of in-class work when discussion and questioning are ongoing and small group work, when they are likely to pause for a longer time than a home-based student, to think through the question and translate a response, and certainly in early assignments and particularly in timed exams.

Socialization issues were very similar to those reported in Part I, including the need to mix and cultural difficulties working with English students. Students find their ability to concentrate and respond to challenge in discussion very difficult if others refuse to work with them. Receiving negative verbal or non-verbal communication from others when they are trying to join in a class with which they are not familiar will act as a negative reinforcement. They will therefore find it more difficult to participate in the future. Students, both home and overseas need some help and guidance when dealing with individuals from other cultures. Home students can be encouraged to act as mentors to overseas students to help them cope with a whole new cultural experience.

49.7   Staff and staff development

Further research was carried out, largely through group discussion, with staff working with overseas students in APU and those teaching on APU validated courses in other countries. The main aim was to determine what kind of difficulties students and staff experience in multicultural learning environments and to identify strategies that have, or could be, developed to improve students' learning experiences.

Most discussions took place in the forum of the 'Professional Development Overseas Group'. This group is a cohesive group of staff many of whom are Malaysian, Indian or non English European. They have used their experiences of being overseas students themselves to help develop effective teaching strategies for current international students. In addition several multi campus staff development sessions were held with a range of staff working with overseas students in a variety of academic areas. It was possible, within these discussion sessions to share experiences, disseminate findings from research and develop suggestions for good practice. These suggestions have ranged from issues relating to preparation, teaching methods and the most effective socialization techniques. Further work is continuing in this staff development area.

49.8   Conclusion

The research undertaken to date has successfully met the main objectives of the study although some of the findings have raised further questions. With respect to approaches to study adopted by overseas students, the results of the ASI in Part I and to a certain extent in

Part II do not appear to match the experiences of the teaching staff. This area is being further researched but it does support, to some extent, Kember and Gow's position. It also suggests that with help and guidance the students may be more open to student centred teaching strategies. This has been confirmed by the experiences of some of the teaching staff and in addition has been reported by the students themselves.

It is also clear from both parts of the study that the more interest and concern shown for the students, whether of an academic or personal nature, the better the overall experience as reported by the students. This adds support to Harris's suggestions. This aspect is also reiterated in the findings of Part I in that the students view their experiences of living and studying in England and in APU as a total experience, i.e. adapting to studying and learning in the UK can not be separated from their other experiences, one aspect influences the other. So when considering the support offered to overseas students it would seem wise not to artificially separate academic, pastoral and day to day living experiences. Therefore in any induction, preparation for study or support system a range of factors need to be addressed including socialization aspects. These aspects could be considered as outside the remit of teaching staff, however the students themselves recognize that if they could 'settle in' more quickly and effectively this would have a positive effect on their studies and therefore their learning experiences.

The students on the whole were very willing to take part in the study and appeared to gain from the experience of further, more in depth contact with a member of the teaching staff. They were also pleased with the recognition of their problems, by the university, that the study represented. The need for adequate preparation for studying in the UK was underlined and results, especially in Part I, also indicated that any preparation that could be undertaken in the students' home institutions also contributed to successful transfer to the UK and APU.

Both parts of the study have resulted in developments which should help to improve the learning experiences of overseas students within APU. They have also identified areas of concern that need to be addressed by the university. This study is the first stage of an extended research programme, it is therefore expected that all relevant issues have not yet been identified and that future research will provide additional guidance on the form that effective support for overseas students should take.

49.9   References

Biggs, J. (1991) Approaches to learning in secondary and tertiary students in Hong Kong: some comparative studies, *Educational Research Journal*, **6**, 27-39.

Biggs, J. (1993) What do inventories of students' learning processes really measure? a theoretical review and clarification, *British Journal of Educational Psychology*, **63**, 3-19.

Bilbow, G.T. (1989) Towards an understanding of overseas students' difficulties in lectures: a phenomenological approach, *Journal of Further and Higher Education*, **13**(3), 85-9.

Crano, S.L. and Crano, W.D. (1993) A measure of adjustment strain in international students, *Journal of Cross Cultural Psychology*, **24**(3), 267-83.

Entwistle, N. (1988) *Styles of Learning and Teaching: An Integrated Outline of Educational Psychology*, David Fulton.

Furnham, A.F. (1993) The adjustment of foreign students, *Higher Education Review*, **26**(1), 11-16.

Harris, R. (1995) Overseas students in the UK university system, *Higher Education*, **29**, 77-92.

Hayes, J. and Allison, C. (1988) Cultural differences in the learning styles of managers,

Management International Review, **28**, 75-80.

Kember, D. and Gow, L. (1991) A challenge to the anecdotal stereotype of the Asian student, *Studies in Higher Education*, **16**(2), 117-28.

Kiley, M. and Meyer, J.H.F. (1996) Indonesian postgraduate students' experiences of and reflections on learning, *Proceedings of the Joint ERA-AARE Conference: Educational Research: Building New Partnerships*, Singapore, 25-29 November.

McNamara, D. and Harris, R. (eds) (1997) *Overseas Students in Higher Education: Issues in Teaching and Learning*, Routledge.

Nulty, D.D. and Barrett, M.A. (1996) Transitions in students' learning styles, *Studies in Higher Education*, **21**(3), 333-45.

O'Donoghue, T. (1996) Malaysian Chinese students' perceptions of what is necessary for their academic success in Australia: a case study at one university, *Journal of Further and Higher Education*, **20**(2), 67-80.

Pong, S.L. (1995) Access to education in peninsular Malaysia: ethnicity, social class and gender, *Compare*, **25**(3), 241-52.

Raaheim, K., Wankowski, J. and Radford, J. (1991) *Helping Students to Learn: Teaching, Counselling and Research*, SRHE

Ramsden, P. and Entwistle, N. (1981) The effects of academic departments on students' approaches to studying, *British Journal of Educational Psychology*, **51**, 368-83.

Ramsden, P. (ed.) (1988) *Improving Learning: New Perspectives*, Kogan Page.

Ramsden P. (1993) Theories of learning and teaching and the practice of excellence in higher education, *Higher Education Research and Development*, **12**(1), 87-106.

Salili, F. and Hau, K.T. (1994) The effect of teachers' evaluative feedback on chinese students' perceptions of ability: a cultural and situational analysis, *Educational Studies*, **20**(2), 223-36.

Samuelowicz, K. (1987) Learning problems of overseas students: two sides to a story, *Higher Education Research and Development*, **6**(2), 121-33.

Sandhu, D.S. (1994) An Examination of the psychological needs of the international student: implications for counselling and psychotherapy, *Journal for the Advancement of Counselling*, **17**, 229-39.

Watkins, D., Reghi, M. and Astilla (1991) The Asian-learner-as-a-rote-learner stereotype: myth or reality, *Educational Psychology*, **11**(1), 21-34.

50 The exploration of tacit knowledge in fashion design education

Alison Shreeve
Senior Lecturer, School of Fashion Design and Technology,
London College of Fashion

50.1   Introduction

Fashion Design education abounds in areas of tacit knowledge (Polanyi, 1958, 1967) linked to skills and the visual hegemony of the design process. The subject is complex including skills of drawing, design, graphic presentation, cutting patterns, making garments, and handling fabrics and machinery to produce an expert finish which is the mark of quality. Many components of these skills can be taught, but there is a fluidity and expertise which is evidenced in a quality performance which cannot be conveyed explicitly (Dormer, 1995).

The primary communication in a design-based activity is visual, with no need for lengthy verbal explanation. This environment does not remain static but evolves in response to technological developments, marketing and retail trends and to style and fashion issues. These are complex, interacting, social contexts which are not explicitly articulated, but within which the designer has to perform.

In education these aspects are presented in a variety of ways, through demonstration, lecture, case studies, simulated industrial experience, practice of skills etc. Much of the teaching employs integrated projects in which the student will design and make in response to a brief. The criteria for success are clearly identified as a list of minimum requirements, together with descriptions which attempt to explain the qualitative criteria. By necessity, these employ a range of words which approximate an indefinite and unarticulated entity which the student has to learn to recognize in order to evaluate and therefore improve their own performance.

We have been attentive to the need to promote the visual display of work in informal and formal situations during the taught day, accompanied by discussion and critical evaluation. Effective feedback is also provided after assessment with the grade conveyed to the student in an academic tutorial with further feedback from group critiques using a selection of successful work which has formed the basis for discussions of quality.

An exercise was devised which attempted to explore the processes which were happening both in the staff assessment of work and the students' learning and recognition of quality in the process of design. It was deemed possible that values could be inculcated by non-verbal means as well as by explicit comments about exemplars. It was decided to employ video to record three members of the course team ranking a selection of flat work (design presentation sheets; sketchbooks; fabric boards) from final-year students in order to illuminate processes involved in recognizing quality.

Eight sets of work with grades covering all assessment bands were used. After the staff ranking the first-year students undertook the same exercise with no peer consultation, following which two discussion groups took place where responses to the work and the exercise of ranking were recorded on video.

Table 50.1 shows the staff rank order of work (represented by letters P-N), Table 50.2 the distribution of students' rank orders in percentage figures and Table 50.3 a ranking from clerical staff undertaking the same exercise. It can be deduced that the recognition of quality is a learned phenomenon; there are clear distinctions between the top and the bottom in regard to quality and that two sets of work in particular (M and R) caused some difficulty in rank evaluation.

1	3	4	5	6	7	8
P/L	M	R	O	Q	S	N

Staff rank order

Table 50.1a

50.2 Indications of tacit knowledge revealed by the video process

Throughout the discussions by both staff and students there were areas which were difficult to express verbally. This is not simply an inability to use language but, probably, it is because verbal language is not the principal conveyor of the information. Students perceive value largely by a tacit, visual learning process. One example of this is provided by a student whose first language is not English who placed S as the lowest rank. When asked why, he made an attempt to justify his decision in plausible critical language, which we deemed an inappropriate explanation. He therefore knew tacitly, but could not express verbally, why he had placed it in the lowest position.

Areas which were difficult to express through words were often hinted at and the sentences were left hanging: 'It's a bit . . .'; 'They're just . . .'; 'There's an element of . . .' . Pauses may be accompanied by gestures suggesting disapproval or an inability to find words, not necessarily implying a value judgement, but seeking others' help in articulating the reasons. Sometimes the help is forthcoming in the expression of support - 'Mmm' - or by placing further suggestions for consideration. Occasionally the gestures are enough to set the value on the work, for example, the dismissive swinging away of a sketchbook which has very little in it except superficial cuttings and careful layout of pasted in material.

A series of phrases emerged which stood as symbols for qualities which were impossible to articulate in any other way. These phrases have to be learned in association with visual qualities and stand for quite complex interpretations. 'In a professional way' conveys a demonstration of presentation and graphic skills to a high standard. The phrase implies that a degree of sophistication was being demonstrated and that there was expert use of tools, materials and concepts.

Phrases were used as a shorthand way to indicate a visual reading and comprehension of the garments as they appeared on paper. These included, 'Design-wise'; 'design ideas'; 'design content'. All the phrases could be used to suggest several things: the way the garments would appear as finished three dimensional products; the aesthetic way they had been considered; the ideas or concepts which the visual structure alluded to; the fashionability of their construction.

		P	L	M	R	O	S	N	Q
highest	1	52	46	2	0	0	0	0	0
	2	35	37	10	12	8	0	0	0
	3	12	4	35	19	17	8	6	0
	4	2	6	29	13	27	13	10	0
	5	0	2	12	13	27	15	27	4
	6	0	4	8	12	12	29	31	6
	7	0	2	4	19	10	21	21	23
lowest	8	0	0	2	12	0	13	6	67

Percentage of students placing subjects P-Q in
ranks 1 - 8

Table 50.1b

	P	L	M	R	O	S	N	Q
1	0	50	0	0	50	0	0	0
2	50	0	17	0	0	0	33	0
3	0	17	17	17	33	17	0	0
4	17	17	17	0	17	0	33	0
5	0	0	0	50	0	17	17	17
6	17	0	17	17	0	17	17	17
7	0	0	33	17	0	50	0	0
8	0	17	0	0	0	0	0	83

Percentage of non students placing subjects P-Q
in ranks 1-8

Table 50.1c

The fundamental aspect of *fashion* design is the notion that it is at the forefront of change. Most design is incremental and in designing for mainstream western fashion markets there are key designers and changes in fabric technology and colour which influence designers. This is the hardest area to pinpoint accurately and 'seeing' whether a design is fashionable is a tacit skill which was indicated by phrases such as 'It's not fashion, but I think there's a market for it'; 'They look dated to me'; 'It's sharper, the most modern of the designs' and 'Its what's happening now', but conversely a similar phrase could be used to indicate non-fashionable design: 'The design is very derivative, it's what's in the shops.' Clearly a balance must be learned by the student in providing designs suited to a commercial context but with a realization of a 'fresh', 'directional' feel.

Other phrases were used to indicate quality and contained complex meanings. For example, 'It's more together' or 'There is that conviction . . . It has a real authority.' At one point a student says of P, one of the highest ranked sets, 'Everything works.' Although the phrases convey positive messages, the cognition in relation to the design activity is tacit. Only a consensual use of such phrases can allow discussion to take place and learning the appropriate use of such phrases must be a part of the design student's increased awareness and articulation of the tacit understanding of quality. It is in learning the appropriate terminology that one may become involved in the explicit demonstration of the professional knowledge which is often tacit, resulting in an increase in confidence (Freeman, 1991). An awareness of how we know what we know allows for greater flexibility in our application and use of that knowledge (Schraw and Moshman, 1995).

A dominant aesthetic quality is indicative of an awareness of fashion. This can be demonstrated in the graphic presentation of the work; by the employment of image and text in certain ways, and by the use of one medium rather than another. This is seldom stated but is contained in words such as 'professional', and in the notion of the fashionable.

Another tacitly understood sense is employed in evaluating, that of touch. The fabric swatches on the design sheets are felt and examined. Their suitability for the accompanying designs are estimated - will the fabric perform in the way the student has suggested, will it make the same shape as the design? The newness or fashionable quality of the fabric is also established both by sight and touch. Is it a fabric which was fashionable several seasons ago or one which is different or in line with the textile predictions? The evaluation by touch is not necessarily accompanied by words.

The reading of design sheets is a complex process and learning would probably improve with more specific discussion. Many of the elements outlined above are part of this 'reading' process, but most fundamental is the ability to visualize the three-dimensional construction of the image as it is presented flat on the page. In a weaker set of work someone says 'She does not understand what she's doing' and 'What does that mean?' This question is accompanied by a gesture which points at the drawing and is asking how the student envisaged constructing the garment. The phrase 'Design-wise one could cut them' implies that one could construct a paper pattern and make the garment from the drawing. This ability to read from the two to the three dimensional may partially account for the erratic positioning of R. Although the verbal and visual messages in the presentation were confusing, the actual garments which constituted the final grades for this work achieved a Distinction. Perhaps those students with a better ability to read the designs placed the work higher. 35% of those students who placed R among the bottom three had been referred in one or more assessments, whereas only 12.5% of similar students placed R within the top three ranks.

The most difficult sets of work to rank were probably those which were not clearly identifiable as high or low. As the discussion above indicates, there were aspects to the work which might have led to confusion and in some cases the presentation of the work was clear, clean and professional which may have been the superficial reason why some students placed it higher, for example, N and O. One of the students in the discussion said that she 'liked' O, it was nicely laid out and easy to see, but as she progressed in her analysis she found less to recommend it and finally said, 'It's a bit boring, it needs more of something to make it more exciting.' The process of having to articulate one's tacit knowing could help to crystallize and possibly to modify one's evaluation. Although there is no clear indication that all tacit knowledge is accessible to conscious reason, it may be feasible to utilize the continuum between the conscious and subconscious to explore such 'knowing' (Reber, 1993). Reading beyond the superficial presentation is so essential to the understanding of the design and it is possibly an area in which much progress could be made to improve learning.

There appears to be no direct correlation between students who achieve high grades and their ability to match the ranking by staff, or an inverse correlation. As there is a very great difference in the pace of learning and in the prior knowledge and experience of students, the correlation may not be evident until the final year of the course, or the ability to 'see' quality may not be fundamental to learning. The study will continue in order to provide a more accurate picture of whether it is the ability to 'see' quality which results in better performance.

50.3   Conclusion

There are areas within fashion design education which are tacit in nature. They belong to the visual and tactile realms, yet are essential components of the realization of quality performance. These tacitly understood qualities are learned and it is possible that the learning process can be improved (Boice, 1993).

The metacognitive process might be explored as an aid to learning. An understanding of the nature of cognition and the tacit dimension could help to increase student self-awareness and to improve self-esteem when effort is employed which often fails to result in improved grades.

The exploration of work which is failing in those areas indicated in the study above could also provide a more accessible comparison than always looking at examples of excellence and might allow self-evaluation of progress which is not solely related to the outcome expressed as a high grade.

More student involvement with the assessment process would also help to improve learning (Ramsden, 1992). Both self- and peer-evaluation are used throughout the course, but greater participation in the examination and evaluation of their own work could improve the use of terminology which is symbolic of those areas of tacit knowledge associated with evaluating quality in the design process. The matching of visual examples with such phrases as 'professional', 'design content' and 'fashionable' could be reinforced; the feedback in such a situation could be immediate.

This study has illuminated areas which require more research and an ongoing reflective examination of the teaching practice in fashion design education is currently being undertaken.

Acknowledgements

I would like to thank Suzi Vaughan, Course Director and Carmel Kelly, for their support and involvement, together with the students of the Fashion Design and Technology course at the London College of Fashion who allowed us to use their work and who took part in the evaluation and discussion sessions. James Rutherford edited and produced the videos used in this study and for presentation at the 5th International Improving Student Learning Symposium.

50.4   References

Boice, R. (1993) Writing blocks and tacit knowledge, *Journal of Higher Education*, **64**(1), 19-54.

Dormer, P. (1994) *The Art of the Maker: Skill and Its Meaning in Art, Craft and Design*, Thames & Hudson, London.

Freeman, D. (1991) To make the tacit explicit - teacher education, emerging discourse and conceptions of teaching, *Journal of Teaching and Teacher Education*,, 7(5-6), 439-54.

Polanyi, M. (1958) *Personal Knowledge*, Routledge & Kegan Paul Ltd., London.

Polanyi, M. (1967) *The Tacit Dimension*, Routledge & Kegan Paul Ltd., London.

Ramsden, P. (1992) *Learning to Teach in Higher Education*, Routledge, London and New York.

Reber, A.S. (1993) *Implicit Learning and Tacit Knowledge: An Essay on the Cognitive Unconscious*, Oxford University Press.

Schraw, G. and Moshman, D. (1995) Metacognitive theories, *Educational Psychology Review*, 7(4), 351-71.

51 The impact of a move to theme or problem-based learning on students' perceptions of their learning

Ranald Macdonald[1]
Centre for Higher Education Practice, The Open University

51.1 Overview

The Breda Business School in the Hogeschool Brabant, Breda, The Netherlands, has taken the decision to adopt a problem- or theme-based approach to learning. In September 1994 the Finance and Accounting Department was the first to make the move, followed by the International Business School in 1996.

This chapter reports briefly on the thinking behind the move but is primarily concerned with the students' perceptions of changes in their learning and how the role of staff has changed. Focus group sessions and questionnaires are being used with students on the programme. The International Management Programme, which is taught in English, enrolled its first students, many of whom are from other European countries, in the new course in September 1996. Most staff are new to the approach and to doing all their teaching in English. The intention is for the study to continue over a period of time to see whether student perceptions of their learning converge or show significant differences.

A separate study is looking at the issues for students learning in another language and under a different educational system. This was reported on at last year's symposium. The research reported in the current chapter is inevitably drawing on the earlier work as theme-based learning may provide a further problem for students for whom studying in English is a challenge in itself.

51.2 Background

The International Management Programme has developed over a number of years in the Breda Business School, Hogeschool Brabant and it is located in the International Business School there. This four-year full-time undergraduate programme is designed to prepare graduates for the increasingly internationalized business world where working with colleagues from different nations, and often in different languages, will become the norm.

The wish to change from a traditional to a problem- or theme-based curriculum was the outcome of discussions by management initiated in 1992 and 1993. The main reason for change was that the old traditional model was no longer seen as providing an effective learning model for individual students. The need to incorporate more communicative/social and professional skills in the study programme emphasized the need for change even further. After extensive discussions at senior management level the members of staff of the Breda Business School were informed and briefed about the proposed change to the educational model.

A clear distinction has to be made between problem-based learning and problem-solving, the former involving the acquisition of knowledge and skills as an integral part of the activities, the latter largely demonstrating what has already been acquired. The model adopted in Breda is closely related to that used at the Maastricht University in The Netherlands.

51.3 The educational model

The educational model used in Breda Business School is based on Problem-Based Learning (PBL) and can best be described as a theme-based approach to curriculum design and delivery. Theme-based learning comprises two elements: problem-based learning, where the emphasis is on the acquisition of knowledge and understanding of theoretical aspects and their application in response to a series of practical problems; and specialist training elements, where students' professional skills and attitudes are developed. The problem-based learning part takes up about 80% of student time (four days a week), the training elements 20%. Additionally, students on the International ManagementProgramme have to study languages.

The Dutch government expects programmes in the Hogescholen to adhere to a set of 'educational requirements' that are drafted after discussion among Heads of Departments, Deans of Business Schools and representatives from business. The educational requirements reflect the outcomes of a graduate leaving from the particular named award.

The contents of the themes are developed by taking the educational requirements and constructing a matrix comprising the elements of the requirements on one axis and eight 'blocks' (themes) on the other. The intention is to cover each element at least once and that a single block forms the basis of a quarter's work.

A block or theme lasts for 10 weeks of which seven are spent on learning activities and the remainder with examinations and, where necessary, reassessment. The learning process is organized in learning cycles, the 'Seven Jump', which start and end with a meeting of a tutorial group, a group of about 12 students and a tutor. The normal length of a learning cycle is about two days (16 hours of study). In the tutor group sessions problems are introduced and discussed, learning objectives are formulated, after which smaller groups of students study theoretical concepts and try to solve the problem. In a second tutor group session, the results are discussed and evaluated .

The student's learning activities are supported by staff with the following additional sessions:

- instructional lectures - two per week;

- training sessions - four hours per week;

- evaluation lectures - one per week.

As a consequence of the limited number of contact hours per week, which have been reduced from an average of 22 previously to 11 now, students are expected to spend about 30 hours per week on self-study, on their own or in small groups.

Whereas previously students had been assessment solely by a final examination, there is now fairly intensive assessment throughout the blocks. For each problem students prepare a group report, one or two will give a presentation and they are given a grade for their contribution to the process. These combine to give half the total mark which is then averaged with the examination mark. Previously students tended to only work hard in the week or so before end of semester examinations. The move to quarters and continuous assessment was partly intended to get them working right from the beginning.

51.4   Methodology

Students were asked to attend specially arranged sessions in their tutor groups at a time when the author was in the Netherlands as he was seen as being neutral by the course team. As a result of this being a time that the students were not used to there was not full attendance. However, four sessions were held to which 36 students in total turned up. The numbers split roughly equally between Dutch and French students with a couple of other nationalities represented.

The purpose of the project was first explained to the students and then they were asked to complete the questionnaire (see Figure 51.1).

Problem Based Learning in Breda Business School

Please answer the questions below **in English**. Your answers will be used in the discussion that will follow. I would like to collect these in at the end.

Thank you for your help.

A. Learning in Problem-Based Learning (PBL)

1.   What do you think of PBL?

2.   How do you learn differently under PBL than under other teaching and learning methods?

B. The role of your tutor in PBL

1.   What is the main role of your tutors in PBL?

2.   How is your tutor's role different from in other teaching and learning methods?

C. Assessment in PBL

1.   How are you assessed in PBL?

2.   How is your learning helped or hindered by the assessment methods used in PBL?

D. Finally: What changes would you like to see made to the system of PBL?

Figure 51.1   Questionnaire

The students took about 20 minutes to complete the questionnaire. The questions were then used as the basis for a focus group session that took a further 20 minutes. The discussion was audio taped and is to be transcribed as the basis for further analysis.

51.5   Initial findings

The raw data was presented to a half-day 'study day' of the staff in Breda who identified areas of strength to be built on and issues which need addressing. A further analysis of the data is being undertaken to theme it more systematically.

Key points which were identified by the students include:

- putting theory into practice;

  A new system which gives you the advantage of not only learning theory but by putting it into practice in the problems or task that you have to solve. I think that you are better prepared for finding a job and that you know more about the reality of these subjects in a job.

- understanding the real world

  I think it is a good way of working, because of concrete cases, we meet the problems as in a company, we learn to work as a team.

- being active, not passive

  It is helped because you now have to be more active, and in this way you learn more.

- learning how to learn

  When putting theory directly into practice you find out that you still don't know everything. You learn by learning and therefore you can better understand the theory.

- freedom in learning

  With PBL we learn by books and ourselves. We can choose what we want to learn. We are more 'free' to study than in normal teaching-learning methods (where the teacher has to be listened to).

- working in groups, giving presentations

  It's a way of studying in which you very much learn how to interact with fellow students and to handle conflicts between each other in order to come to a good result: the report. It is also more interesting than sitting in class and listening to a lecturer, so it keeps you motivated. Motivation is also increased by control on your performance by your fellow students. It learns you to work in a team, to give a good presentation and communication skills, which prepares you better for your career.

- able to make mistakes and learn from them

  My learning is helped by knowing what I'm doing wrong and well and I can develop myself.

- assessment is part of the learning

  We have a clear idea of how we are doing at the moment and this regular assessment makes us able to correct our mistakes.

- the tutor's role is very different

  He doesn't teach us in a formal way, he gives us the direction and then we have to see what we have to learn.

- less content, better learning

  I think we learnt less subjects, but each of them much deeper than with the normal teaching.

Areas of concern or suggestions for change include:

- too little theory

  You learn less theory and it's as if you don't learn anything.

- not enough feedback

  The feedback given during the instruction lecture is not enough and the theory is not well explained.

- the role of the tutor

  The tutor is really involved in the group if he knows about the subject, but when he doesn't know anything about it he is most of the time nearly useless in the progress of the group.

- the number and type of problems

  A bit more practical, it is supposed to reflect problems in real life business. I think it is still too much business school and not really practical cases.

- ending up with a fragmented view of the problem

  Because working in a group you don't get to know every element, just deal with one part of the assignment.

- assessment

  If they want to make it a real PBL system they should abandon the exams and give us a problem which we must solve using all our books and info we can get.

51.6 Future work

The quotations above obviously give only a flavour of a wide spread of both positive and negative views. They may reflect the fact that some students had experienced problem-based learning for a longer period and were more comfortable and that others found it a stark contrast with their previous experiences; this is particularly true for the French. However, it is probably also a reflection of the fact that for the staff it is a new method of teaching and they are taking to it with varying degrees of enthusiasm and commitment.

The exercise of using questionnaires and focus group discussions is to be continued for at least a further two years. This chapter has reported on the views of Year 2 students in 1996/97. Further studies will involve years 2 and 3 in 1997/98 and years 2, 3 and 4 in 1998/99. While it will not be possible to compare individual student's views over time, it should be possible to identify whether students as a group change their views and whether a particular year expresses different views. In particular, it will be interesting to see whether the views of the Year 2 students change, perhaps as a result of staff becoming more comfortable and expert with the approach.

Senior management have expressed a commitment to the continuation of this work as part of their concern to improve the quality of the student learning experience and to be able to justify the change to those who doubt its efficacy.

51.7 Conclusions

This chapter reports what is very much 'work in progress'. The data has yet to be systematically coded and analysed. But even in its raw form it has proved useful in staff development activities with the staff as well as highlighting issues for management of the Business School.

What it has also shown is that some students naturally have a vocabulary that allows them to articulate the experience of learning under a problem-based system which is very similar to the way in which the characteristics of course design for a deep approach to learning are described. The elements of motivation, active learning, student interaction and integrated learning come through clearly in the questionnaires, particularly when contrasted with the descriptions of students' other experiences of learning.

However, there are enough negative comments in the questionnaires to have caused concern for some staff and their managers and it is hope that the continuation of this study will identify improvements over time.

Notes

1. This work is being carried out with Jan Broersma, Head of the International Business School, Hogeschool Brabant, Breda, The Netherlands. The author is on secondment from the Learning and Teaching Institute, Sheffield Hallam University until February 2000.

52 Evaluating the success of a university 101 course designed to encourage students to become strategic, self-directed university students[*]

Allyson Fiona Hadwin, Gary Poole and John Reed
Simon Fraser University, Canada

52.1 Overview

In the Fall of 1996, an Introduction to University course was offered through General Studies for the first time at Simon Fraser University. Through engagement in a range of activities, this course was intended to support students to become strategic, self-directed university students. In this chapter, we: (a) discuss the ways in which course objectives, activities, and assigments were evaluated through student reflections, instructor reflections, surveys, questionnaires, and assignments administered both during and upon completion of the course; and (b) report our findings regarding the success of this course. This chapter provides valuable tips for designing, teaching, and evaluating introduction to university 101 courses.

52.2 Introduction

52.2.1 Course background

In April, 1995, within the context of the President's Committee on University Planning's recommendations for undergraduate students, the Dean of Arts, struck a committee with broad university representation to discuss the institution of a 'University 101' course at SFU. University 101 courses seek to address transition, completion and competency issues faced by students, as well as retention issues faced by post-secondary institutions. The Committee was asked to comment on the components of such a course and to indicate a procedure for implementation. The Committee unanimously endorsed the creation of a General Studies 101 course and also concluded that, because of SFU's situation as a commuter campus with a trimester system, the students who could most benefit from the initial pilot course offering would be incoming high-school graduates. The Committee identified other target student groups who would benefit from such a course, but suggested that in the present economic climate the first course should be targeted toward those in greatest need – incoming students who have just completed high school. In July, 1995, the Dean of Arts approved the proposal from the General Studies 101 Committee to offer a three-credit Introduction to University Studies course in 1996–97.

An instructional team was assembled consisting of each of the authors of this chapter (Gary Poole, John Reed and Allyson Hadwin). Over the course of eight months, we met on a weekly basis to design and develop the course which was offered and evaluated in fall semester 1996. In addition to designing the curriculum, we wanted to embed programme evaluation into the development of the course, making it part of the regular course curriculum. In other words, we discussed the design, development, and integration of programme evaluation as a concurrent and integral part of the programme development. This approach to evaluation design can be very effective because the programme informs the evaluation and, reciprocally, the discussion about the evaluation informs the design of the programme.

Programmes designed to ease the transition to university should strive to embed research and evaluation into their efforts. In a recent paper Hadwin and Winne (1995) suggest that if only 10–15% of the study skills courses now being offered started to collect such data, it would make a significant contribution to our understanding of the effects such courses have and the effectiveness of study skills education in general. It is essential that methods of programme evaluation are built into this type of course. This means that student engagement is monitored and evaluated. Data on changes in attitudes about learning, knowledge about learning, motivation, general knowledge about the university and academia, and course performance should also be collected, along with data about the programme's structure and functioning. This type of evaluation provides the information required to improve the course each time it is offered. We used this philosophy as a frame with which to design and collect evaluation measures throughout the course.

In this chapter we describe five simple evaluation measures that can be adapted to any course. In addition, we report on our evaluation findings in this *Introduction to University* course. Our intent is to inform course evaluation practice, as well as the design and evaluation of transition to university courses.

52.2.2   General course description

This course introduced students to the academic community, resources, support networks and services at Simon Fraser University. Students participated in activities designed to encourage effective and strategic learning. Through course presentations and assignments, students learned about university life and achieved a knowledge of the academic options and goals of Simon Fraser University. Course content was linked wherever possible to academic content and student needs in other courses. This course was structured to provide close teacher–student and student–student interaction using class time and computer conferencing.

52.2.3   Goal and objectives

Our goal in this course was to help students develop skills and strategies necessary to become more independent learners in order to maximize the benefits of their university education. More specifically, we had seven objectives: (a) to provide students with a guided and productive exploration of your methods of learning and task completion so that they may improve upon those methods and choose the ones that are best suited for a variety of academic challenges; (b) to develop a community of learners among students through structured group tasks, class activities, and informal support networks; (c) to introduce students to the professional and personal resources that can enhance their experience at university; (d) to help students develop an understanding of the many facets of the Simon Fraser University community; (e) to provide practice and feedback in the craft of university writing and critical thinking; (f) to develop perspectives and philosophies regarding what higher education is and should be; (g) to pursue learning in ways that recognize the value of diverse perspectives and sources of knowledge.

52.24 Rationale for evaluating the course

As university instructors, we have a number of roles and responsibilities in our university communities. Collectively we share a common goal creating and developing courses that will continually develop and change over time. We are also interested in sharing what we have learned so that other students, instructors, administrators and researchers can benefit from our experiences. As course instructors, we all participate in research of some sort. Instructors continually use the feedback provided by students' assignments, grades and comments to make decisions about course content and processes. This chapter describes six ways in which course evaluation data can be gathered and provides a synthesis of our findings in GS101: *An Introduction to University*.

We augmented the official course evaluation substantially via specific, comprehensive assessment of course: (1) objectives, (2) activities, and (3) general impressions, and with (4) weekly reflections and evaluations on the part of the instructors, and (5) a final reflection by students. These data were collected and analysed with the consent of students in the course. Twenty-eight students enrolled in GS 101, 25 students provided consent to use their evaluation data.

52.3 Objective-based evaluation

One measure of the effectiveness of this course is an objective-based assessment. Our course activities, assignments and readings were oriented toward seven specific course objectives.

Course Objective	Mean Response	% responses indicating yes
To provide students with a guided and productive exploration of their methods of learning and task completion so that they may improve upon those methods and choose the ones that are best suited for a variety of academic challenges.	0.76*	100%
To develop a community of learners among students and their classmates through structured group tasks, class activities, and informal support networks.	0.96	100%
To introduce students to the professional and personal resources that can enhance their experience at university.	1.36	100%
To help students develop an understanding of the many facets of the Simon Fraser University community.	1.20	92%
To provide practice and feedback in the craft of university writing and critical thinking.	0.76	88%
To develop perspectives and philosophies regarding what higher education is and should be.	0.68	92%
To pursue learning in ways that recognize the value of diverse perspectives and sources of knowledge.	0.48	78%

*Scale: -2= not at all, -1=poorly met, 0=somewhat met, 1=well met, 2=very well met)

Table 52.1   Student ratings and mean responses regarding the degree to which course objectives were met for them

These objectives were stated clearly at the beginning of the course and guided significant portions of the instructional design. At the end of the course, we wanted to know if students thought these objectives had been met for them, as individual consumers of the course.

We asked students to rate each of the course objectives indicating how well that objective was met for them (-2 = not at all, -1 = poorly met, 0 = somewhat met, 1 = well met, 2 = very well met). Overwhelmingly, students indicated that all objectives had been met for them, as illustrated by mean responses greater than 0 and by the percentage of responses indicating that objectives had been met to some degree (see Table 52.1). In written comments, students were able to identify course activities and assignments that addressed each objective, and provided rich descriptions about why these objectives were important to them.

The instructors ratings of objectives were very similar, however we judged the finally two objectives more critically, and made several suggestions regarding improvement in meeting those objectives.

In addition to rating each objective, we asked students to indicate what class assignments and activities related to each objective. We collected this data because we were interested in: (a) what class activities and assignments students remembered; and (b) students' perceptions about the ways in which objectives and activities were interwoven. Findings suggest that students were able to link many of the class activities and assignments to specific objectives in the course (see Table 52.2). They also recognized that many activities and assignments were directed towards multiple objectives. The data from this objective-based evaluation has been invaluable in making changes to the current offering of this course. Specifically, we have built in some structured activities that more directly address the final two objectives.

Course Objective	Sample of Related Assignments & Activities (listed by students)
To provide students with a guided and productive exploration of their methods of learning and task completion so that they may improve upon those methods and choose the ones that are best suited for a variety of academic challenges.	• group project • collaboration in and out of class • talk about strengths and weaknesses • peer interviews • reflection exercises • essay • plan of attack for exams
To develop a community of learners among students and their classmates through structured group tasks, class activities, and informal support networks.	• group project • class working together to generate understandings • computer conferencing • interview assignment
To introduce students to the professional and personal resources that can enhance their experience at university.	• library • computer work • visiting professors • group project • visit from the president
To help students develop an understanding of the many facets of the Simon Fraser University community.	• visiting professors • group project
To provide practice and feedback in the craft of university writing and critical thinking.	• Janet Giltrow • essay
To develop perspectives and philosophies regarding what higher education is and should be.	• essay • custom courseware
To pursue learning in ways that recognize the value of diverse perspectives and sources of knowledge.	• in class discussions • group work • guest speakers

Table 52.2   Course assignments and activities that students associated with each objective

52.4 Evaluating course activities and assignments

After the objective-based evaluation, we asked students to rate all the course activities and assignments indicating how valuable they were. Collecting specific ratings and comments about the contents of the course was intended to provide direction for lesson planning in future offerings in the course. This coupled students' recollections of various activities and assignments and their correspondence with course objectives, provided a powerful means with which to critique our instructional design. Students indicated that they found each of

Activities and Assignments	Mean Response	% responses indicating "keep this" (1 or 2)
• procrastination talk by Dr. Steedman	1.91*	96%
• use of computer	1.80	96%
• student presentations	1.48	92%
• visit from president 2	1.43	87%
• visit from president 1	1.42	87%
• effective academic writing	1.40	92%
• first class conference groups	1.36	84%
• reflection exercise 1	1.36	84%
• faculty views of scholarship	1.27	82%
• essay planning assistance in class	1.26	78%
• learning about working in groups	1.24	80%
• exam action plan	1.21	71%
• essay outline template	1.20	80%
• learning about self-regulated learning	1.04	72%
• exam analysis template	.96	67%
• essay about university	.92	60%
• recommendations for self	.76	64%
• reflecting on strengths & weaknesses	.72	52%
• strategic learning questionnaire	.44	36%
• interview summary	.22	43%
• interviewing each other	.20	44%

*scale: -2=definitely dump this, -1=dump this or modify significantly, 0=neutral,

1=keep this and modify slightly, 2=definitely keep this

Table 52.3   Student ratings of activities and assignments (rank ordered)

the activities and assignments to be important parts of the course (see Table 52.3). Mean responses between 0 and 1 indicate that students did not think these activities should be removed from the course, but were neutral about their importance. Responses close to 1 indicate that students thought the activity or assignment should be part of the course but needed some revisions, and responses close to 2 indicate that students thought the activity or assignment should remain part of the course with few to no revisions.

We are in the process of analysing detailed comments and suggestions students made regarding each of the activities and assignments so that this information can be used in the design and delivery of this course in the future. The instructors' ratings of activities and assignments were very similar, and articulated several suggestions for improving these activities and their integration in the course.

52.5   Students' general impressions and evaluations

Students were also asked a number of questions about the course in general in both a general evaluation form we designed, and the standard course evaluation. These questions paralleled issues that are targeted in most standard course evaluation forms. Responses to these questions were on a three-point scale: yes, not sure, no (see Table 52.4). These general impressions and evaluations were accompanied by rich explanations and comments by students. In general, students thought this course should be a graded 3-credit course. They also believed that this course would help them to receive better grades and succeed at SFU in the future, but not necessarily in the concurrent semester. This information played a critical role in shaping our proposal to the university for continued funding. Based on these findings, we proposed, and received approval for four sections of a 3-credit, graded course.

100% of students	indicated that they attended classes almost always (no-one missed more than 2 classes)
92% of students	indicated that this course provided them with an understanding of SFU as a post-secondary institution
88% of students	indicated that this course should be a 3-credit course.
86% of students	indicated that they thought the course content ranged from mid way to very valuable
80% of students	indicated that they feel more competent in their use of computers than they did prior to enrolling in the course.
78% of students	indicated that the course text and readings were mid way to very relevant.
76% of students	indicated that this course would will help them to get better grades in the future
71% of students	indicated that the course provided them with skills to help them succeed at SFU
68% of students	indicated that the course difficulty was mid-way between too easy and too difficult
68% of students	indicated that this course made their first term better
64% of students	indicated that this course should be a graded course in the future.
57% of students	indicated that the amount of work required in the course was mid way between too little and too much (31% thought it leaned toward too much)
56% of students	indicated that they didn't know if the course helped them to get better grades this term
24% of students	indicated that they thought the course should be kept as a pass/fail course

Table 52.4   Students' general impressions and evaluations of the course

52.6   Evaluating success based on student generated goals

Introduction to university courses are somewhat atypical university courses. They are similar to other courses in that they consist of activities and assignments that are grounded in a set of instructional goals and objectives; however, they differ in that those goals and objectives relate to students learning to identify their own needs as learners, and successfully pursue self-generated goals. To evaluate our success in designing and continually adapting a course that would meet the diverse needs of all enrolled students, we asked students to reflect upon their own success toward a set of goals. At the beginning of the course, students were asked to write a reflection to their on-line conference groups discussing their goals as well as what they wanted to learn about in this course, and identifying questions they had about SFU and university in general. At the end of the course they re-read these reflections and wrote a final reflection indicating whether or not they had met their goal/s and discussing their preparedness to pursue those goals independently. Students were also asked to generate a goal for next term.

In the first week of the course, all students identified a wealth of studying skills and strategies as directions and goals for the course. These students recognized a need to develop better learning strategies within their first week of classes, and related concerns were reiterated throughout the course. Over 50% specifically mentioned learning to use computers, the Internet, and e-mail when asked to generate their own goals for the course. Over 80% of students indicated that they had met their goals in this course. Furthermore, all of the students who had not met their goals indicated that they were well on their way to meeting these goals and would continue to pursue them over the course of their university careers. As illustrated below, student comments evidenced thoughtfulness, self-reflection, and an understanding about strategic self-regulated learning.

> No, I would say that I have not fully realized my goal yet. I learned the steps to achieving this goal and its just up to me to use those steps to achieve my goal. I think I will meet my goal of studying better and adjusting over time.

> I know most of what I wanted to know. Anything that I'm still not sure about now, I at least know where to find it or start looking for it. I've learned a lot in this course and will apply it in the future. I'm sure of that.

> Yes, I know how to use the computer. I know that time management is a personal thing and that I must be motivated and be able to recognize my weaknesses and strengths in order to improve myself. I expected the course to manage my time (which is not possible), but I learned how I can organize my time myself.

52.7   Reflections by the instructional team

Throughout the course, the instructional team met once each week to discuss and record perceptions, reflections, questions, concerns and suggestions regarding the course. Detailed critiques of activities and assignments were made in weekly team and individual written reflections. These reflections helped the instructional team refine the course and will be used in conjunction with student comments and evaluations to continue to shape future offerings.

Our written reflections suggest that we could have easily spent the entire course focusing exclusively on learning and writing skills and strategies. For many students, there was great need in this area. At the same time, most students struggled with the learning-to-learn activities and required extensive one-to-one feedback and support to analyse their own learning difficulties, generate solutions and recommendations, and evaluate the effectiveness of those solutions. The instructors provided much-needed extensive feedback and most students were asked to do the assignments a second time based on this feedback. Consequently, there was a significant increase in course assignment load with a concomitant limitation placed on the breadth of activities covered in class. Also, the time spent grading and supporting students on their learning skills and strategies extended well beyond what would be reasonable under ordinary circumstances (i.e. larger classes and one, rather than three, course instructors).

52.8   Summary and conclusions

This chapter overviews five simple methods for evaluating the success of a university course. Throughout this chapter, we have provided specific examples of evaluation measures and findings in order to illustrate that: (a) thorough course evaluations are relatively simple to conduct when course goals and objectives have been clearly articulated; (b) data collected from these types of evaluations provides detailed feedback oriented toward shaping and improving future offerings of a course; and (c) ongoing reflections and evaluations help to guide instructional decision-making throughout a course in order to more effectively weave together student needs and instructional goals

The first offering of GS101 was successful in the following ways:

1. GS101 met each of its seven learning objectives;

2. students found the course activities and assignments to be valuable;

3. students general impressions and evaluations of the course were positive;

4. over 80% of the students indicated that they had met their own goals for the course;

5. weekly written reflections by the instructional team provided a wealth of data for further development and improvement of the course.

Based on the findings from this course evaluation and the indications that the course was successful, we recommended strongly that:

1. the course be expanded to accommodate the needs of a number of student groups we feel would benefit tangibly from a course following the GS101 model;

2. GS101 should be a graded course, rather than pass/fail;

3. GS101 should be expanded to respond to the needs of a broader group of students including incoming high-school graduates, diverse-qualification high-school graduates, college transfer students, students On Academic Probation, and early pre-admission high-school graduates;

4. administration and teaching of GS101 should draw on the expertise of a staff member experienced with both academic and student resources, teaching, counselling and advising, and an instructor combining a solid background in educational and learning theory with practical teaching experience.

Data collected from this extensive evaluation process has been invaluable. It provided direction for instructional planning the following year, and confirmed that this type of course is invaluable for first-year students. Data generated through the evaluation process provided justification for recommendations regarding, budgeting, funding, staffing, course structure, grading. Furthermore, grounding recommendations in concrete data gathered from the participants in the course contributed final university approval for offering four sections of this three-credit, graded course. And finally, conducting an extensive course evaluation provided students with an opportunity to participate in the development and improvement of the course over the course of their own semester, and through to future offerings.

Note

* We would like to thank the first-year students who enthusiastically participated in the first offering of GS101: An Introduction to University Studies as participants and collaborators on this research. Their thoughtful and genuine contributions to the evaluation process are evidenced throughout this chapter and have contributed greatly to the evolution of our course. Support for this research was provided through a research stipend from the Centre for University Teaching.

52.9   Reference

Hadwin, A.F. and Winne, P.H. (1996) A review of recent research on study skills in higher education, *Journal of Higher Education*, **67**, 692–715.

53

Tutors learning about students learning: a course for tutors involved in an induction course in computer science and engineering

Shirley Booth[i] and Marita Christmansson[ii]
(i) Educational Development, Chalmers University of Technology, Göteborg; (ii) Lindholmen Development, Göteborg

53.1   Background

A course for new students in computer science and engineering has been designed to open the field to view from the start, to train in the tools and ways of working that will be useful in the coming programme and in professional life. The course, Computer Science and Engineering in Context (abbreviated in future to CSEC), is reported elsewhere (e.g. Booth and Petersson, Chapter 40 in this volume). It runs for the first term, in parallel with courses in mathematics and programming techniques, and the central feature is a project which the students work on in groups of eight, guided by a tutor,[1] culminating in a written report and oral presentation. The tutors are all graduate students of subjects allied to computer science and engineering and do this work as part of their normal 20% teaching for their departments. There are some 100 students, ranging in age from 19 to late 30s, coming directly from high school or from experience in the workplace.

This chapter is being written after the second year of the course by the course co-ordinator (Marita Christmansson), herself a tutor from the first year of the course, and an educationalist (Shirley Booth) from the university centre for educational development, who has been involved in the overall programme reform from the start as a member of the executive board for the project. They designed and ran the course for tutors that is to be described and evaluated here.

53.2   The first year: Autumn 1995

CSEC ran for the first time in the autumn of 1995, and in preparation the tutors went to a course on the writing process and writing project reports. During the term they met regularly in confidential meetings with a member of the course administration when difficulties and common problems could be aired.

In the evaluation of its first year considerable light was cast on how the students and the tutors (all graduate students) had experienced CSEC, and the results it had in relation to its goals (Booth, Petersson and Bayati, in press).[2]

The interviews with the students showed that they had felt a sense of confusion about what the course had been getting at. Their sense of where the course was pointing was summed up in three qualitatively distinct categories:

- the course points nowhere;
- the course points inwards, towards its parts;
- the course points forwards, towards the coming education and profession.

The first was rarely expressed, for example by a student who had already decided to leave the programme and, in passing, by another as his first reaction. The second, however, dominated: the course was seen either as comprising a number of separate elements, or being primarily about writing and presenting a report. The third, in keeping with the goals of the course but also rather rarely alluded to, indicates the course's lending an insight into the world of computer science and engineering, whether as an educational programme or as a professional field of work and to the role that computer engineering has to play in society at large.

It was hypothesized by the then co-ordinator that the tutors had been prepared somewhat inadequately, and misleadingly, by the course on the writing process. The course was excellent in itself and the tutors appreciated it; the students, too, found the practice of writing valuable and the reports in the first year were generally of a high standard. But, the hypothesis ran, it focused attention too firmly on the report that would close the course, rather than on the elements that went to make up the report – the group work, the investigation, the project organization, the glimpses of computers in society and in the workplace, the computer engineer's role in projects, the *learning*. This, it was felt, prevented the students from seeing the course as integrated into the programme and into their own lifestyles, but had the effect of closing the course in on itself and focusing on its parts – as in the dominant second category above.

While the tutors collectively expressed the goals of the course quite clearly, tending towards the third category, in particular gaining insights into the coming programme, they also admitted a lack of knowledge about the *programme as a whole and its goals*. This implies an emptiness in the interpretation of the course's goals. The goal of learning to work independently and in groups was tackled differently by the tutors; they had adopted different approaches to organizing their groups and the project work, and felt unsure of their effectiveness. They would have liked more preparation, in addition to the course they had on the writing process and the monthly meetings.

A modified form of the Course Experience Questionnaire (CEQ) (Ramsden, 1992) was administered to the students to gauge their experience of the course as a whole. The items that make up the normal collective items of 'clarity of goals', 'appropriate workload', 'appropriate assessment', 'good teaching' and 'sense of independence' were adapted to apply to the course. 'Good teaching' became, for example, 'good tutoring' with adapted items such as 'the tutor tried his or her best to understand any difficulties we had'. A collective item was created to refer to the experience of working in groups and the support they lend to learning. Single items were inserted to refer to general satisfaction with the course, motivation to do well, and insights gained into the working life of a computer engineer. It was administered a few days after the course ended by distributing it on paper through the internal post system. But when that only yielded a handful of replies it was sent by email. Altogether just over half the students replied.

A first explorative analysis of the data obtained showed an alarming relation between general satisfaction with the course and the clarity of the goals experienced – which can be interpreted as the students who did not feel the course was coherent or leading anywhere also felt a frustration. A simple analysis of the correlations between the items is illustrated in Figure 53.1, the left-hand side showing correlation coefficients (all significant) and the right-hand side showing a hypothetical interpretation in which the interviews were taken into account.

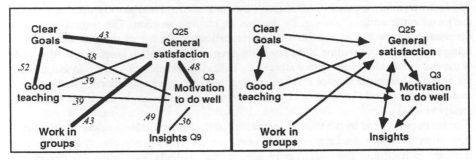

Figure 53.1   A simple model for the relationships between items of the CEQ

The hypothesis is that students who experience a sense of clear goals and good teaching in the course (and these are felt to go hand in hand) feel a sense of satisfaction with the course and are motivated to do well, and this is related to gaining insights into the education and/or future profession. Perceiving working in groups as supporting learning is a complementary factor, which heightens the satisfaction (or dissatisfaction) with the course.

53.3   Towards the second year: summer 1996

Based on the student interviews, the tutors' own reports and strengthened by the above analysis, a decision was taken that in parallel with the CSEC course in its second year a course (for credit) would be held for the tutors. The goals of the tutors' course were stated as follows:

> The goal of the course is that participants should become more aware of the interpersonal processes and learning processes at work in a learning group, by studying relevant theories while at the same time reflecting over the experience of tutoring a group.
>   This is considered to be an important aspect of, on the one hand, working within the course Computer Science and Engineering in Context, and, on the other hand, the participant's own development as a university teacher.

The means to be employed were stated as follows:

- participation in workshops;
- participation in regular tutor meetings where current problems are discussed together with the course leaders;
- study of relevant literature;
- maintaining a log-book during the course;
- regular status reports for tutor-group discussion;
- a written course report.

On a wonderfully sunny day in late August the tutors, the course leaders and the authors drove to the fishing village of Rönnäng on the idyllic island of Tjörn, just north of Göteborg, for a two-day workshop, in preparation for the start of term. Their presentations and discussions were interwoven in a joint effort to hammer out the goals of CSEC and the whole programme, both as envisioned by the course designers and conceptualized by the students and tutors the previous year. Aspects of student learning were taken up and discussed in the context of the student interviews that discussed how they had experienced learning in groups. The role of the tutor was discussed starting in the tutor and student interviews where these roles were expressed.

The goal of this part of the course for tutors was not to bombard them with information and research findings, but rather to give them cause for reflection over their own situation, grounded in the description that had been obtained in the evaluation of the previous year. This was seen as a necessary starting point for a continued reflection over the experiences that they would meet during the coming term. Note that the writing process was removed from this tutor course, even though it was seen as a valuable asset for the tutors; the motivation was that half of the tutors remained from the previous year and, it was felt, their experience would infiltrate the work of the other tutors through the regular meetings that would be held.

In the weeks that followed there were further workshops, though more mundanely held on campus. Group psychology and group processes was the subject of the first, before the start of term, intended to strengthen the tutors' confidence of handling the group and supporting its formation into a well-functioning group (Jaques, 1992; Lennéer-Axelson and Thylefors, 1991). The philosophy and methods of scientific investigation was the subject of the third, intended to support the tutors in advising their groups on reasonable ways of tackling their chosen projects (Rubenowitz, 1980; Carlsson, 1990). A seminar held later on took up different perspectives on learning, contrasting the learning that students experience, and especially in groupwork, with that experienced by working groups who are changing their structure, organization or tasks (Booth, Petersson and Bayati, in press; Wistedt and Martinsson, 1996).

A demand of the course for tutors was that they document their reflections in various ways. First, they kept private log-books of their observations and thoughts. These were distilled once a month into a confidential report that was discussed internally with the course co-ordinator and gave rise to discussions around common difficulties or worries. There was a concerted effort to get the tutors to reflect over what they experienced in the group meetings and try to discuss it in terms of the theories they met in the literature and workshops. After CSEC ended, in order to count the course for credit, they had to write an essay intended to consolidate their reflection by illuminating personal experiences, as recounted in their log-books, with the theoretical perspectives they had met in the course. The goal was to describe how they had experienced working as tutor for the group, how the group had functioned as a learning group, and relate their observations to theory.

53.4 The results: students on CSEC

The overall motivation for the tutor course was to improve learning for the students. In its second year the CSEC course was generally reported to go more smoothly than in the first year. To a large extent this can be accounted for in that the some of the tutors were the same and the co-ordinator had been a tutor the previous year, as well as there now being established routines and clearer deadlines. The second year the course was given was almost bound to be better organized than the first year – though in terms of overall satisfaction such smoothness might be weighed against the rough but fresh feel of the entirely new course.

The same adapted CEQ was run as in the first year, a major difference being that it was administered to all the students while they met in their groups, and almost all were returned. Figures 53.3 to 53.6 show simple comparisons of the collected items of the CEQ for the two years, and Figure 53.2 shows the responses to the single statement 'On the whole I was pleased with the quality of this course.'

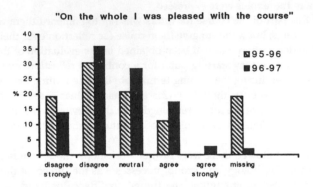

Figure 53.2 Comparison of overall satisfaction with the course

Overall satisfaction is still not overwhelmingly high, but considerably better than the previous year, almost 50% being neutral or positive compared with just above 30%. One goal for the second year was that the course would become more goal-oriented for the students, and as Figure 53.3 shows this appears to have succeeded.

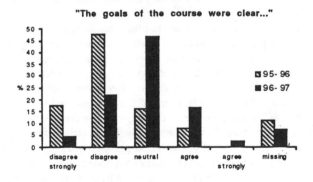

Figure 53.3 Comparison of the clarity of the course's goals

Figures 53.4 and 53.5 indicate a greater degree of satisfaction with the tutoring, 65% neutral or positive going up to more than 80% in the second year, but a similar drop in satisfaction with the groups for working, studying and learning. While this can be seen as a drop in effectiveness of the groups' ways of working, when taken with the previous result it can be interpreted as meaning that in the first year, when the course was experienced as somewhat pointless and the tutors were not clear about their roles, the group took on a greater significance for the individuals in it.

Finally, the CSEC course lead to a much greater degree of insight into the coming programme and the profession of computer engineer than in the previous year, rising from 30% to 65% in the neutral to positive range of the collective item.

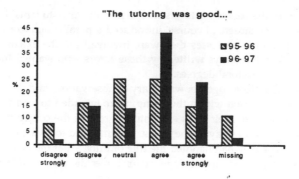

Figure 53.4 Comparison of the satisfaction with tutoring

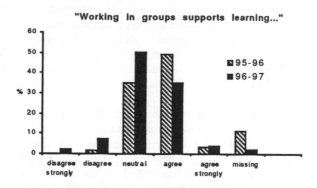

Figure 53.5 Comparison of satisfaction with groups for learning

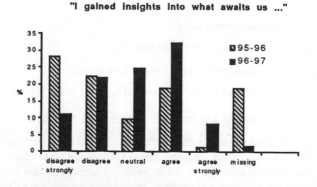

Figure 53.6 Comparison of the degree of insight into the future programme and profession

The results are not sufficient to lead to complacency – there is room for improvement! But the trend is encouraging, and speaks well for the effects of the tutor course.

53.5   The results: tutors on the experience of tutoring

While the main effort of the course for tutors was to improve the students' learning in the CSEC course, the medium chosen, of course, introduced a parallel aim to raise the tutors' awareness of the educational processes they were involved in. The extent to which this succeeded can be seen in the essays written by those tutors who wanted the two weeks' study credit towards their doctoral degrees.

The workshops and literature, together with diary of observations and thoughts and with regular reporting and discussion within the group, were intended to lead the tutors more deeply into a consideration of their roles and into the role of the course in the students' learning as a whole. Writing an essay on the course was intended to give the participants the opportunity to show how they had handled the role of tutor, what they had learned about their students and their learning, and their reflections over the ideas and literature met in the course.

The tutor course was given under three main headings: student learning, group dynamics, and project design and organization. A minimum criterion for the essay was that these three parts of the course were all discussed, from two perspectives: on the one hand, experience and observations from the course and, on the other, what is to be found in the literature. This basic level was met by all reports. A second criterion was that the report was well-structured and correctly written – this is actually the least one can ask of any essay and was not always met at first; however, it is a fault that is readily corrected. As long as the essay was brought up to a reasonable standard in this regard, they were all found acceptable.

More important was the issue of the extent to which the reports gave an indication of quality of participation in the course, hence a quality of learning about being a tutor, and hence a potential for being a better tutor (and indeed, teacher) in future.

Having read the reports, three different ways of writing them were discerned, which reflect, we believe, three different ways of handling the role of tutor. Note that we did not categorize reports as such – one or two of them could be put partly into one and partly into another category. Nor did we categorize the quality of tutoring. What we did say was that the three categories form a hierarchy with respect to reflection over what being a tutor in the CSEC course and being a participant in the tutor course meant, and in this certain categories are more desirable than others.

The three sorts of report were found to be:

- reporting on being a tutor and about the literature;

- reporting on being a tutor *with reference to* the literature;

- reporting *critically* on being a tutor with *critical reference* to the literature.

53.5.1   Reporting on being a tutor and about the literature

This form of report separated its two focuses. Either one half of the report was about being a tutor, observations made and ideas for improvement, while the other discussed the three main parts of the course with reference to the literature. Alternatively, the three parts were treated separately and observations and experiences of being a tutor were described under the three headings.

Such a report can be taken to indicate that the author has both taken the role of tutor seriously and has taken time to study relevant parts of the literature. It can be a thorough and useful account of experience and theory, and can be useful for reference in future. However, it is not at all clear that observations and ideas have been the subject of genuine reflection, or that experiences have been thought about and an attempt has been made to make sense of them. It is not clear that the course as such has had any effect on the participant as a tutor, and that any change had taken place, or might take place in future. If we see *learning* as a change in the way in which one experiences important and relevant aspects of the world (as we do, at the deepest level), then it is not obvious that such a report reflects *learning* about being a tutor.

Note that we do not claim that such a report shows that such learning has *not* taken place. We relate it more to an unwillingness to take the writings and ideas of others (educationalists and psychologists) and make them one's own.

53.5.2   Reporting on being a tutor *with reference to* the literature

This form of report described the experience of being a tutor and referred to the literature in an integrated manner.

Such a report showed that the author had tried to make sense of the experiences in terms of the literature and vice versa. This is more of an indication of a pondering over problematical experiences and a searching for sense by looking at them from different perspectives. It will be useful for reference in future, and will enable the author to recall the ideas and experiences and thereby to go further in understanding aspects of teaching and learning. Such essays can also be used for supporting new tutors, to give them an idea of how they might understand their own experiences and where they might look for support in the literature.

Note that we did not say that such a report is *evidence* for learning (as described above) having taken place, but that there is a better *indication*.

53.5.3   Reporting *critically* on being a tutor with *critical reference* to the literature

This form of report is similar to the previous one, in that the structure is an integration of personal experience and relevant literature from the course, with a clear intention of making sense of both. The significant difference between this form of report and the others is that the authors gave their own experience the same status as the theories in the books; they have 'problematized' both experience and theory. They questioned the theory and they questioned their own observations and they came up, in a few cases, with new ways of seeing things. One told, for example, of meeting a difficulty within their group, finding a possible way of tackling it from the literature, and then questioning the outcome of the attempt. Another told not only of trying to identify the stages of the group's development as a group, but suggesting reasons why it appeared to deviate from the model given in the literature. A third related the experiences not only to the literature but also to earlier experience of leading groups in a research-based company.

We found this form of report exciting. Here were found new ideas and seeds for further development of the theory in the framework of the CSEC course. Such an essay can be used for development of other tutors in future, maybe not at the start of their work but later on when they have started to collect their own impressions.

53.5.4   What was learned?

There is good reason to believe that all the reports indicate that aspects of being a tutor had been scrutinized from the perspectives of experience and theory, and that different degrees of integration and problematizing had been achieved. It can be supposed that all participants had learned about being a tutor, about learning and teaching, about working in groups, and about working with projects, though this learning might have different qualities. The reports are useful, both for reference in future and for inclusion in a portfolio of documents that can be used to show involvement and quality as a teacher when applying for promotion.

What we as course organizers learned was that better advice can be given to participants in such a course, when they ask what a report should look like. We came to see better what reflection means for the participants, and see the need to encourage them to 'problematize' what they see, hear and read, to try to make sense of their experience and the literature, and to respect the conclusions they arrive at.

Two of the seven essays submitted were refused first time and sent back for further work. One of them was simply sloppily written, falling well into the first category. When returned it was of an altogether different quality, falling into the third category and being exemplarily written. The other report came from a young graduate student for whom this was the first teaching assignment, and who got a difficult group with drop-outs and conflicts. After a worrying period as tutor the essay became a very personal outpouring of everything that had gone wrong, with little room for reflection over the process. However, discussion of why it was unreasonable to leave the course with such a negative document that, in any case, did not reflect the whole situation resulted in a worthwhile revision that was less colourful but more measured. It fell into the first category but the two together were felt to indicate a more thorough reflection than either of them alone.

53.6   Conclusion: the way forward

As indicated in the main text, while improvements were seen in the students' perceptions of the course and tutoring, there is room for further improvement, and the effort has continued into the next generation of tutors. A course has been held again and the tutors have been encouraged to keep log-books and write a final essay for credit , as before. As this chapter is being written the CSEC course is coming to an end and another year's results can be reviewed.

As the role of tutor becomes better understood by the graduate students at large, and as the story spreads that it is much more fun than most forms of graduate assistant teaching, a loyal and enthusiastic group of tutors has evolved. The two-day workshop that started the tutor course this year (held at Särö, another coastal town once the favourite of the Swedish court, and again in brilliant summer weather) was noticeably more driven by questions from the newer tutors, and discussed with support and insights from the more experienced tutors.

The way forward is to look at student learning more closely, in the context of the course and with some of the tutors as prime investigators. Some groups have been video-filmed by their tutors and will be interviewed as a result of what is seen there. While CEQ can give certain indicators of how students experience their environment and by implication approach the learning tasks they are involved with, interviews and observations can give a more complete and qualitatively interesting picture of the leaning process in action.

From the perspective of educational development at Chalmers, it seems that here we have the core of a new generation of lecturers and professors who are not afraid of getting close to the students they are teaching and examining the learning they are engaged in. Deliberate innovation and a questioning approach to its outcomes might be the long-term consequences of such an initiative – rather than a taken-for-granted maintenance of the teaching status quo, as is so common, or a blind implementation of the latest fad teaching method.

In the mean time, the tutors are meeting and facing new challenges – at the same time as finding their teaching fun.

Notes

1. We use the word tutor in the special sense of a graduate student who meets the group regularly (once a week) and is available at other times. The tutor is not expected to have specialist knowledge of the project topic, but is expected to assist the group in working on the project in a satisfactory way.

2. Accessible at www.pedu.chalmers.se/shirley/CSECTOC.html

53.7 References

Booth, S., Petersson, J. and Bayati, Z (in press) *Computer Science and Computer Engineering in Context: Evaluation and Development of an Induction Course to a Computer Science and Engineering Degree Programme*, Göteborg: Scripta series on Educational Development at Chalmers.

Börjesson, S. and Liander, K. (1995) *Metod PM för arbetsorganisation* (Notes on the organization of work), manuscript.

Carlsson, B. (1990) *Grundläggande forskningsmetodik* (Basic methods of research), Stockholm: Liber Utbildning.

Jacques, D. (1992) *Learning in Groups* Kogan Page.

Lennéer-Axelson, B. and Thylefors, I. (1991) *Arbetsgruppens psykologi* (The psychology of working groups), Stockholm:Natur & Kultur.

Ramsden, P. (1992) *Learning to Teach in Higher Education*, London: Routledge.

Rubenowitz, S. (1980) *Utrednings- och forskningsmetodik* (Methods of investigation and research), Stockholm: Esselte Studium.

Wistedt, I. and Martinsson, M. (1994) *Kvaliteter i elevers tänkande över en oändlig decimalutveckling* (Qualities of pupil thinking about an infinitely recurrent decimal), Stockholm: Stockholms Universitet, Dept of Education.

54 Learning, assignments and assessment

Dai Hounsell
University of Edinburgh

54.1 Introduction and background

In a study of essay-writing in the arts and social sciences which I undertook at the beginning of the 1980s, I felt justified in depicting essay-writing as an Amazon for undergraduates in those disciplines, since the processes of studying seemed to proceed along a great river of coursework essays (Hounsell, 1984, p. 103). And if I had enlarged the scope of that enquiry to include assignment work by science and engineering students, it would probably have been necessary only to complement my focus on essays with a concern for laboratory and practical reports.

In the late 1990s, however, an interest in undergraduate coursework which simply confined its focus to essays and reports would look rather narrow and traditionally minded, since it appears from the literature of assessment (see, for example, Brown and Pendlebury, 1992; Brown et al., 1994; Gibbs, 1995, Knight, 1995) that coursework assignments in higher education have become much more varied and diverse. Yet neither the scale nor the scope of this apparent diversification have been firmly pinned down. We can be fairly certain that striking examples of diversification have taken place, but it is not clear to what extent these represent the efforts of a few lone innovators or have been much more widespread. And although diversification seems to have been taking place along a variety of fronts, we seem to lack a systematic picture of what kinds of diversity are being practised and how these might interrelate.

In this chapter, my aim is to attempt to remedy that lack by drawing on the findings of a project which has sought to identify, document and disseminate the variety of ways in which assessment practices have been changing in Scottish universities and colleges. ASSHE (Assessment Strategies in Scottish Higher Education) is a two-year project which was set up in August 1994 and was undertaken by a joint University of Edinburgh/Napier University, Edinburgh team, working under the auspices of the Committee of Scottish Higher Education Principals and with the generous financial support of the Scottish Higher Education Funding Council.

As part of the project's dissemination programme, a series of newsletters has been distributed, a selective inventory of changing practices has been published (Hounsell, McCulloch and Scott, 1996), a national conference has been mounted alongside a variety of conference and workshop presentations, and the project's database is being made available electronically via the Internet in downloadable form. A monograph analysing and reviewing the project's findings is in preparation.

The main work of the project involved a survey of changing assessment practices in all the higher education institutions in Scotland – the 21 universities and colleges funded by the Scottish Higher Education Funding Council, together with the Open University in Scotland. In the course of the survey, we attempted to contact all teaching staff in the 22 institutions, drawing on the advice of a network of institutional link-persons. Those surveyed were invited, if they had recently embarked on a change in their assessment practices, to complete a specially designed pro forma which asked them to describe the initiative concerned, to provide important background information (e.g. on the course concerned and the number of students involved), and to outline how students and colleagues had responded to the initiative. It was made clear that the project was interested in changes of all kinds in assessment practices, including changes in what was being assessed, changes in how students were assessed, changes in when and where assessment was taking place, and changes in who was involved in evaluating and assessing students' work.

By the conclusion of the survey phase of the project in summer 1996, a total of 310 completed pro formas had been returned for inclusion in the ASSHE database, while a further 460 members of staff had formally registered interest in being kept abreast of the project's findings. The completed pro formas were drawn from across all 22 institutions surveyed, and from a very wide spectrum of disciplines and subject areas.

54.2 Key findings

54.2.1 Core themes

Although the 310 database entries cover a very large array of changing assessment practices, several 'core' themes have emerged from the analysis which account for the majority of the initiatives documented. These core themes comprise: changes in tests and examinations; changes in coursework assignments; involvement of students in assessment; involvement of non-course colleagues, professional peers and others in assessment; assessing presentation, group- and teamwork and other skills; and applications of computing and information technology in assessment.

The present chapter focuses only on three of these themes: the remarkable diversification in coursework assignments, the rise of group and teamwork, and the growing practice of involving students in assessment. The two latter themes are discussed primarily in relation to their implications for coursework assignment practices, which are represented in about three-quarters of the 310 initiatives documented in the ASSHE database.

54.2.2 Coursework assignments

What the ASSHE database reveals is a very substantial burgeoning and diversification in coursework assignments, standing in stark contrast to the conventional image of coursework assessment in higher education as in the main a combination of essays (particularly for students in the humanities and social sciences), laboratory and practical reports (mainly undertaken by science and engineering students) and the less frequent project or final-year dissertation. Part of that conventional image may be attributable to the fact that any kind of assignment is to a crucial extent discipline- as well as course-specific, and books on teaching and assessment in higher education have largely concentrated on a small number of relatively generic forms of assignment at the expense of a more complex typology which celebrates rather than overrides particularization. Underpinning the analysis reported here therefore was a concern to create an appropriately rich and precise topography, though within certain practical limits, the most important of which was that of working as far as possible with and from the terminology used by those responsible for these initiatives (and thus in turn accepting that no consensus exists on terminology in this field).

Figure 54.1a Types and Forms of Coursework Assessment

In arriving at an appropriately illuminating level of analysis, it was also essential to differentiate between modes of expression and communication, since the initiatives documented extend far beyond the written mode which has hitherto predominantly – not to say overwhelmingly – characterized coursework assignments in higher education. The results of the analysis for individual assignments, which are shown in Figures 54.1a and

	MIXED MODE	ORAL

INDIVIDUAL	advertisements
	displays & exhibitions
	presentations
	  • art & design presentations
	  • conference presentations
	  • poster presentations
	  • video presentations
	seminar or tutorial papers
	slide interpretations
		discussion, seminar & tutorial
		    contributions
		interviews (videotaped)
		leading guided walks

	case-based tutorials case conferences case studies	oral defence oral presentations • mock presentations seminar presentations tutorial presentations

	computer-based assignments
	disk-based assignments
		negotiations
		  • simulated (audio or videotaped)
		  • via electronic mail

	design exercises fieldwork, field visits & field-based assignments independent study learning agreements & contracts open learning packs orchestral conducting placements & workplace assessments pleadings portfolios problem-solving exercises product design & development remedial study scheme proposals task-based assessments tutorial assignments	

	projects
	  • audit projects
	  • design projects
	  • integrative projects
	  • mini-projects
	  • research projects
	  • study projects	

	peer appraisal exercises role play self-appraisal simulations	hypotheticals leading seminars, tutorials or discussions mooting
GROUP	group displays & exhibitions group exercises group posters group projects team portfolios	group debates paired presentations group presentations student conferences videotaping of meetings

Figure 54.1b Types and Forms of Coursework Assessment (continued)

54.1b, therefore rest on a differentiation between written, oral and 'mixed mode' types of assignment, where the latter refers either to assignments which are a mixture of written and oral modes (e.g. a project which is assessed on the basis both of an oral presentation of findings and a written report) or of other audio and/or visual or graphic modes (e.g. videotapes, poster displays). Within each mode, the figures also record a very large array of types and sub-types, broadly ranged in a sequence from relatively straightforward to relatively complex and demanding assignments.

54.2.3 Assessing group and teamwork

Another remarkable finding of the ASSHE project concerns the pervasiveness of group- and team-based assignments in contemporary assessment practice in Scottish higher education. The most obvious stimulus for such a radical shift away from assessing students solely as individuals has been heightened government concern in Britain with the inculcation of 'personal transferable skills' – especially communication and interpersonal and teamwork skills – allied to targeted curriculum development funds under such schemes as the Enterprise in Higher Education Initiative (see for example, Denicolo *et al.*, 1992). Undoubtedly, however, another contributory factor (see for example, Gibbs and Jenkins, 1992; Hounsell, 1994) has been the pressing need to recast teaching-learning practices in the face of fast-rising class sizes coupled with a significant decline in the unit of resource – a development which has inevitably had a considerable impact on small-group teaching strategies and approaches to assessment, both of which are particularly labour-intensive.

The lower part of Figures 54.1a and 54.1b shows the typology of group- and team-based assignments arising from the ASSHE survey, again categorized in terms of three main modes of communication. In fact, in the ASSHE database, there are 35 examples of group-based written assignments, but interestingly there are also 30 examples of group-based oral assignments and some 52 examples of group-based mixed-mode assignments. Note, however, that while the range of types of such assignments appears to be much less marked than for individual assignments, this may simply be a function of ease of nomenclature on the part of those initiating developments of this kind: finer-grained differentiation becomes more cumbersome when the label for an assignment type has already been enlarged by the addition of 'group' or 'team'.

54.2.4 Student involvement in assessment

The term 'student involvement in assessment' – rather than the more customary 'student self- and peer-assessment' (Boud, 1986, 1995) – is used here as the umbrella term to refer to all those instances in which students take part in some way or other and to varying extents in the processes of determining assessment criteria, making evaluative judgements about the quality of their own or of other students' work, or deploying the latter to provide or contribute to comment and feedback. The former term seems a rather more appropriate one since – with respect at least to the ASSHE findings – students are seldom being asked to take on anything like the full mantle of the tutor-as-assessor.

Within the ASSHE database, almost one in four of the 310 initiatives entail student involvement in assessment in some form or other – a noteworthy finding in itself since it would suggest that involving students in assessment is no longer confined to a very small band of enthusiastic innovators. Indeed it appears to be fast-becoming a relatively well-established and widespread practice across Scottish higher education as well as across a wide spectrum of disciplines and fields of study.

The various forms which student involvement takes fall into three broad groupings (Hounsell, 1997) :

- initiatives which involve students in dialogue, consultation and negotiation concerning the criteria to be applied in evaluating and grading or marking the quality of a given assignment; involvement of this kind is of course essentially formative in purpose, and may or may not lead to a substantive student role in applying the criteria concerned;

- initiatives in which students' judgements about the quality of their own work or that of other students play a material part in feedback and comment, but do not contribute to determination of the grade or mark awarded: e.g. in feedback discussions between tutor and student(s), or in feedback discussions solely among students; and either following an evaluative judgement or the award of a grade, or at an interim stage where feedback has the potential to influence a subsequent revision or re-presentation of the assignment and thus to attain a higher level of quality;

- initiatives in which students evaluate the quality of their own and other students' work; these evaluations do not necessarily entail formally proposing an overall mark or summative grade (i.e. they may only take the form of qualitative comments, delivered orally or in written form, or a series of ratings against a checklist of criteria), and there is no recorded instance in the ASSHE database where students are at liberty to award themselves or other students a grade without subsequent confirmation and validation by the tutor or tutors concerned.

Analysis also indicates that peer-assessment is far more commonplace in these initiatives than is self-assessment. This finding may in part be a reflection of the growth in group and team-based assignments, but it seems unlikely that this is the only reason. Other possible factors are first, fewer concerns on the part of tutors about the validity and reliability of students' assessments in situations where more than one student contributes, and secondly, the potential for higher learning outcomes arising from dialogue between students and across student groups about criteria and their application in evaluative judgments (which is at base a characteristically intersubjective process linked to a grasp of norms for academic discourse – see for example Hounsell, 1987, 1988).

54.3   Review and discussion

In order both to encapsulate these changing directions in the nature of coursework and to review their implications, it is illuminating to try and analyse them in terms of a much wider framework applicable to written and other forms of communication of the kind shown in Figure 54.2 (see Hounsell and Murray, 1992, pp. 48ff).

As traditionally practised, forms of written communication commonly set in assignment work – the archetypal essay or practical report – have had a high degree of homogeneity (not to say blandness), and even where there is variation within characteristic forms (e.g. different types of essays or reports), the conventions of academic discourse in the subject or discipline concerned are likely to be the paramount ones. Similarly, the audience for completed assignments is almost invariably the tutor-as-examiner – someone who usually and paradoxically knows more about the topic or theme than any of the students who have undertaken the assignment (Hounsell, 1984) – and there are concomitant constraints upon the purposes for which the writing has been undertaken. And, needless to say, authorship

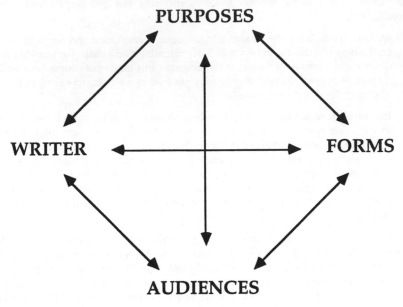

Figure 54.2   A framework for thinking about writing skills

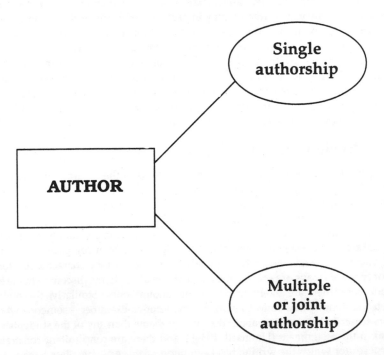

Figure 54.3a Towards a revised framework for analysing assignments in terms of authorship

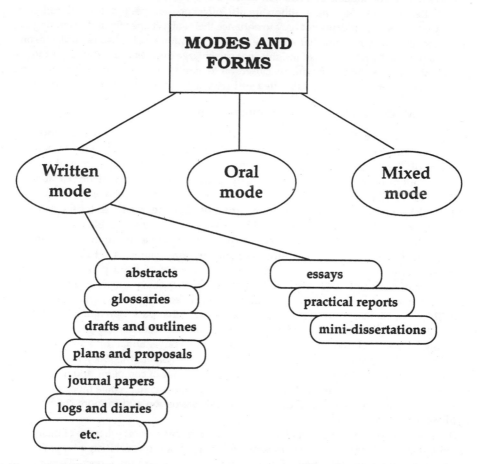

Figure 54.3b Towards a revised framework for analysing assignments by mode and form of communication

has almost universally been confined to the individual student or lone scholar. Such relative invariance – though legitimate in pursuit of traditional and typically self-contained academic goals – provides thin soil for the cultivation of what we might call communicative versatility, i.e. the breadth and depth of communicative expertise which is expected of the graduate of the late 1990s and beyond.

54.3.1 Authorship

The sheer scale of the diversification of coursework revealed by the ASSHE findings, however, is thrown into sharp relief when mapped against such a framework. First and perhaps most obviously (see Figure 54.3a), students are being given opportunities to learn how to communicate as part of a team or group, rather than having sole responsibility for authorship.[1] This therefore serves to intensify and broaden the nature of the communicative challenge, offering students the opportunity of learning how to review and recast what they have to say to accommodate and respond to the thoughts, ideas and observations of their peers. Collaborative and multiple authorship also offers possibilities (e.g. through collective scrutiny of drafts) for students not only to enhance their subject-specific understanding but also to become much more familiar with one another's communicative habits, strategies and styles – a potentially rich source of insights that can enlarge the communicative repertoire of individuals, yet one which is frequently closed off to many students in conventional course settings where work is privately submitted and returned and seldom shared with others.

54.3.2   Modes and forms of communication

Secondly, as Figure 54.3b shows, greater diversity extends both across modes of communication – so that students gain worthwhile practice in communicating in oral and mixed-media forms as well as in writing – and across a much wider spectrum of types of communication, even within the traditionally predominant written mode. In addition therefore to contributing to the development of a much broader portfolio of communication skills (which employers for one will prize on grounds of greater readiness for the demands of the workplace), it also seems reasonable to suggest that there is likely to be some accompanying impact on students' communicative expertise even in more familiar communicative tasks. Drafting an abstract or summary for example, is not simply an act of synthesis: reviewing the skeleton of an argument, a series of main points, or, say, the delineation of a concept, often also entails re-appraisal of questions of coherence, clarity of presentation and sequencing, leading in turn to a more effective presentation of the material in its full form. Similarly, keeping a regular log or diary that puts a premium on personal reflections and the distillation of experiences may enhance students' capacity to generate their own ideas and thoughts when tackling more conventional forms of academic discourse, where private and institutional conceptions (Galbraith, 1980) may be more directly in conflict. And to take a third example, the challenge of compiling and maintaining a rolling glossary of key terms and concepts may help students to become more alert to the need for precision in the use of these terms in both discussion and in more conventional written assignments.

There may also be valuable spin-offs where students have to report the fruits of their work in more than one mode – e.g. when making an oral or poster presentation on a project for which they also have to submit a more comprehensive written report. Certainly, as academics, many of us can recall how responding to the demands of a conference presentation yielded insights which were beneficial in revising the accompanying written paper, just as there were spin-offs for what had first been conveyed as a seminar presentation or informal lecture when we confronted the task of writing it up for publication.

54.3.3   Audience

The ASSHE findings also reveal a marked shift away from the traditional preoccupation with the 'tutor-as-examiner' (cf. Britton *et al.*, 1975), opening up opportunities for students' work to be read, heard, viewed, evaluated and commented on by a much broader constituency, comprising not only fellow-students but in some instances other faculty members or postgraduates not directly involved in the course concerned, or individuals and groups outside the higher education institutions in workplace or community settings (Figure 54.3c). However, it is not just the nature of the audience for coursework which has opened out but also the role which wider audiences may be invited to play:

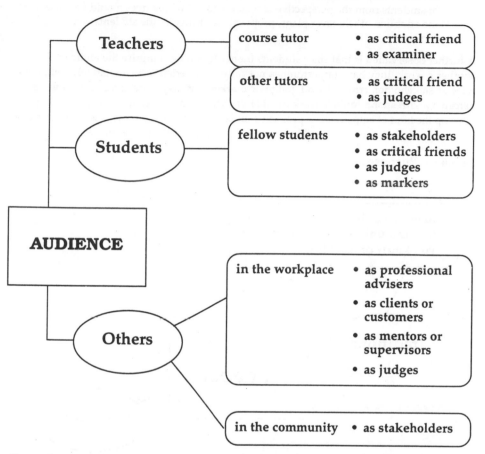

Figure 54.3c Towards a revised framework for analysing assignments by audience

- where other faculty members or postgraduates form part of an audience, for instance, they make be invited to take the role of 'critical friends' (i.e. providing helpful feedback) or of 'judges' (i.e. commenting on the quality of the work – and perhaps also contributing to its summative evaluation – without having responsibility for determining the mark or grade to be awarded);

- fellow-students may be 'stakeholders' (where they are also joint authors), critical friends (where their main role is to offer feedback), or, where they have a more overt role in the assessment process, judges – or even 'markers' in the relatively small number of cases where students are invited to propose grades or marks;

- in the workplace setting, employers or private- and public-sector practitioners may have roles as relatively informal 'professional advisers', or as 'mentors' in a more formal supervisory role, or as 'clients' or 'customers' in projects where the students have been asked to respond to a brief, a problem or a need within a specified context and under given resource constraints;

- in community settings, concerned individuals may be invited to consider the work of students from the perspective of 'stakeholders' whose lives would be affected by the adoption of whatever plans, proposals or strategies the students were to put forward.

A further observation is that since students themselves may comprise the audience for one another's work, they have opportunities not only to experience such relatively unfamiliar roles as stakeholder, critical friend, judge or marker, but also to get a sense of how others perceive and respond to their work (or that of their group or team), and thus perhaps to develop the kind of empathetic or projective understanding which is the truer touchstone of a 'sense of audience' and a desirable attribute of the accomplished communicator.

54.3.4 Purposes

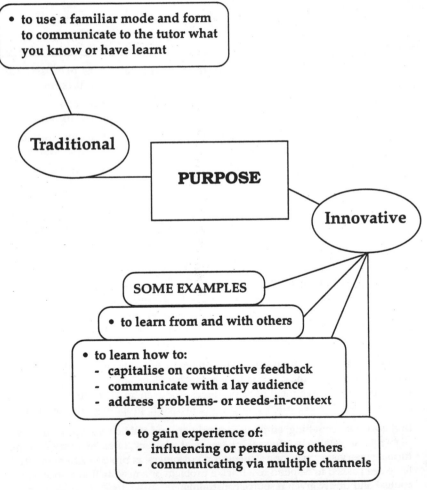

Figure 54.3d Towards a revised framework for analysing assignments by purpose

And finally, to purposes, which are much harder to capture easily without reference to the particular subject-matter of a given assignment and its context, the boundaries to the task-as-assigned, and the course and institutional setting. In broad terms, however, a workable distinction can be drawn between 'traditional' and 'innovative' approaches to assignments in term of their purposes for the students concerned (Figure 54.3d). The purposes of the traditional undergraduate assignment – at obvious risk of caricature – may therefore be characterized as communicating to the tutor what you know or have learnt, by means of a mode or form of communication (e.g. an essay or report) with which you have long been familiar.

Many innovative assignments, however, have fundamentally different purposes. The aim may be, for example, to display your capacity to learn from and with others in the setting of a group or team, as well as on your own, or to show how you might respond appropriately to, and thus capitalize upon, constructive feedback. It may be to venture beyond the conventional essay-writing purposes of exposition, analysis and argument, and towards influencing and persuading others. Or it may be to begin to learn how to communicate with a hitherto unfamiliar audience (within or outside your university) whose members have no specialist knowledge of the subject or field of study concerned, but are perhaps able to bring to bear their everyday understanding and experiences or, say, knowledge of a practical and professional (but not necessarily academic) kind. A purpose of this latter kind may well also entail tackling a set of problems or needs which arise from and are firmly grounded in a specific setting or context, and which therefore call for an approach which is very different from that which might be feasible were the problems of a more customary theoretical or abstract kind. And finally, the underlying purpose of an assignment may be to gain practice in communicating information and ideas through, say, a combination of a poster or short oral presentation and an extended written report, and thus via multiple channels.

54.4   Concluding comments

The application of an analytical framework to changing coursework practices, it would appear, is highly illuminating in underscoring the nature and scope of the diversification which underpins these various changes, which collectively amount to a comprehensive recasting of the hitherto established (and often tacit) conventions of the coursework assignment. What is also intriguing is that some of these changes – e.g. those which involve communicating to lay audiences and via forms of communication which are more typical of industrial, commercial or professional than of higher education contexts – entail stepping beyond the traditional boundaries of academic discourse as conventionally conceived (see for example Hounsell, 1988).

Furthermore, viewed in the round it is difficult to see the consequences of such far-reaching diversification as anything other than pedagogically enriching. For they seem to suggest a welcome enhancement in the breadth and depth of the learning challenges confronting students in their coursework. Two caveats therefore need to be made, however reluctantly. First, any assignment which places relatively new and unfamiliar demands upon students is likely to call for careful consideration of what kinds of guidance, briefing and support may be essential if students are not to be left to sink-or-swim – and potential sources of help such as study guides and manuals, with their predominant focus on the staples of undergraduate studying such as academic reading, essay and report-writing, and note-taking, are unlikely to help bridge this gap in the short term. Second, although the teaching staff responsible for these initiatives see them as for the most part a very worthwhile step forward, we lack systematic evidence of the impact of these changes in practices upon the quality of student learning. Equally, we lack an empirically grounded understanding of the potentially different ways in which students may conceive of and approach such new forms of assignments as, for instance, client-centred reports, poster presentations, or group displays and exhibitions. Remedying each of these gaps will be necessary before we can point with real confidence to improvements in students' learning.

Note

1. The term 'authorship' is of course being used generically here. Strictly speaking, it would be necessary to refer as appropriate to 'writers', 'designers', 'planners', 'speakers', 'producers' and so on.

54.5   References

Boud, D. (1986) *Implementing Student Self-Assessment*, HERDSA Green Guides, no. 5, Kensington, NSW: Higher Education Research and Development Society of Australasia.

Boud, D. (1995) *Enhancing Learning through Self-Assessment*, London and Philadelphia: Kogan Page.

Britton, J. *et al.* (1975) *The Development of Writing Abilities*, London: Macmillan Education, 11–18.

Brown, G. and Pendlebury, M. (1992) *Assessing Active Learning*, Sheffield: CVCP Universities' Staff Development Unit (now UCoSDA), Parts 1 and 2.

Brown, S., Rust, C. and Gibbs, G. (1994) *Strategies for Diversifying Assessment in Higher Education*, Oxford: Oxford Centre for Staff Development.

Denicolo, P., Entwistle, N. and Hounsell, D. (1992) *What Is Active Learning?* (Effective Learning and Teaching in Higher Education, Module 1), Sheffield: CVCP Universities' Staff Development and Training Unit (now UCoSDA).

Galbraith, D. (1980) The effect of conflicting goals on writing: a case study, *Visible Language*, 14(4), 364–75.

Gibbs, G. (1995) *Assessing Student-Centred Courses*, Oxford: Oxford Centre for Staff Development.

Gibbs, G. and Jenkins, A. (eds) (1992) *Teaching Large Classes in Higher Education: How to Maintain Quality with Reduced Resources*, London: Kogan Page.

Hounsell, D. (1984) Learning and essay writing. In Marton, F., Hounsell, D. and Entwistle, N. (eds), *The Experience of Learning*, Edinburgh: Scottish Academic Press, 103–23. (Subsequently republished in a revised form under the new title 'Contrasting conceptions of essay-writing', *The Experience of Learning*, 2nd edn, (Scottish Academic Press, 1997, 106–25.

Hounsell, D. (1987) Essay-writing and the quality of feedback. In J.T.E. Richardson et al. (eds), *Student Learning: Research in Education and Cognitive Psychology*, Milton Keynes: SRHE & Open University Press, 109–19.

Hounsell, D. (1988) Towards an anatomy of academic discourse: meaning and context in the undergraduate essay. In Saljo, R. (ed.), *The Written World: Studies in Literate Thought and Action*, Berlin: Springer-Verlag, 161–77.

Hounsell, D. (1994) Educational development. In D. Watson and J. Bocock (eds), *Managing the University Curriculum in the Year 2000*, Milton Keynes: Society for Research into Higher Education and Open University Press, 89–102.

Hounsell, D. (1997) Reviewing changes in assessment practices: a survey of Scottish higher education. Paper presented at the 7th Conference of the European Association for Research into Learning and Instruction, Invited Symposium on New Assessment Methods, Athens, August 1977, 26–30.

Hounsell, D. and Murray, R. (1992) *Essay Writing for Active Learning*, Sheffield: CVCP Universities' Staff Development Unit (now UCoSDA), Parts 1 and 2.

Hounsell, D., McCulloch, M. and Scott, M. (1996) *The ASSHE Inventory: Changing Assessment Practices in Scottish Higher Education*, Edinburgh and Sheffield: Edinburgh and Napier Universities and the Universities' and Colleges' Staff Development Agency (UCoSDA).

Knight, P. (ed.) (1995) *Assessment for Learning in Higher Education*, London: Kogan Page.

55 Skills for learning: the system!

Viv Anderson and Julia Douglas
Faculty of Cultural and Education Studies, Leeds Metropolitan University

No strategy designed to improve students as learners can afford to neglect the crucial importance of efficient and effective study skills as part of this process. Over the academic year 1996–97 development funds were made available at Leeds Metropolitan University to carry out a major project to design a coherent university-wide approach to the development of study skills in students. A project team of people from all seven academic provision areas, including the five faculties, plus colleagues from the library and computing services was set up.

The first identified aim of the project was to provide a 'working definition' of Study Skills. This definition moved rapidly from concentrating on what might be termed 'mechanical skills' to include more generic transferable skills. The team wished to identify the nature of skills which students need in order to study efficiently and effectively, and those skills required to enable students to transfer their learning beyond their university experience into employment and/or lifelong learning. It was agreed that three main aspects to effective learning can be identified: the ability to study, personal development and 'employability'.

Any working definition of study skills had to take into account additional factors such as the external environment, other work being carried out in the university and a definition which could be used and delivered across the University. It was also felt that the term 'study skills' did not accurately reflect the breadth of skills which had been identified, and therefore the term 'Skills for Learning' was adopted. A crucial aspect of the ethos underlying this project was the recognition that this was primarily a development for students. There was a concern to ensure that different styles of learning and different interest groups were catered for and that students were supported in all aspects of their academic life. Given this focus, steps were taken to ensure student participation and direct involvement in the project. Each stage of the project was evaluated by students and the design of large parts of the user interface was given over to students.

The only efficient means of providing the system across the University was by developing it on the Intranet. In the first instance a comprehensive 'signposting' system was envisaged which would inform students of the availability of already existing study support materials. However the project became much more ambitious not only because the Intranet would provide an effective and flexible electronic delivery system, but it would also offer the opportunity to respond to different learning styles and different learning needs. To facilitate this, a range of materials has been developed which includes: on-line material which is downloadable, interactive software and packages available through Windows 3.11. Hard copy materials are held in red filing cabinets in the Learning Centres.

It was decided that 'Skills for Learning' could be deemed to encompass seven primary broad skill areas or themes. These were:

- assessment;
- employability skills;
- group skills;
- personal development;
- study skills;
- teaching and learning;
- using IT.

Each member of the project team was assigned a theme or part of a theme for which they were responsible. A small study was carried out to ascertain whether or not the themes chosen by the team made ense to students. This was a fairly informal procedure, and students were asked which topics they would want information on if looking for support for study on a computer network; whether the proposed headings covered what they would expect to see and what sort of topics they would expect to see under which heading. From this it was clear that the themes identified had resonance with students and it was therefore agreed to proceed with the original seven.

As well as an academic underpinning, however, it was important to keep in mind the main focus of the work, which was to develop a central resource delivery system. Developing the system for delivery over the Intranet affected the way in which the skills needed to be categorized into a manageable framework. It was necessary to take into account logical arrangement, manageability and a consideration of where and how students might look for items of interest. It became clear, for example, that the Study Skills theme was too bulky for easy navigation, and it was therefore divided into two areas: Study Skills and Information and Research.

A detailed diagram of the final framework can be found in Appendix 55.1.

The Skills for Learning system was clearly becoming quite complex. It was agreed therefore that a database would be built to manage the system. The original specification of the database and subsequent prototype were based on a number of issues:

The rationalization of data: many references are applicable to different cognate areas. With a database the principal resource data need only be entered once, along with the appropriate link information to indicate details of individual references, and to which topic(s) the references relate.

The categorization of available information: providing both generic and contextualized materials to individual students means that web pages have to be dynamically created. This requires the storage and management of data to assist in the tailoring of information to courses, modules or individuals.

The management of content: the system is organic and materials/resources will change regularly. References to resources can be stored in the database, with formatting information either stored in the database or provided by the software used to extract the data. By also providing reliable, accessible, information about the status and usage of resource data, systematic reviews of the resources can be easily managed. These procedures will be implemented using a standard on-line form, as well as a fault reporting mechanism for the site.

There were a number of features for consideration in relation to the design of the system given the large range of competence in using computers. A front-end was created which students would find easy and intuitive. It was also crucial that the system had to be attractive to use – firstly because students need to feel it is designed for them to use and secondly because there is likely to be competition from other web sites. Students can be very critical! It was also important to take into account the needs of students with dyslexia in the design of the user interface, notably fonts and colour combinations.

A second design issue was the development of appropriate navigation tools. One problem with 'surfing the web' is that it is very easy to get lost. Two students designed 'navigation maps' for each theme so that users could move easily from topic to topic within a theme. There are also explicit links forward and back within themes, across to other relevant themes and across the other sites.

Extensive on-line help is also important and therefore a general guide to using the system both navigating round the system and making use of the materials was made available. Many students, and indeed some staff, are still very wary of using computers and do not have a good grasp of computing conventions. Context-sensitive help is being developed for particular pages and for specific resources as well as an index to provide fast access to the system.

Once the system was available in outline form on the Intranet, a small pilot study was carried out to establish how students reacted to the concepts of such a system, as well as the quality of the system. Each member of the team was asked to identify two courses within their faculty with which to pilot the system and the pilot was run over a two week period. Questionnaires were available in hard copy and, by the end of the first week, on-line. Staff in the university were also invited to comment.

The questionnaire was based on contemporary instruments developed for considering aspects of usability in technology orientated learning environments (see Ravden and Johnson, 1989; INUSE, 1996). It consisted of 41 items relating to the following aspects of the system:

- learnability;
- helpfulness;
- navigability;
- quality of the system interface;
- controllability;
- speed;
- workload;
- precision/explicitness;
- likeability.

It mixed open and closed responses on a five-point Likert scale. Respondents were asked to indicate their level of agreement with a series of question statements. They were also asked for comments on a number of particular features, for example on specific navigation maps, colour combinations, and any general views.

In addition to this structured part of the questionnaire, many respondents took the time to answer the more open ended questions. The positive responses clearly out weighed the negative ones. Two comments summarized many of the others:

Keep working on it, it is an excellent idea.

Presentation beautiful. Use of attractive and friendly graphics and nice to see some humour in a teaching/informative package.

The main criticism was the speed of the system to respond. In addition, many respondents felt it would be useful to have a leaflet or booklet, or a clear introduction to the use of the system and further instructions on how to download to a floppy disk.

The results of this pilot were extremely encouraging. Although only a small number of students took part, the level of agreement and the positive responses were remarkable. It clearly demonstrated that students supported the concept of the system. In addition, there was consistent praise for the quality of the system itself. Since the process is a dynamic one, many of the suggestions which were made in the responses to the questionnaire have already been acted upon. The system has been further developed and now includes an extended Help function, as well as an index to help users navigate through the system. There are also additional materials in the filing cabinets.

Furthermore, colleagues who have accessed the system are in general agreement that this is an appropriate approach to take to the development of study skills support and many staff have been happy to have their materials included. Naturally enough, there are some concerns – particularly from staff who do not feel confident technologically themselves, as well as a concern that some students will need support to enable them to use the computers in the first place. There will be particular issues for part-time students. This is clearly an area for future research and development.

This project has proved to be an innovative and exciting contribution to the university's teaching, learning and assessment strategy. It is notoriously difficult, across large institutions, to generate university-wide initiatives. Colleagues tend to work in self contained ways within their schools and faculties. This project was able to harness the skills, expertise and enthusiasm of colleagues to produce a high quality result. Almost without exception, colleagues both within the project team and across the university have expressed interest in and support for the project. The system which has been developed is being seen as an extremely useful tool which can be adopted and adapted by colleagues to provide high quality study skills support for students at all levels.

The system was demonstrated at the 5th International Improving Student Learning Symposium. Colleagues, both national and international, were impressed at the university-wide nature of the project and the breadth of our definition of 'study skills'. Student involvement in the design was highly appreciated and the 'navigation maps' were voted fun to use.

55.1   References

INUSE, World Wide Web page – http://www.npl.co.uk/inuse

Ravden, S. and Johnson, G. (1989) *Evaluating Usability of Human–Computer Interfaces: A Practical Method*, Ellis Horwood.

SKILLS FOR LEARNING PROJECT

TEACHING & LEARNING

Teaching Methods
Lectures
Seminars
Tutorials
Group Work
Laboratories
Workshops
Role Plays
Problem Solving
The Problem Solving Cycle
Problem Solving Techniques
Mind Maps
Learning
Theory & Nature of Language
Language Learning
Learning Styles
Independent Learning
Group Learning
Ethics
Creativity
The Importance of Creativity
How To Be More Creative

PERSONAL DEVELOPMENT

Confidence
Giving/Receiving Criticism
Time Management
Assertiveness
Stress Management
Discrimination

USING I.T.

Word Processing   Databases
Spreadsheets   Powerpoint
Email   World Wide Web

STUDY SKILLS

Reading
  Efficient Reading
  SQ3R
  Speed Reading
  Reading Skills for International Students
Numeracy

Listening
  Listening Skills for International Students
Oral
  Tutorials
  Seminars
  Presentations
  Oral Skills for International Students
Written
  Use of Language
  Reports
  Dissertations
  Essays
  Notes
  Projects
  Writing for International Students
  References
  Instruction Words
  Types of Writing
  Confused Words
  Paragraphs & Punctuation

Information for Students with Dyslexia

Planning & Organising Your Study
Action Planning

GROUP SKILLS

Why Groups are Formed
What Groups Can Offer
Team Roles
Potential Problems with Groups
Effective Group Conditions for
  Good Problem Solving
Advantages & Disadvantages of
  Group Decision Making
Groups vs Individuals
Participative Management
Decision Making Styles
Group Problem Solving Techniques
Networking

EMPLOYABILITY SKILLS

Getting to Know Yourself
  Your Skills, Talents & Abilities
  Career Ideas
  Career Planning & Expectations
Finding Out About...
  Sources of Occupational Information
  Sources of Job, Study & Voluntary Opportunities
  Careers in the 21st Century
Communicating with Employers
  Written Applications - including letters, CVs &
    application forms
  Interview Techniques
Preparing for Placement
Assessment Centres & Psychometric Testing

ASSESSMENT

Purpose of Assessment
Prepare for Assessment
  Self Assessment
  Accreditation of Prior Learning
  Peer Assessment
Assessment Methods
  Portfolios
  Learning Logs
  Learning Assignments
  Learning Diary
  Records of Achievement
  Exams
  Assignments
  Case Studies
  Assessment Criteria

INFORMATION & RESEARCH

Using the Library
  Catalogue
  Literature Searching Principles
  Indexes, Abstracts & Bibliographies
  Audio-Visual Resource
  Electronic Information
  Harvard System of Referencing
Research Skills
  Research Methods
  Dissertations
  Data Collection & Analysis
  Bibliographies
  Statistics

56 CoNoteS: a software tool for promoting self-regulated learning in networked collaborative learning environments[*]

Allyson Fiona Hadwin and Philip H. Winne
Simon Fraser University, Canada

56.1 Introduction

Educators and employers lament that many post-secondary students lack skills for lifelong learning and problem-solving in today's complex world. As a result, institutions of higher learning are increasingly challenged to provide students with opportunities to (a) develop studying skills while enrolled in regular academic courses, (b) enhance expertise in complex, multifaceted curricula, (c) participate in communities of learning where authentic problems are addressed using collaborative expertise, and (d) learn to use software tools and information systems to support critical thinking, learning, and communicating.

While post-secondary institutions are striving to address these calls, research suggests their efforts may fall short. Hattie, Biggs, and Purdie's (1996) review found that study skills training tends to be more effective when students learn new studying skills in the context of actual courses, and when study skills training obliged students to be actively metacognitive. Our review (Hadwin and Winne, 1996) of study skills training indicates that interventions satisfying Hattie *et al.*'s criteria may falter if they fail to support students in two features critical to effective self-regulated learning: setting goals and monitoring learning. To develop skills for coping with complex problems that challenge the grasp of any one individual, students can profit from opportunities to participate in communities of learning where authentic problems are encountered, expertise is shared and distributed among peers, and collaborative approaches to constructing knowledge and solving problems are encouraged (Brown and Campione, 1994; Rogoff, 1994). These features, however, are rare in post-secondary settings.

In this chapter, we describe a state-of-the-art, multicomponent software tool, called CoNoteS (Collaborative Notes System), that we are developing using an authoring system for building adaptive learning systems (STUDY; Field and Winne, 1997). CoNoteS is a collaborative notetaking system designed to support students to (a) analyse task requirements and resources, (b) set goals strategically, (c) monitor the implementation and utility of study tactics they use to approach goals, and (d) metacognitively adapt studying methods. CoNoteS can be used for solo studying or collaborative work in small learning communities. CoNoteS' features include methods for organizing information, hyperlinking and indexing material, and tracking successive updates to course content and projects. Our system is distinguished by its capabilities to (a) observe how a student uses study tactics, (b) provide feedback to students about the correspondence between plans and actual studying, and how useful various tactics have been, and (c) support students in developing skills and strategies for collaborating. The interface and functionality of CoNoteS is strategically grounded in theories of self-regulated learning (e.g. Butler and Winne, 1995; Borkowski and

Thrope, 1994; Garcia and Pintrich, 1994; Pintrich, 1995; Winne and Hadwin, 1996; Zimmerman, 1994), situated cognition (Brown, Colins and Duguid, 1989; Lave and Wenger, 1991; Salomon, 1993), and collaborative learning (Brown, Campione, Webber and McGilly, 1992; Brown, Collins and Duguid, 1989; Lave and Wenger, 1991). In the following, we introduce theories of self-regulated learning, situated cognition, and collaborative learning and illustrate ways in which CoNoteS' interface has been designed to promote contextually grounded, self-regulated learning in networked collaborative learning environments.

56.2   Self-regulated learning

The notion that higher education should strive to promote independent, lifelong learning has become popular recently. Many instructional innovations in higher education are moving away from didactic, instructor-centred approaches to more interactive student-centered approaches. This shift reflects an attempt to engage students actively in searching for information relevant to their goals and in cognitive processing with which knowledge is constructed. The ultimate goal is to provide opportunities for students to develop skills, strategies, attitudes and behaviours that contribute to becoming independent lifelong learners.

Successful self-regulating learners approach learning strategically. They critically assess learning situations and assigned tasks, supplementing instructional cues and support that may be provided in their learning environment. They synthesize their knowledge of: a task's conditions, beliefs and experiences as learners, long-term goals, and conditional knowledge about content and strategies. The result of this first phase of engagement are goals and standards they generate about engaging with the task. As they begin working on the task per se, self-regulating learners update all these types of information to strategically select, adapt, and generate learning tactics (Butler and Winne, 1995; Hadwin and Winne, 1997; Winne and Hadwin, in press). Such learners develop and adaptively refine skills and strategies useful in continuing their learning across a variety of contexts.

Learning how to monitor and control processes and behaviours associated with learning is a complex process. It involves much more than learning sets of prescribed tactics and methods (Butler and Winne, 1995). Difficulties students experience may arise in many parts of the learning process (Winne, 1995, 1997). Students may struggle with understanding, monitoring, or controlling: (a) the way they define or interpret academic tasks (Briggs, 1990), (b) goals they set or ways they plan to engage in the academic task (Morgan, 1985), (c) qualities of tactics and strategies they use to engage the task (for a review, see Hattie *et al.*, 1996), or (d) whether and how they use internal and external evaluations of their engagement in the task to update knowledge about the task and about themselves as learners (Winne, 1997; Winne and Hadwin, in press).

We (Hadwin and Winne, 1997; Winne and Hadwin, in press) suggest that studying unfolds across four dynamic and recursively linked phases: task understanding, goal setting and planning, enacting study tactics and strategies, and metacognitively adapting studying now and in the future (see also Simpson and Nist, 1984). Productively self-regulating students metacognitively monitor their performance across each of these phases of studying (see Figure 56.1). As a result, they generate cognitive evaluations about the task, themselves as learners, and discrepancies between desired and actual accomplishments. These students use the evaluations generated through metacognitive monitoring to enact metacognitive control. As a result, they may choose alternative tactics, or they may adapt the tactics themselves or their understanding of those tactics.

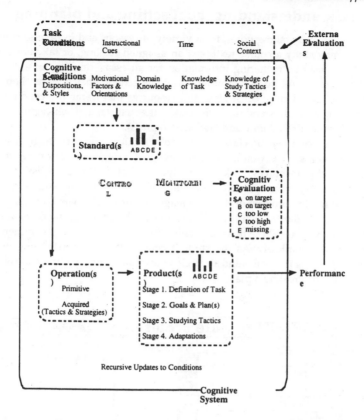

Figure 56.1 A model of recursively updated, self-regulated studying – from "Studying as Self-Regulated Learning" by P. H. Winne and A. F. Hadwin, 1998, in D. J. Hacker, J. Dunlosky, & A. C. Graesser (Eds), *Metacognition in Educational Theory and Practice*, Hillsdale, NJ: Erlbaum. Copyright 1998 by Lawrence Erlbaum Associates

Despite obvious complexities (e.g. see Winne, 1997), students can learn to become strategically self-regulating. Students can learn to become self-regulating (monitoring and controlling their own behaviour, motivation, and cognition) when they are given opportunities to: (a) receive feedback about their own learning; (b) examine their strengths and weaknesses as learners; (c) experience success through their own efforts and persistence; (d) see metacognition, problem-solving, and learning strategies modelled; and (e) practice and receive feedback on their task understanding, goal setting, planning, and evaluation across tasks and spanning time (adapted from Pintrich, 1995, and Winne and Hadwin, in press). In each of these events, metacognitive monitoring and control are keys to self-regulated learning (Winne, 1995; Butler and Winne, 1995). We designed the CoNoteS system with these challenges mind. CoNoteS is an innovative electronic notebook designed to promote metacognitive monitoring, control, and evaluation as students engage in all four phases of studying as self-regulated learning. CoNoteS' interface design provides implicit and explicit cues to support students' metacognitive monitoring and control of learning processes as learners navigate these four phases of studying.

56.3   Task understanding, goal setting and planning

Students study, often by taking notes, for a variety of reasons and in diverse contexts. For example, they may study a course textbook, an assigned reading, or take notes in a class discussion. They may be gathering information for an essay, drafting an assignment, or preparing for an exam. As studying unfolds, students generate perceptions about what the studying task is, and identify constraints and resources that frame the conditions of that task. Constructing an understanding of the task is the first stage of self-regulated studying (Hadwin and Winne, 1997; Winne and Hadwin, in press).

We hypothesize that five main classes of variables influence this first stage of studying as well as subsequent stages. Conditions include goal orientation, learning styles, time constraints, available resources, task knowledge, subject matter expertise, and interest. Processes are basic cognitive operations as well as learned tactics and strategies that create task understanding, the product of this first stage of studying. Goals governing processes are represented as standards, such as grading criteria and past performance. Evaluations are judgments students makes about their understanding of the task, such as confidence, clarity, completeness, and complexity. As the student constructs an understanding of the task, methods for addressing it – tactics and strategies – are automatically retrieved from memory and selected, thereby creating a plan.

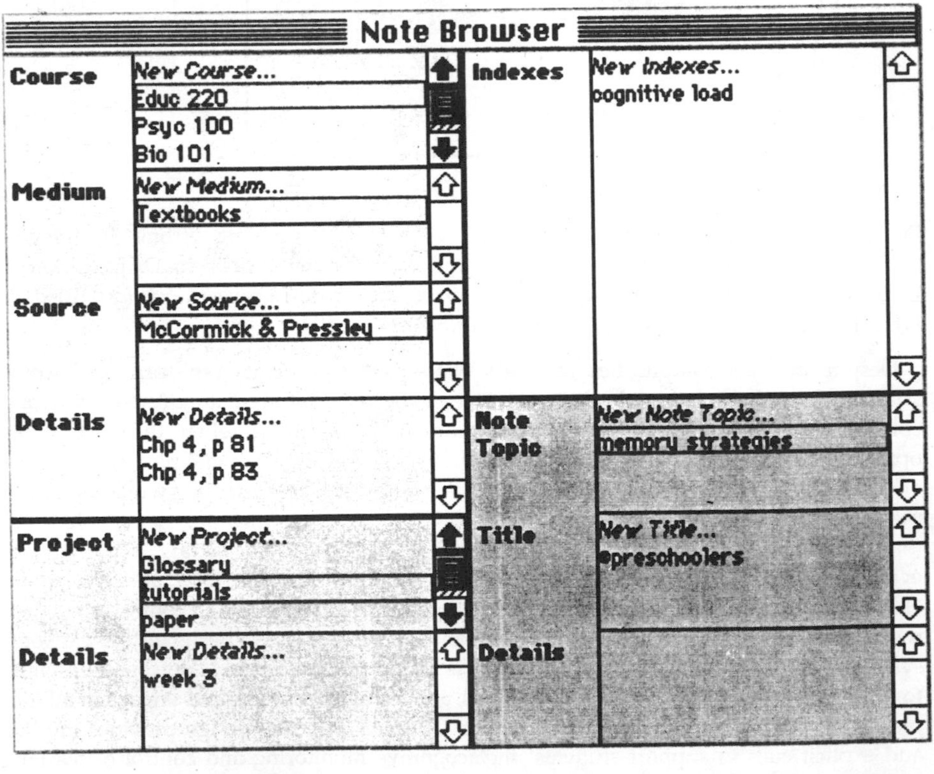

Figure 56.2   CoNoteS' catalogs browser

CoNoteS has been designed to support students at both global and detailed levels as they construct perceptions of note taking tasks associated with a course; as they set goals for notetaking and studying to address various purposes, and as they plan their notetaking activities and tactics. In the first notetaking session for a course, students are invited to use information about the course and its resources (e.g. texts, library reserves, assignments) to develop labels that constitute a multidimensional catalogue of course content and tasks (see Figure 56.2). These labels can be linked to individual notes and later be used to classify and search for notes particular to a label. One catalogue identifies the course, media that convey information, sources of information from which students are taking a note, and any details of that source the student considers useful, such as page numbers or a world wide web URL. A second catalogue records the students' entries about projects in the course, for example, tutorials, a term paper, the midterm exam, self-scheduled reviews, and so forth. For each project, students may also label details (or outlines). A third catalogue identifies all notes in a given course using a three-tiered system: topic, title, and details. A fourth catalogue allows the student to create index terms for individual or sets of notes, and hyperlink those indexes directly to the relevant notes.

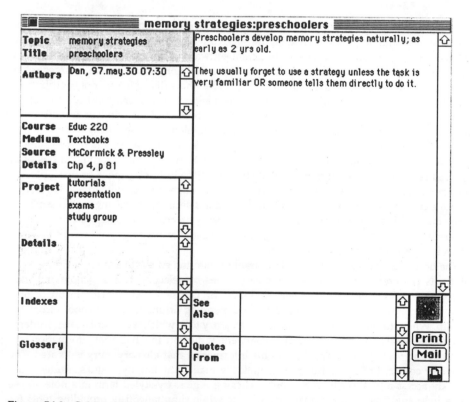

Figure 56.3 CoNoteS' note window

Organizing information about a course according to these four multidimensional catalogues serves three instructional purposes. First, as students choose labels to enter in these directories, they are invited to consider questions such as 'What do I have to do in this course?' (projects), 'Where might information come from?' (media and sources), 'What topics we will cover?' (note topics), what are basic terms for organizing and differentiating this information (indexes). Thus, students are encouraged to address features of a course (conditions, processes, and standards) and generate perceptions about the course in terms of resources, assignments, topics, and ways to index that material. Second, assigning labels and categories to these catalogues generates a labelling system with which students can organize and access information, thereby inviting them to engage in meta-classification of content.

Third, the interface invites students to continuously re-visit their meta-classification of content as they proceed with the course, rehearsing and elaborating earlier plans for studying and addressing assignments. Overall, CoNoteS encourages students to think about assignments, resources, and topics as components of larger themes that can and should be metacognitively re-examined in continuous planning every time they study with CoNoteS. Metacognitively engaging in this type of task analysis, goal setting, and planning is a pivotal component of self-regulated learning.

56.4 Metacognitive monitoring of notetaking and study tactics

CoNoteS was designed to support students in metacognitive monitoring and control in the midst of their studying. As shown in Figure 56.3, each note contains several distinct regions (identified by colour backgrounds in the actual software). The first is the note itself. To the right of a note's text are reflections of how that note is organized within a larger set of information: (a) the topic and title of the note, (b) its authors (listed in order of contributions to the note), (c) the 'location' of the note's information in the course, and (d) projects to which the note's information contributes. Along the bottom of the window are four other regions that invite the student to monitor the note in relation to organizing features of the course (Indexes), cross-references to other unique notes (see also, a list of note topics-titles), Glossary terms used in this note, and notes from which verbatim information has been Quoted From. Implicitly, information that students place in these regions or that CoNoteS automatically records (for example, when a student links a current note to another one to create a cross reference) invites students to engage in selecting, organizing, and assembling information. These cognitive operations afford deeper processing and support the creation of a rich associative system for accessing, monitoring and evaluating relationships between ideas in a course that are recorded in notes.

The note's text itself also provides important monitoring cues (not shown in Figure 56.3). Students can create index terms or glossary notes by selecting text in a note and then choosing an option on a popup menu to 'Index' or 'Glossary' that selected text. CoNoteS then automatically bolds or colours the text depending on the tool they choose from the popup. When studying definitions using the glossary tool, which we describe later, students can quickly revisit the context of that glossary entry, the note in which that information was created, and visually identify where in the information that glossary entry is located. The styled or coloured text in notes are automatically made into 'hot' hyperlinks. Students can quickly access a glossary term by double clicking a glossary-styled term in a note. These links help students review domain knowledge while simultaneously providing tools for students organize information.

Another feature of CoNoteS is that when students copy text from one note or source into another note (a sink), CoNoteS automatically styles the information that is copied in another distinctive way and places a reference to the source note in the sink note's Quotes From region. That reference is also a hyperlink. Should the student want, in a later studying session, to review all of the information in a note from which a sample was quoted, they can retrieve that sink note by double clicking its topic-title entry in the Quotes From region.

By styling verbatim copy differently than normal note text, CoNoteS implicitly cues students to attend to the degree to which they copy material rather than paraphrase it. Entries in Quotes From panel not only keep track of original sources so that students can easily collate information, but also implicitly show that other topics and titles for notes relate to a current note.

CoNoteS was designed to collect data about all these linking activities. We are designing methods by which this data can be used to give explicit feedback to students about selecting, assembling, and translating information. For example, CoNoteS might provide guidance (when relevant) to students who spend the majority of their exam studying activities cutting and pasting notes from other sources rather than engaging in deeper and more effective cognitive processing, such as paraphrasing 'on their own'.

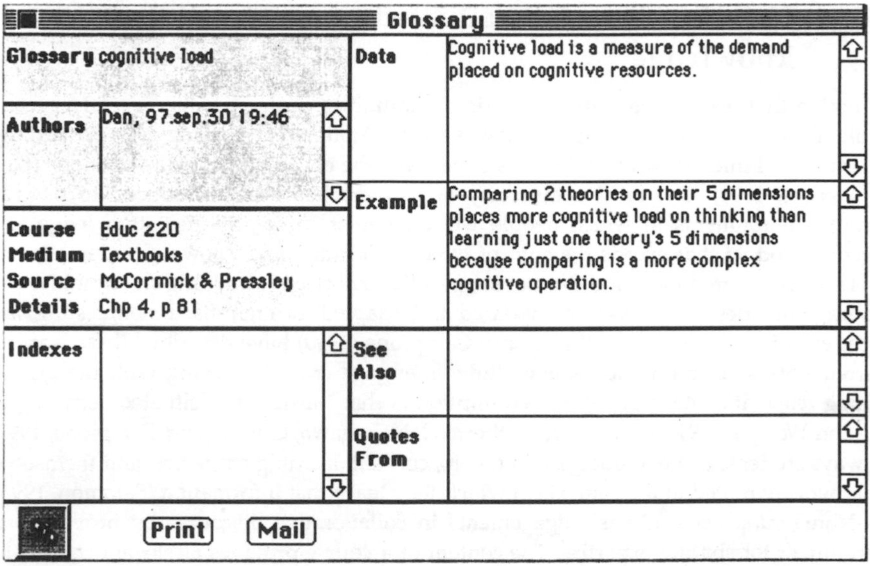

Figure 56.4   CoNoteS' Glossary Template

56.5   Metacognitve control of notetaking and studying tactics

One of the intended effects of metacognitive monitoring is that students use products of self-evaluations to update their knowledge about study tactics, and to employ and strategically adapt processes for analysing tasks, setting goals and planning, applying tactics, and monitoring and evaluating features of their engagement in the studying. CoNoteS has been designed to support students in these activities. It invites students to experiment with different types of note taking templates and to design new templates. For example, students can choose between an array of questioning templates that provide 'stock' prompts for generating questions and recording answers. They can index these questions according to function (to review, to answer, and so forth), and catalogue these types of notes in Project-Details according to types of exam questions they represent.

Templates may also provide implicit cues about tactics. For example, a glossary template displayed in Figure 56.4 provides separate notetaking locations for a glossary description and an example. The latter cues the student about the potential utility of generating an example to supplement the glossary entry itself. CoNoteS can also accommodate students' requests for more explicit instruction or explanation about how glossary templates might be structured and about the benefits of each type of glossary template. For example, we can add to the Glossary template a button that will display another window that provides guidance and rationale for generating one's own examples. In this vein, we are currently developing tools to assist students to develop tactics such as self-questioning, comparing and contrasting, time management, and summarizing. We intend that these tools will be presented in such a way that students can adapt them as they collaborate to analyse challenges to their learning and co-construct new study tactics and strategies.

56.6 Learning as socially situated co-construction of knowledge

The notion that learning is fostered within communities of practice has recently become popular in education. Underlying this view is an assumption that learning develops through dynamic social interactions and that it is situated in the context of those interactions (Lave and Wenger, 1991). The label community of learners has been introduced to describe learning environments in which people work together to co-construct knowledge as a collective product that exeeds the sum of what each individual knows (Scardamalia and Berieter, 1994). Scardamalia and Bereiter suggest that knowledge building communities also encourage theories and ideas to be updated and adapted through discussion, testing, and critical examination. Similarly, Brown and Campione (1990) have described these learning environments as communities where students engage critical thinking with the goal of learning relevant content. A second assumption is that learning is a situated activity (e.g. Lave and Wenger, 1991; Brown, Ash, Rutherford, Nakagawa, Gordon and Campione, 1993). The ways students come to understand theory, content, learning strategies, and themselves as learners are rooted in the contexts in which they learn that information (Salomon, 1993).

CoNoteS supports students' engagements in collaborative discourse by providing an environment for sharing expertise. The content of a course provides a relevant context for note taking, cataloguing, and monitoring activities. As students share their notes, not only can they become active participants in discussions about content, but they can also address how they assemble, index, and organize that content. That is, both content and studying tactics can become focuses for conversations that build up collaboratively shaped knowledge of both topics and about collaborators.

We are now designing methods that will allow students to attach notes to email sent using the software application Eudora so that students can electronically share notes from their notebooks. Upon completion of this project, when a student receives a note, there will be an implicit invitation to make decisions about the degree and nature of collaboration. For example, a student may import a received note, cataloguing its Source as email and the Detail as the name of the sender. Thereafter, the student may link that received note to their own Projects, and classify it using their own labels for Note Topic, Title, and Details. When students save a received note in this way, CoNoteS 'locks' the text of the note so that it can not be altered, though it can be copied into other notes. This type of collaboration is akin to sharing source information. When students use this approach they are distributing ideas to each for one another to 'borrow' rather than truly collaborating to generate a communal product.

An alternative to this form of collaboration is the case where a student merges a peer's note. In this case, CoNoteS automatically adds the sender's note into the receiver's notebook according to the sender's catalogue labels for Projects, Indexes, and Note Topic, Title, and Detail. When CoNoteS identifies that one of the sender's catalogue labels does not exist in the receiver's catalogue, CoNoteS will add the sender's label in a distinctive colour. This marks the new cataloguing system as merged from the sender. In addition, the receiver may add new catalogue labels, such as Index terms or links to the sender's Projects. As senders and receivers use merging operations over an academic term, they are co-constructing content as well as systems for assembling and organizing content.

Beyond collaborating about content *per se*, CoNoteS also affords collaboration about the process of learning, of designing projects, of indexing notes, and so forth. Students who exchange notes about how and why they organize information as they do will be participating in a socially situated dialogue about how they define and address tasks. In this venue, CoNoteS provides tools for constituting a community of practice in which dialogues are jointly about content and procedures for learning.

56.7   CoNoteS as a research tool for examining self-regulated learning in networked collaborative learning environments

In addition to the aforementioned instructional properties, CoNoteS collects complete and precise data every time students interact with the interface. Every entry they make in a catalogue, every change to a note, every styling of text, is logged as to what was done and tagged with a time marker. Collecting this type of data is critical for investigating how students develop effective forms of self-regulated learning over time in collaborative learning environments. When coupled with a full record of the content of notes students make individually and collaboratively, these logs of how students study provide extensive resources for examining (a) what students set as study goals and plans, (b) how study, (c) and whether and under what conditions students change goals, plans, and studying tactics over time. That is, the data that CoNoteS gathers provides raw materials for modelling what studying means to students and how they enact it. This opportunity for analysis helps to bridge social constructionism and cognitive constructivism (Martin and Sugarman, 1996) by investigating how private cognition and sociocultural engagement intertwine as students' construct knowledge about course content in unison with adapting study tactics and collaborative skills that can support lifelong learning.

56.8   Conclusion

CoNoteS is an innovative notetaking system that has potential to promote self-regulated learning in networked collaborative learning environments. It implicitly affords and explicitly provides students with tools and enviroments in which to generate feedback about their learning, a critical resource for metacognitively monitoring and controlling their motivation and cognition. Pintrich (1995) and Winne (1997) suggest that students have greater likelihood of learning to become self-regulating when provided such opportunities to engage in metacognitively guided studying.

Situating an interface designed to promote self-regulated learning in a networked collaborative notetaking system enhances opportunities for students to model metacognition, problem solving, and learning strategies for one another. Students also are invited to share their expertise about course content and engage in penetrating discourse about those notes. Together, these conditions invite co-constructing understandings about course content, and how and why it has the shape it does, as described the language students generate for organizing notes through indexing and cataloguing. In short, beyond merely a sophisticated scaffold for learning, CoNoteS has potential to involve students in discussions about their cognitive engagement. Finally, CoNoteS' data collection features support our work as researchers as we investigate how students learn to co-construct understandings and become productively self-regulating learners.

Note

* Support for this research was provided by a grant to Philip H. Winne from the Social Sciences and Humanities Research Council of Canada (#410-95-1046), and a Social Sciences and Research Council of Canada doctoral fellowship awarded to Allyson Fiona Hadwin. Thanks to Dan Field, our programmer, and to Vivian Rosner and Rob McTavish for providing funding and technological assistance from the Lohn Lab. Correspondence should be addressed to: Allyson Hadwin or Philip H. Winne, Faculty of Education, Simon Fraser University, Burnaby, BC, Canada, V5A 1S6.

56.9   References

Borkowski, J.G. and Thrope, P.K. (1994) Self-regulation and motivation: a lifespan perspective on underachievement. In D.H. Schunk and B.J. Zimmerman (eds), *Self-regulation of Learning and Performance: Issues and Educational Implications*, Hillsdale, NJ: Lawrence Erlbaum.

Brown, A.L. and Campione, J.C. (1990) Communities of learning and thinking, or a context by any other name, *Contributions to Human Development*, **21**, 108–26.

Brown, A.L. and Campione, J.C. (1994) Guided discovery in a community of learners. In K. McGilly (ed.), *Classroom Lessons: Integrating Cognitive Theory and Classroom Practice*, Cambridge, MA: MIT Press.

Brown, A.L., Ash, D., Rutherford, M., Nakagawa, K., Gordon, A. and Campione, J.C. (1993) Distributed expertise in the classroom. In G. Salomon (ed.), *Distributed Cognitions: Psychological and Educational Considerations*, New York, NY: Cambridge University Press.

Brown, A.L., Campione, J.C., Webber, L.S. and McGilly (1992) Interactive learning environments: a new look at assessment and instruction. In B.R. Gifford and M.C. O'Connor (eds), *Changing Assessments: Alternative Views of Aptitude, Achievement and Instruction*, Boston, MA: Kluwer Academic Publishers.

Brown, J.S., Collins, A. and Duguid, P. (1989) Situated cognition and the culture of learning, *Educational Researcher*, **18**, 33–42.

Butler, D.L. and Winne, P.H. (1995) Feedback and self-regulated learning: a theoretical synthesis, *Review of Educational Research*, **65**, 245–81.

Field, D. and Winne, P.H. (1997) STUDY: An environment for authoring and presenting adaptive learning tutorials (version 3.1) [computer program].

Garcia, T. and Pintrich, P.R. (1994) Regulating motivation and cognition in the classroom: the role of self-schemas and self-regulatory strategies. In D.H. Schunk and B.J. Zimmerman (eds), *Self-regulation of Learning and Performance: Issues and Educational Implications*, Hillsdale, NJ: Lawrence Erlbaum.

Hadwin, A.F. and Winne, P.H. (1997) Goal setting in studying as self-regulated learning: making sense of disparate literatures. Paper accepted for presentation at the *Annual Meeting of the Canadian Society for the Study of Education*, June, St John's, Newfoundland.

Hadwin, A.F. and Winne, P.H. (1996) Study strategies have meager support: a review with recommendations for implementation, *Journal of Higher Education*, **67**, 692–715.

Hattie, J., Biggs, J. and Purdie, N. (19??) Effects of learning skills interventions on student learning: a meta-analysis, *Review of Educational Research*, **66**, 99–136.

Lave, J. and Wenger, E. (1991) *Situated Learning: Legitimate Peripheral Participation*, New York, NY: Cambridge University Press.

Martin, J. and Sugarman, J. Bridging social constructionism and cognitive constructivism: a psychology of human possibility and constraint, *Journal of Mind and Behavior*, **17**, 291–30.

Morgan, M. (1985) Self-monitoring of attained subgoals in private study, *Journal of Educational Psychology*, **77**, 623–30.

Pintrich, P.R. (1995) Understanding self-regulated learning, *New Directions for Teaching and Learning*, **63**, 3–12.

Rogoff, B. (1994) Developing understanding of the idea of communities of learners, *Mind, Culture, and Activity*, **1**, 209–29.

Salomon, G. (1993) Editor's introduction. In *Distributed Cognitions: Psychological and Educational Considerations*, New York, NY: Cambridge University Press.

Scardamalia, M. and Bereiter, C. (1994) Computer support for knowledge building communities, *Journal of the Learning Sciences*, **3**, 265–83.

Simpson, M.L. and Nist, S.L. (1984) PLAE: a model for independent learning, *Journal of Reading*, **28, 218–23**.

Winne, P.H. (1995) Inherent details in self-regulated learning, *Educational Psychologist*, **30, 173–87.**

Winne, P.H. (1997) Experimenting to bootstrap self-regulated learning, *Journal of Educational Psychology*, **89, 397–410.**

Winne, P.H. and Hadwin, A.F. 1998 Studying as self-regulated engagement in learning. In D. Hacker, J. Dunlosky and A. Graesser (eds), *Metacognition in Educational Theory and Practice*, Lawrence Erlbaum.

Zimmerman, B.J. (1994) Dimensions of academic self-regulation: a conceptual framework for education. In D.H. Schunk and B.J. Zimmerman (eds), *Self-regulation of Learning and Performance: Issues and Educational Implications*, Hillsdale, NJ: Lawrence Erlbaum.

57 The development and multi-site application of an inter-active multi-media study skills program for undergraduate students

David Ellis, Gabriel Jezierski and Phil Rees
University of Wales Institute, Cardiff

57.1 Introduction

The presentation at the Improving Student Learning Conference of the interactive Study Skills program being developed at the University of Wales Institute, Cardiff (UWIC) was primarily a hands-on demonstration. This chapter is based on that presentation and outlines the context and rationale of the project, the planning and content development, and the instructional design and technical aspects of the program. The chapter concludes by looking at how the project will be further developed, taking into account both comments received at the ISL Conference and internal evaluation at UWIC.

57.2 Context

UWIC is a large university sector higher education institution, catering for approximately 8,000 students, the large majority of whom are undergraduates.

It has for many years been the policy of UWIC that all undergraduates should be provided on entry with a study skills course in order to maximize their learning and achievement in higher education. In the past different faculties and courses have approached this task in individual ways and generally in a piecemeal fashion; they have tended to present similar content, but with little co-ordination between courses and faculties, thus duplicating effort. Additionally, the emphasis has tended to be on 'teaching' study skills through traditional delivery methods rather than focusing on students' learning and development of transferable skills. Initiated by the Faculty of Education and Sport, UWIC is now addressing these issues by developing an innovative and interactive multi-media package for all its incoming undergraduate students.

Beyond this immediate need UWIC is also attempting to address the demand for increased exploitation of Communications and Information Technologies (C&IT). One of the critical issues in this quest is the is the need to convert lecture notes into learning materials suitable for electronic delivery. The development of the Study Skills program has been, in effect, a testbed of this process; it has become a production model for enabling academic staff to produce learning materials easily and in a consistent format for self access by students anywhere and at any time, that is by putting it on to the web/Internet.

57.3 Purposes

The specific purposes of the new study skills program are thus to:

- provide a generic and uniform program of study skills, which is accessible to all undergraduate students electronically across all faculties;

- create an approach which is based on specific learning outcomes and which ensures students do acquire, and are able to demonstrate, the required skills;

- provide an efficient and effective means of maximizing students' learning during their undergraduate period at UWIC.

57.4 Development of the program

The development of the Study Skills program is the first cross-university project at UWIC in which the recently created Learning and Teaching Division has become involved. The project had been agreed by, and has the support of the Teaching and Learning Strategies Advisory Group.

To avoid unnecessary work and the reinventing of wheels, a search was made initially of existing study skills packages that are available, for example from Teaching and Learning Technology Program (TLTP) as well as commercial sources. Several were obtained for evaluation purposes. However, at the time of the evaluation none were available for web-based delivery, a key criteria for UWIC.

Due to this situation and the fact that the main intent was to use the project as a means of developing a general approach for the production of web-based learning materials, it was agreed to develop a specific UWIC Study Skills program from 'scratch'. From the outset there was a consensus that this should contain 'home grown' material already in existence within the university, which would be copyright free, thereby avoiding the biggest drawback of using other institutions' material.

The project plan agreed finally is:

- 1996–97 – input of raw data and text and template experimental period;

- 1997–98 – piloting of version one and development of interactive exercises/activities;

- 1998–99 – piloting of version two including in built student tracking and upgrading of presentation through, for example, the use of audio and video material;

- 1999–2000 – full implementation of the program, exploration of joint ventures with other institutions, marketing etc.

As with most such projects there has been a mixture of formal planning along with 'adjustments' and changes being made along the way; a kind of rapid prototyping approach with several revision cycles.

57.5 Content development

The study skills units written to date include:

- About this program

- What to expect at university

- What about you?

  - How to get yourself organized

  - How to be a good learner

- Getting the information
    - Getting the most out of lectures
    - Effective reading
- Thinking about and discussing what you are learning
    - Critical thinking
    - How to give a good seminar
    - What are tutorials for?
- Applying what you have learned
    - Writing better assignments
    - Report writing
    - Citation and referencing
    - Doing your best in exams
- What's it all for? How does it feel when it's all over? (Graduation Day)

It is also intended to add shortly:

- Using language
- Using numbers and statistics
- Chemical formulae and equations

Each unit is self-contained and includes a number of compulsory self-assessment exercises, designed to ensure student learning occurs. The program is being so designed that students have to proceed step by step and make correct responses before continuing. If a student makes an error, then an explanation is given as to why the answer is incorrect or guidance about where to seek help is provided in order to make an improved response. If a student is unable to proceed for any reason then an email can be sent to the appropriate tutor or a fellow student, asking for assistance. Under normal circumstances a unit cannot be successfully completed unless all exercises are fully correct, although a 'read only' or browsing facility will be available in a later version for students simply to 'dip into' or audit a unit to meet their specific needs at a particular time or to return to any part of the program for revision purposes. It is envisaged that when a unit is finished an automatic record will be made and dispatched to the relevant tutor by email. Exercises will thus not have to be marked, only checked that they have been completed successfully; this process will enable tutors to track students' progress through the program.

The implications of these requirements for the design of the program, especially from the technical point of view, and how this is to be achieved are described below.

57.6   Design of the program – learning environments

In this section some of the technical choices made when putting together the learning system are outlined. Some of the characteristics of the specifications requested and how UWIC wished the system to behave are then described, along with information on how the online systems work and some of the problems initially encountered. The actual technologies used in the system are then explained.

57.6.1 Specification

One of the first tasks in the project was to identify a set of desirable characteristics for the learning environment.

57.6.2 Responsiveness

The time between a learner taking an action and getting a response should be as short as possible. This might be the time taken to navigate from one page to another, or the time taken to have a multiple choice question answered.

57.6.3 A consistent 'look and feel' with easy navigation

The learner needs to be free to concentrate on the learning material without being distracted by the learning environment. the environment should be consistent within itself, and consistent between different learning units.

57.6.4 Questions and answers

The system should be able to support a range of multiple choice questions and free text exercises that are computer marked or self-assessed as appropriate.

57.6.5 Standards base

The technologies and code should conform to agreed standards.

57.6.6 Multi-media

The system should be capable of presenting audio, video and animation.

57.7 Problems with earlier learning systems

Until a few years ago the use of computers for the presentation of learning materials was largely confined to dedicated machines that had exotic devices such as laserdisks and video controllers attached to them.

At that time there was a confusing array of standards. There was a number of competing hardware standards which meant that a particular piece of courseware might run on one machine, but would not work at all on a similar machine with a different make of player.

The equipment costs were high, over five thousand pounds for a laserdisk system, and production costs were also high with many pieces of courseware having development budgets running into six or even seven figures. Once they were produced the materials were relatively inflexible, and could only be adapted by programmers.

This meant that the course materials were:

- high cost;
- restricted access;
- not easily adaptable.

This situation was improved a little by the introduction and standardization of CD-ROM formats, which allowed learning materials of a similar quality to laserdisks to be developed and delivered at lower costs.

Perhaps the most significant long-term development has been in networking and the Internet.

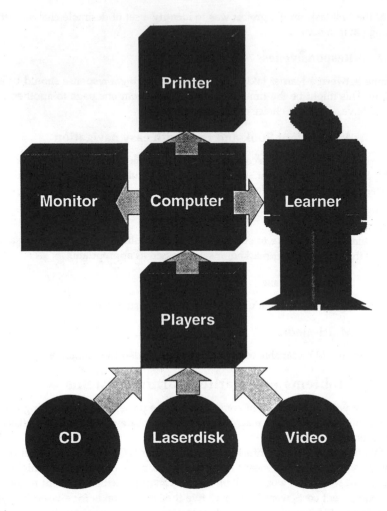

Figure 57.1

Here there are two different types of computer. A server, where information and programs are stored, and a client, that requests, interprets and displays the information it held on the server. This configuration has substantially reduced the costs of producing, distributing and updating materials. Learning materials are stored centrally (on the server), which means that they are cheaper and easier to deploy. Materials are stored on the server's hard disk instead of being pressed to a CD or laserdisk. This means that the materials can be revised more frequently and distributed more easily. There are thus:

- lower production costs;
- flexible (or continual) development;
- higher interaction;
- group learning;
- closer monitoring.

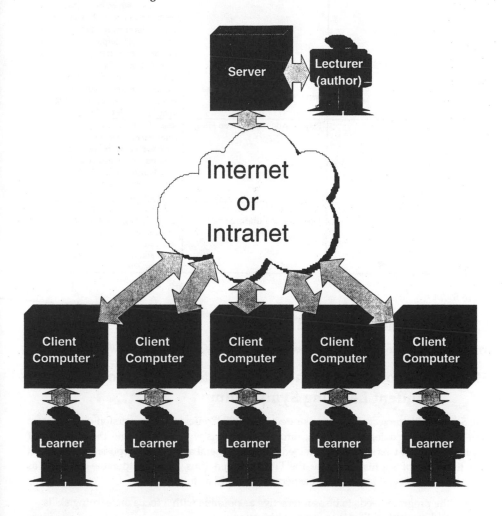

Figure 57.2

Technology	Used For	Comments
Microsoft Word Word Internet Assistant	Preparing Web Pages	Microsoft Word is the standard word processor, used by all UWIC staff.
Javascript	Navigation Interactive Questions	This is a scripting language built in to a web browser. It handles the logic of which information is displayed and controls when and how media clips are played. Because it is interpreted by the web browser, it greatly improves the speed with which multiple choice questions are marked as it does not have to wait for a server connection or for a plug in or Java applet to load.
Real Player	Playing Audio and Video Files	Real player technology compresses video and audio information, which means that files are a more manageable size. It also streams the file, which means that playing starts more quickly.
Macromedia Flash	Animations Diagrams and Illustrations	This is used for preparing complex diagrams and illustrations. These can contain interactive animations, annotations and can be zoomed to show details.

Table 57.1

57.8 Technologies used

The Study Skills program has been developed using the technologies shown in Table 57.1:

57.9 Responses from the 5th International Improving Student Learning Symposium

The Study Skills project was demonstrated at the ISL Conference. The version-one program was available for delegates to work through. This was well received and the audience of approximately 20 was suitably impressed with the general approach, purposes of the project and the level of sophistication of the IT developed thus far. Considerable advice was received from several international experts in the field as follows:

- the program needs to be as interactive as possible with a focus on learning skills and concepts rather than information giving;

- the supporting text needs to be updated in places;

- more responses saying why an answer is wrong would be helpful and assistance needs to be given if a user cannot proceed rather than simply being told an answer is wrong;

- similar materials being developed at other universities should be viewed;

- open-ended as well as closed tasks should be included in order to develop students' independent and reflective learning skills;

- a wide variety of media should be used in order to maintain student interest and to meet the specific objectives of each unit and task.

57.10   Where are we now?

Since the ISL Conference, the Study Skills program is currently available on UWIC's four sites in Cardiff over the network. While it still has a number of shortcomings, students can either access it as a resource for self study or be directed to it by a tutor.

It is UWIC's first main step into developing a significant program of resource-based materials that can be accessed electronically. It has already proved very beneficial for one course where an increase in student number targets, along with a number of other factors, caused it to be taught through different means. This led to a major review of the course and the subsequent validation of the Study Skills program as half a module. This was mounted on a server and the students have been evaluating their learning experience as a set assignment on the course. This will provide valuable data for evaluating the student experience of this small but significant step toward exploiting Communications and Information technologies at UWIC.

58 Communicating through computers: changing teaching changing times?

Robert Fox and Allan Herrmann
Teaching Learning Group, Curtin University, Western Australia

58.1 Overview

Great expectations surround the new and emergent electronic technologies and it is assumed that the use of new electronic technology will result in more efficient and effective teaching and learning in higher education. The volume of the rhetoric calling for full utilization of electronic communications technologies in distance education, to some extent masks the underlying assumptions regarding the complex relationships between teaching and learning and technology and the contexts in which they exist. This chapter reviews perceptions of electronic communications technology and identifies some the costs and some of the basic skills which teachers must develop in this environment. Within this context, some strategies for the development of appropriate courseware for web-based delivery are identified, which in turn leads to strategies for academic staff development appropriate for improving skills in courseware development and teaching and learning.

58.2 Introduction

Information technology resources – email, the Internet and the World Wide Web (WWW), and multimedia – are increasingly common components of the instructional experience for students: 'having an email address is, at least for some as important as having a mobile telephone' (Bigum, 1997). In this sense, getting online is seen as essential for getting on.

The publication of the Dearing inquiry (1997) into higher education in UK, was closely followed by a one-day colloquium on the implications of the report's pronouncements concerning the use of communication and information technologies (C & IT) and was published shortly afterwards (Fraser, 1997). The Dearing inquiry into C & IT recorded its main concern as costs in terms of time and funds and the relative scarcity of materials where value of the content outweighs the difficulties inherent in its mediation by computer.

58.3 The impact of costs

Fraser makes the point that the

> development of computer-based materials is . . . always expensive and any economic benefits, at least, are notoriously difficult to identify . . . The use of C & IT in learning and teaching might result in a better quality of learning: it might result in a more efficient means of learning: it always results in higher costs.
>
> (Fraser, 1997)

Further, his report on the Dearing committee's findings also mentions the costs associated with staff development and training. However, the main debate surrounded issues concerning the availability or otherwise of worthwhile and cost effective learning resources. In America, Becker (1996) conducted a more detailed costing of introducing information technology into education. His estimates are that an additional US $2,000 to $2,500 is needed to fund each student in their studies. The bulk of these costs (two-thirds) are human, primarily the need for staff development, training and for providing technical support. Green (1997) in his annual survey into computers in higher education notes that most public and private American universities charge their students to cover shortfalls in IT funding. Each student, on top of other payments, is now charged on average US $140 per year to meet the spiralling IT costs (1997).

Todd Oppenheimer (1997) raises a number of controversial issues concerning the importance of computers in schools.

> There is no good evidence that most uses of computers significantly improve teaching and learning, yet school districts are cutting programs – music, art, physical education – that enrich children's lives to make room for this dubious nostrum, and the Clinton Administration has embraced the goal of 'computers in every classroom' with credulous and costly enthusiasm.

> (Oppenheimer, 1997)

Nevertheless, the technological imperative is apparently unstoppable and the pressures to incorporate new technologies into higher education teaching and learning contexts seems inevitable (Holt and Thompson, 1995). At the same time, it is essential to monitor the impact technology is having on shaping work within institutions. This chapter is based on case-study research into using the web in distance education and focuses on attitudes towards the use of communications technologies to improve teaching and learning in varied contexts.

58.4   The Curtin context

The motivations and strategies for web-based teaching at Curtin University vary widely. Curtin Learning Link (Learning Link) located: http://www.curtin.edu.au/learn/ provides distance teaching staff at Curtin University, Western Australia with such an environment for supplementing, changing and replacing existing distance education materials.

Learning Link was trialled in 1996 as a web-based computer mediated communication system for Curtin distance students. During the trials, staff and student involvement was monitored and participants surveyed and interviewed in an effort to begin to develop understandings of the perceptions of, and meanings attributed to the web environment and its use by the participants.

Given that for the most part, 'tried and proven' distance teaching text materials already existed in electronic form, the temptation was to transfer them straight onto the web. This has also been the case for a number of courses which have, what are perceived to be, good lecture notes. A number of assumptions either explicitly or implicitly underlie the intention to 'load' print-based materials onto the web and are embedded in the assumption of the neutrality of technology. For the most part they are reflected in the much used Clark metaphor, 'mere vehicles that deliver instruction but do not influence student achievement any more than the truck that delivers our groceries causes change in our nutrition' . . .

'Basically, the choice of vehicle might influence the cost or extent of distributing instruction, but only the content of the vehicle can influence achievement' (Clark, 1983, p. 445).

The discussion arising from Clark's assertion continues, including the latest technology the web, listing papers challenging the 'no significant difference' position (1995). Carter (1996), in revisiting the argument as to whether or not technologies impact on the instructional message in the context of distance education, provides an insightful review of the arguments in the literature and concludes by renewing the Evans and Nation challenge for distance educators to contextualize their study of media/technology in the broader social and political environment within which learners live.

In a similar way the understanding that dominant classes and genders influence the development of media, also re-contextualizes the discussion. In supporting the need for more contextualized studies, the current investigation approaches Curtin Learning Link from the broader perspective and in the first stage endeavours to identify lecturer perception of its meaning for them; examples of the 'basic skills' which are necessary for them to work in this environment and how this impacts on the staff development activities of the distance education specialists.

58.5   Perceptions and meanings

Although Henri and Parer (1994) suggest that the challenge of computer-mediated communication will be to transfer theories of learning and pedagogical practice into applications of this technology, in practice none of the teaching or tutoring staff focused on this challenge. They were willing to accept that Leaning Link originated within the context of a distance education programme with a considerable investment in existing (largely) print-based materials. They therefore accepted that Curtin Learning Link has as its central focus communication. This was not to deny its roles in presenting content and accessing resources. However, in a country the size of Australia the provision of another option for communication was deemed to be a high priority. Clearly, the fact that this was the intention of the designers had some impact on the users.

Lecturers' perceptions of Learning Link were also revealed in the metaphors which they used. The use of the term 'virtual classroom' while introduced by a number of staff, has not been seen as helpful by the designers as it brings with it a set of social constructs and teaching strategies more appropriately left in the traditional classroom.

However, from the outset, three perceptions of lecturing staff regarding Learning Link became apparent. While they were not mutually exclusive, lecturers tended to identify with:

- a delivery perception (of university teaching and learning as an 'information transference' process and Learning Link as merely another method of delivery);

- a somewhat naive economic (cost-effectiveness) perception (using it to allow students to access the study materials – excluding copyrighted readings – and submit assignments and questions electronically, thereby reducing or re-allocating some of the costs);

- a communications channel perception (an attempt to provide a more 'interactive' learning experience for distance learners).

The main outcome of the first two perceptions was a 'load-up the existing materials' approach. These perceptions are embedded in an 'education as product' philosophy and saw Learning Link as merely a delivery mechanism.

The third perception could be typified as coming from a more 'process' view of education and in some cases was associated with more constructivist approaches and resulted in the lecturer endeavouring to include more discussion opportunities for learners to interact with her/himself and other learners and construct their own content meanings.

As outlined above, the Learning Link designers anticipated the most benefit for distance learners arising from the improved communications and discussion opportunities and for the most part were able to influence the agenda in this direction.

One lecturer conscientiously tried to incorporate both a comprehensive materials delivery site and a full communication/discussion facility and perhaps significantly was the only one out of five, with whom a post-offering debriefing was held, who felt that too much effort was required to use Learning Link as a teaching and learning environment.

The use of synchronous communications options was considered but quickly eliminated due to student locations across a number of time zones and because of a desire not to reduce the flexibility distance education provides. Research into asynchronous web-based discussion groups has been limited (e.g. see Schwan, 1997; Evans and Green, 1995) and therefore important for us to report on the teaching and learning environments within this project. With respect to the use of asynchronous communication options, three were canvassed: email, list servers and web-based discussion groups. Each unit incorporated the possibility of students being able to email staff and other students separately. The choice to use a web-based discussion group rather than a list serve was based on a number of factors. One primary reason was that the majority of students were not online for extended periods of time and therefore the advantages of a 'push' type technology like list servers were not available as students would check the more passive discussion groups each time they went online. This, together with the visual reinforcement of the discussion room structure and the ability to manipulate the messages to provide at least a minimal evaluation of individual participation, underscored our decision to provide at least one discussion room for each unit.

58.6 Basic skills

While the typing skills of lecturers may increase the output in terms of the number of web pages, and their knowledge of html or one of the proliferating web development software packages may improve the technical and design sophistication of the page, it is to a large extent, the meaning which is placed on the web as a teaching and learning tool which can impact most on the educational outcomes. As the designers' position, outlined above, provided the context within which much of the Learning Link development had taken place, the primary skills needed by lecturers must be understood within this context.

Student volunteered perceptions, surveys, interviews and discussions regarding the use of Learning Link indicate that distance students, the majority of whom are mature aged part-time, will not undertake activities related to their study without receiving a 'pay-off'. This does not necessarily have to be of any great magnitude, but must provide a significant return on the extra time and resources invested. In terms of this study, this means that they will not participate in Learning Link unless they perceive some meaningful benefit. Students involved in the earliest trial of Learning Link responded that: when they first linked in, they wished to view and interact with new 'content', not merely a re-presentation of the print materials which they had already received. However, as the semester progressed, the interaction with the tutor and other students provided greater interest and the majority of respondents agreed, proved more rewarding. Coupled with this is the finding by the School of Information Systems at Curtin University that approximately 80% of students responding to a survey indicated that they had printed off instructional web pages to take away to read. This range of responses from students reinforces the position that a key skill for a lecturer developing a web presence is being able to balance the presentation and discussion/interaction components and the integration or otherwise between the web and other teaching and learning materials Taylor *et al.* (in press) in a case study within this Learning Link case study develops this 'balancing' discussion further.

Staff development was needed to enable lecturers to design and select content in a way meaningful and useful to the learners. As mentioned above, simply converting lecture notes or even quality distance materials implies that a change in media would not benefit from content changes. While the need for a 'paradigm shift' was not argued, lecturers were encouraged to re-think their curriculum and consider new strategies in the web component development and implementation.

Staff need to be able to design and manage on-line discussions and communication (Kaye and Mason, 1988). Ensuring that groups work effectively is an important component of this skill, because as Evans and Nation point out 'humans in communication are engaged actively in the making and exchange of meanings . . . not merely about the transmission of messages' (1989, p. 37). The manner in which email is used by some staff make the understanding of these possibilities difficult to attain.

58.7   Strategies for academic staff development

Experience with academic staff development in other types of distance education media has lead to a move from one-off skills development workshops to selecting staff with whom to work more closely over the longer term. The two main reasons for this are low attendance at workshops and low levels of skills retention when the skills learned at the workshop are not able to be practised immediately. To this end a three-strand approach has been taken.

First, in working directly with selected staff specific discipline areas can be targeted. These staff already have evidenced high levels of interest and enthusiasm, or have been recognized as having potential to do so and can act as role models and supports within their teaching schools.

Secondly, from their feedback and with their co-operation, exemplary materials can be developed, as can work practices relevant to those disciplines to which other academic staff in that discipline can more easily relate (and indeed adopt or adapt).

Thirdly, by recording their 'stories' we can contextualize the development process for future colleagues and make the content more relevant for them. This is not a simple or short term project. It is based on the perceived need for staff to have a sense of 'ownership' of their Learning Link activities.

To a large extent, it is the lecturers' decision as to whether they undertake the technical work of page design and development themselves or use the development support services which can be provide at little or no cost to them. As with most distance materials development, effort is expended is at the 'front-end' in an attempt to reduce work at the delivery point. The lecturer is asked to examine which outcomes are required of the student and how best these can be achieved, keeping in mind cost-effectiveness for the university and learner and equity and access requirements. Where Learning Link provides suitable options it is used, contributing to the repertoire of teaching and learning opportunities. There are, of course, many subjective 'professional judgements' involved in this process which provide the opportunity of enhancing the skills of the teaching staff.

Another of the specific skills is that of establishing and managing discussions in the Learning Link environment. The lack of cues and rewards available in the face-to-face mode contributes to anxiety in both staff and learners. As is the case for technologies such as audio conferencing the lack of visual feedback proves to be a significant difficulty. Again, modelling possible alternatives and providing discipline specific examples is a most productive way of dealing with these difficulties. As an added support, the project co-ordinators are examining the possibility of setting up an exemplar 'unit' to enable exchange of ideas experiences between participating staff.

Lecturers are encouraged to conceptualize their unit of study in terms of content rather than time e.g. two hours per week of lecturers and two hours of tutorials, so that discussion groups can be constructed around the issues allowing learners to visit and contribute to various groups, a number of times throughout the semester. This has had the effect of reducing the linearity of the students discussion and while requiring more focus of the lecturers and learners, affords the opportunity to show more clearly the content relationships within the unit.

58.8   Conclusion

Clearly there are more issues involved in assisting lecturers to use the web-based Curtin Learning Link as part of their distance teaching than can be canvassed in this chapter. However, the issue of the need to re-conceptualize the course for developing a Learning Link web component has become evident. Simply moving content from one medium to another without taking into account problematic issues which arise misses the point. The position taken in this paper has been that technology is not and cannot be neutral or value-free that the ever increasing inclusion of electronic technology into the curriculum will impact and change the curriculum and will inevitably lead to a shift which now includes the technology as an entity in its own right in the curriculum (Green, 1996). And further, that ever increasing familiarity with the technology will also hide the impact and influencing factor of the technology on the message (Ihde, 1982 and 1990). That communicaiion and information technology is selected and is seen to be not merely 'non critical' to those 'reductively predisposed' as 'metaphysically similar but potentially literally identical to the human mind' (Ihde, 1982, p. 229) and that technology and its impact is complex and enormous and does affect change and in order to understand it and influence what happens and how it is used we need to understand and appreciate the multitude of non neutral effects the structures of texts and/or sounds and images; the impact of juxtaposing texts and/or sounds and images have on various social groups, on age, on gender, etc.

Feedback from learners and lecturers, therefore is critical to providing valuable information for enhancing future teaching and learning technology developments. These enhancements will then need to be implemented through working closely with specific lecturers and their students and involving lecturers in reflective development by contextualizing the process within disciplines.

58.9   References

Becker, H.J. (1996) How much will a truly empowering technology-rich education cost? In R. Kling (ed.), *Computerization and Controversy: Value Conflicts and Social Choices*, 2nd edn, San Diego: Academic Press, 190–6.

Bigum, C. (1997) Boundaries, barriers and borders: teaching science in a wired world. Keynote address for *CONASTA 46. Annual conference for Australian Science Teachers Association*, 29 June–4 July, http://www.ed.cqu.edu.au/~bigumc/papers/boundaries_borders_and_bar.html

Carter, V. (1996) Do media influence learning? Revisiting the debate in the context of distance education, *Open Learning*, **11**(1), 31–40.

Clark, R.E. (1983) Reconsidering research on learning from media, *Review of Educational Research*, **53**, 445–9.

Dearing Report, The National Committee of Enquiry into Higher Education (1997) http://www.leeds.ac.uk/educol/ncihe/

Fraser, M. (1997) Dearing and IT: some reflections, *CTI Textual Studies*, http://info.ox.ac.uk/ctitext/publish/comtxt/ct15/fraser.html

Holt, D. and Thompson, D. (1995) Responding to the technological imperative: the experience of an open and distance education institution, *Distance Education*, **16**(1), 43–64.

Ihde, D. (1982) The technological embodiment of media. In M.J. Hyde (ed.), *Communication Philosophy and the Technology Age*, Tuscaloosa, Alabama: University of Alabama.

Ihde, D. (1990) *Technology and the Lifeworld: From Garden to Earth*, Bloomington: Indiana University Press.

Evans, T. and Green, B. (1995) Dancing at a distance? postgraduate studies, 'supervision', and distance education. In *Proceedings of the 'Graduate Studies in Education: Innovation in Postgraduate Research and Teaching' Symposium at the 25th Annual National Conference of the Australian Association for Research in Education*, Hobart.

Evans, T. and Nation, D. (1989) *Critical Reflections on Distance Education*, Falmer Press: London.

Green, K. (1997) *Campus Computing Survey: A National Study of the Use of Information Technology in Higher Education*, Claremont Graduate University: Center for Educational Studies.

Green, B., Gough, N. and Blackmore, J. (1996) *The Australian Educational Researcher*, **23**(3).

Henri, F. and Parer, M. (1994) Computer conferencing and content analysis. In T. Nunan (ed.), *Distance Education Futures: Selected Papers from the 11th Biennial Forum of the Australian and South Pacific External Studies Association*, 21–23 July 1994, Adelaide.

Kaye, A. and Mason, R. (eds) (1988) *Mindweave: Communications and Distance Education*, Oxford: Pergamon Press.

No Significant Difference Phenomenon (1995) Fourth edition, http://tenb.mta.ca/phenom/phenom.html

Oppenheimer, T. (1997) The computer delusion, *The Atlantic Monthly*, **280**(1), 45–62, http://www.TheAtlantic.com/issues/97jul/computer.htm

Schwan, S. (1997) *Media Characteristics and Knowledge Acquisition in Computer Conferencing*, Tubingen, Deutsches Institut f.r Fernstudienforschung und der Universita Tubingen.

Taylor, P., Geelan, D., Fox, R. and Herrmman, A. (in press) Perspectives and possibilities: electronic interactivity and social constructivist teaching in a science, mathematics and technology teacher education program: what works and why?, *The Australian Society for Computers in Learning in Tertiary Education (ASCILITE) December, 1997 Conference.* http://www.curtin.edu.au/conference/ascilite97/papers/139.html

59 No time for students to learn important skills? Try 'unstuffing' the curriculum

Robert Fox and Alex Radloff
Teaching Learning Group, Curtin University of Technology,
Perth, Australia

59.1 Overview

Higher education is currently facing major challenges – a move from elite to mass education, an explosion of knowledge across disciplines, the need for accountability to stakeholders, competition between universities for students, globalization of education and work, rapid technological development, and resource constraints. One outcome of these challenges is the 'overstuffed curriculum' – courses which have too much content and not enough opportunity for learners to develop transferable, lifelong skills such as critical thinking, problem-solving, communication and interpersonal skills, all of which are demanded by employers and needed and valued by students.

The consequences of a curriculum which stresses content over process is lack of opportunity for students to develop skills which will help them be more effective learners and increase their chances of employment in a rapidly changing and globally competitive workplace. Faced with an 'overstuffed curriculum', students may adopt a surface approach to learning, rely on tricks and short-term memory to cope with assessment, and complain about an unmanageable workload. Teachers lack time for reflection or adequate planning to meet student needs, rely on the 'quick fix' to solve instructional problems, and may end up cynical and burnt out.

This chapter is based on a workshop which addresses the symptoms of the overstuffed curriculum and the consequences for student learning. In it we offer strategies to help teachers who are 'clinging to the content' to rethink the way they plan and teach their courses to make room in the curriculum for lifelong learning skills.

59.2 Introduction

One issue facing learners and lecturers in higher education is having to learn and teach more in less time. This can result in an overstuffed curriculum in which courses have too much content and a reliance on student 'busy work' to comply with assessment demands. The overstuffed curriculum leaves little opportunity for learners to acquire a deep understanding of the subject, or to develop learning to learn skills and 'generic' lifelong skills such as critical thinking, problem-solving, communication and interpersonal skills.

Most students, especially first year students, need help to become effective learners. Such help is most useful when it is offered in the context of subject learning (Chalmers and Fuller, 1995). Unfortunately, teachers often assert that there is no room in the curriculum for learning to learn and lifelong skills because discipline content must take precedence. As a result, many students may struggle (and fail) to meet the intellectual challenges of tertiary study because they have not been provided with the opportunity to learn how to learn. In the same way, the development of 'generic' lifelong learning skills may also be neglected as teachers attempt to 'cover' more and more discipline-specific content.

In order to avoid the problems associated with an overstuffed curriculum and to achieve a quality education, tertiary teachers must answer the following questions: 'How can we ensure that students are effective learners – active and reflective about their work and responsible for their own learning?'; 'How can we encourage learning for understanding and transfer?'; and 'How can we encourage positive attitudes to, and skills for, lifelong learning?'

In this chapter, we provide practical suggestions to address these questions. The suggestions are based on our own teaching experiences and our work in academic staff development, instructional design and distance education. They are also supported by research on student learning and tertiary teaching (Angelo, 1993; Gibbs and Lucas, 1995; Ramsden, 1993; Shuell, 1990). Underlying these practical suggestions is an assumption about the general approach to teaching which tertiary teachers adopt. We believe that effective teachers are systematic in the way they conceptualize and plan their courses and teaching, adopt a reflective approach to their work, and seek and value feedback about their courses and teaching.

We focus on ways in which we can 'unstuff' the curriculum and encourage quality learning under two broad headings: Course planning and design; and Instructional activities and strategies. The ideas we provide are offered as practical suggestions which can be implemented.

59.3   Course planning and design

59.3.1   Identify the learners

Develop an overall map or profile of your students. This may be a difficult task, but it will help you to focus on the content of the course and how the content will be treated. The main categories to guide you are: age range, gender mix, cultural backgrounds and diversity, student expectations of the course, their expectations of their role and that of the lecturer, previous study experiences, especially within the subject area and discipline culture of the course, the numbers taking the course and the mode of study (full-time or part-time, on-campus, off-campus or mixed-mode). This sketch becomes more complex as variations in students increase. Rowntree (1994, pp. 41–5) provides a useful checklist and a sample profile of a 'typical' learner.

59.3.2   Gauge the workload of the course

You need to consider what the course is worth in terms of its study load and time you expect students to devote to this course in relation to their total study load. A useful guide is to match the number of similar or equivalent courses students are required to take per semester. In very general terms, a full time equivalent undergraduate student may take four courses of study per semester. How many hours of study, on average do you expect students to be studying per week? Divide these hours by four to gauge the hours per week your students can be expected to spend on your course.

Another guide is to match the credit points the course is worth to find a benchmark for study load. In some universities, dividing the credit points by two will provide a general guide to hours of study expected (e.g. Curtin University Handbook, 1997, p. 67). It is interesting to note that a number of research findings suggest that we poorly match our expectations of workload with the time students require to study (for example Svinicki, 1990; Chambers, 1992; MacDonald-Ross and Scott, 1995). Feedback from distance education students at Curtin also supports this view (DESSE, 1997).

How realistic is the expected student workload, not only in relation to the course objectives, assessment and credit points but also in terms of students' other commitments. Research into how students spend their time outside class (de la Harpe, Radloff and Parker, 1997) points to a worrying trend with many students reporting spending more time in paid work than in study.

59.3.3 Clarify the rationale and context for the course of study

Ask yourself these questions and answer them in three or four sentences. Why is this course worth studying? How does it fit into the programme(s) of which it is part? How does the course relate to other courses in the programme(s)? Are there pre-requisite courses to this course? Is this course a pre-requisite to other courses? Are there other courses that parallel this course and should be taken at the same time?

By answering these questions you get a clearer idea of the underlying rationale for the course and where the course fits within a larger context. It then becomes possible to isolate or pinpoint more accurately the parameters of the particular course you are working on.

59.3.4 Identify the learning objectives and outcomes

Ask yourself what you want your students to know and be able to do after completing this course and what you imagine or believe students will want to know and be able to do when they have finished this course. Write no more than three or four outcome statements in terms of knowledge, skills and attitudes. By sticking to a few key statements on outcomes, you will find it easier to maintain a firm grasp on the general focus of the course. Ensure that learning to learn and lifelong learning skills are included in the objectives.

59.3.5 Develop assessment criteria to match the overall objectives

The assessment tasks should match the objectives and outcomes you have identified. The weighting of different assignments and the examination should also reflect the importance of the corresponding objectives and outcomes.

Develop a marking scheme which outlines how you will assess student learning. Clarify the main levels of marking based on overall objectives and outcome statements. Later, when you develop details about the course, you will be able to elaborate on assignments and the marking scheme. At this stage, however, generate a series of key concepts/issues/skills etc. that make up the essence of the course.

59.3.6 Decide what to include and exclude in the course

It is often difficult to determine what to keep in and what to leave out of a course. Try writing a list of all items, issues, topics, concepts, etc. you would want to include in the course taking into account the three or four outcomes you listed in the paragraph: Identify the learning objectives and outcomes, divide your list into three columns: essential, recommended and supplementary. The limitations of a semester course mean that despite your desire as the subject specialist to include more than is realistic your main task is to pare down the curriculum to its essential elements. The essential list must include the key issues mentioned earlier in this paper regarding a range of transferable generic and lifelong learning skills. All too often, these skills and strategies are left out or squeezed out as the course discipline content increases. Candy *et al.*'s (1994, pp. 65–6) description of how this happens at present and how they advocate placing life long learning skills in the centre of the course is illustrated in Figure 59.1. Radloff (1996) recommends a strategy to avoid this squeezing, by integrating all discipline content with lifelong learning skills, as shown in Figure 59.2.

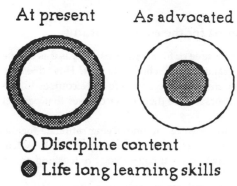

At present   As advocated

○ Discipline content
◉ Life long learning skills

Figure 59.1   Simplified after Candy et al. (1994, p. 66)

○ Discipline content
◉ Life long learning skills

Figure 59.2   Radloff (1996)

59.3.7   Determine the conceptual framework

Develop a conceptual framework to show how various components in the course interrelate and how the overall course relates to other courses and the program(s) of which the course is a part. Look for unifying or fundamental concepts, skills and ideas and make these explicit in your outline. Develop a strategy that enables you to refer students frequently back to this conceptual framework during the semester. One useful strategy is to produce a visual representation of the course such as a flow chart or 'mind map' and refer to it regularly throughout the semester.

59.3.8   Structure the content around key concepts

Review your list of essential components discussed in the paragraph: Decide what to include and exclude in the course, and group these in some way that helps students understand how the course is structured. A course can be organized in the following ways: related topics; theoretical domains to more practical or applied positions; simple, familiar concepts to more complex, less familiar ideas; major themes to more specific themes or issues; or in chronological order. Different subjects lend themselves to different strategies for organizing content and these need to be addressed specifically within the context of the various disciplines and their associated cultures.

59.3.9   Organize the course systematically

Consider how the content in the paragraph: Structure the content around key concepts will be covered in the semester. Draw up an overall plan of when various parts of the course will be covered and how the course is organized including times/dates for class contact, assignment due dates, examinations, field work, collaborative project work, etc. to be undertaken. Remember to schedule in public holidays and class-free-from-contact times. Ensure that you build in enough time for regular review and reflection and time to integrate the various components in the final weeks leading up to the examinations. Remember to build in time for out of class activities, group work, reading and research.

59.3.10   Select texts and readings in line with course objectives

Students are often expected to read a great deal and to cover too much ground (MacDonald-Ross and Scott, 1995) and this can lead to a superficial approach to studying (Säljö, 1982). It is therefore important to make an appropriate selection of texts and readings for students to work through. Carefully consider what students will gain from the text. For example, will the text reinforce the course content, elaborate or extend class activities, or provide contrast to class activities etc.? How does the text relate to the overall aims of the course, how should students use the texts and readings and what should they do with the information once they have read it?

Also consider the suitability of the selected text in terms of user-friendliness and readability. Hartley (1994), Hemmings and Battersby (1989) and Wright (1987) provide useful guidelines for selecting textbooks and readings. Finally, how you present prescribed reading influences student behaviour. Research carried out at Curtin across a number of disciplines has shown that student reading behaviours are influenced by the emphasis the lecturer places on the importance of reading per se for learning and on the perceived value of particular reading for mastering the course content (Kirkpatrick and Mulligan, 1996).

59.4   Instructional strategies and activities

59.4.1   Encourage active student involvement in learning

Select learning activities which require students to engage with the content (Wang and Palincsar, 1989). Activities such as paired problem-solving, jigsaw, reciprocal teaching, question generation and role play can be used as part of regular class activities to encourage student participation in learning (Meyers and Jones, 1993). Allow time in lectures for short self-marked quizzes, buzz groups and pauses for reflection. When setting reading assignments, provide specific questions to guide student reading.

59.4.2   Encourage students to work co-operatively

Help students to learn with and from one another by encouraging co-operative learning as an integral part of your course (Bossert, 1988). Set group learning tasks and provide opportunities for students to work together on activities outside class time. Discuss with students how to maximise group learning and overcome common problems in working with others. Encourage students to form informal study groups or set up a 'study buddy' or a student mentoring system. Make explicit the connection between working effectively in groups and the skills needed to be a successful team member in future professional life.

59.4.3   Structure class times carefully to maximize learning

Students learn most in classes in which they are actively involved. Traditional lectures are least likely to provide opportunities for active student involvement (Gibbs, 1992) so consider dispensing with the traditional one-way delivery lecture and use the lecture time for small group work, self-instruction perhaps using self-paced or computer-based material, or for working in pairs on a specific topic or on problems or case studies using resources such as textbooks, journals, audio-visual material and other forms of information technology.

59.4.4   Increase feedback but reduce formal assessment

An effective teaching programme requires two-way communication between students and teachers. Therefore provide opportunities for regular feedback about learning and teaching throughout the semester. The Five Minute Exam or Half Sheet Response are both quick and easy ways to monitor progress even in large classes. These and other strategies for assessing student learning are described in Angelo and Cross (1993). Encourage students to seek feedback from a variety of sources including peers and provide opportunities for students to develop skill and confidence in self-assessment as part of regular class activities. Help students distinguish between formative and summative assessment.

59.4.5   Emphasize the importance of learning to learn and lifelong learning

Build into your classes explicit instruction and opportunity for practice with feedback, in strategies such as strategic reading, effective writing and study strategies necessary for successful learning of your subject. Include also 'generic' strategies such as goal setting, time and self-management. Discuss how 'experts' in your field think and learn. Make transparent and model the strategies you use for acquiring understanding and skill in your subject. Provide opportunities during class for students to talk about how they learn and the strategies that work for them. Emphasize the 'how to' and not just the 'what' of the subject.

59.5   Conclusion

The suggestions we have made for improving the quality of tertiary teaching and learning by 'unstuffing' the curriculum are for the most part, neither radical nor difficult to implement. Nor do they necessarily have major resource implications. Rather, they require a systematic approach to course design and planning and thoughtful application of what we know about learning and instruction to foster effective learning and ensure that students become effective, lifelong learners. Most importantly, they depend on ? genuine interest in, and professional commitment to, teaching and a concern and respect for students.

59.6 References

Angelo, T.A. (1993) A teacher's dozen – 14 general research-based principles for improving higher learning in our classrooms, *American Associate for Higher Education Bulletin*, April.

Angelo, T.A. and Cross, K.P. (1993) *Classroom Assessment Techniques: A Handbook for College Teachers*, 2nd edn, San Francisco: Jossey-Bass.

Bossert, S.T. (1988) Co-operative activities in the classroom, *Review of Educational Research*, 15, 225–50.

Candy, P., Crebert, G. and O'Leary, J. (1994) *Developing Lifelong Learners through Undergraduate Education*, AGPS: Commissioned Report No. 28, National Board of Employment, Education and Training.

Chalmers, D. and Fuller, R. (1995) *Teaching for Learning at University*, Perth, WA: Edith Cowan University.

Chambers, E.A. (1992) Workload and the quality of student learning, *Studies in Higher Education*, 17(2), 141–53.

Curtin University Handbook and Calendar 1997 (1997) Perth: Curtin University, http://www.curtin.edu.au/curtin/handbook/overview/units.htm

de la Harpe, B., Radloff, A. and Parker, L. (1997) Time spent working and studying in the first year: what do students tell us? Paper presented at the *Teaching Learning Forum. Perth: Murdoch University*, http://cleo.murdoch.edu.au/asu/pubs/tlf/tlf97/harpe73.html

Distance Education Support Services Evaluation, DESSE (1997) Teaching Learning Group, Curtin University, Western Australia. Unpublished raw data.

Hartley, J. (1994) *Designing Instructional Text*, 3rd edn, London: Kogan Page.

Gibbs, G. (1992) Control and independence. In G. Gibbs and A. Jenkins (eds), *Teaching Large Classes in Higher Education*, London: Kogan Page, 37–59.

Gibbs, G. and Lucas, L. (1995). Using research to improve student learning in large classes. Paper presented at the *3rd International Improving Student Learning Symposium: Using Research to Improve Student Learning*, Exeter University, England, 11–13 September.

Hemmings, B. and Battersby, D. (1989) Textbook selection: evaluative criteria, *Higher Education Research and Development*, 8(1), 69–78.

Kirkpatrick, A. and Mulligan, D. (1996) Cultures of learning in Australian universities: reading expectations and practice in the social and applied sciences. Paper presented at the *Applied Linguistics Association of Australia*, *21st Annual Conference, Worlds of Discourse*, Sydney, New South Wales, October.

MacDonald-Ross, M. and Scott, B. (1995) *Results of the Survey of OU Students' Reading Skills. Text & Readers Programme*, Technical Report No. 3. Milton Keynes: Institute of Educational Technology, The Open University.

Meyers, C. and Jones, T. B. (1993) *Promoting Active Learning: Strategies for the College Classroom*, San Francisco: Jossey-Bass.

Radloff, A. (1996) Integrating life long learning skills into the curriculum. Unpublished raw data.

Ramsden, P. (1993). What is good teaching in higher education? In P.T. Knight (ed.), *The Audit and Assessment of Teaching Quality*, Birmingham: Standing Conference on Educational Development, March, pp. 43–52.

Rowntree, D. (1994) *Preparing Materials for Open, Distance and Flexible Learning*, London: Kogan Page.

Säljö, R. (1982) Learning and understanding, *Goteburg Studies in Educational Sciences*, **41**, Gothenburg: Acta Universitatis.

Shuell, T.J. (1990) Phases of meaningful learning, *Review of Educational Research*, **60**(4), 531–47.

Svinicki, M.D. (1990) So much content, so little time, *Teaching Excellence*, **2**(8).

Wang, M.C. and Palincsar, A.S. (1989) Teaching students to assume an active role in their learning. In M.C. Reynolds (ed.), *Knowledge Base for the Beginning Teacher*, Oxford: Pergamon Press, 71–84.

Wright, D.L. (1987) Getting the most out of your textbook, *Teaching at the University of Nebraska, Lincoln*, **8**(3), 1–3.